Handbook of Research on Unemployment and Labor Market Sustainability in the Era of Globalization

Füsun Yenilmez
Eskişehir Osmangazi University, Turkey

Esin Kılıç
Eskişehir Osmangazi University, Turkey

A volume in the Advances in Finance, Accounting, and Economics (AFAE) Book Series

IGI GLOBAL
DISSEMINATOR OF KNOWLEDGE

www.igi-global.com

Published in the United States of America by
IGI Global
Business Science Reference (an imprint of IGI Global)
701 E. Chocolate Avenue
Hershey PA, USA 17033
Tel: 717-533-8845
Fax: 717-533-8661
E-mail: cust@igi-global.com
Web site: http://www.igi-global.com

Library of Congress Cataloging-in-Publication Data

Names: Yenilmez, Füsun, 1969- editor. | Kiliç, Esin, 1984- editor.
Title: Handbook of research on unemployment and labor market sustainability in the era of globalization / Füsun Yenilmez and Esin Kiliç, editors.
Description: Hershey : Business Science Reference, [2017]
Identifiers: LCCN 2016052311| ISBN 9781522520085 (hardcover) | ISBN 9781522520092 (ebook)
Subjects: LCSH: Labor market. | Unemployment. | Migrant labor. | Globalization--Economic aspects.
Classification: LCC HD5706 .H3624 2017 | DDC 331.1--dc23
LC record available at https://lccn.loc.gov/2016052311

This book is published in the IGI Global book series Advances in Finance, Accounting, and Economics (AFAE) (ISSN: 2327-5677; eISSN: 2327-5685)

British Cataloguing in Publication Data
A Cataloguing in Publication record for this book is available from the British Library.

Advances in Finance, Accounting, and Economics (AFAE) Book Series

Ahmed Driouchi
Al Akhawayn University, Morocco

ISSN:2327-5677
EISSN:2327-5685

Mission

In our changing economic and business environment, it is important to consider the financial changes occurring internationally as well as within individual organizations and business environments. Understanding these changes as well as the factors that influence them is crucial in preparing for our financial future and ensuring economic sustainability and growth.

The **Advances in Finance, Accounting, and Economics (AFAE)** book series aims to publish comprehensive and informative titles in all areas of economics and economic theory, finance, and accounting to assist in advancing the available knowledge and providing for further research development in these dynamic fields.

Coverage

- Borrowing and Lending
- Auditing
- Investments and Derivatives
- Theoretical Issues in Economics, Finance, and Accounting
- Economics of Migration and Spatial Mobility
- Accounting information systems
- E-Accounting
- Finance
- Interest Rates and Annuities
- Economic Policy

IGI Global is currently accepting manuscripts for publication within this series. To submit a proposal for a volume in this series, please contact our Acquisition Editors at Acquisitions@igi-global.com or visit: http://www.igi-global.com/publish/.

The Advances in Finance, Accounting, and Economics (AFAE) Book Series (ISSN 2327-5677) is published by IGI Global, 701 E. Chocolate Avenue, Hershey, PA 17033-1240, USA, www.igi-global.com. This series is composed of titles available for purchase individually; each title is edited to be contextually exclusive from any other title within the series. For pricing and ordering information please visit http://www.igi-global.com/book-series/advances-finance-accounting-economics/73685. Postmaster: Send all address changes to above address.

Titles in this Series

For a list of additional titles in this series, please visit: www.igi-global.com

Tools and Techniques for Economic Decision Analysis
Jelena Stanković (University of Niš, Serbia) Pavlos Delias (Eastern Macedonia and Thrace Institute of Technology, Greece) Srđan Marinković (University of Niš, Serbia) and Sylvie Rochhia (Université Côte d'Azur, CNRS, GREDEG, France)
Business Science Reference • copyright 2017 • 305pp • H/C (ISBN: 9781522509592) • US $205.00 (our price)

Corporate Espionage, Geopolitics, and Diplomacy Issues in International Business
Bryan Christiansen (PryMarke, LLC, USA) and Fatmanur Kasarcı (PryMarke Business Academy, Turkey)
Business Science Reference • copyright 2017 • 374pp • H/C (ISBN: 9781522510314) • US $210.00 (our price)

Handbook of Research on Globalization and the International Political Economy
Abdulkadir Isik (Namik Kemal University, Turkey)
Business Science Reference • copyright 2017 • 397pp • H/C (ISBN: 9781522508526) • US $265.00 (our price)

Handbook of Research on Global Indicators of Economic and Political Convergence
Ramesh Chandra Das (Katwa College, India)
Business Science Reference • copyright 2016 • 616pp • H/C (ISBN: 9781522502159) • US $345.00 (our price)

Global Perspectives on Trade Integration and Economies in Transition
Vasily Erokhin (Moscow University of Finance and Law, Russia)
Business Science Reference • copyright 2016 • 407pp • H/C (ISBN: 9781522504511) • US $210.00 (our price)

Handbook of Research on Social Entrepreneurship and Solidarity Economics
José Manuel Saiz-Álvarez (Tecnológico de Monterrey, Mexico)
Business Science Reference • copyright 2016 • 606pp • H/C (ISBN: 9781522500971) • US $230.00 (our price)

Economic Modeling, Analysis, and Policy for Sustainability
Anandajit Goswami (The Energy and Resources Institute (TERI), India) and Arabinda Mishra (ICIMOD, Nepal)
Business Science Reference • copyright 2016 • 388pp • H/C (ISBN: 9781522500940) • US $210.00 (our price)

Financial Market Regulations and Legal Challenges in South Asia
Amit K. Kashyap (Nirma University, India) and Anjani Singh Tomar (Gujarat National Law University, India)
Business Science Reference • copyright 2016 • 346pp • H/C (ISBN: 9781522500049) • US $200.00 (our price)

IGI GLOBAL
DISSEMINATOR OF KNOWLEDGE
www.igi-global.com

701 E. Chocolate Ave., Hershey, PA 17033
Order online at www.igi-global.com or call 717-533-8845 x100
To place a standing order for titles released in this series, contact: cust@igi-global.com
Mon-Fri 8:00 am - 5:00 pm (est) or fax 24 hours a day 717-533-8661

List of Reviewers

Tolga Aksoy, *Yıldız Technical University, Turkey*
Samir Amine, *Université du Québec en Outaouais, Canada*
İsmail Aydoğuş, *Afyon Kocatepe University, Turkey*
Gökhan Aykaç, *Gazi University, Turkey*
Mustafa Kemal Biçerli, *Anadolu University, Turkey*
Ati Cahayani, *Atma Jaya Catholic University, Indonesia*
Şadan Çalışkan, *Uşak University, Turkey*
Fatih Çemrek, *Eskişehir Osmangazi University, Turkey*
Gökçe Cerev, *Fırat University, Turkey*
Banu Demirhan, *Afyon Kocatepe University, Turkey*
Erdal Demirhan, *Afyon Kocatepe University, Turkey*
Etem Hakan Ergeç, *Istanbul Medeniyet University, Turkey*
Sevgi Gerek, *Anadolu University, Turkey*
Nuray Girginer, *Eskişehir Osmangazi University, Turkey*
Feride Gönel, *Yıldız Technical University, Turkey*
Giray Gözgör, *Istanbul Medeniyet University, Turkey*
Özlem İnanç-Tunçer, *Işık University, Turkey*
Mustafa Karabacak, *Uşak University, Turkey*
Müge Kart, *Ankara University, Turkey*
Hüseyin Kaya, *Istanbul Medeniyet University, Turkey*
Bengül Gülümser Kaytancı, *Anadolu University, Turkey*
Özge Kama Masala, *Yıldız Technical University, Turkey*
Oytun Meçik, *Eskişehir Osmangazi University, Turkey*
Maria Pavlis-Korres, *Hellenic Open University, Greece*

Zehra Bilgen Susanlı, *Işık University, Turkey*
Tulus Tambunan, *Trisakti University, Indonesia*
Hüseyin Tatlıdil, *Hacettepe University, Turkey*
Metin Toprak, *Istanbul University, Turkey*
Bora Yenihan, *Sakarya University, Turkey*
Christos Zagkos, *Center of Educational Policy Development (KANEP/GSEE), Greece*

List of Contributors

Table of Contents

Detailed Table of Contents

International Labor Organization (ILO) has been encouraging countries to implement international labor standards since 1919. With the help of international labor standards, ILO aims to improve the quality of human life and dignity. In order to reach this aim, the ILO's 1998 Declaration on Fundamental Principles and Rights at Work sets out four core labor standards that are binding on all ILO member states. Although developed countries ratified many standards, developing countries and especially Muslim countries are lagging behind. In this paper, we attempt to document the labor standards in Muslim countries by using ILO's Information System on International Labor Standards and compare their position with the rest of the world.

At a time when the Indian subcontinent is beset with a burgeoning population, rapid urbanization, and high disposable incomes, the Indian economy is at a precarious stage of balancing demand uncertainties with pressures to minimize bottom line costs. As a consequence, there is great reliance on a dynamic workforce, which comprises of temporary, contract, and casual laborers referred to as the contingent workforce. A talent war is looming on the horizon and employers need to buckle up their workforce armory with an unparalleled employee value proposition, making the business landscape a tricky vehicle to maneuver. A robust strategic framework bolstered by prudent workforce management will aid an organization to fulfill its goals while isolating it from any legal liability. Technology can be used to leverage data analytically for job assessment and aid in seamless project execution. In sum, an approach sensitive to the legal, technological and psychological pillars of managing workers provides a comprehensive mechanism to counter issues associated with contingent workforce management.

Since the date it was founded to the present day, International Labour Organization (ILO) has been working on developing policy proposals about the problematic areas emerging in working life. Though unemployment is regarded across the world as the source of major problematic areas of economies, the thought of the need for taking the new 'invisible' work types into the spotlight also as problematic areas is considered significant. This chapter acknowledges this need and is about the fight against modern slavery; in this context, the chapter takes the assessments and reports of ILO on forced labor. Thus, the purpose is to put forth the necessity and importance of fighting against the modern forms of slave labor, expanding on the efforts of the Organization which can cause significant pressure on the government/state level.

This article aims to provide an analytical and critical reading of the state of knowledge on legislation relating to employment protection (EPL) and its impacts on unemployment, jobs creation, productivity and more generally efficiency of the labor market. We show that the construction of indicators of EPL adopted by the OECD is incomplete and does not take into account local specificities of each labor market. We also show that the dominant idea among liberals that any regulations impeding freedom of the labor market generates unemployment and loss of effectiveness is not so obvious to verify empirically and can even be contradicted. In this analysis, we rely on a critical review of theoretical and empirical studies which have examined the effects of EPL. We also discuss some alternatives such as bonus-malus system or the single contract that have been put forward to address the limitations of a relatively strict EPL.

Free mobility of labor has been the core element of the European integration process. The aim of this chapter is to analyze the effects and challenges of the labor mobility within the EU. The analysis then focuses on the recent trends in labor mobility. Cross-border labor mobility remains low in the EU. The main reasons behind the low levels of labor mobility in the EU include linguistic and cultural reasons, as well as non-tariff barriers such as pension rules, recognition of professional qualification or social security differences. Removal of impediments to free mobility of labor and improvement of flexibility of the European labor markets will strengthen the EU's labor market integration.

Women take part in working life less in proportion to men due to the reasons such as the value judgments of the societies in which they live, the roles of motherhood and housewifery which the society have imposed on them, and social gender inequality. Making use of the economic potential of the country fully and effectively depends on increasing the employment rates of women which remain behind the male employment for various reasons. In this study, it was tried to reveal differences of OECD countries in each other in terms of women's labor force variables. To realize this aim, 9 indicators of women's labor force pertaining to 32 countries, which were received from OECD Employment Outlook 2015, OECD Labor Statistics Book and OECD official website www.oecd.org, were compared with the help of Multidimensional Scaling. The study was carried out for 32 countries both two dimensionally and three dimensionally. Additionally, Factor Analysis was utilized. Determining the most remote countries together in dimensions, variables leading to differences were shown in graphics.

The female labor participation is recently considered as one of the factors leading to economic development in developing countries by amplifying total labor force as qualitative and quantitative. In this study, the authors investigate the factors affecting female labor participation in developing countries, applying panel data model for 83 developing countries over the period of 1990-2014. Empirical results indicate that u-shaped and incompatibility hypotheses are valid in the developing countries. Additionally, improving education levels and increasing male participation in labor markets lead women to more participate in labor markets. These results show the importance of enhancing education level and therefore the policies towards providing it.

Women have been seen as cheap labor and have participated in the economic life less than their male counterparts since the Industrial Revolution, where they joined the waged labor pool. Though the reasons for the women's low participation in the workforce are various; Turkey's current social structure in particular and the social gender perception which acts as the base of this structure emerge as key determinants. For this reason, establishing the general status of female labor in Turkey and comparing the international and national statistical data from a global perspective around the social gender inequality and the distribution of labor based on social gender is the purpose of this study.

Unemployment and poverty are problems experienced especially by developing countries. The higher level of unemployment and poverty will lead the higher level of crime. The unemployment rate in Indonesia in August 2014 is 5.94% or 7,244,905 people, and 4% of Indonesian people living on less than $1.25 a day. One of the things that can reduce the unemployment rate and the percentage of poor people is entrepreneurship. This chapter wants to explain that the level of unemployment and poverty can

rates would increase in the host countries, or that immigrants would depress wages of native workers. However, these perceptions do not find confirmation in the previous research on this literature. The evidence is, at best, mixed. Although the magnitude of the impact depends on time and space, in general, results of the previous literature indicate that immigration has only very small or no effect on employment and wages of resident workers. The aim of this chapter is to provide an overview of immigration-labor market relation for different countries and time intervals with some significant policy implications with regards to state officials.

Preface

Economics is a science that researches the effective utilization of scarce resources. When considered in this context, resources are the basic determinants of individual wealth in a microeconomic sense and of economic welfare in a macroeconomic sense. From the macroeconomic perspective, resources of a country are termed as its factors of production. Among the basic factors of production, labor attracts a great deal of attention. The reason why labor is particularly highlighted is because it is basically a factor of production based on human. Labor is human activity that is utilized during the production of goods and services and it is composed of physical and mental contributions of those who realize the production. The term 'employment' is widely used to express the use of labor in the production process.

Underutilization of factors of production which determine a country's production capability is an important problem in terms of the effective use of resources that are deemed to be scarce. Full employment of labor as a factor of production enables the economy to reach its potential GDP level; production levels below this level correspond to inefficient production levels. Thus, unemployment of workforce who wants to be employed is seen as an idle resource that is not used for the production which creates added value for the economy. However, the unemployment of labor is a more important problem than the underutilization of other factors of production. The reason why labor that is not employed in the production of goods and services is much more problematic is that labor, unlike other factors of production, cannot be stored. Underutilization of other factors of production such as capital and land does not lead to a notable depreciation in their useful economic life while it is the opposite for labor. Thus, the unemployment of labor being an unstorable factor of production has the potential to be a more important problem when compared with the underutilization of other factors of production.

Efficient and full utilization of resources, especially in the short run, and technological improvement, in the long run, are of great importance in terms of economic growth. In this context, unemployment creates a negative impact on the growth performance of economies. As stated by Okun's Law, a one percent decrease in the unemployment rate increases economic growth by about 2%. For this reason, it is seen that full employment takes an important place among the main objectives of economic policies of countries. Other economic policy objectives, such as price stability and financial stability, are also important corresponding with the target of full employment in the long term. Thus, in order to maintain full employment, using appropriate monetary policy is essential as well.

From the macroeconomic perspective, unemployment is surely a crucial problem. But at the same time, all of the changes observed in the labor market are of particular concern to the business world in terms of costs of production and selection of production method. The wage level determined in labor market -where suppliers and demanders of labor interact-, regulations for the wage and labor productivity are among the main issues that are followed closely by employers. Also, the fact that labor demanders cannot find the skilled labor they need not only increases unemployment but also poses production challenges for the business world. Thus, labor market-related problems have been an important research field in both microeconomic and macroeconomic contexts, and along with many academic studies, a large number of reports has been published by labor and employer's unions, national and international organizations in this field. These problems, effects of them on the macroeconomic and microeconomic environment and recommendations for solutions to them are discussed separately in this book with their economic and production aspects.

Unemployment and other labor market-related issues create not only economic but also social and psychological problems. When these problems are evaluated together, it is better understood how unemployment is a major problem. In order to effectively solve these unemployment-driven social and psychological problems, it is necessary to investigate the labor market carefully and carry out required reforms consistent with the findings. When doing this, the structure of unemployment should also be analyzed. At this point, the indicators pertaining to the status of women and youth in the labor market deserves a special emphasis. As a matter of fact, policy makers should put a lot of effort into developing policies to regulate the labor market and to eliminate disparities, discrimination, and inequalities.

Although problems related to labor market create different economic and social effects on every country due to having different socio-economic structures and development levels, these problems have an important place in the agenda of all countries. Developing countries are struggling to reduce unemployment, which is one of their main problems. After the crisis that began in 2008 and still continues to make its effects felt in some countries, one of the most important problems that the developed countries face and need to solve is also unemployment. Besides, immigration from Syria and developing countries to many European countries including Turkey have been considered in terms of its disruptive effects on the labor market of the migration-receiving countries. One of the aims of this book is the evaluation of the changes in the labor market in light of these late developments using current data and the effects of them with an academic approach. This approach helps holistic evaluation of labor market and makes the book a reference source.

With the effects of globalization and improvements in the technology, the labor market has transcended national boundaries and gained an international structure. Therefore, unemployment arising from excess labor supply or lack of labor demand stands as a major problem not only for the national labor market but also for the global labor market. Due to the dynamics that lead to increases in unemployment in the world, the objective of achieving full employment has become more important with regard to macroeconomic policies in the era of globalization.

The economic and social changes that negatively impact labor market deepen existing problems and require the development of new policies. These policies should be not only about economic growth but also about economic development. Training policies aimed at increasing productivity of labor are also important to overcome challenges of unemployment. By taking into consideration the effects of changing social, economic and production structure on national and global labor market, the chapters of this book also recommend various policy implementations based on the evaluation of the labor markets by examining current data and latest developments affecting the labor market.

Structuring economic and social policies and effective creation of legal regulations require a thorough examination of the developments affecting labor markets, which are important in many aspects. This book aims to evaluate the challenges of unemployment and labor market sustainability of in the era of globalization and examine today's labor markets from different perspectives. It contains 21 carefully selected chapters that discuss different academic questions and aim to provide a different viewpoint to the policy makers and researchers who carry out academic studies on labor markets.

In Chapter 1, the authors aimed to document how Muslim countries consider labor rights in terms of core and the total labor standards of International Labour Organization. The chapter is designed to clarify these issues; an overview of international labor standards, analyses fundamental labor standards in Muslim countries and Turkey, importance of legal systems, respectively. Accordingly, an analysis in the chapter indicates that on average Muslim countries ratified much fewer numbers of conventions than other countries. Also, there is considerable heterogeneity across Muslim countries. For example, richer Muslim countries ratified fewer conventions than the poor ones; African Muslim countries ratified more conventions than the Asian Muslim countries and civil law Muslim countries ratified more conventions than the Islamic law ruled Muslim countries and the countries which have mixed legal system.

The second chapter of the book is related to 21st-century labor paradigm. The author of Chapter 2 investigated the contingent workforce phenomenon of about the growing reality of in the Indian economy. Especially in India, outsourcing of work finds its genesis in the cheap buying of labor with minimal employer liability as it has known. Through this aspect, this chapter is a piece has strived to comprehensively cover all problem areas related to Indian contingent workforce management. The chapter contains the titles about the necessary legal compliances, technology ecosystem in labor management, strategies for proactive engagement with contingent workers, industrial relations, cultural integration and also the ethics of labor management.

Chapter 3 clarifies the concept of modern slavery. Certainly, to examine the concept of modern slavery in a global perspective and develop common global policies are seen important. Because it is estimated that modern slavery is spreading rapidly and the problem will get deeper unless necessary precautions are taken; therefore, modern slavery must be understood. The importance of roadmaps drafted and operations run by the international community for the struggle to eliminate modern slavery can be seen clearly in this regard. Accordingly, the chapter uses International Labour Organization's practices as its base and expands on them, because it is the most efficient organization in the fight against towards the elimination of modern slavery in the world. The chapter concludes though the undertakings at the international organizations and international community levels yield efficient results, the importance of the need for national activities and regulations should not be ruled out; states/governments should develop precise and urgent action plans towards the elimination of forced labor.

Employment protection is a popular and interesting concept related to the labor market. Chapter 4 provides an analytical and critical reading of the state of knowledge on legislation relating to employment protection and its impacts on unemployment, jobs creation, productivity and more generally efficiency of the labor market. As a result of the chapter, some alternative policies have suggested which seek to empower the employer in its human resources management and thus give some protection to the employee without constituting an excessive obstruction of the labor market.

As it is known, free movement of people is one of the founding principles of the European Union's internal market. This principle gives all citizens of member countries the right to travel, live and work wherever they wish within the EU. Free movement of labor across the EU has become a controversial issue in several member countries and highlights the major challenge of economic and social convergence of the EU. The main aim of Chapter 5 is to analyze to what extent freedom of movement of labor is realized at the EU level. In this context, this chapter describes the key features of free movement of labor and to makes an assessment of the trend of flows of labor within the EU, by taking into account the current developments such as the recent enlargements and the economic crisis. And then it indicates the costs and benefits of labor mobility at the EU level and discusses the obstacles to the free movement of labor within the EU's internal market. As a consequently, Chapter 5 shows the completion of a fully-functioning single market is generally considered as a response to current challenges of the EU. The chapter emphasizes the cross-border labor mobility not only increase employment and economic welfare but also overcome divergence in labor markets. At the same time, it reduces unemployment differences between the member countries and contributes to an optimal allocation of labor resources within the EU. So, it is obvious to see the labor mobility is of crucial importance for the EU's economic integration process and the challenges that arise from the labor mobility need to be addressed directly.

Women employment is a crucial issue related to the labor market all over the world. In a similar manner, there is huge literature about women employment and women labor force. Chapter 6 is aimed to evaluate indicators of OECD countries in terms of female labor with Factor Analysis performed, which is commonly used for this purpose. The results of analyses evaluating the women's employment in OECD countries led to results associated with countries' level of development. Also, the analysis showed that developed countries have placed in the same group in terms of used variables.

One of the biggest problems of developing countries is the lack of resources, namely production factors. Obviously, the insufficient capital and labor amount impedes the development of these countries and therefore makes difficult to reach the level of developed countries. As previously described, the women's employment in the economy is important for the stability of economic growth. Accordingly, Chapter 7 is determining the factors affecting female labor force participation leads policy makers to implement effective policies towards increasing women's employment by allow policy makers to select the primary tools with the limited public budget, which is a common problem seen in developing countries. As a result, the chapter shows the empirical support for the u-shaped hypothesis, in the first stages of economic development, economic growth decreases the female labor force participate in labor markets but decreases it at the later stages.

Chapter 8 drives a framework for the general status of female labor in Turkey and comparing the international and national statistical data from a global perspective around the social gender inequality and the distribution of labor based on social gender. The brief of the chapter describes the equality between men and women and total participation to social and working life carry major significance for a country's economic growth, social development, and social justice. It is clear that the social and economic gaps between men and women have widened; thus, in order to understand the importance of gender differences the subject needs to be analyzed from a social gender viewpoint.

Unemployment and poverty are problems experienced by all countries of the world. Especially, developing countries usually face heavy problems of unemployment and poverty, including Indonesia which has a population of around 300 million is facing quite heavy problems of unemployment and poverty. Chapter 9 wants to explain that the level of unemployment and poverty can be overcome by the spirit of entrepreneurship of housewives and youths, who have a micro, small, or medium business. The chapter is including an important suggestion such as housewife and youths who are not considered as workers also can help reduce poverty and help reduce unemployment.

As generally accepted unemployment is associated with loss of well-being. In particular, youth unemployment problem in some countries like Turkey has received much attention, because youth unemployment rates are persistently higher than the OECD average. Definitely, the importance of youth unemployment is better understood if the demographic transition of Turkey is taken into consideration. Turkey has a "Window of Opportunity" from 2000 to 2025, and during that period, the working-age population is expected to reach its peak, which will provide favorable conditions for economic growth.

Chapter 10 aims to explore the nature and causes of youth unemployment in Turkey by taking into account its gender dimension. Thus it reviews the policies and programs to tackle the youth unemployment problem and discusses their effectiveness.

Similarly, Chapter 11 aims to analyze and profile youth unemployment problem in the Turkish economy. The chapter contains three main issues such as conceptual framework of unemployment, unemployment problem in Turkey and youth unemployment profile in Turkey. Herewith, it is possible to emphasize that Turkey has needed that a new holistic employment strategy and policy should be built where all classes' views are taken into consideration.

Another youth employment issue is discussed in Chapter 12. This chapter aims to explore diverse factors of precarious youth employment in the tourism sector with particular focus on Bangladesh. Also, the chapter seeks to justify information and communication technology as a possible solution to the persistent precarious youth employment situation in Bangladesh.

Work is undoubtedly a fundamental and inalienable social right, won through labor and political struggles, as well as class and social conflicts. Concerning the thorny issue of unemployment, vulnerability and social exclusion, Chapter 13 attempts to crystallize and analyze young people's attitudes towards unemployment as a social phenomenon, but also towards the ways and forms of this phenomenon configuration and, at the same time, to determine their degree of confidence in what is called welfare state in the context of the Greek economic crisis.

It is generally argued that as intermediary financial institutions, the Islamic banks may provide positive impacts to the financial system. They have the potential of increasing acceleration of economic development. There are a number of studies in the literature suggesting that these institutions make positive contributions from different aspects. There are too many studies in the empirical literature which try to examine the relationship between Islamic banking and the real economy. In this context, Chapter 14 reviews the linkage between bank loans and employment in the Turkish economy. For this purpose, the causal relationship between the loans offered by banks for these sectors and employment has been analyzed in the chapter.

Another sectoral research is related to construction industry. Construction industry both plays an important role in the global economy as it has 15% share of the world's GDP and depends more on labor compared to other industries. In addition, the construction industry has higher multiplier effects compared to other industries. Thus it is absolutely an important sector in terms of the labor market. Chapter 15 examines the global trends in the construction industry with employment dimension. As clearly seen, globalization of the construction labor market resulted in changing labor profile as well as in the emergence of the multilingual and multicultural project and construction teams. Globalization of the construction industry increased opportunities and expanded markets where construction labor can work. In this way, the chapter is expected to contribute to the literature with respect to the challenges construction industry will face due to the global trends as well as with respect to the changes in the workforce profile, skills, and talents in the construction industry.

Economic structural transformation, which has been referred to quite often in economic literature in recent years, influences countries and their markets in many ways. As it is known, structural transformation first requires transformation from agriculture to manufacturing and then from manufacturing to services. To realize sustainable growth and development objectives, countries have to succeed in structural transformation. In Chapter 16, changes in the employment structure of South Korea and Japan, both of whom have successfully completed the structural transformation, were studied in terms of economic complexity and product space theory.

As the basic economic indicators of the modern economy, the concepts of unemployment, inflation, and economic growth are major macroeconomic variables which are often analyzed. Whereas an economic growth could occur as a result of financial activity level in an economy, there could also be observed a chart which shows an inflationary setting and/or high unemployment rates. Chapter 17 is aimed to analyze the relationship among variables about annual economic growth in the period of 1960-2014, inflation rate and unemployment data in Turkey. Thus it is possible to present political suggestions for the economy of Turkey in the light of the analysis findings. Herewith, it easy to see that to keep the growth process sustainable, the economy of Turkey should be built in a manner of promoting growth dynamics; based on technology and meanwhile not only importing technology but also producing it. So, as highlighted in the chapter, it is obvious that it will bring new requirements in the context of the labor market, quality and productivity increase.

Innovation is an important driving force for the development of countries as it boosts the productivity of physical and human capital. Obviously, today's highly competitive technological markets, innovation plays a substantial role in countries' strategies as it is the most important factor for sustainable development and competitive superiority. Chapter 18 aims to assess the innovation performances of EU countries and Turkey to determine prominent drivers that affect the innovative activity of innovation efficient countries. Consequently, human capital and employment related drivers are the factors that foster innovation efficiency the most on a country level compared to research and development expenditure, intellectual property rights, application, infrastructure and environmental indicators, within most innovation efficient EU countries.

Chapter 19 investigates the Indonesian experience with economic growth and changes in labor market segmentation and labor productivity for the period 1990-2015. This chapter is particularly important for Indonesian economic growth for two main reasons. First, along with accumulation in physical investment and technology progress, labor productivity growth is also a major determinant of long-term economic growth. Second, like in other developing countries, the labor market in Indonesia is also segmented with a large share of informal workers, and it may have a negative impact on the country's economic growth.

As it is known, economies in transition from centrally planned economy to liberal economy characterized as transition economies. The countries that are deemed transition economies in the literature shift to an environment where the prices are determined by the free market instead of a central organization during the process of economic liberalization. Chapter 20 discusses the relationship between trade openness and unemployment for transition economies between the period of 1998-2014 with dynamic panel data analysis methods. The chapter emphasizes that in transition economies trade openness rates have a reducing effect on the unemployment rates. Accordingly, it is interpreted as the positive result of commercial liberalization on the labor market in terms of employment.

The relationship between labor market and immigration is very strong. So, this relationship needs to be explored. The last chapter concerned with an analysis of the impact of immigration on labor market of receiving countries, focusing on employment and wages. It is obvious that the effect of immigration on the welfare of the native population is an important issue in public debate. Chapter 21 concludes that immigration may have both positive and negative impacts on the labor market.

Chapter 1
Why Do Labor Standards Differ Across Muslim Countries?

Özge Kama Masala
Yıldız Technical University, Turkey

Tolga Aksoy
Yıldız Technical University, Turkey

ABSTRACT

International Labor Organization (ILO) has been encouraging countries to implement international labor standards since 1919. With the help of international labor standards, ILO aims to improve the quality of human life and dignity. In order to reach this aim, the ILO's 1998 Declaration on Fundamental Principles and Rights at Work sets out four core labor standards that are binding on all ILO member states. Although developed countries ratified many standards, developing countries and especially Muslim countries are lagging behind. In this paper, we attempt to document the labor standards in Muslim countries by using ILO's Information System on International Labor Standards and compare their position with the rest of the world.

INTRODUCTION

As the world gets more and more globalized, some regional/state issues like working conditions become matters of the international audience. Worldwide connections and increased information techniques have helped to increase individual awareness. Many developed countries have created different programs to encourage better working conditions for their citizens. The issue has been on the agenda of not only economists but also governments and non-governmental, humanitarian organizations for some time. There has been progress on the issue, partly by reason of International Labor Organization's (ILO) endorsement of these labor rights as human rights thus the majority of countries have ratified the core labor rights throughout the last decade.

Concerns about the labor rights came into question for the first time in the United Kingdom during the Industrial Revolution. Recognizing rights and enforcing standards universally is crucial for achieving global social justice. Even though the need for an international organization to regulate labor rights

DOI: 10.4018/978-1-5225-2008-5.ch001

was obvious no major steps were taken until the end of First World War. In 1919, ILO was established as a special branch of the United Nations, with an aim to establish internationally recognized human and labor rights, to persuade nations to recognize these rights and to resolve disputed issues regarding their implementation.

The issue of labor standards can be analyzed from different aspects. One aspect of studying labor rights is to relate labor rights with human rights. Implementation of basic rights surely helps to protect human dignity and promotes social justice, but it does so at the expense of an increase in labor costs. As the globalization expands to more countries, competition between and within countries intensifies in a great manner. The increase in competition puts workers in danger since labor is not as mobile as capital, and therefore regarded as the primary production factor whose costs could be diminished easily. This in return provides labor cost advantage/disadvantage to countries with weak/strong civil liberties since countries with better civil liberties tend to have higher labor standards. Considering the fact that labor standards may cause labor costs to increase, some developing countries tend to rule them out, and many of them race to the bottom to attract foreign direct investment (Davies & Vadlamannati, 2013).

Another line of research explores the relationship between labor standards and export performance (Felbermayr, Prat, & Schmerer, 2008; Hur, 2009; Duanmu, 2014). If labor standards are cost-push factors, then in countries where labor is well protected, export goods would be more expensive with respect to the countries where labor is less protected. Thus, the former group of countries would have a lower level of economic growth than the latter one. In addition, governments, especially in lower income regions of the world, might tolerate poor working conditions to attract foreign direct investment, stating another case of a race to the bottom.

However, labor standards are not necessarily linked only to cost-push factors. Considering especially the fundamental labor standards (FLS) which we discuss in detail below, can be accepted as the foundations of basic human rights. Since human capital is the engine of growth in modern economies, it is not reasonable to think that human capital accumulation can be achieved without protecting labor properly. Preventing and protecting child labor, for instance, is crucial for human capital development. Furthermore, human capital is an important production factor for both attracting (Blomström & Kokko, 2003; Noorbakhsh, Paloni, & Youssef, 2001) and reaping the benefits of foreign direct investments (Aksoy & Gönel, 2016; Xu, 2000). Hence a counter argument is that well-protected labor rights are, quite the contrary, a prerequisite for human capital development and long-run economic growth.

Various countries differ in the implementation of labor rights for different reasons, but from a moral point of view, labor rights can be seen as a complementary to human rights and it becomes important to emphasize the relationship between ILO and international human rights law. The Universal Declaration of Human Rights of 1948 was adopted by the United Nations General Assembly and is a milestone document in the history of human rights. Article 23 of the Declaration asserts: “everyone has the right to work, to free choice of employment, has the right to equal pay for equal work and has the right to form and join trade unions for the protection of his interests”. As can be seen, this Article has close relations with ILO’s aim of improving the quality of life by improving working conditions for employees. To fulfill this aim, the ILO`s 1998 Declaration on Fundamental Principles and Rights at Work sets our four core labor standards that are binding on all ILO member states.

The aim of this study is to investigate how well ILO’s FLS are implemented in Muslim countries. This paper is structured as follows: Section 2 provides an overview of international labor standards. Section 3 analyses FLS in Muslim countries and Turkey. Section 4 discusses the importance of legal systems. Finally, section 5 concludes.

AN OVERVIEW OF INTERNATIONAL LABOR STANDARDS

Since its foundation, ILO has been encouraging countries to implement international labor standards in order to improve labor conditions. ILO's conventions compromise a wide range of worker rights, from rights related to freedom of association, collective bargaining, and industrial relations to rights regarding seafarers. Hence the type and total number of conventions that a country ratifies are very likely to change depending on the income level, geographical conditions, political structure and culture as well as religion of that particular country. Recognizing that economic growth alone is not enough to provide social justice around the world; ILO issued a declaration and defined FLS which apply to all people in all states regardless of the level of economic development in 1998. The declaration commits member states to respect and promote eight fundamental rights defined in four categories:

1. **Union Rights:**
   a. Freedom of association and right to organize convention,
   b. Right to organize and collective bargaining convention.
2. **Child Labor:**
   a. Minimum wage convention,
   b. Worst forms of child labor convention.
3. **Forced Labor:**
   a. Forced labor convention,
   b. Abolition of forced labor convention.
4. **Discrimination:**
   a. Equal remuneration convention,
   b. Discrimination (employment and occupation) convention.

These rights can also be seen as a crucial factor in strengthening human capital in countries. For example, with the abolition of child labor in the second category, the ILO is hoping to improve the education, health, and motivation of children[1]. However, it is very difficult to solve such an endemic problem just by law. For instance, Doepke and Zilibotti (2009) suggests that imposing international labor standards in developing countries might be counterproductive and jeopardize child-labor problem. Hence child labor prohibition laws should be accompanied by anti-poverty policies and by improving schooling costs and conditions.

Collective bargaining is generally considered as a cost increasing factor since it enables unions to force firms to increase wages above the competitive wage level and/or improve working conditions with the threat of a strike. In this case, the firms have to share profits with unions based on the bargaining power of the parties. Nonetheless, unions and collective bargaining can be efficiency enhancing. The first reason is collective bargaining provides peaceful coordination between employer and the employee which in return would influence their workplaces environment. Another factor might be the formal or informal bargaining between the parties enables the labor market to respond to shocks more effectively and move the economy towards a new equilibrium (Aidt & Tzannatos, 2005). Certainly, how these conditions affect the firms, and the economy would also depend on the bargaining power of the unions.

Elimination of forced labor and the equity rationale (third and fourth categories) can be related to human rights. Where all human being is born free and equal in dignity and rights, they cannot be forced to work for any reasons. The same logic can be applied to equity, where everybody is equal discrimination in respect of employment and occupation should be abandoned. Studying all these core rights, one can claim that these provide a process, not a particular outcome or more clearly they give people freedom to choose (McCrudden & Davies, 2000).

Even though 185 of the 193 United Nations member states are also members of the ILO, it does not mean that all of the core standards are entirely ratified by all member states. 179 countries ratified the convention concerning the Prohibition and Immediate Action for the Elimination of Worst Forms of Child Labor. This convention is also the most ratified convention among core standards. Unfortunately, only 153 countries have accepted the Freedom of Association and Protection of the Right to Organize Convention.

It is also worth mentioning that since ILO has no sanctioning power on member countries, it cannot force them to ratify all the standards that ILO formalized. In addition, even though ILO's supervisory bodies- the Committee of Experts on the Application of Conventions and Recommendations (CEACR) and the Conference Committee on the Application of Conventions and Recommendations- have the authority to monitor conformance with labor standards, ILO review and complaint mechanisms mainly function to bring to lights the violations and to shame those who commit them (Anner & Caraway, 2010). In line with these observations, Peksen and Blanton (2016) casts doubt on the idea that ratifying ILO conventions promote the protection of labor rights.

INTERNATIONAL LABOR STANDARDS IN MUSLIM COUNTRIES

Countries have applied different legal systems according to their needs, cultures, and colonial conditions. The choice of their labor laws can be related to their legal origins and economic systems. Common and civil law countries utilize different strategies for dealing with market failures: common law relies on contract and private litigation and civil law on direct supervision of markets by the government. Thus, their legal origins have created differences in their labor regulations. For instance, according to Botero, Djankov, La Porta, Lopez-de-Silanes and Shleifer (2005), Socialist and French legal origin countries have sharply higher levels of labor regulations than do common law countries.

We have tried to follow a similar attitude with core labor rights. By examining the ratified conventions in details, we aim to identify the standpoint of the countries[2]. Despite the importance of fundamental labor standards, there stands a gap between Muslim countries and others. As Table 1 demonstrates, among the 45 countries in which Muslim population is the majority, only 27 of these nations ratified all of the conventions by the year of 2013. However, none of the Muslim countries refused to sign all of the FLS, and there is a lack of willingness in Muslim countries in participating in conventions especially related to union rights. It appears that only 29 Muslim countries ratified Right to Organize and Collective Bargaining Convention and 36 Muslim countries ratified Freedom of Association and Protection of the Right to Organize Convention. Considering the other FLS, equal remuneration convention is the one which is ratified by the least number of Muslim countries.

Labor laws, like other institutional structures, are very diverse all around the world. They are affected by different mechanisms like legal, political, economic and cultural conditions of a country. As the policies are carried out by politicians, an investigation on labor laws will shed some light on government's perceptions on the issue. Even though ratifications are not mandatory, we believe signing a convention is an indication to comply with the rules.

Table 1. Ratification of ILO fundamental labor standards (as of 2013)

No.	ILO Convention	Year of Adoption	Number of Muslim Countries
Union Rights			
87	Freedom of Association and Protection of the Right to Organize Convention	1948	29
98	Right to Organize and Collective Bargaining Convention	1949	36
Forced Labor			
29	Forced Labor Convention	1930	43
105	Abolition of Forced Labor Convention	1957	43
Child Labor			
138	Minimum Age Convention	1973	41
182	Worst Forms of Child Labor Convention	1999	44
Discrimination			
100	Equal Remuneration Convention	1951	39
111	Discrimination (Employment and Occupation) Convention	1958	42

Source: Authors' estimate based on ILO data (ILO, 2015).

Left-hand side of the Figure 1 depicts the evolution of FLS in countries where the majority of the population is Muslim (51% or more), or the majority is from another religion. We observe that during the sample period, Muslim countries on average have a lower level of FLS with respect to the other countries. In the right-hand side of the Figure 1 we investigate the same issue by examining total labor standards (TLS). There are 189 conventions in total labor standards, and here we try to analyze the ratified conventions by time across countries separating them according to the majority of their population being either Muslim or from another religion. Compared to the FLS, the difference is now more striking. There is a clear difference between the number of labor standards that are ratified by Muslim and non-Muslim countries. The total number of ratification decreases a few in the middle of 1990s and 2000s, but the difference is about ten, and it does not change dramatically during the period. As we have mentioned above even though ILO does not have any sanctioning power, FLS can be considered as the basis of all labor laws. So from this perspective, we can understand why both Muslim and non-Muslim countries are close in FLS, and there stands a gap on TLS.

In Figure 2, we analyze the Muslim countries according to their geographical location. In the left-hand side of the Figure 2, we observe that from the 1960s to 2010, African Muslim countries have a greater number of FLS than the Asian Muslim countries. Although the number is equalized at the beginning of 2000, on average, African countries ratified a larger number of FLS by the end of 2013. In the the right-hand side of the Figure 2, we compare TLS. In this case, there is a clearer difference during the whole period. It appears that African Muslim countries attach more importance to ILO's labor standards than the Asian Muslim countries. The difference between the total labor standards is increasing from 1960 to 1993. Although the difference decreases after that year, by the end of the sample period, African countries ratified more conventions than the Asian Muslim countries.

Next, we decompose Muslim countries according to income level. Based on World Bank classification, Muslim countries classified as low-income, middle-income, and high-income countries. In the

Figure 1. International labor standards in Muslim and non-Muslim countries

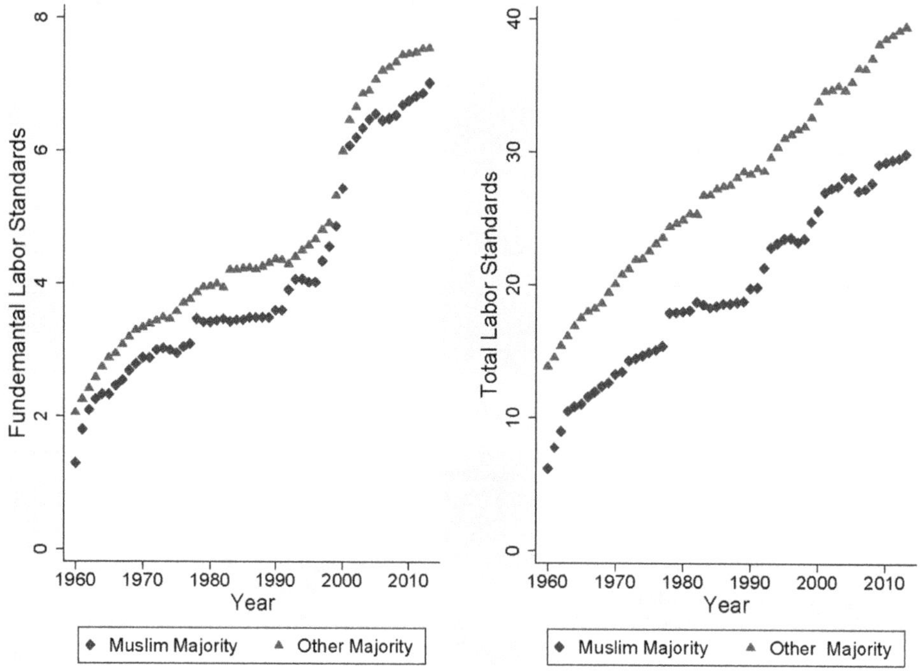

Figure 2. International labor standards in Muslim countries (by region)

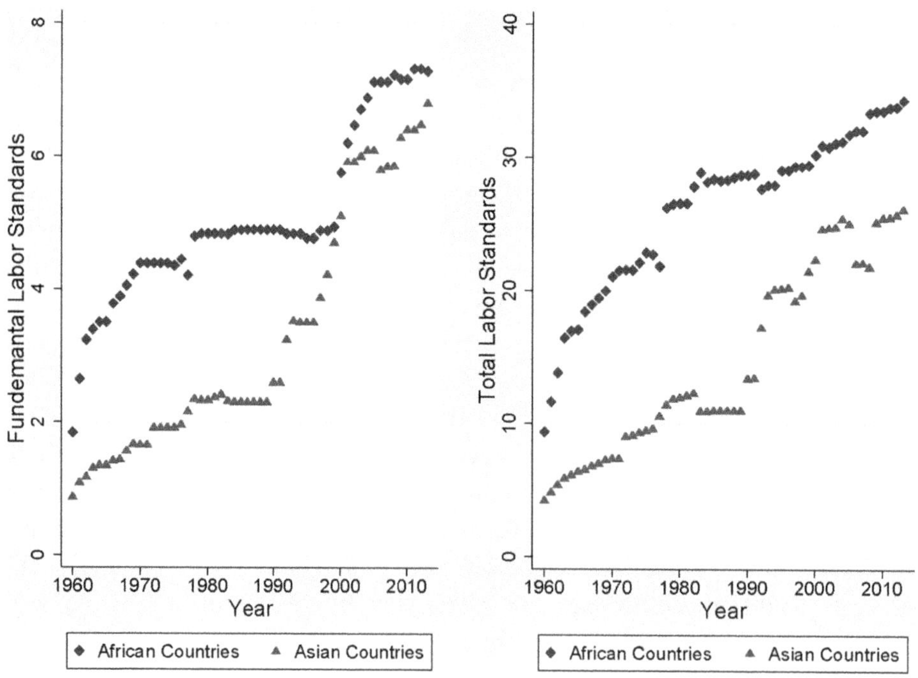

the left-hand side of Figure 3, we depict FLS based on income classification. The figure shows a very interesting observation. It appears that low-income Muslim countries ratified more FLS than the middle and high-income Muslim countries. There is a very evident difference between low and middle-income Muslim countries and high-income Muslim countries. On the other hand, low-income Muslim countries start with a bit lower level of FLS than the middle-income Muslim countries but then until 2000, they have a greater level of FLS. By 2013 low-income Muslim countries have a slightly higher number of FLS than middle-income Muslim countries, and both groups of countries has greater number of FLS than high-income Muslim countries. In the right-hand side of the Figure 3, we compare Muslim countries according to the TLS. It seems that the trend for FLS is also prevalent for TLS. Low and middle-income Muslim countries start from the same level, then we observe a separation from the mid-1960s to 2000, and they reach the same level again. However, the total number of ILO ratifications is much lower in the high-income Muslim countries during the whole period.

Finally, we decompose Muslim countries according to the legal origin in Figure 4. By splitting the countries according to their legal origin, we try to reveal the link between institutional background and labor standards. Muslim countries are classified according to whether they are ruled by Shari'a (Islamic law), by a mixed system (Islamic and another legal system e.g. common law) or by a civil law system. In order to specify the legal origin in Muslim countries, we used data from the CIA Factbook whether the country had Common Law/Civil Law/Shari'a Law or mixed systems. Here we have to construct our own data relying on CIA Factbook due to some inconsistencies in La Porta, Lopez-de-Silanes, Shleifer, and Vishny (1997) data. The main problem emerges that their data and CIA Factbook legal origin does not fit. La Porta et al. (1997)'s classification of countries into legal origin depends on Rene David's classification, and their classification is widely criticized (Licht, 2005). Their data accepts Shari'a Law

Figure 3. International labor standards in Muslim countries (by income)

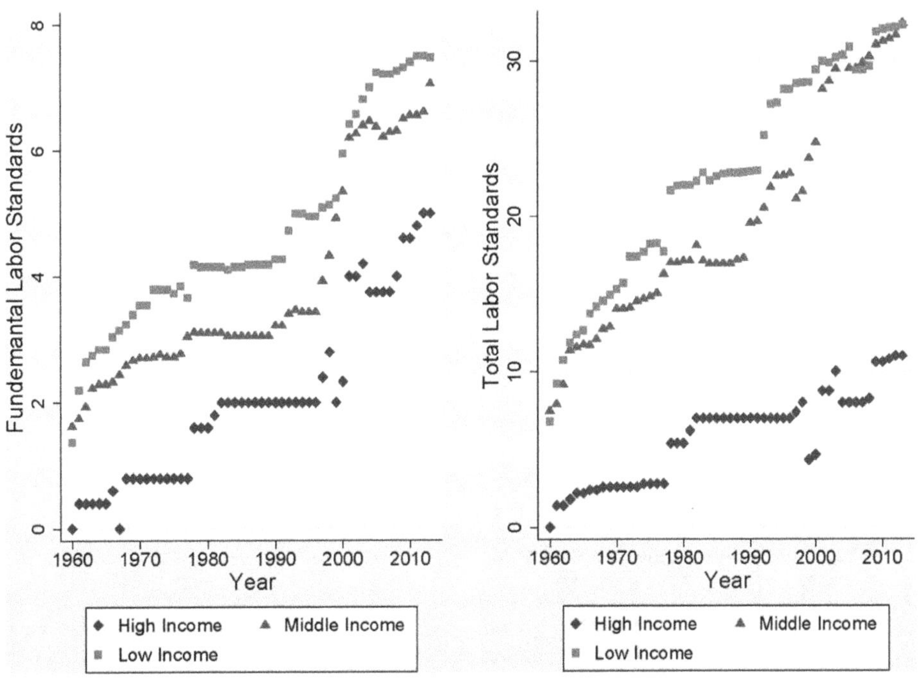

countries as common law countries, but we think they should be analyzed separately. Analyzing the legal origin data and countries in detail, we decided that using CIA Factbook would be more convincing.

The left-hand side of the Figure 4 represents the evolution of FLS. It shows that during the whole period, civil law countries have the highest share of FLS than the Islamic law countries and mixed system countries. By 2013, civil law countries have FLS almost equal to 8, mixed around 7 and sharia countries 6.2. Considering the total number of labor standards in the right-hand side of the Figure 4, we observe that civil law and mixed countries start from the same level. Although, the lines intersect at some periods, by 2013, civil law Muslim countries have a greater number of TLS than the mixed Muslim countries. In addition, both groups of countries ratified much more ILO conventions than Islamic law countries during the whole period. By 2013, the difference between civil law and Islamic law countries is equal to 15 conventions.

The Case of Turkey

Turkey and ILO have a long history since Turkey became a member state of ILO in 18.07.1932. This date demonstrates the early petition of labor rights in a Muslim country, and it can be linked to the ideology of the country at that time. After the establishment of Turkish Republic, the legislators have codified its civil law followed the example of the Codes of Switzerland in 1927. In line with these policies, the state had started to enact social laws in line with Ataturk's statist policies (the legislators have codified its civil law followed the example of the Codes of Switzerland in 1927 and the state had started to enact social laws in line with Ataturk's statist policies). These rights include the protection of public health, national and public holidays. Even though these rights had connections with labor laws, they were not

Figure 4. International labor standards in Muslim countries (by legal system)

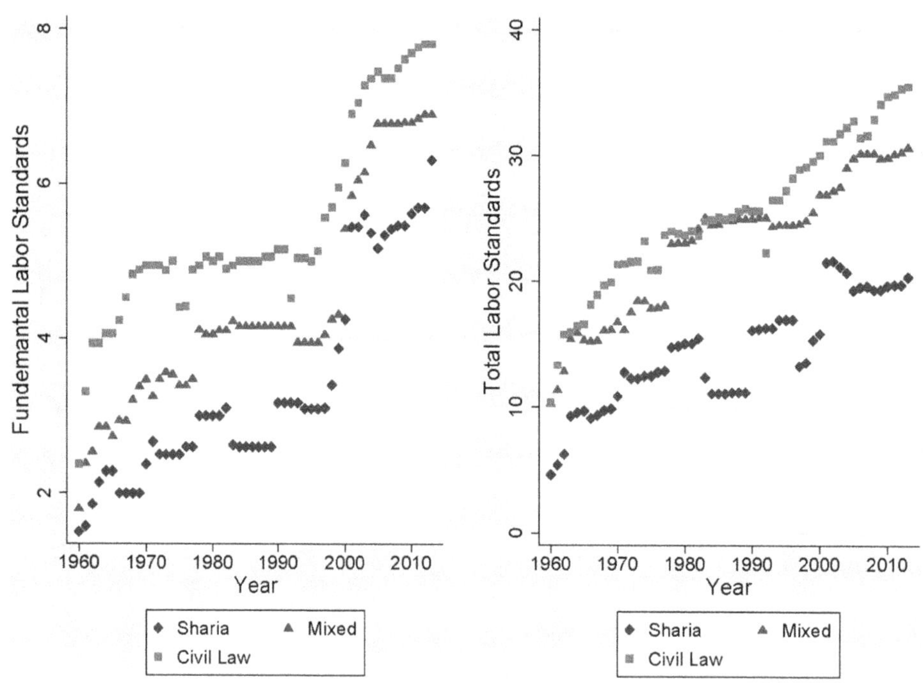

recognized by a direct labor law at that time. It might be argued that due to war conditions and limited industrial production, the government did not want to strengthen labor forces on purpose. There were several attempts on different occasions, but a well-established labor law was not enacted until 1937 (Demir, 2007).

The first Turkish Labor Act (Nr. 3008) can be considered as a modern document for the fact that it was prepared according to the agreements of ILO and for the first time the lives and rights of workers were safeguarded and institutionalized by the state. But there were still some missing encounters because the act did not recognize the employees' right to engage in collective bargaining and had tightened the existing restrictions on strikes and locks out by introducing penal sanctions. One reason for such and act was the protection of newly founded state enterprises.

First ratified convention with ILO was on C045- Underground work (women) convention in 1938. No female, whatever her age, shall be employed on underground work in any mine. Primarily this convention can be criticized on the grounds of gender discrimination but considering the traditional and religious background of the country signing this petition seemed to fit, and no criticism was made at the time of ratification.

In 1946 the Ministry of Labor was established, and just a year later Turkey's first Trade Unions Act was passed. More conventions signed between ILO and the new ministry e.g. C014- Weekly rest convention and Workmen's Compensation (occupational diseases). In 1952, Right to Organize and Collective bargaining convention was enacted. An interesting milestone in Turkish labor history is the constitution of 1961, which was prepared after a coup by armed forces and intellectuals. The constitution was important because it highlighted economic and social development while emphasizing the importance of basic rights of minimum wages and social security (Viner, 1992). It also guaranteed the right to strike and to bargain collectively by the constitution. In the following years, Abolition of Forced Labor in 1961 and Equal Remuneration and Discrimination conventions in 1967 were ratified. Unfortunately, due to political instability and economic crisis the country confronted another coup in 1980 which also abolished the 1961 Constitution.

Compared to 1961 Constitution, 1982 Constitution was more detailed and restrictive. Despite the restrictions an important core convention was ratified, Freedom of Association and Protection of the Right to Organize, in 1993. During the 1990s, Turkey tried to increase the length of its mandatory education, and in line with this policy, the government ratified another core ILO convention on the Minimum Age for Employment in 1998, Forced Labor convention in 1999 and Eliminating the Worst Forms of Child Labor in 2001. The law on trade unions and collective labor agreements have amended once more in 2012 replacing the much criticized earlier legislation. By 2013, Turkey ratified 59 conventions out of 189 labor standards. Hence Turkey does not appear to be very different from other countries in which Muslim population is the majority but compared to their average of 32 conventions the country's position is relatively better.

EXPLAINING THE DIFFERENCES BETWEEN MUSLIM COUNTRIES

As can be seen from the previous section, the evidence reveals that in Muslim countries ILO's FLS are ratified below the average, and they are even less ratified in the countries which are located in Asia, which are richer and where Islamic legal system is accepted. This result brings us to the question of why there stands an obvious gap between the Muslim countries. In this section, we will try to answer the reasons behind this fact. We think the practice of law might have a significant effect on Muslim countries. As we have mentioned before the data about the legal origin comes from the CIA Factbook, and it is differentiated according to their data on Common Law/Civil Law/Islamic Law or mixed countries. Before proceeding further, it might be useful to take a closer look at the Muslim countries.

Many people assume that most Muslim people live in the Middle East but in fact, this region constitutes about 35 percent of the total world Muslim population. Most populous Muslim states, Indonesia, Pakistan, Bangladesh, and India, are all outside the Middle East. Only 19 of the Muslim countries can be found in the Middle East, and not all of these countries have Arab populations. Most of this region was under the Ottoman Rule for centuries, and traces of Ottoman ruling can be seen even today. This fact can be related to major legal reforms, including the replacement of Islamic law with civil law in almost all areas (Moors, 1999). But as we all know, countries cannot choice their legal origin rationally. Legal origins are adopted mainly through conquest and colonization. This logic also explains how civil law is extended to Near East, northern and sub-Saharan Africa, Indochina, and Oceania during the colonial era. As mentioned before we have analyzed the Muslim countries according to their geographical location and our results have revealed that African countries have ratified more conventions than Asian Muslim countries. There is no rational reason to think that geography is related to ratifying labor standards. In addition, the fact that richer Muslim countries ratify fewer labor standards seems contradictory in the beginning; however, looking deeply we see that these countries are oil-rich countries such as Kuwait and Saudi Arabia. Hence workers are not very likely to demand high labor standards. Therefore, we believe that the primary suspect behind the disparity is the legal system of Muslim countries.

The impact of legal origin on countries' economic growth emerged basically in the late 1990s. By focusing on the explanation of differences between common and civil law traditions, Glaeser and Shleifer (2002) point out that civil law can become a control instrument of a bad government and hence have adverse consequences for the security of property rights which may be widened to other rights as well. Here the country's legal system is crucial because regulations in the labor markets are shaped by it. Normally, common law can be related to England and its colonies and the main differences between civil law and common law is; civil law relies on professional judges, legal codes, and written records, while common law relies on judges, case studies and oral arguments which give judges an active role in developing rules (Glaeser & Shleifer, 2002). Our findings reveal that more labor laws are ratified in civil law countries. Analyzing these civil law countries we have seen that they are also more democratic than the other Muslim countries. This can be evaluated that rights are better protected in this countries since in more democratic countries politicians have an interest to enhance the labor rights to get votes to be elected. On the contrary to our findings, La Porta, Lopez-de-Silanes, Shleifer, and Vishny (1998) argue that historically, common law countries tended to protect property rights more and limit governmental interferences, for the fact that judges in common law countries are relatively more independent. Here the difference might arise because of our limited focus on the countries. But we have to add one interesting fact about their study, which is in their data they accepted Shari'a/Islamic Law countries as common law countries. We, however, think countries that have accepted Islamic Law and English common law are very diverse and cannot be analyzed under the same classification.

The principles of labor law can be found in Muslim legal discourse as early as the first years of the Islamic faith. In some Muslim countries, issues related to labor are solved according to Islamic law. Islamic law is comprised of the two Islamic sources of religious law: Qur`an (Koran) and Prophetic Tradition. For questions not directly addressed in the primary sources, the application of sharia is extended through consensus of the religious scholars thought to embody the consensus of the Muslim community (ijma) and the Qiyas. Qiyas is a method of analogical reasoning that aims to govern a new situation with an old rule as long as this new situation is similar to that governed by the old rule (Elsaman, 2011).

Unfortunately, literature on Islam and labor laws is very limited, and Islamic law influences the lives of Muslims differently according to their established legal system. Some Muslim countries have Islamic (the Sharia) law, some French civil law and a few of them have English common law tradition. One might think that the legal origin can be related to the percentage of Muslim people living in the community but it does not have a significant effect on countries legal origin. Another interesting situation occurs in the application of legal laws in Muslim countries. Some countries have chosen to integrate Islamic law with their traditional law or French civil law. In these mixed legal systems, Muslim countries have chosen to keep their marriage and personal status laws based on the Islamic law.

In this study, we have focused on eight fundamental rights defined in four categories in Muslim countries and our research has given us a perspective to clarify the situation in these countries. Except the United Arab Emirates and Somalia, all the countries have ratified Worst Forms of Child Labor Convention. Considering the Islamic view on child, it is no surprise that this convention is the most ratified one. Islamic law prohibits oppression of children and any kind of abuse, insult, and exploitation. The rights specific to children's conditions are considered divine (Abdulrazzak, 2014) and safeguarded in Islam. The problem of child labor is not just related to legal origin. Despite the ILO's aim to eliminate the worst forms of child labor by 2016, by just looking at sub-Saharan Africa this objective will not be easy to fulfill.

The least ratified convention is Freedom of Association and Protection of the Right to Organize Convention. The Islamic texts prohibit the economic exploitation of workers, and the employer-employee relationship is based on a brotherhood relationship. Moreover, Al-Faruqi (1985) argues that the aims of both Islam and trade unions are justice, so not only are compatible, but Islam encourages unionism. According to Elsaman (2011), applying the general principle founded by the Qur'an on freedom of assembling and cooperation, and the examples driven by the Muslims' history, the recent local employment laws of almost all Muslim countries provide for the right to collective bargaining and freedom of association. Hence there seems to be a contradiction in terms of workers' rights in Muslim countries. Depending on this, it would not be surprising to have more countries ratifying this convention in the future.

CONCLUSION

Protecting labor rights is a very controversial issue since it has many aspects that need to be studied from basic human rights to production costs. For this reason, there are remarkable differences across countries in terms of labor market institutions, law and practice regulations. Implementing labor standards is going to prove the countries' respect for its own citizens and also improve their life quality. However, nobody can deny the realities of a more competitive world where some governments close their eyes for the race to the bottom in order to decrease production costs and attract more foreign investment.

In this study, we aimed to document how Muslim countries consider labor rights in terms of core and the total labor standards of ILO. The descriptive analysis indicates that on average Muslim countries ratified much fewer numbers of conventions than other countries. In addition, there is considerable heterogeneity across Muslim countries. Richer Muslim countries ratified fewer conventions than the poor ones; African Muslim countries ratified more conventions than the Asian Muslim countries and civil law Muslim countries ratified more conventions than the Islamic law ruled Muslim countries and the countries which have mixed legal system.

Although Islamic rules tend to protect labor, the evidence based on ILO data reveals the opposite. There is a high heterogeneity across Muslim countries, and this heterogeneity arises from the legal origin. The application of legal origin theory in economics has been extensively used recently. It is for sure that this theory has created strong criticism but despite its flaws, looking at our evidence, we think that there stands a significant relationship between the legal origin and labor rights in Muslim countries. Our analyses have shown us that Muslim countries with civil law tradition tend to sign more labor conventions than common law tradition, probably because of the fact that these countries are also more democratic than the other Muslim countries. This result reveals that politicians have an interest to protect the rights of the workers to bc rcclcctcd.

REFERENCES

Abdulrazzak, N. L. (2014). *My rights are divine: A closer look at children's rights in the Muslim Arab world.* Bloomington, IN: AuthorHouse.

Aidt, T., & Tzannatos, Z. (2005). *The cost and benefits of collective bargaining: A survey.* Cambridge Working Papers in Economics, No 0541. Cambridge: Cambridge University.

Aksoy, T., & Gönel, F. (2016). Revisiting FDI-led growth hypothesis: The role of sector characteristics. *The Journal of International Trade & Economic Development, 25*(8), 1144–1166. doi:10.1080/09638199.2016.1195431

Al-Faruqi, I. R., & Al-Banna, G. (1985). *Towards Islamic labour and unionism: Three papers.* Cairo: International Islamic Confederation of Labor.

Anner, M., & Caraway, T. (2010). International institutions and workers rights: Between labor standards and market flexibility. *Studies in Comparative International Development, 45*(2), 151–169. doi:10.1007/s12116-010-9064-x

Basu, K. (1999). Child labor: Cause, consequence, and cure, with remarks on international labor standards. *Journal of Economic Literature, 37*(3), 1083–1119. doi:10.1257/jel.37.3.1083

Blomström, M., & Kokko, A. (2003). *Human capital and inward FDI.* EIJS Working Papers Series, 167. Stockholm: The European Institute of Japanese Studies.

Botero, J., Djankov, S., La Porta, R., Lopez-de-Silanes, F., & Shleifer, A. (2005). The regulation of labor. *The Quarterly Journal of Economics, 119*(4), 1339–1382. doi:10.1162/0033553042476215

Davies, R. B., & Vadlamannati, K. C. (2013). A race to the bottom in labor standards? An empirical investigation. *Journal of Development Economics, 103*, 1–14. doi:10.1016/j.jdeveco.2013.01.003

Demir, F. (2007). Atatürk dönemi çalışma hayatımız. *TÜHİS İş Kanunu ve İktisat Dergisi, 20*(4), 1–20.

Doepke, M., & Zilibotti, F. (2009). International labor standards and the political economy of child-labor regulation. *Journal of the European Economic Association, 7*(2-3), 508–518. doi:10.1162/JEEA.2009.7.2-3.508

Duanmu, J. L. (2014). A race to lower standards? Labor standards and location choice of outward FDI from the BRIC countries. *International Business Review*, *23*(3), 620–634. doi:10.1016/j.ibusrev.2013.10.004

Elsaman, R. (2011). Corporate social responsibility in Islamic law: Labor and employment. *Yonsei Law Journal*, *2*(1), 64–93.

Felbermayr, G., Prat, J., & Schmerer, H. J. (2008). *Globalization and labor market outcomes: Wage bargaining, search frictions and firm heterogeneity*. IZA Discussion Paper, 3363. Retrieved from http://digital.csic.es/bitstream/10261/44732/3/Globalization%20and%20labor%20market.pdf

Glaeser, E., & Shleifer, A. (2002). Legal origins. *The Quarterly Journal of Economics*, *117*(4), 1193–1229. doi:10.1162/003355302320935016

Hur, J., & Zhao, L. (2009). Labor standards, labor-management bargaining and international rivalry. *Journal of Economic Behavior & Organization*, *71*(2), 259–272. doi:10.1016/j.jebo.2009.04.002

International Labour Organization. (2015). *Ratifications of fundamental conventions by country*. Retrieved from http://www.ilo.org/dyn/normlex/en/f?p=NORMLEXPUB:10011:0:NO:P10011_DISPLAY_BY,P10011_CONVENTION_TYPE_CODE:1,F

La Porta, R., Lopez-de-Silanes, F., Shleifer, A., & Vishny, R. W. (1997). Legal determinants of external finance. *The Journal of Finance*, *52*(3), 1131–1150. doi:10.1111/j.1540-6261.1997.tb02727.x

La Porta, R., Lopez-de-Silanes, F., Shleifer, A., & Vishny, R. W. (1998). Law and finance. *Journal of Political Economy*, *106*(6), 1113–1155. doi:10.1086/250042

Licht, A., Goldschmidt, C., & Schwartz, S. H. (2005). Culture, law and corporate governance. *International Review of Law and Economics*, *25*(2), 229–255. doi:10.1016/j.irle.2005.06.005

McCrudden, C., & Davies, A. (2000). A perspective on trade and labor rights. *Journal of International Economic Law*, *3*(1), 43–62. doi:10.1093/jiel/3.1.43

Moors, A. (1999). Debating Islamic family law: Legal texts and social practices. In M. L. Meriwether & J. E. Tucker (Eds.), *A social history of women and gender in the modern Middle East* (pp. 141–176). Boulder, CO: Westview Press.

Noorbakhsh, F., Paloni, A., & Youssef, A. (2001). Human capital and FDI inflows to developing countries: New empirical evidence. *World Development*, *29*(9), 1593–1610. doi:10.1016/S0305-750X(01)00054-7

Peksen, D., & Blanton, R. G. (2016). The impact of ILO conventions on worker rights: Are empty promises worse than no promises? *The Review of International Organizations*. doi:10.1007/s11558-015-9241-9

Viner, J. (1992). Turkey, the EEC and labor law: Is harmonization possible. *Northwestern Journal of International Law & Business*, *13*(2), 445–476.

Xu, B. (2000). Multinational enterprises, technology diffusion, and host country productivity growth. *Journal of Development Economics*, *62*(2), 477–493. doi:10.1016/S0304-3878(00)00093-6

KEY TERMS AND DEFINITIONS

Child Labor: The employment of children in an industry or business, especially illegal or considered exploitative.

Discrimination: The practice of unfairly treating a person or group of people differently from other people or groups of people.

Forced Labor: Any work or services which people are forced to do against their will under the threat of some form of punishment.

International Labor Organization: ILO is a United Nations agency dedicated to improving labor conditions and living standards for men and women.

International Labor Standards: Standards refer to conventions agreed upon by international actors.

Labor Law: Those areas of law which appertain to the relationship between employers and employees and between employers and trade unions.

Labor Rights: Are a group of rules pertaining to working people and their organizations.

Labor Union: An association, combination of employees who band together to secure favorable wages, improved working conditions and better working hours.

ENDNOTES

1 See Basu (1999) for an extensive review of the international labor standards and child labor nexus.

2 See Table 2 in the appendix for the details of FLS in Muslim countries.

APPENDIX

Table 2. Core labor standards in Muslim countries

Country	Muslim Population (%)	C029 (1930)	C087 (1948)	C098 (1949)	C100 (1951)	C105 (1957)	C111 (1958)	C138 (1973)	C182 (1999)
Afghanistan	99.3				1969	1963	1969	2010	2010
Albania	56.7	1957	1957	1957	1957	1997	1997	1998	2001
United Arab Emirates	94.9	1982			1997	1997	2001		
Azerbaijan	93.4	1992	1992	1992	1992	2000	1992	1992	2004
Burkina Faso	60.5	1960	1960	1962	969	1997	1962	1999	2001
Bangladesh	89.5	1972	1972	1972	1998	1972	1972		2001
Bahrain	70.3	1981				1998	2000	2012	2001
Brunei Darussalam	78.8							2011	2008
Comoros	98	1978	1978	1978	1978	1978	2004	2004	2004
Djibouti	94	1978	1978	1978	1978	1978	2005	2005	2005
Algeria	99.1	1962	1962	1962	1962	1969	1969	1984	2001
Egypt	90	1955	1957	1954	1960	1958	1960	1999	2002
Guinea	85	1959	1959	1959	1967	1961	1960	2003	2003
Gambia	90	2000	2000	2000	2000	2000	2000	2000	2001
Indonesia	87.2	1950	1998	1957	1958	1999	1999	1999	2000
Iran	99.4	1957			1972	1959	1964		2002
Iraq	99	1962		1962	1963	1959	1959	1985	2001
Jordan	97.2	1966		1968	1966	1958	1963	1998	2000
Kazakhstan	70.2	2001	2000	2001	2001	2001	1999	2001	2003
Kyrgyzstan	75	1992	1992	1992	1992	1999	1992	1992	2004
Kuwait	76.7	1968	1961	2007		1961	1966	1999	2000
Lebanon	54	1977		1977	1977	1977	1977	2003	2001
Libya	96.6	1961	2000	1962	1962	1961	1961	1975	2000
Morocco	99.4	1957		1957	1979	1966	1963	2000	2001
Maldives	99.9	2013	2013	2013	2013	2013	2013	2013	2013
Mali	94.8	1960	1960	1964	1968	1962	1964	2002	2000
Mauritania	99.4	1961	1961	2001	2001	1997	1963	2001	2001
Malaysia	61.3	1957		1961	1997			1997	2000
Niger	80	1961	1961	1962	1966	1962	1962	1978	2000
Oman	85.9	1998				2005		2005	2001
Pakistan	96.4	1957	1951	1952	2001	1960	1961	2006	2001
Qatar	77.5	1998				2007	1976	2006	2000

continued on following page

Table 2. Continued

Country	Muslim Population (%)	C029 (1930)	C087 (1948)	C098 (1949)	C100 (1951)	C105 (1957)	C111 (1958)	C138 (1973)	C182 (1999)
Saudi Arabia	98.8	1978			1978	1978	1978		2001
Sudan	73	1957		1957	1970	1970	1970	2003	2003
Senegal	94	1960	1960	1961	1962	1961	1967	1999	2000
Sierra Leone	60	1961	1961	1961	1968	1961	1966	2011	2011
Somalia	99.8	1960				1961	1961		
Syrian Arab Republic	89.6	1960	1960	1957	1957	1958	1960	2001	2003
Chad	53.1	1960	1960	1961	1966	1961	1966	2005	2000
Tajikistan	85	1993	1993	1993	1993	1999	1993	1993	2005
Turkmenistan	89	1997	1997	1997	1997	1997	1997	2012	2010
Tunisia	99.4	1962	1957	1957	1968	1959	1959	1995	2000
Turkey	99.2	1998	1993	1952	1967	1961	1967	1998	2001
Uzbekistan	88	1992		1992	1992	1997	1992	2009	2008
Yemen	99.5	1969	1976	1969	1976	1969	1969	2000	2000

C029: Forced Labor; C087: Freedom of Association and Protection of Right to Organize; C098: Right to Organize and Collective Bargaining; C100: Equal Remuneration; C105: Abolition of Forced Labor; C111: Discrimination; C138: Minimum Age; C182: Worst Form of Child Labor

Chapter 2
Redefining the 21st Century Labor Paradigm:
Role of Contingent Workforce in the Indian Economy

Shaurya Sharma
Xavier School of Management, India

Shivankar Sharma
Shardul Amarchand Mangaldas & Co, India

ABSTRACT

At a time when the Indian subcontinent is beset with a burgeoning population, rapid urbanization, and high disposable incomes, the Indian economy is at a precarious stage of balancing demand uncertainties with pressures to minimize bottom line costs. As a consequence, there is great reliance on a dynamic workforce, which comprises of temporary, contract, and casual laborers referred to as the contingent workforce. A talent war is looming on the horizon and employers need to buckle up their workforce armory with an unparalleled employee value proposition, making the business landscape a tricky vehicle to maneuver. A robust strategic framework bolstered by prudent workforce management will aid an organization to fulfill its goals while isolating it from any legal liability. Technology can be used to leverage data analytically for job assessment and aid in seamless project execution. In sum, an approach sensitive to the legal, technological and psychological pillars of managing workers provides a comprehensive mechanism to counter issues associated with contingent workforce management.

INTRODUCTION

As per a survey conducted by The Associated Chambers of Commerce of India (ASSOCHAM) in 2013, the contingent workforce has seen an increase at a rate of 39% (Associated Chambers of Commerce of India [ASSOCHAM], 2014). Changing work styles, low-key government involvement (with relaxed regulatory framework) and emphasis on consumer-driven economy have been instrumental in driving

DOI: 10.4018/978-1-5225-2008-5.ch002

the growth of the Indian market. According to India Brand Equity Foundation, the Indian fast-moving consumer goods (FMCG) market alone is expected to increase at a compound annual growth rate (CAGR) of 14.7%, reaching $110.4 billion during the period 2012-2020 (India Brand Equity Foundation, 2016). Even though the manufacturing sector is facing a turbulent time, it is still the most labor-intensive industry (barring agriculture where disguised employment often distorts the employment figures), thereby providing employment to large scores of contingent workers. In such an environment, a number of business processes are dependent on out-of-payroll talent. This, in turn, warrants strategic management of such a workforce to meet the heightened human capital requirements of both the organization and potential employees.

BACKGROUND

In India, the proportion of the labor workforce to the overall population stands at 56% as compared to the world average of around 64%. The mismatch between male and female participation is glaring due to prevailing socio-economic factors, and the female labor force stands at a dismal 31% (among the lowest in the world) (Institute for Human Development, 2014). The informal sector (comprising of unincorporated and unorganized business units) employs an overwhelmingly large percentage of workers, and approximately 92% of the total workforce is engaged in enterprises ranging from small factories (SMEs) to pushcart vendors and agricultural labor (Planning Commission of India, 2007) (Korgaokar & Myrstad, 1997). Every second worker is self-employed in a small-scale economic activity, and every one out of three workers seeks employment on a day to day basis. Even among the 18% of the workers who are regular, less than 8% have a full-time employment which has a social protection scheme in place (Institute for Human Development, 2014).

The informal workers have negligible employee guaranteed social protection but the situation is changing due to recent intervention by the Government in the form of various national and state level social schemes (such as the Annapurna, Antyodaya Anna Yojana and Pension Schemes). However, most of the Indian labor laws apply to the formal sector, leaving the informal workers bereft of any legal safeguards.

Figure 1. Striking a delicate balance in the labor market

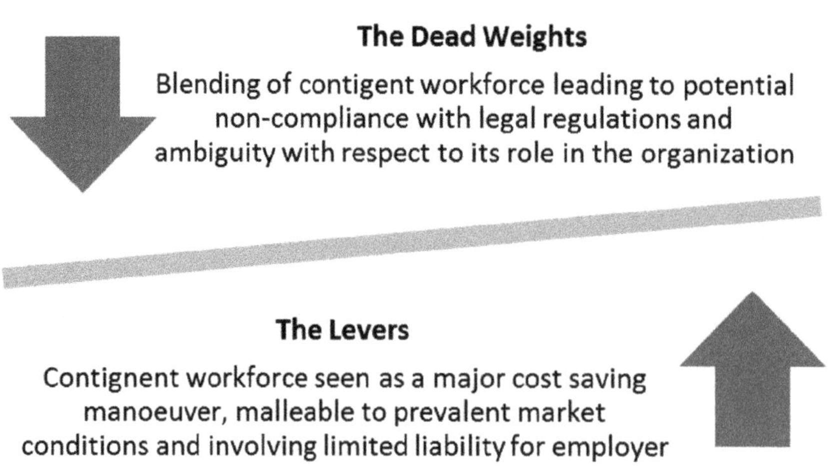

Poor education infrastructure combined with an unchecked growth of unorganised economy have led to rampant child labour (around 2% of children in the age group 5 to 14 were involved in labour in 2010) and debt bondage (Brown, 2008; International Labour Organization, 2008; Ministry of Statistics and Programme Implementation, 2014). A majority of laborers are uneducated, with approximately 30% of the workers having completed secondary education and only 10% of the workers having received any formal or informal vocational training (Swaminathan, 1991). The scarcity of regular employment makes access to skill acquisition programs limited, leading to an overlap between poverty and sub-standard employment quality (Chakrabarti, 2009). The labor scenario is further exacerbated by the fact the disadvantaged social groups (such as Scheduled Castes and Tribes) are disproportionately employed as low paid casual labors, especially in the low-productivity sectors, namely, agriculture and construction.

CONTINGENT WORKFORCE 2.0

Contingent workforce refers to those employees who fall either outside the norm of traditional hourly/salaried permanent employees or who are employed on a contingent basis. It includes eight major categories which are: temporary workers, part-time workers, outsourced workers, offshore workers, independent contractors, interns and consultants (Henson, 2008). The combined spending by companies on contingent workforce has been estimated to be $300 billion per year, with many economists predicting an accelerating rate in the near future (Gartside, Silverstone, Farley, & Cantrel, 2013). In 2012, the top Fortune 500 companies had 26% of their total workforce as contingent workers and by 2020 almost half of the private workforce would either be independent or contract workers at some point in their professional lives (MBO Partners, 2013; Dwyer, 2013).

There are broadly two classes of contingent workers: high skilled and low skilled workers; with each having different motivations and surrounding circumstances to take up contingent assignments. In today's rapidly evolving society, the global contingent workforce is incorporating well-educated workers who voluntarily take up flexible roles (which involve high skilled high-value work) while maintaining the same level of organizational engagement (Gartside et al., 2013). Nevertheless, the extended workforce in developing countries is still largely comprised of a weakly unionized workforce involved in low skilled work. India falls in this category with ManpowerGroup ranking India second in the world, only after China, in terms of availability of contingent workforce (India Business Insight, 2014). The Indian labor workforce primarily belongs to the unorganized sector where work exploitation is rampant and governmental regulation is abysmal (National Statistical Commission, 2012). The unorganized labor sector, having low productivity and high poverty, accounted for only 57% of India's national domestic product in 2006 even when it comprised of 94% of the total labor in India (Kulshreshtha, 2011; Bhalla, 2003; Kochhar, 2012).

The fundamental problems with contingent employees are low employee engagement and motivation arising largely because of lack of clarity on job role and assessments. Appealing to psychological requirements of the contingent employees thus goes a long way in ensuring the productivity of the employees. In addition, compliance with legal requirements is of paramount importance since non-compliance can have far reaching consequences for an organization's profitability and brand image. Therefore, human management of the Indian contingent workforce demands a deviation from traditional human resource management practices (Tetteh, 2016).

Figure 2. Proposed management framework for a productive contingent workforce

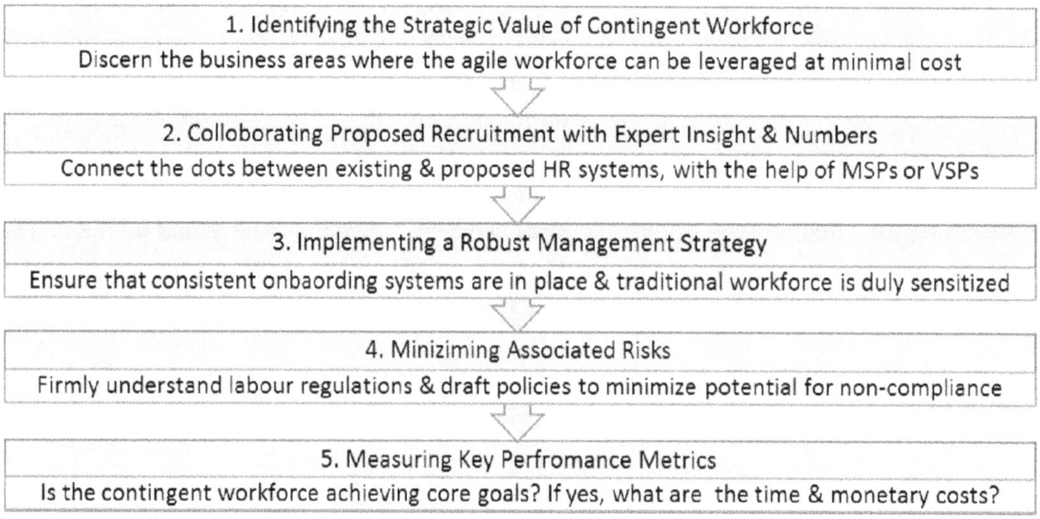

READING BETWEEN THE LINES: NECESSARY LEGAL COMPLIANCES

At the outset, organizations should view extended workforce as a key talent source and not a labor arbitrage. The channels and structures encompassing an extended workforce should go beyond the confines of mere compliances with labor laws and involve all the functional areas working as talent brokers in tandem (Smith, Gartside, Sloman, & Marshall, 2014). Organizations should strive to ensure that the Ten Principles of the UN Global Compact apply to the extended workforce and that it is engaged with not on an external but on a similar footing as an internal workforce. However, at the same time, a clear distinction in the role of authority has to be defined in order to not misconstrue the prevailing employer-employee relationship (Reardon, 2011).

Sham and Camouflage

The Supreme Court, on a reading of the Indian Contract Labour (Regulation and Abolition) Act, 1970, has laid down that contingent workers, on the fulfillment of certain conditions, are eligible to be regularized, essentially losing their contingent character and being on par with regular workers. Additionally, in cases where the contingent workmen employed by the contractor perform the same or similar kind of work as the workmen directly employed by the principal employer of the establishment, Rule 25(2)(v) (a) of the Indian Contract Labour (Regulation and Abolition) Rules 1971 states that organisations have to ensure a parity between the two subsets of workmen in terms of the wage rates, holidays, hours of work and other conditions of service.

Being mindful of the above legal dispositions and relevant case laws *(International Airports Authority Employees Union Case, 1997; Bharat Heavy Electricals Ltd. Case, 2003; National Thermal Power Corporation Ltd. Case, 2003),* the establishment in cases of same or similar kind of work, should clearly segregate the job profiles of the contingent and permanent workforce while vying for social integration of the two. The organization in light of the Supreme Court judgments should not interfere in the direct employer and employee relationship existing between the contractor and contingent workmen since instances of doing so could result in a possible sham contract emerging between the principal employer and the contractor. The focus of the management should instead be on enhancing the contractors' capabilities by specifying the employee types, real-time project portfolio apart from proactive project planning and consistent tracking of project expenses (Shahstree, 2013).

Retrenchment of Temporary Workers

While a temporary workman is categorically defined in the Industrial Employment (Standing Orders) Act, 1946 and the Model Standing Orders framed thereunder, there is an ambiguity on whether there is a need for an employer to give notice when the temporary worker's contract expires or when the employer chooses not to renew the contract. In order to maintain congenial relations with the local populace, it is advisable for the employer to follow a last-come-first-go employment policy in which the last one to be hired becomes the first to be laid off during a downturn while ensuring that the retrenched workers are paid a subsistence wage, which includes retrenchment and gratuity payments.

ENABLING THE TECHNOLOGY ECOSYSTEM IN LABOUR MANAGEMENT

A particular tool of handling contingent workforce which has not been extensively utilized is data management. More are the contingent workers employed by an organization, more difficult it becomes for the employer to grapple with the task of identifying and distinguishing them. Therefore, every organization should have an employee management system in place for holistic talent management (Gibson, 2015). Within such systems, employers can have complete visibility into all enterprise projects involving robust performance tracking of permanent and contingent workers (including contractors), headcount tracking, project management and employee system access. In addition to making sure that payments are promptly made to contractors, cloud-based softwares protect employers from non-compliance repercussions while enabling them to recognize high performance, negotiate better rates and delineate clear-cut project criteria. While there is a plethora of data management systems available to organizations ranging from vendor on premises (VOP) to managed service providers (MSP), stand-alone vendor management systems (VMS) provide the most simplified solutions of the lot.

To put in place such elaborate data crunching mechanisms, HR needs to play the critical role of a collaborator and needs to be analytics focused. In order to leverage data points effectively, HR and the in-house analytics team must be trained to collect, manage and interpret data in shortest spans of time. In the case of low employee engagement or productivity among the contingent workforce, it must be conveyed that the key is to identify the chief organizational behavior and psychological characteristics and try to establish a correlation with the existing data to determine any causal relationship. To ensure a hassle-free management of the workers (in terms of a single snapshot of the entire number of contingent workers employed at any time), it is essential to include a contingent workforce based management system under the ambit of the overall employee management system. The obtained employee details, demographic characteristics and job roles can be highly useful in solving several problems encountered in contingent workforce employment, which are listed as follows:

Figure 3. VMS as a holistic talent management tool
ManpowerGroup Solutions.

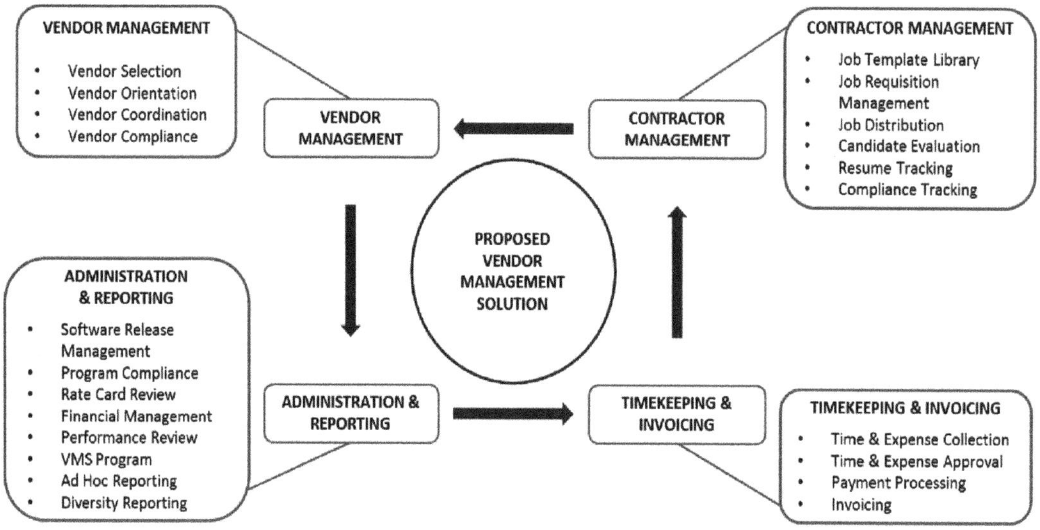

1. Categorization of workers under:
    a. Temporary,
    b. Contract,
    c. Casual,
    d. Others.
2. Analysis of workers' respective skills,
3. Snapshot of workers' past working experience, organizations, etc.,
4. Credible contractors/agencies for future association.

Numbers

Getting the right number of workers for a given task and/or an organization at any point of time is an onerous task. Data analysis of the past records will help forecast future requirement based on season, production levels and demand fluctuations in the market. A workforce analysis of the contingent workers with respect to their productivity can be done, and an optimal number may be reached which will aid in achieving the optimal utilization of the required number of contingent workers. A comprehensive management system should be employed to take care of official paperwork and maintenance of records, thereby ensuring smooth completion of any legal requirement (Daly, 2013). Any outlier spikes in particular time periods may be identified with adequate reasons and future preventive measures be subsequently employed.

Role Stressors

One reason of disengagement and hence lowered productivity of contingent workers is a lack of role clarity and increased stress. The nature of work getting distributed in *ad hoc* periods leads to imbalance and stress in both physical and mental terms. Data management systems should record the number of hours which have been put in by the contingent workers and work allocation should be accordingly calibrated to reduce any instances of employee stress. Further, a detailed analysis of a worker's unique skillset will aid in allocating him/her to the best-suited job while maintaining the required workplace satisfaction (Etheredge, Dorf, & Thakkar, 2009).

Contractors/Agencies

Due to the presence of a number of contractors it becomes imperative to identify the best ones arranged as per the desired competencies. Mapping workers to their contractor and measuring their aggregate productivity level plays a crucial role in identifying a credible contractor workforce. In addition, customized demands of the organization and proper documentation of contractors' work can pinpoint priority contract points for any future commitment (ASSOCHAM, 2014).

Figure 4. Detailed management strategies for ICs (Independent Contractors)
Source: Dwyer, 2012.

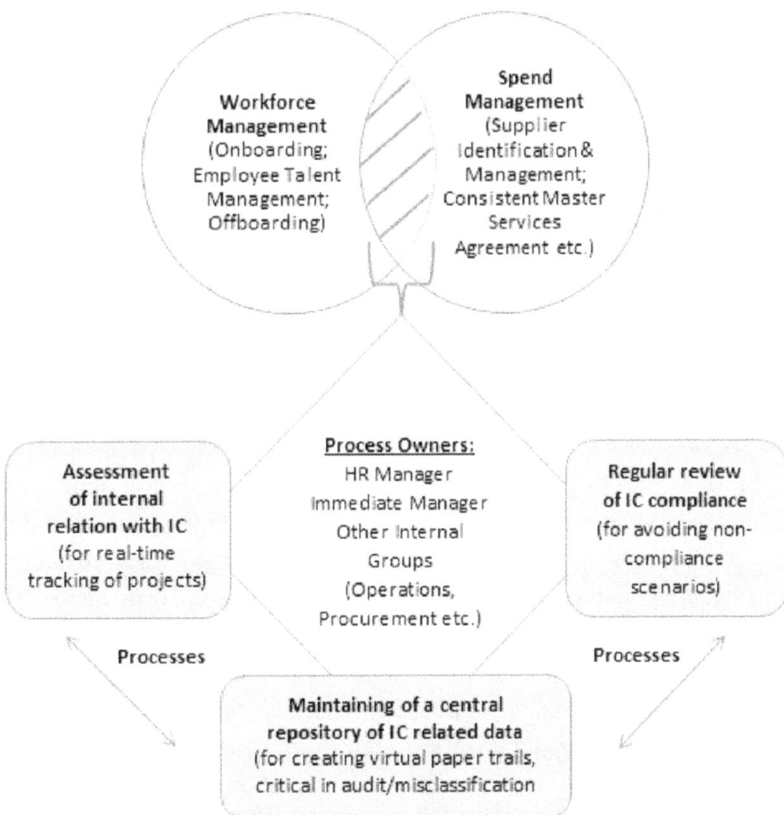

PROACTIVE ENGAGEMENT WITH CONTINGENT WORKERS

Previously, workers were hired on a temporary or contract basis in order to gain a cost advantage, but it is now widely understood that the true gains lie in creating synergy for this volatile talent base. There must be clear communication from the employer's side to the permanent employees regarding their job security before contingent talent is brought into the organization. Permanent employees should be reassured that the contingent workforce serves as a partner in furthering the goals of the organization (in cases of contract labor) or acts as a buffer during lean periods (in cases of temporary and casual labor). Meanwhile, to keep the contract and temporary employees motivated, the length of their employment should be increased while reducing the number of workers in a specific role to a minimum. Furthermore, the competency models adopted by the organization (or the contractor), which are used to map job profiles to required competencies, need to clarify the differentiating parameters vis-à-vis knowledge, technical skills, and behavioural traits required of the contingent workforce as opposed to those required of the permanent workers for all job profiles (LeBleu & Sobkowiak, 1995).

To project oneself as an employer or partner of choice, the organization needs to proactively embark on branding and reward strategies that pay competitive compensation packages. Global MNCs need to tweak their global HR policies to suit the local culture in an endeavor to address the internal division of labor within the organization (Edwards & Kuruvilla, 2005). All on-site contingent employees across industries should be included in the organization's engagement activities such as festivals or feasts. The high skilled workers look for flexibility in their professional or personal lives and thus there is some level of dissonance. On the other hand, the low-skilled workers' value monetary rewards the highest and can hence adhere to unfavorable work standards. Since the contingent workforce is not directly employed by the firm they work for, the low-skilled workers sometimes feel alienated and perceive a step-motherly treatment from the management. Targeted employee communication at specific groups or individuals along with 360-degree feedback and employee surveys (undertaken by contractors in case of contract labor) is essential for gaining valuable insights as to the needs of the contingent workforce (Oracle, 2010). Thus, tailor made employee engagement strategies at each level of workers' hierarchy need to be established for the seamless working of organizations.

Every employer seeks to have a workforce which is not only productive but is also loyal to the organization. In this light, it is quite surprising that only 30-35% of companies conduct background checks of contingent workers even when $50 billion is lost annually to employee theft and fraud. It has been documented in a recent HireRight survey that contingent employees are 92% more likely to have a criminal record than their permanent counterparts and 50% more likely to have a drug history (HireRight, 2015). Moreover, hiring through outsourcing agencies and contractors may not meet the screening standards of the organization, thereby making it vulnerable to miscreants who can bypass the internal checks of the organization. To place the above facts colloquially, while one needs to have a security check and an escort in order to visit the CEO of an organization, a cleaning vendor often has unfettered access, with no prior background screening done. Background screening should be made a standard hiring policy under the supervision of a central security division and should be applicable to the entire workforce including the temporary, casual and contractual hires. Nevertheless, the employer shouldn't discriminate against contingent hires under the garb of being overly cautious against the hiring of anti-social elements. Everyone enjoys the right to equal employment as prescribed by the Indian Constitution and thus he or she should be allowed to avail of it in practice.

INDUSTRIAL RELATIONS AND CULTURAL INTEGRATION

Plants are most vulnerable to the simmering tension between workers and management. India has traditionally been a welfare state, and its manufacturing sector can be best described as a place of tense calm. In 2012, the nation was shaken to the core when a general manager of human resources was charred to death in a workers' triggered violence at Maruti Suzuki's Manesar Plant (Press Trust of India, 2012). The unfortunate event brought to the fore, the importance of trust between the employer and the employee, especially in cases where there is a great amount of information asymmetry. The key lesson to draw is that the employer shouldn't explicitly interfere in the internal politics of the workforce as it may lead to further alienation of workers. Instead, the prudent strategy for the management is to ensure that it has the upper hand at the negotiation table vis-à-vis the workers' unions. In order to achieve this, the employer should recognize only those unions which are bereft of a violent past and enjoy the support of the majority of members. In addition, workers are more inclined to be a part of a union which has the power and authority to engage in participatory management. Thus, the employer not only succeeds in establishing a channel of communication with the workers but also keeps the militant unions fragmented from the overall functioning of the plant. To enforce strict discipline within the plant premises, the employer needs to:

1. Identify violent/distrustful workers and closely monitor them for pre-emptive action,
2. Educate workers of the plant's standing orders and make them visible for one and all,
3. Fast track disciplinary inquiry against guilty workers (in case of any dispute),
4. Maintain a regular contact with the local police station and seek its advice,
5. Objective qualifying parameters for background screening of potential workers.

To foster sustainable relationships with unions at the nascent stage, the employer needs to contextualize the social capital and workers' motive with respect to changing times (Hyman, 2007). For instance, a representation driven union operates under a leadership model (i.e. socialist) which is different from that of a service driven union (i.e. modern day capitalist) (Ewing, 2005). Notwithstanding the adopted ideology of the unions, the employer has to aid them in understanding the nuances of workforce politics and indirectly mentor them in framing the charter of demands for two reasons:

1. Newly formed unions are immature and thus doesn't have either the political mileage or experience to translate workers' angst into demands that are both tangible and pragmatic.
2. Employer can influence the decision-making process as there are no formal/concrete demands.

The management should recognize unions by holding elections at the earliest opportunity since with passage of time, militant unions are bound to act as a hindrance to the process by feeding off the insecurity of workers. To uphold the trust of the workforce and ensure that deserving candidates win the election, employer should prevent the following scenarios from taking place-

1. **Vicious Election Atmosphere:** There should be no booth capturing or under the table deals.
2. **Horse Trading:** Candidates shouldn't be allowed to jump ships for vested interests.
3. **Result Distortion:** Fence sitters should be encouraged to vote on the basis of deliberate decisions rather than superficial interests or ad-hoc inclinations.

To address the leadership gap in unions, the employer should apprise unions on the need to have honorary members who bring with them a deeper understanding of the industry. As a sign of goodwill, the employer should waive off their membership fees but at the same time ensure that the external members don't have a violent background or powerful political sponsors. The employer should provide an ecosystem for the leadership of the union to effectively:

1. Identify critical requirements (economic, social and political) of the members.
2. Assess alternatives based on best practices insight within the time and resources constraints.
3. Design robust internal feedback loops for the members to provide their insights/recommendations.
4. Develop non-negotiables that link to specific processes under the prevailing organization culture.
5. Establish a governance system that tracks accountability and enables an ownership culture.

THE ETHICS OF LABOUR MANAGEMENT

In India, outsourcing of work finds its genesis in the cheap buying of labor with minimal employer liability. Nevertheless, such a financial rationale is not devoid of unethicality since the workers are often exploited and subjected to working conditions which they never gave their consent to. Workers are forced into servitude due to the skewed demand-supply mechanisms of the unorganized labor market. Machiavellian styled "ends justify the means" models which are quoted in defense (whereby cost reduction as the end objective is used to justify corporate level strategy) violate ethical principles and entail high human costs (Breslin, 1999). In addition, the notion of global outsourcing has significantly contributed to contingent workers earning less than their permanent counterparts without health, life, disability, post-retirement or any other social security benefits (Geiger, 1999). Therefore, even when an organization cannot ensure permanent job stability to the contingent workforce and bring it at par with the permanent workforce, it should heavily invest in making the contingent workers become aware of their rights and various government sponsored social welfare schemes. But such benevolence can back fire if the organization doesn't factor in its role as a principal employer, thereby leading to unintended legal consequences (such as forceful regularization of contract labor). To prevent such a scenario from unfolding, it would be wise for the management to marry its CSR initiatives with its will to ameliorate the pitiful conditions of the contingent workers while restricting itself from operating within the purview of the employer-employee relationship.

FUTURE RESEARCH DIRECTIONS AND ADDITIONAL READING

India has traditionally been a welfare state and is a signatory to various multilateral labor bodies (including the International Labour Organization). The Indian labor laws impart to workers the undeniable right to fair and humane employment, right against discrimination, right to form trade unions and right to participation in management. Nevertheless, the innumerable laws have been accused by corporates and scholars as a hindrance to smooth transaction of business and economic activity, leading to labor market rigidity (Aghion, Burgess, Redding, S, & Zilibotti, 2008; Besley & Burgess, 2004; Hasan, Mitra, & Ural, 2007a). The informal sector has largely been left out of the legal purview and thus the reader may be interested in how the Indian government plans to bring the informal workers under the scope of legal safeguards without becoming an impediment in day to day business activities. Furthermore, the stringent labor laws have lead entrepreneurs to employ casual and contract workers (Sen, Saha, & Maiti, 2010; Hasan, Mitra, & Ramaswamy, 2007b). Therefore, while the Government attention in the informal sector is warranted, the reader may like to enquire as to what alternate plans of action should the policy makers devise in order to prevent business owners in shifting their employment base to a new kind of workforce (and even automation), so that the vulnerable workers aren't deprived of their sources of employment. Lastly, the question of underground economy is ever-pertinent in the Indian labor debate (Djankov & Ramalho, 2009; Boeri, Helppie, & Macis, 2008) and the reader may desire to delve deeper into the subject.

CONCLUDING REMARKS

There is a growing realization among the Indian business community that contingent workforce can be a significant source of human capital. In an industry, which strives to evolve from a commodity based entity to a talent focused one, traditional management systems can no longer suffice. Employers should be attentive to the value and potential of the contingent workforce in enabling an organization to meet its goals. This research piece has strived to comprehensively cover all problem areas related to Indian contingent workforce management. As contingent workers aren't on an organization's payroll, employers need to go through a separate process to ensure that they are paid and treated in a fair manner. Moreover, to ensure efficient decision-making processes based on sound rationale, employers need to collate historical and marketplace data in robust management systems. Employee management, as a preventive measure to worker alienation, needs to be extended to include the category of contingent workforce. Internal security checks in organizations leave a room for improvement in the case of background checks and thus employing of contingent workers should be preceded by diligent internal scrutiny wherein it is ensured that rules relating to employment practices are duly followed. The crucial issue of low motivation plaguing the contingent workers should be addressed by using policies that enable their engagement with the organization in a manner similar to those used to deal with permanent workers. An overarching philosophy is, thus, required to motivate both permanent and temporary workmen by providing them with defined career paths and regular training opportunities. To achieve synergy in the workforce, the human resource department needs to act as a strategic liaison that clearly communicates its vision of change management to all the concerned stakeholders (refer to appendix). Lastly, ethics as a management notion is fast losing its currency in today's business environment and the employers should, hence, treat the issue of labor arbitrage from not only a legal or an economic perspective but also from a moral prism.

REFERENCES

Aghion, P., Burgess, R., Redding, S., & Zilibotti, F. (2008). The unequal effects of liberalisation: Evidence from dismantling the license raj in India. *The American Economic Review*, *94*(4), 1397–1412. doi:10.1257/aer.98.4.1397

Associated Chambers of Commerce of India. (2014). *Rise of contract workers by 39% in 2013*. Retrieved 31 November, 2015, from http://www.assocham.org/newsdetail.php?id=4379

Besley, T., & Burgess, R. (2004). Can labour regulation hinder economic performance? - Evidence from India. *The Quarterly Journal of Economics*, *119*(1), 91–134. doi:10.1162/003355304772839533

Bhalla, S. (2003). *The restructuring of unorganized sector in India*. Planning Commission, Government of India.

Bharat Heavy Electricals Ltd. vs. State of Uttar Pradesh. (2003). *Supreme Court Cases (SCC) 528.*

Boeri, T., Helppie, B., & Macis, M. (2008). *Labor regulations in developing countries: a review of the evidence and directions for future research*. World Bank.

Breslin, D. A. (1999). *On the ethics of outsourcing: a philosophical look at A-76*. Defence Acquisition Industry.

Brown, D. K., Deardorff, A. V., & Stern, R. M. (2008). Child labor: Theory, evidence, and policy. In K. Basu (Ed.), *International labor standards: History, theory, and policy options*. Hoboken, NJ: Blackwell Publishing Ltd.

Chakrabarti, S. (2009). *Gender dimensions of the informal sector and informal employment in India.* Global Forum on Gender Statistics.

Daly, K. A. (2013). *Managing the contingent work force: lessons for success*. Queen's University Industrial Relations Centre.

Djankov, S., & Ramalho, R. (2009). Employment laws in developing countries. *Journal of Comparative Economics*, *37*(1), 3–13. doi:10.1016/j.jce.2008.10.003

Dwyer, C. J. (2012). *Contingent workforce management: The next-generation guidebook to managing the modern contingent workforce umbrella*. Aberdeen Group.

Dwyer, C. J. (2013). *The state of contingent workforce management 2014: A framework for success.* Ardent Partners.

Edwards, T., & Kuruvilla, S. (2005). International HRM: National business systems, organizational politics and the international division of labour in MNCs. *International Journal of Human Resource Management*, *16*(1), 1–21. doi:10.1080/0958519042000295920

Etheredge, K., Dorf, S., & Thakkar, T. (2009). Optimize your contract labor. *Supply Chain Management Review*, *13*(5), 50–51.

Ewing, K. D. (2005). The function of trade unions. *Industrial Law Journal*, *34*(1), 1–22. doi:10.1093/ilj/34.1.1

Gartside, D., Silverstone, Y., Farley, C., & Cantrel, S. M. (2013). *Trends reshaping the future of HR: The rise of the extended workforce*. Accenture.

Geiger, J. J. (1999). The new emerging temporary workforce. In *Proceedings of the Academy of Strategic and Organisational leadership.*

Gibson, N. (2015). *Five ways employers can better manage contingent workers.* Retrieved 15 March, 2016, from http://www.thestaffingstream.com/2015/09/01/five-ways-employers-can-better-manage-contingent-workers/

Hasan, R., Mitra, D., & Ramaswamy, K. (2007b). Trade reforms, labor regulations, and labor-demand elasticities: Empirical evidence from India. *The Review of Economics and Statistics, 89*(3), 466–481. doi:10.1162/rest.89.3.466

Hasan, R., Mitra, D., & Ural, B. (2007a). Trade liberalisation, labour market institutions and poverty reduction: Evidence from India states. *India Policy Forum, 3*, 71-122.

Henson, R. (2008). Contingent workforce: beyond the four walls. In K. V. Beaman (Ed.), *HR frontiers: Shifting borders and changing boundaries* (pp. 211–226). IHRIM Press: Futura Publishing.

HireRight. (2015). *Employment screening benchmarking report.* Retrieved 24 January, 2016, from http://www.hireright.com/benchmarking

Hyman, R. (2007). How can trade unions act strategically? *Transfer: European Review of Labour and Research, 13*(2), 193–210. doi:10.1177/102425890701300204

India Brand Equity Foundation. (2016). *Indian consumer durables and FMCG industry analysis.* Retrieved 22 February, 2016, from http://www.ibef.org/industry/fmcg-presentation

India Business Insight. (2014). *India ranks second in contingent workforce availability (stands at the top in cost efficiency).* Informatics India Limited.

Institute for Human Development. (2014). *India labour and employment report 2014: Workers in the era of globalization.* New Delhi: Academic Foundation.

International Airports Authority Employees Union vs. Airport Authority of India, (1997). *Supreme Court Cases (SCC) 754.*

International Labour Organization. (2008). *Child labor - causes.* United Nations.

Kochhar, K., Mitra, P., & Nayar, R. (2012). More jobs, better jobs. *Finance & Development, 49*(2), 48–51.

Korgaokar, C., & Myrstad, G. (1997). *Protecting children in the world of work.* International Labour Organization.

Kulshreshtha, A. C. (2011). Measuring the unorganized sector in India. *Review of Income and Wealth, 57*, 123–134.

LeBleu, R., & Sobkowiak, R. (1995). New workforce competency models. *Information Systems Management, 12*(3), 7–12. doi:10.1080/07399019508962980

ManpowerGroup Solutions. (n.d.). *Valuable contributors to contingent workforce management.* White Paper.

Ministry of Statistics and Programme Implementation. (2014). *Labour and employment statistics.* Government of India.

National Statistical Commission. (2012). *Report of the committee on unorganised sector statistics*. Government of India.

National Thermal Power Corporation Ltd. v. Karri Pothuraju. (2003). *Supreme Court Cases (SCC) 384*.

Oracle. (2010). *Successfully executing and managing a contingent workforce strategy*. E-Business Suite Human Resources Management System.

MBO Partners. (2013). *The state of independence in America*. Third Annual Independent Workforce Report.

Planning Commission of India. (2007). *Labour laws and other labour regulations*. The Government of India.

Press Trust of India. (2012). Maruti's Manesar plant GM(HR) burned to death, 91 workers arrested; government says business confidence intact. *The Times of India*.

Reardon, G. (2011). *How to manage contingent workers*. Littler Mendelson, P.C.

Sen, K., Saha, B., & Maiti, D. (2010). *Labour market institution and flexibility in Indian manufacturing*. University of Manchester.

Shahstree, A. (2013). *Contract Labour (R&A) Act, 1970: Practices, problems & perspectives with respect to manufacturing industry*. Legal Services India. Retrieved 15 December, 2015, from http://www.legalservicesindia.com/article/article/perspectives-on-contract-labour-act-1452-1.html

Smith, D., Gartside, D., Sloman, C., & Marshall, B. (2014). *Managing the extended workforce: A skills strategy for business agility. Outlook Point of View*. Accenture.

Swaminathan, M. (1991). *Understanding the informal sector: A survey*. WIDER Working Papers.

Tetteh, V. A. (2016). Management of human resources. *Research Starters Business,* 1-5.

KEY TERMS AND DEFINITIONS

Contingent Workforce: A group of provisional workers who work on a non-permanent basis (temporary, part-time, outsourced and offshore workers, independent professionals, interns, and consultants).

Data Management: Design and development of systems, policies, and procedures for effectively managing an organization's information lifecycle needs.

Employee Engagement: The degree to which employees relate to their jobs and are committed to the organization, thereby putting additional effort into their current work/task.

Employer-Employee Relationship: Workplace relation between the employee and employer, covering psychological, financial and socio-legal aspects.

Information Asymmetry: One party has more or better access to information than the other, thereby creating a power imbalance in economic/social transactions.

Job Description: Formal documentation of an employee's work tasks and responsibilities.

Labour Arbitrage: Movement of jobs to countries with inexpensive labor and cost of doing business, as a result of negligible barriers to international trade.

Participatory Management: Empowering employees to contribute in the organizational decision-making process.

Sham Contract: An employment relationship deliberately disguised as an independent contract, wherein the worker is engaged as an employee.

APPENDIX

Table 1. Template for management communication

<table>
<tr><th>Strategy</th><th>Objective</th><th>Result</th><th>Theme</th><th>Tools</th><th>HR Role</th><th>Frequency</th><th>Metrics</th></tr>
<tr><td colspan="8">Platform: Intranet</td></tr>
<tr><td>Home Page</td><td>Business metrics dashboard</td><td>To apprise managers of progress</td><td>Plant-wide HR initiatives</td><td rowspan="3">IT systems (desktops etc.) along with a dedicated IT function to direct the flow of data</td><td>Update data regularly</td><td>Daily</td><td rowspan="3">• No. of hits on website
• Queries raised by employees in town hall, one to one & one to many meetings</td></tr>
<tr><td>Function Page</td><td>Department dashboard & contracts</td><td>To apprise employees of progress</td><td>Function-wide HR initiatives</td><td>None</td><td>Daily</td></tr>
<tr><td>Project Page</td><td>Project KPI dashboard & budgets</td><td>To appraise team members of progress</td><td>Project level HR initiatives</td><td>None</td><td>Daily</td></tr>
<tr><td colspan="8">Platform: E-Mail</td></tr>
<tr><td>Information Bulletins</td><td rowspan="3">Inform & engage employees by creating initial buzz on change management</td><td rowspan="3">To make employees understand purpose & progress of proposed HR initiatives</td><td rowspan="3">To connect employee & incorporate ground realities to proposed HR philosophy</td><td rowspan="3">IT systems (desktops etc.) & rooms (for any personal meets)</td><td rowspan="3">Consult, develop & publish any required data</td><td rowspan="3">Weekly or monthly depending on the urgency</td><td rowspan="3">No. of meaningful replies and queries raised to e-mails</td></tr>
<tr><td>Messages from Leaders</td></tr>
<tr><td>Activity reports</td></tr>
<tr><td colspan="8">Platform: Meetings</td></tr>
<tr><td>Lunch with Leaders</td><td rowspan="2">Inform, clarify & exchange views</td><td rowspan="2">To reduce information asymmetry in the plant</td><td rowspan="2">To facilitate a dialogue that fine tunes the HR philosophy</td><td rowspan="5">Rooms & other logistical issues (including catering, corporate branding)</td><td rowspan="5">Plan, announce & attend sessions to ensure maximum employee audience</td><td>Bimonthly</td><td rowspan="2">• Employee surveys
• Leaders' observations</td></tr>
<tr><td>Informal Connects</td><td>Varies</td></tr>
<tr><td>Town hall Meetings</td><td rowspan="3">Open-for-all doubt clearing & brainstorming sessions</td><td rowspan="3">To involve & encourage employees in effectively implementing HR initiatives</td><td rowspan="3">To ensure that the process is tailor made for all work levels across the plant</td><td>Weekly</td><td rowspan="3">• No. of attendees
• Employee surveys
• Leaders' observations</td></tr>
<tr><td>One to Many Meetings</td><td>Monthly</td></tr>
<tr><td>One to One Meetings</td><td>Biannually</td></tr>
<tr><td colspan="8">Platform: Documents</td></tr>
<tr><td>News Magazine</td><td rowspan="3">To connect employees to their colleagues, plant, and the job</td><td rowspan="3">To inform employees about past HR plans & their implications</td><td rowspan="3">To apprise employees on how & why the new HR philosophy was developed</td><td rowspan="3">IT systems, printing press & access to the storage room, etc.</td><td rowspan="3">Develop, collate & publish data for workers</td><td>Monthly</td><td rowspan="3">• Readership
• Employee surveys
• Active involvement (articles etc.)</td></tr>
<tr><td>Decision Logs</td><td>Weekly</td></tr>
<tr><td>Firm Documents</td><td>Varies</td></tr>
</table>

Table 2. Governance model for communication of HR philosophy

Action Item	Owner	Approver	Executor	Audience
Teaser E-mails, Newsletter, Danglers & Posters	HR Head	HR Head	HR Team	All Employees
Emails from HR Head, Plant Head & IR Executive	HR Head	Plant Head	HR Head	All Employees
Town hall Meetings led by Plant Head	HR Head	HR Head	Plant Head	Leaders
One to Many Connects led by Function Heads	Leaders	HR Head	Leaders	Managers
One to One Sessions led by HRBPs & Managers	HR Head	Managers	HR Team	Workers

Owner: Leads Process; Approver: Designs & Decides Process; Executor: Delivers Process.

Chapter 3
The Role of International Labour Organization in the Fight Against Modern Slavery

Halise Duygu Özalp
University of Turkish Aeronautical Association, Turkey

ABSTRACT

Since the date it was founded to the present day, International Labour Organization (ILO) has been working on developing policy proposals about the problematic areas emerging in working life. Though unemployment is regarded across the world as the source of major problematic areas of economies, the thought of the need for taking the new 'invisible' work types into the spotlight also as problematic areas is considered significant. This chapter acknowledges this need and is about the fight against modern slavery; in this context, the chapter takes the assessments and reports of ILO on forced labor. Thus, the purpose is to put forth the necessity and importance of fighting against the modern forms of slave labor, expanding on the efforts of the Organization which can cause significant pressure on the government/ state level.

INTRODUCTION

International Labour Organization (ILO) states that the number of modern slaves is 20.9 million, based on its study in 2012. According to the 2016 data of Global Slavery Index (GSI), however, there is a total of 45.8 million modern slaves in 167 countries on a global scale (Walk Free Foundation [WFF], 2016). In any case, it is clear that slave labor is still a matter of fact. In addition, a historical look at the surveys on modern slavery, together with the fact that the number of people working at the level of modern slavery has started to increase steadily, dictates the importance of the efforts toward the elimination of modern slavery.

Firstly, information about the concept of modern slavery and its usage is discussed in the chapter. When we say 'slavery', the word may sound antiquated, but it can be clearly seen that the modern world has created its own form of slavery. The studies made on a global scale carry an important role in the

DOI: 10.4018/978-1-5225-2008-5.ch003

creation of this visibility. The studies of academics, establishments/institutions, and non-government organizations take an essential place in defining the concept of modern slavery and increasing international awareness.

After the conceptual explanations on the subject, the dynamics of the emergence of slave labor in today's world are addressed, and the typologies and/or classifications regarding slave labor are discussed. Moving on from this point, modern slavery's position in the existing labor/economic relations will be mentioned taking into consideration its place in the global economy in terms of the economic value gained from slave labor.

Though slavery is banned by means of national legal measures in many countries, it is clear that national anti-slavery measures and interventions are inefficient; in this context, studies aim to take modern slavery into the hand in a global perspective and develop common global policies are seen important. The importance of roadmaps drafted and operations run by the international community for the struggle to eliminate modern slavery can be seen clearly in this regard. Because it's the most efficient organization in the struggle towards the elimination of modern slavery, this chapter uses ILO's practices as its base and expands on them.

THE CONCEPT OF MODERN SLAVERY

Though it is accepted that there are various difficulties in defining modern slavery, the presence of violence and coercion are seen as the most fundamental determinants of the concept. This phenomenon is defined as the exploitation of people via coercion, fraud or deceit for a certain period of time (Brooks, 2014, p. 243). One of the important points here is the limitation on people's freedom areas.The literature on the subject states that not all work which includes coercion can be seen as slavery; seizure of people's ID cards and/or passports and restriction of their right of movement are important for slavery and/or slavery-like work's definition.

On the other hand, it can be seen that terms like, slavery-like labor, forced labor, and compulsory labor are used to replace the term of modern slavery. In any case, though the term forced labor is used instead of modern slavery[1], the fundamental documents for the definition of modern slavery are the Forced Labour Convention No.29 and the Abolition of Forced Labour Convention No.105, drafted by ILO.

In the Convention No.29, forced labor is defined as all work or service which is exacted from any person under the menace of any penalty and for which the said person has not offered himself voluntarily. In addition, ILO connects forced labor with voluntariness and punishment, defining it with dependency, presence of coercion/oppression at the time of recruitment and impossibility to leave the employer (International Labour Organization [ILO], 2014a, p. 31).

Modern slavery is defined by terms like forced labor, debt bondage, human trafficking, sex slavery and forced or slave marriage in the Global Slavery Index reports. A similar definition is made by Crane (2012, p. 3), stating that modern slavery still exists in various forms that include traditional slavery, bonded labor, human trafficking and forced labor.

Another important definition of modern slavery comes from Bales (Bales, 2002, p.10). Bales states that unlike slavery of the past, people are not owned directly in modern slavery but instead, are under complete domination; following this, he reports that people are used as disposable tools for the sake of greater profit. Bales (2002, p. 27) also adds emphasis to the enslavement of people via violence and their involuntary constraint for exploitation when explaining the emergence of modern slavery.

CAUSES OF MODERN SLAVERY

The processes that create and/or lead to modern slavery are generally considered around socio-economic factors/parameters. In addition, ILO's studies – particularly the report published in June 2014 – carry importance for acutely revealing the causality between poverty and modern slavery. The report, which studies forced labor in terms of supply and demand, presents concrete evidence on the relationship between forced labor and poverty for the first time (ILO, 2014a).

When the socio-economic factors are observed, it is stated that forced labor is generally seen in the sectors and industries that employ underqualified and undereducated workers. Aside from poverty and deprivation from social protection, ignorance and the lack of education are seen to be counted among the causes of slave labor in the ILO reports. Among the risk groups of forced labor, undereducated people and their children are reported to carry a high risk. The low level of education forces people to accept the poor working conditions imposed upon them.

Aside from these causes, migration, both in national borders and between countries, is regarded as an important cause of falling into forced labor. The 2014 ILO report mentions labor abuse cases of immigrants. Gender, in addition, is also an important factor in forced labor. According to ILO's global calculations, roughly 55% of all the forced labor victims in the entire world consist of women and girls. The report points out that most forced workers subjected to sexual abuse and household work are women and girls, while men and boys have the tendency to be used proportionately more in the other economic activities (ILO, 2014a, p. 46).

While slavery may appear in culturally various foundations and forms in different regions, it stems from fundamentally similar social and economic problems. It can be said that factors like poverty, the rapid increase in global population, unemployment, discriminatory norms and practices that trigger inequality –particularly towards women and children–, instrumentalization of religion, popularization and internalization of abuse via the ethical disorganisation of the state and the economy lie behind the extensity of today's modern slavery.

MANIFESTATIONS OF MODERN SLAVERY

It can be seen that there are different classifications in the literature regarding the manifestations of modern slavery. For example, while Bales counts modern slavery types as chattel slavery, debt bondage and contract slavery, ILO handles the subject as state-imposed forced labor, forced sexual exploitation and forced labor exploitation (International Labour Organization [ILO], 2012c). Aside from these classifications, modern slavery is also explained also by ILO with topics like children's exploitation, women's exploitation, and labor exploitation.

Bales states that the manifestations of modern slavery are mobile and mercurial and that slavery must be studied from every possible aspect (Bales, 2002, p. 26). Though in this chapter ILO's works the definition of and fight against modern slavery are the main focal, Bales' classification – though criticized in a lot of ways which is accepted to have played a pivotal role in creating international awareness about modern slavery – is also included here.

Bales, in his classification, alleges that chattel slavery is the most similar manifestation of modern slavery to traditional slavery. A relationship of personal property is dominant in this type of slavery; people are enslaved by birth, being sold or other ways, being forced to a perpetual state of slavery. Debt bondage is the most common form of modern slavery and is generally included in the definition of modern slavery. Because of poverty, difficulties in making a living and underqualification, people put their own beings as assurance in return of the money they borrow in to escape the financial hardships they are in. Subjects like the context of the service/labor expected from people or the duration of the service are not clarified at the beginning of the relationship between 'modern slaves' and 'their masters'; thus, the debt becomes the primary factor of servitude, in other words, sustained slavery.

The slavery that shows itself as contract work is important in showing how the factors of modern labor relationships are utilized in order to hide slavery in the modern society. Bales (2002, p. 27) states that, even though the contracts appear to be documents drafted in order to secure a workshop or factory job, the workers find themselves enslaved when they reach the actual workplace. In other words, the contracts, which are utilized as tools here, both lay the groundwork for deceiving people and serve as written documents that give legitimacy to slavery.

An important matter to mention in Bales' classification, also stated by himself, is the interconnected structure of these slavery types. Modern slavery, in its pure and unaltered form, may not be included in any single classification directly; in other words, one type of slavery may carry the properties of several other types. For example, contracts may be drafted in order to hide chattel slavery, while the chattel slavery hidden by a contract may be based on debt bondage.

It's also possible to access the classifications regarding the types of forced labor in the reports by ILO. The types of modern slavery included in the 2005 Report by ILO. As stated in the report, the classification adopted by ILO is divided into two groups as forced labor imposed by the State and by private enterprises/agencies; commercial sexual exploitation and forced labor exploitation are considered under the topic of forced labor imposed by private enterprises and agencies. Additionally, Belser states commercial sexual exploitation and economic exploitation which are imposed upon human trafficking victims in the report (Belser, 2005).

THE ECONOMY OF MODERN SLAVERY

It can be said that with the disorganization/corruption in the state structures, the increase in population and impoverishment, the modern world has created its own kind of modern slavery. The comparison of this modern slavery with traditional slavery carries importance in the context of understanding its modern structure. For example, it appears that the cost of owning a slave in traditional slavery is higher compared to modern slavery. While this situation can be associated with the increase in population, meaning an approach that goes as 'the more the potential slaves, the less they cost' the buying and selling of slaves, the longer term of the interrelation and the relatively higher importance of their bodily/physical health makes traditional slavery costlier.

The biggest difference between traditional and modern slavery comes from the magnitude of profit gained over slavery/slave labor. The assessment of the profit generated in terms of the number of people affected/exposed shows that there are a total of 45.8 million modern slaves in 167 countries on a global scale according to the 2016 GSI data (GSI, 2016). In ILO's reports and working papers, such as ILO's 2012 report titled "Measurement of Forced Labour: Opportunities and Challenges" – despite that it is an earlier study – the number of modern slaves in the world is reported to be 20.9 million. One can argue that the difference in numbers is the result of different measurement methods and variables. However, since

ILO's work is taken as a base for the study, particularly the data on the economy of modern slavery, the number of slaves is accepted as 20.9 million people (International Labour Organization [ILO], 2012b).

Another topic as striking as people exposed to slavery is the fact that forced labor has generated a profit of more than US$150 billion worldwide, as stated in "Profits and Poverty: The Economics of Forced Labour", a report published by ILO in 2014. In other words, the report declares that the profit generated from the labor of 20.9 million slaves is over US$150 billion.

In the report, ILO considers the types of slavery as commercial sexual exploitation and economic exploitation and looking at the distribution of the said profit of US$150 billion from this perspective; it states that nearly two-thirds of it – US$99 billion – comes from commercial sexual exploitation. Moving on, it becomes possible to say that the economy of modern slavery is mostly based on the commercial sexual exploitation of women and girls. The exploitation of women and girls does not revolve around commercial sexual exploitation only; since the rest of the profit – US$51 billion– includes domestic servitude, agriculture, and other economic activities, the extent of exploitation becomes even more visible.

This level of profit generated over slavery constitutes the key point of developing efficient action plans in the fight against slavery. In other words, the fact that the profits are this high despite relatively low costs must be taken into account in the fight against slavery.

THE FIGHT AGAINST MODERN SLAVERY IN ILO PAPERS

Modern slavery may have various different names such as forced labor, compulsory labor or bonded labor, but it can be seen that the international community is efficient in developing and spreading awareness about this struggle. There are many non-governmental organizations operating against modern slavery in a global scale. ILO, Anti-Slavery International, Human Rights Watch (HRW), Walk Free Foundation (WFF), End Slavery Now and Free The Slaves are at the forefront of these organizations. When considered on the basis of resulting in national legal regulations of countries – efficiency, in other words – it can be said that the works of ILO are the most efficient among these organizations.

In this context, studies conducted and reports published by ILO, whose defining role in setting the doctrines and principles compatible with human dignity is accepted within the whole international struggle, can be considered as fundamental guidelines. Moving on from this point, ILO's definitions of forced labor types that it regards as the manifestations of modern slavery and its studies to picture the current situation are touched upon; also, activities and studies that aim to eliminate forced labor, slavery/slavery-like work, in other words, are discussed in a global context.

Studies by ILO both constitute a roadmap for the governments in order to develop national policies and provide a basis for the defense of the fundamental rights regarding working life by increasing the awareness in the international community.

As mentioned previously, despite the appearance of the term modern slavery in ILO papers, forced labor is the more generally used term. In this part of the study, activities by ILO that aim to create awareness about forced labor and eliminate all work that consists forced labor are considered under two sub-topics. In this context, Conventions which are the basic regulatory instruments of the Organization are covered first, followed by reports, and finally, the suggestions and considerations made within this scope. The aim here is to clarify the activities and reports by ILO and their importance.

Conventions

Conventions come first and foremost among ILO's important regulations on the working life. Signatory countries guided via these conventions to pass the necessary national legislations. Forced labor is clearly stated in the ILO Conventions, as well as other work types that are connected with it like bonded labor and compulsory labor.

Forced labor, as defined by the Organization, goes beyond low-paid jobs with bad conditions and is considered to violate many human rights.

The Organization has two fundamental conventions on forced labor: Forced Labour Convention No.29 and Abolition of Forced Labour Convention No.105. Aside from these two fundamental conventions, Worst Forms of Child Labour Convention No.182, which is one of ILO's eight conventions on fundamental rights, is also handled in the context of forced labor regulations (International Labour Organization [ILO], 2012a).

In accordance with United Nations (UN)'s works towards the abolition of forced labor, the Organization published the Forced Labour Convention No.29 in 1930. The convention means with the term forced or compulsory labor all work or service which is exacted from any person under the menace of any penalty and for which the said person has not offered himself voluntarily (No.29, Article 2). Each Member which ratifies the Convention will undertake to suppress the use of forced or compulsory labor in all its forms within the shortest possible period (No.29, Article 1).

In the 1950s, pro-forced labor political views had started to be punished, and different manifestations had emerged along with earthbound/agricultural feudalism. In 1956, UN was conducting studies towards the abolition of slavery; following this, ILO published Abolition of Forced Labour Convention No.105 in 1957. The Convention No.105, which can be considered a complementary part of Convention No.29, aims to prepare a basis for the signatory countries to guarantee that they will never resort to forced labor under any circumstance and in turn, totally eliminate forced labor. Accordingly, each state that ratifies the Convention undertakes to suppress and not to make use of any form of forced or compulsory labor as a means of political coercion or as a punishment for holding or expressing political views or views ideologically opposed to the established political, social or economic system; as a method of mobilising and using labor for purposes of economic development; as a means of labor discipline; as a punishment for having participated in strikes; as a means of racial, social, national or religious discrimination. (No.105, Article 1).

Convention No.182 is about child labor. It was published within this scope in 1999, as a result of the endeavors to prevent and eliminate child labor under 18 years of age with poor working conditions. Each member country which ratifies the Convention is obliged to take immediate and effective measures to secure the prohibition and elimination of the worst forms of child labor as a matter of urgency (No.182, Article 1). The Convention is among the eight fundamental/core conventions of the Organization. The term 'the worst forms of child labor' comprises all forms of slavery or practices similar to slavery, such as the sale and trafficking of children, debt bondage, and serfdom, and forced or compulsory labor, including forced or compulsory recruitment of children for use in armed conflict; the use, procuring or offering of a child for prostitution, for the production of pornography or for pornographic performances; the use, procuring or offering of a child for illicit activities, in particular for the production and trafficking of drugs as defined in the relevant international treaties and the work which, by its nature or the circumstances in which it is carried out, is likely to harm the health, safety or morals of children (No.182, Article 3).

Reports

Aside from conventions, reports by ILO are also efficient in both creating/actualizing national and international action plans and guiding national governments and the international community. It can be seen that the need for ILO's reporting activities arose at the end of the 1990s and regular reporting on the subject has followed this awareness.

While the assessments in the first reports on forced labor were of a rather qualitative nature, the following reports focus on the depth/extent of the problem, setting off on a search for quantitative data.

1998 Declaration: Declaration on Fundamental Principles and Rights at Work

When we look at the reporting activities conducted by ILO, it can be seen that the first study of the Organization that includes regulations that raise concern over and eliminate forced labor is the "Declaration on Fundamental Principles and Rights at Work" published in 1998. The principal emphasis of the Declaration is that all members - even if they have not ratified the Conventions in question - have an obligation to promote and realize the principles and rights in the four categories below:

- Freedom of association and the effective recognition of the right to collective bargaining;
- The elimination of all forms of forced or compulsory labor;
- The effective abolition of child labor;
- The elimination of discrimination in respect of employment and occupation. (International Labour Organization [ILO], (1998).

With this Declaration published, the universal status and application to all people in every country, regardless of economic development level, is confirmed clearly.

The Declaration states that forced labor includes a manner of work, imposed by the will and power of states or persons, that threatens workers by creating severe deprivations like cuts on food or payments, physical violence or sexual exploitation, limitations on the freedom of movement or confinement. When we look at the Declaration for exemplification of forced labor, we can see the example of retention of the identification documents of a household worker who has fallen into forced labor, denying him/her from going outside and threatening him/her with corporal punishment or no payment.

Moving on from this example, the principle dynamics of forced labor are also touched. It is also possible here that the worker is retained for an intolerably low payment, but this reflects a different situation than forced labor. The primary indicator of forced labor, as stated in the Declaration, is defined by the person's right to leave. If people have the right to leave the workplace, the situation will be exploitation, not forced labor.

In addition, the Declaration remarks that people being pushed to debt bondage, occurring in many developing countries, is a common form of forced labor; moreover, it is also pointed out that human/labor trafficking may lead to forced labor, setting the base for the subject's connections which carries importance for further reporting activities.

2001 Report: Stopping Forced Labour

The Declaration of 1998, while being not limited to forced labor, is regarded important as the fundamental text that draws attention to the subject of forced labor. The Declaration's significance is not only limited to this, as the follow-up reports and the fact that it presents a base for the reporting activities on forced labor give it importance.

Following the Declaration, after the 89th International Labour Conference (ILC) in 2001, a report was published under the title of "Stopping Forced Labour". The report carries significance on the basis of in-depth assessment of forced labor. Forced labor and compulsory labor are handled in the report from a global perspective, with the current situation of forced labor, compulsory labor and bonded labor experienced in different countries being handled together with conceptual assessments.

The 2001 Report comes forward in the sense of handling forced labor as a topic that needs to be exposed and fought against and containing detailed analyses on a country by country basis. The report draws attention to the fact that forced labor, even though banned in a global perspective, still exists in different forms, from traditional and modern slavery to debt bondage and human trafficking. In this context, the report includes national/local organizations, national governments, worker and employer organizations and the international community as the respondents/parties of the topic.

The report both handles common types of forced labor and contains the history of the undertakings by international organizations level in the fight against forced labor. The first chapter of the report handles the concepts of forced and compulsory labor in a broad perspective. The report states here that labor based on slavery and abduction is a perpetual problem, along with including the still changing manifestations of forced labor. Later, subjects of forced labor in public work, forced labor and compulsory recruitment in agriculture and rural areas – with reference to the forced labor types in the rural areas of Brazil –, domestic servitude, bonded labor, forced labor in armed forces, forced labor related to human trafficking and forced labor in prisons – forced labor in relation to conviction – are examined in sub-topics.

The second chapter of the report contains supporting work conducted by ILO for the abolition of forced and compulsory labor. In this context, it can be seen that UN steps forward in the areas of drafting a legislation regarding working types including forced labor and the fight against forced labor. UN's endeavors on the subject had started in the period following the First World War, the 1920s in other words. Keeping in mind this period that the works on the subject had started, the report frequently underlines that forced labor still exists, despite being condemned both by ILO Conventions and other documents published.

The third and final chapter of the report states the need to prepare an action plan against forced labor, detailing the contents of the suggested action plan. ILO's principle emphasis in this perspective is towards the need of a compatible action plan, followed by the inclusion of the contents for future action plans. This chapter first states that forced labor, in its current form, cannot attract the attention of the world yet and underlines the fact that it's a subject that needs to be focused and worked on. Within this framework to eliminate forced labor, increasing awareness and defining the problem is seen as the first step of the action plans that will be/may be developed. It is seen imperative that the global community understands that the elimination of every form of forced and compulsory labor is a prerequisite for the success of broader development goals such as sustainable agriculture and poverty reduction for women and men in all sectors, forced labor is a continuing problem of serious proportions, rather than a relic of a bygone age and action will be required on several fronts (ILO, 2001, p. 96).

2004 Report: Forced Labour: Definitions, Indicators, and Measurement

"Forced Labour: Definitions, Indicators and Measurement", published in 2004, is another report that comes forward among the works of ILO conducted in order to draw attention to forced labor and combat it by creating awareness on a global scale. The report explains the various existing forms of forced labor, summarizes/discusses the various measurement methods and provides guidelines for future studies.

From a general perspective, the report focuses on the subjects of handling forced labor together with topics that are known to create this form of labor, like human trafficking, and its definition and measurement in order to fully summarize its extent – the number of people exposed, clarifying regional statuses, the profits generated, etc. In this context, forced labor is first explained in the report from a conceptual perspective.

Accordingly, the report considers the concept of forced labor in particular relation to the conceptual categories of poverty and states that poverty and social exclusion still triggers forced labor, despite the changes and developments in its economic frame. The important point to be mentioned here, however, is that poverty, social exclusion and denial of human rights are necessary, but not sufficient conditions for forced labor. In other words, though the relation between these concepts can be seen clearly, the report cannot pass a precise judgment on whether there is a causality between them or not.

The following chapter discusses the indicators of forced labor. The considerations on the indicators are discussed in relation to the status of countries in complying with the core labor standards. In this context – with reference to the previous works –, it is stated that compliance with the core labor standards depend on the income capacity of countries, namely the average level of national income and income distribution; in addition, having an educational, health and political capacity is seen necessary since these are in close relationship with social awareness. The report sees whether countries have ratified the ILO conventions on forced labor – Convention 29 and 105 – as the key indicator for Formal Forced Labour index (FFLI). In this context, it is examined from the periodical charts that most of the ILO member countries have ratified both conventions, a few have ratified only one and approximately 5% of the members have ratified neither of them. This leads FFLI scores to range from 0 to 1, with a score 0.5 being assigned to countries that ratified one convention and not the other.

The fact that implementing the necessities from the Convention to national legislations is as important as ratification/signing of the Convention itself is not ruled out. Since the reality and practical application in each country may be different, the Real Forced Labour Index (RFLI) is being developed. The reported violations in forced labor conventions are the basis for this measurement, where the magnitude of forced labor in a country is quantified by assigning it a value between 1 (possible) and 5 (very serious). The Forced Labour Index (FLI) is the result of the average of combined data from FFLI and RFLI.

The report's chapter regarding the measurement of forced labor contains the method used by Bales for determining the people exposed to forced labor. The report states that Bales' work helps locate the juncture difficulties in obtaining numbers for forced labor, and can be used at the initial stage to measure the incidence of forced labor.

It is stated that Bales has reached the number of 27 million in 2002 with his process and going over the distinct aspects of this method would be helpful (Ruwanpura & Rai, 2004).

2005 Report: Forced Labour and Human Trafficking - Estimating the Profits

It is clear that ILO's 2005 report titled "Forced Labour and Human Trafficking: Estimating the Profits" has a particular importance among other reports on forced labor. The importance attributed to the paper comes from the fact that ILO has published its estimations on forced labor for the first time in 2005.

The report handles forced labor in relation to human trafficking and states that according to the basic calculations, profits made from forced laborers reach a total of US$ 44.3 billion every year in a global scale, US$ 31.6 billion of which coming from trafficked victims. Furthermore, it is pointed out that more than US$15 billion generated by the exploitation of trafficking and forced labor victims comes from the developed countries.

A general perspective on forced labor is provided in the paper, as its definition, forms and ILO's previous works on the subject are studied in a historical frame. Following this comes the calculation of the profit, and then the labor types and the profits generated are evaluated under the topics of Forced Economic Exploitation (EE) and Commercial Sexual Exploitation (CSE), based on the adopted differentiation.

According to the global calculations of ILO in 2005, there are 12.3 million forced estimated labor victims around the world. The distribution of these 12.3 million shows that 2.5 million are forced to work by the state, the army or rebel military groups; while a total of 9.8 million people are exploited by private agents and enterprises, 7.8 million of which in forced economic exploitation and 1.4 in commercial sexual exploitation.

2012 Report: Measurement of Forced Labour, Opportunities, and Challenges

With the 2012 report, titled "Measurement of Forced Labour, Opportunities and Challenges", ILO brings explanations on the current status of forced labor according to the quantitative data gathered. The report states that the number of forced laborers by 2012 is 20.9 million. The distribution of these people shows that 68% of forced laborers are subjected to labor exploitation, 22% to sexual exploitation and 10% to state-imposed forced labor (ILO, 2012b).

The report lines up the subjects and the data required to clarify the national extent of the problem; accordingly, the report underlines following should be known at a national level: how big is the problem, who are the people and the victims in risk, in which industries and occupations do they work, how do the recruitment processes work, and what does the term coercion mean – the forms in which coercion appears –. It is stated that the statistics of identified victims and estimations based on qualitative research are required in this process.

Forced labor is defined as a manner of work which is conducted involuntarily and includes punishment, and has three constituents: non-paid employment, coercion during the course of work and the inability to leave the employer. Afterward, coercion is defined as the presence of penalties or the threat of penalties to the laborer and/or the family/relatives of the laborer. In this context, the term coercion is detailed around the following circumstances:

- Violence and threat of violence,
- Restriction on the laborer's freedom of movement,
- Debt bondage,

- Withholding of wages (at the source),
- Retention of identification and/or travel documents (i.e. passports),
- Exploitation/abuse of vulnerability.

As mentioned previously, in ILO documents forced labor is classified into the forms that forced labor imposed by State and forced labor imposed in the private economy either for sexual or for labor exploitation.

When the manifestations of forced labor are observed, it is stated that of the total number of 20.9 million forced laborers, 18.7 million (90%) are exploited in the private economy, by individuals or enterprises. Out of these, 4.5 million are victims of forced sexual exploitation and 14.2 million are victims of forced labor exploitation, in economic activities such as agriculture, construction, domestic work and manufacturing (ILO, 2012c).

2014 Report: Profits and Poverty - The Economics of Forced Labour

The most recent report by ILO on forced labor is "Profits and Poverty: The Economics of Forced Labour", published in May 2014. The paper includes old data on the number of forced laborers in a global scale and states that there are roughly 21 million (20.9 million) forced laborers globally. What's new in the report, however, is the emphasis on a new phase in global forced labor.

As mentioned before, according to the report, global profit from forced labor is a total of US$150 billion, of which US$99 billion from commercial sexual exploitation and US$51 billion from domestic servitude, agriculture, and other economic activities. This rise in the numbers, combined with the ever-increasing visibility and the more people falling into forced labor, brings along a new and urgent call for action. In addition to uttering this call, compelling legal measures are being taken, by making substantial amendments in the Convention No.29, in order for the countries to develop national policies. The Protocol to the Convention No. 29 and Recommendation No.203 have been ratified during the meeting held after the publication of the report.

Accordingly, with the "Protocol to the Forced Labour Convention", all transitional articles of the Convention No.29, with the exception of articles regarding the definition of and exceptions of forced labor and the criminalization of this action are abolished.

"Recommendation on Supplementary Measures for The Effective Suppression of Forced Labour No.203" contains prevention, protection and solution methods regarding forced labor and detailed explanations of the Protocol clauses regarding the access to justice, implementation and international cooperation.

The Protocol aims to provide the development of active policies in the fight against forced labor by imposing on the member countries the obligation to prevent and eliminate forced and compulsory labor, develop appropriate and effective solutions for the victims of this action including protection and reparations and impose sanctions on the perpetrators of these crimes.

A causality relationship can be established between forced labor and human trafficking, in fact, sometimes these terms are used interchangeably. The Protocol also covers these subjects, stating that the precautions taken in accordance with the Protocol must also contain special actions towards human trafficking which has forced labor purposes. It is stipulated that each member country must develop a national policy and an action plan in this direction (ILO, 2014b).

The reporting activities conducted by ILO during the period between the end of the 1990s and present day contain measurement methods, aside from the definition of forced labor. It's possible to say that by using these methods, the number of forced laborers and the magnitude of profits generated from this manner of labor – the present status on a global scale in other words – can be correctly specified. Ensuring efficient participation of both national governments and national/international non-governmental organizations in the fight against forced labor are also among the fundamental goals of the reports.

CONCLUSION

It is estimated that modern slavery is spreading rapidly and the problem will get deeper unless necessary precautions are taken; therefore, modern slavery must be understood. Clearly defining the subject in order to determine the target of the struggle by minimizing conceptual differences appears important for the outset of the fight against forced labor.

From a historical perspective, though it can be seen that some regulations have been made in the states and/or regional organizations level regarding the fight against modern slavery, it is possible to say that the most efficient role in the struggle against this manner of labor has been played by ILO. The Organization, having conducted operations towards the betterment of labor life, is regarded as an important guide in terms of international prestige for conducting and regulating the activities of the international community.

It should be said here, however, that local differences are an important subject. Though the undertakings at the international organizations and international community levels yield efficient results, the importance of the need for national activities and regulations should not be ruled out; states/governments should develop precise and urgent action plans towards the elimination of forced labor. Another significant point for the importance of national action plans is, even though in the global sense the socio-economic reasons are similar, that different modern slavery types may have cultural roots; therefore, local anti-slavery policies can only be efficiently employed by taking this cultural difference into consideration.

Another reflection of the global activities of ILO occurs at the international community level. Non-governmental organizations, through their entities, conduct operations aiming the abolishment of modern slavery and stand as elements of pressure for states/governments and international bodies. The primary emphasis of ILO and the international community can be considered within this frame. The states/governments should take active roles in the struggle against modern slavery, completely prohibit these manners of labor and ensure swift punishment in the case of their occurrence.

To summarize, all the activities, operations, and/or reporting show that the real struggle is to point out that modern slave labor is still present even despite its assumption to be non-existent in the modern society and to abolish slavery and all similar manners of labor. Even though the efforts of the international community are important by themselves, the significance of the establishment and functionality of control mechanisms in order for these efforts to have a real significance is also clear.

REFERENCES

Bales, K. (2002). *"Kullanılıp atılanlar": Küresel ekonomide yeni kölelik* (P. Öğünç, Trans.). İstanbul: Çitlembik Yayınları. (Original work published 2000)

Bales, K. (2010, February). *How to combat modern slavery?* Retrieved from http://www.ted.com/talks/kevin_bales_how_to_combat_modern_slavery

Belser, P. (2005). *Forced labour and human trafficking: Estimating the profits*. Geneva: International Labour Office.

Brooks, R. L. (2014). Postconflict justice in the aftermath of modern slavery. *The George Washington International Law Review*, *46*(2), 243–303.

Crane, A. (2012). Modern slavery as a management practice: Exploring the conditions and capabilities for human exploitation. *Academy of Management Review*, *38*(1), 49–69. doi:10.5465/amr.2011.0145

International Labour Organization. (1930). *Forced labour convention* (No.29). Retrieved from http://www.ilo.org/dyn/normlex/en/f?p=NORMLEXPUB:12100:0:NO:12100:P12100_INSTRUMENT_ID:312174:NO

International Labour Organization. (1957). *Abolition of Forced Labour Convention* (No.105). Retrieved from http://www.ilo.org/dyn/normlex/en/f?p=NORMLEXPUB:12100:0:NO:12100:P12100_INSTRUMENT_ID:312250:NO

International Labour Organization. (1998). *About the declaration*. Retrieved from http://www.ilo.org/declaration/thedeclaration/lang--en/index.htm

International Labour Organization. (1998). *Declaration on Fundamental Principles and Rights at Work: Declaration overview*. Retrieved from http://www.ilo.org/wcmsp5/groups/public/---ed_norm/---declaration/documents/publication/wcms_095898.pdf

International Labour Organization. (1999). *Worst Forms of Child Labour Convention* (No.182). Retrieved from http://www.ilo.org/dyn/normlex/en/f?p=NORMLEXPUB:12100:0:NO:12100:P12100_INSTRUMENT_ID:312327:NO

International Labour Organization. (2001). *Stopping forced labour*. Geneva: International Labour Office.

International Labour Organization. (2012a). *21 million people are now victims of forced labour, ILO says*. Retrieved 28 January, 2016, from http://www.ilo.org/global/about-the-ilo/newsroom/news/WCMS_181961/lang--en/index.htm

International Labour Organization. (2012b). *Measurement of forced labour: Opportunities and challenges*. Geneva: International Labour Office.

International Labour Organization. (2012c). Global estimate of forced labour: Results and methodology (Special Action Programme to Combat Forced Labour [SAP-FL]). Geneva: International Labour Office.

International Labour Organization. (2014a). *Profits and poverty: The economics of forced labour*. Geneva: International Labour Office.

International Labour Organization. (2014b). *The Protocol to the Forced Labour Convention*. Retrieved from http://www.ilo.org/wcmsp5/groups/public/---ed_norm/---declaration/documents/publication/wcms_321414.pdf

Ruwanpura, K. N., & Rai, P. (2004). *Forced labour: Definitions, indicators and measurement*. Geneva: International Labour Office.

Walk Free Foundation. (2016). *The Global Slavery Index 2016*. Walk Free Foundation Publications.

KEY TERMS AND DEFINITIONS

Commercial Sexual Exploitation (CSE): Commercial sexual exploitation refers to the sexual harassment/abuse a child – both girls and boys – and/or a woman by an adult, mostly as a result of human trafficking.

Economic Exploitation (EE): Economic exploitation refers to forced labor in traditional economic sectors mostly in agriculture into ILO documents. ILO has estimated that there are about 8.1 million people in forced labor in various labor-intensive sectors.

Forced Labor Index (FLI): Forced Labor Index (FLI) is constructed by ILO specialist. It consists of two elements which are the Formal Forced Labor Index (FFLI) and the Real Forced Labor Index (RFLI). The FFLI is developed to evaluate the legal aspect of a country's compliance in terms of formal respect of the ILO Conventions No. 29 and No. 105. Since the reality and practical application in each country may be different, the RFLI is being developed as a measure of forced labor conventions violations. The FLI is the result of the average of combined data from FFLI and RFLI.

Global Slavery Index (GSI): Global Slavery Index is ranking of slavery conditions in worldwide. The index published by the Walk Free Foundation (WFF). The first annual index was published in 2013. Researchers collect data by quantitative methods and work in consultation with the experts from their partners. From 2014, they have conducted surveys with Gallup Inc.

International Labour Organization (ILO): Since the date, it was founded to the present day, ILO has been working on developing policy proposals about the problematic areas emerging in working life. One of the ILO's priorities in existing forms of forced labor includes combatting these types of enslavement.

Modern Slavery: The most fundamental determinants of modern slavery are the presence of violence and coercion. One of the important points here is the limitation on people's freedom areas. The literature on the subject states that not all work which includes coercion can be seen as slavery; seizure of people's ID cards and/or passports and restriction of their right of movement are important for slavery and/or slavery-like work's definition.

State-Imposed Forced Labor: When states exploit individuals' bodies for their own gain, it's named as state-imposed forced labor. According to the ILO researches, of the total number of victims of forced labor, 2.2 million are in this form of forced labor – for example in prisons, or in work imposed by the state military or by rebel armed forces includes child soldiers which is one of the worst forms of child labor.

ENDNOTE

1 Though the term 'forced labor' is preferred instead of 'modern slavery' in the studies of ILO, the latter term can be also seen in recent ILO documents.

Chapter 4
The Labor Market Regulation

Samir Amine
Université du Québec en Outaouais, Canada

ABSTRACT

This article aims to provide an analytical and critical reading of the state of knowledge on legislation relating to employment protection (EPL) and its impacts on unemployment, jobs creation, productivity and more generally efficiency of the labor market. We show that the construction of indicators of EPL adopted by the OECD is incomplete and does not take into account local specificities of each labor market. We also show that the dominant idea among liberals that any regulations impeding freedom of the labor market generates unemployment and loss of effectiveness is not so obvious to verify empirically and can even be contradicted. In this analysis, we rely on a critical review of theoretical and empirical studies which have examined the effects of EPL. We also discuss some alternatives such as bonus-malus system or the single contract that have been put forward to address the limitations of a relatively strict EPL.

INTRODUCTION

Persistent unemployment and rising wage differences at the expense of low-skilled workers characterize the labor market in most Western countries, particularly those in Europe. These, with the exception of England, are deemed to be rigid in terms of public policies considered generous for workers and binding for firms.

Moreover, since the last financial crisis in 2008, countries such as France, noted the difficulty of their institutions to quickly adapt to changes caused by the economic situation. In this sense, some studies have pointed out that a dual labor market, where the insiders are protected from much larger job than outsiders would generate negative externalities on job creation (Kirat, 2006). Thus, under the recommendations of the Organisation for Economic Co-operation and Development (OECD), more rigid economies have started a process of reforms aimed at increasing the flexibility of the labor market and reducing persistent inequalities, so questioning the rigid nature of the employment protection legislation (EPL).

This article aims to provide an analytical and critical reading of the state of knowledge on legislation relating to employment protection (EPL) and its impacts on unemployment, jobs creation, productivity and more generally efficiency of the labor market. We show that the construction of indicators of EPL

DOI: 10.4018/978-1-5225-2008-5.ch004

adopted by the OECD is incomplete and does not take into account local specificities of each labor market. We also show that the dominant idea among liberals that any regulations impeding freedom of the labor market generates unemployment and loss of effectiveness is not so obvious to verify empirically and can even be contradicted. In this analysis, we rely on a critical review of theoretical and empirical studies which have examined the effects of EPL. We also discuss some alternatives such as bonus-malus system or the single contract that have been put forward to address the limitations of a relatively strict EPL.

MAIN FOCUS OF THE CHAPTER

Indicators of EPL According to the OECD

The OECD EPL covers all legislative provisions that impose costs on employers when they wish to make labor adjustments (Organisation for Economic Co-operation and Development [OECD], 2013). These provisions are grouped into three categories. There is at first, the rules governing the protection of regular workers in the event of individual dismissals. This component is divided into sub-categories: procedural constraints, notice period, indemnity for the individual dismissals without fault, and difficulty dismissing. So, to be able to assess the rigor of this component, the OECD study including provisions on notification procedures, the duration of the notice period and the definition of a justified or unfair dismissal (Organisation for Economic Co-operation and Development [OECD], 2014).

Then, the second component is the regulation of temporary contracts (OECD, 2014). The latter is divided into two categories: fixed-term contracts and temporary contracts. For this category, OECD estimates, for example, the maximum number of successive fixed-term contracts that can make a firm and the types of jobs that temporary contracts are allowed (OECD, 2014).

Finally, the third category represents obligations relating to collective redundancies. To evaluate this component, the OECD based its analysis in particular on the definition of collective redundancy, on the obligations additional notifications to individual dismissals and on the specific costs for the employer for this type of dismissal (OECD, 2014).

Each of these three components, with respective weights (5/12, 5/12, 2/12) in the composition of the synthetic indicator, allows assessing the rigor of an EPL for a country. From 21 criteria classified into the three categories mentioned above, the OECD built in 2013 a summary indicator of EPL for each member of the G20. This composite index ranges from zero to six. When a country is close to "zero", it means that it has a slightly restrictive EPL when the score "six" lead a very strict EPL. By compiling data from the OECD, we get Figure 1 which represents the overall indicators for the different countries.

According to this analysis, we see that Canada is among the countries with low EPL. Moreover, its synthetic index of 0.97 is widely found below the average of OECD member countries (which is of the order of 2.2). We also find the United States close to the Canadian situation with an index of 0.82. In contrast, we note that the indicator of EPL in France amounting to 3.2 is significantly higher than that of Canada. This finding is not surprising since the French legislation on employment protection is highly protective and restrictive for firms wishing to conduct workforce adjustments. One of the lessons of this graph is that, in general, Europe has a much stricter EPL on dismissal and use of temporary contracts than in North America. In fact, the OECD (2013) class two groups of countries according to strictness of EPL: firstly, the common-law countries (including Canada) who have no rigor facing to temporary

Figure 1. Global synthetic index of EPL according to the OECD
Source: OECD, 2014.

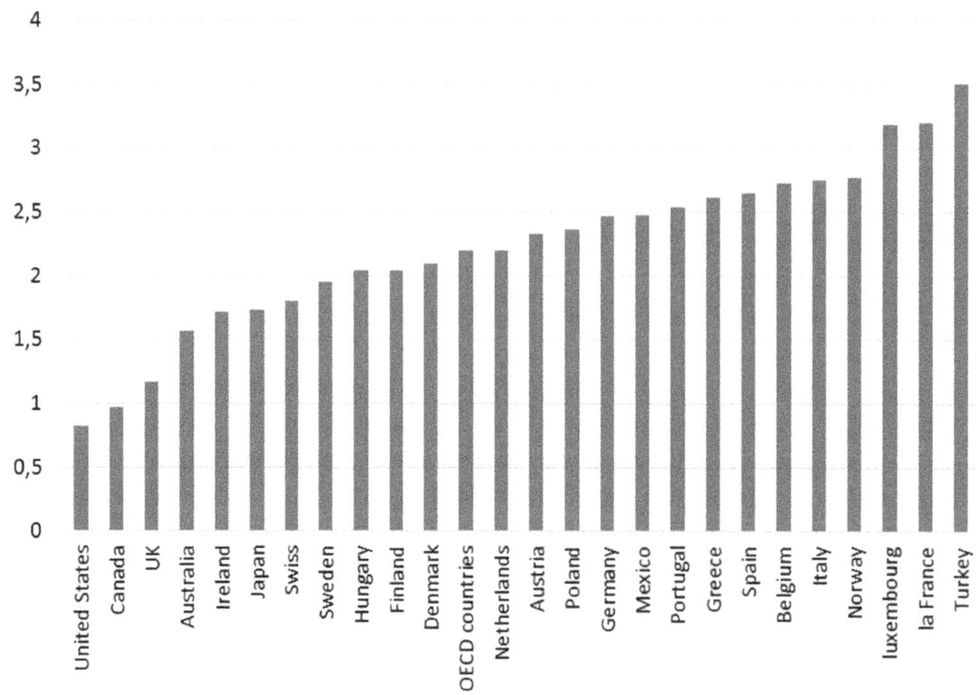

job and offering a "low to medium" protection for employees in the event of individual dismissals and the other, those who have a "medium to very restrictive" regulations on temporary contracts and individual dismissals. Moreover, we find that in the vast majority of the rigid or flexible country in terms of EPL (including Canada), there is a much greater protection for collective redundancies that individual dismissals.

Moreover, we must emphasize that the models presented in this article do not represent a complete list of models that have been developed to assess the employment protection in several countries. In this sense, Block (2007) mentions that the analytical models do not have the same scope and the same level of coverage as defined given to the EPL.

To assess the degree of severity of labor standards in the United States and the European Union, Block et al. (2003) developed a model based on 10 variables: the minimum wage, overtime, vacation pay, employment insurance, workers compensation, collective bargaining, discrimination in employment, dismissal or unfair dismissal, health and safety and the notice for mass layoffs. They found that in general labor standards were higher in the EU than at the United States. Deakin et al. (2009) reach the same conclusion as part of their analysis model using the same variables on a sample of 25 countries between 1995 and 2005.

What Does the Literature Say?

Although the debate on the EPL has been accentuated with the economic crisis, the craze about this subject does not date from yesterday. In fact, since the 90s, the literature was interested in the effects of

EPL on labor market so in theory as empirically. Several studies have attempted to measure the impact of EPL on various economic indicators such as unemployment, the employment rate, mobility of labor, productivity, innovation, etc.

Theoretical Effects Rather Negative but Not Unequivocal in Particular Long-Term

Boeri and Garibaldi (2007) showed, using a dynamic model of labor demand, that the transition, from a system where the EPL is rigid to a system with "two-speed", increased the employment growth. These "two-speed" reforms, called partial or "at the margin", were characterized by liberalization of temporary contracts (fixed-term contracts) while maintaining unchanged the protection on permanent contracts (permanent contracts). According to the authors, this growth would be largely due to the increase in temporary jobs that allow greater flexibility to firms. However, this growth is related to a "honeymoon" effect, that is to say, a temporary effect, since the gains in creating jobs disappear over time because of the decline in permanent jobs (Boeri & Garibaldi, 2007, p. 358). Indeed, long-term, temporary employment growth decreases the level of permanent jobs because of the substitution process that occurs. In other words, whereas the costs associated with temporary contracts are much lower than those associated with permanent contracts, companies tend to replace them with fixed-term contracts that allow them a much wider flexibility. Similarly, Kugler and St. Paul (2004) show that the more redundancy costs are high, most firms tend to practice discrimination in hiring unemployed seeking job. In fact, they explain that firms prefer to hire a candidate who is already in employment since this type of candidate (seen as the "good employee") is subject to less dismissal than the bad or unproductive worker. Thus, based on the applicant's status (unemployed or employed), the firm provides productivity thereof. It minimizes the risk of having to dismissal in the months or years after hiring.

Some research has also focused on the impact of EPL on unemployment. However, the theoretical conclusions related to this relationship are not yet fully conclusive. Moreover, Blanchard and Wolfers (2000) report that the influence of EPL on unemployment is ambiguous. Moreover, from a matching model with endogenous job destruction, L'Haridon and Malherbet (2003) demonstrate that "the total effect of the EPL on the unemployment rate, although negative, is very limited or negligible" (p. 31). Their results, however, indicate that the costs associated with dismissal imply an increase in the average duration of unemployment. They also note that "the strengthening of employment protection for permanent jobs promotes workforce retention on stable contracts (and therefore a reduction of inflows to unemployment from these contracts) but at the same time induces an increase in the rate of destruction of unstable jobs (and therefore an increase in unemployment of inflows from these contracts)" (L'Haridon & Malherbet, 2003, p. 40). Thus, we see that when the EPL is rigorous, it is mainly temporary contracts to workers who are most affected by unemployment, although not all are protected from long-term unemployment. Indeed, Postel-Vinay and Saint-Martin (2004) find that the EPL can cause a feeling of insecurity for the employees in the sense that when EPL is strict, it limits the reallocation of labor (market rigidity), which means that employees expect a difficulty finding a new job if they are made redundant, and thus, retain the status of unemployed for a long time.

Other studies have also attempted to link the dualism in the labor market and the strictness of EPL. Among others, L'Haridon and Malherbet (2003) point out that in the presence of a highly restrictive EPL, flexibility is widely assumed by temporary workers. These often find themselves having to walk from a fixed-term contract to another fixed-term contract to meet companies' needs for flexibility, but they generally have difficulty in landing a permanent contract. Saint-Paul (1996) also adds that it is the young and the unqualified workers who are most affected by this problem of dualism in the labor market.

In regard to the impact of EPL on the mobility of the workforce, L'Haridon and Malherbet (2003) note that when the employment protection increases, the flows into and out of unemployment tend to decrease. Indeed, when several legislative constraints are imposed on firms to adjust their workforce, these are reducing their dismissal and in turn hires. However, when the EPL increases, the authors find that job to job flows are increasing since essentially firms rely on their internal flexibility. In other words, when firms are in the presence of a highly protective EPL, they promote the labor rotation within the firm rather than laying off and hiring significantly (L'Haridon & Malherbet, 2003, p. 32).

Some work has also been done on the effects of the EPL in terms of the level of firm's productivity. Poschke (2009) attempts to assess how the costs of layoffs, reflecting the rigor of an EPL, would influence the growth of aggregate productivity. To do this, he develops an endogenous growth model based on the effect of selection and on the effect of imitation. In other words, he explains that the selection effect occurs when only the most productive firms remain on the market, and the very low productivity firms have no choice but to leave it in the context of pressure. While imitation effect is achieved when the new firms entering the market attempt to mimic existing firms that are most productive. Through its theoretical analysis, Poschke (2009) finds that the costs of layoffs will not only create a bad reallocation of labor and discourage the entry of new firms, but these costs also discourage exit of firms less productive. Specifically, the author shows that when companies leaving the market are subject to the rules governing the costs of layoffs, they are perceived as an exit tax. Therefore, these costs discourage the exit of low productivity firms and in turn reduce productivity growth due to the weakening of the selection effect (more marginal firms remain on the market). Conversely, when companies leaving the market are exempt from the cost of redundancies and that only companies remaining on the market must pay the adjustment costs, it causes a drop in the value of maintaining the market relative to the output value. It thus encourages firms with low productivity to leave the market, while reinforcing the selection effect that is manifested by an increase in productivity growth. Moreover, the author explains that new companies entering the market are necessary for the growth of productivity since they can replace companies that have left and that with greater productivity, as they try to imitate the more productive firms. Finally, Poschke (2009) argues that the effect of firing costs on productivity is more pronounced in the services sector. In sum, we can learn from this work that EPL that imposes costs of layoffs to companies leaving the market can have a negative impact on the growth of aggregate productivity since it would impede the exit of low productivity firms.

On the other hand, with the aid of a theoretical model, Belot et al. (2007) show that when benefits are important, so when we are dealing with a highly protective EPL, workers tend to invest more efforts in their work since they hold a job security. This phenomenon would tend eventually to increase the company's productivity level. However, the authors note that a small threat of dismissal may also help to deter workers to invest maximum efforts since essentially latter know that their employer does not lay off easily. Some authors (Suedekum & Ruehmann, 2003) also refers to this phenomenon called "lethargic" effect of severance pay.

Even the theoretical point of view, the relationship between innovation and the EPL has also been the subject of study. Saint-Paul (2002) provides, inter alia, in light why Europe would be less high-tech than the United States. Thus, from a theoretical approach, the author shows that rigid economic structures where the costs associated with redundancies are high as many European structures, would be more inclined to invest in secondary innovation (improve existing products located at an advanced stage in their life cycle), rather than in primary innovation (produce new products). Indeed, whereas the primary innovation requires, in general, more labor adjustments, high innovation proves much cheaper for the company that is installed in a country where EPL is strict. Moreover, Saint-Paul (2002) points out that the costs of layoffs would reduce welfare in case of secondary innovation do not increase productive efficiency in a major way. Bartelsman et al. (2002) also added that countries with a restrictive EPL combined with an intermediate trading scheme would lead to a low innovation activity and be less inclined to experiment with new technologies offering high productivity potential.

Empirical Evidence Not Always Robust and Sometimes Contradictory

By analyzing the literature, we find that the empirical results generally support those theoretical, cited above. However, the arguments made by this empirical light still insufficient to settle this debate on the effects of the EPL.

Although part of the literature has made the observation that there was no significant effect of EPL on employment (Organisation for Economic Co-operation and Development [OECD], 2007, 2013), some studies have suggested that high protection employment could have negative effects on employment. Indeed, Lazear (1990) shows, using data from 22 developed countries between 1956 and 1984, that greater rigor on severance payments has the effect of reducing the employment-population ratio. Specifically, the transition from a situation where no severance pay is required to a situation where compensation represents 3 months salary for an employee with seniority of 10 years would reduce the employment-population ratio of about 1% (Lazear, 1990, p. 725). Moreover, it notes that the obligation to provide severance pay would encourage companies to replace full-time jobs with part-time jobs, which is a way for companies to evade the law. In fact, this phenomenon is illustrated through the negative impact has the obligation of severance pay on the average hours worked. More recently and in the same vein, Di Tella and McCulloch (2005) made the observation that countries with more flexible labor market have a higher employment rate. In reaching these conclusions, the authors drew on data from World Competitiveness Report that collect the views of managers can assess market flexibility. Conscious of the subjective nature of the data, they show that if France had a similar level of market flexibility than the United States, the employment rate would increase by 1.5% in the short term and 3.6% long term (Di Tella & McCulloch, 2005, p. 1237). They also add that the flexibility of the labor market would have a positive and significant relationship with the participation rate. Thus, according to these authors, greater flexibility is associated with a higher participation rate.

While most empirical studies agree to say that the EPL would have a negative impact on unemployment, results, in general, do not seem significant and robust enough. Among these studies, we find that of Lazear (1990) argues that the compelling companies to pay severance pay increase unemployment. Indeed, from scratch, an increase of three months severance pay would increase the unemployment rate to 5.5% for the US (Lazear, 1990, p. 725). However, the scope of its results is limited because its research is based on an employee who has a seniority of 10 years. Furthermore, the study takes into account only the rigor of severance pay and notice periods. These two aspects do not represent the entire employment protection. Di Tella and McCulloch (2005) find, in turn, through their analysis that countries with high labor market flexibility would lower unemployment and would be associated with a small proportion of long-term unemployed. More flexibility would also be correlated with a low vacancy rate. Blanchard and Wolfers (2000) adds, relying on data from 20 OECD countries and by focusing on the interactions between economic shocks and configuration of market institutions, a highly protective EPL may make it a difficult adjustment of an economy following a macroeconomic shock. In other words, the authors show that the same economic impact, but occurring in a country whose employment protection is low and a country with a rigid EPL has significantly different effects on unemployment. Thus, in the countries where employment protection is low, the economic shock result in a smaller increase in unemployment than if that same shock occurred in the presence of strict EPL.

As for the mobility of the workforce, Boeri and Jimeno (2005) show, by studying the case of Italy and using the double difference method, particularly that EPL would reduce hiring but would not affect job growth thereof. Millán et al. (2013) reached the same conclusions by studying more specifically small firms: strict EPL results in a low-level redundancy, but also low hiring because of the costs associated with layoffs and hirings, reducing mobility labor that can affect productivity growth. Thus, based on data ranging from 1994 to 2001 from the Community panel survey of European households (PCM), they note that EPL has a negative impact on the probability that an individual password self-employed to employer because of the high costs of hiring in a context of strict EPL. Specifically, they find that a decrease of 0.43 of the EPL indicator increases the probability of hiring new employees by 2.9% (Millán et al., 2013, p. 447). Thus, it is possible to deduce that a more flexible EPL encourages more hiring. As for layoffs, they note that a decrease in the indicator of 0.43 LPE increased from 3.1% the probability that an employer becomes self-employed. Therefore, it follows that a less rigid EPL causes more layoffs a stricter EPL. However, the authors emphasize that we cannot reach final conclusions on the fact that layoffs decisions are more predominant than hiring at a low EPL. The reverse is also true. One can, however, assert that EPL with low indicator fact increase the mobility of the workforce is an important source of productivity of a country. Haltiwanger et al. (2014) show, also using the double difference method, a strong legislative rigor on layoffs and hiring would reduce the efficiency of the allocation of labor, and that, particularly in industries where the rotation of employment is high. However, Di Tella and McCulloch (2005), through their study, find no positive influence of the flexibility of the labor market on employment inflows, that is to say, hiring.

Regarding the effects of EPL on productivity, some works such as Van Schaik and Van de Klunbert (2013) showed, by making estimates of OLS using data between 1960 and 2005 from 21 member countries of the OECD, that during the 60s, the EPL would have a significant positive effect on productivity. However, in the following years, its effect would have decreased to ultimately have a negative impact on productivity growth from 1980. The authors offer an explanation for this phenomenon. The EPL would have a positive impact on productivity growth when countries apply a strategy based on investment in their convergence process (between 1950-1960 and 1970). However, the EPL would have a negative effect on productivity growth when countries should implement a strategy based on innovation in a context where potential growth by imitation ran out (either from 70-80 years) (Van Schaik and Van de Klunbert, 2013, p. 976). Therefore, the authors argue that strong EPL now perhaps is not so relevant and adapted to the market as it was before because it comes hamper productivity largely driven by innovation. Moreover, Autor et al. (2007) by looking at the case of the US, demonstrate that not only the implementation of the clause of wrongful dismissal through various states resulted in a reduction in the mobility of labor, and, particularly in the manufacturing sector where staff turnover is high, but the same clause also induced a reduction in total factor productivity.

The study of Auer et al. (2005) sheds a different light against the link between EPL and productivity based on the age of the workers. The authors show a clear positive and significant correlation between EPL strictness and the proportion of workers with seniority of 10 years. Therefore, strict EPL encourage longer tenure among workers. Specifically, by performing an econometric analysis between variables labor productivity and seniority from 13 European countries between 1992 and 2002, Auer et al. (2005) suggest that the age of a worker may contribute positively to productivity but within limits. In other words, according to their analysis, workers with four to ten years of experience would contribute most to productivity. Following the concept of specific human capital business, they show that "seniority allows companies to invest in their workforce over the long term, as it reduces the risk that workers leave the company" (Auer, Berg & Coulibaly, 2005, p. 347). In addition, "the value of the marginal product of the worker increases with time through on-site training" (Auer et al., 2005, p. 347). They, therefore, conclude that "seniority prompting the company to train its workers and the compensation structure encourages them to stay in business and not to shirk" (Auer et al., 2005, p. 348). Therefore, it can increase the overall productivity of the firm. However, their results show that a long tenure (more than 10 years, but especially those over 15 and 20 years) or short (less than a year) would hurt productivity. They come to the conclusion that seniority is beneficial to 13.6 years for productivity, then have a more nuanced, even negative impact. Although this data is very specific, the authors mention that the optimal length is difficult to accurately assess and may vary from one country to another and even from one area to another. From this, the authors believe that Europe is not meeting productivity problems (Auer et al., 2005, p. 345), since none of the European countries surveyed had an average length greater than 13.6 years. Admittedly, this may, for cons, prove to be incorrect if one looks at individual, sectoral or company. Finally, the authors add that "the countries where seniority has an intermediate duration, and which also invest in labor market policies to support transitions between jobs, seem to achieve the best results in this area, they also record the higher proportion of quality jobs " (Auer et al., 2005, p. 336).

Muller and Berger (2013), show, by using statistical regression analysis, that there would be a moderately significant and positive relationship between EPL strictness on the part of individual dismissals (permanent contracts) and total labor productivity of an economy. That is, when the rigor on individual dismissals increased by 1 point, total labor productivity increases of 0.22 in 2008 (Muller & Berger, 2013, p. 8). The authors attribute this to the fact that worker, under a protective EPL, feels secure and motivated in their jobs since the chances of layoffs are lower, which contributes to higher productivity. This explanation is therefore in the same direction as the result of Belot et al. (2007).

In terms of innovation, Griffith and Macartney (2014), through their empirical analysis of 12 European countries have studied the behavior of patenting regarding multinationals. They conclude that EPL would not discourage companies to conduct general innovation activities. However, they first argue that strict EPL particularly patents encourage innovation in secondary since companies are constrained in their labor adjustment due to there being associated costs. They show as companies prefer to implement their radical innovation in countries where EPL is low since this type of innovation usually requires a complete renewal of the workforce knowing that the workforce already in place do not have the skills necessary for the implementation of the new technology.

DISCUSSION

Despite the extensive research on the effects of the EPL, certain limits emerge from the current literature. First, we find that most empirical studies do not take into account the indirect effects of other labor market institutions that act inevitably on firm flexibility in terms of hiring and firing. In fact, we believe that firms' decision to dismiss or hire for economic reasons, not solely the EPL strictness, but multiple factors. We can also think of the contributions to be paid by firms to Employment-Insurance that can influence the decisions of dismissal. One should take into account different regulations and policies to ensure the safety of workers in assessing the rigor of employment protection (Betcherman & Whitehead, 2002). Moreover, it is also important to incorporate into studies of the EPL, the effect of other non-legislative elements such as social security system which also provides protection against loss of employment (Ochel, 2009). While, we recognize the difficulty of measuring the effect of the various institutions on firms decisions relating to workforce adjustment in the empirical analysis. However, by further integrating these indirect effects, this could make the results on the relationship between EPL and more robust economic indicators (Blanchard & Tirole, 2003).

In a similar vein, the definition of EPL given by the OECD is also restrictive in the sense that it is limited only to legislation imposing costs on employers during a labor adjustment, as layoffs and the use of temporary contracts. Some authors, like Deslauriers et al. (2009), in their Canadian study of the EPL, suggested expanding the definition by including quantitative variables (minimum wage and measures of employment assistance services), the variables from provincial standards (working time legislation and legislation on the protection of employment) and certain laws relating to industrial relations (rigorousness in the accreditation process and the process surrounding the strikes). Moreover, note that the adopted weights (5/12, 5/12, 2/12) in the construction of indicators of EPL are not explicitly justified and do not necessarily take account of local conditions of each labor market (Kirat, 2006). Consequently, international comparisons are difficult to conduct. We can actually compare indicators of EPL between countries, but largely dilutes the quality of the comparison since the synthetic indicator does not reflect the social, cultural and legal procedures unique to each country. These procedures may be notably more or less time-consuming depending on the country in which we find ourselves. Although there are efforts to try to reduce the differences between countries in the studies, the complexity of interactions and discrepancies remain high in an attempt to succeed in making a perfect-modeled international comparison. So simple international comparisons between EPL indicators are incomplete.

Moreover, we note that the current EPL indicators do not include new job failure modes such as voluntary redundancy plans and the devices providing secure the career as the portability of acquired rights (Martin, Du Marais, & Dehaze, 2013). Indeed, in some countries like Canada, the employer may decide to set up a voluntary redundancy plan rather than making redundancies. With a view to downsizing, this process is to provide the entire staff or certain categories of employees to voluntarily leave the company under certain conditions negotiated amicably between the employee and the employer (Niel, 2009). As for the portability of acquired rights, the career security can take many forms such as the individual right to training in France (Pereira, 2010). We consider that to take account of these new modes of rupture job in assessing EPL rigor would certainly bring more nuances facing the classification made by the OECD between countries.

Considering the current debate on EPL strictness and the need to reconcile security for workers and flexibility wanted by firms in a highly competitive global environment, it would be appropriate to consider other devices, namely, the bonus-malus system and the single employment contract progressive rights.

Bonus-Malus System

This device, which is currently used in the United States, is based on the rule of polluter-pays that companies must contribute to the Unemployment-Insurance according to their history of layoffs for economic reasons. In other words, a company that lays off massively must contribute more to the unemployment insurance fund by another. This system would possess certain advantages such as making firms face dismissal. Indeed, layoffs generate high costs not only for the individual but also for society, especially when we think of social security schemes to which the individual uses the following dismissal. Given the similarities in the economic and institutional level, this instrument could also apply to the Canadian context in which the EPL is relatively low, and companies do not internalize the costs associated with job losses. Nevertheless, we should not forget that imposing a severance tax on firms whose financial health is fragile, could lead to closures and termination of activities (Margolis & Fougère, 1999). Hence the need to modulate the rate and establish a ceiling for contributions for not harms these businesses in financial difficulties.

Although this device allows to overcome the drawbacks of an EPL too few or too strict, some limitations should be highlighted. Indeed, it is reasonable to expect that, imposing a termination fee, some companies might exert undue pressure on the employee that he voluntarily leaves his employment. In this case, the role of the judiciary is important for control these undesirable behaviors. Moreover, this tax could also increase the risk of employment discrimination to the detriment of certain at-risk workers such as unskilled (Blanchard & Tirole, 2003).

Single Employment Contract to Progressive Rights

The only contract to progressive rights is intended to replace the permanent and fixed-term contracts into one single contract. This alternative was notably advanced by Blanchard and Tirole (2003) to address certain issues in the labor market such as youth unemployment. Whereas the difference, between the costs associated with the protection of fixed-term contracts and costs related to the protection of permanent contracts, is high, they propose the following process. First, they recommend that a trial period in which the employer may terminate the employment without obligation. Then the idea is to gradually increase, depending on the age and experience of the worker, the rights, and obligations of the couple "employer-employee". This method then reduces the threshold effect generated by the transformation of a fixed-term to permanent contract.

This contract would reduce existing inequalities between *insiders* and *outsiders* and provide better employment opportunities for the most vulnerable groups in the labor market. However, this unique contract requires a complete overhaul of the legislation in the labor law and requires accompanying measures that reduce the risk of insecurity associated with fixed-term contracts.

CONCLUSION

By browsing through the literature on the EPL, we see very little Canadian research has been done on this subject. Indeed, very few studies have attempted to empirically confirm or deny the relevance of the indicator as the OECD attributes to Canada. In addition, although recent indicators of EPL made by OECD in 2013 now include devices from national and regional collective bargaining and case law, it is observed that the clauses negotiated at the local level (which is the case for the majority of unions in Canada) are not considered in the assessment of the severity of the EPL, despite the fact that the country is, therefore, unionization rate (30% in 2012). We, therefore, find that the OECD does not take into account the extent of the protection offered by the Canadian collective agreements which are broader than the minimum standards set by the laws.

On the other hand, we find that most of the research has mainly concentrated on the negative effects of EPL without considering the possible benefits of such protection, from an economic point of view, social or cultural. Now we have shown through this literature review, the evidence of a negative effect of EPL on the labor market was not so blatant as one would expect and that empirical studies have even sometimes put in evidence some positive effects. Finally, we identified some alternative policies, which seek to empower the employer in its human resources management and thus give some protection to the employee without constituting an excessive obstruction of the labor market. Despite having highlighted the imperfections such alternatives, this research integration of employee protection in a free labor market shows, we believe, that many experts in the labor market, even fundamentally liberal recognize significant positive effects on employee protection, positive effects, although generally identified in many studies, we seem insufficiently valued today.

REFERENCES

Auer, P., Berg, J., & Coulibaly, E. I. (2005). Une main-d'œuvre stable est-elle bonne pour la productivité?. *Revue internationale du Travail, 144*(3), 335-361.

Autor, D. H., Kerr, W. R., & Kugler, A. D. (2007). Does employment protection reduce productivity? Evidence from US States. *The Economic Journal, 117*(521), 189–217. doi:10.1111/j.1468-0297.2007.02055.x

Bartelsman, E., Bassanini, A., Haltiwanger, J., Jarmin, R., & Scarpetta, S. (2002). *The spread of ICT and productivity growth: Is Europe really lagging behind in the new economy?* Oxford, UK: Oxford University Press.

Belot, M., Boone, J., & Van Ours, J. (2007). Welfare effects of employment protection. *Economica, 74*(295), 381–396. doi:10.1111/j.1468-0335.2006.00576.x

Betcherman, G., & Whitehead, T. (2002). Règlementations de protection d'emploi: Règles d'embauche et de licenciement. *Banque Mondiale: Cahiers de la politique de l'emploi, 1*, 1-8.

Blanchard, O., & Tirole, J. (2003). *Protection de l'emploi et procédures de licenciement*. Paris: La documentation française.

Blanchard, O., & Wolfers, J. (2000). The role of shocks and institutions in the rise of European unemployment: The aggregate evidence. *The Economic Journal, 110*(462), 1–33. doi:10.1111/1468-0297.00518

Block, R. N. (2007). Indicators of labour standards: An overview and comparison. In D. Kucera (Ed.), *Qualitative Indicators of Labour Standards* (pp. 27–56). Dordrecht, Netherlands: Springer. doi:10.1007/978-1-4020-5310-8_2

Block, R. N., Berg, P., & Roberts, K. (2003). Comparing and quantifying labour standards in the United States and the European Union. *International Journal of Comparative Labour Law and Industrial Relations, 19*(4), 441–468.

Boeri, T., & Garibaldi, P. (2007). Two tier reforms of employment protection: A honeymoon effect? *The Economic Journal, 117*(521), 357–385. doi:10.1111/j.1468-0297.2007.02060.x

Boeri, T., & Jimeno, J. (2005). The effects of employment protection: Learning from variable enforcement. *European Economic Review*, *49*(8), 2057–2077. doi:10.1016/j.euroecorev.2004.09.013

Deakin, S., Armour, J., & Singh, A. (2009). Law, finance and development indices, 1970-2005. UK Data Service. SN: 6260.

Deslauriers, J., Dostie, B., & Gagné, R. (2009). L'impact économique de la législation du marché du travail. *Centre sur la productivité et la prospérité*, 1-42.

Di Tella, R., & MacCulloch, R. (2005). The consequences of labor market flexibility: Panel evidence based on survey data. *European Economic Review*, *49*(5), 1225–1259. doi:10.1016/j.euroecorev.2003.11.002

Griffith, R., & Macartney, G. (2014). Employment protection legislation, multinational firms, and innovation. *The Review of Economics and Statistics*, *96*(1), 135–150. doi:10.1162/REST_a_00348

Haltiwanger, J., Scarpetta, S., & Schweiger, H. (2014). Cross country differences in job reallocation: The role of industry, firm size and regulations. *Labour Economics*, *26*, 11–25. doi:10.1016/j.labeco.2013.10.001

Kirat, T. (2006). *Les indicateurs de protection de l'emploi (OCDE et Banque Mondiale)*. Document de travail pour le Projet « Évaluation du droit du travail ».

Kugler, A., & Saint-Paul, G. (2004). How do firing costs affect worker flows in a world with adverse selection. *Journal of Labor Economics*, *22*(3), 553–584. doi:10.1086/383107

L'Haridon, O., & Malherbet, F. (2003). Protection de l'emploi et performance du marché du travail. *Revue française d'économie, 17*(4), 21-83.

Lazear, E. P. (1990). Job security provisions and employment. *The Quarterly Journal of Economics*, *105*(3), 699–726. doi:10.2307/2937895

Margolis, D., & Fougère, D. (1999). *Moduler les cotisations employeurs à l'assurance-chômage: Le système américain de l'experience rating*. Rapport au Commissariat Général du Plan.

Martin, J., Du Marais, B., & Dehaze, A. (2013). *Mise en perspective des difficultés dans la mesure du droit du travail, Direction générale du Trésor*. Retrieved from http://www.tresor.economie.gouv.fr/File/405741

Millán, A., Millán, J. M., Román, C., & Van Stel, A. (2013). How does employment protection legislation influence hiring and firing decisions by the smallest firms? *Economics Letters*, *121*(3), 444–448. doi:10.1016/j.econlet.2013.09.021

Muller, L., & Berger, D. P. (2013). The impact of a country's employment protection legislation on its economic prosperity. *International Journal of Humanities and Social Science*, *3*(12), 1–13.

Niel, S. (2009). Comment développer un plan de départ volontaire pour motif économique?. *Les cahiers du DRH, 155*, 27-33.

Ochel, W. (2009). Employment protection: Concepts and measurement. *CESifo DICE Report*, *7*(2), 30–38.

Organisation for Economic Co-operation and Development. (2007). *Des emplois plus nombreux, mais moins productifs? L'impact des politiques du marché du travail sur la productivité. In Perspective de l'emploi de l'OCDE 2007*. Éditions OCDE.

Organisation for Economic Co-operation and Development. (2013). *Protéger l'emploi, renforcer la flexibilité: Un nouveau regard sur la législation sur la protection de l'emploi. In Perspectives de l'emploi de l'OCDE 2013*. Éditions OCDE.

Organisation for Economic Co-operation and Development. (2014). *Les indicateurs de l'OCDE sur la protection de l'emploi*. Retrieved from http://www.oecd.org/fr/emploi/emp/lesindicateursdelocdesurla-protectiondelemploi.htm

Pereira, B. (2010). Libéralisation du marché du travail: Vers une flexisécurité à la française. *Management & Avenir*, *4*(34), 81–106. doi:10.3917/mav.034.0081

Poschke, M. (2009). Employment protection, firm selection, and growth. *Journal of Monetary Economics*, *56*(8), 1074–1085. doi:10.1016/j.jmoneco.2009.10.013

Postel-Vinay, F., & Saint-Martin, A. (2004). Comment les salariés perçoivent-ils la protection de lemploi? *Economie & Statistique*, *372*(1), 41–59. doi:10.3406/estat.2004.7266

Saint-Paul, G. (1996). Labor market institutions and the cohesion of the middle class. *International Tax and Public Finance*, *3*(3), 385–395. doi:10.1007/BF00418951

Saint-Paul, G. (2002). Employment protection, international specialization, and innovation. *European Economic Review*, *46*(2), 375–395. doi:10.1016/S0014-2921(01)00093-9

Suedekum, J., & Ruehmann, P. (2003). Severance payments and firm-specific human capital. *Labour*, *17*(1), 47–62. doi:10.1111/1467-9914.00221

Van Schaik, T., & Van de Klundert, T. (2013). Employment protection legislation and catching-up. *Applied Economics*, *45*(8), 973–981. doi:10.1080/00036846.2011.613784

KEY TERMS AND DEFINITIONS

Bonus-Malus System: Bonus-malus system is based on the rule of polluter-pays that companies must contribute to the Unemployment-Insurance according to their history of layoffs for economic reasons.

Collective Dismissals Obligations: All elements related to the definition of collective redundancy, the obligations additional notifications to individual dismissals and to the specific costs for the employer for this type of dismissal.

Employment Protection Legislation: Employment protection legislation covers all legislative provisions that impose costs on employers when they wish to make labor adjustments.

Individual Dismissals Obligations: All elements related to the definition of individual redundancy, the notifications and to the specific costs for the employer.

Regular Workers Protection: Regular workers protection includes procedural constraints, notice period, indemnity for the individual dismissals without fault, and difficulty dismissing.

Single Employment Contract: Single employment contract is intended to replace the permanent and fixed-term contracts into one single contract.

Temporary Workers Protection: Estimates the maximum number of successive fixed-term contracts that can make a firm and the types of jobs that temporary contracts are allowed.

Chapter 5
The EU's Internal Market and the Free Movement of Labor: Economic Effects and Challenges

Zeynep Kaplan
Yıldız Technical University, Turkey

ABSTRACT

Free mobility of labor has been the core element of the European integration process. The aim of this chapter is to analyze the effects and challenges of the labor mobility within the EU. The analysis then focuses on the recent trends in labor mobility. Cross-border labor mobility remains low in the EU. The main reasons behind the low levels of labor mobility in the EU include linguistic and cultural reasons, as well as non-tariff barriers such as pension rules, recognition of professional qualification or social security differences. Removal of impediments to free mobility of labor and improvement of flexibility of the European labor markets will strengthen the EU's labor market integration.

INTRODUCTION

Free movement of people - alongside free movement of goods, services, and capital - is one of the four founding principles of the European Union's (EU) internal market. It gives all citizens of member countries the right to travel, live and work wherever they wish within the EU. In a broad sense, it includes the rights of movement and residence for labor, the rights of entry and residence for family members, and the right to work and be treated on an equal footing with nationals of that member state. However, barriers have affected the free movement of labor within the EU. Furthermore, free movement of labor across the EU has become a controversial issue in several member countries and highlights the major challenge of economic and social convergence of the EU.

The main aim of this paper is to analyze to what extent freedom of movement of labor is realized at the EU level. In this context, the purpose of this paper is twofold: (i) to describe the key features of free movement of labor and to make an assessment of the trend of flows of labor within the EU, by taking into account the current developments such as the recent enlargements and the economic crisis. (ii) to indicate

DOI: 10.4018/978-1-5225-2008-5.ch005

the costs and benefits of labor mobility at the EU level and discuss the obstacles to the free movement of labor within the EU's internal market. In this framework, the paper consists of six sections. The first section reviews the theory of international economic integration. The next two sections introduce the development and the structure of the EU's single market by introducing the main principals and barriers. The fourth section deals with the recent trends and developments of labor mobility. The next section discusses the costs and benefits of labor mobility at the EU level. The sixth section highlights existing problems related to the free movement of labor by taking into account the recent debates on the issue. The final section concludes.

BACKGROUND

International economic integration, often termed as regionalism, is defined as the institutional combination of sovereign economies into larger economic blocs (Robson, 1998, p. 1). Such initiatives between separate national economies have been claimed as one of the most prominent developments in international trade policy after the mid-twentieth century. Indeed, as indicated by Jovanovic (1998), international economic integration has touched most of the countries, and it became an unavoidable part in most international economic policy decisions.

As introduced by Balassa (1961), international economic integration may take several forms that represent varying stages of integration. These stages include free trade area, customs union, common market, economic union and complete economic integration. In a *free trade area*, all tariffs and quantitative restrictions subject to trade between member countries are eliminated, but each nation retains its national trade policy against the non-member states. A *customs union*, by contrast, involves the equalization of customs tariffs in trade towards non-members. A *common market* involves not only the integration of product markets through trade liberalization that results from customs union but also the free movement of factors of production within the bloc (Robson, 1998, p. 72). Member countries introduce common regulations on the movement of factors of production with third countries (Jovanovic, 1998, p. 10). A more advanced form of integration is economic union. An *economic union* requires the harmonization in many areas of economic policy such as monetary, fiscal, industrial, regional, transport, etc. Finally, a *total economic union* calls for the unification of economic policies and setting up of a supranational authority with great economic authority. The most prominent achievement in this sense is the establishment of organizations in the developed world such as the European Union (EU) which has evolved from a customs union to a monetary union and from six to twenty-eight member states. The main goal of the European integration initiative from the beginning has been the deepening of economic, political and social linkages between the nations and regions of Europe.

The EU was founded on four basic principles: free movement of labor, capital, goods, and services. These "four freedoms" were set out in the Treaty of Rome, and the main purpose was to promote European economic integration and take advantage of multiple economic benefits. The economic theory suggest that economic integration: (i) increases trade between participating countries, although some trade may be diverted to and from the non-members; (ii) increases competitive pressures on domestic markets; (iii) improves productivity; (iv) creates benefits to consumers through reduced prices, greater choice and increased quality; (v) benefits businesses through greater technical and allocative efficiency; (vi) allows technology transfer across national borders; and (vii) greater economies of scale and increased specialization.

In economic literature, it is largely concluded that the free movement of factors of production leads to a more efficient use of economic resources if necessary actions are taken in order to perverse movements of productive factors (Balassa, 1961, p. 98). Within the EU, the economic rationale behind the establishment of a well-functioning and effective internal market aimed to boost welfare, stimulate growth and increase European competitiveness (Mariniello, Sapir, & Terzi, 2015, p. 1). Moreover, in the context of economic crisis, labor mobility is considered as an adjustment mechanism which received considerable attention in the literature. Indeed, Mundell (1961) asserted the need for greater labor and capital mobility as a shock absorber within a monetary union. He argued that high factor mobility, especially labor mobility, is the crucial defining characteristic of an optimum currency area.

THE DEVELOPMENT OF THE EU'S INTERNAL MARKET

The Treaty of Rome, signed in 1957, provided for the establishment of a customs union and a common market (now an 'internal market')[1] across the member states to boost trade and increase welfare. Articles 2 and 3 of the Treaty directly state that the primary concern is to create a common market and specify the necessary measures that must be undertaken to achieve this target. The first crucial step on the way the common market was the creation of the customs union among six member states on 1 July 1968, 18 months earlier than planned in the Treaty of Rome. A common labor market which guarantees the free movement of labor was also established in 1968. Although member states completed the creation of a customs union by 1968 but did not complete the creation of a common market until the 1990s.

The failure to not to complete the common market during the 1970s and 1980s was considered to have resulted in significant economic costs. In response, European Council approved the aim of creating a fully-fledged internal market in March 1985 and asked the European Commission to prepare a program and timetable for implementation. A White Paper on Completing the Internal Market was published in June 1985. It detailed 300 legislative proposals, including measures to eliminate a series of physical, technical and fiscal non-tariff barriers. Later in 1988 an extensive analysis of the potential impact of the market integration was conducted by the Cecchini Report. The Report indicated that the establishment of the internal market would create major opportunities. The Single European Act, the first major treaty amendment[2] in 1987, set a deadline for completing the internal market by 31 December 1992.

Between 1986 and 1992, the EU adopted nearly 280 pieces of legislation to allow 12 sets of national regulations to be replaced by one common European law which would be agreed to in all member states. As a consequence, on 1st of January 1993, internal border controls between the member states were abolished, and a common market based on the free movement of goods, services, capital and people became a reality. Since its creation, single market eliminated trade barriers, increased competition and created new job opportunities. More recently, The Single Market Act I and II was put forward in 2011 and 2012 respectively, aiming to exploit further opportunities within the EU market to boost employment and growth. However, European Commission (2013) recalled that 20 years after its establishment, EU's internal market integration has not yet been fully completed, primarily because member states have not fully transposed or implemented the approximately 1500 directives and around 1000 regulations.

THE MAIN PRINCIPLES AND THE BARRIERS OF THE EU'S INTERNAL MARKET

The internal market, as one of the EU's greatest achievements, refers to the EU as a territory without internal frontiers or any regulatory barriers to the free movement of goods, services, labor and capital- the so-called four freedoms. These four freedoms are the core elements of the EU's market integration.

- **The Principle of Free Movement of Goods:** Originally, free movement of goods was seen as an extension of the customs union involving the abolition of customs tariffs, quotas and measures having equivalent effect on trade, and the establishment of a common external tariff towards non-members. Later, the emphasis was laid on eliminating all remaining barriers to free mobility of goods with a view to creating the internal market - an area without internal borders, in which goods could move as freely as on a national market. Trade within the internal market is essential for the growth of the European economies. In this context, the EU aims to ensure the free movement of goods within the market.
- **The Principle of Free Movement of Services:** The free movement of services is an essential element for the well-functioning of the EU's internal market. Over the post-war period, there has been a sectoral shift from manufacturing towards a service economy. In a similar manner, the size of the services sector in Europe has expanded consistently over the last decades. Thus, services are also crucial to the EU economy and account for over 70% of its GDP and a similar proportion of its employment. Intra-EU trade in services is approximately 28% of total intra-EU trade. However, many non-tariff barriers still exist, and the free mobility of services is less mature than the free mobility of goods. Thus, the level of integration for services continues to be significantly lower than for goods.

Provision of services is technically complex and covers both temporary movement to provide services as well as to freedom of establishment. The provisions on *freedom of establishment* are set out in Articles 49-55 of the Treaty on the Functioning of the EU (TFEU). This provides the right for persons to establish themselves permanently in another EU member as self-employed and for companies to establish themselves as a branch or subsidiary. Articles 56-62 of the TFEU cover the provisions on *freedom to provide services* which give EU nationals or firms the right to provide services across the EU.

- **The Principle of Free Movement of Capital:** Economic theory suggests that the free movement of capital leads to an optimal allocation of resources and enables integrated, open, competitive and efficient European financial markets and services. A system for the free movement of capital has been in place since 1 July 1990 and constitutes the first stage in the preparations for the European Monetary Union. From 1 January 1994, all restrictions on capital movements and payments between EU and between EU states and third countries were removed, and financial markets within the EU were then completely liberalized. Thus, the liberalization of capital movements to and from third countries is also extended. Articles 63-66 of the TFEU deal with the free movement of capital (Art. 63 (1) of the TFEU) and payments (Art. 63(2) of the TFEU) and financial operations within the internal market.
- **The Principle of Free Movement of Labor:** Free mobility of labor is at the heart of the internal market and is one of its 'four freedoms'. The principle of free movement of labor is considered as part of free movement of persons. The principle of free movement of labor facilitates the mobility

of workers within the EU and allows any citizen of the EU member states is allowed to go to another member state for work and have equal treatment as the nationals. This required the lowering of various legal and administrative obstacles and introducing the mutual recognition of professional qualifications of other EU states.

Figure 1 shows a summary of four freedoms of the EU's internal market. The above-mentioned freedoms and thus the completion of the internal market required the elimination of a number of barriers, limitations, and difficulties that hamper the free mobility within the EU. As stated in European Commission's (1985) White Paper on the Single Market, the completion of the internal market requires the gradual removal of three types of barriers to free mobility: physical, technical and fiscal barriers.

- **Physical Barriers:** The physical barriers were the controls carried out on goods and persons which cover the customs checks, the immigration controls, the passport controls and the occasional search of personal baggage. The removal of these barriers is crucial to trade, industry, and businesses that they impose an unnecessary burden and damage competitiveness of the EU economies. All border controls within the EU on goods together with customs controls on people eliminated completely on 1 January 1993. While the physical barriers were abolished within the internal frontiers and they were repositioned at the external borders.
- **Technical Barriers:** The technical barriers to trade involve the national rules and regulations, which varied among member states in a large number of areas. EU countries have adopted the principle of mutual recognition of national rules for the majority of products. Thus, if a product is lawfully produced and sold in a member state, it should be sold freely in all EU markets. However, free mobility can be subject to certain constraints in some areas such as the protection of human health and life and of the environment.

Figure 1. A summary of four freedoms of the EU's internal market

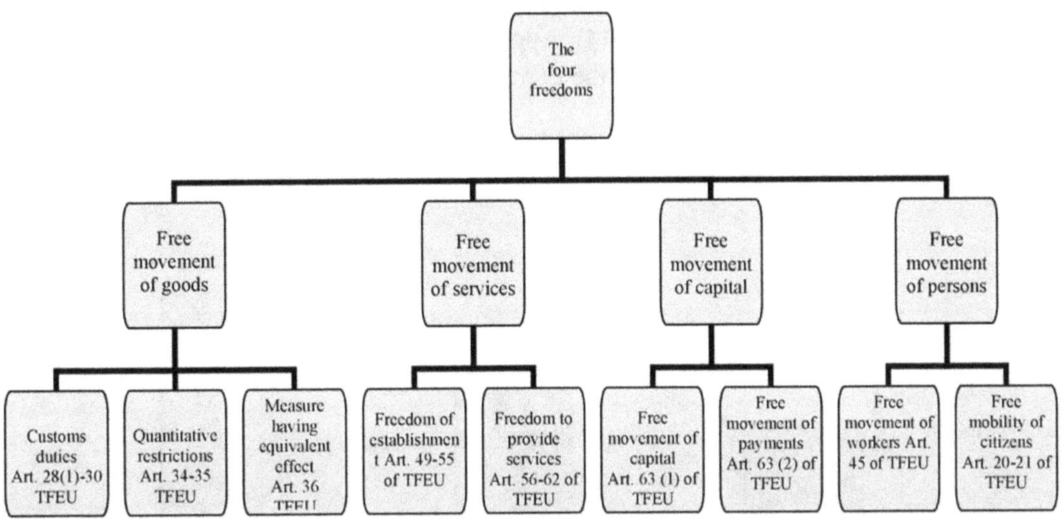

- **Fiscal Barriers:** Fiscal barriers have been reduced through the partial approximation of national VAT rates. However, the lack of fiscal harmonization at the EU level still affects intra-EU economic activities.

The major obstacles to internal mobility included physical border controls, technical and fiscal barriers. Jovanovic (2009) indicate that although many barriers to internal trade in the EU has been removed, there are others that still persist, making the internal market imperfect. He adds that while standards at the EU level are being developed, the guiding principle should be mutual recognition of national standards. Thus, along with the elimination of physical, technical and fiscal barriers, principles of mutual recognition, and promotion of standardization is crucial in order to continue the completion of the internal market.

THE RECENT TRENDS IN EU'S LABOR MOBILITY

The idea of labor mobility was first introduced with the Treaty of Paris of 1951 which enables the mobility of workers employed in coal and steel industries. The free mobility of workers was extended to all sectors of the member countries with the signing of the Treaty of Rome in 1957. Thus, the EU workers have benefited from labor mobility since the 1950s. Almost 40 years later, in 1992, the principle of free mobility was introduced for all EU citizens, whether they are economically active or not. While the free movement of people is one of the four basic freedoms of the EU, the labor mobility within the EU is not high enough. In other words, the Single European Labor Market is still far from completion.

Since its establishment, the single market has grown from 345 million citizens in 1992 to over 500 million in 2015. Approximately 8.1 million EU citizens work and live in another member country, representing 3.3% of the total EU labor force (Andor, 2014; Dhéret, Lazarowicz, Nicoli, Pascouau, & Zuleeg, 2013). Figure 2 shows that there are sharp increases in mobility since 2004. Prior to 2004 enlargement, this ratio was only about 1.4% of the total labor force in the EU.

Additionally, around 1.1 million EU citizens were living in one country but working in another country (frontier or cross-border workers) and around 1.2 million EU citizens each year are posted to another country (European Commission, 2014). Approximately, 78% of EU's active population residing in another EU country is employed, and their employment rate is around 68% (3% higher than the

Figure 2. Economically active EU citizens living in another member state (% of total EU labor force)
Source: European Commission, 2015.

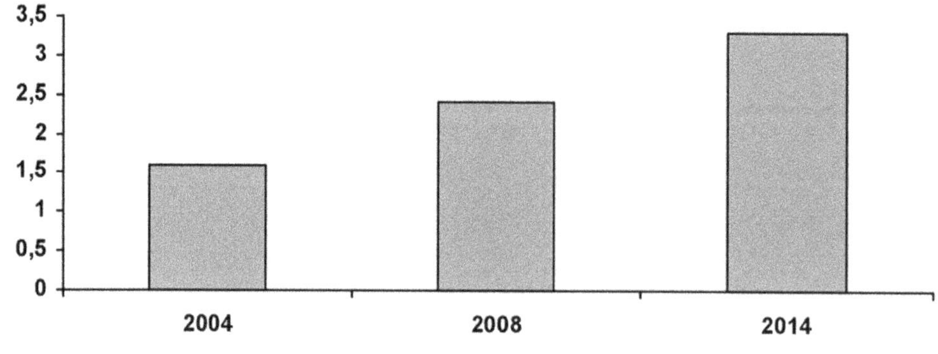

average among those residing in their country of citizenship) (European Commission, 2014). As seen in Figure 3, mobile EU citizens have a slightly higher unemployment rate than nationals of the host countries. But the key difference is that mobile EU workers are employed at a significantly higher rate (68%) than nationals of the host countries (65%).

Over the last decade, two developments shaped the labor mobility patterns within the EU. According to Andor (2014), the first development is the recent enlargements of the EU. The number of EU member countries has risen from 15 to 28 over the last decade which turned the internal market into a lot bigger and much more diverse economy. These recent enlargements accelerated the East-West mobility along with the traditional South-North mobility trend. As a result of the latest EU enlargements, the number of EU-12 citizens residing in EU-15 has increased from 1.7 to 5.6 million[3] (European Commission, 2014). Heinz and Warmendinger (2006) also indicate that East-West mobility includes a large number of temporary workers, some of whom work illegally. It is also crucial to note that future economic growth and social development in Eastern European countries will likely to reduce labor flows to the West. Secondly, the recent Eurozone crisis has acted as a stimulus for intra-EU mobility (European Commission, 2014). Andor states that the recent economic crisis has increased the imbalances in the EU labor markets and created new pressures for labor outflows from the peripheral Eurozone countries Greece, Portugal, Ireland, Spain, and Italy. He concludes that while the East-West mobility remains predominant, South-North mobility is also on the rise.

Table 1 shows the top five countries of residence for EU-28 mobile citizens as well as EFTA and third country nationals. Germany is the main country of residence of movers followed by UK, Spain, France and Italy. It is crucial to note that while in the long run free mobility applies equally to all EU citizens, this is not the case for third country nationals. However, the number of third-country nationals is higher than that of EU-28 mobile workers. While the share of third-country nationals is around 58%, EU movers make up around 41% of EU nationals.

Most EU-28 movers are of working age in the main receiving countries. Thus, the EU-28 movers aged between 15-64 are just above 78% of the EU-28 population. Among the top five countries, France is home to older EU-28 movers, with a percentage of people aged 65 years or above 20%. Table 2 shows that young workers are relatively mobile and EU labor mobility decreases with age. In terms of citizenship of the EU- 28, Romanians, Poles, Italians, Portuguese and Germans together make up 58% of the EU movers. It is interesting to note that some of the top countries of residence are also among the most represented countries of citizenship, such as Germany and Italy (Canetta et al., 2014).

Figure 3. EU mobile citizens by employment and economic activity
Source: European Commission, 2015.

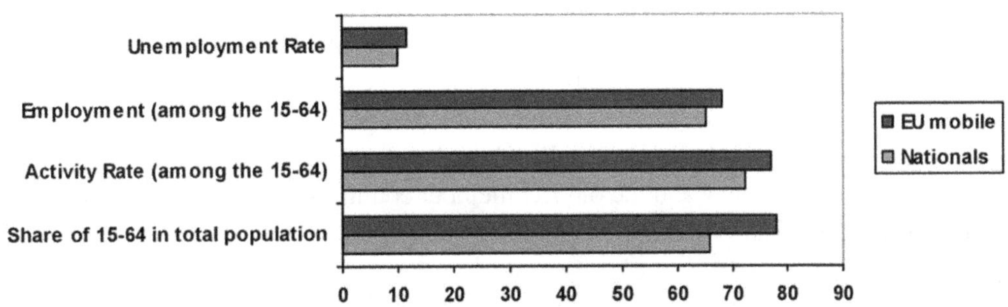

Table 1. Top 5 countries of residence of EU-28 movers, 2013

	EU-28		EFTA		Third Country Nationals		Total Foreign Population
	Total ('000)	%	Total ('000)	%	Total ('000)	%	
Germany	3 259	42,3	50	0,7	4 387	57,0	7 696
UK	2 421	49,1	33	0,7	2 475	50,2	4 930
Spain	2 062	40,7	32	0,6	2 978	58,7	5 073
France	1 407	34,4	52	1,3	2 631	64,3	4 089
Italy	1 304	29,8	9	0,2	3 074	70,1	4 388
EU-28	14 032	41,2	273	0,8	19 783	58,0	34 089

Canetta, Fries-Tersch, & Mabilia, 2014.

Table 2. Age structure of EU-28 movers, 2013

	Under 15		15-24		25-64		65 or Above		Total ('000)
	Total ('000)	%	Total ('000)	%	Total ('000)	%	Total ('000)	%	
Germany	234	7,2	352	10,8	2290	70,3	368	11,3	3259
UK	383	15,8	288	11,9	1570	64,9	179	7,4	2421
Spain	218	10,6	200	9,7	1413	68,5	233	11,3	2062
France	171	12,2	107	7,6	845	60,1	283	20,1	1407
Italy	198	15,2	144	11,0	932	71,4	30	2,3	1304
EU-28	1644	11,7	1486	10,6	9464	67,5	1395	9,9	14029

Canetta et al., 2014.

THE COSTS AND BENEFITS OF LABOR MOBILITY IN THE EU

From a macroeconomic point of view, labor mobility reduces unemployment differences between the member countries and contributes to an optimal allocation of labor resources within the EU. Nevertheless, European mobility remains low (European Commission, 2012). This is even more interesting given the huge disparities in unemployment rates between EU members. Moreover, within the EU, foreign trade policy and foreign exchange rates have lost their significance as instruments of economic flexibility as a result of the creation of the customs union and monetary union respectively. These developments have increased the importance of the existence of flexible labor markets in the EU (Zimmerman, 2009, p. 1). Labor mobility ensures a quick adjustment of labor markets at the EU level. Indeed, in the absence of national monetary and exchange rate policies, low levels of labor mobility hamper the adjustment mechanism within the monetary union (Heinz & Warmendinger, 2006). Jauer, Liebig, Martin and Puhani (2014) show, for example, that intra-EU migration flows could be able to absorb up to one-fourth of the asymmetric shocks to unemployment induced by the recent economic crisis. Thus, the increased mobility of labor between the new and the old EU member countries is an important issue in particular on its impact on European labor markets.

Labor mobility can be a solution for labor shortages and skills gaps by allowing a more efficient matching of workers' skills with job vacancies and facilitating the general upskilling of the EU's labor force (Heinz & Warmendinger, 2006). Labor mobility is crucial also for increasing social and cultural integration and strengthening EU identity among the citizens of the member states (Krause, Rinne, & Zimmermann, 2014). Since its implementation, free movement of citizens and labor has become a symbol of European integration. A Eurobarometer survey shows that 56% of citizens see the free movement of people as the most positive outcome of European integration (European Commission, 2014).

However, there are some major concerns about the free movement of labor within the EU. First, as a result of labor mobility, the general labor supply increases. The increase in labor supply accompanied by a constant labor demand may put downward pressure on wages in the receiving countries. Secondly, migrants may take away jobs from the native citizens. Especially the flows of young and skilled workforce may pose a risk on receiving economies. Migrants might also find it difficult to integrate into the local societies if they have very different social or cultural backgrounds.

Migrants place a heavy strain on the social security systems of the receiving countries. A Eurobarometer survey shows that the respondents most concerned with access to various social benefits abroad and portability of pension rights are generally higher in Northern countries and continental Europe where the welfare state is well established (Table 4). In a similar manner, the fear of losing acquired entitlements from their more generous social welfare systems may limit the mobility from these welfare states (Eurofound, 2014). All these concerns led some receiving countries to apply restrictions on mobility or limit access to their social security systems after the recent enlargements.

TOWARDS A EUROPEAN SINGLE LABOR MARKET: EXISTING PROBLEMS

Free mobility of labor has been one of the most controversial and challenging issues for the deepening of the EU's integration process. Labor mobility is regulated by a complex mix of national and EU regulation. European Commission has taken various numbers of initiatives to boost labor mobility within the EU. Any discrimination between labor based on nationality is prevented by EU legislation. Over decades, several significant steps have been made, but a number of obstacles remained to be overcome. Within the EU, a number of factors can explain the persistent low levels of labor mobility (Barslund, Busse, & Schwarzwälder, 2015; Zimmerman, 2009; Heinz & Warmedinger, 2006).

The main impediment to cross-border mobility in the EU is the *language and cultural barriers*. Most member countries have the English language as their first foreign language on the primary school curriculum. As a result, in terms of proficiency levels, there are huge differences between the best and the worst performer countries (Barslund et al., 2015). Thus, poor language skills and cultural differences present the most important barriers to geographic labor mobility in Europe. The aim of improving labor mobility at the EU level may give new impetus to the learning more than two foreign languages. Cultural barriers also play a role in the low levels of migration. Some EU citizens may be reluctant to move to another member state if history, popular culture, and the simple everyday life functions are different from their home country (McCormick, 2008, p. 148).

Harmonization of social security systems is one of the fundamental tools to ensure the labor rights which are employed in at least two different member countries. However, *the lack of harmonization of social security benefits* including pension rules is a crucial barrier to the free movement of the labor. Some member countries concern that high numbers of incoming workers and job seekers become a burden on their social security systems. Indeed, recent debates, especially in the United Kingdom, have focused on "benefit tourism" which allows foreign citizens using their right to move freely in the EU with the intention of exploiting generous social security systems.

Another barrier is the *insufficient recognition of professional qualifications* at the EU level. The EU aims to allow mobility for all types of labor by ensuring the best possible match between the requirements of workers and employers. In this respect, facilitating the recognition of professional qualifications for professionals, such as doctors, architects, engineers, electricians, accountants, teachers and a host of other professions is crucial. Thus, defining rules for the recognition procedures and simplifying the recognition of professional qualifications is necessary. Furthermore, education and training requirements for obtaining such professional qualifications can differ among the member states. Thus, *disparate education systems and policies* need to be harmonized at the EU level, and educational exchange programs should be strongly promoted.

Another reason for the low level of labor mobility is *the insufficient transparency of the European job market and online job search engines.* Indeed, effective tools and measures to match workers and employers across member countries can contribute to a true labor market. The availability and transparency of more EURES tools and services will further facilitate the mobility of workers. This will help reduce the mismatch of labor with positive effects on employment levels and economic output (European Commission, 2012).

The recent *transitional restrictions* on labor mobility from older member states to newer members (Bulgaria, Romania, and Croatia) contradict with the principle of free movement. According to transitional provisions, restrictions on the free movement of labor may apply to workers from EU countries for a transitional period of up to 7 years after they become members of the EU. Although the rationale for temporary restrictions is to ensure that labor flows from sending country did not have sudden and adverse effects on receiving country's economy, such barriers or restrictions lessen efficiency gains from the use of human capital and reduces the ability of adjustments of national labor markets during asymmetric shocks (Heinz & Warmedinger, 2006).

The transitional restrictions were split into three phases (Gower & Hawkins, 2013): For the first two years after accession (1 Jan. 2007-31 Dec. 2008) Bulgarian and Romanian workers' access to labor markets in other member countries depended on those states' national laws and policies. Romania and Bulgaria faced restrictions on access to labor markets in Belgium, Germany, Ireland, France, Italy, Lux-

Table 3. The phases of transitional restrictions on labor mobility

Transitional Arrangements	Bulgaria and Romania	Croatia
Phase 1: From the date of accession to 2 years after accession. Other member states may apply their own national rules when it comes to allowing access to the labor markets for workers from the new member state.	Jan. 1, 2007-Dec. 31, 2008	July 1, 2013-June 30, 2015
Phase 2: From 2 to 5 years after accession. Other member countries may only apply their own national rules after having notified the European Commission.	Jan. 1, 2009-Dec. 31, 2011	July 1, 2015-June 30, 2018
Phase 3: From 5 to 7 years after accession. Other member states may only apply their own national rules in case of serious disturbances in their labor market and after having notified the European Commission.	Jan. 1, 2011-Dec. 31, 2013	July 1, 2018-June 30, 2020

Canetta et al., 2014.

embourg, the Netherlands, Austria, the UK, and Malta. These countries could continue to apply their national restrictions for a further three years (1 Jan. 2009-31 Dec. 2011) if they notified the European Commission of their intention to do so. Moreover, the restrictions could be applied for a further two years (1 Jan. 2012-31 Dec. 2013) if they experienced or anticipated serious disturbances in their labor markets, and notified the European Commission.

Moreover, barriers such as the cost of moving and inefficient housing markets prevent not only mobility but also lead to potentially negative effects. Most of these barriers and limitations distinguish the European situation from the labor market in the United States (US), where mobility is much higher. Importantly, US mobility is not only higher than within Europe, but also higher than within European countries (Bonin et al., 2008). They explain the low levels of mobility in the EU by the differences in language, culture, and institutions. Zimmermann (2004, p. 1) indicate that interregional migration plays a much greater role in adjustment in the US than in the EU and this leads to the relative success of the US economy.

A Eurobarometer survey on labor market mobility provides detailed information particularly on barriers and limitations to mobility within Europe (European Commission, 2010). Survey data shows that half of the respondents perceive that language differences are the main barrier to cross-border mobility. Language and cultural barriers could be eliminated by the promotion of language capacity and education in both the sending and receiving member countries. Finding a job and suitable housing are the two other impediments. Adapting to a different culture continues to be the main barrier to mobility for 16% of respondents. The other sources of concern for the EU citizens range from the recognition of qualifications to pension rights.

FUTURE RESEARCH DIRECTIONS

Two recent developments have changed the evolution of labor mobility in the EU: recent enlargements and economic crisis. These two crucial developments have changed the direction of the labor mobility flows within the EU countries. Along with these developments, another crucial event took place with the UK's decision on leaving the EU, the so-called Brexit. Free mobility of labor within the EU has been one of the most sensitive issues in the period leading up to the Brexit. How the Brexit will change the labor

Table 4. Practical difficulties encountered or expected in relation to working abroad (% of respondents)

Barriers to Labor Mobility	Share	Barriers to Labor Mobility	Share
Lack of language skills	52%	Finding a job for one's partner/spouse	10%
Finding a job	24%	Recognition of educational and professional qualifications	10%
Finding suitable housing	16%	Transfer of pension rights	9%
Cultural adaptation	16%	Problems with returning home and integrating into work or private life	6%
Dealing with the administrative formalities	13%	Problems with income taxes or similar	4%
Accessing health care or other social benefits	11%	Access to child care, school or university for the children	4%
Obtaining a work permit	10%	Other	2%

European Commission, 2010.

mobility patterns within the EU seems to be one of the most controversial issues for policy makers in the coming years. Analyzing how these developments will be affecting the labor mobility and how the EU will respond to these challenges remains an important subject for future research.

CONCLUSION

Free mobility of labor – as one of EU's 'four freedoms'- is the cornerstone of the EU's internal market. A complete internal market enables goods, services, capital and people to move as freely as within a single country. In order to create an internal market, a huge number of physical, technical, and fiscal barriers to free movement between the EU's member countries have been abolished. Many obstacles remain, however, especially in cross-country mobility of labor. Within the EU, national labor markets are not very integrated, and the challenges to labor mobility are among the highly debated issues within the EU. The main reasons behind the low levels of labor mobility in the EU are obviously linguistic and cultural reasons, but also because of non-tariff barriers such as pension rules, recognition of professional qualification or tax and social security differences. In this respect, mutual recognition plays a crucial role in the functioning of the internal market. This does not mean that there should be the same rules in every country, but that labor, as well as other factors of production, should be able to move freely within the EU.

Completion of a fully-functioning single market is generally considered as a response to current challenges of the EU. Cross-border labor mobility not only increases employment and economic welfare but also overcome divergence in labor markets. Moreover, it reduces unemployment differences between the member countries and contributes to an optimal allocation of labor resources within the EU. In this respect, labor mobility is of crucial importance for the EU's economic integration process and the challenges that arise from the labor mobility need to be addressed directly. A better functioning labor markets not only at national but also at the EU level is needed. An increase in the number of mobile workers could help address labor market imbalances, thus divergences in labor market performance across the EU countries and achieve a Single European Labor Market.

REFERENCES

Andor, L. (2014). *Labor mobility in the EU: Challenges and perspectives for a genuine European labor market*. Press Release. Retrieved May 1, 2016, from http://europa.eu/rapid/press-release_SPEECH-14-491_en.htm

Balassa, B. (1961). *The theory of economic integration*. Homewood, IL: Richard D. Irwin.

Barslund, M., Busse, M., & Schwarzwälder, J. (2015). *Labor mobility in Europe: An untapped resource?*. CEPS Policy Brief, No. 327, March.

Bonin, H., Eichhorst, W., Florman, C., Hansen, M. O., Skiöld, L., Stuhler, J.,... Zimmermann, K. F. (2008). *Geographic mobility in the European Union: Optimising its economic and social benefits,* IZA Research Report No.19. Bonn: Institute for the Study of Labor.

Canetta, E., Fries-Tersch, E., & Mabilia, V. (2014). *Annual report on statistics on Intra-EU movers.* Network Statistics FMSSFE.

Dhéret, C., Lazarowicz, A., Nicoli, F., Pascouau, Y., & Zuleeg, F. (2013). *Making progress towards the completion of the Single European Labor Market. EPC Issue Paper No. 75*. Brussels: European Policy Centre.

Eurofound. (2014). *Labor mobility in the EU: Recent trends and policies*. Publications Office of the European Union. Luxembourg: European Commission.

European Commission. (1985). *White Paper on completing the internal market*. COM (85) 310, 14 June. Brussels: European Commission.

European Commission. (2010). *Geographical and labor market mobility. Special Eurobarometer, 337/ Wave 72.5*. Brussels: European Commission.

European Commission. (2012). *Single Market Act II–Together for new growth. Communication from the Commission to the European Parliament, the Council, the European Economic and Social Committee and the Committee of the Regions, COM(2012) 573 final*. Brussels: European Commission.

European Commission. (2013). *Labor market developments in Europe 2013. European Economy Series 6/2013*. Brussels: European Commission.

European Commission. (2014). *Labor mobility within the EU*. MEMO, Press Release Database 25 September. Retrieved May 1, 2016, from http://europa.eu/rapid/press-release_MEMO-14-541_en.htm

European Commission. (2015). *Labor mobility in the EU: Facts, figures and the labor mobility package*. DG Employment, Social Affairs and Inclusion Free Movement of Workers and Coordination of Social Security Systems.

Gower, M., & Hawkins, O. (2013). *Ending of transitional restrictions for Bulgarian and Romanian workers*. Standard Note SN/HA/06606, House of Commons Library.

Heinz, F. F., & Warmedinger, W. M. (2006). *Cross-border labor mobility within an enlarged EU*. ECB Occasional Paper Series No. 52. Frankfurt: European Central Bank.

Jauer, J., Liebig, T., Martin, J. P., & Puhani, P. A. (2014). *Migration as an adjustment mechanism in the crisis? A comparison of Europe and the United States*. IZA Discussion Paper No. 7921. Bonn: Institute for the Study of Labor.

Jovanovic, M. N. (1998). *International economic integration: Limits and prospects*. London: Routledge.

Jovanovic, M. N. (2009). *Evolutionary economic geography: Location and production and the European Union*. Oxfordshire, UK: Routledge.

Krause, A., Rinne, U., & Zimmermann, K. F. (2014). *How far away is a Single European Labor Market?* IZA Discussion Paper No. 8383. Bonn: Institute for the Study of Labor.

Mariniello, M., Sapir, A., & Terzi, A. (2015). *The long road towards the European Single Market*. Bruegel Working Paper, 2015/01.

McCormick, J. (2008). *Understanding the European Union: A concise introduction* (4th ed.). Palgrave Macmillan.

Moussis, N. (2011). Access to European Union: Law, economics, policies (19th ed.). Rixensart.

Mundell, R. A. (1961). A theory of optimum currency areas. *The American Economic Review*, *51*, 657–665.

Robson, P. (1998). The economics of international integration (4th ed.). London: Routledge.

Studer, R. (2015). How important is an integrated European market? Some insights from history, Perspectives on Europe. *Autumn, 45*(2), 14-19. Retrieved May 13, 2016, from http://councilforeuropeanstudies.org/files/Perspectives/Autumn%202015/s4_Studer.pdf

Zimmermann, K. F. (2004). *European labor lobility: Challenges and potentials. IZA Policy Paper No. 69*. Bonn: Institute for the Study of Labor.

Zimmermann, K. F. (2009). *Labor mobility and the integration of European Labor Markets*. IZA Discussion Paper No. 3999. Bonn: Institute for the Study of Labor.

ADDITIONAL READING

Baldwin, R. E., & Wyplosz, C. (2012). *The economics of European Integration* (4th ed.). London: McGraw-Hill.

El-Agraa, A. E. (2011). The European Union: Economics and policies (9th ed.). United Kingdon: Cambridge University Pres.

Ilzkovitz, F., Dierx, A., Kovacs, V., & Sousa, N. (2007). *Steps towards a deeper economic integration: the Internal Market in the 21st century.* A contribution to the Single Market Review, European Economy No. 271.

Sapir, A. (2011). European integration at the crossroads: A review essay on the 50th anniversary of Bela Balassas theory of economic integration. *Journal of Economic Literature*, *49*(4), 1200–1229. doi:10.1257/jel.49.4.1200

Studer, R. (2015). *How important is an integrated European market? Some insights from history, Perspectives on Europe, Autumn, 45*(2), 14-19. Retrieved May 13, 2016, from http://councilforeuropeanstudies.org/files/Perspectives/Autumn%202015/s4_Studer.pdf

KEY TERMS AND DEFINITIONS

Cecchini Report: A report prepared by a group of experts, chaired by Paolo Cecchini, examining the benefits and costs of establishing a common market in the EU.

Economic Integration: Economic integration is an economic arrangement between two or more nations, marked by the reduction or elimination of barriers to trade that prevent the flows of goods and services.

Enlargement: The EU has gone through several phases of expansion since its establishment in the late 1950s. The biggest wave was in 2004 when 10 countries joined, eight of them being Central and Eastern European countries. Currently, the EU has 28 member states.

European Union: European Union is an economic and political body aiming at achieving closer economic and political union among its member states. As of 2016, the European Union has 28 member countries.

Four Freedoms: Four freedoms denotes free mobility of goods, services, capital and persons in the EU's internal market.

Internal Market: An economic area without internal borders in which the free movement of goods, persons, services and capital is ensured.

Labor Mobility: The easiness of which workers are able to move freely within an economy or between different economies.

Single European Act: The Single European Act, signed in 1986, set a deadline of end 1992 for the establishment of the common market. Within the EU, the common market was launched on 1 January 1993.

ENDNOTES

1 The concepts of *common market*, *single market* and *internal market* are used mostly synonymously but they have significant nuances of meaning. *Common market* is a stage in the regional economic integration process, which, aims to remove all the barriers to intra-regional trade with a view to the merger of national markets into a *single market* giving rise to conditions as close as possible to a genuine internal market. Treaty of Lisbon (Art. 26) ignores the concepts of the "single market" and the "common market" and replaces the *internal market*, as an area without internal frontiers in which the free movement of goods, persons, services and capital is ensured. For more details see Moussis (2011).

2 Treaty of Rome –the founding treaty of the EU- was signed in Rome in 1957. Since then a series of treaties has extended the scope and the objectives of the EU. The amending treaties are: Single European Act (1987); Treaty of Maastricht (1993), Treaty of Amsterdam (1999), Treaty of Nice (2003) and Treaty of Lisbon (2009).

3 The EU-12 refers to the new member states that joined the EU in 2004 and 2007 enlargements. The EU-2 comprised the following countries: Bulgaria, Republic of Cyprus, Czech Republic, Estonia, Hungary, Latvia, Lithuania, Malta, Poland, Romania, Slovakia, and Slovenia. The EU-15 refers to the number of member countries in the EU prior to the accession of ten candidate countries on 1 May 2004. The EU-15 comprised the following countries: Austria, Belgium, Denmark, Finland, France, Germany, Greece, Ireland, Italy, Luxembourg, Netherlands, Portugal, Spain, Sweden, and United Kingdom. The EU-28 refers to: Austria, Belgium, Bulgaria, Croatia, Republic of Cyprus, Czech Republic, Denmark, Estonia, Finland, France, Germany, Greece, Hungary, Ireland, Italy, Latvia, Lithuania, Luxembourg, Malta, Netherlands, Poland, Portugal, Romania, Slovakia, Slovenia, Spain, Sweden and the UK.

Chapter 6
Statistical Analysis of Women's Labor Force Data of OECD Countries

Fatih Çemrek
Eskişehir Osmangazi University, Turkey

Füsun Yenilmez
Eskişehir Osmangazi University, Turkey

ABSTRACT

Women take part in working life less in proportion to men due to the reasons such as the value judgments of the societies in which they live, the roles of motherhood and housewifery which the society have imposed on them, and social gender inequality. Making use of the economic potential of the country fully and effectively depends on increasing the employment rates of women which remain behind the male employment for various reasons. In this study, it was tried to reveal differences of OECD countries in each other in terms of women's labor force variables. To realize this aim, 9 indicators of women's labor force pertaining to 32 countries, which were received from OECD Employment Outlook 2015, OECD Labor Statistics Book and OECD official website www.oecd.org, were compared with the help of Multidimensional Scaling. The study was carried out for 32 countries both two dimensionally and three dimensionally. Additionally, Factor Analysis was utilized. Determining the most remote countries together in dimensions, variables leading to differences were shown in graphics.

INTRODUCTION AND PURPOSE

Women's taking an active role in social and economic development process and increasing women participation in the labor force are quite important issues to enhance sustainable development from a social perspective. In this context, more female participation in the labor force will prevent female poverty, and promote better living conditions (Korkmaz, Alacahan, Cesim, Yücel, & Aras, 2013, 1847).

Even if the rates of women's employment have increased in the globalization period, this increase is seen mostly at works which are low paid and deprived of social security and legal protection. Women

DOI: 10.4018/978-1-5225-2008-5.ch006

are employed mainly in the service sector. This situation is related to both implemented policies and the role which the society has imposed on women. This case is expressed with the concept of "gender mainstreaming". Gender roles are behaviors which have come up until today since the first communities, having the characteristics of cultural inheritance.

Furthermore, the wage differences between men and women are also an issue in question. The secret behind unequal positions of women in work, career, economic and political participation lies in the definition of women as housewives socially (Mies, 1994).

It is generally possible to handle the reasons of women's participation in the labor force economically and socially. Lack of income, changes in marital status, having a child or not and level of education are ranked among the reasons why women labor force participated in work life. Taken into consideration sociologically, gaining prestige or self-realization comes to the front (Öztürk & Çetin, 2009).

On looking into the rates of women employment in OECD countries in 2015, the average of OECD is found out as 45.13%. Estonia and Finland are seen with 48.90% in the first place. Among 34 countries, Turkey is in the last place with a 29.60%. Above Turkey, the country in the 33rd place, Mexico takes place with a 33% rate.

Over time, women's labor market positions and way of working have also changed. How this change happened on sectoral basis is an important subject since the sectoral distribution of employment in a country is the significant indicator of the developmental level of that country. While the employment together with the development has been decreasing in the agricultural sector, it has been increasing in non-agricultural sectors. This condition prevails exactly in the women employment. Whereas women labor force in developing countries is concentrated in the agricultural sector, in developed countries it is concentrated in the service sector. Correspondingly, in developed countries, paid woman labor takes the place of unpaid family labor in developing countries (Berber & Yılmaz Eser, 2008). When it is evaluated from this perspective, women's labor force participation is an important issue for sustainable development.

Considering the sectoral distribution of the women workforce in OECD countries; the women employment rate in the agricultural sector OECD average stood at 4.8. Turkey is in first place with 41.70% in this classification. Poland takes the second place with 14.20% proportion. The United Kingdom takes in the last place with 0.5%. Looking at these figures, we can say that nearly half of women employment is in the agricultural sector in Turkey.

Looking into the rates of women employment in the industrial sector, OECD average stood at 13.74%. In this classification, Czech Republic is located in the first place with 26%. The Slovak Republic comes in the second place with a rate of 24.10%. In the last rank located the United Kingdom with a rate of 7.40% as well as in agricultural sector.

Looking at the women employment rate in the services sector; OECD average stood at 81.63%. The United Kingdom is located in the first rank with 91.20% in this classification. Norway comes in the second place with a rate of 90.50%. Turkey takes the last place with a rate of 43%.

On studying the researches about women's labor force participation, it is stated that schooling rate, age, marital status and the number of children are the main factors which influence women's decision to take part in the labor force (Dayıoğlu, 2000; Dayıoğlu & Kasnakoğlu, 1997; Tunalı & Ercan, 1998; Tunalı, 1997). Çınar (1994) indicates that "security" concerns affecting the women's working decisions led them to prefer to work at home in comparison to formal working. Yenilmez and Işıklı (2010), comparing the rates of women labor force participation in Turkey with the ones in the other countries taking place in different groups, detected that in this ranking, Turkey stood at the last ranks in the list of many countries such as OECD, EU and Islamic countries took place.

The studies which examine the income differences between men and women found out significant differences between hourly incomes of men and women as well (Kasnakoğlu & Dayıoğlu, 1997; Tunalı & Ercan, 1998; Tansel, 1994, 1999; Dayıoğlu & Tunalı, 2003).

In another group of research, it was examined the effects of the industrial system changing with structural adjustment policies on women's employment (Çağatay & Berik, 1990; Çağatay & Özler, 1995). These studies found evidence related to the feminization of labor force following 1980 structural adjustment program which adopts export-oriented growth strategy.

Women employment is one of the overemphasized subjects in Turkey as well as in the world. Killingworth and Heckman (1986), focusing on western economies in their studies, reviewed theoretical and empirical studies about the women labor force supply. Gustafsson and Jacobsson (1985), explaining the increasing women participation rate, pointed out the wage difference decreasing in reference to the gender in Sweden. Similarly, Shimada and Higuchi (1985) exposed that the improvements in women's education and wages led to a significant increase in paid women employment. Michale (1985) analyzed the relationship between fertility and marital status and labor force participation in his study. Psacharopoulos and Tzannatos (1993) examined the women labor force participation in 15 Latin American countries and stated that women labor force participation increased despite unfavorable economic conditions. Lim (2000), researched the influences of cyclical fluctuations in women employment and concluded that East Asia economic crisis had a different impact on women employment.

As revealed by the studies, it is observed major interzonal differences between the rates of men and women employment in the world. According to the United Nations' statistics, In the world, it is observed that there are huge differences in areas with respect to female –male employment rates (United Nations, 2012). 2012 Global Social Gender Gap Report by World Economic Forum also supported the United Nations' data. It is stressed that social gender inequality about participation into the economy continued in all of 135 countries involved in the report (Hausmann, Tyson, & Zahidi, 2012, pp. 7-20). Women do not have the same employment opportunities as men do in most parts of the world. On the other hand, the rates of women and men employment are viewed as close to each other in non-agricultural employment in the developed regions including North America and Europe together with Caucasians and Central Asia (United Nations, 2012).

This study aimed to evaluate indicators of OECD countries in terms of female labor. To achieve this goal, factor analysis performed, which is commonly used for this purpose. According to the results of factor analysis, OECD countries have been ranked in means of these criteria. The score values of the countries have been calculated in terms of obtained three factors, so, the countries have been ranked according to this score values. Highness of factor scores shows the country's good condition in terms of female employment indicators. The multidimensional scaling (MDS) analysis is applied as a secondary analysis to display the countries by graphically in all dimensions. The results of this analysis and the results of factor analysis showed similarity. The aim of the study is to examine the women employment in the light of the data related to the women labor force of 32 countries, members of OECD. In this context, the analysis of 32 countries will be compared with the factor analysis and multidimensional scaling.

On literature review for the method of this study, a number of studies on variety of issues such as animal husbandry, energy, labor, finance, education, health have been identified, which applied factor analysis and multidimensional scaling analysis (Cheung & So, 2005; Sığırlı, Ediz, Cangür, Ercan, & Kan, 2006; Ersungur, Kızıltan, & Polat, 2007; Şahin, Abay, & Miran, 2008; Ersöz, 2009; Çakır, Sözen, & Yücesu, 2009; Albayrak, 2010; Bülbül & Köse, 2010; Karacaer & Kapusuzoğlu, 2010; Akküçük, 2011; Gevrekçi, Ataç, Takma, Akbaş, & Taşkın, 2011; Akın & Eren, 2012; Arslan & Tatlıdil, 2012; Beyhan

Acar, 2013; Demiray Erol, 2013; Çakır Zeytinoğlu & Sadıç, 2013; Kapusuzoğlu & İbicioğlu, 2013; Aydın, 2013; Tezcan, 2014; Çelik, 2015; Ersöz, Türkoğlu Elitaş, & Ersöz, 2015; Yenilmez & Girginer, 2016).

THE METHOD

In this study; using statistical data of the OECD countries about the women labor force with MDS analysis, it is aimed to demonstrate their similarities and differences graphically, and on the basis of these statistical data, to make the ranking of countries with the help of factor analysis.

For this aim, the data on women labor force indicators of 34 countries were obtained from Organisation for Economic Co-operation and Development (OECD, 2015) and Organisation for Economic Co-operation and Development (OECD, 2016). Nevertheless, Switzerland and the USA was left out of the scope of the analysis since the observations by some variables could not be reached, so the study has been conducted in 32 countries.

Variables and Definitions

The variables examined in this study;

X_1: Employment rate of college graduate women (aged 25-64) (%)
X_2: College graduate women's labor force participation rate (%)
X_3: College graduate women's unemployment rate (%)
X_4: Women's employment rate (%)
X_5: Part-time working female ratio (%)
X_6: Labor force participation rate among women (aged 15-64)
X_7: Women's employment rate in the agricultural sector (%)
X_8: Women's employment rate in industrial sector (%)
X_9: Women's employment rate in the service sector (%)

Techniques

Factor Analysis

The base of factor analysis, commonly applied in many areas, mainly in social sciences were laid by Charles Spearman. Spearman developed the factor analysis in order to investigate the relationship between the success in various lessons and the intelligence level of students in 1904 (Sharma, 1996, p. 90).

The aim of factor analysis is to find out a new unrelated variable in limited number, called factor, among the variables associated with each variable in an event with p variable. This analysis tries to make dimension reduction and to resolve the dependency structure (Tatlıdil, 2002, p. 167).

Standardizing X_{pxn} raw data matrix, Z_{pxn} standardized data matrix is used. Linear model showing the relationship between common factors and variables Z_j is expressed as follows:

$$z_{ii} = a_{i1}f_1 + a_{i2}f_2 + \ldots + a_{im}f_m + b_i u_i \quad (1)$$

a_{jim} : *j*. The load or weight of the variable on factor *m*

f_m : Factor *m*

u_i : Residual factor

b_i : Coefficient for residual factor

It is also possible to write equation (1) in the form of matrix as follows:

$$Z = AF + BU \tag{2}$$

After factor analysis is applied, with factor conversion;

- Dimension reduction,
- Perpendicularity or ensuring independence,
- The conceptual significance is provided.

In factor analysis, factors in the minimum number are defined, which explain the correlations between variables the best or taking them into account; with factor rotation, the most reasonable factor solution is found out; loads of factors are estimated; comment is made for the common factor or factors; If necessary, factor scores are estimated (Anderson, 1984; Sharma, 1996, p. 99; Johnson & Wichern, 2007; Stevens, 2009; Härdle & Simar, 2012).

Multidimensional Scaling (MDS)

With multidimensional scaling, it is aimed to expose an image which reveals the positions and the structural relationship among these objects in multidimensional space, using the specified distance values determined in reference to *p* variable among the objects (individual or observation) in n number (Özdamar, 1999, p. 479).

The general purpose of multidimensional scaling analysis is to reveal the structure of objects, in small dimensions, closely to the original shape (using distant values). MDS is one of the Q-analysis techniques like cluster and discriminant analysis; moreover, it takes place among R analysis techniques due to the dimension reduction feature (Tatlıdil, 2002, p. 353). This analysis is a graphical representation which stands for the distances between the objects with a minimum of errors and aims to identify their distances via any functions (Oğuzlar, 1995).

MDS is a type of multivariable statistical analysis which is applied to the analysis of behavioral data such as personal preferences, attitudes, tendencies, beliefs, and expectations. The geometric meaning of multidimensional scaling analysis is that the related individuals or stimulants are shown as points in space in which each variable is a dimension (Kurtuluş, 1998, pp. 436-438). It is involved in classification and grouping analyses such as cluster analysis and discriminant analysis (Hair, Anderson, Tahtam, & Black, 1998; Tatlıdil, 2002; İpekçi Çetin, 2003).

MDS is divided into metric and non-metric scaling techniques. A similar approach to the implementation of the basic components of the metric scaling techniques is used. When distances between the objects in the number of n are given as matrix *S*, the object is represented by *n* point in *(n-1)* dimensional *E* space. S_{ij} values in here,

$$S_{ij} < S_{ik} + S_{kj} \text{ for all } i, j \text{ and } k \tag{3}$$

provides the condition.

The geometric model of each *n* objects which fulfills this requirement can be established. The problem encountered here is that the model is represented by a small number of dimensions. For this reason, when scaling to reduce the number of dimensions, it is calculated d_{ij} values which will represent these values in new space in place of S_{ij} values.

The steps followed in the implementation of non-metric scaling techniques:

$$d_{r_1 s_1} < \ldots < d_{r_m s_m},\ m = (1/2)n(n-1) \tag{4}$$

- All the elements of *D* similarity matrix (except for diagonal elements) are ranked.
- The stress value, which is an expression of the difference between the actual figure in multidimensional space and the estimated figure in reduced dimensional space, is calculated, and this process continues until the smallest stress value is obtained (Kalaycı, 2005, pp. 380-381; Jobson, 1992, pp. 568-580).

The stress value has emerged as an important criterion for determining whether the number of dimensions is fit, which was used in graphical representation acquired as a result of multidimensional scaling analysis. The stress measure, the measure of concordance or goodness of fit, has an extensive usage in multidimensional scaling analysis.

For the coefficient of stress, which is the measure of conformity of the acquired figure with the actual figure, the following tolerance proportions developed by Kruskall are applied. Accordingly;

- If stress>0.20, weak concordance,
- If stress=0.10, medium concordance,
- If stress=0.05, good concordance,
- If stress=0.00, complete concordance is considered to be (Tatlıdil, 2002, p. 363).

Application

Descriptive statistics of the data which are in relation to the variables used in the study, obtained by the countries, were provided in Table 1.

The Results of the Factor Analysis

Sample Sufficiency Test and Sphericity Test

Table 2 gives information about two hypotheses of factor analysis. From the Table 2, according to Kaiser-Meyer-Olkin (KMO) sampling adequacy test results, KMO value is 0.765. This value is higher than 0.70, and it means a good result. Besides, Bartlett's sphericity test (H_0: all correlation coefficients are equal to 0) rejects/rejected the hypothesis at 0.05 significance level. In addition, supposition test of sphericity

Table 1. Descriptive statistics of the variables

Variable	Minimum	Maximum	Mean	Std. Deviation
X_1	62.30	88.30	78.5094	6.65865
X_2	64.10	91.60	83.1250	6.00446
X_3	1.80	22.70	5.7406	4.39184
X_4	29.60	48.90	45.0625	3.82595
X_5	56.80	80.10	67.8437	6.99119
X_6	33.60	84.20	66.5219	9.96017
X_7	0.50	41.70	4.2844	7.61921
X_8	7.40	26.00	13.7406	5.33061
X_9	43.00	91.20	81.6281	10.02716

Table 2. KMO and Bartlett's test

Kaiser-Meyer-Olkin Measure of Sampling Adequacy.		0.765
Bartlett's Test of Sphericity	Approx. Chi-Square	344.433
	df	36
	Sig.	0.000

Table 3. Eigenvalues and variance explanation ratios of the factors

Factor	Eigenvalue	Variance Explanation Ratio (%)
1	4.632	51.47
2	1.295	14.38
3	1.200	13.34
Total	-------	79.19

by the Bartlett test (H_0: All correlation coefficients are not quite far from zero) is rejected on a level of statistical significance $p<0.0005$ for approx. ChiSquare=344.433. Consequently, the coefficients are not all zero, so that the second acceptance of factor analysis is satisfied. As a result, both acceptances for the conduct of factor analysis are satisfied, and we can proceed to it.

As a result of factor analysis application, 3 numbers of the eigenvalue, of which eigenvalues are greater than 1, were obtained. Total variance explanation ratio was found to be 79.2% for these three factors. This means that approximately 21% variance loss is a matter of discussion by obtaining 3 factors from 9 original variables.

In Table 3, the first factor explains %51.47 of total variance; the second factor 14.38%, and the third factor 13.34%.

By looking at the component matrix demonstrated in Table 4, it can be decided that the analyzed variables take place in which factors.

As seen in Table 4, It cannot be exactly determined that variables X_2, X_5, take place in which factors. For this reason, the values in Table 5 were obtained by applying VARIMAX rotation, one of the factor rotation techniques.

From Table 5, it is easily determined that each variable takes place in which factor. In reference to this, factors and variables falling within each factor are shown in Table 6.

According to Table 6, X_1 (employment rate of college graduate women (aged 25-64) (%)), X_2 (college graduate women's labor force participation rate (%)), X_4 (women's employment rate (%)), X_6 (labor

Table 4. Component matrix

Variable	Component		
	1	2	3
X_6	0.907	0.183	-0.035
X_4	0.894	0.118	-0.063
X_1	0.819	0.420	-0.263
X_9	0.815	-0.424	0.351
X_7	-0.758	0.441	-0.028
X_2	0.692	0.647	0.168
X_5	0.489	-0.451	-0.246
X_3	-0.398	0.222	0.732
X_8	-0.474	0.158	-0.615

Extraction Method: Principal Component Analysis a. 3 components extracted.

Table 5. Rotated component matrix

Variable	Component		
	1	2	3
X_2	0.931	**0.166**	**-0.178**
X_1	0.900	**0.077**	**0.316**
X_6	0.782	**0.397**	**0.298**
X_4	0.730	**0.404**	**0.348**
X_9	**0.267**	0.905	**0.277**
X_8	**-0.183**	-0.745	**0.197**
X_7	**-0.239**	-0.674	**-0.508**
X_3	**-0.192**	**0.131**	-0.830
X_5	**0.061**	**0.350**	0.614

Extraction Method: Principal Component Analysis. Rotation Method: Varimax with Kaiser Normalization. a. Rotation converged in 4 iterations

Table 6. Variables falling within each factor

Factor	Variable
1	X_1, X_2, X_4, X_6
2	X_7, X_8, X_9
3	X_3, X_5

force participation rate among women (aged 15-64) (%)) take place in the 1st factor. The 1st factor is comprised of the general women employment rates.

The variables in the 2nd factor are respectively X_7 (women's employment rate in the agricultural sector (%)), X_8 (women's employment rate in the industrial sector (%)), X_9 (women's employment rate (%)). The 2nd factor shows the sectoral distribution of women employment.

Variables X_3 (college graduate women's unemployment rate (%)) and X_5 (part-time working female ratio (%)) have taken place in the 3rd factor. The 3rd factor is comprised of non-employment rates of women.

As a result of factor rotation, factor score coefficient matrix was obtained as in shown in Table 7.

When viewed from the Table 7, it has the same result as obtained in Table 5 according to the coefficient factor of the variables. This means that the variables with the most weight to factors still have not changed.

As can be seen from Table 8, as for the first factor by the score values of countries, the most remote countries each other is determined as Sweden and South Korea. As for the second factor, on looking at score values of countries, Greece and Turkey are most remote countries each other. For the 3rd factor, the most remote countries each other can be viewed as Hungary and Mexico.

In Table 8, the ranking of countries is included in terms of the first factor scores. When looked at this ranking, Sweden has the highest score value whereas Korea has the lowest one.

Table 7. Factor score coefficient rotation matrix as a result of factor rotation

Variable	Component		
	1	2	3
X_1	0.369	-0.208	0.073
X_2	0.441	-0.083	-0.301
X_3	0.008	0.255	-0.586
X_4	0.206	0.028	0.071
X_5	-0.148	0.107	0.376
X_6	0.241	0.019	0.029
X_7	0.119	-0.283	-0.221
X_8	0.051	-0.450	0.287
X_9	-0.122	0.456	0.015

Extraction Method: Principal Component Analysis. Rotation Method: Varimax with Kaiser Normalization. Component Scores.

Multidimensional scaling analysis was conducted for 9 variables in order to analyze the women employment data of 32 countries, members of OECD. MDS was conducted as 2 and 3 dimensionally, and the stress value was obtained smaller (stress value=0.022653) in three dimensions as well, and also a graphic providing a concordance close to the complete concordance was found out. For this reason, the results of 3 dimensional MDS analysis were presented, and the comments were made on these results. The results are shown in Table 9.

The graph handling the results in Table 9 is shown in Figure 1.

When countries are ranked according to the first dimension, Table 10 is obtained. According to Table 10, it can be seen that Greece and Turkey are the most remote countries each other in the first dimension. The variables leading to differences between these two countries are presented in the graphic in Figure 2.

When countries are ranked according to the second dimension, Table 11 is obtained. According to Table 11, it can be seen that Greece and Turkey are the most remote countries each other in the first dimension. The variables leading to differences between these two countries are presented in the graphic in Figure 2.

According to Figure 2, in comparison Turkey with Greece (two most remote countries each other in the 1st and 2nd dimensions), the variables that cause differences between these two countries most are variables X_7 (women's employment rate in the agricultural sector (%)), X_9 (women's employment rate in the service sector (%)).

At the beginning of the study, it was noted that the sectoral distribution of employment in the country is an important indicator of the level of development of the country. While the employment together with the development has been decreasing in the agricultural sector, it has been increasing in non-agricultural sectors. This condition prevails exactly in the women employment. Whereas women labor force in developing countries is concentrated in the agricultural sector, in developed countries it is concentrated in the service sector. Accordingly, since X_7 (women's employment rate in the agricultural sector (%)) is higher in Turkey than in Greece, Turkey is regarded as a developing country. Rather, X_9 (women employment rate in the service sector (%)) in Turkey is relatively low in comparison to Greece, so in reference to these variables, Greece is assessed as a developed country.

Table 8. VARIMAX factor score values for countries as a result of factor rotation

Country	f_1	Country	f_2	Country	f_3
Sweden	1.51262	Greece	1.96517	Hungary	1.41129
Iceland	1.49447	Spain	1.29301	Slovak Republic	1.35844
Portugal	1.33458	Ireland	1.08247	Turkey	1.23013
Denmark	1.16536	United Kingdom	1.02337	Ireland	1.11453
Slovenia	1.11461	Canada	0.85929	Netherlands	1.1075
Norway	1.10967	Belgium	0.76543	Luxembourg	1.04241
Netherlands	0.85588	Israel	0.75578	Iceland	0.75852
Finland	0.77284	Australia	0.75386	Sweden	0.61422
Estonia	0.6933	France	0.4973	Australia	0.59896
Poland	0.6264	Iceland	0.45312	New Zealand	0.46789
Germany	0.60802	Italy	0.44556	United Kingdom	0.41193
New Zealand	0.48178	Norway	0.42802	France	0.28734
France	0.30709	Netherlands	0.42494	Finland	0.27928
Israel	0.27468	New Zealand	0.33544	Poland	0.1777
Canada	0.17137	Sweden	0.32194	Germany	0.16208
Austria	0.01423	Austria	0.25036	Italy	0.0674
Spain	-0.08303	Japan	0.24621	Japan	0.03954
United Kingdom	-0.08782	Finland	0.21652	Israel	0.03187
Belgium	-0.10714	Chile	0.17984	Spain	0.00605
Australia	-0.20347	Korea	-0.0105	Czech Republic	-0.02561
Slovak Republic	-0.21002	Denmark	-0.02122	Norway	-0.20195
Luxembourg	-0.2364	Germany	-0.16621	Greece	-0.2188
Czech Republic	-0.28639	Mexico	-0.24917	Estonia	-0.25476
Hungary	-0.54055	Estonia	-0.69702	Korea	-0.29255
Chile	-0.56858	Luxembourg	-0.74537	Portugal	-0.33363
Ireland	-0.57406	Hungary	-0.84223	Slovenia	-0.40241
Italy	-1.03499	Portugal	-0.86454	Chile	-0.45387
Greece	-1.25045	Slovak Republic	-1.06405	Belgium	-0.48907
Mexico	-1.56077	Czech Republic	-1.46108	Canada	-1.42887
Japan	-1.599	Poland	-1.51532	Denmark	-1.82391
Turkey	-1.74801	Slovenia	-1.92052	Austria	-2.39183
Korea	-2.44621	Turkey	-2.74039	Mexico	-2.8498

When countries are ranked as to 3rd dimension, Table 13 is obtained. As to Table 13, Czech Republic and Mexico are the most remote countries each other. The variables causing differences between the Czech Republic and Mexico are identified by the graphic in Figure 3.

Table 9. Coordinate values of each country in dimensions in 3 dimensional MDS

Country	Dimension			Country	Dimension		
	1	2	3		1	2	3
Australia	0.6256	0.173	-0.0329	Italy	-0.2776	-0.0252	-0.1099
Austria	0.3078	0.1246	-0.0198	Japan	1.4429	0.4334	-0.0055
Belgium	-0.2752	-0.0605	-0.0554	Korea	1.0864	0.3603	-0.0589
Canada	1.1087	0.3076	-0.0095	Luxembourg	-0.3239	0.0407	-0.0064
Chile	-0.4613	-0.1374	-0.0393	Mexico	-0.285	-0.0898	-0.2458
Czech Republic	0.0414	0.2769	0.5088	Netherlands	-0.2521	-0.0927	-0.0078
Denmark	0.6262	0.1111	0.0397	New Zealand	0.0204	-0.0177	-0.0092
Estonia	0.123	0.0135	0.0584	Norway	0.1055	-0.0043	-0.0128
Finland	0.7475	0.174	0.0095	Poland	-1.4097	-0.419	0.01
France	0.0314	0.0189	-0.0252	Portugal	-0.661	-0.304	0.0609
Germany	0.2367	0.0783	0.0669	Slovak Republic	0.7391	0.2049	0.0837
Greece	2.2246	0.6306	-0.0815	Slovenia	-1.0348	-0.3345	0.0744
Hungary	0.2309	0.1527	0.0206	Spain	0.8117	0.2279	-0.0835
Iceland	0.8066	0.1518	0.0516	Sweden	0.712	0.0566	0.0285
Ireland	0.3809	0.1302	-0.1582	Turkey	-8.3595	-2.439	0.0244
Israel	0.2601	0.0606	-0.0393	United Kingdom	0.6705	0.1964	-0.0366

Figure 1. 3 dimensional MDS graphic

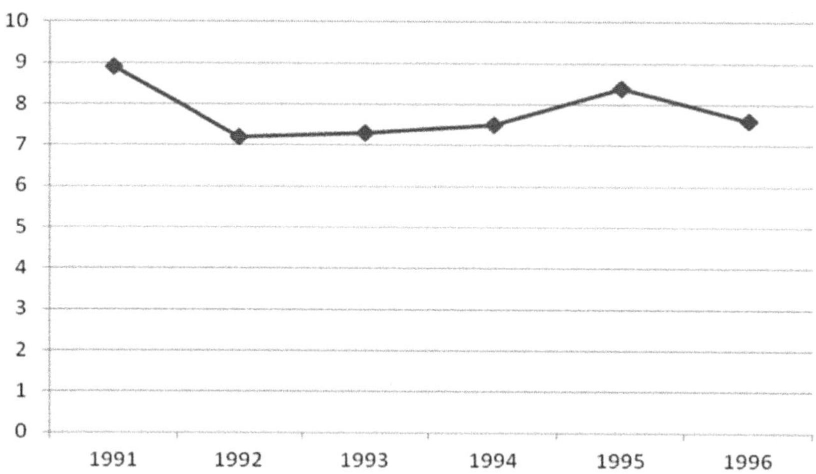

According to the Figure 3, The variables causing differences between the Czech Republic and Mexico most are variables X_5 (part-time working female ratio (%)), X_6 (labor force participation rate among women (aged 15-64) (%)) and X_8 (women's employment rate in industrial sector (%)).

As shown in the evaluation results, the Czech Republic, also an EU country, is better off than Mexico in terms of stated variables. This can be explained by that Czech Republic is a developed EU country.

Table 10. Coordinate values of countries ranked as to 1st dimension

Country	Coordinate Value	Country	Coordinate Value	Country	Coordinate Value	Country	Coordinate Value
Greece	2.2246	Sweden	0.712	Hungary	0.2309	Italy	-0.2776
Japan	1.4429	United Kingdom	0.6705	Estonia	0.1230	Mexico	-0.2850
Canada	1.1087	Denmark	0.6262	Norway	0.1055	Luxembourg	-0.3239
Korea	1.0864	Australia	0.6256	Czech Republic	0.0414	Chile	-0.4613
Spain	0.8117	Ireland	0.3809	France	0.0314	Portugal	-0.6610
Iceland	0.8066	Austria	0.3078	New Zealand	0.0204	Slovenia	-1.0348
Finland	0.7475	Israel	0.2601	Netherlands	-0.2521	Poland	-1.4097
Slovak Republic	0.7391	Germany	0.2367	Belgium	-0.2752	Turkey	-8.3595

Table 11. Coordinate values of countries ranked as to 2nd dimension

Country	Coordinate Value	Country	Coordinate Value	Country	Coordinate Value	Country	Coordinate Value
Greece	0.6306	Finland	0.1740	Israel	0.0606	Belgium	-0.0605
Japan	0.4334	Australia	0.1730	Sweden	0.0566	Mexico	-0.0898
Korea	0.3603	Hungary	0.1527	Luxembourg	0.0407	Netherlands	-0.0927
Canada	0.3076	Iceland	0.1518	France	0.0189	Chile	-0.1374
Czech Republic	0.2769	Ireland	0.1302	Estonia	0.0135	Portugal	-0.304
Spain	0.2279	Austria	0.1246	Norway	-0.0043	Slovenia	-0.3345
Slovak Republic	0.2049	Denmark	0.1111	New Zealand	-0.0177	Poland	-0.419
United Kingdom	0.1964	Germany	0.0783	Italy	-0.0252	Turkey	-2.439

Figure 2. The comparison graphic for Turkey and Greece

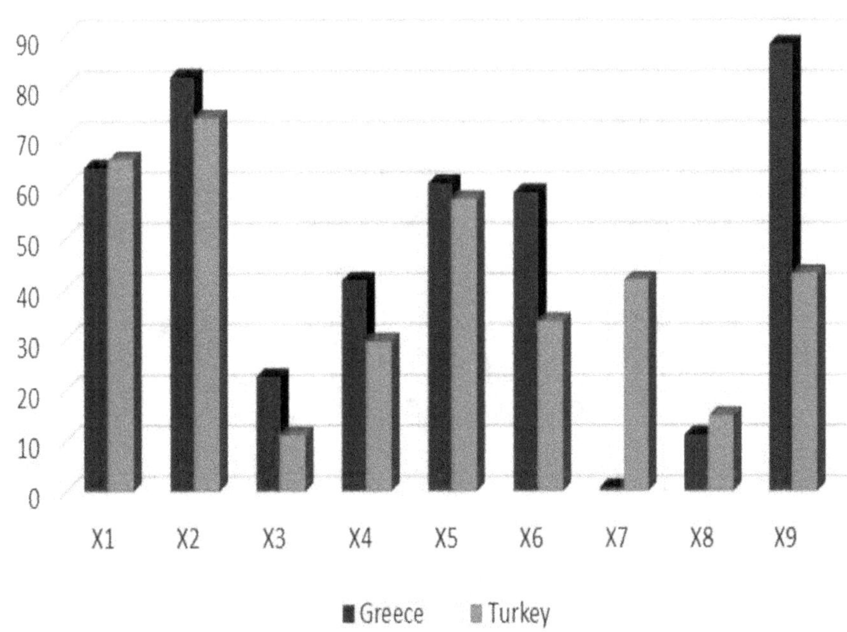

Table 12. The data on Greece and Turkey, the most remote countries each other as to 1st and 2nd dimensions

Country	X_1	X_2	X_3	X_4	X5	X_6	X_7	X_8	X_9
Greece	63.90	81.80	22.70	41.70	60.80	59.00	0.80	11.10	88.20
Turkey	65.50	73.70	11.10	29.60	57.70	33.60	41.70	15.00	43.00

Table 13. Coordinate values of countries ranked as to 3rd dimension

Country	Coordinate Value	Country	Coordinate Value	Country	Coordinate Value	Country	Coordinate Value
Czech Republic	0.5088	Sweden	0.0285	New Zealand	-0.0092	Chile	-0.0393
Slovak Republic	0.0837	Turkey	0.0244	Canada	-0.0095	Belgium	-0.0554
Slovenia	0.0744	Hungary	0.0206	Norway	-0.0128	Korea	-0.0589
Germany	0.0669	Poland	0.0100	Austria	-0.0198	Greece	-0.0815
Portugal	0.0609	Finland	0.0095	France	-0.0252	Spain	-0.0835
Estonia	0.0584	Japan	-0.0055	Australia	-0.0329	Italy	-0.1099
Iceland	0.0516	Luxembourg	-0.0064	United Kingdom	-0.0366	Ireland	-0.1582
Denmark	0.0397	Netherlands	-0.0078	Israel	-0.0393	Mexico	-0.2458

Table 14. The data for Czech Republic and Mexico

Country	X_1	X_2	X_3	X_4	X_5	X_6	X_7	X_8	X_9
Czech Republic	77.30	79.60	2.90	43.50	70.50	65.60	2.20	26.00	71.70
Mexico	71.40	75.20	5.00	38.00	56.80	46.80	3.70	16.20	79.60

Figure 3. The comparison graphic for Czech Republic and Mexico

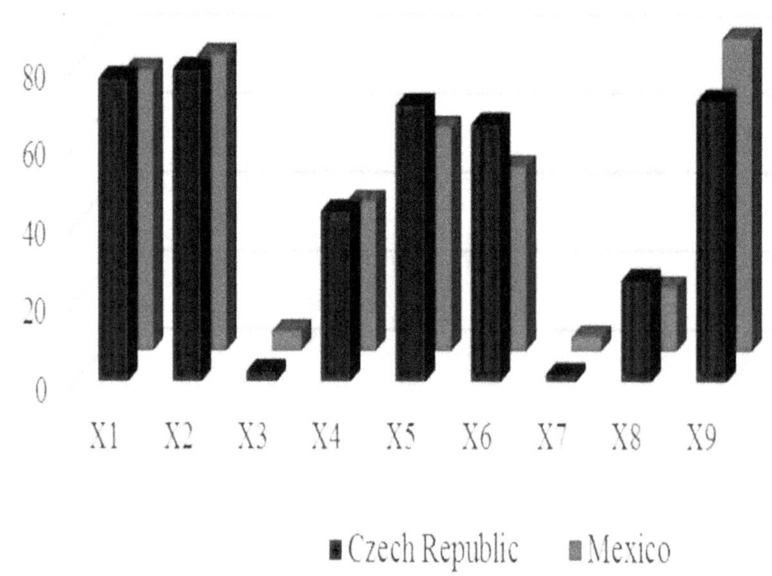

CONCLUSION AND RECOMMENDATIONS

Integration of women into the labor force, thereby to the economy will be an important factor in accelerating the benefits, development, and growth for the country. In this respect, it is necessary to take the necessary measures to ensure the participation of women in the workforce.

In this regard, firstly, gender perception in society should be changed, and the policies promoting women's labor force participation should be developed. Many responsibilities attributed to women by society such as household chores and childcare should be shared by members of the family. Pre-school education institutions should be increased. Besides, since raising the level of formal education for women increased women labor force, it is important to encourage especially women in rural areas to have formal and vocational education.

By legal regulations, women should be included in the labor force working life. In this regard, it is required to ensure the social security of women who are employed unrecorded and as unpaid family workers. However, it is seen that women have been working intensively in the services sector and also unrecorded in urban areas in recent years.

In this study in which OECD countries were compared according to women labor force statistics, first, ranking of aforementioned countries was made as to the factor analysis, then meanings of the positions determined by points on three-dimensional graphic were explained Switzerland and the USA were left out of the scope of the analysis since the data could not be obtained for some variables related to women labor force. In this study, the data was obtained for 9 variables related to women labor force and employment. When the number of indicators has increased, the results may vary.

Before to implementation factor analysis, KMO and Bartlett's tests were applied. It was found that sample sufficiency index KMO by Kaiser-Meyer-Olkin, which compares the sizes of the observed correlation coefficients to the sizes of the partial correlation coefficients for the sum of analysis variables is 76.5%, and it is reliable because it overcomes 70% by far. In addition, supposition test of sphericity by the Bartlett test (H_0: All correlation coefficients are not quite far from zero) is rejected on a level of statistical significance $p<0.0005$ for approx. ChiSquare=344.433. Consequently, the coefficients are not all zero, so that the second acceptance of factor analysis is satisfied.

According to factor analysis, the three factors were obtained of which eigenvalues are greater than one. The variance explanation ratio was found as 79.2% in total for these three factors. As it cannot be determined exactly that variables X_2 (college graduate women's labor force participation rate (%)) and X_5 (part-time working female ratio (%)) were located in which factor, VARIMAX rotation was conducted. As a result of factor analysis, it is determined that variables X_1 (employment rate of college graduate women (aged 25-64) %), X_2 (college graduate women's labor force participation rate (%), X_4 (women's employment rate (%), X_6 (labor force participation rate among women aged 15-64 (%)) were located in 1st factor. In the 2nd factor, variables X_7 (women's employment rate in the agricultural sector (%)), X_8 (women's employment rate in the industrial sector (%), X_9 (women's employment rate in the service sector (%)) were respectively located. Finally, variables X_3 (college graduate women's unemployment rate (%)) and X_5 (part-time working female ratio (%)) fell within the 3rd factor.

It was identified that two most remote countries each other were Sweden and South Korea by their score values for the first factor. When the score values of countries were viewed as the second factor, it was seen that Greece and Turkey are two most remote countries each other, Hungary and Mexico were two most remote countries each other as for the 3rd factor.

In order to express graphically the positions of countries determined by points according to the variables examined in the study, 0.023 rate of stress value was found out with metric scaling technique, applying multidimensional scaling analysis, and it was achieved a graphic which gave an image close to complete concordance. In reference to this stress value, it was determined that Greece and Turkey were the most remote countries each other in the first and second dimensions of this three-dimensional scaling. The variables causing differences between these two countries most are variables X_7 (women's employment rate in the agricultural sector (%)), X_9 (women's employment Rate in the service sector (%)). In the third dimension, the most remote countries are the Czech Republic and Mexico. It was determined that the variables causing differences between these two countries most were variables X_5 (part-time working female ratio (%)), X_6 (labor force participation rate among women (aged 15-64) (%)) and X_8 (women's employment rate in the industrial sector (%)).

The results of both of the analyses evaluating the women's employment in OECD countries led to results associated with countries' level of development. It was observed that developed countries have placed in the same group in terms of used variables. Meanwhile, developing countries are grouped in their own. This result suggests that increasing of the female labor force depends on increasing the educational level of women.

To sum up, although women employment is highly important for economic development, it is a fact that women employment is rather low. This may be said to be resulting from many different factors such as gender, education, policies, family life and etc. The problem of the less women taking part in the labor force can be solved through legal, political, and social regulations as well as economic conjuncture.

REFERENCES

Akın, H. B., & Eren, O. (2012). OECD ülkelerinin eğitim göstergelerinin kümeleme analizi ve çok boyutlu ölçekleme analizi ile karşılaştırmalı analizi. *Öneri, 10*(37), 175-181.

Akküçük, U. (2011). A study on the competitive positions of countries using cluster analysis and multidimensional scaling. *European Journal of Economics, Finance and Administrative Sciences, 37*, 17–26.

Albayrak, A. N., & Erkut, G. (2010). Türkiye'de bölgesel rekabet gücü analizi. *Megaron, 5*(3), 137–148.

Anderson, D. F. (1984). *An introduction to multivariate statistical methods* (2nd ed.). New York: John Wiley and Sons.

Arslan, N., & Tatlıdil, H. (2012). Defining and measuring competitiveness: A comparative analysis of Turkey with 11 potential rivals. *International Journal of Basic and Applied Sciences LJBAS-LJENS, 12*(2), 31–43.

Aydın, D. (2013). Bankaların 2012 yılı sermaye yeterlilik rasyolarına göre kümeleme analizi ve çok boyutlu ölçekleme sonucu sınıflandırılma yapıları. *Bankacılık ve Sigortacılık Araştırmaları Dergisi, 1*(5-6), 29–47.

Berber, M., & Yılmaz Eser, B. (2008). Türkiye'de kadın istihdamı: Ülke ve bölge düzeyinde sektörel analiz. *İş Güç Endüstri İlişkileri ve İnsan Kaynakları Dergisi, 10*(2), 1-16.

Beyhan Acar, A. (2013). İşgücü piyasası temel göstergeleri bakımından çok boyutlu ölçekleme analizi ile Türkiye ile diğer OECD ülkelerinin karşılaştırılması. *İstanbul Üniversitesi İşletme Fakültesi İşletme İktisadı Enstitüsü Yönetim Dergisi, 24*(75), 121-144.

Bülbül, S., & Köse, A. (2010). Türkiye'de bölgelerarası iç göç hareketlerinin çok boyutlu ölçekleme yöntemi ile incelenmesi. *İstanbul Üniversitesi İşletme Fakültesi Dergisi, 39*(1), 75-94.

Çağatay, N., & Berik, G. (1990). Transition to export-led growth in Turkey: Is there a feminization of employment? *The Review of Radical Political Economics, 22*(1), 115–134. doi:10.1177/048661349002200110

Çağatay, N., & Özler, Ş. (1995). Feminization of the labor force: The effects of long- term development and structural adjustment. *World Development, 23*(11), 1883–1894. doi:10.1016/0305-750X(95)00086-R

Çakır, M. T., Sözen, A., & Yücesu, H. S. (2009). Türkiye'nin sosyo-ekonomik göstergeleri ile enerji göstergeleri arasındaki ilişkinin çok değişkenli veri analizi ile irdelenmesi. *Uluslararası İlişkiler, 5*(20), 27–56.

Çakır Zeytinoğlu, F., & Sadıç, Ç. (2013). Türkiye'deki illerin turizm verileri açısından çok boyutlu ölçekleme analizi ile incelenmesi. *Trakya Üniversitesi Sosyal Bilimler Dergisi, 15*(2), 77–94.

Çelik, Ş. (2015). Çok boyutlu ölçekleme analizi ile hayvancılık açısından Türkiye'de illerin sınıflandırılması. *Erciyes Üniversitesi Fen Bilimleri Enstitüsü Dergisi, 31*(4), 159–164.

Cheung, K. W., & So, H. C. (2005). A multidimensional scaling framework for mobile location using time-of-arrival measurements. *IEEE Transactions on Signal Processing, 53*(2), 460–470. doi:10.1109/TSP.2004.840721

Çınar, M. (1994). Unskilled urban migrant women and disguised employment: Home-working women in İstanbul, Turkey. *World Development, 22*(3), 369–380. doi:10.1016/0305-750X(94)90128-7

Dayıoğlu, M. (2000). Labor force participation of women in Turkey. In F. Acar & A. Güneş-Ayata (Eds.), *Gender and identity construction: Women of Central Asia, the Caucasus and Turkey* (pp. 44–73). Leiden: Brill.

Dayıoğlu, M., & Kasnakoğlu, Z. (1997). Kentsel kesimde kadın ve erkeklerin işgücüne katılımları ve kazanç farklılıkları. *METU Studies in Development, 24*(3), 329–361.

Dayıoğlu, M., & Tunalı, I. (2003). *Falling behind while catching up: Changes in the female-male wage differential in urban Turkey, 1988 to 1994. Manuscript*. Koç University.

Demiray Erol, E. (2013). Türkiye ve Avrupa Birliği üyesi ülkelerin sosyoekonomik gelişmişlik düzeylerinin karşılaştırmalı analizi. *Sosyal ve Beşeri Bilimler Dergisi, 5*(1), 198–208.

Ersöz, F. (2009). Avrupa inovasyon göstergeleri (EIS) ışığında Türkiye'nin konumu. *İstanbul Teknik Üniversitesi Sosyal Bilimler Dergisi, 6*(1), 3-16.

Ersöz, T., Türkoğlu Elitaş, M. N., & Ersöz, F. (2015). OECD ülkelerinde biyokütle enerji üretiminin çok boyutlu ölçekleme analizi ile incelenmesi. *TÜBAV Bilim, 8*(3), 1–11.

Ersungur, Ş. M., Kızıltan, A., & Polat, Ö. (2007). Türkiye'de bölgelerin sosyo-ekonomik gelişmişlik sıralaması: Temel bileşenler analizi. *Atatürk Üniversitesi İktisadi ve İdari Bilimler Dergisi, 21*(2), 55–66.

Gevrekçi, Y., Ataç, F. E., Takma, Ç., Akbaş, Y., & Taşkın, T. (2011). Koyunculuk açısından Batı Anadolu illerinin sınıflandırılması. *Kafkas Üniversitesi Veterinerlik Fakültesi Dergisi, 17*(5), 755–760.

Gustafsson, S., & Jacobsson, R. (1985). Trends in female labor-force participation in Sweden. *Journal of Labor Economics, 3*(1), 256–274. doi:10.1086/298084 PMID:12267649

Hair, J. F., Anderson, R. E., Tahtam, R. L., & Black, W. C. (1998). *Multivariate data analysis*. Prentice-Hall.

Härdle, W. K., & Simar, L. (2012). Applied multivariate statistical analysis (3rd ed.). Springer. doi:10.1007/978-3-642-17229-8

Hausmann, R., Tyson, L. D., & Zahidi, S. (2012). *The global gender gap report*. Geneva: The World Economic Forum.

İpekçi Çetin, E. (2003). Çok değişkenli analizlerin pazarlama ile ilgili araştırmalarda kullanımı: 1995-2002 arası yazın taraması. *Akdeniz İ.İ.B.F. Dergisi, 5*, 32–47.

Jobson, J. D. (1992). *Applied multivariate data analysis*. New York: Springer-Verlag. doi:10.1007/978-1-4612-0921-8

Johnson, R. A., & Wichern, D. A. (2007). *Applied multivariate statistical analysis* (6th ed.). Englewood Cliffs, NJ: Prentice-Hall.

Kalaycı, Ş. (2005). *SPSS uygulamalı çok değişkenli istatistik teknikleri* (2nd ed.). Ankara: Asi 1 Yayın Dağıtım Ltd. Şti.

Kapusuzoğlu, A., & İbicioğlu, M. (2013). Portföy çeşitlemesi: İMKB'de sektörel endeksler üzerine bir analiz. *Muhasebe ve Finansman Dergisi,* 119-138.

Karacaer, S., & Kapusuzoğlu, A. (2010). İMKB turizm sektöründe entellektüel sermayenin firma değeri üzerindeki etkisinin analizi. *Anatolia: Turizm Araştırmaları Dergisi, 21*(1), 98–108.

Kasnakoğlu, Z., & Dayıoğlu, M. (1997). Female labor force participation and earnings differentials between genders in Turkey. In J. M. Rives & M. Yousefi (Eds.), *Economic dimensions of gender inequality: A global perspective* (pp. 95–117). Westport, CT: Praeger.

Killingsworth, M., & Heckman, J. (1986). Female labor supply: A survey. In O. Ashenfelter & R. Layard (Eds.), *Handbook of labor economics* (Vol. 1, pp. 103–204). Amsterdam: North- Holland.

Korkmaz, M., Alacahan, N. D., Cesim, D. T., Yücel, A. S., & Aras, G. (2013). Türkiyede kadın istihdamının Amerika Birleşik Devletlerindeki kadın istihdamı ile karşılaştırılması. *Turkish Studies, 8/9*(Summer), 1845–1863. doi:10.7827/TurkishStudies.5494

Kurtuluş, K. (1998). Pazarlama araştırmaları (6th ed.). İstanbul: İstanbul Üniv., İşletme Fakültesi Yayınları, No: 28.

Lim, J. Y. (2000). The effects of the East Asian crisis on the employment of women and men: The Philippine case. *World Development, 28*(7), 1285–1306. doi:10.1016/S0305-750X(00)00023-1

Michael, R. T. (1985). Consequences of the rise in female labor force participation rates: Questions and probes. *Journal of Labor Economics, 3*(1), 117–146. doi:10.1086/298078

Mies, M. (1994). Gender and global capitalism. In L. Sklair (Ed.), *Capitalism and development* (pp. 107–122). London: Routledge. doi:10.4324/9780203201961_chapter_6

Oğuzlar, A. (1995). Çok boyutlu ölçekleme ve kümeleme analizi arasındaki ilişkiler. *Uludağ Üniversitesi İ.İ.B.F. Dergisi, 18*(2).

Organisation for Economic Co-operation and Development. (2015). *OECD employment outlook 2015*. Paris: OECD Publishing. doi:10.1787/empl_outlook-2015-en

Organisation for Economic Co-operation and Development. (2016). *OECD labour force statistics 2015*. Paris: OECD Publishing. doi:10.1787/oecd_lfs-2015-en

Özdamar, K. (1999). *Paket programlarla istatistiksel veri analizi*. Eskişehir: Kaan Kitabevi.

Öztürk, M., & Çetin, B. I. (2009). Dünyada ve Türkiye'de yoksulluk ve kadınlar. *Journal of Yaşar University, 3*(11), 2661–2698.

Psacharopoulos, G., & Tzannatos, Z. (1993). Economic and demographic effects on working women in Latin America. *Journal of Population Economics, 6*(4), 293–315. doi:10.1007/BF00599040 PMID:12286863

Şahin, A., Abay, C., & Miran, B. (2008). Tarımsal ve sosyo ekonomik özellikler açısından Türkiye'nin AB'ne uyum olanaklarının değerlendirilmesi: Bir MDS uygulaması. *Finans Politik ve Ekonomik Yorumlar Dergisi, 45*(5), 17–59.

Sharma, S. (1996). *Applied multivariate techniques*. New York: John Wiley & Sons Inc.

Shimada, H., & Higuchi, Y. (1985). An analysis of trends in female labor-force participation in Japan. *Journal of Labor Economics, 3*(1), 355–374. doi:10.1086/298089 PMID:12267652

Sığırlı, D., Ediz, B., Cangür, Ş., Ercan, İ., & Kan, İ. (2006). Türkiye ve Avrupa Birliği'ne üye ülkelerin sağlık düzeyi ölçütlerinin çok boyutlu ölçekleme analizi ile incelenmesi. *İnönü Üniversitesi Tıp Fakültesi Dergisi, 13*(2), 81-85.

Stevens, J. P. (2009). *Applied multivariate statistics for the social sciences* (5th ed.). Taylor & Francis Group.

Tansel, A. (1994). Wage employment, earnings and returns to schooling for men and women in Turkey. *Economics of Education Review, 13*(4), 305–320. doi:10.1016/S0272-7757(05)80054-8

Tansel, A. (1999). *Public-private employment choice, wage differentials and gender in Turkey*. Yale University Economic Growth Center Discussion Paper, No. 797.

Tatlıdil, H. (2002). *Uygulamalı çok değişkenli istatistiksel analiz*. Ankara: Ziraat Matbaacılık A.Ş.

Tezcan, N. (2014). OECD ve BRIC ülkelerinin enerji göstergeleri açısından çok boyutlu ölçekleme analizi ile karşılaştırılması. *İstanbul Üniversitesi İşletme Fakültesi İşletme İktisadı Enstitüsü Yönetim Dergisi, 25*(77), 119-134.

Tunalı, I. (1997). To work or not to work: An examination of female labor force participation in urban Turkey.*Proceedings of the 4th Annual Conference of the Economic Research Forum.*

Tunalı, I., & Ercan, H. (1998). Labor market segmentation in Turkey. In T. Bulutay (Ed.), *Main characteristics and trends in the Turkish labor market* (pp. 85–127). Ankara: Turkish Statistical Institute.

United Nations. (2012). *The millennium development goals report 2012*. New York: United Nations.

Yenilmez, F., & Girginer, N. (2016). Comparison of indicators of womens labour between Turkey and EU member states by employing multidimensional scaling analysis and clustering analysis. *Applied Economics*, *48*(13), 1229–1239. doi:10.1080/00036846.2015.1096005

Yenilmez, F., & Işıklı, B. (2010). The comparison of labor force participation rate of women in Turkey with the world country groups. *Anadolu University Journal of Social Sciences*, *10*(3), 77–92.

KEY TERMS AND DEFINITIONS

Economic Development: The process by which a nation improves the economic, political, and social well-being of its people.

Factor Analysis: A statistical method used to describe variability among observed, correlated variables in terms of a potentially lower number of unobserved variables called factors.

Gender Mainstreaming: The public policy concept of assessing the different implications for women and men of any planned policy action, including legislation and programs, in all areas and levels. Mainstreaming essentially offers a pluralistic approach that values the diversity among both men and women.

Multidimensional Scaling: Multidimensional scaling (MDS) is a means of visualizing the level of similarity of individual cases of a dataset. It refers to a set of related ordination techniques used in information visualization, in particular to display the information contained in a distance matrix.

OECD Member Countries: The Organization for Economic Co-operation and Development (OECD) is an intergovernmental economic organization with 35 member countries, founded in 1961 to stimulate economic progress and world trade. It is a forum of countries describing themselves as committed to democracy and the market economy, providing a platform to compare policy experiences, seeking answers to common problems, identify good practices and coordinate domestic and international policies of its members.

Women Labor: The participation of women in social production. The character of their participation is determined by the socioeconomic structure of the society. In an exploitative class society, private ownership of the means of production gives rise to social inequality for women, including job discrimination. The liberation of women and their full equality with men are possible only with the establishment of public ownership of the means of production and the abolition of the exploitation of one man by another.

Chapter 7
The Determinants of Female Labor Force Participation:
Evidence from Aggregated and Disaggregated Panel Data of Developing Countries

Banu Demirhan
Afyon Kocatepe University, Turkey

Erdal Demirhan
Afyon Kocatepe University, Turkey

ABSTRACT

The female labor participation is recently considered as one of the factors leading to economic development in developing countries by amplifying total labor force as qualitative and quantitative. In this study, the authors investigate the factors affecting female labor participation in developing countries, applying panel data model for 83 developing countries over the period of 1990-2014. Empirical results indicate that u-shaped and incompatibility hypotheses are valid in the developing countries. Additionally, improving education levels and increasing male participation in labor markets lead women to more participate in labor markets. These results show the importance of enhancing education level and therefore the policies towards providing it.

INTRODUCTION

International Labour Organization (ILO, 2016) defines labor force participation rate as "... a measure of the proportion of a country's working-age population that engages actively in the labor market, either by working or by looking for work", therefore, it demonstrates the relative size of the supply of labor available in labor markets. In this context, an increase in female labor force participation (FLFP) boosts the supply of female labor, leading to higher labor inputs and faster economic growth. Additionally,

DOI: 10.4018/978-1-5225-2008-5.ch007

following the economic growth, women's capabilities typically improve and thus this enables women to engage in work outside the home. In other words, female labor supply is considered as both a driver and an outcome of development (Verick, 2014).

One of the biggest problems of developing countries is the lack of resources, namely production factors. The insufficient capital and labor amount impedes the development of these countries and therefore makes difficult to reach the level of developed countries. Hence, development strategies tend to increase the amount of capital and labor in developing countries. On the other hand, the structure of labor markets in developing countries exhibits male dominant feature, as a result of being considered male workers as primary earners. In general, women are generally employed less in comparison to men in all countries and work at lower wages (Yenilmez & Girginer, 2016). An increase in women's labor force participation may contribute to economic growth in developing countries. Additionally, female labor force can increase the growth potential in the economies where skilled female labor is abundant (Kinoshita & Guo, 2015).

In fact, the argument that an increase in FLFP can boost economic growth by increasing labor supply is the rationale of improving the participation of women in labor markets. In this context, determining the factors affecting female labor force participation leads policy makers to implement effective policies towards increasing women's employment by allow policy makers to select the primary tools with the limited public budget, which is a common problem seen in developing countries. In this context, employing panel data method, we aim to investigate empirically the factors behind FLFP. In the econometric estimations, we use several models to analyze the impact of all variables on FLFP. We, also, divide the developing countries into sub-groups to determine the differences in estimations across the country groups. We apply panel data method for developing countries covering the period 1990-2014. The paper is organized as follows: section 2 provides an overview of the determinants of FLFP. Section 3 describes the data and econometric methodology. Section 4 presents the estimation results and Section 5 sets out conclusion.

LITERATURE ON THE DETERMINANTS OF FEMALE LABOR FORCE PARTICIPATION

Reviewing the literature, we find that the studies investigating the determinants of FLFP mainly focus on various factors. According to Shah and Al-Qudsi (1990), they are divided into two groups that are background and intervening. Background factors consist of demographic and socio-cultural ones, influencing the supply factors, and intervening factors consist of supply and demand ones. While socio-cultural factors include protective norms, non-desirability of specific jobs, and status considerations; demographic ones include age, family size, age of youngest child, marital status, household headship, and family type. Supply factors consist of husband's income, occupation, and income, which are related to husbands, and women's education, skill level, and motivation to work are the main ones, which are related to women. The availability of child care and attractiveness of jobs can also be considered as the variables including in the supply factors. The demand factors affecting FLFP include the variables related to the demand for female workers such as rate and character of economic development, the size of the informal sector, discrimination against the female employment, and regulations about wages and sex discrimination in hiring. In this study, considering the factors explained above, we select the variables used in the econometric models, which can be accounted for as follows:

Fluctuations in Economic Activity

The relationship between FLFP and economic growth may be u-shaped, which means that the negative effect on FLFP turns to positive in the later development periods. (Tsani, Paroussos, Fragiadakis, Charalambidis, & Capros, 2013; Lechman & Kaur, 2015). In the declining part of the u-shaped curve, there is a shift from a subsistence agriculture economy to an industrialized and labor-intensive economy. If this transformation leads to greater demand for male workers than female ones, there is a trade-off between economic growth and FLFP. On the other hand, once economic development continues, this trend is reversed, implying that there is a transition from the industrial sector to service ones. Additionally, economic growth, accompanied by declines in fertility rates and increases in their education level, raises FLFP, implying increasing portion of the u-shaped curve (Lechman & Kaur, 2015). The effect of economic growth on female employment may vary across the sectors. Economic growth may have an adverse impact on women's employment in agriculture sector if the female labor shifts to other sectors such as industry or service. Although such tendency is expected in agricultural female employment, it is not certain for industry and service sectors (Haghighat, 2002). Moreover, higher household income and increasing social protection lead to withdrawing of women from the market for domestic work and childcare. As the economy grows, labor force participation increases due to better education, lower fertility rates, access to labor-saving household technology, and the availability of market-based household services (International Monetary Fund [IMF], 2013). This situation reflects the other explanation of u-shaped FLFP curve. In the empirical literature, Haghighat (2002) and Tansel (2001) find a u-shaped relationship between economic growth and female labor participation.

The impact of economic fluctuations may also lead to a change in unemployment rate. Several studies (Osterholm, 2010; Layard, Nickell, & Jackman, 1991; Murphy & Topel, 1997; Gustavsson & Osterholm, 2006) focus on the relationship between unemployment and FLFP. If the firms are closed, the workers become unemployed or give up working. However, when the new investment areas are created, unemployed workers canalize to new creating jobs, and the workers not in the labor force may decide to enter labor markets (Liu, 2014). Therefore, changes in unemployment rate affects FLFP. In general, changes in unemployment rate have two effects on FLFP. The first is called the "discouraged worker effect", which argues that people are discouraged by recession periods because they prefer to stay out labor markets due to long periods of job searching. If economic activities rise, then discouraged people are willing to take the job, increasing labor participation. The second is called the "added worker effect", which implies that the husband's labor market status significantly influences the wife's labor market behavior (Prieto-Rodriguez & Rodriguez-Gutierrez, 2003). "added worker effect" argues that if primary earners become unemployment during economic downturns, then other members of households turn towards labor markets o maintain family income. This hypothesis also accounts for why female labor force participation increases in the periods of economic recession. In contrast, an increase in economic activity might lead to a decrease in the number of additional family members since primary earners again enter the labor market.

To sum up, the negative impact of unemployment on FLFP means that higher unemployment rates are associated with lower labor participation rates, which can be expressed as discouraged worker effects. However, if the effect is positive, it can be interpreted that high unemployment rates lead women to enter the labor force to add to household income. Finally, the unemployment invariance hypothesis suggests that the long-run unemployment rate is independent of the labor force (Emerson, 2011). In the literature, several studies, such as Osterholm (2010) and Darby, Hart, and Vecchi (2001), supports discouraged-worker effects.

Education

Women's education levels are one of the most significant factors influencing participation of women in the labor force (Yenilmez & Girginer, 2016). The higher education level has an impact on FLFP in several ways. *First,* education can both enlarge job opportunities in the labor market and encourage women to work in the markets instead of homemaking (Besamusca, Tijdens, Keune, & Steinmetz, 2015). Especially married female education is related to domestic work and market work. An increase in the education level of married women may reduce domestic work. However, its effect on market work is uncertain due to income effect. Therefore, women's educational attainment has an impact on the composition of domestic work and market work as suggested by Becker (1991), which is named the household production theory. *Second,* the earnings from labor market are also a key factor for women to participate in labor markets. An increase in wages increases the opportunity cost of staying out of the labor market, and therefore women make more effort to participate in the labor market. Once making the assumption that higher education brings about higher wages, we expect that an increase in education level increases the opportunity cost of unemployment, leading to an increase in female employment (England, Gornick, & Shafer, 2012). Since earning losses increase when wages go up, it is expected that an increase in wages encourages women to enter labor markets. Therefore, an increase in wages has a role that creates an incentive effect on FLFP. In the standard monopsony model of minimum wage effects, minimum wages increase wages and employment levels but lead to lower levels of firm welfare (Flinn, 2006). In this context, the level of reservation wage is crucial importance for women who decide to enter the labor market. In a simple search model where individuals are homogenous, individuals who draw wage offers above the reservation wage choose to work. However, individuals who draw offers below the reservation wage do not work (Devereux, 2004). The other issue about this factor is wage inequality, which can be expressed as a growing male-female pay gap. The widening gap that is low relative wages discourages female labor force participation (Hare, 2016). Moreover, the social norms against female employment lead to low wages of women workers (Göksel, 2013). Higher education levels of women contribute to abolishing the attitudes against women's employment. *Third,* the effect of educational attainment on labor force participation can be twofold. An increase in educational attainment leads to a drop in female labor force participation because of the youngest female in the educational system; training may keep school age women out of the labor market, which primarily occurs if the number of students increases in higher education. On the other hand, an increase in the number of students in the secondary level leads to an increase in labor force participation because the standard knowledge that is necessary for the labor markets can be obtained in the secondary education process. This situation becomes apparent once the students completing the secondary school do not continue to higher education. *Fourth,* female education contributes to FLFP by decreasing fertility since an increase in fertility leads women to leave out of labor markets. Black, Devereux, and Salvanes (2008) and Kırdar, Tayfur, and Koç (2009) argued that compulsory-schooling reduces fertility at young ages. *Fifth,* the social norms against female employment are a barrier for women to have a high level of education and therefore to enter labor markets (Göksel, 2013). In this context, attitudes against the women worker increase the adverse effect of lower education level on female employment. However, with higher educational attainment, the social norms against women's employment change for entering women to labor market since education leads the mechanisms increasing women's employment to move. Finally, it is worth noting that in many developing countries, the relationship between education attainment and FLFP is u-shaped. In poorer countries, uneducated women participate in subsistence activities and informal employment, but women with a high school education may stay out of the labor force. Once women have more than a secondary level education, higher wages encourage women to join the labor force, particularly if appropriate jobs are available (Verick, 2014). In the empirical literature, the studies, accordance with the theory, commonly argue the positive effect of education on FLFP (See. Hare, 2016). In the literature, Tansel (2001) and England et al. (2012) can be given as examples finding the positive impact of education on female employment.

Fertility

The fertility, which can be measured by the existing number of children (Smith-Lovin & Tickamyer, 1978) or the number of births (Desai & Waite, 1991), leads women to stay away from the labor market. In general, it is expected that the fertility has an adverse impact on FLFP (Willis, 1987; Hotz, Klerman, & Willis, 1997) because fertility makes it difficult to balance between work and parenting duties, which is called incompatibility hypothesis (Stycos & Weller, 1967). In this context, the burdens on women such as domestic and care work impede women to enter labor markets. Therefore, the larger the time demand is, the smaller women's capabilities will be to participate in the labor force (Besamusca, et al., 2015). Although the negative effect on FLFP, higher fertility can be associated with higher FLFP rate because women workers have the income to pay for childcare services, which encourages them to enter labor markets, called societal response hypothesis (Rindfuss & Brewster, 1996; Givord & Marbot, 2015). However, childcare costs determine the women's decision towards participating in the labor market (Connelly, 1992). It is worth noting that FLFP affects fertility negatively because the working status of mother conflicts with childbearing (Miah & Mizan, 1995). In the empirical literature, several studies such as Rica and Ferrero (2003) find the negative effect of fertility on FLFP. However, the studies such as Vlasbom and Schippers (2004) find mixed results that both effects are valid for different countries.

Health

The health conditions of women may have an effect on FLFP by changing the workers' preferences between leisure and work. A deterioration of health causes the need of more leisure, reducing labor supply. Moreover, once employment has a negative effect on individuals' health, or individuals may use health conditions to justify their labor force status, which is called as justification hypothesis, then the health is treated as an exogenous variable in labor supply models (Cai, 2010). Worsening of health occurs not only as physically but also as mental. The inverse relationship between mental illness and productivity (Chatterji, Alergria, Lu, & Takeuchi, 2007; Kessler & Frank, 1997; French & Zarkin, 1998) determines the negative effect of mental illness on FLFP. In this context, worsening mental health leads workers, regardless of female or male, to out of the labor market due to decreasing of the productivity of labor (Vecchio et al., 2014).

DATA AND ECONOMETRIC METHODOLOGY

In this study, we use the data on developing countries for the period of 1990-2014. Female labor force participation rate, which is used as dependent variable in the econometric models, varies considerably across developing countries, and there is a decline in developing Europe and Central Asia, East Asia and Pacific, and South Asia. In particular, the decline in developing East Asia & Pacific is noteworthy because it dropped from 69.37% in 1990 to 62.65% in 2014. On the other hand, there are increases in the rates in Latin America and Caribbean, the Middle East and North Africa, and Sub-Saharan Africa. The highest growth occurs in developing Latin America and Caribbean, which rises from 40.70% in 1990 to 54.69 in 2014. Moreover, among developing countries, the Middle East and North Africa has the lowest rates (20.20%), and Sub-Saharan Africa has the highest rates (63.76%) in developing region in 2014 (Figure 1).

In this study, we use panel data regression models to estimate the effects of the factors on female employment and female labor force participation. The models are designed for 83 developing countries over the period of 1990-2014. All variables are obtained from World Bank (2016). The definitions of the variables and their descriptive statistics are displayed in Table 1. Additionally, the countries used in the econometric estimations are reported in Table 5 in the Appendix. The data are not available for all countries or years. Therefore, the panel data are unbalanced. The number of observations is different for each model due to the choice of explanatory variables. This study uses six models which consist of benchmark and augmented ones. In the benchmark model, primary (*PRMY*), secondary (*SCND*), and tertiary (*TRTR*) school enrollment rates, gross domestic product (GDP) per capita (*GPER*), and male labor force participation rate (*MLFP*) are used. In the augmented models, age dependency ratio (*AGDR*), life expectancy at birth (*LIFE*) and Fertility rate (*FRTL*) is used. *PRMY*, *SCND*, and *TRTR* variables stand for the education. The *GPER* variable is a proxy for economic activity and used to investigate u-shaped relationship between economic growth and female labor participation. The *LIFE* variable is considered as proxy for the health conditions. *MLFP* variable is taken to indicate the effect of male labor force participation rate on *FLFP*. *AGDR* and *FRTL* variables, mostly used in the empirical literature, are also included in the econometric models. In selecting of these variables, we considered the factors affecting female labor force participation in the macroeconomic framework, which are mentioned in the previous section.

To analyze the determinants of the FLFP in developing countries, we apply the panel data method. The following panel regression equation is estimated in this study:

$$FLFP_{it} = \beta_{0i} + \beta_{1i}EDU_{it} + \beta_{2i}GPER_{it} + \beta_{3i}GPER2_{it} + \beta_{4i}MLFP_{it} + \beta_{5i}CV_{it} + \varepsilon_{it} \quad (1)$$

Figure 1. Female labor force participation rates in developing area (1990-2014)
Source: World Bank (2016).

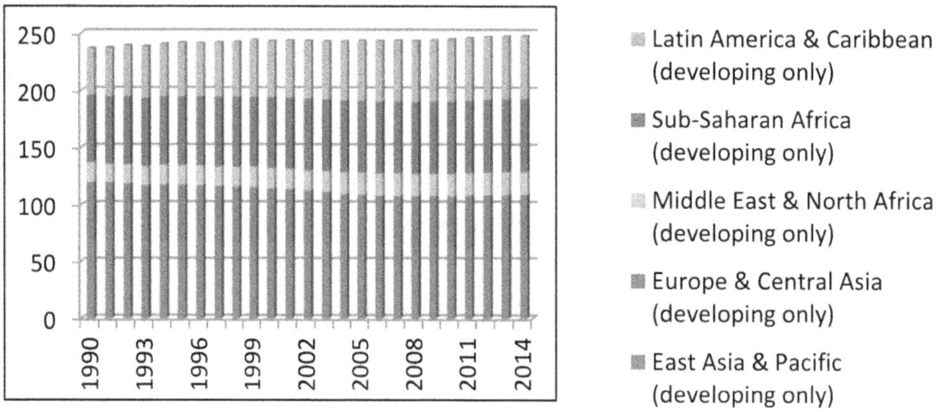

**For a more accurate representation of this figure, please see the electronic version.*

Table 1. Variable definitions and summary statistics

Variable	Definition	Obs.	Mean	Std. Dev.	Min	Max
FLFP	Labor force participation rate, female (% of female population ages 15+)	2075	52.23	19.75	9.20	90.80
GPER	GDP per capita (constant 2005 US$). Expressed in logarithmic form.	2016	7.07	1.04	4.73	9.08
PRMR	School enrollment, primary, female (% gross)	1775	95.32	23.02	17.82	148.24
SCND	School enrollment, secondary, female (% gross)	1410	58.14	30.53	2.42	123.60
TRTR	School enrollment, tertiary, female (% gross)	1258	21.86	22.22	0.10	150.70
MLFP	Labor force participation rate, male (% of male population ages 15+)	2075	77.21	7.99	43.30	92.30
FRTL	Fertility rate, total (births per woman)	2068	3.79	1.74	1.08	8.60
LIFE	Life expectancy at birth, female (years)	2067	66.01	10.05	30.00	81.91
AGDR	Age dependency ratio (% of working-age population)	2075	72.64	19.71	34.49	118.77

Source: World Bank (2016).
The countries in the sample are demonstrated in the Appendix in Table 5. The period used in the empirical models covers the 1990-2014.

where the subscript i ($i=1,...N$) denotes countries, the subscript t indicates the time ($t=1,...,T$), and ε_t is a stochastic error term. The *EDU* variable indicates several education levels of women such as primary, secondary, and tertiary school enrollment rates. *GPER* variable is real GDP per capita, and *GPER2* is the square of real GDP per capita to test the validity of the u-shaped hypothesis. *MLFP* is male labor force participation rate, and *CV* denotes the variables used in the augmented models, such as fertility rate, life expectancy at birth, and age dependency ratio. The method used in estimating equation 1 is selected by carrying out several pre-tests, providing knowledge about which estimator should be chosen among fixed effect, random effect and pooled estimators. The F test suggested by Moulton and Randolph (1989) is employed to make a choice between fixed effect and pooled models. The selection of random effects and pooled models requires applying several tests such as Breusch and Pagan (1980) LM, Adjusted LM, Score (Bottai, 2003), Honda (1985), and King and Wu (1997). Following pre-tests, if it is concluded that pooled estimators are not preferred then to compare the fixed effects and random effect models we apply Hausman (1978) test. Following Wooldridge (2002), we construct the equation for fixed-effects as follows:

$$y_{it} = \beta_0 + \beta_k x_{kit} + a_i + \mu_{it} \tag{2}$$

where, i represents cross-section units (countries), t represents each time period (with $t=1,2,..., T$); and μ_{it} is the idiosyncratic error term or time-varying error term, and represents unobserved factors that change over time and affect y_{it}. y_{it} is the *FLFP* variable for each country (i) at each time period t, x_{kit} is set of k variables, and a_i is unobserved, time-constant factors. In fixed-effects model, the main assumption is that every unobserved effect has correlation with each explanatory variable. The other approach used in panel data analysis, random effect model, is estimated by using equation (3).

$$y_{it} = \beta_0 + \beta_k x_{kit} + \nu_{it} \tag{3}$$

where, $v_{it}=a_i+\mu_{it}$, represents composite error term. The main assumption in random effect analysis is that every unobserved effect is not correlated with each explanatory variable [$Cov(y_{itj}, a_i)=0, t=1,2,...,T$ and $j=1,2,...,k$.]. Preference in between fixed-effects model and random-effects model is made by using Hausman (1978) test.

EMPIRICAL RESULTS

Selecting appropriate model, we applied several pre-tests accounted in the methodology section. For this purpose, we first construct fixed and random effects models and estimate parameters and then test the hypotheses using model selection. Table 2 reports the results of the tests that are applied for the model selection for six models. The first panel of Table 2 shows the F tests that are used the selection between pooled model and fixed effects model. The test results indicate the rejection of null hypothesis for all models, meaning fixed effects model should be preferred against the pooled model. The selection between pooled model and random effects model can be made by using several tests such as Breusch and Pagan (1980) LM, Adjusted LM, Score (Bottai, 2003), Honda (1985), and King and Wu (1997), reported the second panel of Table 2. For all tests, the null hypothesis is rejected for all models that is random effects models are preferred against pooled models. Ultimately, we apply Hausman (1978) test to determine which model should be used between fixed effects and random effects models. According to the results of Hausman (1978) test, the null hypothesis is rejected for all models, pointing out the fixed effects model should be used in the estimations.

After specifying the appropriate model for the estimations, we estimate the factors affecting FLFP by using fixed effect models and apply the specification tests to determine whether the estimators are inconsistent and unbiased. The estimates of the fixed effect model are not reported to converse space. As is known, to obtain consistent and unbiased estimators, there should not be autocorrelation and heteroscedasticity in the residuals. In this study, we use Modified Wald tests (Greene, 2000) for determining heteroscedasticity and both Bhargava, Franzini, and Narendranathan (1982) Durbin-Watson test and Baltagi-Wu (1999) locally best invariant (LBI) tests for determining autocorrelation. If Modified Wald statistics is statistically significant, the null hypothesis of no heteroskedasticity is rejected. Moreover, if Bhargava et al. (1982) Durbin Watson and Baltagi-Wu (1999) LBI statistics close to two, we reject the

Table 2. The tests for model selection

Variable	Model 1	Model 2	Model 3	Model 4	Model 5	Model 6
F test	643***	636***	683***	594***	607***	565***
B-P LM	15706***	13935***	11746***	9381***	8306***	6296***
ALM	14115***	12377***	10652***	8312***	7364***	5443***
Score	4.5e+07***	8.7e+07***	3.8e+07***	5.6e+07***	3.4e+07***	6.6e+07***
Honda	125.32***	118.04***	108.38***	96.85***	91.14***	79.34***
King-Wu	125.32***	118.04***	108.38***	96.85***	91.14***	79.34***
Hausman	50.72***	111.88***	34.80***	85.10***	38.38***	106.09***

Source: Author's calculations.

*** Indicates significant at 1% level, ** 5%, and * 10%. B-P LM denotes Breusch and Pagan (1980) LM test. ALM denotes Adjusted Lagrange Multiplier test.

null hypothesis of no autocorrelation. In this context, test results reported in Table 3 indicate that there are autocorrelation and heteroscedasticity in the residuals, indicating fixed effects estimators inconsistent and biased.

Detecting the problem of autocorrelation and heteroscedasticity in the residuals, we estimate the parameters with robust standard errors, reported in Table 4. According to Table 4, *GPER* and *GPER2* variables have negative and positive sign in all models except model 5. The parameters of these variables are also statistically significant. This finding indicates the association between real GDP per capita and female labor participation is negative initially but positive later. The negative association is illustrated on the downward half of the u-shape and indicating that a higher real GDP per capita is initially associated with lower female labor participation. Positive association is represented on the upward half of the u-shape and suggesting that a higher real GDP per capita is associated with higher female labor participation. In other words, the negative effect of real GDP per capita on *FLFP* turns to positive in the later periods. These findings show the validity of u-shaped hypothesis in developing countries.

The parameters of *PRMR* and *SCND* variables, which are two of three education levels, are statistically significant in the benchmark models but not significant in augmented models. The other education level indicator, *TRTR*, is not statistically significant in both of benchmark and augmented models. These results indicate that female primary and secondary school enrollment are an important role for women to participate in labor markets. One percentage point increase in *PRMR* increases the *FLFP* by 0.06 points. This positive effect is greater when *SCND* variable is taken as education level indicator; one percentage point increase in *SCND* increases the *FLFP* by 0.14 points. Therefore, secondary school enrollment rate has more positive impact than primary one on *FLFP* in developing countries. The parameter of *MLFP* variable has a positive sign and statistically significant, showing that men participation increases women involvement in labor markets. *FRTL*, which is expected to affect *FLFP* negatively, have negative statistically significant for all models; one unit increase in *FRTL* decreases *FLFP* by at least 2.26 points. The parameters of other variables (*AGDR* and *LIFE*) in the augmented models are not statistically significant although they have the signs that are accordance with the theory. Therefore, it is concluded that both life expectancy at birth and age dependency ratio have no effect on *FLFP* in the developing countries. In the point of policy implementation, these conclusions verify the opinion that the policies aiming to increase women labor participate in labor markets should tend to improve education levels and enhance economic growth.

After applying the fixed effect model for developing countries using aggregated data, the estimations will be performed by constructing the previous models by country groups. Hence, it can be determined which factors come to the forefront across developing country groups. For this purpose, we use five

Table 3. The specification tests for the fixed effect models

Heteroscedasticity	Model 1	Model 2	Model 3	Model 4	Model 5	Model 6
M-Wald	5.4e+05 ***	3.3e+05 ***	3.3e+05 ***	3.6e+05 ***	4.7e+06 ***	2.4e+06 ***
Autocorrelation	**Model 1**	**Model 2**	**Model 3**	**Model 4**	**Model 5**	**Model 6**
Bhargava et al. DW	.139	.150	.202	.204	.205	.221
Baltagi-Wu LBI	.404	.425	.604	.613	.690	.679

Source: Author's calculations.

*** Indicates significant at 1% level, ** 5%, and * 10%.

Table 4. The estimation of fixed effects model with robust standard errors (Aggregated data)

Variable	Model 1	Model 2	Model 3	Model 4	Model 5	Model 6
GPER	-27.8***	-32***	-20.6**	-28.5***	-7.49	-24.3***
GPER^2	2.11***	2.21***	1.35**	1.86***	.626	1.63***
PRMR	.0593**	.0078				
MLFP	.642***	.803***	.791***	.879***	.661***	.801***
FRTL		-3.02***		-2.26***		-3.03***
AGDR		-.0161		-.0341		-.0113
LIFE		.0796		.0621		.0412
SCND			.141***	.0622		
TRTR					.0327	.0133
_cons	86**	110***	58.7*	93.2***	20.9	87.3***
N	1745	1744	1383	1382	1243	1243
F	17.2	19.5	47.9	34.7	7.92	26.3
r2	.276	.449	.433	.517	.273	.468

Source: Author's calculations.

*** Indicates significant at 1% level, ** 5%, and * 10%.

developing country groups: Europe and Central Asia, Middle East and North Africa, Latin America and Caribbean, Sub-Saharan Africa, and East Asia and Pacific. The estimation results are reported in the Appendix in Table (6-10). According to estimations from the sub-groups of countries, the u-shaped hypothesis is valid in Europe and Central Asia, the Middle East and North Africa, and Sub-Saharan Africa countries. Inverse u-Shaped, however, is valid only in Latin America and Caribbean for model 3. The impact of economic growth on *FLFP* is greater in the Middle East and North Africa countries than in other country groups. At the first stages of economic development, economic growth decreases *FLFP*, and when the economy continues to grow, the effect turns to positive (Table 7).

Considering the effect of *PRMR* on *FLFP*, although the effect is positive in the estimations from aggregated data, we obtain mixed results in the estimations from disaggregated data; the effect is negative for the Middle East and North Africa and East Asia and Pacific country groups, but positive for other country groups, in particular in the benchmark models. Among the countries where the coefficient of *PRMR* is positive, Latin America and Caribbean has the highest value, which is 0.183 (Table 8, Model 1). The other education variable *SCND* is positive and statistically significant for all country groups except East Asia and Pacific, confirming the estimations from aggregated data reported in Table 4. The highest parameter of *SCND* is found in the Latin America and Caribbean country group, which is 0.211 (Table 8, Model 3). *TRTR* variable, the highest education level, has a positive effect on *FLFP* in the Middle East and North Africa and Sub-Saharan country groups. This effect reaches its highest value with 0.342 in the Sub-Saharan country group. It is worth noting that the *TRTR* variable has no effect on *FLFP* in the estimations from aggregated data. In the framework of the estimations from disaggregated data, we conclude that an increase in education levels leads women to labor participate in labor markets, confirming the findings from aggregated data.

The effect of *MLFP* variable, similar to the findings from aggregated data, has a positive impact on *FLFP* for all country groups, indicating the male participation to labor markets contribute to female participation positively. The most positive effect is seen in Latin America and Caribbean group, which is 1.24 (Table 8, Model 4). *FRTL* variable, which is used in the augmented models, has a negative effect on *FLFP* almost in all country groups. The highest negative effect is seen in Sub-Saharan Africa country group, which is 4.04 (Table 9, Model 2). Assessing these results with the findings from aggregated data, we can conclude that fertility rate is one of the crucial factors affecting FLFP. The *AGDR* variable is negative effects on the Middle East and North Africa, Latin America and Caribbean, and East Asia and Pacific country groups but positive effect on only in Sub-Saharan country group. These findings are different from the estimations from aggregated data reported in Table 4, which shows that *AGDR* has no statistical effect on *FLFP*. *LIFE*, the last variable used in the models, has no statistical effect on *FLFP* in the estimations from aggregated data; it has a positive sign for Latin America and Caribbean, East Asia and Pacific, and Sub-Saharan country groups but negative for the Middle East and North Africa country groups.

CONCLUSION

In this study, we investigated the factors leading women to participate in labor markets in developing countries. We used the data of 83 developing countries over the period of 1990-2014 and employed panel data methods for developing country groups. We obtained the empirical support for the u-shaped hypothesis; in the first stages of economic development, economic growth decreases the female labor force participate in labor markets but decreases it at the later stages. This argument is confirmed in Europe and Central Asia, the Middle East and North Africa, and Sub-Saharan Africa countries. This finding is consistent with Haghighat (2002) and Tansel (2001). Among the education indicators, secondary school enrollment rate has a positive effect on female labor participation in developing countries when aggregated data is used. This positive effect is also valid once the econometric analysis is done by country groups. Although varies by country groups, the effect of the primary and tertiary school enrollment rates also have positive effects on female labor participation in general. These findings indicate improving education level increases the female participation to labor markets by enhancing job opportunities, verifying the findings from Tansel (2001) and England et al. (2012).

In this study, the other striking result is the relationship between male participation and female participation. Empirical findings suggest that male participation leads women to participate in labor markets. Occurring this result implies that husbands encourage their wives to participate the markets to maintain or increase family income. Also, with working in the labor markets, men may change their thoughts against the women employment. According to empirical findings obtained from the econometric estimations, for both aggregated and disaggregated data, the fertility rate has negative effect on female labor participation. This finding confirms the study of Rica and Ferrero (2003). Therefore, we find a strong evidence for the validity of incompatibility hypothesis in the developing countries. The possible reason behind this finding may be the expansion of women's responsibility due to child rearing. On the other hand, it is worth noting that this negative effect smoothens over the later periods due to improving child care services.

Considering the other variables, such as age dependency ratio and life expectancy at birth, we find no statistically significant effects of these variables on female labor participation. When considering the empirical results together, we suggest economic policies improving education levels. Also, fewer fertility rates imply more women's participation in labor markets in developing countries. In this context, improving and increasing child care services may increase the women's participation in developing countries. The investigating of this topic empirically may contribute to the literature. Moreover, using time series methods on the determinants of female labor participation may capture the country-specific factors. Finally, the estimations from the models suggest that further investigations with different methods and micro based variables can be realized. In particular, the effect of education and fertility variables on female labor force participation can be investigated on the regional and industrial basis.

REFERENCES

Baltagi, B. H., & Wu, P. X. (1999). Unequally spaced panel data regressions with AR(1) disturbances. *Econometric Theory*, *15*(06), 814–823. doi:10.1017/S0266466699156020

Becker, G. S. (1991). *A treatise on the family*. Harvard University Press.

Besamusca, J., Tijdens, K., Keune, M., & Steinmetz, S. (2015). Working women worldwide. Age effects in female labor force participation in 117 countries. *World Development*, *74*, 123–141. doi:10.1016/j.worlddev.2015.04.015

Bhargava, A., Franzini, L., & Narendranathan, W. (1982). Serial correlation and the fixed effects model. *The Review of Economic Studies*, *49*(4), 533–549. doi:10.2307/2297285

Black, S., Devereux, P., & Salvanes, K. (2008). Staying in the classroom and out of the maternity ward? The effect of compulsory schooling laws on teenage births. *The Economic Journal*, *118*(530), 1025–1034. doi:10.1111/j.1468-0297.2008.02159.x

Bottai, M. (2003). Confidence regions when the Fisher information is zero. *Biometrika*, *90*(1), 73–84. doi:10.1093/biomet/90.1.73

Breusch, T. S., & Pagan, A. R. (1980). The lagrange multiplier test and its applications to model specification in econometrics. *The Review of Economic Studies*, *47*(1), 239–253. doi:10.2307/2297111

Cai, L. (2010). The relationship between health and labour force participation: Evidence from a panel data simultaneous equation model. *Labour Economics*, *17*(1), 77–90. doi:10.1016/j.labeco.2009.04.001

Chatterji, P., Alergria, M., Lu, M., & Takeuchi, D. (2007). Psychiatric disorders and labor market outcomes: Evidence from the national Latino and Asian American study. *Health Economics*, *16*(10), 1069–1090. doi:10.1002/hec.1210 PMID:17294497

Connelly, R. (1992). The effect of child care costs on married womens labor force participation. *The Review of Economics and Statistics*, *74*(1), 83–90. doi:10.2307/2109545

Darby, J., Hart, R. A., & Vecchi, M. (2001). Labour force participation and the business cycle: A comparative analysis of France, Japan, Sweden and United States. *Japan and the World Economy*, *13*(2), 113–133. doi:10.1016/S0922-1425(00)00049-9

Desai, S., & Waite, L. (1991). Womens employment during pregnancy and after the first birth: Occupational characteristics and work commitment. *American Sociological Review, 56*(4), 551–566. doi:10.2307/2096274

Devereux, P. J. (2004). Changes in relative wages and family labor supply. *The Journal of Human Resources, 39*(3), 696–722. doi:10.2307/3558993

Emerson, J. (2011). Unemployment and labor force participation in the United States. *Economics Letters, 111*(3), 203–206. doi:10.1016/j.econlet.2011.02.022

England, P., Gornick, J., & Shafer, E. F. (2012). Women's employment, education, and the gender gap in 17 countries. *Monthly Labor Review, 13*(4), 3–12.

Flinn, C. J. (2006). Minimum wage effects on labor market outcomes under search, matching, and endogenous contact rates. *Econometrica, 74*(4), 1013–1062. doi:10.1111/j.1468-0262.2006.00693.x

French, M., & Zarkin, G. (1998). Mental health, absenteeism and earnings at a large manufacturing worksite. *The Journal of Mental Health Policy and Economics, 1*(4), 161–172. doi:10.1002/(SICI)1099-176X(199812)1:4<161::AID-MHP21>3.0.CO;2-I PMID:11967394

Givord, P., & Marbot, C. (2015). Does the cost of child care affect female labor market participation? An evaluation of a French reform of childcare subsidies. *Labour Economics, 36*, 99–111. doi:10.1016/j.labeco.2015.07.003

Göksel, İ. (2013). Female labor force participation in Turkey: The role of conservatism. *Womens Studies International Forum, 41*, 45–54. doi:10.1016/j.wsif.2013.04.006

Greene, W. (2000). *Econometric Analysis*. Upper Saddle River, NJ: Prentice-Hall.

Gustavsson, M., & Osterholm, P. (2006). The informational value of unemployment statistics: A note on the time series properties of participation rates. *Economics Letters, 92*(3), 428–433. doi:10.1016/j.econlet.2006.03.032

Haghighat, E. (2002). Culture, development and female labor force participation: Disaggregating different sectors. *International Review of Sociology, 12*(3), 343–362. doi:10.1080/0390670022000041376

Hare, D. (2016). What accounts for the decline in labor force participation among married women in urban China. 1991–2011? *China Economic Review, 38*, 251–266. doi:10.1016/j.chieco.2016.01.004

Hausman, J. A. (1978). Specification tests in econometrics. *Econometrica, 46*(6), 1251–1271. doi:10.2307/1913827

Honda, Y. (1985). Testing the error components model with non-normal disturbances. *The Review of Economic Studies, 52*(4), 681–690. doi:10.2307/2297739

Hotz, V. J., Klerman, J. A., & Willis, R. J. (1997). The economics of fertility in developed countries. In M. R. Rosenzweig & O. Stark (Eds.), *Handbook of population and family economics* (pp. 275–347). Amsterdam: Elsevier. doi:10.1016/S1574-003X(97)80024-4

International Labour Organization. (2016). *Key Indicators of the labour market* (8th ed.).

International Monetary Fund. (2013). *Women, work, and the economy: Macroeconomic gains from gender equity*. IMF Staff Discussion Note, SDN/13/10.

Kessler, R., & Frank, R. (1997). The impact of psychiatric disorders on work loss days. *Psychological Medicine*, *27*(4), 861–873. doi:10.1017/S0033291797004807 PMID:9234464

King, M. L., & Wu, P. X. (1997). Locally optimal one sided tests for multiparameter hypotheses. *Econometric Reviews*, *16*(2), 131–156. doi:10.1080/07474939708800379

Kinoshita, Y., & Guo, F. (2015). *What can boost female labor force participation in Asia?* IMF Working Paper, WP/15/56.

Kırdar, M. G., Tayfur, M. D., & Koç, İ. (2009). *The impact of schooling on the timing of marriage and fertility: Evidence from a change in compulsory schooling law*. Ankara: Department of Economics, Middle East Technical University.

Layard, R., Nickell, S. J., & Jackman, R. (1991). *Unemployment: Macroeconomic performance and the labour market*. Oxford, UK: Oxford University Press.

Lechman, E., & Kaur, H. (2015). Economic growth and female labor force participation- verifying the u-feminization Hypothesis. New evidence for 162 countries over the period 1990-2012. *Economia e Sociologia (Evora, Portugal)*, *8*(1), 246–257.

Liu, D.-C. (2014). The link between unemployment and labor force participation rates in Japan: A regional perspective. *Japan and the World Economy*, *30*, 52–58. doi:10.1016/j.japwor.2014.02.004

Miah, M. M. R., & Mizan, A. N. (1995). Labor force participation and fertility: A study of married women in Bangladesh. In M. S. Das & V. K. Gupta (Eds.), *Social status of women in developing countries* (pp. 125–140). New Delhi: M D Publications PVT Ltd.

Moulton, B. R., & Randolph, W. C. (1989). Alternative tests of the error components model. *Econometrica*, *57*(3), 685–693. doi:10.2307/1911059

Murphy, K. M., & Topel, R. (1997). Unemployment and nonemployment. *The American Economic Review*, *87*, 295–300.

Osterholm, P. (2010). Unemployment and labour-force participation in Sweden. *Economics Letters*, *106*(3), 205–208. doi:10.1016/j.econlet.2009.12.002

Prieto-Rodriguez, J., & Rodriguez-Gutierrez, C. (2003). Participation of married women in the European labor markets and the added worker effect. *Journal of Socio-Economics*, *32*(4), 429–446. doi:10.1016/S1053-5357(03)00050-7

Rica, S., & Ferrero, M. D. (2003). The effect of fertility on labor force participation: The Spanish evidence. *Spanish Economic Review*, *5*(2), 153–172.

Rindfuss, R. R., & Brewster, K. L. (1996). Childrearing and fertility. *Population and Development Review*, *22*, 258–289. doi:10.2307/2808014

Shah, N. M., & Al-Qudsi, S. S. (1990). Female work roles in a traditional, oil economy: Kuwait. *Research in Human Capital and Development*, *6*, 213–246.

Smith-Lovin, L., & Tickamyer, A. (1978). Nonrecursive models of labor force participation, fertility behavior, and sex role attitudes. *American Sociological Review*, *43*(4), 541–557. doi:10.2307/2094778 PMID:707913

Stycos, J. M., & Weller, R. H. (1967). Female working roles and fertility. *Demography*, *4*(1), 210–217. doi:10.2307/2060362 PMID:21279773

Tansel, A. (2001). *Economic development and female labor force participation in Turkey: Time-series evidence and cross-province estimates*. ERC Working Paper, 01/05.

Tsani, S., Paroussos, L., Fragiadakis, C., Charalambidis, I., & Capros, P. (2013). Female labour force participation and economic growth in the South Mediterranean countries. *Economics Letters*, *120*(2), 323–328. doi:10.1016/j.econlet.2013.04.043

Vecchio, N., Mihala, G., Sheridan, J., Hilton, M. F., Whiteford, H., & Scuffham, P. A. (2014). A link between labor participation, mental health and class of medication for mental well-being. *Economic Analysis and Policy*, *44*(4), 376–385. doi:10.1016/j.eap.2014.11.006

Verick, S. (2014). *Female labor force participation in developing countries*. IZA World of Labor.

Vlasbom, J. D., & Schippers, J. J. (2004). Increases in female labor force participation in Europe: Similarities and differences. *European Journal of Population*, *20*(4), 375–392. doi:10.1007/s10680-004-5302-0

Willis, R. K. (1987). What have we learned from the economics of the family? *The American Economic Review*, *77*(2), 68–81.

Wooldridge, J. M. (2002). *Introductory econometrics: A modern approach* (2nd ed.). South-Western Cengage Learning.

World Bank. (2016). *World Development Indicators 2016*. Retrieved February 15, 2016, from http://databank.worldbank.org/data/reports.aspx?source=world-development-indicators

Yenilmez, F., & Girginer, N. (2016). Comparison of indicators of womens labour between Turkey and EU member states by employing multidimensional scaling analysis and clustering analysis. *Applied Economics*, *48*(13), 1229–1239. doi:10.1080/00036846.2015.1096005

KEY TERMS AND DEFINITIONS

Age Dependency Ratio: The ratio of dependents (people younger than 15 or older than 64) to the working-age population (aged 15-64).

Fixed-Effects Model: The model that represents the observed quantities in terms of explanatory variables that are treated as if the quantities were non-random.

GDP per Capita: Gross domestic product divided by mid-year population.

Gross Primary or Secondary School Enrolment Ratio: The number of children enrolled in a level (primary or secondary), regardless of age, divided by the population of the age group that officially corresponds to the same level.

Labor Participation Rate: The proportion of the population ages 15 and older that is economically active.

Life Expectancy at Birth: The number of years newborn children would live if subject to the mortality risks prevailing for the cross-section of population at the time of their birth.

Total Fertility Rate: The number of children that would be born per woman if she were to live to the end of her child-bearing years and bear children at each age in accordance with prevailing age-specific fertility rates.

APPENDIX

Table 5. Developing country groups used in the econometric estimations

Country Groups	Countries
East Asia and Pacific	Cambodia, China, Fiji, Indonesia, Lao PDR, Mongolia, Myanmar, Philippines, Thailand
Europe and Central Asia	Albania, Azerbaijan, Belarus, Bulgaria, Georgia, Kazakhstan, Kyrgyz Republic, Macedonia FYR, Moldova, Montenegro, Romania, Serbia, Tajikistan, Turkey, Ukraine, Uzbekistan
Latin America and Caribbean	Belize, Colombia, Costa Rica, Cuba, Dominican Republic, El Salvador, Guyana, Honduras, Jamaica, Mexico, Nicaragua, Panama, Paraguay, Peru
Middle East and North Africa	Algeria, Egypt, Iran, Jordan, Lebanon, Morocco, Syria, Tunisia, West Bank and Gaza, Yemen
Sub-Saharan Africa	Benin, Botswana, Burkina Faso, Burundi, Cabo Verde, Cameroon, Central African Republic, Chad, Comoros, Congo, Dem. Rep., Congo, Rep., Eritrea, Ethiopia, Ghana, Guinea, Kenya, Lesotho, Madagascar, Malawi, Mali, Mauritania, Mauritius, Mozambique, Namibia, Niger, Rwanda, Senegal, South Africa, Sudan, Swaziland, Tanzania, Togo, Uganda, Zimbabwe

Source: World Bank (2016).

Table 6. The estimation of fixed effects model with robust standard errors (Europe and Central Asia)

Variable	Model 1	Model 2	Model 3	Model 4	Model 5	Model 6
GPER	-27.8***	-32***	-20.6**	-28.5***	-7.49	-24.3***
GPER²	2.11***	2.21***	1.35**	1.86***	.626	1.63***
PRMR	.0593**	.0078				
MLFP	.642***	.803***	.791***	.879***	.661***	.801***
FRTL		-3.02***		-2.26***		-3.03***
AGDR		-.0161		-.0341		-.0113
LIFE		.0796		.0621		.0412
SCND			.141***	.0622		
TRTR					.0327	.0133
_cons	86**	110***	58.7*	93.2***	20.9	87.3***
N	1745	1744	1383	1382	1243	1243
F	17.2	19.5	47.9	34.7	7.92	26.3
r2	.276	.449	.433	.517	.273	.468

Source: Author's calculations.
*** Indicates significant at 1% level, ** 5%, and * 10%.

Table 7. The estimation of fixed effects model with robust standard errors (Middle East and North Africa)

Variable	Model 1	Model 2	Model 3	Model 4	Model 5	Model 6
GPER	-43.1***	-33.6**	-64.7***	-66.4***	-20.1	-52.7***
GPER²	3.38***	2.37**	4.71***	4.62***	1.69*	3.82***
PRMR	-.038**	-.0616***				
MLFP	.306***	.465***	.53***	.54***	.676***	.73***
FRTL		.446		-.256		-1.61***
AGDR		-.2***		-.193***		-.0684
LIFE		-.198		-.519***		-.565***
SCND			.0405*	-.0136		
TRTR					.0558***	.0292
_cons	131**	135**	195***	269***	23	195***
N	210	210	190	190	171	171
F	33	49.4	28.5	37.9	31.5	31.1
r2	.403	.642	.393	.605	.445	.586

Source: Author's calculations.

*** Indicates significant at 1% level, ** 5%, and * 10%.

Table 8. The estimation of fixed effects model with robust standard errors (Latin America and Caribbean)

Variable	Model 1	Model 2	Model 3	Model 4	Model 5	Model 6
GPER	20.7	-23.9	69.4**	-3.03	15.2	22.7
GPER²	-.058	1.91*	-3.66**	.436	-.193	-1.36
PRMR	.183***	.0827***				
MLFP	.629***	1.1***	1.02***	1.24***	.393**	1.07***
FRTL		1.85		1.92		3.37**
AGDR		-.482***		-.406***		-.346***
LIFE		.521**		.562**		1.68***
SCND			.211***	.1***		
TRTR					.0293	.0228
_cons	-186**	2.41	-372***	-87.2	-96.9	-249**
N	281	281	237	237	186	186
F	89.1	137	124	110	29.6	59.6
r2	.576	.787	.694	.78	.413	.717

Source: Author's calculations.

*** Indicates significant at 1% level, ** 5%, and * 10%.

Table 9. The estimation of fixed effects model with robust standard errors (Sub-Saharan Africa)

Variable	Model 1	Model 2	Model 3	Model 4	Model 5	Model 6
GPER	-34.1***	-30.2***	-9.04*	-23.1***	10.7	-8.75
GPER²	2.72***	2.15***	.42	1.48***	-.954	.297
PRMR	.0644***	.00547				
MLFP	.579***	.643***	.713***	.782***	.523***	.623***
FRTL		-4.04***		-3.39***		-3.67***
AGDR		.106***		.0738*		.0659
LIFE		.059*		.0387		.0214
SCND			.176***	.0532*		
TRTR					.342***	.208***
_cons	116***	123***	40***	92.8***	-9.13	67.7***
N	738	738	544	544	470	470
F	74.9	71.6	91.4	69.5	37.5	50.9
r2	.3	.418	.42	.491	.258	.454

Source: Author's calculations.
*** Indicates significant at 1% level, ** 5%, and * 10%.

Table 10. The estimation of fixed effects model with robust standard errors (East Asia and Pacific)

Variable	Model 1	Model 2	Model 3	Model 4	Model 5	Model 6
GPER	8.65	-7.67	8.11	-14.3	3.95	-9.29
GPER²	-.775*	.00869	-.792	.593	-.369	.558
PRMR	.0071	-.0673***				
MLFP	.284***	.209**	.256**	.143	.502***	.713***
FRTL		.841		1.1		-1.05
AGDR		-.0782		-.0267		-.12***
LIFE		.715***		.852**		-.394
SCND			-.00382	-.065**		
TRTR					.00273	.00575
_cons	14.9	57.5*	23.2	63.7*	13.5	80.8**
N	171	171	136	136	124	124
F	21.2	27.2	26.1	24.3	24.5	17.8
r2	.348	.55	.457	.584	.466	.533

Source: Author's calculations.
*** Indicates significant at 1% level, ** 5%, and * 10%.

Chapter 8
The Outlook of Female Labor in Turkey in the Context of Social Gender Perception from a Global Perspective

Eda Kılıç
Uludağ University, Turkey

ABSTRACT

Women have been seen as cheap labor and have participated in the economic life less than their male counterparts since the Industrial Revolution, where they joined the waged labor pool. Though the reasons for the women's low participation in the workforce are various; Turkey's current social structure in particular and the social gender perception which acts as the base of this structure emerge as key determinants. For this reason, establishing the general status of female labor in Turkey and comparing the international and national statistical data from a global perspective around the social gender inequality and the distribution of labor based on social gender is the purpose of this study.

INTRODUCTION

The biological differences between man and woman from the beginning of humanity have always rooted together with socialization and have surrounded every aspect of the lives of both genders. For this reason, especially women, have been struggling to take a place in the society they live in without being able to shed their gender identity, formed by the social gender perception. Unfortunately, the quantitative equality between men and women has not been actualized at the point of participation to the social and economic life. Women have constantly been struggling to bring themselves and their rights into view in every corner of the world. While this struggle has resulted in great achievements in some societies, women still keep their secondary status in others. Explaining the women's low labor force participation and high unemployment levels with reasons like economic growth, development level, economic resources or political regimes would not be enough, particularly in the labor market – the fundament

DOI: 10.4018/978-1-5225-2008-5.ch008

of the economy which is one of the primary constituents of the society. In Turkey, women's labor force participation rates are increasing, but this increase is far from meeting the expectations compared with other OECD countries.

For this reason, establishing the general status of female labor in Turkey and comparing the international and national statistical data from a global perspective around the social gender inequality and the distribution of labor based on social gender is the purpose of this chapter.

THE HISTORICAL DEVELOPMENT OF FEMALE LABOR IN THE WORLD AND TURKEY

Women have been participating in the economic production throughout the ages. They had worked together with men and maintained their lives both in the hunter/gatherer and agricultural societies.

But the women's participation in waged labor, which means the sale of their labor, was actualized with the Industrial Revolution, which is considered a global revolution. In other words, it was possible in this period for the women, being finally considered as workers, to be paid in return for their labor. Substantial developments like the invention of the steam engine, the ease of transportation made possible by the use of these engines in ships and locomotives and similarly, the mechanization of the textile production starting from second half of the 1800s, brought a need for the mass workforce.

This mass workforce wasn't limited to the male population, as it included female and child labor to satisfy the emerging needs. In particular, the use of machines simplifying the production techniques, labor division, specialization and the developments in the textile sector have increased the need for women's labor (Altan & Ersöz, 1994, p. 21). While the small wages paid in return for the working times up to 20 hours worsened the living conditions of all the workers, women and children were the most heavily affected; for these participated in working life for wages even less than the men were being paid.

Women have entered the labor market with industrialization; but even though the conditions were improved due to the social policies, protective laws, and regulation mechanisms over the course of time, the secondary status of ill-paid labor under heavy working conditions still remains to this day.

In female labor has seen a decrease with the industrial production focusing on chemicals and heavy metals starting from the 19th century. The Second World War years, though, were the breaking point in the labor history of women. Until this period, women were in a 'reserved labor' position and did not enter the labor market unless it was unavoidable. The employment of a married woman was an indication that her husband was not able to take care of her properly, particularly in England. However, when the Second World War erupted, a serious labor vacancy came with the conscription of the men, resulting in the women getting back to the workforce. The increase in female labor was not only the result of the decrease in male labor due to men going to the war; it was also because the housework had decreased and women were responsible for providing for their families. When the war ended, many women chose not to withdraw from the labor market.

Following this period, female labor participation rates have increased all over the world, and with this increase, the female labor rate caught up to the male labor rate in the developed countries (Mincer, 1958, pp. 288-300).

Starting from the 1950s, the female labor participation rate kept increasing. Though the Second World War is considered as the breaking point, it can be said that many factors like the increase in female education levels, technological advancements, pay growth and decreasing birth rates have influenced this increase in the following years.

During these years, the working-age women constituted 50% of the population in the developing countries and 47% of the population in the developed countries. Meanwhile, 87% of the women in the developing countries labored in the agriculture sector, while this rate was 47% in the developed countries. In 1985, participation in the workforce was 49% in the developing countries, while the rate went up from 47% to 58% in the developed countries. The developed countries saw an increase in both non-agricultural employment and female labor participation (Koray, 1992, p. 93). An expanding service sector is, without a doubt, one of the reasons for an increase this speeding in the developed countries. However, nearly all of the countries in the world went on to legislative regulations for the protection and support of the women working under their roof, while international agreements accelerated these regulations (Koray, Demirbilek, & Demirbilek, 2000, pp. 214-215).

Historically, for our country, the start of the working life of women actually takes place during the reign of the Ottoman Empire. This course was naturally in parallel with the industrialization process. The legal steps, however, were taken during the Republic period (Önder, 2013, p. 37).

The woman, who mainly participated in the agricultural production up until the Imperial Edict of Reorganization, started to work for wages in direct proportion to her qualifications and her social class. The city-dwelling and well-educated women were employed in health and education sectors under better conditions; yet the underqualified, low income and city-dwelling women labored for 14 to 15 hours a day for little payment in small workshops. The women in the rural areas participated in the working life by weaving carpets and rugs, aside from unpaid family labor (Aslan, 2006, pp.120-121).

Between 1913-1915, the employment statistics for the production sector in large cities like Istanbul and Izmir show that the 32% of the women were employed in 1913, while the rate was 29% in 1915. On the other hand, 90% of the workers in cotton and silk weaving and 50% of the workers in tobacco production were women. İnan (1982) argued that the primary reason for the women to be employed in these sectors was, like the rest of the world, that they were employed for a smaller wage than the men. Another important cause was the gender-based distribution of labor (as cited in Önder, 2013, p. 38).

Though female labor was used both during the reign of the Ottoman Empire and the early years of the Republic of Turkey, the heavy work conditions and long working hours that come into question for all workers were paid with low wages, but the payments of the women were even less than their male counterparts (Makal, 2010, pp. 24-26).

To compensate for the lack of workforce caused by the conscription of the men in the Balkan War in 1915, the necessity for more women to join the workforce arose. This necessity increased even further during the First and Second Worlds Wars; so much so that during the First World War, the women were employed in the frontline, the garrisons and the cities (Berber & Eser, 2008; Çitçi, 1982, pp. 122-129). However, when the war ended, most of the women working withdrew from employment and returned home to carry on with the housework (Berber & Eser, 2008).

With the Republic, the legislative regulations lacking concrete footing up to that point gave way to the Civil Law in 1926, which secured the woman as an entity; thereby, the women acquired equal rights with men in subjects like marriage, divorcement, inheritance, and custody. In addition to these rights, they also gained the right of suffrage over time. With the Village Institutes and the steps taken in the field of education, women's education levels were increased, and their inclusion in work life was ensured. Starting from the early years of the Republic, the labor rights of the women were also put under protection with law. The foremost of these legal regulations were the General Health Protection

Law, Law No. 394 of 1925 and Law No. 2739 of 1935, aiming to secure all the workers' rights, not just women, under legal assurance.

According to the Industrial Census, which was taken in 1927 and took into account the distribution of workers by gender in the industrial enterprises employing four or more workers, the ratio of the women workers was 25.58%. The primary reason for this relatively high ratio of women in the workforce in this period was that the women concentrated in the sectors they had traditionally been employed; another reason was the decrease in the male labor due to the wars and the last reason was that the women were forced to work because of losing their husbands in the war (Makal, 2010, pp. 21-23).

The women would have taken their place in the industrialization struggle during the 1930s. Despite these developments, the women had been showing low participation rates to the workforce until the 1950s. During this period, the rural-urban migration and the urbanization that came with it resulted in the increase in the women's participation in the workforce. Despite the service sector's development in the same period, women still preferred to work in the industrial sector; however, the service sector created new job opportunities and a trend toward itself.

With the arrival of the 1950s, the use of female labor had started in the non-agricultural sectors, textile and leather industries in particular; this development accompanied the transition to urban life. Though the women's participation rate in the workforce had reached 72% during these years, by the 1960s it started to decrease to a participation rate of 56%.

By the 1970s, the women's willingness to work had increased; but with the inability of the industry to provide enough employment and the service sector's inadequacy starting with the 1980s, this desire to work could not be acceded (Ecevit, 1995, pp. 120-121). In addition, due to the rural-urban migrating women's lack of proper education and qualification, some opted to be housewives while others tended towards working informally in unregistered jobs. Neoliberal policies introduced flexible work types to the working life and women again were employed in these types of work. With the development of the service sectors like banking, tourism, and health, the areas of employment have shifted to these sectors.

However, the inclusion of women in the working life has added new layers to the problems regarding the inequality between men and women. Women did not have the chance to establish the price of their own work in the face of the free market's economic conditions. Because of the rapid increase in population and the low level of education, female labor had become the sole resource that is both abundant and cheap. This situation provided an accumulation of capital as part of the outward-looking development strategies. With her bargaining power and right of association eliminated with the coup, the woman's power in the working life had diminished severely. Female labor's shift to the service sector meant a severe depreciation of women's labor, a definition of the low paid and low-status jobs - which especially are temporary and without job security - as women's jobs and the use of female labor in the shadow (informal) sector (Berber & Eser, 2008).

In time, the increase in the educational levels of women allowed them to stand out in respected job positions - teachers, doctors, judges, academics, etc. Likewise, they had shown success in the other jobs of the service sector, becoming preferable to their male counterparts in the previously male-dominated jobs like banking and insurance.

Today, two major problems show up regarding the existence of women in the workforce: The low participation rates of female labor and the high rate of unemployment. Gender inequality lies at the bottom of these two problems. In the following sections, the impact of gender inequality and the reasons of the aforementioned problems will be explained while trying to put forth the status of the female labor force in Turkey with the help of national and international statistics.

SOCIAL GENDER INEQUALITY AND WORKING LIFE

Gender is a status acquired by birth. The individual is a part of the society from the moment he/she comes to life. Social gender, however, consists of the social positions, roles and the way of social relationships attributed to being a man or a woman by the society in which the individual lives. Because of this, social gender manifests as a cultural product. The differences between men and women, as a result of the fabrication of the social gender, show themselves as inequalities in nearly every aspect of social life. While the extent of these inequalities differs from society to society and culture to culture, a society in which the men are at a disadvantage doesn't exist. Dominant concepts like power, status, money, and prestige are identified mostly with men. Providing for the family is mainly the man's responsibility, while the woman's primary responsibility is doing the housework and to raising the children. Most feminist theoreticians (Walby, 2001; Hartman, 1992; Harding, 1981) explain this situation with a patriarchal system of relations.

Walby (2001) argued that the primary factor carrying the social gender inequality from the household to the public life is capitalism (as cited in Giddens, 2013, p. 521). Female labor became the center of interest for capitalism, due to the fact that women can be employed informally and in flexible schedules because of the limited time they can spare to paid work from the household responsibilities they are encumbered with (Yaman Öztürk, 2008). Walby (2001) also argued that capitalism has been feeding from the patriarchy by means of gender-based labor distribution as a result of this patriarchy (as cited in Giddens, 2013, p. 521). The partnership of patriarchy and capitalism has become a consensus/conflict which feeds and transforms the both parties, devalues the female labor and solidifies the secondary status of the woman (Harding, 1981, pp. 136-137). According to Hartmann (1992, p.142), the sources of patriarchy are the men's block and restraint on women's access to the production resources and control over the women's participation in the workforce; or, in short, the domination of men over female labor. The conflict between capitalism and patriarchy, on the other hand, stems from the fact that capitalism weakens the patriarchal systems control over the women at some points (Ferguson & Folbre, 1981, p. 314). The interaction between patriarchy and capitalism can thus be defined as patriarchal capitalism. It can be said that this interaction is the primary factor that defines the female labor's form, value and participation rate to the labor market; or, in a nutshell, the main reason for the social gender inequality.

According to the studies made on whether gender inequality has any effect on the working life of women, the primary factor which shapes their decision to enter the labor market is the social role imposed on them by the society's gender perception (Alkan, 1995; Özar & Günlük-Şenesen, 1998; Eyüboğlu, Özar, & Tanrıöver, 2000; Erman, 2001; Kasnakoğlu & Dayıoğlu, 2002; Gündüz-Hoşgör & Smits, 2006; Pancaroğlu, 2006).

From the society's gender perception, in general, the women are responsible for the household work like cleaning, ironing and dishwashing and caring for their husbands, children or even the elderly and sick residents of the house. Their participation in the working life is frowned upon by the family and the society. Though the rise in educational levels, the heightened awareness of men and women and the democratization process has transformed the social gender perception, the present inequalities keep showing themselves in every area of society.

As stated in the World Economic Forum (WEF, 2015), Turkey is ranked 130th in a total of 145 countries. According to the index, a value of 1 denotes total equality and a value of 0 denotes total inequality, a value lower than 1 denotes the existence of inequality. Based on this index, Turkey's score is 0.601.

At the top of the rank, Iceland sits with a score of 0.881. As can be seen from Table 1, Turkey is well behind in the general rankings and is in the last place among the European and Central Asian countries.

It is, naturally, impossible to appraise a country in terms of gender inequality by means of a mere score and thus, the countries' scores of gender inequality have been put under the light in four other areas comprising of several various constituents.

The indexing areas, Turkey's scores in these areas and its rankings among 145 countries are as follows:

- 0.459 points and 131st rank in terms of economic participation and opportunity,
- 0.957 points and 105th rank in terms of educational attainment,
- 0.980 points and 1st rank in terms health and survival,
- 0.103 points and 105rd rank in terms of political empowerment.

The most relevant part of WEF (2015) report is without a doubt the sub-area of economic participation and opportunity. The status of this sub-era is shown in Figure 1.

Table 1. Global ranking, 2015

Country	Global Index		Economic Participation and Opportunity		Educational Attainment		Health and Survival		Political Empowerment	
	Rank		Score		Rank		Score		Rank	
Iceland*	1	0.881	5	0.836	1	1.000	105	0.970	1	0.719
Norway*	2	0.850	1	0.868	32	1.000	70	0.974	3	0.559
Finland*	3	0.850	8	0.815	1	1.000	1	0.980	2	0.607
Sweden*	4	0.823	4	0.836	54	0.996	71	0.974	5	0.486
Ireland*	5	0.807	26	0.777	44	0.998	56	0.979	6	0.474
Switzerland*	8	0.785	17	0.798	69	0.993	74	0.974	18	0.376
Slovenia*	9	0.784	24	0.778	29	1.000	79	0.973	16	0.385
New Zealand*	10	0.782	30	0.768	1	1.000	105	0.970	15	0.390
Germany*	11	0.779	38	0.737	88	0.987	56	0.979	11	0.413
Netherlands*	13	0.776	39	0.732	1	1.000	104	0.970	13	0.401
Denmark*	14	0.767	20	0.788	1	1.000	107	0.970	29	0.309
France*	15	0.761	56	0.699	1	1.000	1	0.980	19	0.365
South Africa*	17	0.759	72	0.670	85	0.987	1	0.980	14	0.400
United Kingdom*	18	0.758	43	0.724	37	1.000	66	0.974	23	0.335
Belgium*	19	0.753	34	0.762	1	1.000	66	0.974	35	0.275
Latvia*	20	0.752	21	0.784	1	1.000	1	0.980	40	0.246
Estonia*	21	0.749	47	0.711	39	0.999	1	0.980	30	0.308
Spain*	25	0.742	67	0.674	47	0.998	93	0.972	26	0.326
United States*	28	0.740	6	0.826	40	0.999	64	0.975	72	0.162
Cuba	29	0.740	119	0.579	26	1.000	63	0.975	12	0.407

continued on following page

Table 1. Continued

Country	Global Index		Economic Participation and Opportunity		Educational Attainment		Health and Survival		Political Empowerment	
	Rank		Score		Rank		Score		Rank	
Canada*	30	0.740	28	0.773	1	1.000	109	0.969	46	0.218
Lithuania*	31	0.740	35	0.759	66	0.994	42	0.979	45	0.227
Luxembourg*	32	0.738	31	0.766	1	1.000	71	0.974	53	0.212
Australia*	36	0.733	32	0.766	1	1.000	74	0.974	61	0.193
Austria*	37	0.733	52	0.705	1	1.000	1	0.980	39	0.246
Costa Rica*	38	0.732	118	0.587	1	1.000	64	0.975	20	0.365
Portugal*	39	0.731	46	0.712	60	0.995	79	0.973	41	0.244
Italy*	41	0.726	111	0.603	58	0.995	74	0.974	24	0.331
Colombia*	42	0.725	37	0.746	61	0.994	42	0.979	64	0.180
Bulgaria	43	0.722	55	0.701	72	0.992	42	0.979	48	0.215
Poland*	51	0.715	75	0.667	38	1.000	42	0.979	52	0.213
Israel*	53	0.712	71	0.671	51	0.996	69	0.974	54	0.205
Mexico*	71	0.699	126	0.545	75	0.991	1	0.980	34	0.281
Russian Federation*	75	0.694	42	0.731	27	1.000	42	0.979	128	0.066
Kyrgyz Republic	76	0.693	80	0.658	81	0.989	79	0.973	76	0.153
Czech Republic*	81	0.687	94	0.636	1	1.000	42	0.979	83	0.134
Greece*	87	0.685	87	0.644	56	0.996	56	0.979	91	0.120
China	91	0.682	81	0.657	83	0.988	145	0.919	73	0.162
Azerbaijan	96	0.675	54	0.701	90	0.984	139	0.950	129	0.063
Slovak Republic*	97	0.675	93	0.638	1	1.000	79	0.973	115	0.087
Hungary*	99	0.672	62	0.685	76	0.991	42	0.979	139	0.035
Cyprus	100	0.671	88	0.643	41	0.998	73	0.974	124	0.069
Japan*	101	0.670	106	0.611	84	0.988	42	0.979	104	0.103
India	108	0.664	139	0.383	125	0.896	143	0.942	9	0.433
Korea, Rep.*	115	0.651	125	0.557	102	0.965	79	0.973	101	0.107
United Arab Emirates	119	0.646	128	0.519	86	0.987	133	0.961	93	0.115
Nigeria	125	0.638	61	0.691	137	0.802	133	0.961	111	0.097
Turkey*	130	0.624	131	0.459	105	0.957	1	0.980	105	0.103
Saudi Arabia	134	0.605	138	0.387	82	0.988	129	0.966	121	0.077
Egypt	136	0.599	135	0.441	115	0.935	97	0.971	136	0.048
Iran, Islamic Rep.	141	0.580	141	0.357	106	0.954	99	0.971	137	0.037
Syria	143	0.568	144	0.279	103	0.965	102	0.970	130	0.059
Yemen	145	0.484	145	0.225	142	0.720	123	0.967	140	0.026

Source: (WEF, 2015).

* OECD countries.

Figure 1. Economic participation and opportunity
Source: (WEF, 2015).

	Rank	Score	Sample average	Female	Male	Female-to-male ratio
ECONOMIC PARTICIPATION AND OPPORTUNITY	131	0.459	0.592			
Labour force participation	131	0.43	0.67	32	76	0.43
Wage equality for similar work (survey)	82	0.62	0.60	—	—	0.62
Estimated earned income (PPP US$)	130	0.39	0.54	10,967	27,836	0.39
Legislators, senior officials, and managers	109	0.15	0.27	13	87	0.15
Professional and technical workers	103	0.59	0.64	37	63	0.59

As can be seen from Figure 1, it seems not possible to say that there is an equality of genders; be it in terms of workforce participation rates, estimated income levels or employment numbers in positions like legislators, senior officials and managers, and professional and technical workers. What's more, the current status remains below the average of the countries. The only variable that is above the average is the wage equality; though the reality of wage inequality in Turkey shows itself in the index. According to this data, however, it also cannot be said that there is equality in wages in the other countries.

THE FACTORS AFFECTING THE WOMEN'S PARTICIPATION IN THE WORKFORCE

High unemployment and low labor force participation rates, meaning the inability to create adequate and quality employment, is a major structural problem of the economy of Turkey ever since the 2000s. The solution to this structural problem is to make extensive growth policies with a potential for providing increased employment in order to end the social gender inequality and support the introduction and commitment of women to the labor market. But, female labor has been seen as a reserve workforce ever since its inclusion in the labor market since the Industrial Revolution and its participation rate cannot reach the desired levels even though it has vital importance in the sustainability of any country's development and growth.

The low participation rate of women in the workforce constitutes one of the major problems in Turkey's labor market and the female labor force participation rates have a decreasing trend over the course of years. The female labor force participation rate, which was at 54% during the 1970s, went down to 40% in the 1980s, to 34% in the October of 1990 and to 30% in 1996. The rate of 1998 was 26%, while it was 28% in 2000 (Koray, Demirbilek, & Demirbilek, 2000, p. 106). In 2010 it was 27.2%, while it was 35.3% in the March of 2016 (Turkish Statistical Institute [TURKSTAT], 2016).

One of the major influence over the decrease in the female labor force participation rates to the workforce starting from the 1970s is the fact of rural-urban migration. The transformation of the industry, the need for male labor in the sectoral distribution and the higher qualification requirements from the previous periods for female labor blocked the women, whose labor had been used for unpaid family labor in the agricultural sector in the past, from participating in the urban workforce to at the desired level. On the other hand, some families did not need the income that the woman would gain in return for her work. Even if the family was in need of extra income, factors like the household responsibilities, childbirth, traditional and social disapproval or even the objection of the husband to the employment of his wife kept the women from entering the work life. Those who started working in order to contribute to the family income could only find a place in the small-scale businesses of industrial and service sectors with informally and low-paid jobs that have no social security – buttonholing, doing lacework and knitting or working as cashiers and sales clerks, etc. Reasons of this nature still remain as of today. Women work unregistered for small-scale businesses, which increased in number with subcontracting becoming commonplace, and as unpaid family workers. Shadow employment and home-based production are the two key dynamics of female employment in Turkey.

One of the primary elements factors of low labor force participation is the fact that Turkey is one of the countries which have lowest female labor force participation rate at the global scale. In this context, this section of the chapter will compare the total and female labor force participation rates in Turkey with the rest of the OECD countries, trying to put forth the defining factors of female labor participation in the light of national data. The labor force participation rates and the education levels of women in the workforce of the OECD countries are shown in Table 2.

As can be seen in Table 2, Turkey has the lowest workforce participation rate among the OECD countries. According to the 2014 data, only the 55.1% of the active population are in the workforce. On the other hand, the country with the highest labor participation rate is Iceland with 86.7%. In Turkey, the participation rate of the women in working age is %33.6; in other words, only one of every three women participates to the workforce. In the case of men, this rate is 76.6%; despite being lower than most of the developed countries, it is considerably higher than the female participation rate in Turkey. The reason for the total workforce participation rate to be this low is that the women supply their labor in a lower proportion of the market. The young women's (aged 15-24) participation rate is 27.7%. Female labor gains weight in the middle-age group, aged between 25-54 years, with a rate of 38.8%. The participation of aged women between 55-64 years is 17.9%.

According to the OECD (2015a) data, when the female labor participation rates are studied in terms of educational levels, 30.2% of women with a pre-secondary level of education, 37.7% of women with a high school degree and 73.7% of women with a higher education degree participate in the working life. As can be seen in Table 3, the rate of participation for women with a higher education degree is 71.3% (TURKSTAT, 2016). According to these statistics, the participation rates are 13.8% for illiterate women, 25.9% for women with less than high school education, 32.3% for high school graduates and 40.3% for vocational or technical high school graduates.

It is clear that the higher education graduates have a higher participation rate than women of other educational backgrounds, but in Turkey – because of its last position after Japan and Korea in terms of labor force participation rates by educational attainment according to Table 2– it can be seen that there is a considerable fraction that does not work even if they have an adequate education. An increase in the education level of the workforce would affect the economic growth and development positively and contribute to the poverty reduction effort (Günsoy & Özsoy, 2012). On the other hand, the longer periods of education coming as a result of a larger portion of the population attending the schools may affect the total labor supply negatively. The positive effects, however, are felt stronger. Education is not only effective for increasing the workforce participation rates. It also helps women to work in more qualified and better-paid jobs and in addition, is effective in weakening the social gender perception imposed by the patriarchal mindset and making the society accept the entry of the women to the working life (Toksöz, 2007a).

Table 2. Labour force participation rates by selected age groups and educational attainment

Country	Labor Force Participation Rates			Labor Force Participation Rates by Selected Age Groups			Labor Force Participation Rates by Educational Attainment (25-64), 2013		
	Total (15-64)	Men (15-64)	Women (15-64)	Youth (15-24) (Women)	Prime Age (25-54) (Women)	Older Population (55-64) (Women)	Women		
	2014	2014	2014	2014	2014	2014	Less than Upper Secondary Education	Upper Secondary Education	Tertiary Education
Australia	76.3	82.2	70.5	66.2	75.9	56.2	56.3	71.5	81.3
Austria	75.4	80.0	70.8	55.4	84.5	37.5	54.9	77.4	86.7
Belgium	67.7	72.4	63.0	28.1	80.6	39.0	43.8	72.4	85.3
Canada	77.8	81.3	74.2	64.6	81.9	59.2	51.4	73.2	83.0
Czech Republic	73.5	81.2	65.6	26.1	81.6	46.3	46.7	73.7	79.6
Denmark	78.1	81.1	75.0	62.0	83.8	60.3	59.4	80.5	89.1
Estonia	75.2	79.3	71.2	37.0	81.8	66.5	57.4	75.3	85.0
Finland	75.5	77.1	73.8	52.5	83.4	65.8	55.6	76.0	85.5
France	71.3	75.3	67.4	33.4	83.5	48.6	55.2	76.2	86.3
Germany	77.7	82.5	72.9	47.7	82.4	62.9	56.7	78.4	86.1
Greece	67.4	76.0	59.0	26.1	75.6	29.9	47.3	63.6	81.8
Hungary	67.0	73.4	60.7	25.9	78.8	37.4	42.6	68.2	78.2
Iceland	86.7	89.1	84.2	78.4	86.3	83.3	72.5	b	91.1
Ireland	69.7	77.1	62.5	35.5	72.6	48.1	40.7	65.9	81.5
Israel	72.2	76.1	68.4	48.5	78.4	60.3	33.7	71.1	85.5
Italy	64.9	74.7	55.2	25.5	66.4	38.3	40.4	67.3	80.4
Japan	75.5	84.9	66.0	43.4	74.5	57.5	c	66.5	71.3
Korea	67.8	78.6	57.0	32.5	64.8	53.0	58.6	59.3	64.1
Luxembourg	70.8	77.2	64.2	23.0	80.9	36.5	58.0	67.3	83.3
Mexico	63.7	82.1	46.8	32.2	54.8	36.9	45.4	57.9	75.2
Netherlands	79.0	84.2	73.8	67.7	81.9	54.3	54.8	78.0	89.1

continued on following page

Table 2. Continued

Country	Labor Force Participation Rates			Labor Force Participation Rates by Selected Age Groups			Labor Force Participation Rates by Educational Attainment (25-64), 2013		
	Total (15-64)	Men (15-64)	Women (15-64)	Youth (15-24) (Women)	Prime Age (25-54) (Women)	Older Population (55-64) (Women)	Women		
	2014	2014	2014	2014	2014	2014	Less than Upper Secondary Education	Upper Secondary Education	Tertiary Education
New Zealand	79.0	84.1	74.1	58.5	79.3	74.2	66.4	75.8	85.2
Norway	78.1	80.2	75.9	56.2	84.1	69.2	61.5	78.7	89.7
Poland	67.9	74.6	61.1	28.7	79.6	35.2	35.8	62.1	86.3
Portugal	73.2	76.7	70.0	33.8	85.8	47.5	66.7	88.1	90.4
Slovak Republic	70.3	77.6	62.8	23.6	80.4	42.1	43.9	71.7	80.1
Slovenia	70.9	74.3	67.3	30.5	88.3	31.1	45.0	71.9	87.7
Spain	75.3	80.7	69.8	37.6	82.0	46.9	60.7	78.9	87.5
Sweden	81.5	83.6	79.3	55.9	88.0	75.2	59.7	84.1	91.6
Switzerland	83.8	88.5	79.0	66.6	85.7	66.5	68.4	79.6	86.7
Turkey	55.1	76.6	33.6	27.7	38.8	17.9	30.2	37.7	73.7
United Kingdom	77.6	83.1	72.1	59.6	80.0	56.4	54.7	76.7	82.6
United States	72.7	78.5	67.1	53.6	73.9	58.8	47.3	67.1	79.0
OECD	71.2	79.7	62.8	43.1	71.9	51.5	52.2	71.6	83.3
Colombia	74.0	85.7	62.9	46.1	73.2	48.3	60.2	73.3	87.1
Costa Rica	68.4	82.0	54.6	38.1	64.9	39.0			
Latvia	74.6	77.8	71.6	35.3	84.0	61.7	55.2	75.1	88.3
Lithuania	73.7	76.0	71.6	29.6	88.7	58.9			
Russian Fed.	73.1	78.6	68.1	34.3	86.1	40.7	45.7	68.9	81.4
South Africa	57.1	63.7	50.7	22.8	66.1	35.4			

Source: Organisation for Economic Co-Operation and Development (OECD, 2015a) and Organisation for Economic Co-Operation and Development (OECD, 2015e).

Table 3. Labour force participation rate by educational attainment

Educational Attainment	Labor Force Participation Rate					
	Total		Male		Female	
	2015	2016	2015	2016	2015	2016
Total	50.4	51.3	70.6	71.5	30.7	31.6
Illiterate	18.2	16.7	31.1	30.3	15.6	13.8
Less than high school	46.9	47.8	67.4	68.2	25.6	25.9
High school	53.8	53.2	70.7	70.0	32.2	32.3
Vocational high school	65.1	66.4	80.6	82.4	40.4	40.3
Higher education	80.3	79.5	86.0	86.5	73.0	71.3

Source: TURKSTAT (2016) April Statistics.

According to the World Bank's study of Turkey's labor market, the real reason for the women's low participation in the workforce is the very low participation rate of the undereducated women in the cities (World Bank, 2006). The reasons of this are of economic and social nature. Among the economic obstacles are the expansion of the shadow sectors, low wages, long working hours and the lack of child care services. The cultural obstacles, on the other hand, are in relation to the familial and social pressure put on women to make them carry out their 'primary' job, housework, and to keep them inside the house. Labor division based on the social gender and the social gender roles shaped by this division keeps the women responsible for the housework and the care of the children, the sick and the elderly, considerably preventing them from entering the labor market. The main reason for the women not participating in the workforce is housework with 54.8%. This rate proves how great an obstacle the social gender-based labor division is for the female participation to the labor force. The women's responsibility for this work, which the men are traditionally exempted, is an important factor that affects the women's decisions to work outside the home (Ecevit, 2008; TURKSTAT, 2016). Family pressure comes forth as a significant obstacle to the undereducated women's entry into the workforce; because the decision for a woman to work in an income generating job is subject to the permission of the male individuals in the family, rather than being a personal decision. The permission in question, if given, is limited to the jobs deemed appropriate for the woman (Toksöz, 2007b, pp. 57-79).

In the case of married women with children, reasons like the lack of a family elder to take care of the children, the limited nature of the public care services and the high cost of the private care services may keep the women from the labor market in order to care for their children. Even if the child care problems are solved with one of the aforementioned alternatives, the woman is still not emancipated from her household responsibilities and the load she bears greatly increases. Being married with children comes forth as a decisive factor on women's entry into the workforce even with the increase in their educational levels. TURKSTAT's Time Use Survey of 2014-2015 shows that the working women spare an average of 3 hours and 31 minutes of their daily time to the household and family care, while in the case of men, this time is 46 minutes (Turkish Statistical Institute [TURKSTAT], 2015).

When the participation rates of the women based on their marital status, on the other hand, the ratio for the married women to enter the labor force in 2013 was 30.5%. This rate is 37.9 for single women, 50.9% for divorced women and 9% for widowed women; it is safe to say that the single or divorced women participate more in the labor force (Toksöz, 2015). It has been estimated that marriage and childbirth cause the 70% of the female employees to quit a job while being used as grounds for dismissal for the 20% of the employers (Ecevit, 1998, pp. 67-72). Single women usually postpone marriage in order to complete their education and secure their place in the labor market. Divorced women, on the other hand, usually enter the working life to reorient their lives and to provide for themselves and their children, if they have any, in the days to come.

The economic obstacles preventing the women from entering into the labor force are the economic depressions, unemployment, low wages and long working hours. The periods of economic depression may affect the female labor participation rate in a positive or negative way. Women may show the desire to work in order to prevent the household income loss, especially during periods of depression and the unemployment that comes with. In the case of a dismissal during an economic depression and fruitless job searches, on the other hand, may cause the women to withdraw from the labor market or give up on their decision to enter the labor market. This case is named the "discouraged worker effect" (Belet, 2013).

The other economic determinant of female labor force participation rate is the inflation rate. The inflation rate, felt stronger with every passing year, causes the women to enter the workforce because of the inability to maintain the living standards with the current household income. At the time of the first entry to the labor market, those who are underqualified and undereducated or those who cannot find a job in accordance with their qualifications are forced to settle for working in small scale and/or unrecorded works for low wages.

The recent developments in the field of social security also affect the female participation to the labor force. By increasing the employees' necessary day count for contribution and raising the age threshold, the period of contribution is extended, and the benefits of the social security system have been reduced by lowering the retirement pensions and making the conditions for a partial pension more difficult in Turkey. The recent legislations have made the women's access to social security and health services even more difficult, increasing the current insecurity and poverty of them. Low female labor participation rates, lower wages than the men and the fact that most women are employed in unregistered jobs show us that the women in Turkey are excluded from the social security system and cannot benefit from health services. It seems very difficult for women, who are paid lower than men, to afford the contributions they are supposed to pay and benefit from individual retirement plans or private health services.

Marriage, on the other hand, becomes a tool for most women to benefit from the social security system or private health services. Women in Turkey can only benefit from the sickness and, to a very limited extent, maternal insurance; they are not under the protection of the social security against cases like old age or disablement as individuals and citizens. Thus, this system puts women under the heavy dependence on their husbands' income. Aside from being punished for taking care of the children, the sick and the elderly by not being able to work for wages, the women also cannot benefit from the future assurance the social security system provides. This causes the household labor of the working women and the labor of the unemployed women to be excluded from the system. The system disregards the familial inequalities between the man and the woman; even some of the rights granted to the women during the period of the previous law are taken back with the new legislation. For example, the conditions to be eligible for a death pension after the insured individual's death have been made more difficult. Moreover, daughters over the age of 25 are faced with the obligation to pay contributions in order for them to benefit from the system after the death of the insured parent. Another example is the equalization of retirement age for women and men after 2048.

The women also need some health services dictated by their sex (i.e., childbirth, treatment of breast and uterine cancers as well as infections); moreover, physical and psychological violence, domestic violence and honor killings pose a serious threat to women's health and survival (Dedeoğlu & Öztürk, 2010, pp. 59-65).

Other reasons for the low labour force participation can be summarized as the decrease of agricultural employment with downward trend in the agricultural area allocation, the ongoing increase in the population, the shortcomings in the employment opportunities in the face of increasing working-age population, early retirement, the decrease in employment in the public due to privatization, alienation of the undereducated women from the labor market because of technological developments, the inadequacy of part-time employment and the income level of the household.

Social gender inequality shows itself in essentially all areas of the society, be it in the field of education, labor force participation or division of the household responsibilities. In the following sections of this chapter, the employment of women and the gender inequalities they actually face during the employment will be studied.

THE OUTLOOK OF FEMALE EMPLOYMENT IN TURKEY

Workforce participation consists of two elements: employment and unemployment. The increase in the working age population is still higher than the increase in the employment areas although the high population growth times are well behind. This means, especially for the women entering the workforce, being employed in jobs incompatible with decent work or facing the danger of unemployment. A long period of unemployment will eventually cause the woman to stop offering her labor to the market. The low rates of participation in the workforce in Turkey result in employment rates lower than the standard.

The difference can be seen when the female employment rate in Turkey is compared to the OECD countries (Table 4). A glance at the statistical data of Organisation for Economic Co-Operation and Development (OECD, 2015d) countries shows that the ratio of female labor to the total civilian workforce is 29.6%. In other words, only 30% of total employment consists of women. This ratio is observed as 45.6% in the Eurozone and 45.7% in the EU according to 2014 data. It can be seen that the country with the lowest female employment rate after Turkey is Mexico with 38%. On the other hand, female employment rates nearing 50% in countries like Estonia, Finland, Portugal and Russia provide a significant indicator for the level of development and social gender equality in the working life (OECD, 2015d).

According to the TURKSTAT Labor Force statistics of March 2016, the total employment rate is 50.4%, the male employment rate is 69.7%, and the female employment rate is 31.1%. The male employment rate is more than the double of the female rate. National data also supports these OECD (2015d) data (TURKSTAT, 2016). The female employment rates this low suggests that the true cause of the employment problems of Turkey stem from the female employment ratio.

Other fundamental reasons for the low employment rate are the economic instability, inadequate investments, the failure of institutionalization in the labor market, a higher working-age population increase than the total population increase, the inability to create adequate employment opportunities for the underqualified workforce coming from agricultural background, the shortage of qualifications for the workforce to satisfy the needs of the economy, the failure to establish the relationship between the labor market and the educational system, the inability to establish the flexibility, the lack of adequate

Table 4. Female employment, self-employment, and part-time employment rates

Country	Female Civilian Employment as a Percentage of Civilian Employment		Female Self-Employment as a Percentage of Female Civilian Employment		Female Part-Time Employment as a Percentage of Female Employment		Female Share of Part-Time Employment	
	2013	2014	2013	2014	2013	2014	2013	2014
Australia	45.8	45.9	8.1	..	38.1	38.3	70.3	69.9
Austria	47.0	47.2	10.6	10.5	33.4	34.9	78.9	78.6
Belgium	45.9	46.4	10.7	12.3	31.4	30.5	80.8	79.1
Canada	47.7	47.6	8.1	8.0	26.7	27.0	66.7	66.6
Chile	40.4	40.9	25.1	25.6	24.3	25.0	59.2	60.2
Czech Republic	43.5	43.5	13.5	12.9	8.0	7.7	71.2	70.5
Denmark	47.5	..	5.6	..	24.7	25.4	61.1	61.0
Estonia	49.5	48.9	5.9	5.7	11.3	10.3	69.3	66.1
Finland	48.8	48.9	8.8	9.4	16.7	16.8	62.2	61.4
France	48.3	..	..	..	22.5	22.3	76.9	75.7
Germany	46.7	46.7	8.1	8.0	38.1	37.5	78.6	78.1
Greece	41.3	41.7	31.9	29.8	15.6	16.2	62.3	60.8
Hungary	46.1	46.0	8.2	7.8	6.3	5.8	62.5	62.8
Iceland	47.9	47.8	8.4	7.8	24.6	23.2	67.5	66.2
Ireland	46.4	45.9	8.1	7.9	36.2	35.4	71.9	72.2
Israel	46.8	47.1	9.0	9.1	21.5	21.8	69.1	69.4
Italy	42.2	42.3	18.3	18.5	32.8	32.9	74.1	73.4
Japan	42.8	..	10.4	..	36.2	37.2	70.3	69.8
Korea	41.9	42.0	25.3	24.6	16.2	15.6	60.5	62.2
Luxembourg	..	..	..	..	27.7	27.7	80.3	80.1
Mexico	38.5	38.0	33.8	32.7	28.4	27.9	57.6	56.8
Netherlands	46.4	..	12.1	..	61.1	60.6	73.2	72.5
New Zealand	47.4	47.3	11.7	11.8	33.5	32.7	73.2	72.0
Norway	47.4	47.4	4.4	4.3	28.8	27.7	69.4	69.8
Poland	44.5	44.7	18.4	17.7	11.8	10.7	67.9	67.1
Portugal	48.6	48.7	17.5	14.9	14.1	12.9	58.0	57.9
Slovak Republic	44.4	44.3	9.8	9.9	5.6	6.4	58.0	58.2
Slovenia	45.4	45.5	13.6	16.0	11.2	12.5	59.1	59.6
Spain	45.8	45.7	13.1	13.0	23.4	23.6	73.4	74.0
Sweden	47.6	47.6	6.2	6.2	18.4	18.3	61.2	61.1
Switzerland	45.3	45.5	10.2	10.0	45.7	45.6	80.0	78.5
Turkey	29.9|	29.6	43.4|	39.8	24.5	20.6	59.9	57.7
United Kingdom	46.9	46.9	9.6	10.6	38.7	38.1	73.8	74.2
United States	47.0	46.9	5.6	5.4	..	..	..	..
OECD - Total	..	..	..	..	26.1	25.9	68.9	68.8

continued on following page

Table 4. Continued

Country	Female Civilian Employment as a Percentage of Civilian Employment		Female Self-Employment as a Percentage of Female Civilian Employment		Female Part-Time Employment as a Percentage of Female Employment		Female Share of Part-Time Employment	
	2013	2014	2013	2014	2013	2014	2013	2014
G7	46.0	..	..	..	26.7	26.8	71.2	71.1
Euro area	45.6	..	11.6	..	29.2	28.6	73.3	72.9
European Union	45.7	..	12.3	..	29.2	28.8	74.3	73.9
Brazil	42.8	..	26.8	..	24.7	..	64.2	..
Colombia	41.5	..	52.1	..	28.4	26.6	66.5	67.5
Russian Federation	48.9	48.8	6.4	6.3	5.8	5.3	65.5	65.1

Source: OECD (2015d).

support for entrepreneurship, the social gender inequality and the discriminative practices the women face over the course of their employment (Devlet Planlama Teşkilatı [DPT], 2006).

When the educational levels of employed women are studied, the results show that 13.5% of illiterate, 24.2% of women with less than high school, 25.7% of high school graduates, 34.1% of vocational and technical high school graduates and 61.3% of higher education graduates are employed (see Table 5).

The emphasis on education in the recent years, with new universities and departments opening regularly, causes an increase in the number of higher education graduates. As stated in the previous section, however, only 70% of the higher-education graduate women participate in the workforce. The increase in the educational levels has not reflected on workforce participation and consequently, employment (TURKSTAT, 2016).

A study of OECD (2015d) data based on the job status shows that 39.8% of the employed women are self-employed. As can be seen from Table 4, the country with the highest rate of self-employment is Turkey. Following Turkey come Mexico with 32.7%, Greece with 29.8%, Chile with 25.6% and Korea with 24.6%.

Table 5. Employment rate by educational attainment

Educational Attainment	Employment Rate					
	Total		Male		Female	
	2015	2016	2015	2016	2015	2016
Total	45.0	46.1	63.8	64.8	26.7	27.9
Illiterate	17.2	15.6	27.5	26.0	15.1	13.5
Less than high school	42.0	43.0	60.4	61.5	22.9	24.2
High school	47.0	46.4	64.2	62.7	25.0	25.7
Vocational high school	57.9	59.6	73.7	75.8	32.9	34.1
Higher education	71.8	71.8	79.7	80.1	61.5	61.3

Source: TURKSTAT (2016) April Statistics.

Self-employment, despite having been divided into 3 different groups as employers, self-employed ones, and unpaid family workers in the TURKSTAT statistics, is considered in the OECD (2015d) data as a single state of employment. The high statistical ratio of self-employment among the employed women presents a negative effect on the labor market of the country in question. Self-employment mainly consists of unpaid family workers. It is a type of labor conducted by those who prefer to work at home or in small workshops on a piecework basis because of the unqualified nature and low qualifications of part-time labor, in order to use the time needed especially for the household work and the care of the elderly, the sick and the children (Dayıoğlu & Kırdar, 2010). It can also be seen that 20% of female labor also consists of part-time workers in Turkey and the ratio of the part-time working women to the total number of part-time workers is 57.7% (OECD, 2016). This case proves both the intensity of the work deemed as 'women's work' by the literature and that the responsibilities laid on the women by social gender inequality only allow them to be employed as part-time labor in Turkey.

As stated before, the biggest obstacle in front of female employment is this responsibility to take care of the sick, the elderly and the children that are laid on the women's shoulders. According to the Regulation on the Working Conditions of Pregnant and Nursing Women, Nursing Rooms and Child Care Homes (2004), it is imperative for every workplace that has 100 to 150 female employees to include a nursing room in order for the children to be kept, cared and nursed; while every workplace that has more 150 female employees must include a child care home for the children of 0 to 6 years of age to be kept and cared and for the nursing of the babies by their mothers. This legislation, by including a lower limit of female employees, both reinforces the view that lays the burden of childcare to the mother and causes the employers to hire limited female labor in order to avoid the obligation to maintain these facilities. Furthermore, most working women can't benefit from this regulation since they are self-employed, while others also remain out of its scope because of their waged or casual work in small scale businesses.

According to the TURKSTAT data, 63.8% of the working women take their place in the working life as waged or casual workers, 1.3% are employers, 9.2% are self-employed, and 25.7% are unpaid family workers in Turkey (See Table 6). In other words, one of every four women is an unpaid family worker. This is a very common labor practice in the rural areas, where the women can both labor in the agricultural lands of the family and spare time for the household and caring duties while contributing to the family income (Özer & Biçerli, 2004). On the other hand, with the rural-urban migration as a result of the disorganization in agriculture, unpaid family labor and agricultural labor in general continues to lose its share in the total employment, while paid and casual labor fails to show an increase in the same proportions.

When the economic activities of the employed women in Turkey are studied, it can be seen that the agricultural employment rate which was 42.1% in 2008 has fallen to 27% by 2016. The ratio of the women employed in the industrial sector by 2008 was estimated as 15.7% in 2008; this rate has fallen to 15.1% by 2016. Under these circumstances, the ratio of female employment in the service sector can be expected to increase by roughly 15%; hence, while 42.2% of the employed women worked in the service sector in 2008, by 2016 this ratio has reached 56.9% (See Table 6).

As known the phenomenon which consists one of the most problematic areas of the employment structure in Turkey is unregistered employment. Unregistered employment means employment that lacks social security and is outside the scope of legal protective measures (Toksöz, 2007a). Unregistered employment is a way of work preferred by many male or female employees for the purpose of keeping the labor cost, which has a significant share in the total production cost, relatively low or forced to them by the employer. When we look at the causes of unregistered employment, we can see the increase in

Table 6. Employment status, economic activity, and unregistered rate on employment

	Total (%)		Male (%)		Unregistered Rate (%) (Male)		Female (%)		Unregistered Rate (%) (Female)	
	2015	**2016**	**2015**	**2016**	**2015**	**2016**	**2015**	**2016**	**2015**	**2016**
Employment status	**100.0**	**100.0**	**100.0**	**100.0**	**27.4**	**28.2**	**100.0**	**100.0**	**45.3**	**43.3**
Regular or casual employee	66.8	67.5	68.9	69.2	16.7	17.2	61.9	63.8	19.0	18.6
Employer	4.3	4.6	5.7	6.1	11.8	15.9	1.1	1.3	10.1	11.2
Self employed	17.3	17.0	20.9	20.5	54.8	57.6	9.0	9.2	86.1	85.2
Unpaid family worker	11.5	10.8	4.5	4.2	83.6	83.6	28.0	25.7	92.0	91.5
Economic activities	**100.0**	**100.0**	**100.0**	**100.0**			**100.0**	**100.0**		
Agriculture	20.0	18.9	15.7	15.3			30.0	27.0		
Industry	20.5	19.6	22.4	21.6			16.0	15.1		
Construction	6.9	7.1	9.5	9.9			0.8	0.9		
Services	52.6	54.4	52.4	53.3			53.2	56.9		

Source: TURKSTAT (2016) April Statistics.

population, unfair distribution of income, poverty, migration, urbanization, high unemployment rates, low educational levels and the lack of information and awareness that comes as a result, high rates and unfair collection of taxes, high labor costs, social security practices like voluntary insurance and the inadequacies in the implementation of the laws and regulations governing flexible work in recorded employment (DPT, 2006).

In Turkey, the total ratio of unregistered labor is 32.9%; but the ratio of unregistered female labor is 43.3% while the male labor of the same nature is 28.2%. 93.9% of the women and 71.2% of the men employed in agriculture are unregistered. The unregistered employment ratio in the female unpaid family labor in agriculture is 94.9%. According to TURKSTAT (2016), women are employed more commonly in unregistered jobs. The cause for the unregistered work ratio in total to be high is, again, unregistered female employment. Unpaid family labor in particular – whether agricultural or non-agricultural – points directly to unregistered labor. Besides, women's home based production labor, paid housework and manual labor, etc. are mostly unregistered. While unregistered female employment in the non-agricultural sectors has a relatively high ratio of 24.6%, the ratio of unregistered and unpaid family labor employed in these sectors is 66.6%. Likewise, the percentages of unregistered self-employed women in the agricultural and non-agricultural sectors are 95.7% and 80% respectively. Social gender discrimination shows itself in unregistered employment. Women who are employed unregistered cannot come under the protection of the social security system and cannot enjoy the rights granted by the Labor Law No. 4857. These circumstances solidify the secondary status of women in the labor market. Working for low wages without job security and social protection either pushes the women out of the labor market or forces them to work under adverse circumstances because of the necessity to generate income (Ecevit, 2008). Aside from the economic hardships, women opt for this kind of employment for various reasons. Young mothers choose jobs with more flexible working hours; while some women can only get their husband's permission to work by choosing this kind of jobs – like daily cleaning work. Other causes include the desire to avert the problems stemming from the negative impression of the society about female labor and to avoid the harassments, wage inequalities, and discriminations in subjects like promotion in the workplace (Çınar, 1994, pp. 369-380).

The problems caused by unrecorded labor on the national economy, aside from its negative effects on female employment, are substantial. Problems like the inability to access quality data in economic indicators, budgetary deficits, a decrease in tax income, unfair competition between businesses and a diminishing in the comprehensiveness of the social security system come to mind. The steps to be taken against unregistered employment include macroeconomic stability, lifting the burden of wages and social contributions from the shoulders of employers, eliminating the legal barriers hampering the spread of flexible working arrangements and creating a labor market that balances flexibility and security.

The other problems faced by female labor are in connection with the fact that social gender equality in Turkey still hasn't been established as of today. The discriminative practices the women are subjected to as soon as they apply for the job – specifying the gender in the job postings, questions during the interview about marital status, current number of children and plans of having children –, having their access to vocational education blocked during their employment, laboring for wages relatively lower than men are paid, the glass ceiling that keep them from reaching their career goals and being subjected to mobbing and verbal or sexual harassment because of their gender; problems like these show that the social gender perception is well established in the working life too.

FEMALE UNEMPLOYMENT IN TURKEY

As mentioned in the previous sections, the major problems of the labor market in Turkey are the low workforce participation rates and high unemployment. These problems are the problems of the labor market itself, but it is clear that the women are more heavily affected from these.

By ILO's definition, unemployment covers all non-institutional persons of working age (15 and up) who, during the reference period, are out of work, want a job, have actively sought work and are available to start working in the case they find a job. Unemployment is generally defined as the state of not being able to find a job with a market-level wage despite possessing the desire and the qualification to work. The causes of unemployment in Turkey include the inability to generate adequate employment even in times of economic growth, agricultural disorganization, the disparity between supply and demand in the labor market, low educational levels and the inefficacy of active labor market policies.

According to the OECD (2015b) data, the female unemployment rate of Turkey in 2014 was 11.8%; this rate is higher than the OECD and EU averages, respectively 7.5% and 10.3%. A look at Table 7 will show the highest female unemployment rates in the European Union countries: Greece with 30.2%, Spain with 25.4%, Portugal with 14.3% and Italy with 13.8%. It's not possible to reach the inferences by interpreting only the unemployment data without considering the workforce participation rates because of the close relationship between them. High unemployment rates are considered more problematic when the country's workforce participation rate is low as well. When we look at women's workforce participation rates in the same countries, we see Greece with 59%, Spain with 69.8%, Portugal with 70% and Italy with 55.2%. Because of the recent economic depression, Greece shows a proportional similarity with Turkey; however, with half of the female population participating in the workforce in the other countries, the levels can be considered acceptable in comparison to Turkey. Turkey's female workforce participation rate, on the other hand, is 33.6%. The high female unemployment rate despite a low participation in the workforce poses a severe problem in Turkey.

Table 7. Unemployment rates by selected age groups and educational attainment

Country	Unemployment Rates (As a Percentage of Labor Force)			Unemployment Rates by Selected Age Groups			Unemployment Rates by Educational Attainment		
	Total	Men	Women	Youth (15-24) (Women)	Prime Age (25-54) (Women)	Older Population (55-64) (Women)	Women 2013		
	2014	2014	2014	2014	2014	2014	Less than Upper Secondary Education	Upper Secondary Education	Tertiary Education
Australia	6.1	6.0	6.2	12.5	5.1	3.8	7.3	5.8	3.0
Austria	5.6	5.8	5.4	9.9	5.0	2.8	7.4	3.6	3.8
Belgium	8.5	9.0	7.9	22.3	7.0	5.1	13.3	7.3	4.4
Canada	6.9	7.4	6.4	11.9	5.5	5.5	11.1	6.6	4.7
Chile	6.4	6.0	6.9	..	..	..	8.3	8.4	4.2
Czech Republic	6.1	5.1	7.4	17.1	7.1	5.4	23.6	7.8	2.9
Denmark	6.6	6.4	6.8	11.5	6.4	4.5	9.3	6.8	4.6
Estonia	7.4	7.9	6.8	10.0	7.2	5.1	11.7	8.9	5.6
Finland	8.7	9.3	7.9	18.0	6.5	6.4	13.1	7.5	4.0
France	10.3	10.5	10.0	22.1	8.7	6.7	13.8	8.8	5.1
Germany	5.0	5.3	4.6	7.1	4.4	4.6	10.3	4.7	2.6
Greece	26.5	23.6	30.2	58.1	29.8	16.4	30.1	34.2	22.7
Hungary	7.7	7.6	7.9	20.9	7.2	6.0	20.9	8.9	3.9
Iceland	4.9	5.0	4.8	6.9	5.0	3.2	6.7	b	4.2
Ireland	11.3	12.8	9.4	25.6	8.3	6.7	15.5	11.7	6.3
Israel	5.9	5.9	5.9	11.1	5.2	3.9	7.7	7.1	4.3
Italy	12.7	11.9	13.8	44.7	13.2	4.4	15.7	10.4	8.3
Japan	3.6	3.8	3.4	5.4	3.5	2.5	c	4.3	3.2
Korea	3.5	3.6	3.5	9.2	3.3	1.9	1.4	2.4	2.7
Luxembourg	5.9	5.9	5.8	18.1	5.1	4.2	10.8	6.8	4.0
Mexico	4.8	4.8	4.9	10.3	4.1	1.7	3.3	4.1	5.0
Netherlands	7.4	7.1	7.7	13.1	6.6	7.2	7.7	5.9	3.3
New Zealand	5.8	5.1	6.6	15.7	5.6	3.1	7.4	5.8	3.6
Norway	3.5	3.7	3.2	6.6	3.2	1.0	5.7	2.3	1.8
Poland	9.0	8.5	9.6	25.5	8.7	6.3	21.0	11.4	5.6
Portugal	13.9	13.5	14.3	35.4	13.4	11.5	16.3	15.9	12.8
Slovak Republic	13.2	12.8	13.6	30.1	12.7	11.7	37.7	13.3	7.2
Slovenia	9.7	8.9	10.5	21.3	10.5	6.6	19.1	11.4	6.6
Spain	24.4	23.6	25.4	52.9	24.1	19.4	34.0	25.1	16.4
Sweden	8.0	8.2	7.7	21.5	5.9	4.6	16.1	6.0	3.7
Switzerland	4.5	4.4	4.7	8.5	4.5	3.1	7.5	3.5	3.4

continued on following page

Table 7. Continued

Country	Unemployment Rates (As a Percentage of Labor Force)			Unemployment Rates by Selected Age Groups			Unemployment Rates by Educational Attainment		
	Total	Men	Women	Youth (15-24) (Women)	Prime Age (25-54) (Women)	Older Population (55-64) (Women)	Women 2013		
	2014	2014	2014	2014	2014	2014	Less than Upper Secondary Education	Upper Secondary Education	Tertiary Education
Turkey	9.9	9.0	11.8	20.4	10.9	2.2	8.6	17.7	11.1
United Kingdom	6.1	6.4	5.8	14.0	4.9	3.8	9.8	5.5	2.9
United States	6.2	6.3	6.1	12.2	5.3	4.2	14.1	7.8	4.1
EU 28	10.2	10.1	10.3						
OECD	7.3	7.3	7.5	14.5	7.0	4.7	13.5	9.0	5.6
Brazil	4.9						6.7	7.4	3.4
China									
India									
Indonesia	5.8								
Russian Federation	5.2	5.5	4.8	14.1	4.2	2.7	11.3	6.2	2.8
South Africa	25.1	23.3	27.2	55.3	24.5	7.1			

Source: Organisation for Economic Co-Operation and Development (OECD, 2015b), OECD (2015c), and OECD (2015e).

The TURKSTAT data of 2016 shows female unemployment rate as 11.8% and the male unemployment rate as 9.3%. This rate, however, considers the unpaid family workers employed because of their employment in the agricultural sector; so the non-agricultural unemployment rates present more realistic data about urban female unemployment. The female non-agricultural unemployment rate in this context is 15.4%, while this rate is 10.5% for the men (TURKSTAT, 2016). While the general unemployment rates do not differ between men and women, the non-agricultural unemployment rates differ greatly; this refers to a difficulty for women to find a job compared to men.

As for the previous jobs, only 4.7% of the unemployed women stated that they worked in agriculture. 17.6% of them entered the workforce in industry and 57.2% of them in the service sector. Women face a higher risk of unemployment in the service sector which includes less secure jobs. The ratio of first-time job seeking women is 10.5%, while the ratio of women who had quitted their jobs prior to the last eight years and still cannot find a new job even if they desire to be employed is 8.7% (TURKSTAT, 2016).

Hidden female unemployment is also a case in Turkey. 68.4% of the female population does not participate in the workforce and the major reason stated for this is full-time household work with a ratio of 54.8%. It is possible, then, to see an increase of roughly 35% in the female workforce participation rate if the major obstacles preventing the women's entry into the working life like household work and child care are lifted. Despite the importance of an increase in the labor participation for progress and development, the failure to create new employment areas will extend the proportions of unemployment.

Table 8. Unemployment rate by educational attainment

Educational Attainment	Unemployment Rate					
	Total		Male		Female	
	2015	2016	2015	2016	2015	2016
Total	10.6	10.1	9.6	9.3	12.9	11.8
Illiterate	5.4	6.2	11.6	14.2	3.0	2.6
Less than high school	10.4	9.9	10.5	9.8	10.3	10.1
High school	12.7	12.8	9.2	10.4	22.3	19.5
Vocational high school	10.9	10.2	8.5	8.1	18.6	16.9
Higher education	10.7	9.7	7.4	7.4	15.8	13.4

Source: TURKSTAT (2016) April Statistics.

When the unemployment rates of female labor compared in accordance with the age groups, youth unemployment appears as another problem in Turkey. The female youth unemployment rate is 20.4%, while middle age unemployment has been estimated as 10.9% (OECD, 2015b). Both the low workforce participation rate due to the increase in education levels and the inadequacy of the labor market cause high unemployment among young women.

An analysis of female unemployment rates based on education levels reveals that 8.6% of the women with pre-high school education are unemployed, while this rate is 11.1% for the higher education graduates. The highest unemployment rate based on the education level belong women with on high-school and other equivalent school degrees with 17.7% (Organisation for Economic Co-Operation and Development [OECD], 2015c). According to TURKSTAT data, these rates are much higher. The rates are 2.6% for illiterate women, 10.1% for women with pre-high school education, 19.5% for high school graduates, 16.9% for vocational and technical high school graduates and 13.4 for higher education graduates.

When the job-searching periods are studied, it can be seen that the 74.8% of the unemployed women are without a job for less than a year, while 25.2% has been searching for 1 year or more, meaning they have been unemployed for a long term. For men, the rate of more than 1 year of unemployment is stated as 19.7% (TURKSTAT, 2016). These rates show that women stay unemployed longer than men. The causes of this are the relative lack of qualifications required for entry to the labor market and men's social role/responsibility of providing for the family (Ecevit, 2008).

This high unemployment rate for female labor breaks disrupts the women's desire to enter the labor market and breaks their courage. The ones who decide to enter the labor market, on the other hand, opt for small scale and/or home based, unregistered, part-time and low-paid jobs either because they think that they cannot be employed in institutional, high-paid jobs with job security where they can be under the protection of the social security system, or because of a refused application to such a job.

CONCLUSION

The equality between men and women and total participation to social and working life carry major significance for a country's economic growth, social development, and social justice. For this reason, women's participation in the workforce has been the main topic of interest. Women's employment has received support with legal regulations, policies and strategies over the course of years; but because of the social gender inequality, women who entered the workforce took on their backs double the workload at home and in the workplace and were employed in worse conditions than men. The household workload has brought an inability to work or withdrawal from the labor market. The social and economic gaps between men and women have widened; thus, in order to understand the importance of gender differences the subject needs to be analyzed from a social gender viewpoint.

Establishing the general status of female labor in Turkey and comparing the international and national statistical data from a global perspective around the social gender inequality and the distribution of labor based on social gender is the purpose of this chapter. Thus, first of all, female labor force participation in Turkey and in the world is examined within a historical perspective in this chapter. Then, comparing several indicators provided by The Global Gender Gap Report, which introduced by the World Economic Forum in 2015, it is shown that Turkey has more gender inequality than most of the other countries. Moreover, the status of female labor in Turkey is evaluated in a global context, by using 2015 OECD labor force statistics, as well as in a national context, by using 2016 TURKSTAT labor statistics. According to the comparisons, there is a major gender inequality between women and men in Turkey, particularly in terms of education, economic participation, and opportunities. Besides, women's labor force participation rate is relatively low, but the female unemployment rate is high in Turkey, compared with other OECD countries. These results refer that one of the obstacles to the participation of women in the labor force is the gender-based distribution of labor.Gender inequality is among the factors that lead to high unemployment rates. In this context, the failure to create appropriate jobs for women, the firms prefer women versus men, wage inequality, relatively low qualifications, training and experience of women are some of the factors that creates unemployment.

Nevertheless, women's participation in the labor force is becoming more and more accepted by the society in the recent years. This is closely related to women's income generating activities which start because of the inadequacy of men's income to provide for the household. It is also clear that the women's education levels have increased. The 2009 report by WB and DPT, on the other hand, states that even when all the city-dwelling women were university graduates, female labor participation rate would only reach 47%. Even this rate is greatly lower than the 60% rate set by the European Union.

For this reason, there is a need for the transformation of the social gender perception, the elimination of gender-based inequalities in social and working life, an improvement of women's vocational skills, their inclusion to the social security system, ensuring equal pay for equal work with their male counterparts, the inclusion of their unpaid household work such as childcare etc. to the social security system and preventing unregistered work with the inclusion of the unpaid family workers in agriculture and manufacture to the social system.

REFERENCES

Alkan, D. (1995). *Women's employment and income distribution by gender in Turkey* (Unpublished master's thesis). Middle East Technical University, Ankara, Turkey.

Altan, Ş., & Ersöz, A. (1994). *Kadının çifte yükümlülüğü* (Vol. 2). Kadın ve Sosyal Hizmetler Müsteşarlığı Kadın Statüsü ve Sorunları Genel Müdürlüğü Bülteni.

Aslan, O. E. (2006). Cumhuriyet ve kadın memurlar. *Amme İdaresi Dergisi*, *39*(4), 117–149.

Belet, N. (2013). Kriz olgusunun kadına yönelik algıya ve kadın işgücüne etkisi. *Gazi Üniversitesi İİBF Dergisi*, *15*(1), 1–28.

Berber, M., & Eser, B. Y. (2008). Türkiye'de kadın istihdamı: Ülke ve bölge düzeyinde sektörel analizi. *İş, Güç. Endüstri İlişkileri ve İnsan Kaynakları Dergisi*, *10*(2), 1–16.

Çınar, M. E. (1994). Unskilled urban migrant women and disguised employment: Home-working women in Istanbul, Turkey. *World Development*, *22*(3), 369–380. doi:10.1016/0305-750X(94)90128-7

Çitçi, O. (1982). *Kadın sorunu ve kamu kesiminde kadın*. Ankara: Todaie Yayınları.

Dayıoğlu, M., & Kırdar, M. (2010). *The determinants of and trends in labor force participation of women in Turkey*. Working Paper, No. 5. Ankara: State Planning Organization of the Republic of Turkey/World Bank.

Dedeoğlu, S., & Öztürk, M. Y. (2010). *Kapitalizm, ataerkillik ve kadın emeği Türkiye örneği*. İstanbul: Sav Yayıncılık.

Devlet Planlama Teşkilatı. (2006). *Orta vadeli program 2007-2009*. Ankara: DPT. Retrieved from http://ekutup.dpt.gov.tr/program/2007-09.pdf

Ecevit, Y. (1988). *Küreselleşme, yapısal uyum ve kadın emeğinin kullanımında değişmeler*. İstanbul: KSSGM ve İnsan Haklarını Geliştirme Vakfı.

Ecevit, Y. (1995). Kentsel üretim sürecinde kadın emeğinin konumu ve değişen biçimleri. In Ş. Tekeli (Ed.), *Kadın bakış açısından kadınlar*. İstanbul: İletişim Yayınları.

Ecevit, Y. (2008). İşgücüne katılım ve istihdam. In *Türkiye'de toplumsal cinsiyet eşitsizliği: Sorunlar, öncelikler ve çözüm önerileri*. İstanbul: TÜSİAD-KAGİDER.

Erman, T. (2001). Rural migrants and patriarchy in Turkish cities. *International Journal of Urban and Regional Research*, *25*(1), 118–133. doi:10.1111/1468-2427.00301

Eyüboğlu, A., Özar, Ş., & Tanrıöver, H. T. (2000). *Kentlerde kadınların iş yaşamına katılım sorunlarının sosyo-ekonomik ve kültürel boyutları*. Ankara: T. C. Başbakanlık KSSGM.

Ferguson, A., & Folbre, N. (1981). The unhappy marriage of patriarchy and capitalism. In L. Sargent (Ed.), *Women and revolution: A discussion of the unhappy marriage of Marxism and feminism* (pp. 313–339). Boston: South End Press.

Giddens, A. (2013). *Sosyoloji* (7th ed.). İstanbul: Kırmızı Yayınları.

Gündüz-Hoşgör, A., & Smits, J. (2006). *Variation in labor market participation of married women in Turkey*. Nijmegen: Radboud University.

Günsoy, G., & Özsoy, C. (2012). Türkiye'de kadın işgücü, eğitim ve büyüme ilişkisinin VAR analizi. *Finans Politik & Ekonomik Yorumlar*, *49*(568), 21–39.

Harding, S. (1981). What is the real material base of patriarchy and capital? In L. Sargent (Ed.), *Women and revolution: A discussion of the unhappy marriage of Marxism and feminism* (pp. 15–164). Boston: South End Press.

Hartmann, H. (1992). Marksizm'le Feminizm'in mutsuz evliliği. In G. A. Savran & N. Tura (Eds.), *Kadının görünmeyen emeği: Maddeci bir feminizm üzerine* (G. Aygen, Trans.). (pp. 128–170). İstanbul: Kardelen.

Kasnakoğlu, Z., & Dayıoğlu, M. (2002). Measuring the value of home production in Turkey. In T. Bulutay (Ed.), *The new developments in national accounts*. Ankara: DİE.

Koray, M. (1992). Çalışma yaşamında kadın gerçekleri. *Amme İdaresi Dergisi, 25*(1), 25–40.

Koray, M., Demirbilek, S., & Demirbilek, T. (2000). *Gıda işkolunda çalışan kadınların koşulları ve geleceği*. Ankara: T.C. Başbakanlık KSSGM.

Macionis, J. J. (2014). *Sosyoloji*. Ankara: Nobel Akademik Yayıncılık.

Makal, A. (2010). Türkiye'de erken cumhuriyet döneminde kadın emeği. *Çalışma ve Toplum, 25*(2), 13–41.

Mincer, J. (1958). Investment in human capital and personal ıncome distribution. *Journal of Political Economy, 66*(4), 281–302. doi:10.1086/258055

Önder, N. (2013). Türkiye'de kadın işgücünün görünümü. *ÇSGB Çalışma Dergisi, 1*(1), 35-61.

Organisation for Economic Co-Operation and Development. (2015a). *Education at a glance interim report: Update of employment and educational attainment indicators*. Retrieved from www.oecd.org/edu/eag-interim-report.htm

Organisation for Economic Co-Operation and Development. (2015b). *Employment outlook 2015*. Paris: OECD Publishing. doi:10.1787/empl_outlook-2015-en

Organisation for Economic Co-Operation and Development. (2015c). *OECD factbook 2015-2016: Economic, environmental and social statistics*. Paris: OECD Publishing. doi:10.1787/factbook-2015-en

Organisation for Economic Co-Operation and Development. (2015d). *OECD labour force statistics 2015*. Paris: OECD Publishing. doi:10.1787/oecd_lfs-2015-en

Organisation for Economic Co-Operation and Development. (2015e). *OECD online employment database*. Retrieved from http://www.oecd.org/employment/emp/onlineoecdemploymentdatabase.htm

Özar, Ş., & Günlük-Şenesen, G. (1998). Determinants of female (non) participation in the urban labour force in Turkey. *METU Studies in Development, 25*(2), 311–328.

Özer, M., & Biçerli, K. (2004). Türkiye'de kadın işgücünün panel veri analizi. *Anadolu Üniversitesi Sosyal Bilimler Dergisi, 3*(1), 55–86.

Pancaroğlu, N. S. (2006). *Problems of women participation in labor force and employment in urban areas: The case of İzmit* (Unpublished master's thesis). Kocaeli Üniversitesi, Kocaeli.

Regulation on the Working Conditions of Pregnant and Nursing Women, Nursing Rooms and Child Care Homes. (2004). Official Gazette, No: 25522. Retrieved from http://www.resmigazete.gov.tr/eskiler/2004/07/20040714.htm#5

Toksöz, G. (2007a). *Türkiye'de kadın istihdamı durum raporu*. Ankara: Uluslararası Çalışma Örgütü Yayını.

Toksöz, G. (2007b). İşgücü piyasasının toplumsal cinsiyet perspektifinden analizi ve bölgeler arası dengesizlikler. *Çalışma ve Toplum Dergisi, 4*, 57-79.

Toksöz, G. (2015). *Bin Yıl Kalkınma Hedefleri açısından Türkiye'de çalışma yaşamında kadınların durumu* [PowerPoint slides]. Retrieved May 10, 2016, from http://www.halksagligi.hacettepe.edu.tr/sunumlar_ve_seminerler/20mart_Sempozyum/GToksoz_trde_calismayasaminda_kadinlar.pdf

Turkish Statistical Institute. (2015). *Labor force statistics*. Retrieved July 17, 2016, from http://www.tuik.gov.tr/PreHaberBultenleri.do?id=18627

Turkish Statistical Institute. (2016). *Labor force statistics*. Retrieved July 17, 2016, from http://www.tuik.gov.tr/PreHaberBultenleri.do?id=21572

World Bank. (2006). *Turkey - Labor market study*. Washington, DC: World Bank. Retrieved from http://documents.worldbank.org/curated/en/869781468310746230/Turkey-Labor-market-study

World Bank. (2009). *Female labor force participation in Turkey: Trends, determinants and policy framework*. Washington, DC: World Bank Group. Retrieved from http://documents.worldbank.org/curated/en/201081468111238047/Female-labor-force-participation-in-Turkey-trends-determinants-and-policy-framework

World Economic Forum. (2015). *Global gender gap report*. Geneva: WEF. Retrieved from http://reports.weforum.org/global-gender-gap-report-2015/

Yaman Öztürk, M. (2008). *Kapitalist toplumda kadının ezilmesinin koşulları: Martha Gimenez'e yanıt*. Manuscript.

KEY WORDS AND DEFINITIONS

Employment: Inclusion to the working life.

Female Unemployment: The lack of job for women who wants to work at current wage.

Flexible Work: A form of work which has not strict working standards related to the working conditions, wages, working hours, and workplace.

Labor Force Participation: Proportion of the population participating in the labor force to the working age population.

TURKSTAT: An institution which is gathering and publishing national data of specific issues in different areas in Turkey.

Undeclared Employment: A form of employment that deprives the employees of the benefit of social security, because they have not been declared to one or more administrative authorities.

Unemployment: The state of people who have the willingness to work but can't find a job providing them adequate conditions to sustain their life.

Chapter 9
The Role of Entrepreneurial Spirit in Indonesian Youths and Housewives to Reduce Unemployment and Poverty Rate

Ati Cahayani
Atma Jaya Catholic University, Indonesia

ABSTRACT

Unemployment and poverty are problems experienced especially by developing countries. The higher level of unemployment and poverty will lead the higher level of crime. The unemployment rate in Indonesia in August 2014 is 5.94% or 7,244,905 people, and 4% of Indonesian people living on less than $1.25 a day. One of the things that can reduce the unemployment rate and the percentage of poor people is entrepreneurship. This chapter wants to explain that the level of unemployment and poverty can be minimized by the spirit of entrepreneurship of housewives and youths, who has a micro, small, and medium business. From six women and youth entrepreneurs who start their micro and small business that described in this book chapter, it can be seen that their effort could empower themselves and make themselves and their family exit from poverty. But, they are facing barriers to starting up. The government must push and encourage Indonesian people to become an entrepreneur by designing entrepreneurship development program, which includes government, educational institution, and family.

INTRODUCTION

Unemployment and poverty are problems experienced by all countries. The higher the level of unemployment and poverty will lead the higher the level of crime. Therefore, the problem of unemployment and poverty should receive serious attention from the government.

Developing countries usually face heavy problems of unemployment and poverty, including Indonesia which has a population of around 300 million is facing quite heavy problems of unemployment

DOI: 10.4018/978-1-5225-2008-5.ch009

and poverty. Indonesian Government realized that Indonesia's large population has great potential for unemployment problems. One of the government's efforts to tackle the problem of unemployment is by opening new work opportunity, especially with the labor-intensive program. October 2015, Indonesian President, Joko Widodo, has launched a labor-intensive program, which is expected could decrease the rate of unemployment (Praditya, 2015). Opening new work opportunity is not an easy thing to do. Indonesian government needs to cooperate with entrepreneurs, including entrepreneurs who have micro, small, medium enterprises (MSME), to open new work opportunity.

But, it must be remembered that the availability of employment is determined by economic growth in the country, including in Indonesia. If a country is not experiencing economic growth, then many companies bankrupt and mass layoff occurs. In the end, it will create a level of unemployment and poverty increased. In Old Order Era, the focus of Government is in politics, and that made the economy condition in Indonesia was bad. In New Order Era, the conditions of Indonesia's economy improve (Subandi, 2006). One of the famous economic development programs at the time of New Order is the Five Years Development (PELITA) and Plan of Five Years Development (REPELITA). That development program that was published to the community was created as a reference for the development that must be achieved within 5 years. In the reformation era, the term is no longer used, but any President in this era has a work plan to improve the Indonesia economy. President Joko Widodo, for instance, issued packages of economy policies to improve the economy in Indonesia (Waluyo, 2015).

One indicator of economic growth is growth of Gross Domestic Product (Sanusi, 2007). Data from BPS (2016b) shows that the growth of GDP Indonesia on 2014 is 3.6%, decline from 4.1% on 2013. The Central Bureau of statistics (BPS) recorded that economic growth in Indonesia is 4.79 percent on an annual basis (year-on-year (yoy)), where this figure is smaller than the previous year's close of 5.02 percent (Gumelar, 2016). The condition of the economy that is not too good makes this unemployment rate and poverty ever hard to be pressed.

The problems of unemployment and poverty increased since Indonesia entered the Era of ASEAN Economic Community since 2015. With the ASEAN Economic Community, the boundaries between countries of ASEAN seemed to be lost, the labor of one country can easily work in other countries in ASEAN, and trade between ASEAN countries has become easier with low import tax. ASEAN Economic Community can be seen as an opportunity or a threat. With the ASEAN economic community, then the opportunities for Indonesia's labor force to work in other countries in ASEAN increased, but also can make the unemployment rate in Indonesia is increasing and ultimately could raise the rate of poverty. With the ASEAN economic community, the market becomes large, but the level of competition and the demand for good quality is high.

This book chapter wants to explain that the level of unemployment and poverty can be overcome by the spirit of entrepreneurship of housewives and youths, who have a micro, small, and medium business. The structure of this book chapter: The first section is the introduction that describes the benefits or the importance of this book chapter; in the second and third sections are explained about important aspect in this book chapter i.e. unemployment and poverty; the fourth section describes the main focus of this book chapter, which is about entrepreneurship in Indonesia; the fifth section describes solution and recommendation, that is entrepreneurship development program in Indonesia; and the sixth section is the conclusion.

EMPLOYMENT, UNEMPLOYMENT, HALF UNEMPLOYMENT

People who categorized as employed are those who worked as paid employees, worked in their own business, or worked as unpaid workers in a family member's business. It also includes those who were not working but who had jobs from which they were temporarily absent because of, for example, vacation, illness, or bad weather (Mankiw, 2007).

Muana (2005, p. 249) said that unemployment is a condition where people who include in workforce category but do not have a job and also not try to find job actively. This condition is also known as open unemployment. Djohanputro (2006) said, there are four types of unemployment: open unemployment, under-employment, people who work actively but less utilized (include: premature retirement, hidden retirement, disguised underemployment), and the impaired. During this time, the government only records the data of open unemployment, as seen in Table 1, because open unemployment is easy to see, and the other three types of unemployment are not clearly visible so the data cannot collect easily.

Indonesia Statistics Center (BPS) shows data that on August 2013, Indonesia has a workforce of 120.2 million people but only 112.7 million people have a job, or it can say that 7.41 million people or 6.17% of the workforce are unemployment. And as shown in Table 1, in August 2014, the unemployment rate has decreased to 5.94% (BPS, 2016a). But according to Indonesia Statistic Center (BPS, 2016e), total unemployment of people with a bachelor's degree are 495,143 in August 2014 or increase from 398,298 in February 2014 as shown in Table 2. This means that workforce whom graduate from college cannot be absorbed in labor market. Those people are called as educated unemployment. Actually, educated unemployment is workforce who graduate from high school or more but jobless (Tobing, 2005).

The educated unemployment that likely to rise by 2014 is caused by two factors: frictional and structural. Those two factors make 2 conditions of unemployment (Mankiw, 2007): frictional unemployment and structural unemployment. Frictional unemployment is the unemployment that results because it takes time for workers to search for the jobs that best suit their tastes and skills and structural unemployment is the unemployment that result because the number of jobs available in some labor markets is insufficient to provide a job for everyone who wants one (Mankiw, 2007). Frictional and structural unemployment

Table 1. Type of activity of Indonesian people above 15 years old

	Type of Activity	2013		2014	
		February	August	February	August
1	Indonesian people above 15 years old	178,130,470	179,967,361	181,169,972	182,992,204
2	Workforce	123,170,509	120,172,003	125,316,991	121,872,931
	a. Rate of workforce participation (%)	69.15	66.77	69.17	66.60
	b. Working/Employment	115,929,612	112,761,072	118,169,922	114,628,026
	c. Unemployment	7,240,897	7,410,931	7,147,069	7,244,905
	d. Rate of unemployment (%)	5.88	6.17	5.70	5.94
3	Non-workforce	54,959,961	59,795,358	55,852,981	61,119,273
	a. Student above 15 years old	15,328,846	14,630,852	15,899,591	16,769,494
	b. Household	32,653, 052	36,036, 779	32,853,393	36,019,249
	c. Others	6,978,063	9,127,727	7,099,997	8,330,530

Source: BPS (2016a)

Table 2. Unemployment data according to educational level

No.	Educational Level	2014	
		February	August
1	Do not have education certificate	134,040	74,898
2	Not graduate from elementary school	610,574	389,550
3	Elementary school	1,374,822	1,229,652
4	Junior high school	1,693,203	1,566,838
5	Senior high school	1,893,509	1,962,786
6	Vocational high school	847,365	1,332,521
7	Diploma I,II,II/Academy	195,258	193,517
8	University	398,298	495,143
	Total	**7,147,069**	**7,244,905**

Source: BPS (2016e)

usually become long-term unemployment. Long-term unemployment creates new problems because the longer a worker is unemployed, the more difficult for him or her to find a job (Hornstein & Lubik, 2010). To overcome this problem, they could be encouraged to develop their own business or become an entrepreneur.

There are those who argue that more women are unemployed than men. But, what is the actual fact? ILO said, in many countries around the world, they are more unemployment women than unemployment man (around 6.2% unemployment women comparing to 5.5% unemployment men) due to discrimination to women (Detik, 2016). How about in Indonesia? Data from Indonesia Statistic Center shows that men are more unemployed than women (men 4.86% and women 3.48%) on 2012 (as shown in Table 3). But in recent data, Indonesian Gender Gap Index from Global Gender Gap Report (World Economic Forum, 2015) shows that women are more unemployed than men (women 6.4% and men 6%).

But on Table 4, it can be seen that for household activity, percentages of women (36.97%) who do household activity are bigger than men (1.63%), and that usual for Indonesian culture that think men as husband and father do work to provide family needs and women as wife and mother do household work.

Indeed, there are groups of people who can help the family economy, although not included in the labor force. They are household and student above 15 years old. From Table 1 and Table 4, it can be seen that households and students above 15 years old (youths) are not considered as workforce or labor force. According to Indonesia Center of Statistics, on August 2014 Indonesia has 36,019,249 household

Table 3. Employment and unemployment by gender on 2012 (percentage)

People on Working Age	Type of Activity		
		Women	Men
		2012	2012
Workforce	Working/Employment	47.91	79.57
	Unemployment	3.48	4.86

Source: BPS (2016d)

Table 4. Non-workforce activity by gender on 2012 (percentage)

People on Working Age	Type of Activity	Women	Men
		2012	2012
Non-workforce	Students above 15 years old	7.94	8.26
	Household	36.97	1.63
	Others	3.70	5.69

Source: BPS (2016d)

and 16,769,494 students above 15 years old (youths) (BPS, 2016a) from 61,119,273 non-workforce. It is a large enough number.

Under the conditions that exist in Indonesia today, the author wants to focus on housewives and youths that are not included in the labor force in reducing unemployment and poverty levels, but from some data that author gets, some of them gain profit from doing some kind of work for instance as part-time entrepreneur or freelance worker. That means they also can help the government to reduce the unemployment rate by open new work opportunity and also reduce the poverty rate.

For the household, the authors only limit on household women (housewives), as the number of household women in Indonesia is much more than a household men (as can be seen in Table 4). But before the author discusses the role of entrepreneurial spirit in housewives and youths, will be presented first a number of definitions of employment, unemployment, half-employment, entrepreneurship and entrepreneurial spirit, and micro, small, and medium enterprises. These definitions should be understood in order to understand this book chapter comprehensively.

POVERTY

Mc Quibria (as cited in Stone, 1992, p. 24), explain about poverty and people who poor socially and economically: "It's the lack of ability to employ assets that cause poverty. If your only asset is labor and you are unemployed, you are poor. If you are in a rural area and you don't own land, then you are also poor." From that definition, it can be seen that people who don't have any assets, and he/she does not work, then he/she is categorized as a poor. But if you have a lot of assets and do not work, you are not categorized as poor. That definition implicitly explains that unemployment usually causes poverty.

Beside the term of poverty in general like Mc Quibria said above, in Economic Studies, it is also known the term of poverty line and poverty rate. Poverty rate is the percentage of the population whose family income falls below an absolute level called the poverty line (Mankiw, 2007). And, poverty line is an absolute level of income set by the federal government for each family size below which a family is deemed to be in poverty (Mankiw, 2007).

What will take to end poverty and improve the lives of the poor? Economic growth will prove paramount, but, beyond growth itself, it must ensure that all members of society share in the benefits of that growth (World Bank and International Monetary Fund [IMF], 2014). In 1966, New Order Era got inherited from the Old Order Era, i.e. inflation amounted to 670% (Sanusi, 2007). Inflation is an increase in the overall level of prices (Mankiw, 2007). Inflation will cause the price of goods, in particular the major commodities, rose sharply, which ultimately makes the purchasing power decreases and economic growth will stagnant. And, that is the reason that inflation is often assumed by people can affect the poverty rate. As mentioned in Section 2, New Order Era makes program PELITA (Five Years Development) and REPELITA (Five Years Development Plan) to develop the economic conditions. And, specifically for poverty alleviation programs, the New Order Era issued a variety of programs, including Presidential Instruction Program for Poor Village, Independent Young Families, and Health Aid Project. In the era of reformation, the Government issued a variety of programs to suppress the poverty, including Direct Cash Assistance (BLT), Smart Indonesia Card, Healthy Indonesia Card, and Prosperous Family Card.

According to data from World Bank and IMF, it can be seen that poverty has been more prevalent in Sub-Saharan Africa and South Asia than in other developing regions, accounting for about 80 percent of the global poor (2014). Data of World Bank and IMF shows that in 2011 there are 4% of Indonesian people living on less than $1.25 a day (2014). $1.25 per day is poverty line. People who spend less than $1.25 per month are considered as poor.

How about poverty in Indonesia in 2015? Data from BPS show that Indonesia has 28,513.57 thousand (11.13% of total population) poor people in the second half of 2015 or the number of poor people decrease from 28,592.79 thousand (11.22%of total population) in the first half of 2015 to 28,513.57 in the second half (BPS, 2016c). The decrease of poverty rate is not significant. Indonesian government still has a lot of things to do to reduce or minimize the poverty rate.

ENTREPRENEURSHIP DEVELOPMENT IN INDONESIA

As mentioned in Introduction Section, Indonesian government needs to cooperate with entrepreneurs to open new work opportunity. In essence, entrepreneurs have an important role in economic growth and prosperity of a country (Salimath & Cullen, 2010). The Indonesian government also must encourage people to be an entrepreneur.

Ciputra said, entrepreneurs in Indonesia are around 0.18 percent or 400,000 entrepreneurs (Ciputra, 2008). On March 2015, Minister of Cooperative and Small-Medium Enterprises Anak Agung Gede Ngurah Puspayoga said that entrepreneurs in Indonesia only 1.65% of total Indonesian population (Republika, 2015).

According to data from Global Entrepreneurship Monitor 2013, Indonesia Report based on APS (Adult Population Survey) survey in their (adults') perception of entrepreneurial activities, three measures were obtained: perceived opportunity (perception of entrepreneurial opportunity), perceived capability (perception of required knowledge, skill, and experience to start business), and fear of failure (of starting your own business) (Nawangpalupi, Pawitan, Gunawan, Widyarini, & Iskandarsjah, 2014). From those three measures, perceived capability gain relatively high percentage, i.e. 62%, and only 46.6% respondents have a perception of entrepreneurial opportunity. And from 46.6% respondents who have a perception of entrepreneurial opportunity, 35% have a fear of failure (Nawangpalupi et. al., 2014). So, it can be seen that there are only a few of Indonesia adulthood whom can see a business opportunity and not be afraid to fail. Global Entrepreneurship Monitor Report on 2013 said that if compared with other countries in South East Asia and Asia Pacific, Indonesia is in the second position under the Philippines (47.9%) for perceived opportunity and also second position under the Philippines (68.4%) for perceived capability, but for fear of failure Indonesia is on number 9 from 11 countries in South East Asia and Asia Pacific (Amorós & Bosma, 2013).

Entrepreneur and Entrepreneurial Spirit

Emzen, as cited by Bulut and Sayin (2010, pp. 559-568), define an entrepreneur as "the person who generally sets up his or her own business and who brings various production factors together and takes risks in order to produce something and subsequently aims to profit." Amorós and Bosma (2013) divide entrepreneur into 2 types: necessity-driven entrepreneur and opportunity-driven entrepreneur. Joardar, Wu, and Chen (2014) said that GEM defined that the two types differ from each other in that opportunity entrepreneur is motivated by opportunity and necessity entrepreneur type is more requirement-based.

Everybody actually can be an entrepreneur, even an uneducated person. The most important thing is that person must have an entrepreneurial spirit. According to Ciputra (2008, p. 19), people with an entrepreneurial spirit have some characteristics, such as innovative, creative, want to take calculated risk. John Kao (Kuratko & Hodgetts, 2007, p. 118) explain about 11 entrepreneurial characteristics: *total commitment, determination and perseverance; drive to achieve and grow; opportunity and goal orientation; taking initiative and personal responsibility; persistent problem solving; realism and a sense of humor; seeking and using feedback; internal locus of control; calculated risk taking and risk seeking; low need for status and power; integrity and reliability*. Stevenson and Gumpert (Kuratko & Hodgetts, 2007, p. 118) said that *imagination, flexibility* and *willingness to accept risk* as the characteristics of those who have an entrepreneurial spirit in the organization. Hornaday in Kuratko and Hodgetts (2007, p.119) explained clearly the 42 characteristics that are often shown inside of an entrepreneur. Are people who want to be entrepreneur must have all those 42 characteristics? Kuratko and Hodgetts (2007) says that the thing that differentiates a successful and reliable entrepreneur with the other ones is the way they process the imagination and creative thinking with the systematic and logical processing ability.

Even though it said that everybody could be an entrepreneur as long as he or she has an entrepreneurial spirit, but actually, there are some barriers to building a new business or known as barriers to starting up. The author know several people who actually want to be entrepreneurs and have an entrepreneurial spirit but do not know how to start a business, do not have enough money to fund their business, and afraid of the risks. Meanwhile, the results of Robertson, Collins, Medeira, and Slater (2003) showed that there are few barriers to starting a business, such as unmotivated, no business idea, no skills, and no confidence, too risky, do not get help, and there are no funds.

Micro, Small, and Medium Enterprises

Usually, people think that entrepreneur must be a rich person with large enterprise or company. But, actually, a person who only makes and sells homemade cupcake is also considered as an entrepreneur. People who only own small grocery store also considered as an entrepreneur. Those businesses are categorized into Micro, Small, and Medium Enterprise.

These are criteria of Micro, Small, and Medium Enterprise according Act No. 20 year 2008, as retrieved from Bank Indonesia website:

1. **Micro Enterprise:**
    a. Net worth maximal Rp. 50,000,000 (around $3,600) per year.
    b. Net sales maximal Rp. 300,000,000 (around $ 21,000) per year.

2. **Small Enterprise:**
    a. Net worth Rp. 50,000,000-Rp. 500,000,000 (around $3,600-$36,000) per year.
    b. Net sales Rp. 300,000,000-Rp. 2,500,000,000 (around $21,000-$178,571) per year.
3. **Medium Enterprise:**
    a. Net worth Rp. 500,000,000-10,000,000,000 (around $36,000-$714,286).
    b. Net sales Rp. 2,500,000,000-50,000,000,000 (around $178,571-$3,571,429).

In 2013, Indonesia has 57,895,721 MSME or increase 2.41% from 2012 and only has 5,066 big enterprises or BE (Department of Cooperative and Small Medium Enterprise, 2016). It can be seen that MSME have almost 99% of market and BE only has less than 1% of the market, as shown in Table 5.

From that data, the researcher assumes that MSMEs in Indonesia play a great role. When Indonesia was faced with a great crisis in 1997, the MSME became the savior for Indonesia people. Around that time, the amount of small business increased drastically, from only 7,000 small businesses in 1980 to 40 million in 2001 (Margiman, 2008). The MSME in Indonesia are dominated by the agriculture, forestry, farming, and fishery sectors (53.5%), and large businesses in the processing sector (35.4%) (Margiman, 2008). Those sectors have been existing for a long time in the Indonesia's. But, now, with the development of knowledge, technology, and managerial skills, new industries start to emerge in the business field, such as creative industry.

The development of technology is not only creating a new industry. The development of technology also creates a new way to do business. Now, people are all familiar with e-business. E-business emerged because of the development of internet technology. With e-business, people can sell and promote their product via the internet; the customers can buy and order things via the internet. With the convenience offered by Internet technology, more and more people could become entrepreneurs in more cheap and easy way. Why? With e-business, people do not need much cost for things, such as for store, for advertising and promotion, and for storage the product. And with e-business, people can do business in more flexible time and way.

Women and Youths Entrepreneurship in Micro and Small Business

Women and youths entrepreneurs have unique characteristics. Cahayani, Gunawan, and Isololipu (2016) quoted research result regarding the entrepreneurial spirit in women entrepreneurs who are also the member of cooperative in Bojonegoro by Iedarwati, Isololipu, and Cahayani. It said that personality characteristic is more prominent if compared to other two characteristics, which are managerial and

Table 5. Data of micro, small, and medium enterprise and big enterprise year 2012 and 2013

Enterprise	2012	2013	Percentage of Increasing
Micro, Small, Medium Enterprise	***56,534,592***	***57,895,721***	***2.41***
Micro Enterprise	*55,856,176*	*57,189,393*	*2.39*
Small Enterprise	*629,418*	*654,222*	*3.94*
Medium Enterprise	*48,997*	*52,106*	*6.35*
Big Enterprise	***4,968***	***5,066***	**1.97**

Source: Ministry of Cooperative and MSME

agent of change. Cahayani et al. (2016) also quoted research result regarding the entrepreneurial spirit in young entrepreneurs who are Business Administration Department alumni by Cahayani, Gunawan, Iedarwati, Isololipu. It said that the characteristics of an agent of change are stronger than the other two characteristics. Despite those research results, this book chapter section wants to describe the role of women and youths entrepreneurs in micro and small business to reduce unemployment and poverty rate.

Indonesia has some famous women entrepreneurship, such as Martha Tilaar (owner of Martha Tilaar Group), Mooryati Sudibyo (owner of Mustika Ratu brand), and Wendy Sui Cheng Yap (President Director and CEO of PT Nippon Indosari Tbk). For youth entrepreneur, Nina Moran and her sisters (owner of Go Girl Magazine) can also be categorized as quite successful youth entrepreneur. All of them already have a lot of employees and absolutely could help government program to reduce unemployment and poverty rate because their business can absorb a lot of people to be their employees. This subsection does not want to describe successful women and youths entrepreneurs. This subsection wants to show the portrait of few housewives and youths that try to do business, even though only part time and micro and small business.

One of the people who talk to the author is a young housewife, lady A. Before she married, she was a career woman, but after married she decided to be a housewife. But after a while, she tried to do something. She tried to do an activity to fill her spare time. She wants it to be a productive activity and not consumptive. At first, she had no idea. But, after talking with her high school friend, she gets an idea, which received orders for screen printing T-shirt. At first, she did not have a brand for her micro and part-time business. But, after a while, she decided to name her business as D'Juno Custom. Her screen printing T-shirt did not last long. After she had quite a lot order, she had difficulties in managing time between business and parenting, and finally, she decided to stop that business.

A few years after that, Lady A tried a new business which still survives today. She makes hairpins and bandanas for children and also brooches for hijabs women with brand Lara Handycraft. The idea of doing this business is obtained after she is invited by her friends to learn how to make hair pin, brooch, and bandana. After being able to make hair pin, brooch, and a bandana, she was challenged by her trainer to try selling her work.

She is doing her micro business in her home when her son has a nap or already falls asleep at night or when she has spare time. She prefers to use e-business because it can reduce the cost of promotion and production. She only makes hairpins, bandanas, or brooches after she receives the order. She always uses Internet technology to promote her products. Usually, she puts the photo of her product on her social media, and it proved to be an effective way to promote their products. And, she also learned new techniques to create a bandana, brooch and hair pin from the internet.

She chooses to be a part-time entrepreneur because it flexible and easy to manage and she also can still do her job as wife and mother. Even though she is not categorized as a poor family, but what she does makes her able to achieve self-actualization.

When asked, who inspired her to try to do business; she said that she was inspired by some people. First is her father who had retired as permanent employees but has a variety of micro-business to fulfill the needs of her family. Second are some of her friends who also are housewives but can still make money by being a part-time entrepreneur.

How about her son, is she teach something about this business skill to her son? Lady A said, one day, she told her five years old son to sell all of his comic books before he can buy new comic books. She and her son made a small garage sale to sell her son's comic books. By doing that, she teaches her son to be entrepreneur unwittingly. And by doing that, she also teaches her son that you must do something first to get what you want or no pain no gain.

A little bit different with Lady A, miss B is a single parent with two teenage girls. Her condition pushes her to do something to earn money, but at the same time, she still has time to do house chores and parenting things. With her skills to make cookies, she decided to accept the orders for making cookies, especially in Eidul-Fitr season and Christmas season. How does she promote her products? She distributed flyers to her neighbors around the house and also to parents of her daughters' school friends. When she is getting a lot of orders, she hires someone else to help her complete that order. She also accepts the orders for daily catering. Miss B who only graduated from high school also is a part-time taxi driver. In short, she will do everything she can to fulfill her two teenage girl's needs. Is she feeling ashamed with what she does? No, she said, she has no time to feel ashamed.

She also said, that her two teenage daughters also help her to bake cakes or make cookies or deliver the catering to customers. So actually, unwittingly, miss B taught her children about entrepreneurship and entrepreneurial spirit. Miss B also taught her children a value of life: no need to feel ashamed doing something legal.

Now, miss B is a full-time entrepreneur and part-time worker, but when she still married, she was a part-time entrepreneur doing her cookies and catering business. At first, she did cookies and catering business as for leisure activities.

Actually, miss B learned to be an entrepreneur from her ex-husband. Her ex-husband has a small business, and she usually helped at administrative things, such as buy the material, do accounting, and some other things. When they divorced, she already has some knowledge to do business and already has entrepreneurial skill and spirit and ready to run her own business as a full-time entrepreneur.

Mrs. C is a young housewife with two little sons. Before married, she already has plans to become a housewife with income. She has a business that can be done at home, such as make cake, cupcake, cookies by order, sell Indonesia traditional crackers and cookies, make Indonesia traditional snack and food by order. How she promotes her business? She uses some ways to promote her business, such as making the web that contains all about her culinary business, joining the bazaar at his son's school, word of mouth, and also giving a sample of cake to her friends or families or neighbor and ask the endorsement.

Mrs. C has the intention to be an entrepreneur since before she married and graduated from university. She has a value that family is number one, and parenting is mother's primary responsibility so she decided to be a housewife with a small business that she can handle in her spare time. She also has a small shop that sells traditional snacks from some province and city of Indonesia. She has a worker that standby at her shop every day, and she only visits her shop occasionally. She also helps her sister in law to do travel business. All those business activities were conducted in her spare time.

D is a young man who still is a student in one of a university in Jakarta. In his spare time, he and some of his friend make and sell traditional cloth from East Nusa Tenggara just for a hobby. They do word to mouth promotions to sell that product. Even he does that just for hobby and cannot sell a lot of cloth up until now, but actually what he does still can help his family because the money that he earned is for his pocket money, so he does not have to ask from his parents. He does not come from rich family, so what he does help his family. Is he wants to become a full-time entrepreneur after he graduates from university? He said he is still not sure about that because he worries that he will not have enough money to fund his business even though he finds that entrepreneurship is an interesting field. He also said, his father does not support him to be a full-time entrepreneur, and that is the reason why he was not chosen major on entrepreneur at his university. But he said, he still want to be a part-time entrepreneur especially in the industry or field that he likes.

Mr. E is a young full-time entrepreneur and already had a business since still in university as a student, which is he tried to sell hamburger. In addition to the hamburger business, Mr. E also opened an "ayam penyet" (fried chicken with traditional chili sauce and some vegetable) diner, joint with his sister/brother in law. When the hamburger shop is closed because of its location contract expired, his "ayam penyet" diner has been running. In addition to the "ayam penyet" diner, Mr. E also has a pizzeria that initially he was peddling in the food truck. In addition to the two types of business, Mr. E had also tried to open a coffee shop but did not last long. Of the several types of business that he started since in university, he has been able to hire a few employees. This means he can create jobs for others and help the government to reduce the unemployment rate.

Mr. E is the risk taker. That is why he runs several businesses at the same time. For him, if there is a chance, then it should be used. That principle makes him runs a business selling hamburgers and "ayam penyet" restaurant. When there is a friend or relative who offered the location, he immediately accepted it, and the idea about hamburger corner came after he accepted that offering. What about with "ayam penyet" restaurant? He accepted the offer from his brother/sister in law to run business "ayam penyet" restaurant though he did not know anything about the business. His actions seem reckless, but entrepreneurs are required to be able to make decisions quickly and precisely in exploiting existing opportunities. He said, after getting married and having children, although more considerations to be made, but he continues to make decisions quickly and accurately.

The last person is Miss F. Miss F is a young lady that already has been a part-time entrepreneur before graduated from university. Now, she is a full-time entrepreneur. She has culinary business made from catfish: meatball catfish, nugget catfish, cracker from catfish skin and catfish bone. She also has business with her friend from her university with brand Salt Factory. Salt Factory produces rice bowl with some topping: catfish salted egg, chicken, and more. Salt Factory has some new menus now, mantau (Chinese bun) that filled with chicken mayo and crabmeat mayo and skelly scallop. She is the determinant and creative person. She always tries to find new recipes to make a new product and new ways to promote and sell his product. She and her friend do not have a permanent store. They usually join event or bazaar to sell their product and accept order via social media. They do this method of business because they still do not enough money to rent or own a store.

Miss F said, she has no intention to be an employee, because she cannot have flexible time, cannot do something that she like, and cannot express and do innovative and creative things without permission from boss or company. Yes, she is a unique young lady that is not afraid to try her idea.

From those six people, it can be seen that A, C, and D who are not included in the labor force could receive income, although not a lot, and help their husbands or parents, which included in the labor force, to fulfill the family needs. Mrs. B even now is a full-time entrepreneur and part-time worker and included in the labor force, but when she started her business, she was doing that as a housewife and not included in the labor force. E and F even though now are full-time entrepreneurs and included in the labor force, but they try to become an entrepreneur when they were still a student and not included in the labor force.

From those six people, it can be seen that all of them have an entrepreneurial spirit, even some of them only housewives and part-time entrepreneurs. And from these data, it can be seen that even entrepreneurs in micro business can hire someone else to help them when they got a lot of orders. They also could have the networking to help buy raw materials or sell their products, so it can also indirectly drive the country's economy. This suggests that entrepreneurs could be a government partner to reduce the level of poverty and unemployment.

So, it can be said that entrepreneurial spirit is the core to reduce the level of poverty and unemployment. Why? Because only housewives and students above 15 years old who have an entrepreneurial spirit are trying to do something to create jobs so they can earn money. It can be seen that people who have an entrepreneurial spirit will show some unique characteristics, such as think creatively, unyielding, and proactive in life. They are also adaptive to the changes, as seen from the results of talking with Miss. B. Those characteristics make people with an entrepreneurial spirit will not just do nothing when fired from the company, or when cannot get a job. They will always find a way out of it by doing their own business.

The entrepreneurial spirit can be owned and developed in various ways. The entrepreneurial spirit can be transferred to people around those six entrepreneurs, either consciously or unconsciously. Miss B learned about the business and the entrepreneurial spirit from her ex-husband, lady A has an entrepreneurial spirit that is learned from her father, and Mr. E that has learned about spiritual spirit from his parent since childhood. The entrepreneurial spirit can indeed be transmitted by the nearest person, but the most influencing person in growing and developing the entrepreneurial spirit are the parents, especially mothers, who care for their children from infancy. So when the children of A, B, C, and E saw their parents own and run a business, even if only part-time, or even when they asked for helping parents in running the business, it is one of the most effective ways to instill and develop an entrepreneurial spirit. Their parents can be their role model. Unmarried young entrepreneurs, such as D and F, can transmit their entrepreneurial spirit to relatives or people closest to them.

Those six people above are just a small sample taken by the author to show that housewives and students who do not include in the labor force could also play a role in the movement of the Indonesian economy, such as reducing unemployment and alleviating poverty, by becoming a part-time entrepreneur. If there are many housewives and students over 15 years old who can own a business, part time or full time, the Indonesian economy can be increased considerably. It is time for the government to empower them, for the improvement of the economy of Indonesia.

ENTREPRENEURSHIP DEVELOPMENT PROGRAM IN INDONESIA

It can be seen above that the entrepreneurial spirit is the core. However, the barrier to start-ups often prevents people from starting trying to do business. Therefore, in addition to empowering entrepreneurial spirit, there are also some programs that must also be taken to deter barrier to start-up.

There are some suggestions that have been expressed by government officials or leaders of companies in Indonesia to empower those who are interested in becoming entrepreneurs but do not know what to do. Former Indonesian Vice President Boediono have been asked a business owner to reach out to young entrepreneurs, who generally still in college, by providing a place for entrepreneurial business practices (business incubator). He said the business practice is important (Kompas, 2013, January 18, p. 20).

But, what about the young entrepreneurs in college or university who do not get a chance to practice in the corporate-owned business incubator? D, E, and F actually do not get a chance to practice in the corporate-owned business incubator. They said, they only learned from the experience and learn from others who run a similar business. It can be said that it is important to gather with the person who also runs a business to find a new idea, new knowledge, new spirit, and new perspective to run a business. D,

E, and F also said, networking is the important thing to face the barrier to start up. They said friendship and wide networking enabling them to learn about how to start a business and can improve business capabilities. And by having a networking and socializing with people who run a similar business, they said, it can also empower their entrepreneurial spirit.

What is the most considered as a barrier to starting up by housewives? They said that the biggest obstacle is the lack of knowledge to start a business. And how about housewives who are interested in becoming entrepreneurs but do not know how to start it? A, B, and C said that they are looking for and get information on the internet and their friends or relatives. After that, they tried to run the business, step by step. In essence, they said, they learned from the experience. That is why, before making and selling a new product, they make sample products to be given to their relatives or friends to get feedback for the product. Usually, they bring their cookies or cake or food to "arisan" (regular social gathering). In Indonesia, many housewives are joining "arisan". Arisan is an activity to raise money or goods of the same value by a few people and then drawn between them to see who will get it, sweepstakes conducted in a regular meeting until all members get it. The authors argue, this regular social gathering could be an activity where the housewives who want to do business to learn to do business by inviting a speaker or trainer who can teach the participants gathering to conduct micro business. It is actually experienced by lady A when she was learning how to make a brooch, bandana, and a hair pin.

For housewives like A, B, C, what they do to empower their entrepreneurial spirit? Miss B said that she has an entrepreneurial spirit although she became an entrepreneur because the conditions forced her to become an entrepreneur. She thanked that condition that forced her to learn to do business and it removes the barrier to start-up. Actually, the author thinks that she has the characteristic of determination and perseverance and does not afraid of change and that condition strengthens her entrepreneurial characteristic and also entrepreneurial spirit. But Miss B also acknowledged that to foster creativity, as one of the characteristics of entrepreneurs, she must learn from a lot of people. She admits that it is important for an entrepreneur to have networking. Similar to Miss B, lady A, and Mrs. C think that they can empower their entrepreneurial spirit by gather with the person who runs a similar business and by having great networking. Based on the statement of A, B, and C, it can be said that "arisan" (regular social gathering) could also serve to empower the entrepreneurial spirit.

In addition to the ways above, there are a few more ways to empower the entrepreneurial spirit and also deter barrier to a start-up that can be done by the government, educational institutions, and parents, especially housewives. First, the government could increase the role of cooperative. Cooperative is a union that aims to meet the needs of its members by selling grocery items at a bargain price (does not intend to make a profit). There are several types of a cooperative. One is specifically aimed at the service or requires its members to save money, in addition, to being able to provide loans to its members. People call it credit cooperative. In Indonesia, there are a lot of a cooperative. Minister of Cooperative and MSME said, on February 2014, they registered 200,808 cooperatives in Indonesia (Sikumbang, 2014, February 1).

In 2010, the author visited a region in East Java, namely Bojonegoro. There, the author meet and talk with members of credit cooperative from various villages in Bojonegoro were all women. They all find it useful because they can obtain loans with much lower interest than the interest from the bank.

Indonesia already has a government ministry specifically address the issue of cooperative, namely a cooperative and MSME ministry. But the socialization of the role of cooperative, especially for youths and women, are less widely applied. Many Indonesian people are familiar with the word "cooperative" but did not know the specific role of the cooperative for its members. This makes many people in Indonesia who have not felt the need to become a member of a cooperative, even Mr. D.

Besides the government, educational institutions, ranging from early childhood education to higher education, will be expected to teach about entrepreneurship, both theory and practice. By always taught about entrepreneurship, it is expected that students will start to have an entrepreneurial spirit and also have an idea of the barrier to start up that they will face when starting a business.

Currently, there are already many kindergartens, elementary schools, junior high schools, and high schools held a business day every year, in which students are asked to sell goods at a school bazaar. It is a good activity to introduce the business practice to students, but not a lot of schools conduct an evaluation of the event for the students, so students do not understand the mistake that they have already done. In addition, many schools and colleges that are not balanced in giving the practice and theory of entrepreneurship. Theories about entrepreneurship cannot be considered trivial because it becomes a basic knowledge of entrepreneurship and also the basis of the philosophy of entrepreneurship.

It is better if the university or college have a business incubator. A business incubator can help students, especially who have an interest in becoming entrepreneurs. The business incubator provides consulting service; help student to liaise with investors and to bridge the relationship between alumni entrepreneurs and students who will become entrepreneurs. Business Incubator will be very helpful for students like Mr. D who are interested in becoming entrepreneurs but still have some doubts.

In addition to government and educational institutions, parents, especially housewives who are fully engaged in early childhood education for their children at home, played a major role in instilling entrepreneurial values to their children. Of interaction in daily life, the housewife can teach their children to be creative and innovative, driven and diligent, and proactive to change and adaptive to whatever environment they encounter. A simple example, the actions of Lady A, who taught her son to sell his comic book before her son could buy a new comic book. The simple action of an entrepreneurial spirit performed by housewives for their children will actually firmly plant in the child mind. And housewives who become entrepreneurs can be a role model in fostering the entrepreneurial spirit within their children. Children can see firsthand the entrepreneurial practice in their home.

CONCLUSION

From the discussion above, it can be concluded that a housewife and students above 15 years old (youths) who are not considered as workers also can help reduce poverty and help reduce unemployment. They can play a role as a pillar of the Indonesia's economy, especially in times of economic crisis and employee firing occurs everywhere. Although they only have a micro business, and only do business in their spare time, but they still have a market and remain able to sustain the country's economy. Imagine if all youths and all housewives who in August 2014 amounted to more than 40 million people have their own business. They certainly also can help the Indonesian economy in the era of the ASEAN economic community when the level of competition increases and the market became wide.

And from those discussions above, it also can be seen that college students who already have started a business, although only as a part-time entrepreneur, have a tendency to continue their business after graduating from college. This is because, at the moment they still have parents to finance their lives, they've tried to do business and face barriers to starting up. When they've finished college, they've managed to face barriers to starting up. And, the entrepreneurial spirit has inherent strongly within them.

Given such conditions, it would better if the government extends the program to empower entrepreneurial spirit and also to deter barrier to starting up for housewives and youths, either with the status of a part-time or full-time entrepreneur, which actually includes the criteria of the owner of Micro, Small, and Medium Enterprises. In an effort to empower the housewives and youths, the government is expected to strengthen the role of a cooperative to help entrepreneurs MSME owners. Educational institutions, parents, especially housewives, and networking have a major role in the empowerment of entrepreneurial spirit and also deter barrier to starting up.

REFERENCES

Amorós, J. E., & Bosma, N. (2013). *Global entrepreneurship monitor 2013*. Retrieved December 20, 2014, from http://www.gemconsortium.org/report

Badan Pusat Statistik. (2016a). *Data masyarakat yang berusia 15 tahun atau lebih dan aktivitas mereka dari tahun 2004-2014*. Retrieved February 28, 2016, from http://www.bps.go.id/linkTabelStatis/view/id/969

Badan Pusat Statistik. (2016b). *Laju pertumbuhan produk domestik bruto per kapita beberapa negara menurut harga konstan (persen)*. Retrieved September 4, 2016, from https://www.bps.go.id/linkTabelStatis/view/id/1244

Badan Pusat Statistik. (2016c). *Persentase penduduk miskin September 2015 mencapai 11.13%*. Retrieved September 6, 2016, from https://www.bps.go.id/brs/view/id/1227

Badan Pusat Statistik. (2016d). *Persentase penduduk usia 15 tahun ke atas menurut* jenis *kegiatan seminggu yang lalu 2009-2012*. Retrieved on March 3, 2016, from http://www.bps.go.id/linkTabelStatis/view/id/1608

Badan Pusat Statistik. (2016e). *Tingkat pengangguran berdasarkan tingkat pendidikan*. Retrieved March 10, 2016, from http://www.bps.go.id/linkTabelStatis/view/id/972

Bank Indonesia. (2016). *Undang-undang Republik Indonesia no. 20 tahun 2008 tentang usaha kecil, mikro, dan menengah*. Retrieved March 10, 2016, from http://www.bi.go.id/id/tentang-bi/uu-bi/Documents/UU20Tahun2008UMKM.pdf

Bulut, Y., & Sayin, E. (2010). An evaluation of entrepreneurship characteristics of university students: An empirical investigation from the faculty of economic and administrative sciences in Adnan Menderes University. *International Journal of Economic Perspectives*, *4*(3), 559–568.

Cahayani, A., Gunawan, A. S., & Isololipu, K. (2016, July). The dimension of entrepreneurial characteristics in young entrepreneurs in the creative industry field in Jakarta. *China-USA Business Review*, *15*(7), 319–329. doi:10.17265/1537-1514/2016.07.00

Ciputra. (2008). *Ciputra quantum leap*. Jakarta: PT. Elex Media Komputindo.

Detik. (2016). *ILO: Pekerja perempuan masih alami diskriminasi*. Retrieved March 10, 2016, from http://news.detik.com/bbc/3160381/ilo-pekerja-perempuan-masih-alami-diskriminasi

Djohanputro, B. (2006). *Prinsip-prinsip ekonomi makro. General Series No. 10.* Jakarta: PPM.

Gumelar, G. (2016). *BPS: Laju ekonomi 2015 banyak terganjal faktor eksternal.* Retrieved September 4, 2016, from http://www.cnnindonesia.com/ekonomi/20160205135559-78-109139/bps-laju-ekonomi-2015-banyak-terganjal-faktor-eksternal/

Hornstein, A., & Lubik, T. A. (2010). *The rise in long-term unemployment: Potential causes and implications.* Richmond, VA: Federal Reserve Bank of Richmond. Retrieved March 8, 2016, from http://search.proquest.com/docview/874210915?accountid=48149

Joardar, A., Wu, S., & Chen, S. (2014). The impact of national culture and type of entrepreneurs on outsourcing. *The International Entrepreneurship and Management Journal, 10*(3), 643–659. doi:10.1007/s11365-012-0247-y

Kompas. (2013). *Wapres imbau dunia usaha menjangkau wirausaha muda.* Kompas, January 18, 2013. Retrieved September, 2016, from http://nasional.kompas.com/read/2013/01/18/04034059/wapres.imbau.dunia.usaha.menjangkau.wirausaha.muda on September 10, 2016.

Kuratko, D. F., & Hodgetts, R. M. (2007). *Entrepreneurship: Theory, process, practice* (7th ed.). Ohio: Thomson South-Western.

Mankiw, N. G. (2007). *Principles of economics* (4th ed.). Ohio: Thomson South-Western.

Margiman. (2008). *Quo vadis kewirausahaan di Indonesia.* Retrieved November 30, 2009, from http://www.ciputra.org/node/95/quo-vadis-kewirausahaan-di-indonesia.htm

Ministry of A Cooperative and Small and Medium Enterprise. (2016). *Data usaha mikro, kecil, dan menengah (UMKM) dan usaha besar (UB).* Retrieved March 3, 2016, from http://www.depkop.go.id/berita-informasi/data-informasi/data-umkm/

Muana, N. (2005). Makro ekonomi: Teori, masalah, dan kebijakan (2nd ed.). Jakarta: PT. Raja Grafika Persada.

Nawangpalupi, C. B., Pawitan, G., Gunawan, A., Widyarini, M., & Iskandarsjah, T. (2014). *Global entrepreneurship monitor 2013, Indonesia report.* Bandung: Universitas Katolik Parahyangan.

Praditya, I. I. (2015, October 5). Tekan pengangguran: Joko Widodo luncurkan program padat karya. Retrieved September 4, 2016, from http://bisnis.liputan6.com/read/2332754/tekan-pengangguran-jokowi-luncurkan-program-padat-karya

Republika. (2015). *Jumlah pengusaha Indonesia hanya 16,5%.* Retrieved September 6, 2016, from http://www.republika.co.id/berita/nasional/umum/15/03/12/nl3i58-jumlah-pengusaha-indonesia-hanya-165-persen

Robertson, M., Collins, A., Medeira, N., & Slater, J. (2003). Barriers to start-up and their effect on aspirant entrepreneurs. *Education + Training, 45*(6), 308–316. doi:10.1108/00400910310495950

Salimath, M. S., & Cullen, J. B. (2010). Formal and informal institutional effects on entrepreneurship: A synthesis of national-level research. *The International Journal of Organizational Analysis, 18*(3), 358–385. doi:10.1108/19348831011062175

Sanusi, A. (2007). Perbandingan laju pertumbuhan ekonomi dan laju pertumbuhan penduduk. *Widya: Majalah Ilmiah, 24*(240), 36-42. Retrieved August 30, 2016, from http://www.atmajaya.ac.id/web/WebHost.aspx?cid=library code: MM47-25 V24 N260 200705 p36 optim.pdf

Sikumbang, Z. (2014). *Menkop: jumlah koperasi dan UMKM terus meningkat.* February 1, 2014. Retrieved March 27, 2016, from http://www.antaranews.com/berita/416949/menkop-jumlah-a cooperative-dan-umkm-terus-meningkat

Stone, E. (1992). Investing in the poor. *Asian Business, April*, 24-32.

Subandi. (2006). *Sistem ekonomi Indonesia*. Bandung: ALFABETA.

Tobing, E. (2005). *Pengangguran tenaga kerja terdidik*. Jakarta: The Prospect.

Waluyo, A. (2015, September 9). *Jokowi umumkan paket kebijakan ekonomi*. Retrieved September 3, 2016, from http://www.voaindonesia.com/a/jokowi-umumkan-paket-kebijakan-ekonomi-/2953846.html

World Bank & International Monetary Fund. (2014). *Global monitoring report 2014/2015: Ending poverty and sharing prosperity*. Retrieved September 10, 2016, from http://www.worldbank.org/content/dam/Worldbank/gmr/gmr2014/GMR_2014_Full_Report.pdf

World Economic Forum. (2015). *Global gender gap report 2015*. Retrieved September 6, 2016, from http://www3.weforum.org/docs/GGGR2015/cover.pdf

KEY TERMS AND DEFINITIONS

Developing Country: A condition where a country has low living standard and low per capita income. The human development index in this kind of country is also considering low.

Entrepreneurial Spirit: A mindset and attitude that own by someone that make them have some traits, such as want to take a risk, accept the challenge, and do not like to wait for something to happen or have act orientation.

Housewife: A married woman who do household management and caring her family as the main occupation.

Poverty: A state of one who lacks a certain amount of material possession or money. This condition could be defined as either absolute or relative.

Unemployment: A condition where someone in labor force group does not have any job.

World Bank: An organization that gives assistance of financial and technical aspect for developing countries all around the world.

Youth: The time of life between childhood and adulthood.

Chapter 10
Youth Unemployment in Turkey

Z. Bilgen Susanlı
Işık University, Turkey

ABSTRACT

This book chapter describes the recent trends in youth unemployment in Turkey by taking into account the causes of unemployment, and the job search methods of the unemployed. Analyses reveal interesting insights. First, inactivity among youth remains high despite the steep decline in the NEET rate during the last decade. Across age groups and genders, females aged between 20 and 24 have the highest NEET rates. Second, there is a widening gender unemployment gap which underscores gender differences in access to jobs. Third, unemployment rates increase consistently with the level of education. Fourth, while temporary jobs coming to an end is the most common reason for unemployment reported by males, a substantial share of unemployed females is first-time jobs-seekers. As far as policymaking is concerned, education policies as well as timely and well-designed training and job assistance programs are essential for facilitating the youth's entry into stable employment.

INTRODUCTION

Labor market conditions deteriorated in many countries during the global recession. Young people were particularly affected by the economic downturn as it became increasingly difficult for them to find or maintain jobs. This generated a heightened interest from policymakers and researchers with the aim of finding solutions to the problems of the youth in the labor market.

It has been well-documented that unemployment lowers well-being (Clark & Oswald, 1994; Winkelmann & Winkelmann, 1998). In addition to the loss of income, unemployment leads to a fall in well-being as it deprives individuals of all the non-pecuniary benefits that come with employment such as self-confidence and self-esteem. Hence, unemployed people, on average, report lower levels of well-being. Unemployment spells earlier in life may leave scarring effects in the sense that there may be lasting effects of job loss on well-being (Clark, Knabe, & Ratzel, 2011; Knabe & Ratzel, 2011). Experiencing unemployment while young is linked with lower levels of happiness, job satisfaction, wages and health (Bell & Blanchflower, 2010; Gregg & Tominey, 2005), and a higher likelihood of engaging in criminal activities in the future (Fougere, Kramarz, & Pouget, 2009). At the macro level, persistent

DOI: 10.4018/978-1-5225-2008-5.ch010

unemployment causes greater income inequality which undermines the confidence in government and hence leads to social unrest.[1]

In addition to the reasons mentioned above, the labor market outcomes of the youth have a pivotal role for Turkey considering its demographic transition. It is estimated that Turkey will go through a demographic period called the "Window of Opportunity" between 2000 and 2025. Accordingly, the working-age population is expected to attain its maximum, which will provide favorable conditions for economic growth.[2]

The youth unemployment rates in Turkey have steadily been higher than the OECD average since 2000. While several studies focused on the subject of youth unemployment in Turkey, the inactivity of the youth measured by the share of youth that is neither in employment nor education and training - the so-called NEET rate - is a much less studied topic. The category of NEETs is of particular importance as Turkey has the highest share of NEETs among OECD countries. As of 2014, the share of NEETs among 15-19 and 20-24-year-olds in Turkey is 21 percent and 36 percent, respectively.

Another salient characteristic of the Turkish labor market is low labor market attachment among women. As of 2014, female labor participation rate in Turkey is 33.6 percent - the lowest among OECD countries. Female labor force participation is typically lower in urban areas due to the predominance of unpaid family work in rural areas. Migration from rural to urban areas is another factor behind the lower participation of females in urban areas as migrant women fail to meet the skill requirements of the jobs in urban labor markets. The labor force participation rate of the female youth is remarkably low - 27.7 percent in 2014. In addition, young women that do participate seem to face difficulties in finding employment. Since the global recession, the gender gap in unemployment rates has widened highlighting the gender differences in access to jobs. As of 2015, the youth unemployment rate in Turkey stands at 18.5 percent with 22.2 percent and 16.5 percent among females and males, respectively (Turkish Statistical Institute [TURKSTAT], 2016).

This book chapter aims to explore the nature and causes of youth unemployment in Turkey by taking into account its gender dimension. The recent trends in the labor market outcomes of the Turkish youth will be reviewed by focusing on the impact of the global recession of 2008-2009. This chapter is organized around seven parts. Part two provides a description of key indicators of the labor market. Part three gives a brief overview of the recent literature. Part four introduces the salient characteristics of the youth labor markets and summarizes the reasons behind the declining labor market prospects of the young people in the aftermath of the global recession. Part five analyses the trends in the main labor market indicators of the youth in Turkey. Part six reviews the policies and programs to tackle the youth unemployment problem and discusses their effectiveness. Part seven makes some concluding remarks.

LABOR MARKET INDICATORS

In describing the outlook of the labor market, labor market indicators are used. Typically, these indicators are produced using data from household labor force surveys conducted by national statistical agencies in each country.

Labor market indicators cover the civilian non-institutional working age population which comprises the population 15 years of age and over within the non-institutional civilian population. The non-institutional civilian population refers to all the population excluding the residents of institutions such as schools, dormitories, kindergartens, rest homes for elderly persons, special hospitals, military barracks and recreation quarters for officers. By using data collected in these surveys, the following indicators are estimated:

- A person is defined to be "at work" if s/he is engaged in any activity during the reference period for at least one hour as a regular employee, casual employee, self-employed or unpaid family worker.
- Employed persons consist of those who are at work, and all self-employed and employers with a job but who are not at work in the reference week due to various reasons.
- Unemployed persons include individuals 15 years and older who were not at work during the reference period except for temporary illness, who were actively searching for a job during the last four weeks, and who are available to start working in two weeks if a job is found.[3]
- Labor force comprises of all employed and unemployed individuals.
- Labor force participation rate equals the labor force as a percent of the non-institutional working age population.

The youth unemployment rate is calculated as the number of unemployed youth as a percent of the number of youth in labor force. Recently, there has been a growing focus on the concept of the NEETs. The NEET youth are defined as those that are not in employment, education or training. While there is no standard for the international definition of the NEETs, the Eurostat, International Labour Office (ILO), and other international organizations have adopted the following definition:

$$Youth\ NEET\ rate\ (\%) = \frac{\left(\begin{array}{c}Number\ of\ 15\text{ - }24\text{ - }year\text{ - }olds\ who\ are\ not\ in\ employment,\\ education\ or\ training\end{array}\right)}{Number\ of\ 15\text{ - }24\text{ - }year\text{ - }olds\ in\ the\ population} * 100$$

The NEET rate has the following advantages over the conventionally used unemployment rate:

1. The unemployment rate may present an incomplete picture of the problems of the youth in the labor market if the majority of the youth in a given labor market remain in education until the age of 24 and the ones that do join the labor force are mostly unemployed.
2. Since the unemployment rate reflects the conditions of those who are participants, it excludes those who are willing to work but who have given up job search as they believe that there is no work available due to various reasons. These are the discouraged individuals that report neither having a job in the reference period nor having searched for one but are willing to work if a job is available. Discouragement from the labor force may be an outcome of individual characteristics as well as economic circumstances. As the discouraged youth leave the labor force, they are no longer included in the labor force statistics.
3. In addition to the discouraged youth, the NEET category also includes different groups of youth that choose to stay out of the labor market due to reasons such as marriage and childbearing, caregiving for the elderly, and sickness and disability. Clearly, these choices are a function of the circumstances in the labor market as much as of individual preferences.

Although the NEET group is a comprehensive category embracing the several groups with problematic labor market transitions, one must be cautious in lumping together the discouraged and the unemployed together with the voluntarily nonparticipating youth.

RELATED LITERATURE

The declining labor market prospects of the youth has spurred much attention from academicians and policymakers. Studies on this subject abound. Hence, this section does not intend to provide a comprehensive survey. Rather, the most common findings from the recent research will be reviewed briefly.

There are two stylized facts of the labor market regarding the youth: (i) the youth experience higher unemployment rates than adults do, (ii) the youth unemployment rates are more sensitive to business cycles than the adult unemployment rates. Dietrich and Moller (2016) propose four explanations for these. The first reason is related to the lower productivity of the young workers compared to adults due to lack of skills and qualifications resulting from lack of job experience. Accordingly, young workers receive lower wages than adults. Second, since young workers are at the start of their working lives, they tend to switch jobs more frequently to find better job opportunities and better matches to their skills and interests. Hence, young workers are more likely to be unemployed at any point in time. The third explanation is related to the Insider-Outsider Theory (Lindbeck & Snower, 2001). In this framework, older workers that are already employed can be viewed as insiders. Due to hiring and firing costs, older workers can command higher wages. In economic downturns, older workers would not have any incentive to compromise, creating barriers for the new labor market entrants to find employment. Fourth, in times of layoffs, younger workers are dismissed before older workers as the latter also serve as trainers for the newly recruited workers. Using data from EU-15 countries for the 1995-2014 period, Dietrich and Moller (2016) examine youth unemployment in the aftermath of the global recession. Their analyses underline the country-specific factors such as institutions, traditions, and structures in explaining differences across European countries. Findings reveal significant disparities in the response of adult and youth unemployment rates to economic activity across countries. They also document that countries in the sample are more similar with respect to adult unemployment than to youth unemployment.

To explain the differential effects of economic downturns on particular groups in the labor market, Cho and Newhouse (2012) identify three potential mechanisms. The first channel refers to differences in sectoral employment across groups. Occupational segregation results from differences in human capital investments as well as discrimination. Along similar lines, gender differences in the impacts of crises may depend on occupational segregation. The second mechanism relates to the perceptions of firms regarding worker productivity and labor market attachment. Accordingly, the young workers may be disadvantaged due to their low productivity and higher job turnover. The third mechanism that may generate differential effects on labor market outcomes may be an outcome of household labor supply decisions. In this sense, the added worker effect refers to the (temporary) rise in the labor force participation of married women when their spouses become jobless. The youth in families facing income losses may make similar choices whereby they enter the workforce to support their families. In the work of Cho and Newhouse (2012), findings from empirical analyses covering 17 countries indicate that the vulnerability of the youth results from disproportionate firings within an industry or their lack of access to jobs after exiting education.

Verick (2009) examines the heterogeneous impact of the global recession on youth and adult unemployment across 24 European Union member states as well as Australia, Canada, Norway, Turkey, and the United States. Main findings reinforce the previous findings of increased vulnerability of the youth. Analyses also underscore the gender dimension of the impact. In particular, the impact on young men was more negative as these individuals were employed in the sectors such as construction and manufacturing that were more heavily impacted by the recession.

Choudry, Marelli, and Signorelli (2012) investigate the effect of financial crises on youth unemployment during the 1980-2005 period for a group of 17 middle-income countries. Their findings yield two important points. First, the effect of financial crises on unemployment last longer than the impact on GDP. Second, the impact on youth unemployment exceeds that on overall unemployment.

It has been argued that the conventional indicators such as employment and unemployment have limited relevance to the problems that the youth face in the labor market. These issues include early school leaving, discouragement, and inactivity. Since the onset of the recession, there has been a heightened focus on the determinants and consequences of the NEET status. Understanding the determinants of becoming NEET is important as these individuals face a high risk of exclusion as they lack access to education and work. Studies on the determinants of NEET status largely agree on a number of key factors such as education, disability and sickness, and family background (Bynner & Parsons, 2002; Eurofound, 2012; Sadler, Akisler, & Burch, 2014). Sadler et al. (2014) propose that low educational attainment may have its roots in poor mental and physical health, and lack of parental commitment to education.

Bäckman and Nilsson (2016) investigate the consequences of being NEET for three different Swedish birth cohorts and report detrimental effects both in the short-run and the long-run. Findings in the work of Bäckman and Nilsson (2016) also suggest that the likelihood of social exclusion due to becoming NEET is higher in the younger cohorts than in older ones. Also, a number of studies from the medical literature report a negative correlation between NEET status and mental health. Baggio et al. (2015) and Benjet et al. (2012) document that substance abuse and poorer mental health are underlying factors of NEET status.

Furlong (2006) identifies both advantages and disadvantages of the NEET concept. While the use of an inclusive concept ensures that the vulnerability of the inactives is also taken into consideration, the lack of an internationally accepted definition for the NEETs makes it harder to make cross-country comparisons. Yates and Payne (2006) also emphasize that caution must be exercised in lumping together various groups of young individuals with different characteristics, facing different challenges and risks.

Studies on the youth unemployment in Turkey have focused mainly on macroeconomic factors. Using data for the 2005-2010 period, Kabaklarlı, Er, and Buluş (2011) examine the determinants of youth unemployment in Turkey. Their findings are suggestive of a long-run relationship between youth unemployment rate and real investment, real output, productivity, and inflation. Sayın (2011) identifies economic growth and enrollment in higher education as long-run determinants of the youth unemployment rates during 1988-2010. Along similar lines, Çondur and Bölükbaş (2014) find that gross domestic product and producer price index are significant determinants of youth unemployment rates between 2000 and 2010. Murat and Şahin (2011) document that incoordination between the education system and the business world, lack of life-long learning strategy, insufficiency of 8-years primary education, and problems with the quality of education are the causes of youth unemployment. Bayraktar and İncekara (2013) also report the lack of human capital and the mismatch between the expected wages and skill endowments of the young job searchers as important factors.

THE DECLINING LABOR MARKET PROSPECTS OF THE YOUTH DURING THE GLOBAL RECESSION

The youth labor market conditions showed substantial progress in the OECD area in the decade leading up to 2008-2009 until the global financial crisis hit the youth labor market. With the onset of the crisis in the second half of 2008, large declines in output caused sharp falls in employment and steep rises in unemployment rates in many countries (Organisation for Economic Co-operation and Development [OECD], 2009). Consequently, the youth were disproportionately affected by the recession as they bore a greater share of job losses. Since then, the problems the youth face in the labor market have been a top policy concern (International Labour Office [ILO], 2011; OECD, 2009).

Table 1 presents the trends in the global labor market for the 2007-2015 period. The number of youth unemployed globally reached 77 million in 2009 amounting to about 39 percent of the total unemployed. Despite the decline in the number of unemployed youth to 73.3 million in 2014, the youth unemployment rate has stagnated around 13 percent since 2009. Five years after the peak of the global recession in 2010, the global youth unemployment rate is still not back to its pre-recession level of 11.7 percent in 2007. An estimated number of 73.4 million youth were unemployed globally in 2015. Figures in Table 1 also indicate that the share of youth in the pool of unemployed displays a steady decline from 41.2 percent in 2007 to 36.4 percent in 2015. While this is favorable, since only one-sixth of the world population is between 15 and 24 years old, the youth are clearly overrepresented in the pool of unemployed.[4] An additional indicator that measures how the youth fare relative to the adults is the ratio of youth to the adult unemployment rate. Since 2007, this ratio has stagnated around 2.8 - 2.9 which implies that the youth are three times as likely to be unemployed as the adults.

The 2008-2009 recession is characterized by a high degree of synchronization of output falls across countries due to sharp declines in production and export demand. However, countries that were exposed to similar magnitudes of shocks to output produced widely varying labor market responses (Organisation for Economic Co-operation and Development [OECD], 2010). One factor behind this is whether employers resorted to shedding labor or to reducing working hours in response to weakening business conditions.[5]

Figure 1 presents the evolution of the youth unemployment rates for selected OECD countries. Following the decline in the previous decade, the OECD youth unemployment rate rose from 11.9 percent

Table 1. Global unemployment and unemployment rates, 2007-2015

	2007	2008	2009	2010	2011	2012	2013	2014	2015
Youth Unemployment (millions)	70.5	72.9	76.6	75.6	74.4	74.3	73.9	73.3	73.4
Adult Unemployment (millions)	100.5	106.1	121.5	120.8	120.9	123	125.7	126.2	128.2
Total Unemployment (millions)	171	179	198.1	196.4	195.3	197.3	199.6	199.4	201.6
Youth Unemployment Rate (%)	11.7	12.2	12.9	13	12.9	13	13	13	13.1
Adult Unemployment Rate (%)	4	4.2	4.7	4.6	4.5	4.5	4.5	4.5	4.5
Total Unemployment Rate (%)	5.5	5.7	6.2	6.1	6	6	6	5.9	5.9
Ratio of youth-to-adult unemp. rate (%)	2.9	2.9	2.8	2.8	2.8	2.9	2.9	2.9	2.9

Source: International Labour Office (ILO, 2015).

Figure 1. Youth unemployment rates in selected OECD countries, 2005-2014
Source: Author's calculations using data from OECD statistics database, http://stats.oecd.org.

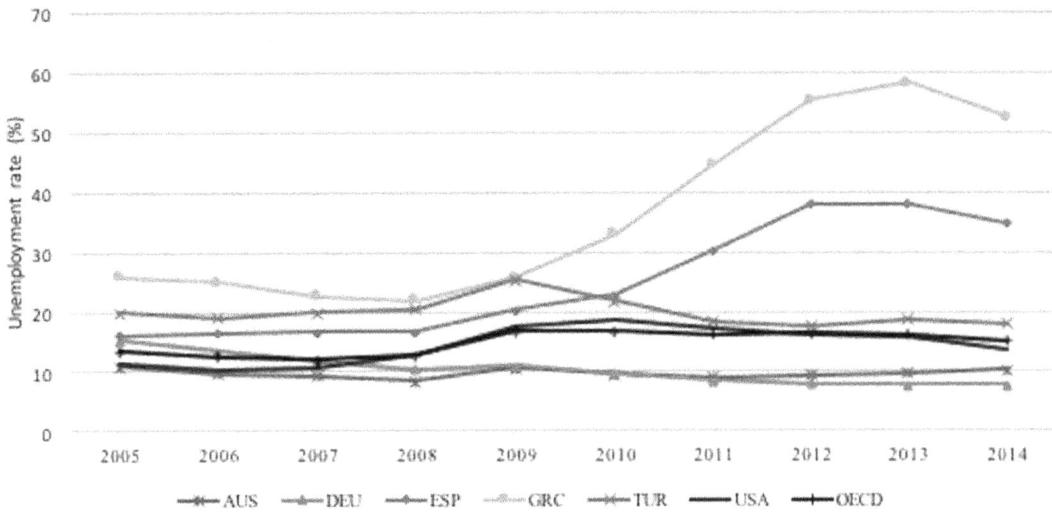

**For a more accurate representation of this figure, please see the electronic version.*

in 2007 to 12.7 percent in 2008, then to 16.7 percent in 2009. While the increase in youth unemployment rate was much steeper in some countries such as Greece, Spain, United States, and Turkey, some countries such as Austria and Germany experienced a mild increase.[6]

The global youth labor force participation rate declined from 50.7 percent to 48.1 percent between 2007 and 2015. This implies that the youth are increasingly staying out of the labor force. The increased withdrawal from the labor force may be reflecting the choice of the youth to remain longer in education implied by the continuous increase in the enrollment in tertiary education in the last decade. At the OECD level, the share of 25-34-year-olds with university education rose from 26 percent to 32 percent between 2000 to 2005, and then to 37 percent and 41 percent in 2010 and 2014, respectively (Organisation for Economic Co-operation and Development [OECD], 2016). While this is a welcome development, it is well-known that a substantial share of the jobless youth is neither in education nor training, hence the NEETs.

Figure 2 presents the share of youth not in employment, education or training among 20-24-year-olds in OECD countries in 2005 and 2010. There are large differences across countries and over time. Reflecting the impact of the global recession, the NEET rates among the 20-24-year-olds increased between 2005 and 2010 in many countries. However, some countries such as the Czech Republic, Germany, Poland and Turkey experienced substantial declines in NEET rates. For example, while the NEET share in Germany declined significantly from 18.7 percent in 2005 to 13.7 percent in 2010, it increased from 19.1 percent to 27 percent in Spain. Despite the fall from 49.7 percent to 43.7 percent, Turkey has the highest share of NEETs among the 20-24 year-olds.

When analyzing the health of the youth labor market, only paying attention to the conventional indicators such as the unemployment rate and labor force participation rate may mask several underlying problems with the quality of jobs held by the youth. Even when the youth do find jobs, they are more likely than adults to be in jobs that are poorly paid, and that mostly lack social security coverage and opportunities for training and career advancement. These jobs are typically informal or temporary jobs. Although a greater share of youth is in informal and temporary employment than prime-age workers

Figure 2. The NEET rates among the 20-24-year-old youth in OECD countries in 2005 and 2010
Source: Author's calculations using data from OECD statistics database, http://stats.oecd.org.

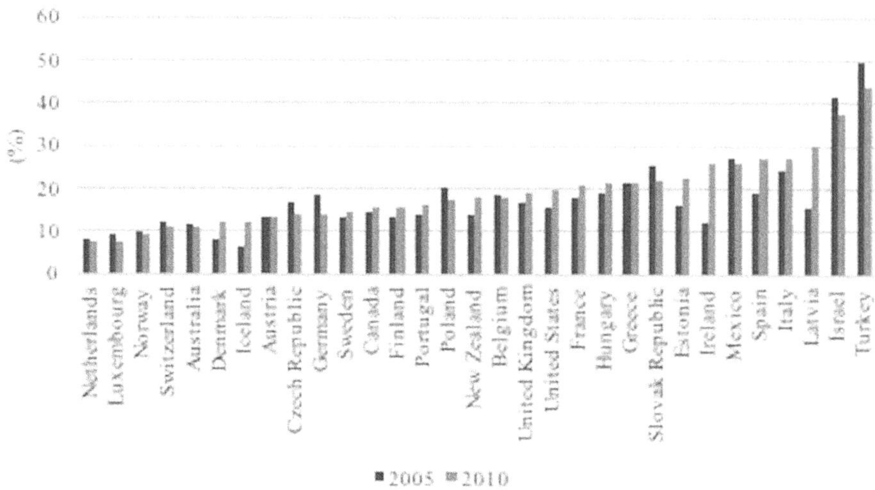

(25-64-year-olds) in many countries, large variations exist across countries (Organisation for Economic Co-operation and Development [OECD], 2014). Informal employment refers to the production of legal goods and services where one or more of the legal requirements regarding employment are not met (Organisation for Economic Co-operation and Development [OECD], 2008). Informal jobs lack social security registration and some or all of the benefits associated with labor contracts such as minimum wages, employment protection, and occupational health and safety standards. These jobs are often low-paid and offer less training and career progression possibilities than formal ones. Similarly, the rise in temporary employment among the young people has been a concern (O'Higgins, 2015). Although temporary jobs may serve as stepping stones to more stable permanent jobs, they may create a segmented labor market if employment protection differs across temporary and permanent jobs.

As this book chapter is being written, the youth are still facing hard times to find jobs in a labor market where they are three times more likely to be unemployed compared to prime-age individuals. In many OECD countries, the youth unemployment rates remain at higher levels compared to pre-crisis levels despite increasing educational attainment and declining cohort sizes.

THE YOUTH LABOR MARKET IN TURKEY

The labor market conditions of the youth in Turkey are of crucial importance considering the demographic transition that started in the early twentieth century. The demographic transition process can be summarized as a shift from high levels of mortality and fertility to lower levels (İçduygu, 2012). The demographic transition is expected to last three to four more decades, and when it is over, the age structure of the population will be much older.[7] Currently, Turkey is faced with a demographic window of opportunity which is defined as a time period when the working-age population constitutes a substantial share of the total population. The ratio of the population aged 0-14 years and of older adults aged 65 years and above to the working age population gives the total dependency ratio. Between 2010 and 2030, the dependency ratio is estimated to be near its minimum. Also called a demographic dividend or demographic bonus, the demographic window presents favorable conditions for economic growth as smaller dependency ratios are expected to raise savings and investments. As of 2015, Turkey's population is about 78.7 million, and the youth constitute 16.4 percent of this, amounting to about 12.9 million. Although Turkey has the highest share of youth among the EU-28 and candidate countries, with the increase in life expectancy and falling total fertility rate, the population will start aging in about ten years (Turkish Statistical Institute [TURKSTAT], 2014). This share is estimated to fall to 15.1 percent in 2023, and to 11.7 percent in 2050. Therefore, to take advantage of the favorable age structure provided by the demographic dividend, it is crucial that the working age population is productively integrated into the labor market. In this regard, low labor force participation rates, especially for women, and high unemployment and inactivity among the youth remain as important obstacles for taking advantage of the demographic bonus.

Historically, the youth unemployment rates in Turkey have been above the OECD average, highlighting the problematic nature of the labor market experience of the Turkish youth. This is especially more so for young women. Figure 3 presents the youth unemployment rates separately for females and males along with the unemployment rates of prime-age men for the period 2000-2015. The prime-age men serve as the reference group as they encounter the fewest obstacles in the labor market. As such, the persistent gap between the unemployment rates of prime-age men and those of the youth marks the difficulties the youth face in the labor market. The unemployment rates for females and males were on the rise after the economic crisis in 2001 until 2003 and peaked at around 25 percent in 2009 due to the decline in GDP. As economic growth picked up after 2009, the unemployment rates for females and males started to decline with that of males declining faster. Since then, there is a widening gender unemployment gap. As of 2015, the unemployment rate for females and males stands at 22.2 percent and 16.5 percent, respectively.

Figure 3. Youth unemployment rates in Turkey, by gender
Source: Author's calculations using data from OECD statistics database, http://stats.oecd.org.

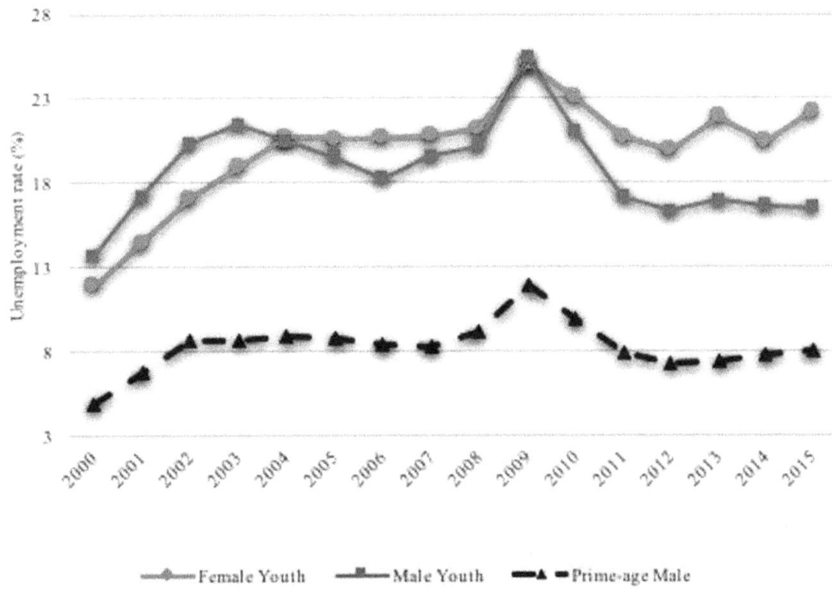

**For a more accurate representation of this figure, please see the electronic version.*

Figure 4 shows the unemployment rates among 15-24-year-olds by education level between 2004 and 2014. The unemployment rate is highest among those with a university degree, and it falls with educational attainment. This underscores the mismatch between the skills and qualifications gained at university and those required in the labor market. Keeping in mind that some of the youth may remain in higher education until the age of 24, the unemployment rates for the university graduates may turn out to be even higher if the 25-30-years-olds are also included in the calculation.

The age groups 15-19 and 20-24 have distinct characteristics regarding labor market attachment. On the one hand, as a substantial share of the 15-19-year-olds transition from high school to university, one would expect falling labor force participation among the 20-24-year-olds as the share of the youth remaining in education rises. On the other hand, the youth aged 20-24 are transitioning from university to either graduate school or the labor market. Hence, one would expect the participation behavior of this age group to be closer to that of the prime-age population. Therefore, to examine such trends, Figure 5 presents the NEET rates between 2000 and 2014 for the two age groups for females and males. As Figure 5 shows, the NEET rates declined for all groups. The downward trend is stronger for the youth aged between 15-19. This may be explained by choice of youth to stay longer in education.[8] Despite the significant decline from 64 percent in 2000 to 51 percent in 2014, the NEET share is the highest among females aged 20-24.

Developing effective solutions for youth unemployment requires understanding the underlying causes of their unemployment. Figure 6 depicts the reasons for unemployment reported by the unemployed youth using data from 2014 Turkish Household Labor Force Survey, (THLFS, hereafter). The figure is constructed using the responses of the jobless youth about their situation when they started looking for employment. About 26 percent of the unemployed are those whose temporary jobs came to an end. This is much higher among males than females (31.7 percent vs. 16 percent). The second most common response is "Others" which includes education, military service, and household chores. These other situations apply to 25.3 percent of the total youth. Lastly, 17.8 percent of the jobless youth report being

Figure 4. Youth unemployment rates by education level, 2004-2014
Source: Author's calculations using TUIK Labor Force Statistics.

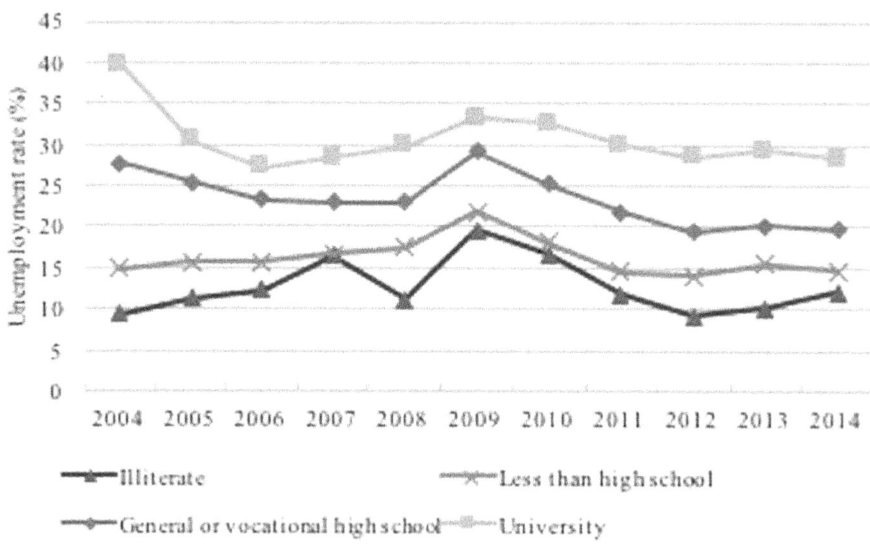

Figure 5. NEET rates, by age group and gender, 2000-2014
Source: Author's calculations using data from OECD statistics database, http://stats.oecd.org.

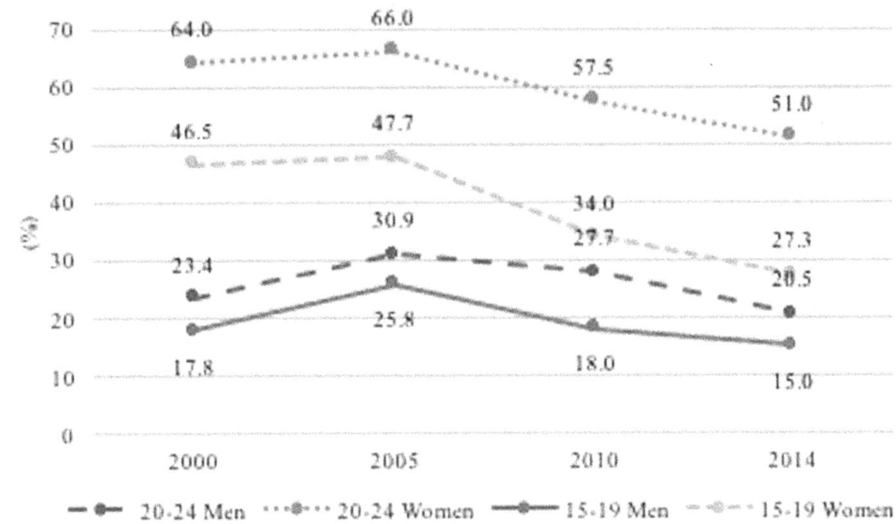

first-time job-seekers. While the share of first-time job-seekers is 13.5 percent among males, it is 24.8 percent among females. This large difference between males and females is another manifestation of gender differences in access to jobs.

It is useful to understand how the youth search for jobs when assisting them in finding employment. In this regard, the THLFS surveys ask jobless individuals which job search methods they use. An unemployed person may report having used more than one job search channel. Data from the 2004-2013 period is summarized in Table 2. The search behavior of the unemployed youth reveals that asking friends and relatives is the most popular method. The second most common method is direct application to employers.

Figure 6. Youth unemployment by reasons, 2014
Source: Turkish Statistical Institute (2015).

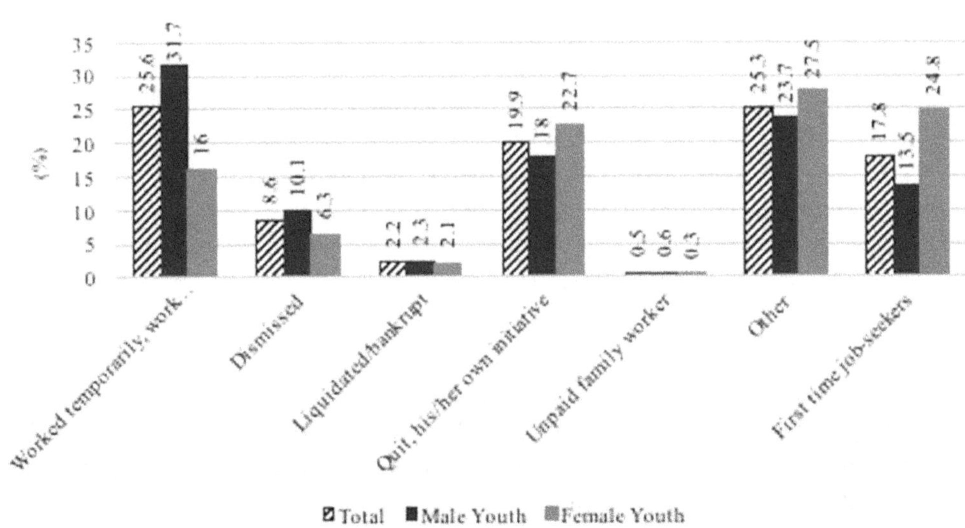

Table 2. Job search methods used by unemployed youth

(%)	2004	2005	2006	2007	2008	2009	2010	2011	2012	2013
Direct application to employers	74.5	72.9	71.9	73.0	73.4	78.0	77.7	76.8	77.1	73.2
Friends and relatives etc.	92.5	93.5	93.4	93.4	94.7	96.0	94.8	93.9	94.0	92.3
Contact with Turkish Employment Office	14.5	13.1	9.5	13.1	9.9	12.0	13.0	15.6	19.7	23.6
Contact with private employment agencies	10.9	9.4	9.7	9.4	9.7	10.2	10.5	9.6	10.1	11.3
Study ads in newspapers or journals	36.5	34.2	35.3	34.4	36.8	29.6	27.6	29.8	31.5	31.1
Insert or answer ads in newspapers	11.1	10.6	9.0	10.8	10.0	10.2	9.1	8.7	8.9	8.0
Used internet	10.8	8.5	8.1	8.7	8.0	7.2	7.9	9.1	10.3	9.3
Take a test, interview or examination	0.8	0.9	0.7	0.9	0.9	1.1	1.2	1.0	0.9	1.3
Look for place or equipment to establish your own business	0.6	0.4	0.5	0.4	0.4	0.9	0.8	0.7	0.8	1.0
Look for credit, license, etc. to establish your own business	6.9	6.8	5.7	6.9	6.1	7.7	8.8	10.5	12.9	17.7
Wait for a call from Turkish Employment Agency	19.8	29.8	35.7	29.8	43.3	40.6	41.8	42.3	39.7	42.8
Wait for the results of an application for a job	10.7	6.8	7.7	6.9	5.9	5.3	5.9	8.9	10.0	8.1
Wait for the results of a competition for recruitment to the public sector	0.3	0.5	0.3	0.5	0.2	1.2	1.8	0.6	0.4	0.5

Source: Author's calculations using THLFS 2004-2013.

The youth also seem to rely increasingly on Turkish Employment Agency (İŞKUR) for job search over the years. Interestingly, an increasing share of the youth report having applied for credit, license, etc. to establish their own business. This rise is more pronounced starting 2009, especially between 2012 and 2013. One potential explanation for this is the expansion of the entrepreneurship training programs as part of the active labor market policies of İŞKUR since 2008. Indeed, İŞKUR has shown significant progress since 2008 by increasing its coverage of training programs from 55,531 trainees in 2008 to 370,385 in 2015. Vocational training courses are designed to improve the skills of the trainees with the intention of enhancing the employability of the participants. Besides, İŞKUR introduced entrepreneurship programs in 2009 with the aim of providing the basics of entrepreneurship and business plans through theoretical and applied modules. As of June 2016, these programs also feature a grant up to 50,000 Turkish Liras.

Even when the youth do find employment, the quality of their jobs is questionable. The jobs of the youth are mostly temporary which have a pre-determined termination date and which typically last shorter than 12 months. The incidence of temporary employment as a percent of all wage and salary employment among the youth is higher in Turkey compared to the OECD average (13.2 percent vs. 11.4 percent in 2015). Also, the incidence of temporary employment is much higher among the youth than older workers (23.4 percent vs. 10.6 percent in 2015). The share of temporary employment in total employment among young men rose from 13.3 percent in 2008 to 15.3 percent in 2009. Among young women, the share of temporary employment increased from 10.9 percent in 2008 to 14.4 percent in 2009. Since 2009, temporary employment shares for both young men and women displayed a continuous increase while those for adult men and women remained roughly stable.

Another widely used measure of job quality in the developing country context is the formality status of employment. This is mainly based on the findings that informal jobs on average pay lower wages to workers with observable earning-related characteristics (El Badaoui, Strobl, & Walsh, 2008; Gong & Van Soest, 2002). Using data from 1994 Household Expenditure Survey for the Turkish labor market, Tansel (1999) finds that there is a wage premium in the formal sector both for women and men. Using more recent data from the THLFS surveys for the 2005-2009 period, Baskaya and Hulagu (2011) detect a wage premium for formal workers of about 15-20 percent. Their results suggest that the wage premium is stronger for younger workers and women. Wages of informal workers are also found to be more sensitive to regional unemployment rates (Baltagi, Baskaya, & Hulagu, 2013). Using Survey of Income and Living Conditions data for the period 2006-2009, Tansel and Kan (2012) estimate the transition probabilities across informal and formal sectors for the wage and salary employed, the self-employed, the unemployed and inactive individuals. They find that the probability of transitions from informal-salaried jobs to formal-salaried jobs is five times that of the transitions in the reverse direction. Their results also indicate that gender and age are important determinants of the transition probabilities and that females are more likely to be informally self-employed and inactive. Taken together, all these findings can be interpreted as evidence for the conventional segmented labor markets theory.[9] In this sense, informal jobs may be thought of as a last resort for those who cannot find formal jobs sector due to entry barriers. However, informal jobs may also be thought of as stepping stones where one accumulates human capital, gain expertise and build professional networks for the purpose of switching to a formal job. In this regard, the presence of a large informal sector may create incentives for some youth to substitute work experience in informal jobs for formal education. Using data from the THLFS for 2012 and 2013, Tumen (2015) finds that the availability of informal employment opportunities in the local labor market is negatively associated with the likelihood of a university degree and positively related with secondary school dropouts.

As of 2015, the share of wage and salary workers without social security registration is about 34 percent and 15 percent of the youth and adults in Turkey, respectively. Young men are much more likely to be informally employed compared to women (36 percent vs. 27 percent). The share of informal workers rose from 43 percent in 2008 to 46 percent in 2009 in response to the impact of the economic downturn. Together with the findings from the aforementioned studies, these may be an indication of the different roles informal jobs play in different economic conditions.

POTENTIAL SOLUTIONS

A vast body of work has been done to address the question of how to assist the jobless youth in the labor market. Devising comprehensive solutions to the youth challenge requires both demand and supply side policies and addressing the cyclical and structural issues. A rise in aggregate demand is vital to creating jobs for the youth. Considering the sensitivity of youth unemployment rates to business cycles, this requires prompt and well-designed counter-cyclical monetary and fiscal policies to manage fluctuations in economic activity.

Another issue to be addressed is the lack of skills of the youth for the case of Turkey. Despite rising educational attainment, the lack of competencies constitutes a major obstacle to finding and keeping jobs. The fact that youth unemployment rate increases with the level of education attained underlines the mismatch of skills and qualifications acquired during education and those demanded by employers in the labor market. Hence, education and training are keys to ensuring that the youth attain relevant skills and qualifications during formal education. Providing policies that are appropriately designed to raise the skills of the youth not only increases the chances of finding a job for the unemployed but also helps the employed to earn higher incomes. Besides, raising educational attainment is also likely to be influential in raising the quality of employment and fighting informality.[10] In addition, quality apprenticeship and internship programs may equip the youth with relevant skills and work experience. Internships may also serve as stepping stones into more stable jobs as long as they are not used as a means to cheap labor by employers.

Other suggestions for tackling youth unemployment are active labor market policies. Active labor market policies (ALMP) are defined as social expenditures (excluding education) which are aimed at enhancing the employability of the unemployed as well as the earning capacity of the employed. ALMPs consist of categories such as training programs, job search assistance, private sector employment schemes, supported employment, direct job creation, and other policies.[11]

Training programs are mainly vocational training programs for the unemployed or those who have a high risk losing their jobs. These measures aim to increase the employability of the participants by enhancing their human capital.

Job-search assistance programs are all measures with the purpose of improving the efficiency of the job search process of the unemployed such as job search assistance, job counseling, and guidance. These measures facilitate the transition of the unemployed into jobs by matching the employers and job searchers more efficiently than they otherwise would. Job search assistance programs are found to be more cost-effective than other ALMPs. However, their effectiveness depends on the availability of jobs. In times of economic downturns with intensive labor shedding, these measures are less likely to be effective.

Private sector employment schemes are employment incentives which are wage subsidies or social security exemptions. These can also serve as effective financial incentives for employers in times of economic downturns since they may lower the cost of labor for the employers by compensating for the low productivity and the lack of skills of the newly hired young workers.

Supported employment refers to subsidies aimed at helping individuals with a reduced capacity to work to obtain and maintain employment.

Direct job creation includes programs that create temporary jobs intended for a specific group of unemployed individuals that are otherwise difficult to place in jobs. These jobs are mainly public or non-profit jobs and would not exist without the policy.

In Turkey, the design and execution of ALMPs are under the responsibility of İŞKUR. These programs have been implemented since the 1990s.[12] Results from a survey of about 5,300 individuals that participated in İŞKUR's vocational training courses reveal interesting insights about the effectiveness of these courses. The survey covers a representative sample of general vocational training courses that took place between December 2010 and June 2011. Survey findings indicate that İŞKUR trainees are younger, have less work experience and higher levels of education than the average unemployed in urban areas (Almeida, Ridao-Cano, Levent, & McKenzie, 2011). Trainees are predominantly young (average trainee is 27 years old) and female (63 percent are female). A large share of participants (37 percent) has no work experience. Average work experience among those with prior experience is five years. While 71 percent of men has had work experience, this is 51 percent among women. It is also noteworthy that about half of the trainees report not having searched for a job in the last four weeks. The evaluation of the impact of the training shows that while the courses have a small impact on the probability of employment, they do have a small but significant effect on the quality of employment (World Bank, 2013). In particular, evaluation results indicate that training increased the likelihood of formal employment by up to three percentage points and earnings from employment by up to 13 percentage points. These survey results highlight the need for job counseling and job search assistance to come before the training programs. Job seekers need to be activated to look for a job and be guided through employment services before they attend any training.

CONCLUDING REMARKS

Creating employment for young people is a critical challenge for today's economic policymaking. With insufficient job opportunities, the youth take up on whatever jobs are available, mostly temporary and informal ones with limited employment protection. Although these jobs may serve as stepping stones into stable employment, they render the youth vulnerable to economic downturns. In this regard, the labor market conditions of the youth in Turkey deserve special attention as Turkey has the highest share of youth that is neither in employment nor in education or training among OECD countries. Analyses reveal interesting insights. First, inactivity, especially among young women, remains high despite the steep decline in the NEET rate in the last decade. As of 2014, more than half of the women between the ages of 20 and 24 are neither in education nor in employment. Second, there is a persistent gender unemployment gap which underscores gender differences in access to jobs. Third, youth unemployment rate rises with the level education attained. The unemployment rate is highest among the youth with a university degree. This points out the lack of qualifications as one of the main obstacles to getting a job. Fourth, while temporary jobs coming to an end is the most common reason for joblessness reported by males, about a quarter of unemployed females are first-time jobs-seekers. An examination of the job search methods of the jobless youth indicates that asking friends and relatives is the most common method. Notably, the youth have tended to rely increasingly on the İŞKUR for finding employment in the recent years. Lastly, even when the youth do get a job, the quality of their jobs as measured by the formality status are questionable. The youth are more than twice as likely to be in temporary and informal employment than adults. In sum, these findings highlight a couple of key issues. First, the global recession undoubtedly exacerbated the labor market conditions of the youth. As such, strong economic growth is vital for creating jobs for the youth. Second, gender differences in access to employment, and the lack of skills and qualifications emerge as important aspects of the youth labor market. As far as policymaking is concerned, education policies play a key role in ensuring that the youth leave education with skills and qualifications valued in the labor market. Accordingly, action must be taken to provide timely and well-designed training and job assistance programs for facilitating the youth's entry into stable employment.

REFERENCES

Almeida, R., Ridao-Cano, C., Levent, A., & McKenzie, D. (2011). *İŞKUR vocational trainees: Profile, job-search behavior and expectations. Baseline report*. Washington, DC: World Bank.

Baggio, S., Iglesias, K., Deline, S., Studer, J., Henchoz, Y., Mohler-Kuo, M., & Gmel, G. (2015). Not in education, employment, or training status among young Swiss men. Longitudinal associations with mental health and substance use. *The Journal of Adolescent Health*, *56*(2), 238–243. doi:10.1016/j.jadohealth.2014.09.006 PMID:25620308

Baltagi, B., Baskaya, Y. S., & Hulagu, T. (2013). How different are the wage curves for formal and informal workers? Evidence from Turkey. *Papers in Regional Science*, *92*(2), 271–283. doi:10.1111/j.1435-5957.2012.00478.x

Baskaya, Y. S., & Hulagu, T. (2011). *Informal-formal worker wage gap in Turkey: Evidence from a semi-parametric approach* (Central Bank of Turkey Working Paper 11/15). Retrieved from http://www.tcmb.gov.tr/wps/wcm/connect/TCMB+EN/TCMB+EN/Main+Menu/PUBLICATIONS/Research/Working+Paperss/2011/11-15

Bayraktar, S., & İncekara, A. (2013). Tükiye'nin genç işsizlik profili. *Çalışma İlişkileri Dergisi*, *4*(1), 15-38.

Bell, D. N. F., & Blanchflower, D. G. (2010). *Youth unemployment: Déjà vu?* (IZA Discussion Paper No. 4075). Retrieved from http://ftp.iza.org/dp4705.pdf

Benjet, C., Hernández-Motoya, D., Borges, G., Méndez, E., Medina-Mora, M. E., & Aguilar-Gaxiola, S. (2012). Youth who neither study nor work: Mental health, education and employment. *Salud Pública de México*, *54*(4), 410–417. doi:10.1590/S0036-36342012000400011 PMID:22832833

Bentolila, S., Boeri, T., & Cahuc, P. (2010). *Ending the scourge of dual labour markets in Europe*. VoxEU.org.

Bloom, D. E., Canning, D., & Fink, G. (2011). *Implications of population aging for economic growth* (NBER Working Paper No. 16705). Retrieved from http://www.nber.org/papers/w16705

Bäckman, O., & Nilsson, A. (2016). Long-term consequences of being not in employment, education or training as a young adult. Stability and change in three Swedish birth cohorts. *European Societies*, *18*(2), 136–157. doi:10.1080/14616696.2016.1153699

Bynner, J., & Parsons, S. (2002). Social exclusion and the transition from school to work: The case of young people not in employment, education or training (NEET). *Journal of Vocational Behavior*, *60*, 289–309. doi:10.1006/jvbe.2001.1868

Cahuc, P., Carcillo, S., Rinne, U., & Zimmermann, K. F. (2013). *Youth unemployment in old Europe: The polar cases of France and Germany* (IZA Discussion Paper No. 7490). Retrieved from http://ftp.iza.org/dp7490.pdf

Caliendo, M., & Schmidl, R. (2016). Youth unemployment and active labor market policies in Europe. *IZA Journal of Labor Policy*, *5*(1), 1. doi:10.1186/s40173-016-0057-x

Card, D., Kluve, J., & Weber, A. (2010). Active labour market policy evaluation: A meta- analysis. *The Economic Journal*, *120*(548), 452–477. doi:10.1111/j.1468-0297.2010.02387.x

Cho, Y., & Newhouse, D. (2012). How did the Great Recession affect different types of workers? Evidence from 17 middle-income countries. *World Development*, *41*, 31–50. doi:10.1016/j.worlddev.2012.06.003

Choudry, M. T., Marelli, E., & Signorelli, M. (2012). Youth unemployment rate and impact of financial crises. *International Journal of Manpower*, *33*(1), 76–95. doi:10.1108/01437721211212538

Clark, A., Knabe, A., & Ratzel, S. (2011). Boon or bane? Others unemployment, well-being and job insecurity. *Labour Economics, 17*(1), 52–61. doi:10.1016/j.labeco.2009.05.007

Clark, A. E., & Oswald, A. (1994). Unhappiness and unemployment. *The Economic Journal, 104*(424), 648–659. doi:10.2307/2234639

Çondur, F., & Bölükbaş, M. (2014). Türkiye'de işgücü piyasası ve genç işsizlik büyüme ilişkisi üzerine bir inceleme. *Amme Idaresi Dergisi, 47*(2), 77–93.

Dietrich, H., & Moller, J. (2016). Youth unemployment in Europe – business cycle and institutional effects. *International Economics & Economic Policy, 13*(1), 5–15. doi:10.1007/s10368-015-0331-1

El Badaoui, E., Strobl, E., & Walsh, F. (2008). Is there an informal employment wage penalty? Evidence from South Africa. *Economic Development and Cultural Change, 56*(3), 683–710. doi:10.1086/533550

Eurofound. (2012). *NEETs – Young people not in employment, education or training: Characteristics, costs and policy responses in Europe*. Luxembourg: Publications Office of the European Union.

Fields, G. (1975). Rural-urban migration, urban unemployment and underemployment, and job search activity in LDCs. *Journal of Development Economics, 2*(2), 165–187. doi:10.1016/0304-3878(75)90014-0 PMID:12265914

Fougere, D., Kramarz, F., & Pouget, J. (2009). Youth unemployment and crime in France. *Journal of the European Economic Association, 7*(5), 909–938. doi:10.1162/JEEA.2009.7.5.909

Furlong, A. (2006). Not a very NEET solution: Representing problematic labour market transitions among early school-leavers. *Work, Employment and Society, 20*(3), 553–569. doi:10.1177/0950017006067001

Gong, X., & Van Soest, A. (2002). Wage differentials and mobility in the urban labour market: A panel data analysis for Mexico. *Labour Economics, 9*(4), 513–529. doi:10.1016/S0927-5371(02)00045-3

Gregg, P., & Tominey, E. (2005). The wage scar from male youth unemployment. *Labour Economics, 12*(4), 487–509. doi:10.1016/j.labeco.2005.05.004

Hoşgör, S., & Tansel, A. (2010). *2050'ye doğru nüfusbilim ve yönetim: Eğitim, işgücü, sağlık ve sosyal güvenlik sistemine yansımalar (Yayın No: TUSIAD-T/2010/11/505)*. İstanbul: Türkiye Sanayicileri ve İşadamları Derneği ve Birleşmiş Milletler Nüfus Fonu.

İçduygu, A. (2012). Demography and immigration/emigration. In M. Heper & S. Sayarı (Eds.), *The Routledge handbook of modern Turkey* (pp. 328–338). London: Routledge.

International Labour Office. (2011). *Global employment trends for youth: 2011 update*. Geneva: ILO.

International Labour Office. (2015). *World employment and social outlook: Trends 2015*. Geneva: ILO.

Kabaklarlı, E., Er, P. H., & Buluş, A. (2011). *Economic determinants of Turkish youth unemployment problem: Co integration analysis*. Retrieved from http://kastoria.teikoz.gr/icoae2/wordpress/wp-content/uploads/2011/10/028.pdf

Kluve, J. (2010). The effectiveness of European active labor market programs. *Labour Economics, 17*(6), 904–918. doi:10.1016/j.labeco.2010.02.004

Knabe, A., & Rätzel, S. (2011). Scarring or scaring? The psychological impact of past unemployment and future unemployment risk. *Economica, 78*(310), 283–293. doi:10.1111/j.1468-0335.2009.00816.x

Lindbeck, A., & Snower, D. J. (2001). Insiders versus outsiders. *The Journal of Economic Perspectives, 15*(1), 165–188. doi:10.1257/jep.15.1.165

Murat, S., & Şahin, L. (2011). Gençlerin istihdamı/işsizliği bakımından Türk eğitim sisteminin değerlendirilmesi. *Çalışma ve Toplum, 3*, 93-135.

O'Higgins, N. (2015). *Youth unemployment* (IZA Policy Paper No.103). Retrieved from http://ftp.iza.org/pp103.pdf

Oren, K., & Şahverdioğlu, H. (2016). Turkiye'de genç işsizliği ve genç işsizliğinin giderilmesinde aktif istihdam politikaları. *Gençlik Araştırmaları Dergisi, 5*(1), 5–37.

Organisation for Economic Co-operation and Development. (2008). Declaring work or staying underground: Informal employment in seven OECD countries. In *OECD employment outlook 2008*. OECD Publishing.

Organisation for Economic Co-operation and Development. (2009). *OECD Employment Outlook 2009: Tackling the jobs crisis*. Paris: OECD Publishing. doi:10.1787/empl_outlook-2009-en

Organisation for Economic Co-operation and Development. (2010). *OECD Employment Outlook 2010: Moving beyond the jobs crisis*. Paris: OECD Publishing. doi:10.1787/empl_outlook-2010-en

Organisation for Economic Co-operation and Development. (2014). Promoting better labor market outcomes for the youth. Report on youth employment and apprenticeships prepared for the G20 Labour and Employment Ministerial Meeting, Melbourne, Australia.

Organisation for Economic Co-operation and Development. (2016). *Population with tertiary education* (indicator). doi: 10.1787/0b8f90e9-en

Pages, C., & Stampini, M. (2009). No education, no good jobs? Evidence on the relationship between education and labor market segmentation. *Journal of Comparative Economics, 37*(3), 387–401. doi:10.1016/j.jce.2009.05.002

Sadler, K., Akister, J., & Burch, S. (2014). Who are the young people who are not in education, employment or training? An application of the risk factors to a rural area in the UK. *International Journal of Social Work, 58*(4), 508–520. doi:10.1177/0020872813515010

Sayın, F. (2011). Türkiye'de 1988-2010 döneminde eğitim ve büyümenin genç işsizliğine etkisinin analizi. *Dokuz Eylül Üniversitesi Sosyal Bilimler Enstütüsü Dergisi, 13*(4), 33–53.

Tansel, A. (1999). *Formal versus informal sector choice of wage earners and their wages in Turkey* (Economic Research Forum Working Paper no. 9927). Retrieved from http://papers.ssrn.com/sol3/papers.cfm?abstract_id=263469

Tansel, A., & Kan, E. O. (2012). *Labor mobility across the formal/informal divide in Turkey: Evidence from individual level data* (IZA Discussion Paper No.6271). Retrieved from http://ftp.iza.org/dp6271.pdf

Tasci, M., & Zenker, M. (2011). *Labor market rigidity, unemployment, and the Great Recession.* Federal Reserve Bank of Cleveland, Economic Commentary.

Tumen, S. (2015). Skill acquisition in the informal economy and schooling decisions: Evidence from emerging economies. *Labour, 29*(3), 270–290. doi:10.1111/labr.12059

Turkish Statistical Institute. (2014). Youth in statistics (Istatistiklerle Gençlik), 2013. Haber Bülteni, No.16055, Ankara.

Turkish Statistical Institute. (2015). *Youth in statistics (Istatistiklerle Gençlik), 2014.* Retrieved from http://www.tuik.gov.tr/Kitap.do?metod=KitapDetay&KT_ID=11&KITAP_ID=251

Turkish Statistical Institute. (2016). Youth in statistics (Istatistiklerle Gençlik), 2015. Haber Bülteni, No.21517, Ankara.

United Nations, Department of Economic and Social Affairs, Population Division. (2013). *World population aging 2013* (ST/ESA/SER.A/348).

Verick, S. (2009). *Who is hit hardest during a financial crisis? The vulnerability of young men and women to unemployment in an economic downturn* (IZA Discussion Paper No.4359). Retrieved from http://ftp.iza.org/dp4359.pdf

Winkelmann, L., & Winkelmann, R. (1998). Why are the unemployed so unhappy? Evidence from panel data. *Economica, 65*(257), 1–15. doi:10.1111/1468-0335.00111

World Bank. (2013). *Final report.* Washington, DC: World Bank Group. Retrieved from http://documents.worldbank.org/curated/en/2013/08/19151577/turkey-evaluating-impact-İŞKURs-vocational-training-programs-vol-1-2-final-report

Yates, S., & Payne, M. (2006). Not a very NEET solution: Representing problematic labour market transitions among early school-leavers. *Journal of Youth Studies, 20*(3), 553–569.

KEY TERMS AND DEFINITIONS

Active Labor Market Policies: Government programs with the intention of helping the unemployed find jobs or increasing the earnings capacity of those already employed.

Household Labor Force Survey: A national survey administered to households with the aim of collecting information to be used in official labor force statistics.

Informal Employment: Jobs that are not, in law or in practice, in compliance with national labor legislation due to several reasons.

Labor Force: The sum of employed and unemployed individuals in a given labor market.

Labor Force Participation Rate: The labor force as a percent of the non-institutional population.

Labor Market: The market that consists of labor supply, labor demand, and all aspects of the employment relationships.

Not in Education, Employment or Training: A concept, also known as NEET, that measures the inactivity of the youth. The number of individuals in the NEET group as a percentage of the 15-24-year-old population is called the NEET rate.

Youth Unemployment: A concept refers to the unemployment of individuals aged 15-24.

ENDNOTES

1 It has been documented that events of social unrest have been more frequent in areas with higher male youth unemployment levels (ILO, 2015).

2 See Hoşgör and Tansel (2010) and İçduygu (2012) for a more in-depth discussion of Turkey's demographic transition.

3 To ensure full compliance with the European Union, in February 2014 Turkish Statistical Institute (TURKSTAT) revised the reference period for job search as four weeks instead of "last three months". This change eliminates comparability with the previous surveys. For details, see http://www.turkstat.gov.tr/MicroVeri/Hia_2014/english/downloads/explanations.pdf

4 Data from the ILO database indicate that as of 2015 there are about 1.2 billion youth which amount to about 16.2 percent of the total world population.

5 Economic theory predicts that more rigid labor markets have lower unemployment rates and lower worker turnover as stricter labor market policies create a disincentive for firings and hirings. A number of papers document that differences in the labor market institutions explain the varying outcomes of the labor markets in response to shocks to the GDP (Dietrich & Moller, 2016; Tasci & Zenker, 2011).

6 The dual apprenticeship system in Germany is one of the factors behind the resilience of youth unemployment to the global recession (Cahuc, Carcillo, Rinne, & Zimmermann, 2013).

7 The economic consequences of aging due to declining working age populations and soaring older population are well-documented (Bloom, Canning, & Fink, 2011; United Nations, Department of Economic and Social Affairs, Population Division, 2013).

8 This is consistent with the increase in the share of the 25-34-year-olds with a tertiary degree from 12.7 percent to 24.8 percent between 2000 and 2014 in Turkey (OECD, 2016).

9 According to Fields (1975), the labor market is segmented along formal-informal sectors. In this framework, the desirability of the jobs only depends on wages, and hence formal sector jobs that come with higher wages are superior to informal ones. Since the number of jobs in the formal sector is limited, those workers who cannot find employment in the formal sector and who cannot afford to search work in the informal sector.

10 Pages and Stampini (2009) and Tansel and Kan (2012) find evidence in mobility patterns that suggests a preference for formal jobs over informal jobs.

11 A large number of studies examine the effectiveness ALMPs. Some examples are Caliendo & Schmidl (2016); Card, Kluve, & Weber (2010); Kluve (2010).

12 For an analysis of İŞKUR's vocational training programs, see Oren and Şahverdioğlu (2016).

Chapter 11
Considerations on the Youth Unemployment Problem in Turkey

Füsun Yenilmez
Eskişehir Osmangazi University, Turkey

Yahya Can Dura
Ministry of Interior, Turkey

Yavuz Hürol Karabilgin
Turkish Revenue Administration, Turkey

ABSTRACT

This paper, aims to analyze and profile youth unemployment problem in the Turkish economy and contains three parts: "Conceptual Framework of Unemployment", "Unemployment Problem in Turkey" and "Youth Unemployment Phenomenon and Youth Unemployment Profile in Turkey", as well as trend analysis over a long time series (1988-2016) created by using TURKSTAT, OECD and World Bank databases. It also analysis youth unemployment problem by evaluating quantitative indicators and their trend data and tries to make recommendations on strategies and policies essential to the solution of the problem.

INTRODUCTION

Unemployment is a major dilemma for the global capitalist economies. In a capitalist economy, all of the production factors constitute the capital of society and labor is considered as a commodity that can be bought and sold in the market. This situation, as a by-product of the liberation of people, is entirely capitalism-specific and created by the lack of means of production.

It is tough to consider this issue from a labor perspective because capital and entrepreneur are major factors, or in other words, focal points of production procedure and distribution affairs. In this regard, we believe that it is necessary to consider the dynamics of distribution affairs while analyzing unemployment problem and the measures that should be taken against it.

DOI: 10.4018/978-1-5225-2008-5.ch011

As a matter of fact, it is not possible to see unemployment as a problem created only by mechanical and objective procedures outside distribution affairs. This problem also requires a class-based analysis and might as well be a case that is fed, supported and ignored by dynamics of profit and accumulation procedures of the capital section. With all these aspects, it is necessary to see unemployment problem as a concept with multi-directions and factors and create strategic and political measures accordingly.

This paper, aims to analyze and profile youth unemployment problem in the Turkish economy and contains three parts: "Conceptual Framework of Unemployment", "Unemployment Problem in Turkey" and "Youth Unemployment Profile in Turkey", as well as trend analysis over a long time series (1988-2016) created by using TURKSTAT, OECD and World Bank databases. It also analyzes youth unemployment problem by evaluating quantitative indicators and their trend data and tries to make recommendations on strategies and policies essential to the solution of the problem.

CONCEPTUAL FRAMEWORK OF UNEMPLOYMENT

We can say that unemployment as a concept can acquire a different character depending on the changes in time and place. The definition of unemployment, which was defined as a state of having no job as a result of the absence of skills in the past highlights personal fault (Bayraktar & İncekara, 2013). This primitive definition of unemployment has evolved into an international standard definition made by ILO, and this new definition is based on three criteria. With the presence of the three criteria: demand, availability and state of being unemployed simultaneously, we can describe a person as unemployed.

Unemployment which is the state of failing to use labor power in manufacturing procedures with desired levels and presence of unemployed job demanding people leads to loss of economic effectiveness on the one hand and the emergence of social problems on the other (Kesici, 2010).

In spite of all economic and socio-politic measures, unemployment which is increasing its effects gradually is the individual and social reality that has a negative impact on economies. We can say that unemployment is a society-centered concept and means wasted human capacities of societies.

Unemployment is a failure by labor factor to participate in production and is a fact created by people who cannot find a job opportunity over the current wage level despite supplying their labor power (Bayraktar & İncekara, 2013). Therefore unemployment is not a problem that can be analyzed outside the distribution affairs and requires class-based analysis. It can also be considered as a topic that is directly affected and ignored by the dynamics of profit and accumulation procedures of production sections.

According to Turkish Statistical Institute:

Out of the unemployed people within the reference term (people who have not worked with/without salary or daily wage or a profit sharing scheme and have no connection with such a job), those who have used at least one of the job seeking channels in the last three months and are available to start working in 15 days are included in the unemployed population on condition that they are in non-corporate working age. (www.tuik.gov.tr)

According to Turkish Employment Agency*:*

They are the people under active register who are in working age and power and willing to work and have no job with an income at the minimum wage level at the time of applying to the Agency. When people who seek better working conditions and who are willing to work at a specific establishment are subtracted from registered workforce, remaining ones are considered as the registered unemployed population. (Sürücü, 2014)

The European Union considers the definition of unemployment from a different perspective and calculates unemployment over the workforce registered at workforce offices; unemployment is defined as "those who have no job at all and ready to switch to another job out of the people who are registered at workforce offices… or worker aid offices" (Sürücü, 2014).

Finally, EUROSTAT and OECD defines unemployment as "unemployed people between 15-24 ages who are available to start working in two weeks and actively searched a job in the past four weeks".

It is possible to make different definitions of unemployment depending on different motives, reasons, and conditions. Therefore we believe that it is important to introduce summaries of basic definitions and concepts related to unemployment. We will first focus on basic concepts of unemployment, and then we will introduce different unemployment types and their definitions.

The share of people who are willing to work in the non-corporate civil population which can also be described as people with and without a job and people who are not included in the workforce is called 'labor force participation share'. The total population of people with and without a job is defined as 'workforce supply' in an economy. The share of unemployed people in the workforce supply gives us 'unemployment'. The share of working people to non-corporate civil population defines 'employment level'.

Unemployment can be classified depending on some of its demographic features and geographical distribution, profession, time and its reasons.

The kind of unemployment created by employed people who have zero or negative contribution to the total production is called 'hidden employment'. Unemployment created by people who are included in the workforce supply but remain unemployed after having searched a job for four weeks is called 'open unemployment'. Open unemployment basically defines current unemployment and has three types which are 'frictional, structural and cyclical unemployment'. The concept 'frictional unemployment' defines those who have recently entered the workforce and the interim period of unemployment status created until finding a new job by people who are in the process of changing their job. Frictional unemployment reflects a short-term condition, and it becomes structural unemployment if it takes a long period of time. Cyclical unemployment happens when there is a recession in the economy. Finally, it will be helpful to make an explanation about the concept of 'natural unemployment'. Obviously, full employment of production factors is not possible to realize without an external intervention to the markets. It is not possible to eliminate unemployment entirely either. In this context, there is an acceptable unemployment rate for all economies. This rate is called natural unemployment rate, and it equals to the total of frictional and structural unemployment.

It is necessary to carefully analyze this issue by its different features, definitions, and classifications and enrich the concept by creating enough data in order to consider unemployment problem as a research area. We can't ignore the fact that unemployment problem is twofold; it can have a deep impact on structures as a social reality, and as a social and economic fact. We can't make solely numeric analysis; we can't forget that this fact is a reality occurring in the individual's, families' and society's lives and that it concerns people's entire life, relations, and essence. Therefore unemployment should not only be analyzed in economic terms, but also as a multi-directional issue related to social policies, education, health, safety and many different disciplines.

UNEMPLOYMENT PROBLEM IN TURKEY

Rapid increase in population, immigration, and workforce flow from rural areas to cities increases the unemployment problem and regional imbalances in Turkey. Low investment level that leads to difficulties in creating new job opportunities are the important problem areas associated with Turkish economy's job creation capacity (Uyar Bozdağlıoğlu, 2008).

In relation to the nature of unemployment problem, the fact that labor force market is expanding with increases in population causes the problem to increase while the existing unemployment problem is a continuing fact (Eser Yılmaz & Terzi, 2008). Urbanization problems, instability, quality incompatibility between workforce supply and demand, insufficiency in support mechanisms for employment creating entrepreneurs are among the factors that make unemployment problem in Turkey more complicated (Özdemir, Ersöz, & Sarıoğlu, 2006).

When we examine unemployment parameters in Turkey from a sector-specific standpoint, we see that non-agricultural sectors have the highest share. Immigration and workforce flow from rural areas to cities are the major reasons for this distribution. High labor supply caused by excessive workforce flow to cities leads to increase in the non-agricultural unemployment rate when there are not enough levels of investment in industry and services sectors, and growth rate is insufficient.

While analyzing unemployment problem in Turkey, we should also define this issue's relations with growth dynamics. In theory, it is widely accepted that there is a negative relationship between growth and unemployment rates, in other words, growth increases employment capacity and reduces the unemployment problem. But sources and character of growth determine the intensity of this relationship. Growth may have occurred in labor-intensive or capital-intensive sectors, or it may depend on domestic-foreign markets. Its source may be high-tech development and research and development investments. Every kind of growth may not provide an employment-friendly growth environment (Eser Yılmaz & Terzi, 2008).

Growth parameters and employment potential in the Turkish economy have always had a fluctuating trend under the effects of the economic and financial crisis. Although it has achieved high growth rates in the post-crisis terms, it has not led to increase in employment opportunities because of sources of growth and internal features of its dynamics, the fragile economy, and perception of stability. Thus unemployment rates increased contrary to the positive growth trend in Turkey between the years 1988 and 2016.

Instabilities in economic structure leading to unstable-fluctuating growth environment heavily affect investment decisions of high scale producers, and they start acting more cautiously. Eventually, a permanent workforce employment can't be created (Eser Yılmaz & Terzi, 2008).

When we show the trends in 1988-2015 term GDP growth rates and unemployment rates in the same chart (Figure 2), we find some interesting results. Keeping in mind that it is necessary to make more reliable and precise econometric analysis on these parameters in terms of the relation's direction, we can say that excessively fluctuating economic growth reality caused by economic and fiscal crisis in the last 35 years of Turkish economy seems to have had an increasing effect on unemployment rates all through the term. Another result we found by this analysis made over annual data is that increase in employment achieved during positive growth does not occur with the same intensity.

As it can be seen in Figure 2, 1993-2002 real GDP growth rate from the beginning to the end of the term is 3.1%. Same rates for the 2003-2014 term is 65.2% and 4.8% respectively. However, increases in employment rates are considerably lower in the same terms; unemployment rates increases up to 10% level with the increase in the population. We can describe the term after 2000 in the Turkish economy as "a growth term with weak employment effect".

Figure 1. Trends in unemployment rate % (1988-2016)
Source: Produced by the author using the TURKSTAT data.

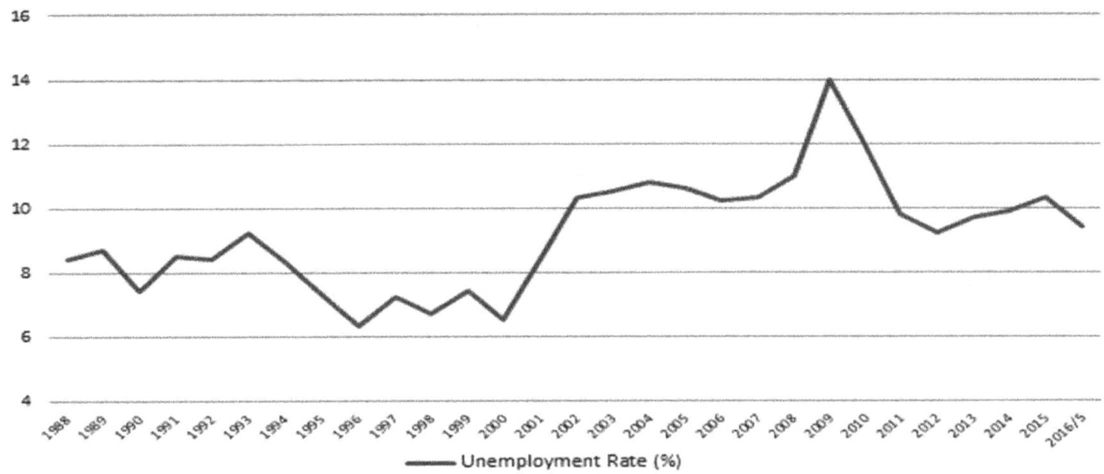

Figure 2. Comparison of unemployment and economic growth trends % (1989-2015)
Source: Produced by the author using the TURKSTAT data.

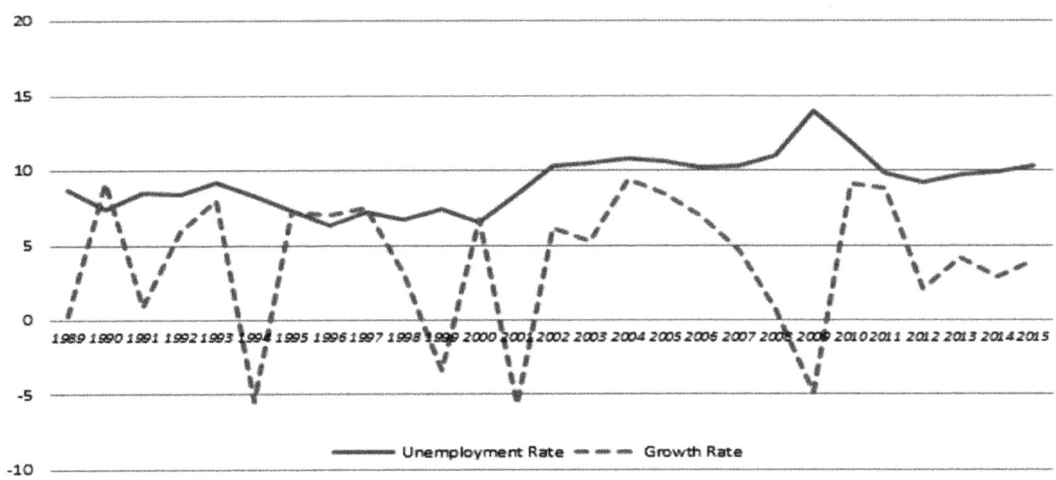

A large number of empirical studies have been made to find the direction of the relationship between growth and unemployment. Göktaş Yılmaz (2005) used Granger causality test and final prediction error and tried to find out the direction of the relationship between growth and unemployment rates in Turkey between the years 1978-2004. The author reached the conclusion that there is no reciprocal causality relationship between growth and unemployment rates. In other words, high or low growth rates have no effect on unemployment (Eser Yılmaz & Terzi, 2008). This result is consistent with trends in growth and unemployment rates for the 1989-2015 term as shown in Figure 2.

The work of Takım (2015) tested the relationship between economic growth and unemployment in Turkey using the data of the 1975-2008 term and Granger causality analysis and found out that they both are reciprocally interacting variables. However, he also expresses that the probability that economic growth will increase employment is lower than the probability that economic shrinkage will reduce employment. Ceylan and Şahin (2010) applied Okun Law, which focuses on the theory that there is a negative relation between real growth rates and the unemployment rate for the 1950-2007 term and found that Okun's coefficient (relation) is unsymmetrical. Consequently, it is shown that real output, reducing the effect of growth on unemployment in expansion times is not the same with its increasing effect in shrinking terms. Şentürk and Akbaş (2014) analyzed the relation between unemployment-inflation and economic growth by using monthly data for the 2005-2012 period. They found that increase in industrial production depends on an increase in capacity utilization rate and technological development and that increase in capacity utilization rate increases workforce demand and unemployment rate decreases. This study found that there is bidirectional causality relationship between industrial production index, inflation rate, and unemployment rate. Çondur and Bölükbaş (2014) analyzed the econometric relationship between youth unemployment and economic growth and by using the quarterly data of the 2000-2014 term, and they determined that there is causality relationship between GDP and youth unemployment. The direction of the relation is from GDP to youth unemployment. In other words, change in growth affects youth unemployment.

It is seen that increases in growth in the Turkish economy do not affect unemployment in the same direction because of some reasons such as effects of the crisis, the reality of a fragile economic structure and lack of a stable environment. Some problem areas in labor markets such as high workforce costs, strict workforce regulations, long working hours, qualifications of human capital and demographic features still exist and have a negative impact on employment opportunities. Unemployment in Turkey which is a widely spread social problem for women and for those who have a low level of education is growing exponentially within the young population between the ages of 15-24. Therefore we believe that youth unemployment fact should be analyzed comprehensively in terms of structural features of workforce markets in Turkey.

YOUTH UNEMPLOYMENT PHENOMENON AND YOUTH UNEMPLOYMENT PROFILE OF TURKEY

In literature, youth unemployment phenomenon is analyzed in terms of its impacts and determinants.

Youth unemployment rate is generally much higher than the adult unemployment rate. What is the reason for this? Employers prefer adult people to young since poor youth labor market performance is related to the low level of human capital (Choudhry, Marelli & Signorelli, 2010).

Youth unemployment has important roles in maintaining investments in education. If people increase their investment in education, two different effects can occur: - Unemployment opportunity cost can decline; - Youth unemployment may have a positive impact on the rate of return to education (Kabaklarlı, Er, & Buluş, 2011).

The job seekers' skills don't match the demands of employers, the educational system in terms of vocational and technical education must be transformed to provide youth unemployed people with relevant skills to adapt to the labor market. Investment in training institutions, which have a functional link with the labour market, is crucial and must be increased. (Kabaklarlı et al., 2011)

Economic activity and productivity are important variables in determining youth unemployment. Economic crises, demographic conditions, and individual characteristics have a negative impact on youth unemployment rates.

Youth unemployment leads to significant social and economic problems: low self-esteem, dependence on family, increasing crime rates, poor social adaptation, and domestic violence. There are also many psychological symptoms (depression and loss of confidence, etc.) caused by youth unemployment (Kabaklarlı et al., 2011).

We know that young people's marginal propensity to consume is higher than adult people. Fort this reason, consumption, investment, and GDP are affected by young unemployment (Kabaklarlı et al., 2011).

Major reasons of employment in Turkey are heavily related to a rapid increase in population. Therefore we can say that workforce supply in the workforce market is pretty high, but employment and labor participation rates are low. The labor market in Turkey is largely occupied by small size enterprises that have the highest share of unemployment and employment potential.

The question we should ask at this point is what the structural reasons are behind a labor market with such characteristics (Ministry of Finance Department of Strategic Development, 2011):

- Population growth rate,
- Youth population,
- Labor force participation rate of women,
- High rate of people that have no high school degree in the total workforce,
- Agriculture's high rate in employment,
- Informal economy,
- Low employment rate.

When we examine some selected population data in terms of age groups in Turkey for the term between 1980-2015 in Table 1, we see that the old population (65+) and the working population between

Table 1. The population parameters (1980-2015)

Year	Total Population	Population Growth Rate (‰)	Age Groups		
			0-14	15-64	65+
1980	44,736,957		39.0	55.9	4.7
1990	56,473,035		35.0	60.7	4.3
2000	67,803,927		29.8	64.5	5.7
2007	70,586,256	-	26.4	66.5	7.1
2008	71,517,100	13.2	26.3	66.9	6.8
2009	72,561,312	14.6	26.0	67.0	7.0
2010	73,722,988	16.0	25.6	67.2	7.2
2011	74,724,269	13.6	25.3	67.4	7.3
2012	75,627,384	12.1	24.9	67.6	7.5
2013	76,667,864	13.7	24.6	67.7	7.7
2014	77,695,904	13.4	24.3	67.8	8.0
2015	78,741,053	13.5	24.0	67.8	8.2

Source: Produced by the author using the TURKSTAT data.

ages 15-64 have an increasing, population between 0-14 ages has a declining trend. Although 15-64 age group's working-age population has as high as 68% share in total population, as it can be seen in Figure 3, parameter trends of 0-14 and 65+ age groups indicate that workforce supply in Turkey will start to decline in the following few decades.

When we analyze the term 1989-2016/5 in terms of labor participation rate which is defined as the share of workforce in non-corporate working age population, it can be seen in Table 2 that there was a stable downward trend from 1989 to 2004, but the trend turned the opposite direction in 2004-2016 term

Figure 3. Distribution of population trends as age groups (1980-2015)
Source: Produced by the author using the Table 1 data.

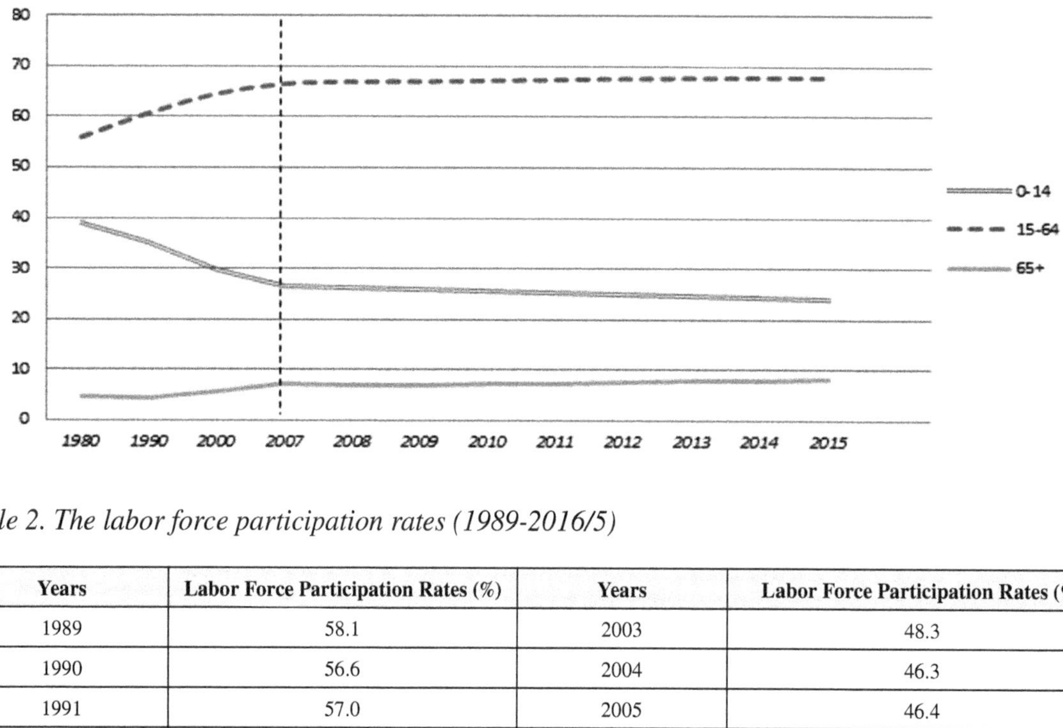

Table 2. The labor force participation rates (1989-2016/5)

Years	Labor Force Participation Rates (%)	Years	Labor Force Participation Rates (%)
1989	58.1	2003	48.3
1990	56.6	2004	46.3
1991	57.0	2005	46.4
1992	56.0	2006	46.3
1993	52.1	2007	46.2
1994	54.6	2008	46.9
1995	54.1	2009	47.9
1996	53.7	2010	48.8
1997	52.6	2011	49.9
1998	52.8	2012	50.0
1999	52.7	2013	50.8
2000	49.9	2014	50.5
2001	49.8	2015	51.3
2002	49.6	2016/5	52.5

Source: Produced by the author using the TURKSTAT dynamic querying data.

and labor participation rate has increased. In fact, we can say that the labor participation rate around 50% is still very low when compared with the OECD countries. However, labor participation rate of college-university degree holders between 15-24 ages has increased to 75% in the past ten years (Turkish Statistical Institute, n.d.).

Table 3 shows young population parameters in Turkey for the term 1988-2016/5. When we analyze workforce, employment, labor participation rates, unemployment and non-agricultural unemployment

Table 3. The young population parameters (1988-2016/5)

Year	Population (15-24) Thousand	Labor Force Thousand	Employment Thousand	Labor Force Participation Rates (%)	Unemployment Rate (%)	Non-Agriculture Unemployment Rate (%)	Employment (%)	Not Included in the Labor Force
1988	10,093	5,653	4,665	56.0	17.5	31.1	46.2	4,440
1989	10,221	5,658	4,686	55.4	17.2	29.0	45.8	4,563
1990	10,144	5,653	4,789	55.7	15.3	26.4	47.2	4,490
1991	11,394	6,200	5,147	54.4	17.0	30.5	45.2	5,194
1992	11,737	6,287	5,236	53.6	16.7	28.5	44.6	5,450
1993	11,945	5,826	4,764	48.8	18.2	29.9	39.9	6,119
1994	12,179	6,192	5,191	50.8	16.2	27.1	42.6	5,987
1995	12,391	6,137	5,198	49.5	15.3	23.5	41.9	6,254
1996	12,552	6,203	5,377	49.4	13.3	23.5	42.8	6,348
1997	12,649	5,958	5,052	47.1	15.2	23.1	39.9	6,691
1998	12,701	6,101	5,228	48.0	14.3	22.7	41.2	6,600
1999	12,701	5,728	4,868	45.1	15.0	22.6	38.3	6,974
2000	12,703	5,401	4,696	42.5	13.1	19.0	37.0	7,302
2001	12,641	5,323	4,460	42.1	16.2	24.4	35.3	7,318
2002	12,520	5,116	4,135	40.9	19.2	26.6	33.0	7,404
2003	12,379	4,753	3,777	38.4	20.5	26.0	30.5	7,626
2004	12,221	4,798	3,856	39.3	19.8	27.0	31.6	7,424
2005	11,840	4,474	3,554	37.8	20.6	26.6	30.0	7,366
2006	11,757	4,436	3,554	37.7	19.9	24.2	30.2	7,321
2007	11,670	4,365	3,533	37.4	19.1	22.5	30.3	7,305
2008	11,583	4,364	3,493	37.7	20.0	23.3	30.2	7,218
2009	11,490	4,381	3,484	38.1	20.5	24.2	30.3	7,109
2010	11,513	4,454	3,328	38.7	25.3	29.8	28.9	7,059
2011	11,548	4,426	3,465	38.3	21.7	25.9	30.0	7,122
2012	11,534	4,529	3,697	39.3	18.4	22.1	32.1	7,005
2013	11,574	4,422	3,647	38.2	17.5	20.9	31.5	7,152
2014	11,724	4,789	3,930	40.8	17.9	21.0	33.5	6,936
2015	11,800	4,958	4,039	42.0	18.5	21.4	34.2	6,843
2016/5	11,848	5,062	4,183	42.7	17.4	20.2	35.3	6,786

Source: Produced by the author using the TURKSTAT data.

rates of 15-24 age group within the scope of a 29-year time series, we can make the following quantitative arguments regarding Turkey's young population:

- Young population increased by 17% from the beginning to the end of the term. Average increase rate is 0.6%.
- Increase rates in the population which are not included in the workforce are higher than increase rates in the young population. The young population which is not included in the workforce increased by 53% from the beginning to the end of the term and the average increase rate is 1.6.
- When we examine the workforce data, we see a reduction around 10% from the beginning to the end of the term. Average increase rate is again negative: -0.31%.
- Employment parameters have similar features parallel to the trend in workforce data. There has been approximately 11% reduction from the beginning to the end of the term. Average increase rate is again negative: -0.26%.

Analysis we made so far regarding 1988-2016/5 term parameters for the population between 15-24 ages in Turkey give us the following results:

- Young population's participation rate in the workforce is declining; the population that is not included in the workforce is increasing.
- Considering the young population increase rate, the downward trend in employment parameters led to an increase in unemployment rates spontaneously.
- Employment falling from 46% level at the beginning of the term down to 35% level at the end shows that young population's employment problem in Turkey is deepening. In fact, this situation is directly related to the increase in the rate of higher education degree holders in the population between 15-24 ages.
- Another finding is that youth unemployment rates in non-agricultural sectors are higher when compared to total unemployment rates. But their proportional difference has dramatically reduced from the beginning to the end of the term. This trend can be explained by the force of employment opportunities created in non-agricultural sectors.

Figure 4 shows the percentage increase in young population in Turkey for the 1989-2016/5 term. Population growth rate had a downward trend between the years 1991 and 2005 while it had an upward trend between the years 2005 and2014. Growth rate had a downward trend in the recent term.

As it can be seen in Figure 5, the share of the young population in total population has decreased in the 2007-2015 term. From the beginning of the term until the end, there has been a reduction by 1.2%.

Making a thorough analysis of unemployment problem in the young population in Turkey depends on making a clear definition of young population's profile of educational level. Because measures against unemployment, efforts to create new job opportunities and training for employment may have different forms depending on young population's level of education.

Table 4 shows the distribution of young population by educational level in the 1988-2013 period. The data contained shows that there have been significant changes in the educational level of the young population from the beginning to the end of the term. The share of higher education degree holders in total young population is 1.4% in 1988 while it went up to almost 8% level in 2013. Rates of high school

Figure 4. The growth rate of young population % (1989-2016/5)
Source: Produced by the author using the Table 3 data.

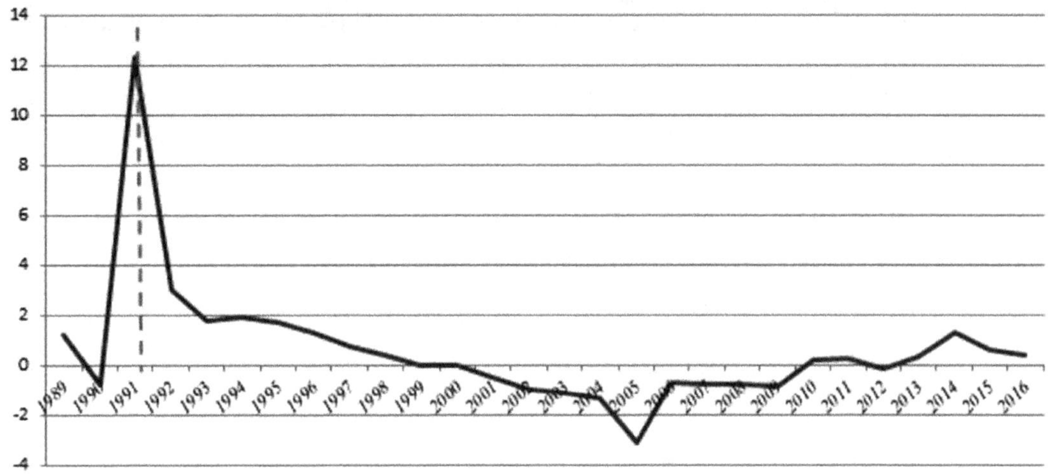

Figure 5. The share of young population in the total population % (2007-2015)
Source: Produced by the author using the Table 3 data.

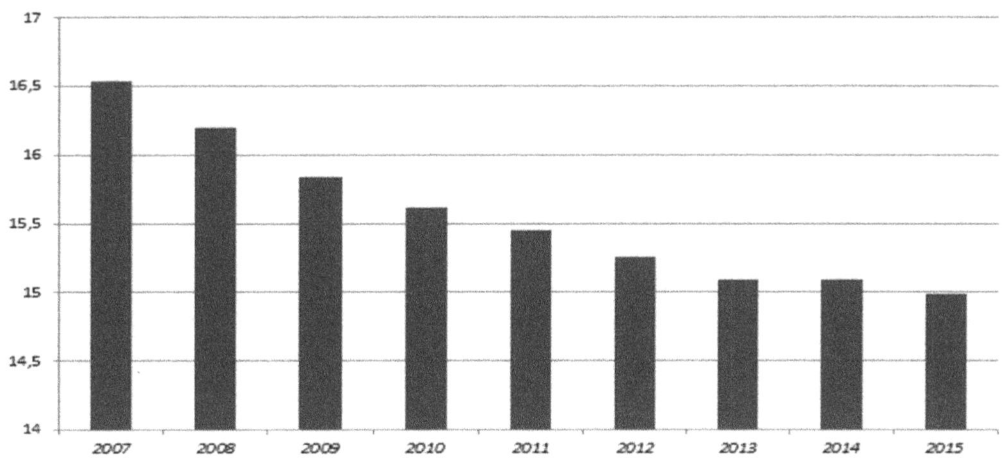

degree holders in the same years are 11% and 30% respectively. As it is seen in the figures in Figure 6, young population in Turkey has become educated exponentially in the last years.

The trend in unemployment rates of the age group of 15-24 in terms of their educational levels for the 1988-2013 period is shown in Table 5 within the scope of a long time series. It is seen that employment opportunities of educated young population have increased. As educational level decreases, employment opportunities also decrease and unemployment increases or decreases with a lower intense when compared to educated social groups.

Figure 7 shows unemployment rates of the young population holding a higher education degree and it is seen that there is a fluctuating downward trend between 1988-2013. This result shows that employment capacity of young population with higher education degree has increased and there has been a change in the quality of the workforce demanded.

Table 4. Educational background of 15-24 age groups population (1988-2013)

Year	Illiterate	Literate (Non-School Degree)	Primary School	Secondary School (and Equivalent Technical School)	High School	Technical School (Equivalent High School)	College-Faculty	Primary Education	Total
1988	887	357	5,597	1,814	999	290	148		10,093
1989	759	371	5,623	1,904	947	267	136		10,009
1990	724	275	5,787	1,935	965	299	131		10,117
1991	763	299	6,548	2,020	1,178	331	164		11,303
1992	724	302	6,432	2,296	1,355	366	178		11,653
1993	585	365	6,401	2,453	1,598	294	174		11,870
1994	568	233	6,488	2,514	1,766	368	181		12,118
1995	485	233	6,111	2,818	2,060	438	199		12,344
1996	472	167	6,101	2,814	2,222	533	207		12,516
1997	450	145	5,965	2,764	2,358	679	268		12,628
1998	433	164	5,700	2,932	2,555	592	316		12,691
1999	395	242	5,619	3,109	2,371	662	308		12,706
2000	522	335	5,375	2,453	2,421	802	371	424	12,703
2001	538	405	5,044	2,185	2,333	935	350	851	12,641
2002	435	420	4,548	2,091	2,401	1,110	396	1,119	12,520
2003	424	522	4,008	1,939	2,403	1,127	473	1,482	12,379
2004	500	654	3,058	1,404	2,399	975	439	2,411	11,840
2005	455	803	2,399	1,085	2,388	1,157	504	2,966	11,757
2006	441	910	1,965	968	2,341	1,186	523	3,337	11,670
2007	418	1,030	1,453	501	2,496	1,184	564	3,938	11,583
2008	406	1,047	1,102	270	2,323	1,142	611	4,589	11,490
2009	435	1,080	666	181	2,072	1,035	621	5,423	11,513
2010	398	1,110	258	78	2,040	967	701	5,996	11,548
2011	351	1,072	84	32	1,983	1,011	759	6,241	11,534
2012	306	986	17	1	1,920	1,120	848	6,377	11,574
2013	278	746	120	117	1,866	1,146	889	6,401	11,563

Source: Produced by the author using the TURKSTAT dynamic querying data.

The trend in youth unemployment rates in Turkey created using World Bank's data can be seen in Figure 8, and it shows that youth employment has a fluctuating but upward trend.

The data on the number and rates of youth unemployment in Turkey in the last 15 years in Table 6 shows that youth unemployment problem still exists. Employment rates of the 15-24 age group which is considered as the young population are higher when compared to 15+ age group unemployment rates.

When we analyze educational levels of young population's unemployment within the range of 15-24 and 20-24 ages, it is seen that rate of higher education degree holders is high within this group of unemployed people. Although unemployment rates of higher education degree holders within the young

Figure 6. Higher graduate young population in the total young population (%) (1988-2013)
Source: Produced by the author using the Table 4 data.

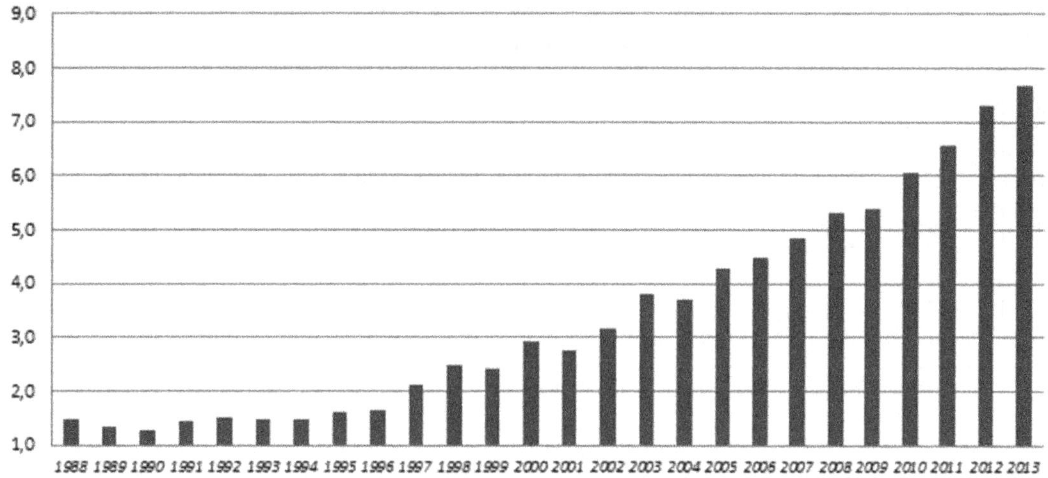

Figure 7. The trend of unemployment rate of higher graduate young population (%) (1988-2013)
Source: Produced by the author using the Table 5 data.

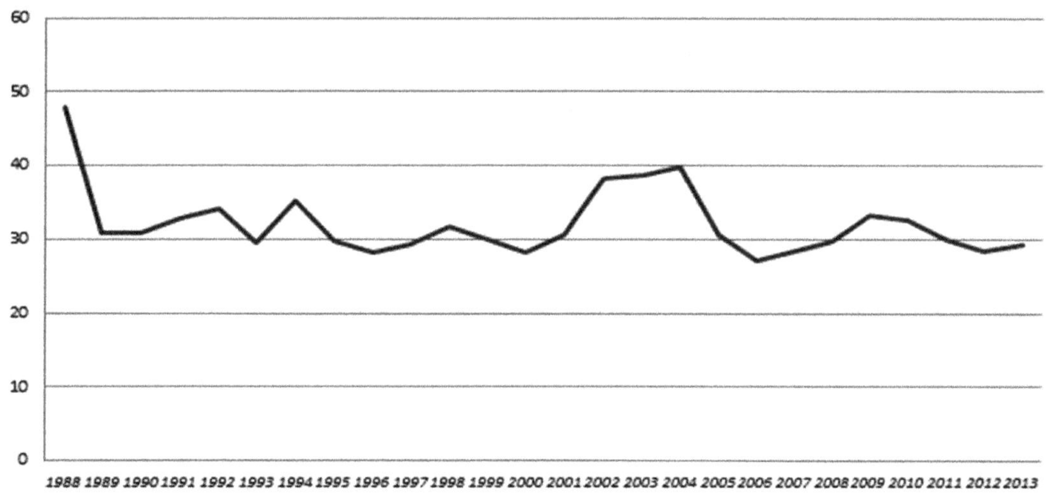

population have a downward trend, this result means that young people who have recently graduated from a university have problems with finding a job and it requires facilitation of procedures for transition from education to employment, developing policies through harmonization of education curriculum and applied education techniques with market requirements (Yentürk & Başlevent, 2007).

15-24 age group which is also considered as young workforce can be assembled into subgroups such as 15-24 and 20-24 age groups. Young workforce and unemployment figures of these groups in years 2014 and 2015 in Turkey are shown in Table 7. This data shows that 20-24 age group workforce and unemployment rates are higher than that of 15-19 age group. The difference between these two groups' unemployment rates is close to 3 points, and unemployment rates of 20-24 age group are 1 point higher than the average unemployment rates of the young population which represents the 15-24 age group.

Table 5. Unemployment rates of 15-24 age groups by education level % (1988-2013)

Year	Illiterate	Literate (Non-School Degree)	Primary School	Secondary School (and Equivalent Technical School)	High School	Technical School (Equivalent High School)	College-Faculty	Primary Education
1988	8.1	12	12.4	27.4	39.5	30.3	47.9	
1989	11.7	15.5	12.5	20.1	38.3	31.4	30.9	
1990	11.3	14.7	11.8	21.2	35.6	28.8	30.9	
1991	5.9	12.4	11.4	21.9	34.2	30.7	32.7	
1992	5	13.8	11.8	21.6	34.3	30.8	34.1	
1993	9.5	16.7	13.3	22.5	34	27.8	29.6	
1994	7.2	14.8	10.9	21.1	31.9	31	35.2	
1995	7.2	13.5	11	18.2	26.4	30.2	29.8	
1996	7.7	7.2	8.5	13.9	26.4	27.4	28.3	
1997	5.6	8.7	7.9	15.3	29.3	27.5	29.4	
1998	6.6	8.5	7.4	15.7	26.9	26	31.6	
1999	6.7	9.3	10	13.9	26.3	24.1	30	
2000	5	11	8.3	13.7	20.6	20.8	28.3	10.3
2001	8.7	14.4	10.6	17.7	24	25.5	30.7	9.6
2002	11.5	15.7	12.4	20.7	26.8	28	38.3	10.7
2003	18.1	30.2	15.3	19.7	25.9	23.8	38.8	11.4
2004	9.6	13	13.4	19.6	26.6	29.3	39.8	13.3
2005	11.3	16.3	14.1	19.2	25.3	25.6	30.5	14.5
2006	12.5	15.3	14.7	17.9	25.2	21.1	27.2	15.2
2007	16.7	17.3	14.7	19.3	23.5	22.6	28.5	16.8
2008	11	19.8	14.3	18.7	25	20.8	29.8	17.9
2009	19.5	23	17.9	21.6	30.6	27.6	33.2	22.4
2010	16.4	18.4	14.9	10.9	27.2	23.1	32.5	18.4
2011	11.2	15.1	11.2	14.1	22.4	21.2	30	14.5
2012	9	14.8	2.5	0	19.8	19.1	28.5	14.1
2013	10.3	15.5	10.9	15.1	21.9	18.6	29.2	15.5

Source: Produced by the author using the TURKSTAT data.

One of the main features of the labor market in Turkey is that youth unemployment rate is higher when compared to the adult unemployment rate. The main reason for 20-24 age group's unemployment rate being higher than 15-19 age group's unemployment rate is that this age group is heavily composed of university and college degree holders and this group differs from the other age groups in terms of experience, professional formation, and salary expectations.

We reach some significant results when we examine the figures of youth employment in terms of gender. It is seen in figures of 2015-2015 in Table 8 that young women's unemployment rates are significantly different from that of the male population. Youth employment rates among women are 4 points

Figure 8. The trend of young unemployment rate (15-24 years) (%) (1991-2015)
Source: Produced by the author using the World Bank database.

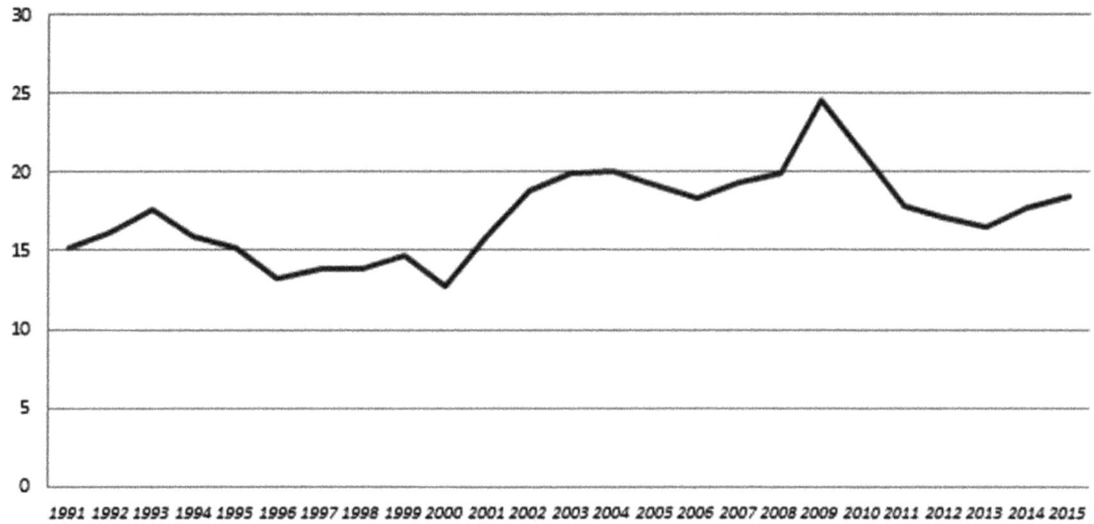

Table 6. The comparison of unemployment figures (15-24 and 15+ age groups) (2000-2015)

Year	Number of Young Unemployed (Thousand) 15-24	Number of Young Unemployed (Thousand) 15+	Unemployment Rate (%)	
			15-24	15+
2000	705	1,497	13.1	6.5
2001	862	1,967	16.2	8.4
2002	980	2,464	19.2	10.3
2003	975	2,493	20.5	10.5
2004	919	2,385	20.6	10.8
2005	881	2,388	19.9	10.6
2006	832	2,328	19.1	10.2
2007	871	2,377	20.0	10.3
2008	897	2,611	20.5	11.0
2009	1,126	3,471	25.3	14.0
2010	961	3,046	21.7	11.9
2011	832	2,615	18.4	9.8
2012	775	2,518	17.5	9.2
2013	857	2,747	18.7	10.1
2014	859	2,853	17.9	9.9
2015	919	3,057	18.5	10.3

Source: Produced by the author using the TURKSTAT data.

Figure 9. Trend of unemployment rates (15-24 and 15+ age groups) (2000-2015) (%)
Source: Produced by the author using the Table 6 data.

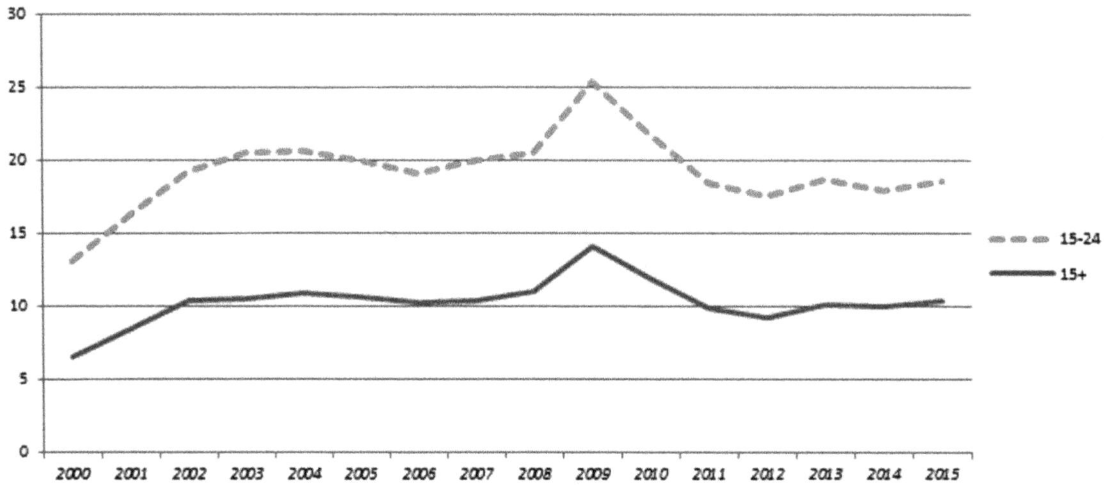

Table 7. Labor, unemployment figures, and rates (15-24 age groups) (2014-2015)

	Labor (Thousand)		Unemployed (Thousand)		Unemployment Rates (%)	
	2014	**2015**	**2014**	**2015**	**2014**	**2015**
15-24	4,789	4,958	859	919	17.9	18.5
15-19	1,741	1,784	281	294	16.1	16.5
20-24	3,048	3,173	578	625	18.9	19.7

Source: Produced by the author using the TURKSTAT dynamic querying data.

Table 8. Distribution of unemployment rates in terms of gender (2014-2015)

	Unemployment Rates (%)			
	2014		**2015**	
	Female	**Male**	**Female**	**Male**
15-24	20.4	16.6	22.2	16.5
15-19	16.1	16.2	18.4	15.6
20-24	22.5	16.9	24.1	17.1

Source: Produced by the author using the TURKSTAT dynamic querying data.

higher than young men's unemployment rates. We can also express that the number of unemployed women within 20-24 age group is higher than that of 15-19 age group.

OECD database displays some other significant figures on the rates of people who are not in education, employment or training (NEETs). Turkey has the last place among OECD countries in the NEET rate for women between 20-24 years old with 47.6%. 15-19 age group women's NEET rate is 24.4% and this figure is also significantly higher than that of men (Organisation for Economic Co-operation and Development, n.d.).

Sectorial conditions of employment are also among the issues that should be addressed while analyzing youth unemployment in Turkey. Considering that employment rates in the agricultural sector are high, it would be meaningful to consider non-agricultural unemployment rates in the analysis for Turkey. The adult unemployment rate in Turkey goes up to 12.7% from 10.3% in terms of non-agricultural unemployment as of 2015. The non-agricultural unemployment rate is 20.2% while it is 17.4% for young unemployment as of May 2016 (See Table 3). It is obvious that unemployment problem is largely seen in non-agricultural sectors. This fact is more visible in women's and youth unemployment figures.

Therefore it is of great importance to deploy economic and social policy measures collectively and create employment strategies for women and young population to fight against unemployment effectively (Yentürk & Başlevent, 2007).

In summary, Turkey's youth employment problem is 1-2 points higher than the average of OECD but lower that many European countries. It is a well-known fact that it is critically important for countries with growth and development goals to create new employment areas for the young workforce which is the dynamic part of the population and engage them in the production process. On the contrary, an increase in youth unemployment rates would soon become an important problem both for young individuals and society. Unemployment would lead to problems in individuals' mental health and societal adaptation and have negative effects on human capital-societal capital accumulation. Development and growth begin with individuals; the dynamic young population is practically the dynamo of economic growth. Therefore it is necessary to take and implement strategy and policy measures targeted at providing high employment opportunities, particularly for the young population.

At this point, we believe that it would be beneficial to analyze the results of "*Skills Matter: Further Results from the Survey of Adult Skills, Country Note Turkey*", an Adults' Skills Research published by the OECD (2016). The Research on Adult Skills (Programme for the International Assessment of Adult Competencies-PIAAC) evaluates skills of adults at/over the age of 16 in literacy, numeracy and problem solving in technology-rich environments. These skills include information processing capabilities that are important for adults to engage in workforce market, education and training, and social and civil life (OECD-PIAAC, 2016).

Findings of this research give us significant insight into the workforce profile and reasons for unemployment problem in Turkey and how this problem should be tackled. Some important findings gathered from "*Skills Matter: Further Results from the Survey of Adult Skills, Country Note Turkey, 2016*" report are as follows:

- *Adults in Turkey show below-average proficiency in literacy, numeracy, and problem-solving in technology-rich environments; a large proportion of these people have weak problem-solving skills in literacy, numeracy and problem solving in technology-rich environments. A small proportion of adults in Turkey has high literacy, numeracy, and problem-solving skills.*
- *Men in Turkey are more proficient than women in all of the three domains assessed – and the difference between the genders is one of the largest observed among all participating countries and economies.*
- *In Turkey, as in other participating countries and economies, adults with higher levels of education are more proficient in information-processing skills.*
- *Younger adults are the most proficient in literacy while older adults are the least proficient.*
- *Workers in Turkey use information-processing skills at work and in their daily lives much less than do workers in other countries.*

- *In Turkey, neither educational attainment nor literacy proficiency is associated with labor market status. But the impact of education on wages is among the strongest in all countries and economies examined.*
    - *In most participating countries/economies, adults who are more proficient in literacy, numeracy and problem solving in technology-rich environments are more likely to participate in the labor market and to be employed, and less likely to be unemployed, than adults who are less proficient, on average.*
    - *In Turkey, neither educational attainment nor proficiency is associated with employment status. Turkey's employment rate remains well below the OECD average, despite a rise from its pre-crisis level, while the unemployment rate remains well above the OECD average. However, the returns to education in Turkey are high: an increase of one standard deviation in years of schooling (around 3.4 years) is associated with a 20% increase in wages.*

The findings of the Research on Adult Skills published by the OECD in 2016 includes many significant aspects related to unemployment/youth unemployment problem in Turkey and strategies-policies to fight against this problem which are the main focuses of this study. First of all, it is seen that proficiency of adult population in literacy, numeracy, and problem-solving in technology-rich environments are considerably low. The report also shows that gender differences (in favor of men) are the highest when compared with other countries. Given the fact that world markets heavily rely on structural features based on competitive and advanced technologies, qualifications and profile of human capital of developing countries are critical for them to achieve high and stable growth trends. Considering its scores in the aforesaid report, Turkey must take prompt measures so as to increase competencies of human capital and eliminate gender differences.

Another interesting finding of the research is that educational level and literacy skills are not directly related to the employment market. But education's effect on salaries is the determining factor when compared to other countries. It is likely that this result is related to structural characteristics of the employment markets in Turkey. The tendency of the sectors with high employment creation capacity towards demanding a certain type of labor can lead to low expectations of competency in these sectors. In order to achieve high and stable growth rate, reduce unemployment rates and increase employment capacity in Turkey, "adults who are more proficient in literacy, numeracy and problem solving in technology-rich environments are more likely to participate in the labor market and to be employed…" finding of the research should be considered substantially.

In summary, it is necessary to evaluate unemployment problem in Turkey both by its labor supply and demand aspects and take measures accordingly. To smooth the school-to-work transition process, to prevent extended spells of unemployment or the complete withdrawal from the labor market, and to promote entry into stable employment relationships, policy makers in many countries resort to active labor market programs (ALMP). Prominent national initiatives include the "New Deal for Young People (NDYP)" in the UK, "Jugend mit Perspektive (JUMP)" in Germany and the "Youth Unemployment Program (YUP)" in Denmark. More recently, the "Youth Guarantee (YG)" adopted by the European Union in 2013 called all member states to set up ALMP programs to ensure that unemployed youth were offered high-quality employment or education opportunities within four months of entering unemployment (Caliendo & Schmidl, 2016).

Cahuc, Carcillo, Rinne and Zimmerman (2013) analyzed youth unemployment and how employment related structures in the EU and the United States responded to the Great Recession in 2008. The findings of their study show that the crisis had a deep impact both on the EU and US in terms of youth employment with the exception of Germany. Although the recession led to economic shrinkage in both regions including Germany, youth unemployment rates in Germany weren't affected by the same magnitude, the Great Recession had only a modest and short-term impact thanks to the avoidance policies in vocational education and training, minimum wages and employment protection and activation measures and labor policies (Cahuc et al., 2013).

We can largely describe some measures as follows (Yentürk & Başlevent, 2007):

- To make the institutions of education, matching and guidance institutions widespread, establish centers particularly designed for education and job matching purposes.
- To make social protection institutions and their implementations widespread.
- To define policies for fighting against unemployment as a separate field particularly for youth unemployment problem and create expertise especially for this field
- Given the fact that women's enrollment in education and participation in employment within the younger population in Turkey is lower in proportion than men's, to develop different strategies targeted at the employment of women and build support mechanisms.
- To create strategies and policies to promote employment in social services and high-tech intensive sectors like transportation/communication where young people have a lower share in employment when compared to adults.
- To provide training consultancy services to young people in order to increase their entrepreneurship and creativity capabilities
- Considering the fact that young population is heavily hired in informal economic activities, to facilitate the inclusion of activities for employment purposes such as part-time professional and practical training in social security.
- To take measures to avoid employment losses that can lead to failure to formalize the informal employment.
- To reduce employment taxes to increase employment of young people, particularly women's employment and implement tax credits for this purpose.

Strengthening of "education capacity, entrepreneurship, vocational training, lifelong learning" are important factors in preventing youth unemployment problem. Government's intervention is the key factor to fight against young unemployment problem. Projects, incentive mechanisms, investment tools and education campaigns with NGOs must be on the state's agenda (Kabaklarlı et al., 2011).

CONCLUSION

This study aims to create the profile of young population and youth unemployment issues in Turkey, and the findings clearly show that there have been long-term unemployment and youth unemployment problems in Turkey. The high rate of population growth is an existing fact, and it is considered that it is Turkish economy's last chance to use its potential of the young population for economic growth because data and trend analysis prove that demographic transition stage will be over in the following few decades. Employment creation capacity and capability of Turkey is low due to some facts such as high population growth rate, qualitative inconsistency between labor supply and demand, problems related to professional training and high rate of immigration from rural areas to cities. Unstable growth trend deepens the impact of the unemployment problem, and it becomes harder to secure an employment-friendly growth environment. While young population still has its potential, it is found that population rate of 65+ and 15-64 age groups have upward, 0-14 age group's population rate has a downward trend. This finding proves that young population is declining and the general population is going to get older in the following few decades in Turkey.

It is seen that participation in the workforce is still low in Turkey although it shows an upward trend in the recent term. Same rate for the young population with a university degree is at the OECD's average. However, when we include other levels of education, participation in workforce rate and employment of young population declines gradually. Although there is a steady difference between young population's non-agricultural unemployment and overall employment, it is possible to say that this difference has declined. While young population's share in total population is gradually declining, unemployment rates of this group have an upward trend. We can say that higher education degree holders within the young population are increasing in ratio and their unemployment rates are declining.

In conclusion, we can say that what Turkey needs is that a new holistic employment strategy and policy should be built where all classes' views are taken into consideration. Employment-based action plans should be implemented considering different societal and economic sectors and different gender groups, dynamic and productive forces of the society should be used to reach growth targets. In this regard, improving education and employment opportunities for the young population should be considered by decision-makers as an important priority and a strategic objective.

REFERENCES

Bayraktar, S., & İncekara, A. (2013). Profile of youth unemployment in Turkey. *Journal of Labor Relations*, *4*(1), 15–38.

Cahuc, P., Carcillo, S., Rinne, U., & Zimmermann, K. F. (2013). *Youth unemployment in old Europe: The polar cases of France and Germany.* IZA Discussion Paper No. 7490.

Caliendo, M., & Schmidl, R. (2016). Youth unemployment and active labor market policies in Europe. *IZA Journal of Labor Policy*, *5*(1), 1–30. doi:10.1186/s40173-016-0057-x

Ceylan, S., & Şahin, B. Y. (2010). Asymmetry in the relationship between unemployment and economic growth. *Journal of Dogus University*, *11*(2), 157–165.

Choudhry, M. T., Marelli, E., & Signorelli, M. (2010). Youth unemployment and the ımpact of financial crises. *International Journal of Manpower*, *33*(1), 76–95. doi:10.1108/01437721211212538

Çondur, F., & Bölükbaş, M. (2014). A study on labor market and the relationship between youth unemployment and economic growth in Turkey. *Public Administration Journal*, *47*(2), 77–93.

Eser Yılmaz, B., & Terzi, H. (2008). The employment problem in Turkey and European employment strategy. *Erciyes University Faculty of Economics and Administrative Sciences Journal*, *30*, 229–250.

Göktaş Yılmaz, O. (2005). The causality relationship between growth and unemployment rates in the Turkish economy. *Economie & Statistique*, *2*, 11–29.

Kabaklarlı, E., Er, P. H., & Buluş, A. (2011). Economic determinants of Turkish youth unemployment problem: Cointegration analysis. *International Conference on Applied Economics – ICOAE*, (pp. 267-272).

Kesici, M. R. (2010). In high growth phase of Turkey economy employment and unemployment. *The Journal of Industrial Relations & Human Resources*, *12*(3), 7–26.

Ministry of Finance Department of Strategic Development. (2011). *Research Report, Problems of the labor market in Turkey and recommendations for solution*. Department of Economic and Sectorial Analysis. Retrieved August 7, 2016, from http://www.maliye.gov.tr

Organisation for Economic Co-operation and Development. (2016a). Skills matter: Further results from the survey of adult skills. *OECD Skills Studies*. Paris: OECD Publishing. 10.1787/9789264258051-en

Organisation for Economic Co-operation and Development. (2016b). Skills matter: Further results from the survey of adult skills. *Country note Turkey*. Retrieved August 22, 2016, from http://www.oecd.org/skills/piaac/

Organisation for Economic Co-operation and Development. (n.d.). *Data set of youth statistics*. Retrieved from www.oecd.org/youth.htm

Özdemir, S., Ersöz, H. Y., & Sarıoğlu, I. (2006). *Supporting SMEs for tackling the unemployment problem*. İstanbul: İstanbul Trade Chamber.

Şentürk, M., & Akbaş, Y. E. (2014). The evaluation of mutual relationship among unemployment-inflation and economic growth: The case of Turkey. *Journal of Yasar University*, *9*(34), 5820–5832. doi:10.19168/jyu.43548

Sürücü, M. (2014). *Passive employment policies to fight against unemployment: The cases of Germany and Turkey. Thesis of Expertise*. Ministry of Labor and Social Security Directorate General of External Affairs and Services for Workers Abroad. Retrieved September 1, 2016, from https://www.csgb.gov.tr/media/1785/mustafasueruecue.pdf

Takım, A. (2015). The relation between economic growth and unemployment in Turkey: Granger causality test. *Dumlupinar University Journal of Social Sciences*, *27*, 315–325.

Turkish Statistical Institute. (n.d.). *Data set of labor statistics*. Retrieved from www.tuik.gov.tr/Dinamik Sorgulama/Isgucu Istatistikleri

Uyar Bozdağlıoğlu, E. Y. (2008). The characteristics of unemployment in Turkey and the policies for fighting it. *Journal of Social Sciences*, *20*, 45–65.

World Bank. (n.d.). *Data set of country statistics (Turkey)*. Retrieved from www.worldbank.org

Yentürk, N., & Başlevent, C. (2007). *Youth unemployment in Turkey*. Youth Research Unit Research Report No 2.

KEY TERMS AND DEFINITIONS

Employment: An agreement in which an employee agrees to work for an employer.

Hidden Employment: The employment type where employed people have zero or negative effect on the total production.

Inflation: Continual increases in the general price level of goods and services in an economy over a specific time period.

International Labour Organization: The UN Agency that works on employment and its international standards, social protection, and job opportunities.

Labor Market: The kind of market created by employees and employers where one provides the supply while the other provides the demand. Labor market is one of the major elements of economies, and it is directly related to the other markets such as the capital market and the market for goods and services.

PIAAC: Programme for the International Assessment of Adult Competencies. The aim of this Programme is to evaluate the key cognitive job skills necessary for people to engage in the community and for growth purposes.

Unemployment: The condition faced by people who would like to have a full-time job but fail to do so.

Youth Unemployment: Defined by UN and ILO as the proportion of unemployed people between the ages of 15-24 in the labor force who are seeking employment.

Chapter 12
Technology Adoption for Addressing Precarious Youth Employment Issue

Azizul Hassan
Cardiff Metropolitan University, Bangladesh

ABSTRACT

This study critically analyzes precarious youth employment in Bangladesh having a specific focus on her tourism industry. Traditionally, the tourism economy of Bangladesh is considered as promising. This research arguably identifies the tourism industry of Bangladesh encouraging conceptual precarious youth employment. From theoretical perspective, this chapter addresses the Theory of Scientific Management of Frederick Taylor (1911) and the Systems Theory of Dunlop (1958) in this context. This conceptual study understands precarious youth employment in the Bangladesh tourism and relates relevance of the two theories mentioned. Based on arguments, this study outlines the role of Information and Communication Technology (ICT) as a latent option to minimize issues generated from precarious youth employment. An in-depth analysis offers policy suggestions for the betterment of youth employment in the Bangladesh tourism industry.

INTRODUCTION

Employment in any area or any economic sector can be granted as rewarding as long as this can produce a positive outcome and can meet the demand of many beneficiary types. However, employment can be precarious and can take diverse shapes and patterns. Youths are a very important part of the national economy of any country, and this is why they deserve regular employment in diverse economic areas. Precarious youth employment is a regular fact and remains present in almost every country of the world including Bangladesh, a South Asian country. Precarious youth employment gets wider attention due to the recent global economic meltdown involving the 'zero hour contract'. Tourism is a rapidly expanding industry and in many cases, acts as the leading economic sector in many countries across the world. In Bangladesh, youth unemployment rate is quite high when the youths occupy a considerable part of the

DOI: 10.4018/978-1-5225-2008-5.ch012

national workforce. Over the last decade, tourism in Bangladesh has flourished due to elevated spending capacities of the peoples, supportive policy implantation and both private and public investments (Hassan & Burns, 2014). This conceptual study aims to explore diverse factors of precarious youth employment in the tourism sector with particular focus on Bangladesh. From a more generic perspective, the country is helping entrepreneurs to come forward and get supported. Literacy rate and the quality of education are massive favors for the development of ICT in a country like Bangladesh. The 'Digital Bangladesh' campaign is an officially supporting this sector to flourish and get expanded to many areas including Small and Medium Enterprises development. The Cabinet of Bangladesh approved a citizen-centric ICT Policy 2009 with 306 action items for all agencies of the government (Government of Bangladesh, 2002). Also, the study seeks to justify information and communication technology (ICT) as a possible solution to the persistent precarious youth employment situation in Bangladesh. This study identifies a knowledge gap in this regard. Thus, the contribution of this study is significant through filling to narrow down this knowledge gap.

METHODOLOGY

The study follows general desk research to collect information and data from internet and library sources. An extensive literature review was performed on the thematic areas including but not limited to areas of precarious job situations, youth unemployment, ethics in workplace, the Theory of Scientific Management of Frederick Taylor (1911), the Systems Theory Dunlop (1958) as relevant theories of this study, information and communication technology (ICT) and policy suggestions. An exercise of scoping with the exploration of key issues and aspects of the research was made to get tourism sector based data on the economic situation and precarious youth employment situation in the identified country of Bangladesh. The research was conducted to collect official data and statistics from the governmental and non-governmental agencies responsible for the tourism sector of Bangladesh. There was a combination of intensive literature reviews followed by personal available information collection on targeted governmental agencies, travel and tourism business owners, current employees, stakeholders and general youth job seekers. Literature based information was also accessed through the use of libraries. In addition, a thorough search on the internet was also carried out. The attempt was clear to avoid complexities of data reliability and duplication carefully.

BACKGROUND

Precarious Employment

Precarious employment is seen as work that is arranged and conditioned with the association of temporary contracts, poor wages or uneven hours (Quinlan, 2012). This is a typical issue that has managed to get more attention in recent times during economic meltdown across the world. The realization is obvious that precarious youth employment needs to be replaced by well-paid and well-deserved employment.

Labour market trends over the last decade, characterized by crises and traditions, mean that young people are more at risk unemployment and insecure employment; facing futures which are more uncertain and precarious than those of recent earlier cohorts' (Fagan, Kanjuo-Mrcela, & Norman, 2012, p. 153). 'Yet, clearly, this is just not an individual struggle: this is an entire cohort of young workers whose access to stable, well-paid and meaningful work is increasingly under threat. However, it is in recognizing the social and structural character of unemployment and underemployment that we can find and advocate for collective, progressive ways to better the lives of young workers. (Foster, 2012, p. 6)

On the critical theoretical ground, the Theory of Scientific Management of Frederick Taylor (1911) and the Systems Theory of Dunlop (1958) as viewed as suitable for this research. The theory of Scientific Management by Frederick Taylor (1911) outlines that, in an organization, employee with specialization and well trained for a particular job has to be selected following proper supervision and organizational hierarchy. On the other side, following the Systems Theory of Dunlop (1958), industrial employment relations are a category of the wider social system and are governed by a set of both formal and informal rules. These rules range from holidays, recruitment, hours, wages, performances and diversified forms of employment. This theory highlights that industrial relations are mostly influenced by numerous factors of environmental contexts for maintaining the process of negotiation and resolving conflicts (Abbott, 2006).

Precarious youth employment is generic by its nature where, the most common features are the unexpected working environment, job insecurity, and low payment. This type employment can mostly be termed as sensitive, and outcomes can appear in forms as something that an individual does not necessarily expect. This type employment is largely undesired that certifies that precarious employment is non-guaranteed, unsafe and ill-paid job type. This is also common that precarious youth employment is a subject of further experimentation to resemble that youth population deserves better employment. These peoples also demand job security and safety at the workplace. However, precarious employment can hardly offer any of these. Employment can be several types where both paid and unpaid works are involved. Employment is a basic human need and is crucial for human existence on earth. This is also important to help continue their survival at the same time. Precarious employment is mostly dominant among youth working class. This is relevant to understand that these peoples form the most important base of a society accelerate socio-economic activities of that identified society. This class is also responsible to shape a society further towards development and remain as an indicator of progression. Employment among youth and young generation can involve diverse factors and based on numerous aspects as related to each other. This is where employment among youths is important to help facilitate socio-economic activities. This is most natural that peoples including youth will take employment mostly in paid form. However, in certain cases, these peoples are forced to take unpaid employment as well. Thus, the common understanding remains dominant that youth peoples are subject to get either paid or unpaid employment.

Precarious Youth Employment and the Recent Tourism Employment Market

After the 1980s, countries with a higher rate of socio-economic development accompanied by formal labor have driven towards casual, precarious or non-standard types of work (Vosko, 2011). Evidently, the scenario in the developing country context is far more depressing with insecure, unpaid or low wage structure followed by exploitation in diverse forms (Bernstein, 2007; Burawoy, 2010). Precarious employment in the tourism and hospitality industry also renders significance. In a recent study, McNamara, Bohle, and Quinlan (2011) have shown that temporary workers have less control over their working patterns accompanied by lower work intensity, excessive working hours with a lower payment and factional relationship in the workplace. Post-war experiences in Asia clearly resemble this pattern.

Precarious employment can be identified by having global challenges and is important to understand the arrangements in workplace and insecurity (Pocock, 2003). The general types of precarious work vary from self, part-time, temporary or even home based employment. International Labour Organization (2013) identifies the precarious employment as 'casual work', 'seasonal work', 'short term work' or types of contract that can be terminated with short notice. However, typically precarious works are characterized by a lower rate of benefits, wages, and security at the workplace. Precarious employment is the outcome of competitive pressure from the capital flow in the industrial nations of the decades of 1960 to 1970 (Harvey, 2005; Harvey, 2010; Hardt & Negri, 2001). Hospitality as a sector is reinforced by the present capitalistic framework to look for lower waged workforce in the typical form of precarious employment (Brown, 2000).

One of the most important trends over the past decades is undeniably the growth of insecurity in the world of work. Worldwide, unimaginable numbers of workers suffer from precarious, insecure, uncertain, and unpredictable working conditions. Unemployment figures alone are cause for concern, but even these fail to capture the larger majority of people who work, but who do not have a decent job, with a decent wage, a secure future, social protection, and access to rights. The universality and dimension of the problem call for coordinated and comprehensive action at the international level. (International Labour Organization, 2011)

In recent years, instability in the employment market has mounted partially due to the economic meltdown in almost all over the world. The situation forced the general workforce specifically the youths to undertake jobs those are most likely can be identified as insecure and precarious. Traditionally, the youths are always considered to be affected by the social unrest and economic upheavals that can have influence in almost all areas of the youth life pattern and on the community (Kalleberg, 2009). *Following* the neoliberalism, growth in the economic sector directs to transition in the labor market connected with shared wealth, social protections and the formal employment (Bacchetta, Ekkehard, & Bustamante, 2009). Offering an agreeable definition of precarious youth employment is difficult and as argued that

... however one defines it, the precariat is far from being homogeneous. The teenager who flits in and out of the internet café while surviving on fleeting jobs is not the same as the migrant who uses his wits to survive, networking feverishly while worrying about the police. Neither is similar to the single mother fretting where the money for next week's food bill is coming from or the man in his 60's who takes casual jobs to help pay medical bills. But they all share a sense that their labour is instrumental (to live), opportunistic (taking what comes) and precarious (insecure). (Standing, 2011, pp. 13-14)

According to International Labour Organization (2014c), the Global Youth Economic Conference – 2012 has urged to invest more to create work opportunities for the youth. Unemployment problem among youths has adverse effects on developed country's economy as well. Recent experiences of riots with the huge involvement of the youths in the United Kingdom have initiated this urge, where the British youths are identified as *'the most unpleasant and violent in the world'* (British Broadcasting Corporation, 2014; The Daily Mail, 2014). According to United Nations Development Programme (2014), in the world, the population of 15 to 24 years group has reached to 1.2 billion. A major part of more than 90 percent of them lives in developing countries and in Asia particularly, the number is 55%. 75 million of the youth workforce will remain unemployed in 2012 that is 12.7% of the total global workforce. From 2008 to 2011, the frequency of temporary employment contract has doubled by 0.9% from the previous year, as a consequence of the global economic crisis. Bangladesh is world's one of the poorest country with a huge number of her workforce remaining unemployed. Youth unemployment in this country has risen to over 47% between the timeframe of 2001 to 2010. The tourism sector accounted for 2.2% of the Bangladesh GDP in 2011 and expected to rise by 7.3% and 6.1%, respectively by 2012 and 2022 even with the serious shortage of skilled workforce (World Travel and Tourism Council, 2014). Tourism is appearing as the single biggest employment generating sector in Bangladesh economy (The Daily Star, 2014).

Precarious Youth Employment and the Bangladesh Tourism Industry Evidence

In a country like Bangladesh with developing economy, precarious youth employment is a known issue in the tourism industry of this country.

Although many young people were aware that many of the jobs they were undertaking were fraught with precarious conditions and pay, these conditions were accepted, because of a realization of the overall lack of jobs and poor employment prospects. Others believed the jobs they were seeking matched their skills, experiences and abilities. Despite the precariousness of the labour market, young people tended to be quite deliberately selective of the sorts of jobs they wanted. (Burrows, 2013)

Precarious employment remains as an unexpected type employment that is commonly taken by peoples in compelling circumstances.

In recent times, jobs in the tourism sector like a brand ambassador, commissioned marketing executive, attendants, receptionists and similar are attracting and employing a huge number of youths, mainly students. Both male and females are involved with these types of work, and such types of works are often insecure, exploitative, discriminative and vulnerable to sexual harassment and do not necessarily follow ethics in the workplace that offer trigger early negative job experiences. Youths those are employed are vulnerable and are forced to undertake low or no paid roles to retain their jobs. Loopholes of the government policies are also supporting to create precarious employment for youths in these identified sectors (Freitag, 1994). One of the very basic reasons is that employing youths with low payment and flexibility offer a better return and profitability for the business organization. The lower literacy rate, poverty, staggering unemployment situation and political instability are forcing the youths to undertake precarious jobs. Clarity in the process of governmental policy formulation and their effectiveness have always remained under questions. In the developing countries, arguably there has never been any specific and highly effective set of policies for helping youths to avoid precarious employment in the particular sector of tourism (Clancy, 1999). Whatever, the jobs are created for the youths in these three countries representing the South Asia in general, are mostly precarious and temporary based.

This is evident that precarious youth employment is gradually shaping as an important issue both inside and outside of Europe,

Further when they do secure employment, young people are more likely to be engaged in positions that are associated with precariousness and the risk of social exclusion. Even the EU admitted recently that fractured transitions between education and employment – with periods of paid work interspersed by unemployment, or withdrawal from the labour market, have been common for young workers, or at least substantial numbers among them. This situation is likely to be exacerbated as the consequences of the financial and economic shock of 2008-9 works its way through economies and labour markets. (Kretsos, 2011, p. 454)

Information and Communication Technology (ICT): A Prospect

The creation of ICT-related jobs and implementing policy frameworks, some sort of prospects remain to be exploited by the identified groups of peoples of society. This helps to progress the socio-economic activities of a society and a nation at the same time. However, this necessarily has to maintain a certain level of standard. The adoption of ICT thus can appear as a way to overcome economic hardship and thus to get out of it. The diversification of employment is beneficial and rewarding in a sense that can produce regular and more accepted job patterns. Information and communication technology can offer benefits to young working class peoples of a country. The role and relevance of information technology in supporting employment generation is actually varied. This finds attachment with the mainstream socio-economic developmental process of a given society that is mainly believed as underdeveloped, in terms of its capacities and potentials.

Information technology can bring positive benefits to young peoples where general interests of this social class largely concentrate on computational activities. The adoption of information and communication technological applications is lucrative for the relatively better return on investment. This also shows possibilities to reveal of certain technological aspects that would otherwise mostly remain inconsistent. ICT and its application are involved with interest generation of specified groups of peoples that are mostly young, active and seek paid employment more than any other class of a particular society. ICT is important in helping to advance a given social system supported by certain features. This is also crucial to believe that the application of ICT would remain as rewarding. There are many scopes and opportunities that need to be exploited and fully utilized. These also can be beneficial to promote and advance a given socio-economic system as per the requirement of its peoples.

This is mostly certain that tourism is a promising industry with capacities to generate opportunities and immense potentials. Thus, this industry in general, can accommodate and create employment to a large section of unemployed youth workers. Youth working class is characteristically hard-working, energetic and reliable. All these features, on a common platform, can offer a huge return on both the individual and the national level investments. This is evident that both tourism and ICT are promising sectors and a possible merger can eventually lead to activate underlying chances. Thus, this helps enhancing potentials and utilizes capacities to create further opportunities for employment generation. Tourism as an industry is offering both direct and indirect benefits to a country like Bangladesh. This is also playing substantial roles to promote a specific destination by bringing development initiatives and creating more opportunities as per requirements of individuals of that area.

Information and communication technology can certainly offer opportunities to those youths remaining as unemployed. There should be a concern that tourism industry needs to be benefitted from the most recent technology adoption. Also, there are scopes and opportunities to overcome specific barriers and to prove that ICT can be a solution for precarious youth employment as an issue. The reason that, youths are more eager to get involved in regular employment, rely on solid earning sources and income generating activities. ICT can also support them moving beyond unexpected job conditions. Relevant data and information are always useful, while understanding the trends of technology adoption in given circumstances also remain crucial. This is encouraging that tourism industry has helped to cater demands of increasing populations that would mostly remain as unemployed.

Again, ICT creates employment and proves that this industry can help reducing unemployment problem. Examples are available in Bangladesh where, rural youths are connected with internet facilities that are helping to get them involved in income generation activities (Kabeer, 2003). Not necessarily these activities are totally tourism-centric but, diverse areas of tourism are actually supported by these. Social media websites as Facebook is supporting youths to stay connected and doing business on this. These types marketing mostly come as social media marketing type. These have differentiated and hardly can be defined as mainstream marketing activities. There are scopes as available for doing business on social media websites on Facebook. Package holiday, tourism destinations, tourism product or services are some examples. Thus this is crucial that opportunities need to be exploited by rural youth populations either to move from precarious to non-precarious employment or to get regular jobs.

Information and communication technology is beneficial for any identified society that mostly remains as underdeveloped, in terms of employment and income generation (Schilderman, 2002). This also becomes a general platform to render the improved capacities aiming to bring out the maximum possible benefits from a given social system. Information and communication technology sector deserve considerable attentions. The service and product of this sector are mostly consumed by general populations by creating chances for more consumption. The benefits of information technology consumption are critical because of its nature to remain active in a competitive market setting. The use and application of information and communication technology vary on certain perspectives. The differences between technology application and their use rely on many factors including capacities and accessibility. That is, a youth worker needs to have certain capacities to purchase or avail technological gadgets. This also needs to remain as acceptable by the relevant industry. On the other side, accessibilities vary on availability and offer of certain technology led products or services.

ICT for Precarious Youth Employment in the Bangladesh Tourism Sector: A Probable Solution

In Bangladesh, youth unemployment rate is relatively higher than any other countries in the world. While the population is growing, this also turns into a perennial situation in employment market with increased number of job seekers. The country with huge population should be the subject of interest generation by individuals and interest groups engaged in business. There are also many other related industries either directly or indirectly benefitted from ICT, tourism, and relevant industries. In tourism industry of Bangladesh, precarious employment is relatively common among almost all age groups including youths. This sector is also important to offer economic benefits to underprivileged populations that are mostly left unattended far below the poverty line. The nature of youth employment in Bangladesh remains largely bleak with almost no progress over decades. In tourism industry particular, the relevance of youth working class denotes massive importance. A satisfied and well-trained group of employees almost always remain as a boon for any economy where Bangladesh can be an answer. The promotion of well-paid employment and to create interests among the youths is crucial for any industry including tourism. This is why tourism as an industry also needs young workers to remain profitable and economically viable.

Development is a massive area that needs proper attention from all of the parties concerned. As well as, this needs to be involved with the input of man, money, management and marketing. This study suggests this ICT as the core of employment market development in the tourism sector of Bangladesh. This is also attached with other relevant aspects as policy support of a country. The public policies of Bangladesh are favoring the development of ICT with huge interests, initiatives, and supports. The government is also offering considerable incentives to help to promote the sector. Logistical and infrastructural supports are also offered by the government to advance the sector. This is also an area to accommodate a huge number of unemployed populations and mainly young populations as they are more likely to be interested computer and its usage. The basic challenge for ICT development and possible job prospects is the language barrier. English has to be an ultimate solution, and this actually takes the time to reach a standard level to become fluent in the English language.

Precarious youth employment is common in the case of Bangladesh. Still, this is widely neglected in the academic with very little attention. This conceptual study aimed to outlines precarious employment status in Bangladesh. There are huge lacks of numeric data and information that can highlight precarious youth employment situation in the country. The study determines that precarious employment among youths in Bangladesh is typical. Thus a strong attention from both academics and researchers are widely deserved. This study should help to attract the attention to place focus on precarious youth employment. Basic expected contribution of this study is to offer a more accepted definition of precarious youth employment that should have relevance in developing economy perspective. Also, this study supports to draw a theoretical platform that is more parallel to the identified research areas. In addition, this study contributes to offering practical implications to bring improvement in the situation that is more likely viewed as discouraging. Recent global experience shows that youth employment can sometimes turn into a serious concern for the society itself. In the country like Bangladesh, the tourism sector is offering huge potentials for economic development. This instigating precarious jobs among youths with reduced ethics in the workplace is always a big question. However, this is a concern to identify the extent to which tourism sector can become able to create substantial employment for youths. Public policies and programs in Bangladesh are supporting to popularize the adoption of technology and to create regular employment for youths. The study validates the application of the Theory of Scientific Management of Frederick Taylor (1911), and the Systems Theory of Dunlop (1958) in ICT led business and employments. Serious lack of data and information on precarious youth employment in Bangladesh was an issue to turn this study as comprehensive and more acceptable. Future research should be directed towards exploring empirical facts on precarious youth employments in developing market contexts.

FUTURE RESEARCH DIRECTIONS

Empirical evidenced as generated through primary data is the basic limitation of this study that possibly could expand research validity and reliability. Future research should focus on combining both primary and secondary data while conducting research in precarious youth employment in the Bangladesh tourism sector.

CONCLUSION

This conceptual study aims to outline precarious youth employment in the Bangladesh tourism sector. ICT is viewed as a possible option to accommodate youth working force and to bring betterment in the employment market in the country. Findings show the presence of precarious youth employment in

Bangladesh as in many other countries of the world. After having analysis, this study suggests that ICT can be a possible solution to overcome precarious youth employment issues in the identified ground of Bangladesh. In reality, the country welcomes investments in ICT and tourism sector with increased attention from both public and private investors. There are already examples of medium to small ICT firms across the country helping to develop this sector and thus to create employments for the purpose. This is certain that tourism sector in Bangladesh is offering opportunities and economic benefits that are widely beneficial for the local population. This sector is also helping to create employment and thus to promote the development of information and communication technology sector. There are massive opportunities to raise potentials of these sectors that can offer benefits to local populations, in terms of both employment generation and socio-economic development. ICT sector depends on technological expertise, and its development supports the Theory of Scientific Management by Frederick Taylor (1911) that outlines that in an organization, employee with specialization and well trained for a particular job has to be selected following proper supervision and organizational hierarchy. On the other side, following the Systems Theory of Dunlop (1958), industrial employment relations are a category of the wider social system and are governed by a set of both formal and informal rules. These rules range from holidays, recruitment, hours, wages, performances and diversified forms of employment. This theory highlights that industrial relations are mostly influenced by numerous factors of environmental contexts for maintaining the process of negotiation and resolving conflicts. In acceptable employment and working environments as ICT and tourism, the possibilities are higher to support the Systems Theory. Examples from Bangladesh show that information and communication technology adoption in a country like this can represent huge potentials. In almost each sector, ICT has immense potentials, and this is where the importance of its adoption really lies. This study suggests that precarious youth employment in Bangladesh can be replaced by ICT-related jobs where emerging market examples as India can appear as an example. Tourism is an industry where the social media marketing can create a new concept. English language adoption needs to be given priority. The very basic advantage of ICT is that it is technology oriented rather than labor. A generic assumption that technology will gradually replace labor-oriented industries and where employees will be more eager to adopt technologies. The tourism sector is also expanding in many other areas and adding more opportunities to serve interests of increased populations who otherwise would be left away from the actual development process. Thus, ICT and its application in the tourism sector can evidently bring prospects of employment generation among the youths in Bangladesh.

REFERENCES

Abbott, K. (2006). A review of employment relations theories and their application. *Problems and Perspectives in Management, 1*, 187–199.

Bacchetta, M., Ekkehard, E., & Bustamante, J. P. (2009). *Globalization and informal jobs in developing countries: A joint study of the International Labour Office and the Secretariat of the World Trade Organization*. Geneva: International Labour Organization and World Trade Organization.

Bernstein, H. (2007). *Capital and labour from centre to margins*. Paper prepared for the Living on the Margins conference, Stellenbosch.

British Broadcasting Corporation. (2014). *French riots: Amiens buildings torched in clashes.* Retrieved September 25, 2014, from http://bbc.in/QxxkGm

Brown, F. (2000). *Tourism reassessed: Blight or blessing?* Oxford, UK: Butterworth Heinemann.

Burawoy, M. (2010). From Polanyi to Pollyanna: The false optimism of global labor studies. *Global Labour Journal, 1*(2), 301–313. doi:10.15173/glj.v1i2.1079

Burrows, S. (2013). Precarious work, neo-liberalism and young peoples experiences of employment in the Illawarra region. *Economic and Labour Relations Review, 24*(3), 380–396. doi:10.1177/1035304613498189

Clancy, M. J. (1999). Tourism and development: Evidence from Mexico. *Annals of Tourism Research, 26*(1), 1–20. doi:10.1016/S0160-7383(98)00046-2

Dunlop, J. T. (1958). *Industrial relations systems.* New York: Holt Rinehart and Winston.

Fagan, C., Kanjuo-Mrcela, A., & Norman, H. (2012). Work young adults navigating European labour markets: Old and new social risks and employment policies. In T. Knijin (Ed.), *Work, family policies and transitions to adulthood in Europe* (pp. 130–154). London: Palgrave Macmillan. doi:10.1057/9781137284198_6

Foster, K. (2012). *Youth employment and un(der) employment in Canada-more than a temporary problem. In Behind the Numbers* (pp. 1–6). Ottawa: Canadian Center for Policy Alternatives.

Freitag, T. G. (1994). Enclave tourism development: For whom the bell tolls? *Annals of Tourism Research, 21*(3), 538–554. doi:10.1016/0160-7383(94)90119-8

Government of Bangladesh. (2002). *National information and communication technology (ICT) policy.* Dhaka: Ministry of Science and Information and Communication Technology.

Hardt, M., & Negri, A. (2001). *Empire.* Cambridge, MA: Harvard University Press.

Harvey, D. (2005). *A brief history of neoliberalism.* New York: Oxford University Press.

Harvey, D. (2010). *The enigma of capital: And the crises of capitalism.* London: Profile.

Hassan, A., & Burns, P. (2014). Tourism policies of Bangladesh – A contextual analysis. *Tourism Planning and Development, 11*(4), 463–466. doi:10.1080/21568316.2013.874366

International Labour Organization. (2011). *Policies and regulations to combat precarious employment.* Retrieved from September 25, 2016, from http://www.ilo.org/wcmsp5/groups/public/---ed_dialogue/---actrav/documents/meetingdocument/wcms_164286.pdf

International Labour Organization. (2013). *Women and men in the informal economy: A statistical picture.* Geneva: International Labour Office, Employment Sector.

International Labour Organization. (2014c). *ILO calls for urgent investment in youth work opportunities.* Retrieved from September 25, 2012, from http://bit.ly/QX0Rd2

Kabeer, N. (2003). *Gender mainstreaming in poverty eradication and the Millennium Development Goals.* London: The Commonwealth Secretariat, the International Development Research Center, and the Canadian International Development Agency. doi:10.14217/9781848598133-en

Kalleberg, A. L. (2009). Precarious Work, Insecure Workers: Employment Relations in Transition. *American Sociological Review*, *74*(1), 11–22. doi:10.1177/000312240907400101

Kretsos, L. (2011). Union responses to the rise of precarious youth employment in Greece. *European Journal of Industrial Relations*, *9*(1), 453–472. doi:10.1111/j.1468-2338.2011.00634.x

McNamara, M., Bohle, P., & Quinlan, M. (2011). Precarious employment, working hours, work-life conflict and health in hotel work. *Applied Ergonomics*, *42*(2), 225–232. doi:10.1016/j.apergo.2010.06.013 PMID:20643398

Pocock, B. (2003). *The work/life collision: What work is doing to Australians and what to do about it.* Annandale: Federation Press.

Quinlan, M. (2012). The pre-invention of precarious employment: The changing world of work in context. *Economic and Labour Relations Review*, *23*(4), 3–24. doi:10.1177/103530461202300402

Schilderman, T. (2002). *Strengthening the knowledge and information systems of the urban poor*. Massachusetts: ITDG.

Standing, G. (2011). *The precariat: The new dangerous class*. London: Bloomsberg.

Taylor, F. W. (2011). *Scientific management*. New York: Harper Row.

The Daily Mail. (2014). *News*. Retrieved December 18, 2014, from http://bit.ly/nBHBst

The Daily Star. (2014). *Tourism: Next job creator*. Retrieved August 7, 2014, from http://bit.ly/GPTuBw

United Nations Development Programme. (2014). *Rio + 20: National report on sustainable development*. Dhaka: Ministry of Environment and Forests, Peoples Republic of Bangladesh.

Vosko, L. F. (2011). *Managing the margins: Gender, citizenship and the international regulation of precarious employment*. New York: Oxford University Press.

World Travel and Tourism Council. (2014). *Bangladesh-key facts at a glance*. Retrieved August 7, 2014, from http://bit.ly/hHqb5P

ADDITIONAL READING

Azim, R., & Hassan, A. (2013). Impact analysis of wireless and mobile technology on business management strategies. *Journal of Information and Knowledge Management*, *2*(2), 141–150.

Dadwal, S., & Hassan, A. (2015). The augmented reality marketing: A merger of marketing and technology in tourism. In N. Ray (Ed.), *Emerging innovative marketing strategies in the tourism industry* (pp. 78–96). Pennsylvania: IGI Global. doi:10.4018/978-1-4666-8699-1.ch005

Hassan, A. (2016). A composition of variable economic activities: Cases of three groups of indigenous of peoples of South Asia. In K. Iankova, A. Hassan, & L. A. Rachel (Eds.), *Indigenous peoples and economic development: An international perspective* (pp. 267–282). Oxon: Routledge.

Hassan, A., Ahmed, M. U., & Shoeb-Ur-Rahman, M. (2015). The development, nature, and impact of medical tourism in Bangladesh. In M. Cooper, K. Vafadari, & M. Hieda (Eds.), *Current issues and emerging trends in medical tourism* (pp. 296–311). Pennsylvania: IGI Global. doi:10.4018/978-1-4666-8574-1.ch021

Hassan, A., & Dadwal, S. (2016). Search engine marketing – An outlining of conceptualization and strategic application. In W. Ozuem & G. Bowen (Eds.), *Competitive social media marketing strategies* (pp. 219–234). Pennsylvania: IGI Global. doi:10.4018/978-1-4666-9776-8.ch011

Hassan, A., & Donatella, P. S. (2016). Google AdSense as a mobile technology in education. In J. L. Holland (Ed.), *Wearable technology and mobile innovations for next-generation education* (pp. 200–223). Pennsylvania: IGI Global. doi:10.4018/978-1-5225-0069-8.ch011

Hassan, A., & Jung, T. (2016). Augmented reality as an emerging application in tourism education. In D. H. Choi, A. Dailey-Hebert, & J. S. Estes (Eds.), *Emerging tools and applications of virtual reality in education* (pp. 168–185). Pennsylvania: IGI Global. doi:10.4018/978-1-4666-9837-6.ch008

Hassan, A., & Rahimi, R. (2016). Consuming ''innovation'': Augmented reality as an innovation tool in digital tourism marketing. In P. Nikolaos & I. Bregoli (Eds.), *Global dynamics in travel, tourism, and hospitality* (pp. 130–147). Pennsylvania: IGI Global. doi:10.4018/978-1-5225-0201-2.ch008

Hassan, A., & Rahimi, R. (in press). Technology use for sustainable coastal tourism in St. Martin's Island of Bangladesh. In A. Jones & M. Phillips (Eds.), *Climate change and coastal tourism*. Bristol: Channelview Publications.

Hassan, A., & Ramkissoon, H. (in press). Augmented reality for visitor experiences. In J. N. Albrecht (Ed.), *Visitor management*. Oxfordshire: CABI.

Hassan, A., & Shabani, N. (in press). Usability analysis of augmented reality for tourism destination promotion. In S. K. Dixit (Ed.), *Routledge handbook of consumer behaviour in hospitality and tourism*. Oxon: Routledge.

Imtiaz, M., & Hassan, A. (2016). The urges of language adaptation for economic development within the Garos of Bangladesh. In K. Iankova, A. Hassan, & L. A. Rachel (Eds.), *indigenous peoples and economic development: An international perspective* (pp. 307–324). Oxon: Routledge.

Sardar, S. M., & Hassan, A. (2015). *Strategic marketing influence on tourism service consumers*. Saarbrücken: LAP Lambert Publication Limited.

KEY TERMS AND DEFINITIONS

ICT: Information and communication technology that is literally related to computer technology.

Precarious Employment: The type of employment for the youth that is unsecured, uncertain, unguaranteed and dangerous.

Precarious: Precarious is something that is dangerous for collapsing or falling and insecurely positioned.

Technology: Scientific knowledge application to meet practical purposes of both of the humans and the industry.

The System Theory: The theory is proposed by Dunlop (1958) that studies phenomena's abstract organization, their substance type, temporal or spatial scale of existence or independence.

The Theory of Scientific Management: The theory is also known as Taylorism that is proposed by Frederick Taylor (1911). This management theory is concerned with both analyzing and synthesizing workflows.

Tourism: The voluntary and temporary movement of people from one place to another for leisure or recreational purpose.

Youth: The time span of human life between childhood and adult age.

Chapter 13
The Puzzle on Unemployment Factors and the Welfare State Role in Greece:
What University Students Believe

Argyris Kyridis
Aristotle University of Thessaloniki, Greece

Christos Dimitrios Tourtouras
Aristotle University of Thessaloniki, Greece

Maria Pavlis Korres
General Secretariat for Lifelong Learning, Greece & Hellenic Open University, Greece

Nikos Fotopoulos
University of Western Macedonia, Greece

Christos Zagkos
Center of Educational Policy Development (KANEP/GSEE), Greece

ABSTRACT

In an era of major technological, digital and scientific achievement, in the modern post-industrial globalized society of great contradictions, problems and conflicts, the unemployment phenomenon, which affects young people to a greater extent, is exacerbated. Greece is the country that was affected more than any other country in southern Europe by the multiple effects of the economic crisis, which among others catapulted youth unemployment to unprecedented levels. This chapter presents a research on views and attitudes analysis of male and female students of higher education in Greece towards unemployment as a social phenomenon, towards stereotypical attitudes on unemployment, as well as towards the ways and forms of the research phenomenon configuration. Subsequently, this research attempts to record, analyze and interpret the students' views and attitudes towards the Greek welfare state, thoroughly studying the correlations of all the above data.

INTRODUCTION

According to Eurostat, unemployment rate for each country is considered the labor force percentage at the age of 15-74 years that do not work, even though they are available, and they were either looking for work during the last month or were about to start work in the next three months. Employees are defined

DOI: 10.4018/978-1-5225-2008-5.ch013

persons at the age of 15 years and over who have either worked on remuneration lately, for at least one hour or have not worked due to leave, whereas economically inactive are defined all other persons who are neither employed nor unemployed.

The lack of a clear policy created severe unemployment problems for young people. The incapacity to provide the necessary services to youth has been documented over and over again and each failure of social programs makes the problem seem much greater (Riessman, 1967; English, 1970). The various youth programs have only dealt with the symptoms, and the rate of youth unemployment will not be reduced until there are changes in the economic and social policies of the countries involved (Fyfe, 1978; Gordon, 1979). Youth unemployment rates across the world are more than double compared to those of adults, which is often interpreted as a lack of decent work opportunities for youth (ILO, 2008).

Work is undoubtedly a fundamental and inalienable social right, won through labour and political struggles, as well as class and social conflicts. The modern bourgeois state, especially in its post-war version - period of the welfare state establishment - has institutionally undertaken to defend the right to work, in an attempt to mediate between the opposing forces of capital and labor – trade union movement. Thus, the unemployed pin their hopes for employment recovery and living conditions improvement on the welfare state, which ought to do what it takes to defend this specific (individual) right of every citizen. However, nowadays, modern states, under the umbrella of neoliberalism, insist on the deregulation strategy of the labor market or on its adjustment and settlement for the benefit of the dominant bourgeois class, which intends to maximize profit through crises creation and "unemployed tanks" augmentation.

Unemployment does not just constitute a macro-economic aggregate, unilaterally determined by the economic conditions on a national or international level. On the contrary, as a socio-economical phenomenon, it is a social malaise indicator, a social cohesion indicator and at the same time a social stratification indicator established in a country. Besides, it is a macro-economic variable which defines the (lower or higher) degree of class conflicts, the reproduction of social classes, the nature of the social division of labor and the welfare indicators we ought to observe in any social formation (Machin & Manning, 1998). Unemployment, at the same time, contains the inherent characteristic of personal and social experience, due to the fact that it is a social phenomenon and not only a generalized and abstract social problem, but it is internalized both individually and by broad social masses, directly affected by the unemployment experience and impact (Dooley & Prause, 2004). Additionally, unemployment causes a wide range of effects, not only economic but also social (Wilson, 1996), psychological (McKee-Ryan, 2005), spiritual (Borrero, 2014; Murphy & Athanasou, 1999;) or even on health (Burgard, Brand, & House, 2007; Kessler et al. 1987).

Unemployment, despite the fact that it influences the entire population spectrum, mainly and almost uncontrollably affects vulnerable social groups that directly or indirectly experience its consequences with great intensity (Smith, 1980). Social vulnerability combined with unemployment creates an explosive social mixture, which deepens recession and paralyzes the social system, thus sharpening social disorganization and pathology. Additionally, they intensify the existing cultural and social classification even more, increasing the symptoms of social pathology phenomena (Smith, 1974). Furthermore, unemployment and especially long-term unemployment leads to brutal social exclusion phenomena (Lawless, Martin, & Hardy, 1998), probably to extreme social differentiation phenomena (Fevre, 1984; Clark & Drinkwater, 2007), as well as antisocial and psychopathological ones which directly affect social cohesion and the sense of social solidarity.

But, how is the unemployment phenomenon linked to the increasing social vulnerability and social exclusion phenomena? It is known that social vulnerability is the obvious result of social and economic inequalities, creating the conditions for possible appearance of phenomena such as poverty, alienation, addictions, lawlessness, introversion and antisocial behavior. For example, if one loses their job and if their social, family and cultural characteristics, do not allow them to easily find another job, then it is very likely to become long-term unemployed. Long-term unemployment will cause serious problems to the family budget and with mathematical precision will lead to basic goods and services deprivation both for himself and his family (Pillinger, 2001). Meanwhile, subsequent social exclusion, structurally appears to be associated with factors as:

1. High and prolonged unemployment,
2. Changes taking place in technological structures and their social impact,
3. National social structures degradation in the context of globalization,
4. Transformation of social values and collective approaches for work,
5. Social fragmentation and ideological disarray tendencies,
6. Spread of the phenomenon of migration flows (Abeledo, n.d.; Kyridis, 2014).

On this basis we could claim that social vulnerability and the consequent social exclusion are "three-dimensional" at their base as they include:

1. Structural factors related to the economic dimension of the problem,
2. Operational factors related to the social dimensions of exclusion, and
3. Subjective factors related to personal attitudes and problems that each person - member of vulnerable groups - experiences (Kyridis, 2014).

As Vatsa (2004) very aptly notes, vulnerability is not directly related to the fact that causes unpleasant effects to a population, but to the percentage of the population who is destined to experience these effects. Consequently, the dominant factor in social reason should not be the type of danger, but by the shielding of the population, so that after its effect the impact is reduced. In other words, vulnerability is not unilaterally connected to which measures will be taken so that the unpleasant danger consequences are mitigated, but (it is connected) to the systemic prevention so that these specific groups, that could potentially be vulnerable, do not finally become vulnerable.

Finally, concerning the thorny issue of unemployment, vulnerability and social exclusion, this research attempts to crystallize and analyze young people's attitudes (Greek universities students) towards unemployment as a social phenomenon, towards stereotypical positions on unemployment, but also towards the ways and forms of this phenomenon configuration and, at the same time, to determine their degree of confidence in what is called welfare state in the context of the Greek economic crisis.

BACKGROUND: THE SITUATION IN GREECE

Regarding the situation in Greece, Eurostat data show that in 2001, year of the euro adoption, total unemployment amounted to 10.5% of the workforce, whereas two years later it dropped to 9.7% (2003) and during the year of the Olympic games (2004) it climbed to 10.6% to give place to a gradual de-escalation, year after year, reaching, in 2008, the record low level of 7.8%, a rate which was very close to the European average of 7,5%. However, as the crisis was setting off, the unemployment rate was increasing, at rapid rates, to 9.6% in 2009, 12.7% in 2010, 17.9% in 2011, 24.5% in 2012 and peaked at 27.5% in 2013. Today (2016) after six years of deep economic recession, general workforce unemployment stubbornly remains at very high levels (24.6% or 1.170.000 persons) leading society to a deep social misery, to an incredible insecurity and unprecedented economic and cultural decline.

Kountentakis (2012) reports that, since the crisis outbreak, high unemployment rates are linked to the efforts in order to make labor market more flexible. Kountenakis considers 2010 as a landmark year, a period when Greek legislation was amended with total deregulation as a result. Thus, together with recruitment reduction and new jobs reduction, layoffs increase was intensified "shooting" unemployment up to stupendous rates. Karantinos, for his part, argues that unemployment in Greece, is mainly cyclical. In particular, he observes that the lack of cumulative product and workforce demand is responsible for the labor market crisis without ignoring structural factors effects, such as the profile of a labor force with low qualifications or no job skills, or a low level of labor mobility. Besides, according to him, ineffective employment policies that aimed at reducing unemployment through wrong measures are also responsible (Karantinos, 2012).

However, the major problem of the country is no other than youth unemployment. In particular, youth unemployment has reached exceptional levels (over 50%), affecting every young man and woman regardless of their qualifications, leading many of them to flee from their country looking for work - often irrelevant to their educational qualifications - to other countries less affected by the economic crisis (Theodoropoulos et al. 2015; Lamprianidis, 2011).

Youth unemployment is a growing problem that has significant long term consequences for individuals, communities, economies and societies. During the last decade, the transition from school to work has become long-term, more complex and turbulent (Schoon & Silberstein, 2009). The National Labour Force Surveys (Hoffman, 2011) show that youth unemployment has increased in all EU countries as the percentage of young people (under 25) who are looking for work ranges from 7% in Austria and 8% in the Netherlands up to 50% in Greece and Spain (EC 2012, EC 2012b). In many countries, therefore, the transition of young people from education to work seems problematic (Keep, 2012). As a result more and more young people, not in education, employment or training, have limited accessibility to job offers, thus joining the emerging vulnerable social group of Neets (Young People Not in Education, Employment and Training). Furthermore, according to the I.L.O. the percentage of young people in the total population is decreasing, while increasingly fragmented or "prolonged" transitions prevail in the European labor market (ILO, 2010a, p. 13), resulting in arrhythmias and dysfunction in the relationship between education-training and labor market. As far as Greece is concerned it is remarkable that 66.6% of a sample of 400 Greek university students said they would definitely or probably leave Greece as soon as they finish their studies, defining the labor market and especially unemployment as the most important reason that leads to this decision (Theodoropoulos, Kyridis, Zagkos, & Konstantinidou, 2015).

MAIN FOCUS OF THE CHAPTER

Concerns and Aim of the Research

In the era of the Greek crisis, it is clear that young men and women are the ones who suffer more than anyone else from the pathology that unemployment generates. It is indeed young men and women who acquire educational qualifications who, under other circumstances, could be integrated more easily into the labor market. They are young people who have worked hard and with their families' economic sacrifices have managed to enter university, expecting this investment (public and private) in effort and money to provide them with a good job, or even a job that ensures a decent living. Contrary to their dreams and expectations, these young men and women today face the spectrum of unemployment which raises an insurmountable obstacle before them. Are they in fact able to recognize unemployment as a major social problem? Do they understand that they would be profoundly affected? Can they understand the structural causes of high unemployment in the country? Do they actually perceive the terms of formation, reproduction as well as the consequences of unemployment? While they are witnesses of the deep economic crisis destroying the country in every aspect of economic and social life, can they feel safe in a weakened and meager welfare state? Do they trust it? Do they recognize their rights? Are they able to assert them?

In particular, the aim of our research spreads in four levels. At the first level the aims are: (A1) to record and analyze the undergraduate and postgraduate students' views and attitudes towards unemployment as a social phenomenon, (A2) to record and analyze their attitudes towards stereotype views on unemployment, and (A3) to record and analyze the ways and forms in which unemployment is formed. At the second level: (B1) to record and analyze the views and attitudes of the students towards the welfare state in general (B2) to record the degree of confidence the students have towards the welfare state, and (B3) to record the students' attitudes towards the Greek welfare state. At the third level (C) to control whether the views and attitudes towards unemployment (A) are related to views and attitudes towards the welfare state (B). Finally, at the fourth level (D) to control whether the respondents' views and attitudes are linked to their demographic and social characteristics.

Methodology and Sample of the Research

The research was conducted in Greece from February 2015 to December 2015. A random and convenience sample consisting of 342 undergraduate and postgraduate students from Greek Universities and Higher Technological Educational Institutions completed anonymously a printed questionnaire. The main reason this particular population was selected is: (a) students are already experiencing or are very close to face the spectrum of unemployment, (b) they are young with presumably higher educational and cognitive skills, and (c) are probably in a period or in the procedure of decision making regarding their future.

As a research tool a questionnaire was used, consisting of three parts: a. Demographic and social data, and the recording of the degree of subjects' politicization in combination with their political and ideological identity, b. An attitude scale towards the phenomenon of unemployment (Cronbach's alpha =.771) and c. An attitude scale towards the welfare state in general and the Greek state in particular (Cronbach's alpha =.774).

During the analyses, carried out as part of Inferential Statistics, in order to check statistical hypotheses and detect statistically significant differentiations between means or statistically significant correlations between variables, non-parametric tests were used, due to the fact that the distribution of the dependent variable was not normal (namely that of the measurement of the degree of agreement/disagreement of the respondents in the various subcategories that correspond to specific attitudes on the question of unemployment and the welfare state). The measurement values of agreement/disagreement on various views and attitudes emerged from a level Likert scale, allowing, by convention, the implementation of quantitative analyses which require scale dependent variables.

Research Results

Descriptive Statistics

Our research sample consisted of 342 young people, the majority of which (65%) were female and the vast majority of which (97%) were enrolled in universities, only 3% in Higher Technological Institutes. Moreover, during the period of the research, 75% were studying at undergraduate level, whereas the remaining 25% at graduate level. 68% were 18 to 22 years and the rest over 23. Only 22% said that they worked while studying, whereas the majority of them stated that their paternal hearth was in Athens-Thessaloniki or another urban center of the country (65% and 17%, respectively), and only 18% in a small town or rural area. Besides, 14% came from families where at least one of the parents was self-employed/scientist, whereas the largest percentage (43%) had parents that were civil servants; the percentage of those whose parents worked as employees in the private sector (16%) was far smaller, approximately 12% had a father with a craftsman profession and a 3% had parents working as merchants. 10% had a father that was laborer or farmer and 3% an unemployed one, whereas 26% had a mother dedicated exclusively to the household.

Regarding the educational level of their parents, we could say that most of them came from family environments with parents who were higher education graduates (51% and 57%, respectively) and 30% with parents who were high school graduates. Only about 10% came from families with illiterate parents or primary school graduates, while the percentage who had parents acquiring a postgraduate diploma (8% of fathers and 5% of mothers) was equally small.

Finally, 53% stated that they ideologically belonged to the wider left (left, extreme left and anarchist) political space, whereas 27% belonged to the centrist and 20% to the right and extreme right space. However, 65% stated a little or completely politically indifferent and 95% totally insecure regarding protection provided by the state.

Regarding how the research subjects express their opinion concerning unemployment (E1-E25) and the welfare state (K1-K19) (Table 1). Generally, it seems that the views of the individuals participating in the sample on the unemployment issue are quite mature, indicating a fairly refined attitude towards a phenomenon that appears to have drawn their attention, and still does, quite highly.

So, they averagely consider that real unemployment is much higher than the one officially reported, they disagree that immigrants are responsible for the unemployment rate increase in the local population; they neither consider government intervention, in order to curb the phenomenon, effective, nor attribute unemployment to individual elements of the personality of the unemployed, for example, to laziness or lack of skills and qualifications.

Instead, they agree that professional racism as well as racism towards the long-term unemployed prevail in our country and, despite the fact that the right to work is inalienable and universal. Also, they consider that there is no proper investment of profits by entrepreneurs in order to create new jobs and they do not accept that flexible working relationships can lead to unemployment reduction. Finally, they reply moderately (neither agree nor disagree) to some views with a dual content or conceptually ambiguous, for example, that "urbanization reduces jobs" or that "the division of occupations into superior and inferior is responsible for increasing unemployment". Regarding the welfare state, we could claim almost the same to what was expressed above in relation to unemployment. However, beyond the given general reflection that our sample's individuals averagely seem to acquire as a whole, a stronger concentration of their preferences in the moderate option of "neither agree nor disagree" is noted in this subject cat-

Table 1. Descriptives in relation to unemployment and welfare state services

Code Thematic Subcategories	Subcategories Thematic Description	N	Mean *	Std. Deviation
E1	Unemployment in the country is much higher than what is shown by the official indicators	341	4.01	, 912
E2	Unemployment contributes to crime rise	342	4.00	, 914
E3	The influx of immigrants has increased unemployment among Greek citizens	341	2.81	1138
E4	Flexible working relationships will lead to unemployment reduction	340	2.56	1,004
E5	Unemployment is directly related to educational level	342	2.49	1,140
E6	State measures to combat unemployment are considered sufficient	340	1.83	1,099
E7	There is racism towards the long term unemployed	341	3.54	, 983
E8	Social welfare measures for the unemployed should be increased	340	4.09	, 886
E9	Unemployment is associated with sloth (laziness)	342	2.40	1,126
E10	Anyone, who wants to find a job, finds one	341	2.60	1103
E11	Unemployment is a phenomenon of social pathology	341	3.71	, 988
E12	The right to work is universal	338	4.38	, 928
E13	Everyone finds a job according to their qualifications	341	2.39	1,042
E14	Today it is more difficult to find a job than in previous decades	342	4.15	, 944
E15	In a fair society there would be no unemployment	342	3.51	1114
E16	Unemployment is a natural consequence of liberalism	339	2.76	1,109
E17	The unemployed hinder the smooth economic growth of the country	340	2.84	1,130
E18	The unemployed are those who cannot meet the labor market modern requirements.	342	2.10	980
E19	Technology development is responsible for the rise in unemployment	342	2.78	1,081
E20	Professional racism is dominant in our country	342	3.65	, 883
E21	The professions division into superior and inferior is responsible for the unemployment increase	341	2.95	1,026
E22	Urbanization reduces jobs	342	3.22	1,010
E23	Entrepreneurs do not productively utilize their profits on investment in order to create new jobs	341	3.67	, 897
E24	The phenomenon of multiple office and overtime exacerbates this serious problem	342	3.62	, 904
E25	Unemployment leads me to occupy myself with something that I do not like in order to cover my basic subsistence needs	342	4.13	938
K1	Vulnerable groups protection is every society's duty	341	4.54	679
K2	The welfare state is currently inexistent	341	3.84	911
K3	Each of us is responsible for our survival	338	3.34	1,081
K4	The welfare state ought to implement the obligations of each society towards its members	338	4.17	, 821
K5	Welfare State should only exist within socialist political systems	340	2.43	, 914
K6	If there is no welfare state, then social inequalities cannot be cured	338	3.86	911
K7	The welfare state implements the principle of social solidarity	340	3.66	, 972
K8	The operation of the welfare state violates the principle of equal rights among all citizens	338	2.52	, 984

continued on following page

Table 1. Continued

Code Thematic Subcategories	Subcategories Thematic Description	N	Mean *	Std. Deviation
K9	The welfare state and liberalism cannot coexist	341	2.73	, 977
K10	Social benefits on behalf of the state are no longer feasible	339	3.19	1,051
K11	The social benefits of the state are associated with the ideology of socialism	340	3.01	905
K12	Modern social inequalities can only be alleviated through the welfare state	341	3.20	, 969
K13	The welfare state should be addressed only to the native vulnerable social groups	340	1.96	, 941
K14	State social benefits to vulnerable groups are sign of a civilized society	341	4.09	, 831
K15	The role of the state is to protect all its citizens, regardless of the economic cost	341	4.23	905
K16	The welfare state acts as a brake on the development of vulnerable social groups	341	2.64	1,010
K17	Unregulated social benefits led the country to its current bad economic condition	341	2.74	1,261
K18	The last to be cut down on by a modern state are social benefits to vulnerable groups	341	3.78	1213
K19	In Greece, social benefits are not only absorbed by vulnerable groups but also by groups that are not entitled to receive them	341	3.87	, 967

* The average concerns the students responses based on a Likert scale with five grades: 1 = totally disagree, 2 = disagree, 3 = neither agree nor disagree, 4 = agree, and 5 = totally agree.

egory, since statements with political content and references to political systems, such as socialism or liberalism, but also class and social inequality issues do not seem to be adequately understood by the average of the research subjects. This could be answered in conjunction with the information obtained above, regarding their low politicization rate, as they themselves declare. Nevertheless, given the above, the respondents' refusal in general to uncritically adopt demanding statements as regards their content is positively surprising, such as that "the operation of the welfare state violates the principle of equal rights among all citizens" or "the welfare state functions as a brake on the vulnerable social groups development" or "every one of us is responsible for their survival". Otherwise, they agree on average that the protection of vulnerable groups is obligation of the state at any price, since they consider that it is, among others, a sign of civilization but do not accept that social protection should be restricted only to native population but it should be extended to all people in need, living in the state's territorial limits. Nevertheless, they are critical and suspicious towards the state operation, highlighting a general concern about the widespread corruption in the Greek state, generally agreeing with the position that social benefits in Greece are supplied to social groups or individuals who do not belong to vulnerable categories, as well.

Statistical Inference

In the Kruskal-Wallis (K-W) analysis conducted, statistically significant differences were found in the means of the attitudes adopted by the students, in specific thematic subcategories according to their ideological integration. In Table 2, it seems that students of right or extreme right ideology and those of the center adopt, to a statistically significantly greater extent, conservative – or even racist type- views that consider immigrants responsible for rising unemployment in the country than students of left ideology. Similarly, individuals of right/extreme right-wing and centrist political hue, statistically, suggest

Table 2. Differentiation in the means of variables regarding unemployment and the welfare state in relation to the political ideology of the students

Thematic Subcategories	Ideological Integration	N	Mean Rank	Kruskal-Wallis	Degrees of Freedom (df)	Monte Carlo Sig. <0.01
E3	Extreme Right /Right	58	195.86	45405	2	, 000
	Centre	78	161.12			
	Left /Extreme Left /Anarchy	152	116.38			
E4	Extreme Right /Right	58	165.32	14540	2	.001
	Centre	79	162.93			
	Left /Extreme Left /Anarchy	152	127.93			
E6	Extreme Right /Right	58	173.95	12310	2	, 003
	Centre	78	145.02			
	Left /Extreme Left /Anarchy	152	133,00			
E8	Extreme Right /Right	57	125.18	9120	2	, 010
	Centre	78	133,26			
	Left /Extreme Left /Anarchy	152	156.57			
E18	Extreme Right /Right	58	139.37	13448	2	.001
	Centre	79	172.47			
	Left /Extreme Left /Anarchy	152	132.87			
E21	Extreme Right /Right	57	118.89	11705	2	, 003
	Centre	79	135,42			
	Left /Extreme Left /Anarchy	152	158.83			
K3	Extreme Right /Right	58	171.87	9771	2	, 007
	Centre	77	144.06			
	Left /Extreme Left /Anarchy	152	133.34			
K8	Extreme Right /Right	58	170.16	13172	2	, 002
	Centre	79	155.14			
	Left /Extreme Left /Anarchy	151	129.08			
K13	Extreme Right /Right	58	187,00	29839	2	, 000
	Centre	78	153.37			
	Left /Extreme Left /Anarchy	152	123.73			
K17	Extreme Right /Right	58	175.36	19463	2	, 000
	Centre	79	160.18			
	Left /Extreme Left /Anarchy	152	125.53			
K18	Extreme Right /Right	58	114.41	16209	2	, 000
	Centre	79	136.19			
	Left /Extreme Left /Anarchy	152	161.25			

significantly more flexible labor relations as a solution to reduce unemployment, focusing on a purely budgetary and financial logic that ignores the social cost, that a corresponding violation of any work established rights left in the labor market area, would entail. Also, the views of students of the above policy hue can become contradictory, since, even though they consider that the State measures to combat unemployment are inadequate, they do not agree, though, that social welfare measures for the unemployed should be increased. The increase of such measures, on the contrary, is statistically significantly more suggested by leftist students. Moreover, the centrist put the blame of unemployment to the unemployed themselves, who are unable to meet market requirements, whereas left-wing students adopt a much more political view that involves all elements of the Marxist political economy and claim that the role and position division in the labor market is responsible for unemployment, wider class stratification and inequality in society.

Regarding the welfare state topic, differentiations in the responses of students of the conservative political space (right /extreme right and centrist) are clear and statistically significant compared to those of the progressive and radical space. The former embrace an individualistic, competitive-type reasoning, that claims that everyone is solely responsible for their survival, a reasoning, where the individual deficit theory regarding those who cannot eventually manage well, is lurking. As an extension to the above, students of this particular political space consider that social type benefits afflict the interests of those who do not need them and do not make use of them, thus violating equality among citizens. Obviously, the basic premise on which the communist philosophy is founded is ignored, a philosophy of solidarity and assistance to those who need it most. In other words, the principle, that we take from everyone according to their ability and give to everyone according to their needs, is ignored. Of course, the racist point of view that social benefits should be addressed exclusively to the native population is not missing in the options of the conservative students of the sample, a rhetoric where the racist approach, nationalism and xenophobia are intensely creeping; as they are all features of the right and extreme right ideology that distinguish people on the basis of other properties, ideologically and politically constructed, and not on their current class position. Therefore, on the basis of a purely neoliberal logic, where all people are treated as commodities, there is obviously no room for foreign workforce entering the country. This force is doomed, in the minds of people who share the dominant ideology, to slide into conditions of absolute incapacity to claim even the most essential benefits for its survival, to be institutionally impeded to absorb even the minimum public and social wealth and, therefore, it is doomed to a situation of social exclusion. Also, the seemingly naive a-political interpretation of the existing socio-economic situation of the country, attests once again to the distorting interpretative dynamics of the neoliberal ideology, which is, of course, embraced by the right and extreme right as well as the centrist students of our sample. So, quite simply, according to them, it is reckless social spending led the country to the current impasse and not the intrinsic, structural and unavoidable crises of the capitalist system itself, which such politically dangerous oversimplifications serve. The argument that irrevocably leads to the contraction of the state in favor of private interests and the free market principles is broadly repeated. Finally, in contrast to the above, left ideology students statistically believe significantly more in the point of view that the welfare state and its benefits are the answer to the handling of poverty and deprivation indiscriminately faced by various vulnerable groups.

Further x^2 analysis supplied us with the information that left ideology students reside at significantly higher rates in the two main urban centers (Athens and Thessaloniki), whereas right-wing ideology students and those of the centrist political space live significantly more in rural areas or small towns (see Table 3). This fact offers more material to the discussion that preceded, since living in large urban

Table 3. Correlation of political and ideological integration of students with their families place of residence

Political-Ideological Integration	Place of Residence				Total
	Athens-Thessaloniki	Urban Center	Town	Rural Area	
Extreme Right/Right	**30**	**8**	**13**	**7**	**58**
% Within Ideological integration	51,7%	13.8%	22,4%	12,1%	100.0%
% Within place of residence	15.7%	17,0%	41,9%	35,0%	20.1%
Adjusted Residual	-2.6	- 6	3.2	1.7	
Centre	**50**	**16**	**9**	**4**	**79**
% Within Ideological integration	63,3%	20,3%	11,4%	5,1%	100.0%
% Within place of residence	26.2%	34,0%	29,0%	20.0%	27,3%
Adjusted Residual	- 6	1.1	2	- 8	
Left/Extreme Left/Anarchy	**111**	**23**	**9**	**9**	**152**
% Within Ideological integration	73,0%	15,1%	5,9%	5,9%	100.0%
% Within place of residence	58,1%	48,9%	29,0%	45,0%	52,6%
Adjusted Residual	2.6	- 5	-2.8	- 7	
Total Count	**191**	**47**	**31**	**20**	**289**

$x^2(6) = 17.647$, $p = 0.007 < 0{,}05$

centers certainly differentiates people's view of social and political reality, particularly enhances their concern on unemployment and social protection issues as well as the necessity or not of the welfare state existence. Life in the province, on the contrary, acquires other qualities that interfere and seem to jointly shape a differentiated general perspective and attitude of people towards issues of social texture.

In the Mann-Whitney (M-W) analysis then performed, several differences in a statistically significant level were detected among the statements that students embraced in relation to their degree of politicization (see Table 4). So, we see from the table that students who claim to be more politicized, appear more suspicious regarding state practices, such as artificial unemployment (less than normal) officially presented. Moreover, students in this category believe that there is racism towards the long-term unemployed and that it is necessary to increase state benefits to them; they consider unemployment as a consequence of neoliberalism and entrepreneurs investments with antisocial orientation. On the contrary, political indifferent or little politicized respondents believe that immigrants are the cause of unemployment, which they also attribute to the indifference and lack of qualifications of those who suffer from it, since in their view, anyone who wants a job, finds one, even equivalent to their qualifications. Regarding the welfare state, more politicized students think that vulnerable groups social protection is the duty of every state regardless of any cost, is a sign of civilization and is interwoven in the socialist ideology. In contrast, politically indifferent students transfer the responsibility of survival to each individual separately, consider that the welfare state is contrary to the principle of citizens equal rights, since some are assisted more than others, and of course, state aid, when provided, should, in their view, be addressed solely to the native population. We could say then, that respondents that belong to the wider political space of the left and claim to be very politicized, are those who are generally in favor of a selfless, al-

Table 4. Differentiation in the means of variables regarding unemployment and the welfare state in relation to the degree of students' politicization

Thematic Subcategories	Politicization Grade	N	Mean Rank	Mann-Whitney (U)	Monte Carlo Sig. <0.01
E1	No politicized/Little politicized/Politically indifferent	219	159.73	10890.000	, 003
	Politicized enough/ Very politicized	120	188.75		
E3	No politicized/Little politicized/Politically indifferent	219	184.47	9971.000	, 000
	Politicized enough/ Very politicized	120	143.59		
E7	No politicized/Little politicized/Politically indifferent	219	159.64	10871.000	, 003
	Politicized enough/ Very politicized	120	188.91		
E8	No politicized/Little politicized/Politically indifferent	218	160.35	11085.500	, 007
	Politicized enough/ Very politicized	120	186.12		
E10	No politicized/Little politicized/Politically indifferent	220	180.79	10715.500	, 002
	Politicized enough/ Very politicized	119	150.05		
E13	No politicized/Little politicized/Politically indifferent	219	179.45	11070.500	, 006
	Politicized enough/ Very politicized	120	152.75		
E16	No politicized/Little politicized/Politically indifferent	217	149.74	8841.000	, 000
	Politicized enough/ Very politicized	120	203.83		
E18	No politicized/Little politicized/Politically indifferent	220	179.60	11197.000	, 007
	Politicized enough/ Very politicized	120	153.81		
E23	No politicized/Little politicized/Politically indifferent	220	161.39	11195.000	, 009
	Politicized enough/ Very politicized	119	185,92		
K1	No politicized/Little politicized/Politically indifferent	219	158.63	10650.500	, 000
	Politicized enough/ Very politicized	120	190.75		
K3	No politicized/Little politicized/Politically indifferent	217	177.53	10952.500	, 008
	Politicized enough/ Very politicized	119	152.04		
K8	No politicized/Little politicized/Politically indifferent	216	178.95		, 003
	Politicized enough/ Very politicized	120	149.69	10703.000	
K11	No politicized/Little politicized/Politically indifferent	218	159.96	11000.500	.004
	Politicized enough/ Very politicized	120	186.83		
K13	No politicized/Little politicized/Politically indifferent	218	177.50	11335.000	, 012
	Politicized enough/ Very politicized	120	154.96		
K14	No politicized/Little politicized/Politically indifferent	219	153.94	9622.000	, 000
	Politicized enough/ Very politicized	120	199.32		
K15	No politicized/Little politicized/Politically indifferent	219	160.74		005
	Politicized enough/ Very politicized	120	186.89	11113.000	

truistic and solidary view of the social problem of unemployment and the social and political issue of the existence or not of a welfare state with benefits to all citizens and particularly to those of the most vulnerable social groups.

A series of further x^2 analyses performed with respect to the degree of politicization of students of the sample gave additional information, very informative in terms of discussion economy. So it seems that a statistically significantly greater percentage of the students that claim to be very politicized are postgraduate male and female students (34.2%) than the percentage of the politically indifferent ones whereas the vast majority of the latter (80%) are of undergraduate level (Table 5). The result is confirmed with further analyses in the course of the discussion.

Also, whether one works or not seems to be related to a statistically significant degree of how politicized they are. So, the students of our sample who claim to be very politicized, and even though they are much fewer (approximately less than half) than those who claim to be politically indifferent, they are, however, overrepresented in the professional sector while studying. In other words, 59,2% of those who work during their studies, claim to be very politicized (see Table 6). The results are possibly affected by the existence of postgraduate male and female students of the sample, who are, as shown above, have a greater degree of politicization than that of undergraduate students, and, moreover, they are more likely to be engaged in some profession while studying. A person's integration, however, in the labor market reasonably increases the chances to deal with policy more and formulate a comprehensive and mature view on various crucial issues of the political space.

Regarding the students' views in relation to their parents professions, no deviations were found on a statistically significant level, apart from the statement that "the welfare state and liberalism cannot coexist". This statement is, therefore, embraced mostly and at a statistically significant level by those respondents that came from artisan, worker and peasant families, a fact that would normally lead to estimations that would be related to greater class awareness of the persons concerned, since they all came from the lower social strata. However, the inconsistent appearance of statistically significant deviations in other similar views on unemployment and the welfare state, removes the possibility of supporting a

Table 5. Correlation of the degree of the students' politicization with their education level during the research period

Politicization Grade	Level of Studies		Total
	Undergraduate	Postgraduate	
No Politicized/Little Politicized/Politically Indifferent	**176**	**44**	**220**
% Within degree of politicization	80,0%	20.0%	100.0%
% Within Study Level	69,0%	51,8%	64,7%
Adjusted Residual	2.9	-2.9	
Politicized Enough/Very Politicized	**79**	**41**	**120**
% Within degree of politicization	65,8%	34,2%	100.0%
% Within Study Level	31,0%	48,2%	35,3%
Adjusted Residual	-2.9	2.9	
Total Count	**255**	**85**	**340**

$x^2(1) = 7573$, $p = 0.006 < 0,05$, with Yates correction.

Table 6. Correlation of the degree of students' politicization with employment/work during their studies

Politicization Grade	Working Status		Total
	Working	Not Working	
No Politicized/Little Politicized/ Politically Indifferent	**31**	**189**	**220**
% Within degree of politicization	14,1%	85,9%	100.0%
% Within employment	40.8%	71,9%	64,9%
Adjusted Residual	-5.0	5.0	
Politicized Enough/Very Politicized	**45**	**74**	**119**
% Within degree of politicization	37,8%	62,2%	100.0%
% Within employment	59,2%	28,1%	35,1%
Adjusted Residual	5.0	-5.0	
Total Count	**76**	**263**	**339**

$x^2(1) = 23.646$, $p = 0.0005 < 0{,}05$, with Yates correction.

similar interpretation. This particular significance should be attributed to a measurement error, since these professional categories do not acquire a sufficient number of people so that any statistical analysis is safely performed. Therefore, it is safer not to evaluate this result.

Regarding the differentiations in the responses among the students of the sample in relation to the educational level of the family of origin, a limited number was detected at a statistically significant level, which is especially difficult to interpret. So, for example, in the K-W analysis conducted, students with fathers who were uneducated or elementary school graduates, but also those with fathers who were post-graduate degree holders, appeared to be more skeptical about the credibility of the official unemployment figures shown by the state. On the other hand it is easier to interpret the greater adherence of those with fathers, that are master holders, to the view that unemployment is directly linked to the educational level, since, for their own families, studying has possibly been proven to be a successful strategy and practice of ensuring better conditions in order to find a job. In locations K6 and K12 which are similar in their conceptual content there is an inconsistency in the respondents' answers, since only those from families with fathers that are Secondary Education graduates steadily converge, in both cases, to agree more with their content which highlights, more or less, the welfare state as a key factor towards social inequalities elimination. The remaining categories of respondents more or less refute themselves as they display an inconsistency in the degree of their agreement or disagreement with the two statements per case (see. Table 7). The different wording of the two, otherwise, similar positions seem to enhance the degree of agreement in the categories of those that initially agreed less. It is possible that the intervention of 5 additional statements (from K6 to K12) relevant to the nature of the welfare state in the corresponding questionnaire, in a way affected the respondents' general concerns. However, any interpretation would be difficult and risky. Regarding their mothers' educational level, it does not seem to play a special role in shaping the respondents' views.

Table 8 depicts the statistically significant differentiations of students in various views and attitudes on unemployment and welfare state, depending on the level of their own studies during the period of the research. The M-W analysis performed, gave similar results to those received from the corresponding analyses in relation to the respondents' degree of politicization and political ideology. In this case we have an identification of male and female postgraduate students with more elaborate views on unemploy-

Table 7. Differentiation in the means of the variables regarding unemployment and the welfare state in relation to their father's level of education

Thematic Subcategories	Education of the Father	N	Mean Rank	Kruskal-Wallis	Degrees of Freedom (df)	Monte Carlo Sig. <0.01
E1	Illiterate/Primary Education Graduate	38	209.45	11364	3	0.01
	Secondary Education Graduate	99	171.69			
	Higher Education Graduate	173	156.45			
	Master Degree	27	182.65			
E5	Illiterate/Primary Education Graduate	38	122.39	11904	3	0,007
	Secondary Education Graduate	100	173.64			
	Higher Education Graduate	173	173.54			
	Master Degree	27	194.59			
K6	Illiterate/Primary Education Graduate	36	133.89	16853	3	0,001
	Secondary Education Graduate	99	195.73			
	Higher Education Graduate	172	157.89			
	Master Degree	27	170,00			
K12	Illiterate/Primary Education Graduate	37	173.95	14265	3	0,002
	Secondary Education Graduate	100	190.83			
	Higher Education Graduate	173	151.18			
	Master Degree	27	195.56			

ment and the welfare state. So, these students neither accept statements that consider unemployment as a cause of crime increase, nor agree that flexible employment contributes to unemployment reduction. Besides, they do not share the view that unemployment is directly related to educational level. Instead, they embrace the views that consider that unemployment is a natural consequence of liberalism and a social pathogenicity index, which would disappear in a just society. Finally, postgraduate male and female students support the necessity and obligation of the existence of the welfare state and social benefits towards vulnerable groups more than undergraduate students. Moreover, they agree with the fact that this is a sign of civilization and must be preserved at all costs, and they neither accept any cuts nor agree with the fact that the existence of the welfare state hinders vulnerable groups development. On the contrary, they agree with the view that the welfare state helps combat social inequalities and that its existence is not consistent with the prevalence of the socio-economical model of the political constitution of liberalism.

Furthermore, pertaining to the above, an additional M-W analysis showed statistically significant differentiations in the statements of the students depending on their age. Older students appear to have more concrete views and attitudes on unemployment and the welfare state. They neither agree with opinions that consider unemployment responsible for rising crime, nor believe that flexible working relations will solve the problem or that everyone can find a job depending on their skills and their educational level. On the contrary, they consider that unemployment is a social pathogenesis and therefore a consequence of liberalism and also that official indicators present lower unemployment rates than the real ones and agree with social measures for the unemployed since they consider the right to work universal. Similarly,

Table 8. Differentiation in the means of the variables regarding unemployment and the welfare state in relation to the educational level of the respondents during the research period

Thematic Sub	Level of Education	N	Mean Rank	Mann-Whitney (U)	Monte Carlo Sig. <0.01
E2	Undergraduate	257	179.35	8905.500	, 002
	Postgraduate	85	147.77		
E4	Undergraduate	255	178,50	8797.500	, 003
	Postgraduate	85	146.50		
E5	Undergraduate	257	178.76	9056.500	, 007
	Postgraduate	85	149.55		
E11	Undergraduate	256	161.06	8334.5	, 000
	Postgraduate	85	200.95		
E15	Undergraduate	257	163.91	8972.500	.004
	Postgraduate	85	194.44		
E16	Undergraduate	256	163.21	8887.000	, 011
	Postgraduate	83	190.93		
K1	Undergraduate	256	164.08	9109.000	.004
	Postgraduate	85	191.84		
K2	Undergraduate	256	161.50	8448.000	.001
	Postgraduate	85	199.61		
K9	Undergraduate	256	163.98	9083.000	, 008
	Postgraduate	85	192.14		
K12	Undergraduate	256	163.51	8961.500	005
	Postgraduate	85	193.57		
K14	Undergraduate	256	163.77	9030.000	005
	Postgraduate	85	192.76		
K15	Undergraduate	256	164.51	9217.500	, 010
	Postgraduate	85	190.56		
K16	Undergraduate	256	180.78	8377.500	.001
	Postgraduate	85	141.56		
K18	Undergraduate	256	162.57	8723.000	, 002
	Postgraduate	85	196.38		

older people consider that the existence of social measures for vulnerable groups is an obligation of any society as well as a sign of civilization and they neither agree with views on discrimination positions that provide social measures exclusively for native vulnerable groups, nor with the idea that the welfare state hinders the development of vulnerable groups. Besides, they do not share the view that reckless social benefits are responsible for the poor economic situation of the country today, as they consider that welfare state and liberalism cannot coexist, thus putting, implicitly, the blame on the prevalence of this policy and the country's economic management model (see Table 9).

Table 9. Differentiation in the means of the variables on unemployment and the welfare state in relation to the age of respondents

Thematic Sub	Age	N	Mean Rank	Mann-Whitney (U)	Monte Carlo Sig. <0.01
E1	18-22 years old	232	159.77	10038.000	, 000
	> = 23 years old	109	194.91		
E2	18-22 years old	233	180.88	10513.000	, 002
	> = 23 years old	109	151.45		
E4	18-22 years old	231	186.61	8869.000	, 000
	> = 23 years old	109	136.37		
E5	18-22 years old	233	187.89	8879.000	, 000
	> = 23 years old	109	136.46		
E8	18-22 years old	231	160.25	10221.000	.001
	> = 23 years old	109	192.23		
E11	18-22 years old	232	159.67	10016.000	.001
	> = 23 years old	109	195.11		
E12	18-22 years old	230	159.32	10077.500	.001
	> = 23 years old	108	191.19		
E13	18-22 years old	232	181,50	10209.000	.001
	> = 23 years old	109	148.66		
E16	18-22 years old	232	162.14	10589.500	, 011
	> = 23 years old	107	187.03		
K1	18-22 years old	232	161.75	10499.000	.001
	> = 23 years old	109	190.68		
K2	18-22 years old	232	162.81	10744.500	, 008
	> = 23 years old	109	188.43		
K9	18-22 years old	232	162.62	10699.500	, 008
	> = 23 years old	109	188.84		
K13	18-22 years old	231	180.39	10306.000	.001
	> = 23 years old	109	149.55		
K14	18-22 years old	232	160.36	10176.500	.001
	> = 23 years old	109	193.64		
K16	18-22 years old	232	182.30	10022.000	.001
	> = 23 years old	109	146.94		
K17	18-22 years old	232	180.38	10468.000	.004
	> = 23 years old	109	151.04		
K18	18-22 years old	232	159.92	10074.000	.001
	> = 23 years old	109	194.58		

The parents' place of residence does not appear to play a role in the views and attitudes of students in our research sample. Only in the statement that manifests that the right to work is universal, we see statistically significant differentiations among individuals with regard to their families' place of residence [KW (3) = 12,494, Monte Carlo Sig. = 0,004 <0,01]. In other words, students from Athens and Thessaloniki show significantly greater identification with this statement, perhaps because work is a major issue in the major urban centers, where the problem of unemployment and survival is particularly acute compared to the smaller regional cities, towns and villages, where survival is perhaps managed more easily through the input of the rest of the community as well, but also because of the comparatively smaller daily requirements and lower cost of living.

Table 10 lists the thematic subcategories, in which significant differentiations are detected among individuals according to their gender. We observe that male students consider that unemployment is linked to the educational level of the individual, whereas female students consider the increase of technology as the root of unemployment, a fact which could be interpreted, if we take into account the observed (but also socially constructed) 'opposition' of the female population towards technology, science and mathematics (Hill, Corbett, and Rose, 2010; Lindberg, Hyde, Petersen, and Linn, 2010; Linn, 2007). Also, female students appear more sensitized to the issue of professional racism and forced (by imposition) "choice" of less or no desired professions due to the general need for survival, as well as to issues regarding the necessity of the welfare state existence, which is not, however, clearly defined in their consciousness, since they think that its establishment is exclusively restricted in socialist political systems.

These differences between men and women may be explained and based on the results of some additional tests carried out on gender. Thus, we see that among women in our sample significantly more female postgraduate students are included than among men (28.8% and 17.5%, respectively) (for the relevant analysis values, see. Table 11). In combination with the respective result of the above analysis, that gave statistically significant differentiations among postgraduate female and male students compared

Table 10. Differentiation in the means of the variables regarding unemployment and the welfare state in relation to the gender of the respondents

Thematic Subcategories	Gender	N	Mean Rank	Mann-Whitney (U)	Monte Carlo Sig. <0.01
E5	Male	120	191.26	10948.500	,002
	Female	222	160.82		
E19	Male	120	154.16	11239.500	,005
	Female	222	180.87		
E20	Male	120	153.43	11151.500	,003
	Female	222	181.27		
E25	Male	120	151.37	10904.500	,001
	Female	222	182.38		
K4	Male	120	150.23	10767.000	,001
	Female	218	180.11		
K5	Male	119	153.07	11075.500	,006
	Female	221	179.88		

Table 11. The x^2 analysis values between gender and level of study

	Value	df	Asymp. Sig. (2-Sided)
Pearson Chi-Square	5,353(b)	1	,021
Continuity Correction(a)	4,763	1	,029
N of Valid Cases	342		

a. Computed only for a 2x2 table
b. 0 cells (,0%) have expected count less than 5. The minimum expected count is 29,82.

to undergraduate students (see Discussion of Table 10), we can presume that the differentiation between women and men is a result of the respective difference in numbers of males and females participating in postgraduate studies.

In addition, we report a statistically significant gender differentiation regarding the sense of security provided by the state to its citizens. We see, then, that women seem to be more insecure, since they find themselves less protected by the state. The insecurity feeling, however, is widespread in the vast majority of the population. Thus, female students declare at a rate of 98.2% that they are not adequately protected by the state, while male students at a rate of 89.1% (for the values of the analysis, see Table 12).

To summarize, we would say that statistically significant differentiations occur in the students' views and attitudes on issues such as unemployment and the welfare state, depending on their gender, political-ideological views and their degree of politicization, but also the level of their studies. Whether they work or not during their studies also plays an important role, as well as their age whereas their father's educational level and their families place of residence are less influential. So, more elaborate and mature views and attitudes are adopted by female, of left ideology and strongly politicized students of older age, that study at the postgraduate level, who are integrated in the labor market and state that their permanent residence is located in the major urban centers of Athens and Thessaloniki.

SOLUTIONS, RECOMMENDATIONS, AND FUTURE RESEARCH DIRECTIONS

Undoubtedly the problem of unemployment and subsequent social vulnerability and social exclusion results, is one of the primary and urgent issues on the agenda of policies concerning training employment and social policy. It is obvious that the prolonged recession and crisis period of the Greek economy

Table 12. The x^2analysis values between gender and sense of security and trust to the state

	Value	df	Asymp. Sig. (2-Sided)
Pearson Chi-Square	13,528(b)	1	,000
Continuity Correction(a)	11,677	1	,001
N of Valid Cases	340		

a. Computed only for a 2x2 table
b. 0 cells (,0%) have expected count less than 5. The minimum expected count is 5,95.

form a negative climate and conditions that indicate the collapse of the citizens' confidence towards the meaning and mission of the modern welfare state. It is clear that fundamental redefinition of the existing structures of education, training, lifelong learning and employment is demanded in an effort to align these areas with the Greek economy demand for productive reconstruction. It is obvious that, the unemployment issue cannot be tackled unilaterally by training or employment policies. It is essential that interventions take into account the conditions of the formation of the new social division of labor in Greece with the following high points:

1. Active confrontation of educational and social inequalities,
2. Technical and vocational training upgrading,
3. Creation of mechanisms for diagnosis and analysis of both production and labor market,
4. Production connection with all forms, types and versions of education-training-lifelong learning,
5. Promotion of advanced sectors emphasizing in areas that contribute to the strengthening of the Greek economy,
6. Flexible integration of policy tools without prejudice and stereotypes of the past (e.g. internship, apprenticeship forms) in order to create real jobs (rather than workforce substitution ones) and a healthy connection between education and work,
7. Development of mechanisms towards the workforce educational strengthening with emphasis on the horizontal skills development,
8. Strengthening and protection of the vulnerable groups,
9. Formation of strong social safety and solidarity networks at local, regional and national level.

It is clear that there are no absolute policy proposals in order to tackle unemployment and its negative effects. Undoubtedly, we face a period of intense upheaval and social mutations absolutely different to the post war era. The challenge, in our opinion lies, with the search for a new balance towards the request for continuous social, economic and cultural development and of social cohesion, solidarity and social justice preservation. Beyond any doubt, uncontrolled hegemony of market forces globally creates the conditions of a fierce economic and socially cruel framework within which labor powers should rearrange and dynamically redefine their perspective In this sense, the search of an "ideal type" for a new welfare state under conditions of neoliberal globalization is the minimum that we should emphasize both politically and in the area of research.

CONCLUSION

Close connection of unemployment, social vulnerability and social exclusion is a key symptom of the economic crisis. At the same time, it signals a series of impacts which leave their indelible traces on the social body, a process reflected in phenomena such as poverty, material deprivation, alienation, violence in all its manifestations, introversion, misery, contemporary barbarism and coercion. These phenomena are aspects of an odious social model which abhors collective rights, undermines social acquisitions, is indifferent to the common good, deregulates any balances achieved so far through class, political, trade union and social struggles. Against this setting, young people, as an immediately and directly affected part of the Greek population, stand with distrust and pessimism resulting in internalization of the economic crisis in a painful, ambivalent and sometimes contradictory way. It is clear how values, certainties and data are not only overthrown but also overshadowed or directly disputed by the sense of insecurity, uncertainty and pessimism. Unquestionably, we ought to stand in a critical and reflective way towards the mosaic of this new era at the same time expressing our solidarity to those categories which are directly affected by marginalization and social exclusion.

REFERENCES

Abedelo, R. (n.d.). *The impact of Lifelong Learning Policies On the Inclusion of Vulnerable Groups.* Retrieved from http://www.prismanet.gr/LLL/downloads/LLL-report.pdf

Bäckman, O., & Nilsson, A. (2011). Pathways to Social Exclusion-A Life-Course Study. *European Sociological Review*, *27*(1), 107–123. doi:10.1093/esr/jcp064

Borrero, M. (2014). Psychological and Emotional Impact of Unemployment. *Journal of Sociology and Social Welfare*, *7*(6), 916–934. Retrieved from http://scholarworks.wmich.edu/jssw/vol7/iss6/12?utm_source=scholarworks.wmich.edu%2Fjssw%2Fvol7%2Fiss6%2F12&utm_medium=PDF&utm_campaign=PDFCoverPages

Burgard, S. A., Brand, J. E., & House, J. S. (2007). Toward a better estimation of the effect of job loss on health. *Journal of Health and Social Behavior*, *48*(4), 369–384. doi:10.1177/002214650704800403 PMID:18198685

Clark, K., & Drinkwater, S. (2007). *Ethnic minorities in the labour market. Dynamics and diversity.* York: JRF.

Dooley, D., & Prause, J. (2004). *The social costs of underemployment: Inadequate employment as disguised unemployment.* Cambridge: Cambridge University Press.

English, J. (1970). Not as a patient: Psychological development in a job training program. *The American Journal of Orthopsychiatry*, *40*(1), 142–150. doi:10.1111/j.1939-0025.1970.tb00688.x PMID:5410676

Feron, A. (2004). *Poverty and social exclusion in Europe and Greece: Notions, perceptions, policies.* Athens: Sakkoulas. (in Greek)

Fevre, R. (1984). *Cheap Labour and Racial Discrimination.* Cambridge: Gower.

Fryer, D. (1992). Psychological or material deprivation: Why does unemployment have mental health consequences. In E. McLaughlin (Ed.), *Understanding Unemployment. New perspectives on active labour market policies* (pp. 103–125). London: Routledge. doi:10.4324/9780203061459.ch6

Fyfe, J. (1978). Youth unemployment: An international perspective. *International Journal of Social Economics*, *5*(1), 51–62. doi:10.1108/eb013820

Gordon, M. (1979). *Youth education and unemployment problems: an international perspective.* New York: Carnegie Council on Policy Studies in Higher Education.

Hill, C., Corbett, C., & Rose, A. (2010). *Why So Few? Women in Science, Technology, Engineering, and Mathematics*. Washington, DC: AAUW.

Hoffman, N. (2011). *Schooling the in the Workplace – How Six of the World's Best Vocational Education Systems Prepare Young People for Jobs and Life*. Cambridge, MA: Harvard Education Press.

ILO. (2008). Global employment trends for youth. Geneva: ILO (International Labour Organization).

Karamesini, M. (2004). Unemployment, poverty and social exclusion in Greece. In M. Petmezidou & C. Papatheodorou (Ed.), Poverty and Social Exclusion (pp. 399-438). Athens: Exantas. (in Greek)

Karantinos, D. (2012). *The Impact of the Crisis on the Greek Labour Market*. European Employment Observatory, Ad Hoc Paper.

Keep, E. (2012). *Youth Transitions, the Labour Market and Entry into Employment: Some Reflections and Questions*. SKOPE Research Paper No. 108. Cardiff, UK: Cardiff University.

Kessler, R. C., House, J. S., & Turner, J. B. (1987). Unemployment and health in a community sample. *Journal of Health and Social Behavior*, *28*(1), 51–59. doi:10.2307/2137140 PMID:3571906

Kountentakis, F. (2012). *Unemployment Dynamics in the Greek Crisis*. University of Crete, Working Paper.

Kyridis, A. (2014). Social vulnerability and social cohesion. The asymptote of a relation. In A. Kyridis (Ed.), *Vulnerable social groups and Lifelong Learning*. Athens: Gutenberg. (in Greek)

Lamprianidis, L. (2011). *Investing in Getaway*. Athens: Kritiki. (in Greek)

Lawless, P., Martin, R., & Hardy, S. (Eds.). (1998). *Unemployment and Social Exclusion: Landscapes of Labour Inequality*. London: Jessica Kingsley Publishers Ltd & Regional Studies Association.

Lindberg, S. M., Hyde, J. S., Petersen, J. L., & Linn, M. C. (2010). New Trends in Gender and Mathematics Performance: A Meta Analysis. *Psychological Bulletin*, *136*(6), 1123–1135. doi:10.1037/a0021276 PMID:21038941

Linn, M. (2007). Women in science: Can evidence inform the debate? *Science*, *317*(5835), 199–200. doi:10.1126/science.1141569

Machin, S., & Manning, A. (1998). *The Causes and Consequences of Long – Term Unemployment in Europe* (Vol. 3, pp. 3085–3139). Elsevier Handbook of Labor Economics.

McKee-Ryan, F. M., Song, Z., Wanberg, C. R., & Kinicki, A. J. (2005). Psychological and physical well-being during unemployment: A meta-analytic study. *The Journal of Applied Psychology*, *90*(1), 53–76. doi:10.1037/0021-9010.90.1.53 PMID:15641890

Murphy, G. C., & Athanasou, J. A. (1999). The effect of unemployment on mental health. *Journal of Occupational and Organizational Psychology*, *72*(1), 83–99. doi:10.1348/096317999166518

Pillinger, J. (2001). *European Foundation for the Improvement of Living and Working Conditions, Quality in social public services*. Luxembourg: Office for Official Publications of the European Communities.

Riessman, F. (1967). New interventions for disadvantaged youth. *The American Journal of Psychiatry*, *123*(7), 880–882. doi:10.1176/ajp.123.7.880 PMID:6066740

Schoon, I., & Silberstein, R. K. (2009). Conceptualising school-towork transitions in context. In Transitions to Work – Globalization, Individualization and Patterns of Delivery. Cambridge, UK: Cambridge University Press.

Smith, D. (1974). *Racial Disadvantage in Employment*. London: Political and Economic Planning.

Smith, D. (1980). How unemployment makes the poor poorer. *Policy Studies*, *1*(1), 20–26. doi:10.1080/01442878008423299

Theodoropoulos, D., Kyridis, A., Zagkos, Ch., & Konstantinidou, Z. (2015). The "Brain Drain" Phenomenon in Greece: Young Greek scientists on their Way to Immigration, in an era of "crisis". Attitudes, Opinions and Beliefs towards the Prospect of Migration. *Journal of Education and Human Development*, *3*(4), 229–248. doi:10.15640/jehd.v3n4a21

Vatsa, K. S. (2004). Risk, vulnerability, and asset-based approach to disaster risk management. *International Journal of Sociology and Social Research*, *24*(10/11), 1–48.

Wilson, W. J. (1996). *When work disappears: The world of the new urban poor*. New York: Alfred A. Knopf.

KEY TERMS AND DEFINITIONS

Economic Crisis: A situation in which the economy of a country experiences a sudden downturn brought on by a financial crisis.

Social Exclusion: The failure of society to provide certain individuals and groups with those rights and benefits normally available to its members, such as employment, adequate housing, health care, education and training, etc.

Social Vulnerability: The inability of people, organizations, and societies to withstand adverse impacts from multiple stressors to which they are exposed. These impacts are due in part to characteristics inherent in social interactions, institutions, and systems of cultural values.

Transition to Employment: It describes the process of having access to the labour market, as well as all the practices and techniques promoting the target of employment.

Unemployment: An unemployed person is defined as: a) someone aged 15 to 74 (in Italy, Spain, the United Kingdom, Iceland, Norway: 16 to 74 years), b) without work during the reference week, c) available to start work within the next two weeks (or has already found a job to start within the next three months), d) actively having sought employment at some time during the last four weeks.

Welfare State: A system whereby the state undertakes to protect the health and well-being of its citizens, especially those in financial or social need, by means of grants, pensions, and other benefits.

Youth Unemployment: Youth unemployment includes all the youth (i.e. people between the ages of 15 and 24, inclusive) who are unemployed.

Chapter 14
Effects of Islamic Banking on Employment:
Turkish Experience

Etem Hakan Ergeç
Istanbul Medeniyet University, Turkey

Bengül Gülümser Kaytancı
Anadolu University, Turkey

ABSTRACT

Islamic Banking (IB) holds the potential of creating positive impacts upon the economy thanks to its governing principles. An extension of this potential is that the employment should be positively affected by Islamic banks. This study comparatively investigates the relationship between Islamic and private commercial banking loan and sectorial employment in Turkish economy through Granger causality method. The loans offered by IBs affect employment in manufacturing and construction sectors whereas such an impact is not identified for others. Therefore, in sectors with the exception of these two, there is no finding suggesting that IBs have positive impacts in respect to employment on real economy.

INTRODUCTION

Because of their working principles, Islamic banks (IBs) play considerable important roles in the economic structures they operate in. It is generally argued that as intermediary financial institutions, the Islamic banks may provide positive impacts to the financial system, more than the conventional banks can do. Also, they have the potential of increasing acceleration of economic development. There are a number of studies in the literature suggesting that these institutions make positive contributions from different aspects. These accounts cite their funding logics, interest-free activities, limited accessibility to global financial markets and avoiding from speculation as major factors for these additional contributions.

Funding logic appears to be the primary factor for this potential impact. Because of their governing principles, IBs, as a financial intermediary, avoid the trade of money. As an extension of this logic, they also tend to avoid interest-based activities. Islamic banking employs financial brokers preferring to deliver

DOI: 10.4018/978-1-5225-2008-5.ch014

loans as they do not reserve the room for interest-bonded assets in their actives. Because the interest-free stock exchange market is less developed than the interest-based stock exchange market, this enables better funding for the private sector in economies where the bank loans are the main means of funding.

Because money is a medium of exchange and not a commodity, its sale and purchase are prohibited in Islam. Prohibition of trade for money means that the loaning activity is more integrated with goods and services. This eventually leads to a linkage between financial flow and productivity. Therefore, the better integration of loans with goods and services means that the loans will have a real direct impact.

One of the loaning forms of these institutions is profit and loss sharing system (PLS). In this system, decisions during loaning are sensitive to the profitability of the investments. Therefore, the PLS systematic also makes sure that the resource allocation takes place more effectively (Khan, 1986; Iqbal, 1997, p. 42). Because of PLS paradigm, Islamic banks can affect productivity more than conventional banks. Because they operate based on the PLS, the Islamic banks have to act carefully in selecting the better projects in an attempt to secure the profitability of the projects; to this end, they should also keep an eye on the customers using loans. Because of only, the most profitable projects would be financed; capital would be transferred to projects which would boost the economy (Dahduli, 2009).

In addition, Islamic banks have to remain careful because they need to be realistic in reporting profits and losses for their investors. Similarly, the customers who deposit their savings with the IBs need to be more careful because of the risk involved in a possible loss in the banking activities. Because there is no predetermined return guarantee on time deposits (profit and loss sharing deposits) in İslamic banking (Chong & Liu, 2009).[1] This indicates that the IBs have to work carefully.

Because loaning transactions are more relevant to the project profitability rather than the financial situation of the bank customer in the PLS logic, it works better for the small investors with profitable ideas. In addition, the sharing of the risks through the PLS logic enables the IBs to offer funds for the projects that hold higher risk but greater revenues in the long term. This may likely positively affect economic development (Mills & Presley, 1999).

Another reason for such a positive contribution includes their protection against fluctuations in interest rates owing to their interest-free activities (Kia & Darrat, 2003; Kassim, Majid, & Yusof, 2009).[2] This means that they become less affected by the interest-rate fluctuations and perform more stable.

Another reason for the possible positive impact upon real economy is the limited access to global financial markets. The current global financial market relies mostly on the interest-based activities. Therefore, it is less deep than other markets. This means that the IBs are less integrated with the global financial markets and that they become less susceptible to the fluctuations in the global financial markets (Zarqa, 2009, pp. 184-185).

Another reason for the positive impact upon the real economy is that the operating principles of the IB require them to stay away from speculations (Al-Jarhi, 2009, p. 14). Because of these principles, it is less likely to see speculative actions in the IBs when compared to the conventional banks.

A number of empirical studies have focused on the practical reflection of the positive impacts of the IBs upon the economy. Likewise, a number of works discovered the response by these banks to the most recent global crisis.[3] It appears that these studies rely on the idea that in times of crisis, the IBs perform better than the conventional saving banks. Because of these positive contributions, causality between the evolution of these institutions and economic development should be expected.[4]

There are too many studies in the empirical literature which try to examine the relationship between Islamic banking and the real economy. Some of this studies are; Furquani and Mulyany (2009), Majid and Kassim (2010) for Malaysia, Goaied and Sassi (2011) for MENA countries, Abduh and Omer

(2012) for Indonesia, Abduh and Chowdhury (2012) for Bangladesh, Abduh, Brahim, and Omar (2012) for Bahrain, Yazdan and Hossein (2012) for Iran and Indonesia, Yusof and Bahlous (2013) for GCC and EA countries, Sarwer, Ramzan, and Ahmad (2013) for Pakistan, Yazdan and Dastan (2013) for 9 countries which has IB. Most of these studies demonstrate a significant relationship between IB evolution and economic development. The IBs have made significant progress in Turkey, compared to the private commercial banks (PCBs) since 2006.[5]Table 1 presents a comparison of this progress between 2006 and 2014. The Table shows that the share of the IBs in terms of loans and actives in the PCBs has increased in this period.

The view that the IBs may create positive impacts upon economy also suggests that the evolution of these institutions may make positive contributions to employment. This study analyzes the relationship between bank loans and employment by comparison of the IBs and PCBs in the Turkish economy. For this purpose, the causal relationship between the loans offered by the banks to the sectors and the sectoral employment has been analyzed to compare the real impact of the loan upon the employment based on the type of the banks and the duration of the loan.

EMPLOYMENT AND LOANS IN TURKEY

Outlook of the Employment in Turkey

In order to evaluate the distribution of labor composition in the Turkish economy, employment figures are presented in Table 2. A review of the table shows that the regular or casual employee group (64%) constitutes the largest share, followed by the self-employed (18%) and the employers with only 4%.

The distribution of the regular or causal employee group, the largest in the employment scheme, by the sectors is given in Table 3. It appears that the manufacturing holds the largest share (24%) among the sectors, followed by wholesale and retail, and construction sectors.

Loans in Turkish Banking System

According to Turkish Banking Law No: 5411, there are three types of banks: deposit banks, participation banks and development and investment banks.[6] (Turkish Banking Law No: 5411, 2005) Other than development and investment banks, the conventional (deposit) and participation banks are allowed to collect a deposit. Figure 1 presents the shares of the banks receiving deposits in the system for the year

Table 1. Share of Islamic banks in Turkish private banking

	2006	2014
Total Loans	5,62	7,60
Total Deposits	5,62	8,90
Total Actives	4,06	7,75

Source: Created based on data from Electronic Data Delivery System (EDDS) of the Central Bank of the Republic of Turkey (CBRT).

Table 2. Outlook of employment in Turkey (2013)

	Thousand	%
Total	25526	
Unpaid Family Worker	3220	12,61
Employer	1178	4,61
Self Employed	4779	18,72
Regular or Casual Employee	16350	64,05

Source: EDDS of the CBRT.

Table 3. Share of sectors in regular or causal employee in Turkey (2013)

	Thousand	%
Manufacturing	4007	24,51
Wholesale and Retail Trade	2138	13,08
Construction	1473	9,01
Education	1230	7,52
Transportation and Storage	953	5,83
Agriculture	587	3,59
Mining	104	0,64
Electricity	163	1,00
Real Estate	143	0,87
Accommodation and Foot	829	5,07
Information and Communication	219	1,34
Financial and Insurance	271	1,66
Professional, Scientific and Technical	398	2,43
Administrative and Support Service	884	5,41
Public Administration and Defense	1462	8,94
Human Health and Social	835	5,11
Arts, Entertainment and Recreation	92	0,56

Source: EDDS of the CBRT.

Figure 1. Share of banks in banking system (2014)
Source: Created based on data from Banking Regulation and Supervision Agency (BRSA).

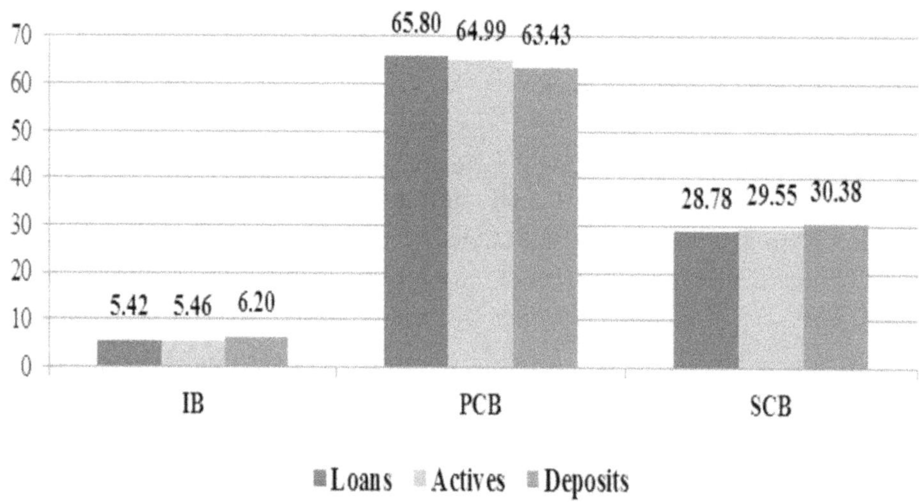

2014. The share of the IBs in the total amounts of loan actives and deposits is around 5%-6%. This is 28%-30% for the state commercial banking and 63%-65% for the private commercial banking.

Table 4 on the other hand, presents some ratios on the loans offered by private commercial banks in the Turkish banking sector for the year 2014. The diversification of these ratios for the dual banking system shows that the means of fund transfer to the real sector has also been diversified for the dual banking system. A review of the table demonstrates that the shares of the consumer loans within the total amounts of loans offered by the banks is smaller in the case of the IBs whereas their share is higher in the category of loans offered for the business enterprises.

A general outlook of the funds offered by the private capital banks in 2014 is presented in Table 5 to assess the commercial loans in the Turkish economy. A review of the table also demonstrates that for the IBs, the funds offered for some sectors within the total amount of funds (A/C) are higher when compared to the share of the IBs in the total loans (7.6%). The share of the funds offered by the IBs for a certain sector in the total amount of funds offered for that sector is 17.77% for construction, 11.93 for wholesale and 15.98% for education. This might indicate that these sectors have the tendency to use more credits higher than IBs. In addition, if the share of the funds offered for some sectors within the total amounts of funds offered by the bank is considered, in some sectors, the IBs show higher figures than the PCBs. The share of the funds for the sector within the bank funds is 25.62% for manufacturing, 20.87% for wholesale and 18.21% for construction.

Figure 2 presents the distribution of the loans offered by Islamic and private commercial banks for the sectors by their maturities.

A review of this trend shows that there are variations across the sectors. Except agriculture and manufacturing, the ratio of the long-term loans in other sectors. This trend is particularly obvious in electricity, transport, real estate and education sectors. A review of the dual banking, on the other hand, reveals that the long-term loan rates by the IBs for the mining, construction, wholesale, transport and education sectors are higher compared to the PCBs. Therefore, the tendency of the IBs to offer medium and long term loans for these sectors is higher compared to the PCBs.

DEVELOPMENT IN ISLAMIC BANKING

The interest-based operations of the conventional banking sector in predominantly Muslim countries have been questioned since the 1950s. For this reason, initial steps have been taken to create an Islamic

Table 4. Share of loans type to loans and actives of banks (2014)

	Share in Loans		Share in Actives	
	IB	**PCB**	**IB**	**PCB**
Consumer Loans	18,78	22,66	11,54	14,21
Commercial Loans	53,56	26,98	32,89	16,92
Import Loans	4,30	0,02	2,64	0,01
Export Loans	2,58	5,35	1,58	3,35
Credit Cards	2,69	9,65	1,65	6,05

Source: Created based on data from BRSA.

Table 5. Loans to sectors in Turkey's private banking sector (2014)

	IB	PCB	Total (IB+PCB)	Share of Banking Type		Share of Sector Loans in Total Loans of Bank's	
	A	B	C(A+B)	A/C	B/C	IB	PCB
Total Loans	64065242	778436926	842502168	7,60	92,40	100	100
Agriculture	879320	15573152	16452472	5,34	94,66	1,37	2,00
Short (Agr)	417223	7878402	8295625	5,03	94,97	0,65	1,01
Long (Agr)	420812	7103124	7523936	5,59	94,41	0,66	0,91
Mining	1033832	12268973	13302805	7,77	92,23	1,61	1,58
Short (Min)	312245	2690354	3002599	10,40	89,60	0,49	0,35
Long (Min)	611334	9270307	9881641	6,19	93,81	0,95	1,19
Manufacturing	16413192	154009651	170422843	9,63	90,37	25,62	19,78
Short (Man)	6402296	72648986	79051282	8,10	91,90	9,99	9,33
Long (Man)	9269943	77487012	86756955	10,68	89,32	14,47	9,95
Electric	1850012	44519377	46369389	3,99	96,01	2,89	5,72
Short (Elec)	371143	3590450	3961593	9,37	90,63	0,58	0,46
Long (Elec)	917802	40890732	41808534	2,20	97,80	1,43	5,25
Construction	11667698	53997819	65665517	17,77	82,23	18,21	6,94
Short (Cons)	3323237	18208558	21531795	15,43	84,57	5,19	2,34
Long (Cons)	7504380	34318666	41823046	17,94	82,06	11,71	4,41
Wholesale	13369476	98677819	112047295	11,93	88,07	20,87	12,68
Short (Who)	5551527	48963620	54515147	10,18	89,82	8,67	6,29
Long (Who)	7339690	46977423	54317113	13,51	86,49	11,46	6,03
Transporting	1592486	35193546	36786032	4,33	95,67	2,49	4,52
Short (Trans)	252209	6817425	7069634	3,57	96,43	0,39	0,88
Long (Trans)	1285740	27843316	29129056	4,41	95,59	2,01	3,58
Real Estate	1640448	32059505	33699953	4,87	95,13	2,56	4,12
Short (Real Est)	284668	5271510	5556178	5,12	94,88	0,44	0,68
Long (Real Est)	1324533	26473229	27797762	4,76	95,24	2,07	3,40
Education	569437	2994558	3563995	15,98	84,02	0,89	0,38
Short (Edu)	61233	896157	957390	6,40	93,60	0,10	0,12
Long (Edu)	506957	2081750	2588707	19,58	80,42	0,79	0,27

Source: Created based on data from BRSA.

banking system in the mid-1970s; these efforts led to the creation of IBs alongside the conventional banks in Muslim countries. In the 1990s, interest-free banking has attracted the attention of international banks which then started to offer service with reference to the Islamic principles in these countries (Türkiye Katılım Bankaları Birliği, March 2015, p. 11).

Figure 2. Share of sectorial loans by maturity type (2014)
Source: Created based on data from BRSA.

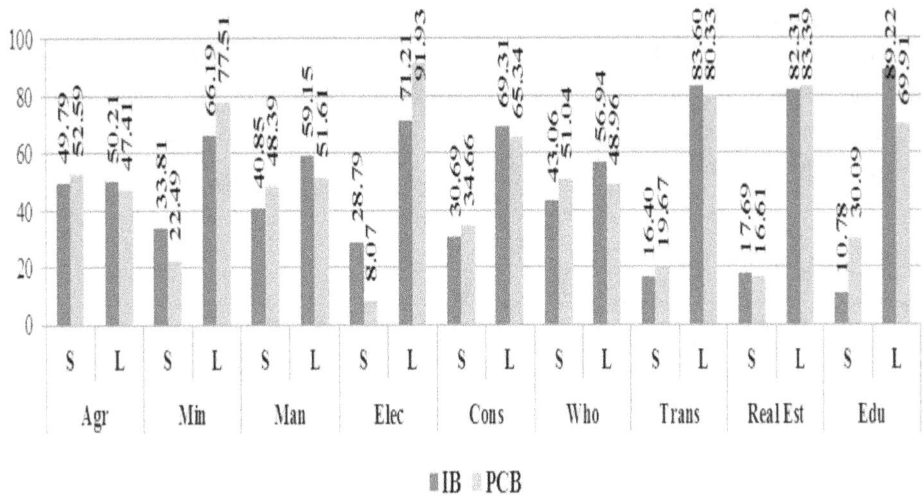

There exist Western banks and institutions that have units operating with interest-free principles; such as Citibank, HSCB, Union Bank of Switzerland, Kleinwort Benson, ANZ Grindlays, and Goldman Sachs (Türkiye Katılım Bankaları Birliği, n.d., p. 8).

In the 2000s, the sector has attracted a great deal of attention in international stage and grown significantly. However, the main factor that contributed to the sector most is the economic crisis in 2008 (Türkiye Katılım Bankaları Birliği, March 2015, p. 11).

The fact that it has become obvious that the IBs are more durable to financial crises led national governments to consider the interest-free banking model and to put investment upon its development. The global Islamic banking system has grown by 17% annually in the last five years; it is also expected that this will remain the main trend in the next five years as well. A number of their total assets is expected to reach $2 trillion by 2019.

According to the Ernst & Youth (2016), 93% of the Islamic banking actives are held in nine main markets including Qatar, Indonesia, Saudi Arabia, Malaysia, UAE and Turkey (QISMUT), Bahrain, Kuwait and Pakistan, QISMUT making up 80% (Ernst & Youth, 2016, p. 12). Estimates indicate that the strong growth in mid run will continue to focus on these markets.

The evolution of the IB sector which now becomes popular thanks to its resistance to the global crisis in 2008 can be traced back to 1980s in Turkey. The first IB institution was created 31 years ago (Türkiye Katılım Bankaları Birliği, 2015, p. 4). They joined the finance sector as Special Finance Institutions in 1985. The finance institutes which remained as special finance institutions up to 2005 were redefined as participation banks under banking law no 5411 published in the Official Gazette 1 Nov 2005 and were granted bank status. The differences between these banks and others were removed by this legislation; as a result, they increased their market share from 1% to 5.2% in 2014. This will likely increase to 20% by 2025 (Türkiye Katılım Bankaları Birliği, March 2015, pp. 5-28).

The participation bank is being supported by the public sector in Turkey. There have been some steps and initiatives to create state-supported participation banks in 2014. In addition to the already existing four participation banks, state-owned Ziraat Participation bank also launched another one in 2015, further joined by Vakıf Participation bank in 2016. Currently, there are six participation banks in Turkey. Table 6 compares the performance of the IBs after 2006, presenting the annual real growth rates of the loans, actives and deposits held by IB and PCBs.

The figures demonstrate that in both average annual growth rate and the total growth rates in the period between 2006 and 2015, the IBs performed better than PCBs. Miscellaneous Information of Banking is shown in Table 7 which indicates that a number of branches, ATMs, and personnel of the IB institutes have grown more than those of the PCBs.

Table 6. Real growth rates of banking

	Loans		Actives		Deposits	
	IB	PCB	IB	PCB	IB	PCB
2007	38,79	17,97	30,02	7,00	22,31	6,68
2008	13,51	14,21	19,99	13,62	16,24	16,38
2009	26,13	-5,58	22,82	3,43	32,01	3,14
2010	20,09	21,43	18,71	11,72	14,10	9,55
2011	17,43	23,41	21,68	15,37	11,32	11,09
2012	14,29	7,55	14,95	2,77	12,21	1,86
2013	20,32	19,61	27,18	15,69	19,03	13,66
2014	-5,12	7,90	-0,25	5,38	-2,27	5,05
2015	4,43	8,69	7,00	8,78	5,61	9,01
Avr.	16,65	12,80	18,01	9,31	14,51	8,49
Growth Rate (%) 2006-2015	265,61	164,62	303,59	103,07	211,19	89,51

Source: Created based on data from BRSA.

Table 7. Miscellaneous information of banking

	Number of Banks		Number of Domestic Branches		Number of ATM		Number of Domestic Staff	
	IB	PCB	IB	PCB	IB	PCB	IB	PCB
2006	4	29	355	4636	380	11462	7.107	98710
2007	4	28	421	5338	500	13296	9.183	111390
2008	4	27	535	6287	679	15848	11.028	122278
2009	4	27	568	6413	801	17104	11.796	121473
2010	4	27	605	6636	924	19756	12.666	125178
2011	4	26	682	6839	1.062	22090	13.838	125568
2012	4	27	825	7066	1.335	23927	15.324	128837
2013	4	27	961	7536	1.886	26993	16.712	136922
2014	4	29	986	7632	2.026	29014	16.207	138664
2015	5	29	1.076	7422	2.137	30356	16.518	136799
Growth Rate (%) 2006-2015			203	60	462	165	132	39

Source: Created based on data from BRSA.

After the announcement of the decision that the public participation banks will join the system, a remarkable increase in the number of branches and staff is also expected. Besides, it is anticipated that conventional private banks will show interest in IB sector and this trend will grow in the near future. (Türkiye Katılım Bankaları Birliği, March 2015, p. 19)

DATA AND METHODOLOGY

This study analyzes the linkage between sector loan variables and the employment. The analyses are performed by reference to the loan durations for both banking systems. The real effect of the credit will be able to contrast by bank type and maturation.

The Granger causality method was used to investigate the causality relationship between loans of and employment of sectors. Further, according to Granger (1969, 1980), this test shows the cause and effect relationship between two series. According to this method, if the expected value of one of the variables at a given time is affected by the past periods of the other series, then the affecting variable is defined as the Granger cause of the affected variable. The hypotheses that were tested using the Granger causality method are stated below.

H_0: Employment is not the Granger cause of Loans.

$$Loan_t = \alpha_0 + \sum_{j=1}^{r} \alpha_j Loan_{t-j} + \sum_{j=1}^{r} \beta_j Emp_{t-j} + v_t$$

H_0: Loans is not Granger cause of the rate of Employment.

$$Emp_t = \alpha_0 + \sum_{j=1}^{r} \alpha_j Emp_{t-j} + \sum_{j=1}^{r} \beta_j Loan_{t-j} + v_t$$

The significance of the causality relationship depends on the coefficient demonstrated by these equations. If the coefficients of the independent variable (β) are significant, it means that the Granger causality runs from the independent variable to the dependent variable.

The sectors reviewed in the study are picked based on their shares in employment. These sectors are manufacturing, construction, transportation, wholesale, and education. The series used in this study are presented in Table 8.

The dataset used in the study is consisting of monthly data which covering the period between Jan 2009 and Jan 2014.[7] The employment figures are retreated from the Electronic Data Delivery System (EDDS) of the Central Bank of the Republic of Turkey (CBRT), and the loan variables from Banking Regulation and Supervision Agency (BRSA). The loan variables are converted into real figures by using consumer price index, and the seasonal impacts are removed from the series. The variables are analyzed after the logarithmic differences are identified. Because the series are stationary at the level, the cointegration relationship is not analyzed; and the Granger causality test involving error terms is not used. To determine the lag length of all models, Akaike Information Criteria (AIC) is used.

Table 8. List of variables

Regular or Casual Employee in Sectors	
LMA_E	Manufacturing Industry
LC_E	Construction Industry
LW_E	Whole and Sale Industry
LED_IS	Education Industry
LTR_E	Transportation Industry
Loans Variables	
LMA_I	Total Loans of IB to Manufacturing
LMA_P	Total Loans of PCB to Manufacturing
LMA_IS	Short Term Loans of IB to Manufacturing
LMA_PS	Short Term Loans of PCB to Manufacturing
LMA_IL	Med.- Long Term Loans of IB to Manufacturing
LMA_PL	Med.- Long Term Loans of PCB to Manufacturing
LC_I	Total Loans of IB to Construction
LC_P	Total Loans of PCB to Construction
LC_IS	Short Term Loans of IB to Construction
LC_PS	Short Term Loans of PCB to Construction
LC_IL	Med.- Long Term Loans of IB to Construction
LC_PL	Med.- Long Term Loans of PCB to Construction
LTR_I	Total Loans of IB to Transportation
LTR_P	Total Loans of PCB to Transportation
LTR_IS	Short Term Loans of IB to Transportation
LTR_PS	Short Term Loans of PCB to Transportation
LTR_IL	Med.- Long Term Loans of IB to Transportation
LTR_PL	Med.- Long Term Loans of PCB to Transportation
LW_I	Total Loans of IB to Whole Sale
LW_P	Total Loans of PCB to Whole Sale
LW_IS	Short Term Loans of IB to Whole Sale
LW_PS	Short Term Loans of PCB to Whole Sale
LW_IL	Med.- Long Term Loans of IB to Whole Sale
LW_PL	Med.- Long Term Loans of PCB to Whole Sale
LED_I	Total Loans of IB to Education
LED_P	Total Loans of PCB to Education
LED_IS	Short Term Loans of IB to Education
LED_PS	Short Term Loans of PCB to Education
LED_IL	Med.- Long Term Loans of IB to Education
LED_PL	Med.- Long Term Loans of PCB to Education

EMPIRICAL RESULT OF ANALYSES

The results of the Granger causality tests between the loans and employment of manufacturing Industries are presented in Table 9. For manufacturing sector which holds the largest share of employment and loans in the banking system, causality from loans towards employment has been identified. But for short term loans, causality for only IBs has been detected. Additionally, causality has been in longer lags for the IBs.

The results of the Granger causality tests for construction industries are shown in Table 10. Similar to the manufacturing sector, causality from loans towards employment has been detected for both banking systems. But it appears that this causality is more visible for the IBs.

The results of the wholesale industry analyses are presented in Table 11. No causality has been detected for the IBs in this sector whereas there is causality in mid and long terms from loans towards employment in PCBs.

The results of the Granger causality test for the education sector are presented in Table 12. A two-way causality has been detected for PCBs whereas only one-way causality has been identified for IBs. In the education sector, employment is the Granger cause of the IB education sector loans.

The results of the causality test between the loans and employment variables for transportation industries are exhibited in Table 13. There is a two-way causality for the PCBs whereas causality is one-way for the IBs. There is causality from employment towards loans in this sector for the IBs.

CONCLUSION

Islamic Banks (IB), in addition to serving as financial intermediaries, also play some significant roles in the economies they operate. It is generally argued that as intermediary financial institutions, the Islamic banks may provide positive impacts to the financial system, better than the conventional banks can do. There are a number of studies in the literature suggesting that these institutions make positive contributions from different aspects. These accounts cite their funding logics, interest-free activities,

Table 9. Granger causality results of manufacturing industry

	Term	Direction of Causality	Lag	F. Stat
Islamic Banking	Sort	Loans does not Granger Cause Employee	4	241831*
		Employee does not Granger Cause Loans		0.06815
	Long	Loans does not Granger Cause Employee	1	159.840
		Employee does not Granger Cause Loans		0.51357
	Total	Loans does not Granger Cause Employee	11	237382**
		Employee does not Granger Cause Loans		135.964
Private Commercial Banking	Sort	Loans does not Granger Cause Employee	2	145.286
		Employee does not Granger Cause Loans		0.06437
	Long	Loans does not Granger Cause Employee	1	424583**
		Employee does not Granger Cause Loans		460535**
	Total	Loans does not Granger Cause Employee	4	306157**
		Employee does not Granger Cause Loans		0.42647

Table 10. Granger causality results of construction industry

	Term	Direction of Causality	Lag	F. Stat
Islamic Banking	Sort	Loans does not Granger Cause Employee	18	179.593
		Employee does not Granger Cause Loans		215.297
	Long	Loans does not Granger Cause Employee	12	319583***
		Employee does not Granger Cause Loans		0.64623
	Total	Loans does not Granger Cause Employee	8	289965**
		Employee does not Granger Cause Loans		123.670
Private Commercial Banking	Sort	Loans does not Granger Cause Employee	18	488010**
		Employee does not Granger Cause Loans		0.68482
	Long	Loans does not Granger Cause Employee	18	112.234
		Employee does not Granger Cause Loans		0.39528
	Total	Loans does not Granger Cause Employee	2	0.11938
		Employee does not Granger Cause Loans		0.52700

Table 11. Granger causality results of whole and sale industry

	Term	Direction of Causality	Lag	F. Stat
Islamic Banking	Sort	Loans does not Granger Cause Employee	3	0.77275
		Employee does not Granger Cause Loans		193.022
	Long	Loans does not Granger Cause Employee	6	0.95118
		Employee does not Granger Cause Loans		170.162
	Total	Loans does not Granger Cause Employee	3	135.933
		Employee does not Granger Cause Loans		0.88470
Private Commercial Banking	Sort	Loans does not Granger Cause Employee	1	0.86512
		Employee does not Granger Cause Loans		0.46181
	Long	Loans does not Granger Cause Employee	7	399244***
		Employee does not Granger Cause Loans		0.42888
	Total	Loans does not Granger Cause Employee	2	0.93374
		Employee does not Granger Cause Loans		0.43896

limited accessibility to global financial markets and avoiding from speculation as major factors for these additional contributions.

Funding logic appears to be the primary factor for this potential impact. Because of their governing principles, IBs, as financial intermediaries, avoid the trade of money or currency. As an extension of this logic, they also tend to avoid interest-based activities. Islamic banking employs financial brokers preferring to deliver loans as they do not reserve a room for interest-bonded assets in their actives. Because the interest-free stock exchange market is less developed than the interest-based stock exchange market, this enables better funding for the private sector in economies where the bank loans are the main means of funding.

Table 12. Granger causality results of education industry

	Term	Direction of Causality	Lag	F. Stat
Islamic Banking	Sort	Loans does not Granger Cause Employee	12	0.76940
		Employee does not Granger Cause Loans		0.54310
	Long	Loans does not Granger Cause Employee	12	133.201
		Employee does not Granger Cause Loans		281736**
	Total	Loans does not Granger Cause Employee	12	103.494
		Employee does not Granger Cause Loans		219899**
Private Commercial Banking	Sort	Loans does not Granger Cause Employee	3	110.217
		Employee does not Granger Cause Loans		502941***
	Long	Loans does not Granger Cause Employee	8	326332***
		Employee does not Granger Cause Loans		239625**
	Total	Loans does not Granger Cause Employee	8	707400***
		Employee does not Granger Cause Loans		258361**

Table 13. Granger causality results of transportation industry

	Term	Direction of Causality	Lag	F. Stat
Islamic Banking	Sort	Loans does not Granger Cause Employee	4	0.98374
		Employee does not Granger Cause Loans		464619***
	Long	Loans does not Granger Cause Employee	2	145.629
		Employee does not Granger Cause Loans		0.67547
	Total	Loans does not Granger Cause Employee	3	0.77965
		Employee does not Granger Cause Loans		339315**
Private Commercial Banking	Sort	Loans does not Granger Cause Employee	1	0.00652
		Employee does not Granger Cause Loans		0.54180
	Long	Loans does not Granger Cause Employee	9	371470***
		Employee does not Granger Cause Loans		196721*
	Total	Loans does not Granger Cause Employee	1	0.10333
		Employee does not Granger Cause Loans		0.15971

Because of the positive impacts by the IBs upon the economy, a causal relationship is expected between the developments of these institutions and economic development. There are many studies in the literature that analyze this relationship. An extension of the idea that the IBs may create positive impacts upon the economy is the possibility that these institutions provide positive contributions upon employment.

It appears that regular or causal employee group holds the largest share (64%) within the total employment in the Turkish economy, followed by self-employed (18%). A review of the distribution of the regular or causal employee group within the sectors of the economy shows that manufacturing sector holds a share of 24%, followed by wholesale and retail sector and construction sector.

The IBs have exhibited relatively higher performance than the PCBs within the Turkish banking system since 2006. Their shares of loans and actives within private capital banking have significantly increased.

A general review of the loans offered by the private capital banks for the Turkish banking sector in 2014 reveals that there is some different for both banking systems. It appears that the shares of the consumer loans within the total loans offered by the bank are smaller for the IBs whereas the shares of the business loans are larger. This indicates that there is a major diversification in terms of transferring fund to the real sector for both banking systems.

Table 14. Summary of the Granger causality results

			Loans Employment
Manufacturing	IB	S	→
		L	
		T	→
	PCB	S	
		L	↔
		T	→
Whole Sale	IB	S	
		L	
		T	
	PCB	S	
		L	→
		T	
Construction	IB	S	
		L	→
		T	→
	PCB	S	→
		L	
		T	
Education	IB	S	
		L	←
		T	←
	PCB	S	←
		L	↔
		T	↔
Transportation	IB	S	←
		L	
		T	←
	PCB	S	
		L	
		T	↔

It also appears that in 2014, the shares of the IBs in loans offered for some sectors including construction, wholesale and education are relatively higher. This may indicate that the tendency of borrowing from the IBs is greater than the other sectors. Besides the share of the credits provided to the sectors such as manufacturing, construction and wholesale is higher in the IBs compared to the PCBs.

A review of the tendency in loans based on loan terms shows that there are variations across sectors. In sectors other than agriculture and manufacturing, the share of the long-term loans is higher. This tendency is particularly obvious in electricity, transport, real estate and education sectors. When the two banking systems are reviewed, for the mining, construction, wholesale, transport and education sectors, the long-term loan rates by the IBs are higher compared to the PCBs. Therefore, the tendency of the IBs to offer medium and long term loans for these sectors is relatively higher when compared to the PCBs.

This study reviews the linkage between bank loans and employment in the Turkish economy. For this purpose, the causal relationship between the loans offered by banks for these sectors and employment has been analyzed. The Granger causality method was used to investigate the causality relationship between loans of and employment of sectors for the period 2009-2014. The analyses are performed based on the loan terms for both banking systems. In this way, the real impact of the loan, according to the bank type and term, has been compared. The study analyzes the manufacturing, construction, transportation, wholesale, and education sectors by referring to the shares of the sectors within employment. Table 14 summarizes the findings of this study.

In some sectors, a two-way causality has been identified for the PCBs whereas such a linkage has not been detected for the IBs. For manufacturing and construction sectors, the loans offered by the IBs affect the employment in causal terms whereas no such impact has been identified for other sectors. Therefore, in sectors other than these, the study offers no findings suggesting that the IBs have the positive impact on the economy in terms of employment for sectors other these ones. Wholesale sector is the one where the causality between loans and employment is the weakest for the IBs.

REFERENCES

Abduh, M., Brahim, S., & Omar, M. A. (2012). A study on finance-growth nexus in dual financial countries: Evidence from Bahrain. *World Applied Science Journal*, *20*(8), 1166–1174.

Abduh, M., & Chowdhury, N. T. (2012). Islamic banking – economic growth nexus: Evidence from Bangladesh. *Journal of Islamic Economics. Banking and Finance*, *8*(3), 104–113.

Abduh, M., & Omar, M. A. (2012). Islamic banking and economic growth: The Indonesian experience. *International Journal of Islamic and Middle Eastern Finance and Management*, *5*(1), 35–47. doi:10.1108/17538391211216811

Ahmed, A. (2010). Global financial crisis: An Islamic finance perspective. *International Journal of Islamic and Middle Eastern Finance and Management*, *3*(4), 306–320. doi:10.1108/17538391011093252

Al-Jarhi, M. A. (2009). *Islamic finance an efficient & equitable option*. Islamic Development Bank, The Islamic Research and Training Institute. Retrieved April 20, 2016, from http://www.iefpedia.com/english/wp-content/uploads/2009/11/ISLAMIC-FINANCE-AN-EFFICIENT-EQUITABLE-OPTION.pdf

Al-Samadi, A. A.-M. A., Hamdan, F., & Almsafir, M. K. (2013). Islamic banking vs. conventional banking, during the global financial crisis: Malaysia as a case. *Journal of Islamic and Human Advanced Research, 3*(1), 27–40.

Aras, O. N., & Öztürk, M. (2011). Reel ekonomiye katkıları bakımından katılım bankalarının kullandırdığı fonların analizi. *Ekonomi Bilimleri Dergisi, 3*(2), 167–179.

Bacha, O. I. (2004). Dual banking systems and interest rate risk for Islamic banks. *The Journal of Accounting, Commerce & Finance – Islamic Perspective, Working Paper, MPRA 12763, 8*(1), 1-42.

Beck, T., Levine, R., & Loayza, N. (2000). Finance and the sources of growth. *Journal of Financial Economics, 58*(1-2), 261–300. doi:10.1016/S0304-405X(00)00072-6

Calderon, C., & Liu, L. (2002). *The direction of causality between financial development and economic growth.* Working Paper No. 184, Central Bank of Chile, Santiago.

Çevik, S., & Charap, J. (2011). *The behaviour of conventional and Islamic bank deposit returns in Malaysia and Turkey.* Working Paper, IMF 11/156. International Monetary Fund.

Chapra, M. U. (2008). *The global financial Crisis: Can Islamic finance help minimize the severity and frequency of such a crisis in the future?* Conference Paper, Islamic Development Bank, Forum on the Global Financial Crisis.

Chong, B. S., & Liu, M.-H. (2009). Islamic banking: Interest-free or interest- based? *Pacific-Basin Finance Journal, 17*(1), 125–144. doi:10.1016/j.pacfin.2007.12.003

Dahduli, M. S. (2009). Islamic banking and economic development. *SSRN Electronic Journal.* doi: 10.2139/ssrn.1616624

Dar, H. A., & Presley, J. R. (2000). Lack of profit loss sharing in Islamic banking: Management and control imbalances. *International Journal of Islamic Financial Services, 2*, 1–9.

Demetriades, P. O., & Hussein, A. K. (1996). Does financial development cause economic growth? Time-series evidence from 16 countries. *Journal of Development Economics, 51*(2), 387–411. doi:10.1016/S0304-3878(96)00421-X

Ergeç, E. H., & Arslan, B. G. (2013). Impact of interest rates on Islamic and conventional banks: The case of Turkey. *Applied Economics, 45*(17), 2381–2388. doi:10.1080/00036846.2012.665598

Ergeç, E. H., & Kaytancı, B. G. (2014). The causality between returns of interest-based banks and interest free banks: The case of Turkey. *International Journal of Islamic and Middle Eastern Finance and Management, 7*(4), 443–456. doi:10.1108/IMEFM-07-2014-0072

Ernst & Young. (2016). *World Islamic Banking Competitiveness Report-2016.* Retrieved April 20, 2016, from http://www.ey.com/Publication/vwLUAssets/ey-world-islamic-banking-competitiveness-report-2016/$FILE/ey-world-islamic-banking-competitiveness-report-2016.pdf

Furqani, H., & Mulyany, R. (2009). Islamic banking and economic growth: Empirical evidence from Malaysia. *Journal of Economic Cooperation and Development, 30*, 59–74.

Goaied, M., & Sassi, S. (2011). Financial development, Islamic banking and economic growth evidence from MENA region. *International Journal of Business and Management Science*, *4*(2), 105–128.

Granger, C. W. J. (1969). Investigating causal relations by econometric models and cross-spectral methods. *Econometrica*, *37*(3), 424–438. doi:10.2307/1912791

Granger, C. W. J. (1980). Testing for causality: A personal viewpoint. *Journal of Economic Dynamics & Control*, *2*, 329–352. doi:10.1016/0165-1889(80)90069-X

Greenwood, J., & Jovanovic, B. (1990). Financial development, growth and the distribution of income. *Journal of Political Economy*, *98*(5), 1076–1107. doi:10.1086/261720

Haron, S., & Ahmad, N. (2000). The effects of conventional interest rates and rate of profits on funds deposited with Islamic banking system in Malaysia. *International Journal of Islamic Financial Services*, *1*(4), 1–7.

Hasan, M. M., & Dridi, J. (2010). *The effects of the global crisis on Islamic and conventional banks: A comparative study.* Working Paper, IMF 10-201. International Monetary Fund.

Iqbal, Z. (1997). Islamic financial systems. *Finance & Development*, (June), 42–45.

Jung, W. S. (1986). Financial development and economic growth: International evidence. *Economic Development and Cultural Change*, *34*(2), 336–346. doi:10.1086/451531

Kaleem, A., & Isa, M. M. (2003). Causal relationship between Islamic and conventional banking instruments in Malaysia. *International Journal of Islamic Financial Services*, *4*(4), 1–8.

Kasri, R. A., & Kassim, S. H. (2009). Empirical determinants of saving in the Islamic Banks: Evidence from Indonesia. *Journal of King Abdulaziz University: Islamic Economics*, *22*(2), 181–201.

Kassim, S., Majid, M. A., & Yusof, R. M. (2009). Impact of monetary policy shocks on conventional and Islamic banks in a dual banking system: Evidence from Malaysia. *Journal of Economic Cooperation and Development*, *30*, 41–58.

Khan, M. (1986). Islamic interest-free banking: A theoretical analysis. *Staff Papers - International Monetary Fund. International Monetary Fund*, *33*(1), 1–27. doi:10.2307/3866920

Kia, A., & Darrat, A. F. (2003). *Modeling money demand under the profit-sharing banking scheme: Evidence on policy invariance and long-run stability.* Working Paper, Department of Economics, Carleton University. Retrieved April 20, 2016, from http://www.mafhoum.com/press7/193E13.pdf

Kınalı, F. (2012). *Faizsiz sistemde bankacılık anlayışı ve kredi işlemleri* (Unpublished master's thesis). T.C. Selçuk Üniversitesi Sosyal Bilimler Enstitüsü İşletme Anabilim Dalı Muhasebe Finansman Bilim Dalı, Konya.

King, R. G., & Levine, R. (1993). Finance and growth: Schumpeter might be right. *The Quarterly Journal of Economics*, *108*(3), 717–737. doi:10.2307/2118406

Levine, R., Loayza, N., & Beck, T. (2000). Financial intermediation and growth: Causality and causes. *Journal of Monetary Economics*, *46*(1), 31–77. doi:10.1016/S0304-3932(00)00017-9

Majid, S. A., & Kassim, S. (2010, August). *Islamic finance and economic growth: The Malaysian experience.* Conference paper, Kuala Lumpur Islamic Finance Forum, Kuala Lumpur.

Mills, P. S., & Presley, J. R. (1999). *Islamic finance: Theory and practice.* London: Macmillan. doi:10.1057/9780230288478

Patrick, H. T. (1966). Financial development and economic growth in underdeveloped countries. *Economic Development and Cultural Change, 14*(2), 174–189. doi:10.1086/450153

Rajan, G. R., & Zingales, L. (1998). Financial dependence and economic growth. *The American Economic Review, 88*, 559–586.

Rosly, S. A. (1999). Al-bay Bithaman Ajil financing: Impacts on Islamic banking performance. *Thunderbird International Business Review, 41*(4-5), 461–480. doi:10.1002/tie.4270410410

Sarwer, M. S., Ramzan, M., & Ahmad, W. (2013). Does Islamic banking system contributes to economy development. *Global Journal of Management and Business Research Version 1.0, 13*(2), 61-68.

Sukmana, R., & Kassim, S. H. (2010). Roles of the Islamic banks in the monetary transmission process in Malaysia. *International Journal of Islamic and Middle Eastern Finance and Management, 3*(1), 7–19. doi:10.1108/17538391011033834

Turkish Banking Law. No: 5411. (2005). *Official Gazette of the Republic of Turkey, 25983 (bis).* Retrieved April 20, 2016, from https://www.bddk.org.tr/websitesi/turkce/Mevzuat/Bankacilik_Kanunu/15405411_sayili_bankacilik_kanunu.pdf

Türkiye Katılım Bankaları Birliği. (2015). *Katılım Bankaları 2015.* İstanbul: Türkiye Katılım Bankaları Birliği. Retrieved April 20, 2016, from http://www.tkbb.org.tr/Documents/Yonetmelikler/KATILIM_2015_TR_final.pdf

Türkiye Katılım Bankaları Birliği. (n.d.). *Katılım Bankacılığı Nedir? Nasıl Çalışır?* Retrieved April 20, 2016, from http://www.tkbb.org.tr/Documents/Yonetmelikler/KATILIM_BANKACILIGI-NEDIR-NASIL-CALISIR.pdf

Türkiye Katılım Bankaları Birliği. (2015, March). *Türkiye katılım bankacılığı strateji belgesi 2015 – 2025 (No: 5).* İstanbul: Türkiye Katılım Bankaları Birliği.

Yazdan, G. F., & Dastan, M. (2013). Analysis of Islamic banks financing and economic growth: A panel cointegration approach. *International Journal of Islamic and Middle Eastern Finance and Management, 6*(2), 156–172. doi:10.1108/17538391311329842

Yazdan, G. F., & Hossein, S. S. M. (2012). Analysis of Islamic bank's financing and economic growth: Case study Iran and Indonesia. *Journal of Economic Cooperation and Development, 33*(4), 1–24.

Yusof, R. M., & Bahlous, M. (2013). Islamic banking and economic growth in GCC & East Asia countries: A panel cointegration analysis. *Journal of Islamic Accounting and Business Research, 4*(2), 151–172. doi:10.1108/JIABR-07-2012-0044

Zainol, Z., & Kassim, S. H. (2010). An analysis of Islamic banks' exposure to rate of return risk. *Journal of Economic Cooperation and Development, 31*(1), 59–84.

Zarqa, M. A. (2009). Stability in an interest-free Islamic economy: A note. In *Issues in the international financial crisis* (pp. 227–235). Jeddah: King Abdulaziz University, Islamic Economic Research Center.

KEY TERMS AND DEFINITIONS

Causality: The causal relationship between two variables.

Interest-Free Banking: The banking system where interests are not used. In this system, banks do not offer a fixed rate of return on deposits and do not charge interest on loans.

Islamic Banking: Banking system compliant with sharia (Islamic Law). Sharia prohibits taking or offering interest. Investment in businesses that provide goods or services considered opposed to Islamic principles (for example, alcohol, pork or tobacco) is also non-halal.

Participation Banking: The name given to Islamic banks in Turkey.

Private Capital Banking: The banking system of which all the shares belong to non-state entities.

Profit And Loss Sharing (PLS): Sharing of risk and profits between the parties. Under the PLS, borrowers share profits and losses with their banks, and banks share profits and losses with their depositors.

Sectoral Loans: Type of commercial loans offered to a specific sector.

ENDNOTES

1. But a number of works indicate that the IBs do not prefer the PLS model in loaning practices. While PLS model is preferred in collecting deposits, they rely on murabaha-based transactions in loaning (Dar & Presley, 2000; Çevik & Charap, 2011 and Chong & Liu, 2009). Therefore, the PLS, originally introduced as the main method, now remains marginal in practice. Only less than 20% of the total financing is being performed through PLS (Kınalı, 2012, p. 149). This is also the case with Turkey. The IBs collect funds through a model partnership (mudaraba) and loan them through murabaha (Aras & Öztürk, 2011).
2. But a number of studies have analyzed the impacts of the interest rates in economic structures with dual banking system upon the IBs and determined this linkage empirically. (Chong & Liu, 2009; Bacha, 2004; Kaleem & Isa, 2003; Rosly, 1999; Haron & Ahmad, 2000; Kasri & Kassim, 2009; Sukmana & Kassim, 2010; Zaionol & Kassim, 2010). Similar empirical results can also be identified in studies focusing on Turkish economy as well (Ergeç & Arslan, 2013; Ergeç & Kaytancı, 2014).
3. For studies on the response by the IB system to the financial crises, see: Chapra, 2008; Hasan & Dridi, 2010; Ahmed, 2010; Al-Samadi, Hamdan, & Almsafir, 2013.
4. The link between financial structure and real economy has always attracted a great deal of attention in the literature. There are a number of scholarly works on the causality between financial system and economic development (King & Levine, 1993; Rajan & Zingales, 1998; Beck, Levine, & Loayza, 2000; Levine, Loayza, & Beck, 2000; Calderón & Liu, 2002; Patrick, 1966; Jung, 1986; Greenwood & Jovanovic, 1990 and Demetriades & Hussein, 1996).
5. Empirical works in the literature compare the Islamic banks and commercial banks in dual banking economies without considering their capital structures. But because the IBs were private capital

banks in the period under review, this study ignores the public-capital banks and instead compares the IBs to the private capital banks.

6 In Turkey; "Participation Banking" notion are used to define these institution; however, they are defined as Islamic or interest-free banking in the international literature. In this study, Islamic banking was preferred to define this banking type.

7 Data restriction on workforce market affected the time interval of the dataset used in the study.

Chapter 15
Global Trends in the Construction Industry:
Challenges of Employment

Begüm Sertyeşilışık
Istanbul Technical University, Turkey

ABSTRACT

Construction industry is a labor-intensive industry contributing to the employment rate of the countries. The state of the country's economy and its construction industry are interdependent. An increase in the unemployment rate in the construction industry can have adverse impacts on the country's economy. Local markets are not local anymore. Even in the domestic markets, there is international competition due to the globalization. For this reason, global changes and new trends as challenges of employment in the construction industry need to be carefully analyzed due to their potential impacts on the employment rate and on the labor profile. This chapter covers construction industry's contribution to the employment rate of the countries; global trends as challenges of employment in the construction industry and as factors influencing professionals' skills needed in the construction industry; ways of adapting the construction workforce and professionals to the global trends in the construction industry.

INTRODUCTION

Construction industry plays an important role in the global economy as it has 15% share in the world's GDP (Gross Domestic Product) (Mazhar & Arain, 2015, p. 434). The global construction market is expected to grow further to USD$15,030 billion in 2025 (Department for Business Innovation and Skills [DEFRA], 2013, p. 5). Construction is a labour-intensive activity, and able to provide employment with low investment (International Labour Organization [ILO], 2001, p. 58). Construction industry depends more on labor compared to other industries (Kim, Kim, Shin, & Kim, 2015, p. 1534). Construction industry contributes to the employment rate of the countries (The World Bank, 2016) as well as to their economy. For this reason, construction industry can contribute to the global unemployment problem as global unemployment increased by 5 million people in 2013and as it is expected to rise by a further 13

DOI: 10.4018/978-1-5225-2008-5.ch015

million people by 2018 (International Labour Organization [ILO], 2014, p. 3). Ernst and Sarabia (2015, p. 24)'s research on structural economic trends in 45 high-income countries, middle-income countries and low-income countries between 1995 and 2009 revealed that the construction sector is crucial for economic growth and employment creation. Similarly, Chiang, Tao and Wong (2015, p. 1)'s study on Hong Kong revealed bidirectional causality links between GDP and construction activities as well as correlations of employment with GDP and construction. Further examples include but are not limited to the construction industries in the UK, Canada, Australia, Portugal, Bulgaria, Spain, Taiwan, United States, and Korea. In the UK, the construction industry contributed to £103 billion in economic output in 2014, and to the 6.2% of total employment in 2015 (Rhodes, 2015, p. 3). Construction industry plays an important role in the economy of Canada (Mazhar & Arain, 2015, p. 434). In Australia, the construction industry employs approximately 9% of the total workforce (Australian Industry Group [AIGROUP], 2015). In Portugal, the construction industry contributes to the 10.7% of total employment and to the 6.4% of GDP (Horta, Camanho, & Costa, 2012, p. 84). Ernst and Sarabia (2015, p. 9)'s research based on the WIOD (World Input-Output Database) (Trimmer, 2012) revealed that the construction industry presented "between 4.5% (Bulgaria) and 10.4% (Spain) of the overall gross output in 1995 and between 4.2% (Taiwan) and 14.6% (Spain) in 2009" and that regarding "total value added, it represented between 4.2% (United States) and 10.1% (Korea) in 1995 and between 2.2% (Taiwan) and 10.8% (Spain) in 2009". The construction industry further contributes to the economy due to "its 'pull' and 'push' multiplier effects on other economic sectors." (Chiang, Tao, & Wong, 2015, p. 1). The construction industry has higher multiplier effects compared to other industries (Ernst & Sarabia, 2015, p. 10). Ernst and Sarabia (2015, p. 24)'s research on 45 countries, based on data obtained through from WIOD and EORA, revealed that construction industry has acted as an employment driver especially in Australia, Czech Republic, Denmark, Finland, France, Germany, Hungary, Italy, Japan, Korea, Malta, Netherlands, Portugal, Russia, Spain, Sweden, Taiwan, United Kingdom, the United States in the 1995-2009 period.

Construction employment trends in countries in the last decade (2005-2015) have been extracted, calculated and adapted from Organisation for Economic Co-operation and Development (OECD, 2016a, 2016b) and Labour Market Statistics (2005-2015a, 2005-2015b) as summarized in Table 1. Accordingly, throughout the world, in 2005, the highest share of the construction employment within the overall employment has been observed in Ireland (12.56%), Spain (12.27%), and Portugal (10.98%) whereas the lowest share has been observed in Israel (5.09%), Netherlands (5.89%), and Sweden (5.91%) (OECD, 2016a, 2016b; Labour Market Statistics, 2005-2015a, 2005-2015b). Furthermore, in 2015 throughout the world, in 2005, the highest share of the construction employment within the overall employment has been observed in Denmark (9.65%), G7 (6.97%), New Zealand (9.45%), Slovak Republic (8.81%) whereas the lowest share has been observed in Netherlands (4.83%), Slovenia (5.77%), and Switzerland (5.84%) (OECD, 2016a, 2016b; Labour Market Statistics, 2005-2016a, 2005-2016b) (Table 1). In the last decade (2005-2015) the highest percentage increase in the construction employment occurred in Estonia (1.74%), Poland (1.53%), Canada (1.3%), Belgium (0.56%), Finland (0.32%), Chile (0.29%), Australia (0.23%), Austria (OECD, 2016a, 2016b; Labour Market Statistics. 2005-2015a, 2005-2015b) (Table 1).

Developing countries' share in the global construction output tends to increase. In 1965 developing countries' share in the global construction output was 10% whereas their share increased to 23% in 1998 (Building Economics Research Unit [BERU], 1972; ILO, 2001, p. 8). Emerging markets and Asia are important markets for the construction industry, and their global market share is expected to increase (DEFRA, 2013, p. 7).

Table 1. Construction employment trends in different countries (2005-2015)

	2005	2015
	Highest Percentages Observed	**Highest Percentages Observed**
Countries (percentage of construction employment)	• Ireland (12.56%) • Spain (12.27%) • Portugal (10.98%)	• Denmark (9.65%) • G7 (6.97%) • New Zealand (9.45%) • Slovak Republic (8.81%)
	2005	**2015**
	Lowest Percentages Observed	**Lowest Percentages Observed**
Countries (percentage of construction employment)	• Israel (5.09%) • Netherlands (5.89%) • Sweden (5.91%)	• Netherlands (4.83%) • Slovenia (5.77%) • Switzerland (5.84%)
	2005-2015	
	Increase in the Construction Employment	**Decrease in the Construction Employment**
Countries (changes in percentage of construction employment)	• Estonia (1.74%) • Poland (1.53%) • Canada (1.3%) • Belgium (0.56%) • Finland (0.32%) • Chile (0.29%) • Australia (0.23%)	• Spain (-6.26%) • Greece (-4.12%) • Portugal (-4.85%) • EU 28 countries (-1.03%) • G7 (-0.86%)

Source: OECD (2016a, 2016b) and Labour Market Statistics (2005-2015a, 2005-2015b).

Globalization and global trends can have an impact on the employment rate and profile in the construction industry. They can challenge the employment as they can influence the demand for construction and the way the construction is performed. Globalization influences social, economic, political, and cultural change (Scholte, 2000; O'Brien & Williams, 2007). Globalization enables different parts of the construction value chain to be performed in different countries (DEFRA, 2013, p. 5). Globalization transforms domestic markets into international ones. Internationalization of domestic markets intensifies competition as local companies, even if they work locally; they need to survive international competition. Similarly, construction employees can work for international or global construction companies within multicultural and multilingual construction teams in their home country or abroad. Global trends in the construction industry can provide challenges as well as opportunities to the construction employment rate, and profile. This chapter aims to investigate global trends in the employment of construction professionals in construction projects in the global construction industry. With this aim, this chapter's objectives were to investigate: construction industry's contribution to the employment rate of the countries; global changes and new trends as challenges of employment in the construction industry; impacts of the global trends in the employment rate in the construction industry as well as on the changes in the professionals' skills and talents needed in the construction industry; ways of adapting the construction workforce and professionals to the future global trends in construction industry.

BACKGROUND

Construction industry employees need to deal with employment challenges in the construction industry due its project and site-based nature. The uniqueness of construction projects and project-based nature of the construction industry affects employment. Each construction project is unique. Construction projects can be mainly classified as residential or non-residential construction projects. Even if technical knowledge needed in different construction project types differ, all construction project types present common challenges regarding employment as they are performed by site based and temporary construction teams working towards the accomplishment of unique construction projects. The site-based nature of the construction projects contributes to the uniqueness of the construction projects. Even if the same design is applied, the site conditions (e.g. soil conditions) may differ. Contractors need to consider site-specific factors which include but are not limited to: availability of local materials, electricity, sanitary systems, and other working conditions (e.g. climate conditions). Furthermore, the location of site influences the availability of skilled and experienced workers locally. Contractors need to decide whether or not to work with local construction workforce as well as whether or not to transport workers from abroad. While employing the staff locally, contractors need to consider their efficiency and experience. They need to compare their efficiency and experience to their man hour wages. Establishment of the construction team is generally achieved precisely upon the main contract award. In each construction project, construction teams can be different mainly due to skills needed, subcontracting/outsourcing, and site-specific factors. Skills needed in the projects mainly depend on the construction project type (e.g. building, bridge, dam, schools, hospitals). Skills, experience, and expertise of the employee need to match with the construction project's needs and requirements. For this reason, uniqueness of the construction projects makes it difficult to the construction workers and employees to keep their employment status in different projects.

Employment rate and conditions in the construction industry are affected by the globalization. Globalization let the introduction of the 'global division of labor' (O'Brien & Williams, 2007, p. 249) which has widespread as global labor consists of the 15% of the world population (Harrod & O'Brien, 2002, p. 13). The global division of labor fosters migration (Stalker, 2001, p. 8), as well as the need for immigrant workers, and peasant workers. Developed countries' dependence on migrant workers increases especially due to increase in the average age of the workers and increase in the retired population in the developed countries (O'Brien & Williams, 2007, p. 250). For example, in the EU (28 countries) percentage of the foreign-born population was 62.1% in 2014 (Organisation for Economic Co-operation and Development [OECD], 2016c).

Employment rate in the construction industry is affected by the volatility in the economy. Construction contributes to the economic growth and is considered as a key barometer of economic conditions as its performance affects and is influenced by economic conditions (Sun, Mitra, & Simone, 2013, p. 5). Local construction markets are influenced by economic crises abroad. For example, the credit crunch in 2008 has affected the global construction industry adversely (DEFRA, 2013, p. 5). Fluctuations in the labour market can occur due to various reasons including: broad business cycle trends for the economy; industry-specific shocks (e.g., changes in productivity, changes in input prices or changes in demand for an industry's output); external forces from the world economy; or local conditions (e.g. government policies) (Campolieti, Gefang, & Koop, 2014, p. 257). Construction industry tends to be affected by the economic crisis relatively later compared to other industries as at the time when a crisis emerges the construction companies generally have ongoing construction projects. In case of prolonged economic crisis, as opportunity for getting new projects becomes scarce, construction companies can be affected adversely upon accomplishment of their ongoing construction projects. Recovery of the construction industry, on the other hand, generally starts just after some period following the economic recovery. The main reason for this is that as the construction projects are expensive, potential clients need to save money before their wish for investing in construction can turn out into a demand.

Employment rate and conditions are affected by the labour-intensiveness or capital-intensiveness of the construction industry. In low-income countries, construction industry is relatively more labour-intensive compared to the construction industry in high-income countries, where construction industry is more capital-intensive as their production relies more on machines, and equipments (ILO, 2001, p. 7). In Europe, labor saving techniques have been observed to have an adverse impact on employment in the short run whereas its positive impact in the long run (Jude & Silaghi, 2016). Even if relying on capital-intensive production can be feasible in high-income countries, it tends not to be feasible in low-income countries due to the high unemployment rate, and low salaries (ILO, 2001, p. 7). Labour-intensive construction is strategically important especially for low-income and lower-middle-income countries due to their lower income, limited capabilities for construction job creation (Ernst & Sarabia, 2015, p. 25).

Employment in the construction industry is affected by the political stability in the country where the construction project is or will be performed. Contractors tend to prefer working in politically stable countries mainly not to encounter payment and safety related problems. Contractors, subcontractors, and suppliers need to take all necessary precautions to keep their staff safe. They need to evacuate the site or country where they operate to keep their staff safe in case of uprisings (e.g. in the Arab Spring, construction companies needed to evacuate their workers safely from Libya) and emergencies. Political stability influences investment rates and reliable work environment. Furthermore, contractors need to consider local laws and regulations on employment and costs associated with them.

IMPACT OF GLOBAL TRENDS ON CONSTRUCTION EMPLOYMENT

Issues, Controversies, Problems

Global construction workforce profile consists of local, and foreign or immigrant workers. Foreign/immigrant workers can encounter with productivity, language, settlement, and cultural adaptation problems. Kim et al. (2015, p. 1535)'s research revealed that in Korea, involvement of foreign workers to the construction process resulted in "decreased labour productivity, increased frequency of accidents, and inferior quality or faulty construction due to language barriers and cultural differences between field managers and foreign workers (Go, Park, Kim, Lim, & Kim, 2009)." (Kim et al., 2015, p. 1535). Similarly, the rapid development of Chinese economy increased demand for construction labor which resulted in peasant workers to work in the construction industry (Zuo, Wang, & Yang, 2012, p. 405). Qatar is an extraordinary example as the number of foreign laborers exceeded the local population. "The country's total population has quintupled since the mid-1980s; moreover, foreign nationals made an estimated 85.7% of all residents and up to 94.1% of all employed population in 2013" (Bel-Air, 2014, p. 3). Labour Force Surveys, 2006 to 2013 and Population Census 2010 revealed that nearly 54.71% of foreign labourers in Qatar work in the construction industry, whereas 18.87% of them work in wholesale and retail trade, 10.38% work in manufacturing, 14.15% in domestic services, and 1.8% in education and that number of foreign labourers in construction quintupled between 2006 and 2013 (Bel-Air, 2014, p. 8). Foreign workers, immigrants, or peasants working as construction workforce need to be adapted to the construction process to overcome the potential difficulties and problems (e.g. health problems, disease, immigration issues, and education problems lack of communication with their colleagues and failure to adjust to the work environment (Ascalon, Schleicher, & Born, 2008; Dong & Liu, 2010; Fontaine, 2007; Kim, et al. 2015, p. 1535). Zuo et al. (2012, p. 411)'s research on the peasant workers in the construction industry with respect to the Maslow's hierarchy of needs theory revealed that they "...have physiological, security and social needs, respected and self-actualization needs" and that "there is need to give priority to the issue of wages, safety in production" (Zuo et al., 2012, p. 411) and their settlement (Kim et al., 2015, p. 1535). Migrant workers generally have poor employment conditions and difficulty in securing enforceable labor rights (O'Brien & Williams, 2007, pp. 250-258). As they need to be equipped with the skills required for performing their job, it is important to "strengthen the compulsory and vocational education to promote the personal qualities of the new generation of migrant workers" (Ji-ying & Yao, 2015, p. 89). Construction employees' ability to keep their employment depends mainly on their productivity, and specialization as low-skilled workers, immigrants having language difficulties, and new entrants tend to be adversely affected by the economic crisis situations (Liu & Edwards, 2015, p. 405).

Globalization of the construction activities fostered the need for global human resources management. Especially, emergence of multinational firms has lead to 'global talent management' in the human resource management to deal with 'global talent challenges' (e.g. talent shortages, talent surpluses, locating and relocating talent) encountered in the rapidly changing, uncertain, and competitive global environment (Schuler, Jackson, & Tarique, 2011, pp. 506-509). Demand for construction workers or employees having certain specialization and competency needs to match with the supplied workforces' specialization and competency (Schuler et al., 2011, pp. 507-509).

Globally and internationally working construction professionals need to be equipped with relevant skills and able to deal with different legal and political aspects in different countries. International construction companies need to comply with requirements of local laws, regulations, and standards in the countries where constructions are carried out. "Construction firms operate in a sector with increasing levels of regulation ranging from health and safety to sustainability and carbon emissions requirements, and they also face increasing global competition." (DEFRA, 2013, p. 12).

Innovations can result in either decrease or increase in the employment rate in the construction industry. Innovations can lead to reduce the employment rate as the quantity of employees needed can be reduced due to enhanced efficiency and effectiveness in work. Innovations, on the other hand, can increase demand for employment of employees possessing certain skills. There might even be scarcity in the skilled employees. Furthermore, the introduction of new technologies/innovations can lead to the emergence of new markets, and new employment opportunities. For example, Kunapatarawong and Martínez-Ros (2016, p. 1218)'s study revealed a positive and significant relationship between employment and firms paying attention to green innovation. Green innovation (fostering sustainability, low carbon economy, green building energy efficiency) is substantial for green economy which can foster employment rate (Cai, Mu, Wang, & Chen, 2014, p. 1155; Engel & Daniel, 2009; Haerer & Pratson, 2015, p. 82; Henriques, Coelho, & Cassidy, 2016, p. 519; Kim & Jeong, 2016, p. 468; Mirasgedis, Tourkolias, Pavlakis,

& Diakoulaki, 2014, p. 275). Ge and Zhi (2016, p. 260) emphasized that green economy has fostered employment in many countries [e.g. Turkey (Cetin & Erican, 2011), Canada (Rutovitz & Atherton, 2009), in the EU (United Nations Environment Programme [UNEP], 2011)]. New employment opportunities arise due to emerging renewable energy technologies (Cameron & Zwann, 2015, p. 160). The International Renewable Energy Agency (IRENA, 2011, 2014)'s annual reviews of global employment in the field of the renewable energy (IRENA, 2014) supported this situation. Similarly, expected growth of the global green and sustainable building industry market (Ibisworld, 2012; DEFRA, 2013, p. 6) and expected increase in demand for retrofitting of existing buildings due to the need for sustainable buildings. (DEFRA, 2013, p. 7) provide new employment opportunities. For this reason, "there is a growing demand for design and construction professionals with sustainability skills…" (Mazhar & Arain, 2015, p. 441). Furthermore, enhancing sustainability requirements performance of constructions as well as construction project management requires construction employees to adopt waste preventing strategies and culture (Ajayi et al., 2016, p. 185). Furthermore, innovations are expected to foster employment complying with the European Commission (2011)'s 'Resource Efficiency Roadmap' aims according to which the Member States are required "to shift their economies onto more sustainable growth trajectories while improving competitiveness and creating more employment." (Cooper, Skelton, Owen, Densley-Tingley, & Allwood, 2016, p. 54).

Innovations in the construction industry have an impact on the employment profile, and rate as innovations have potential of influencing productivity as well as the way construction project management and constructions are carried out. There are two main innovation areas in the construction industry, namely: Innovations in construction project management and in construction processes, as well as innovations in the field of the construction materials. Innovations in construction materials mainly aim to dematerialize constructions, to reduce their environmental footprint, to enhance their sustainability performance as well as to accelerate construction processes and to reduce their costs. Innovations in construction project management and in construction processes, on the other hand, are mainly carried out to enhance the efficiency and effectiveness of the construction project management and can result in reduced cost, accelerated and lean processes as well as reduced environmental footprint. Construction project management is becoming more IT-intensive. The nature of the construction project management is becoming more and more interdisciplinary, IT-based and complex especially due to its highly fragmented and geographically dispersed nature as well as due to increased competition requiring fast and high-quality construction. For example, BIM (Building information modeling) is expected to be used widely in the construction industry as it is expected to reduce the need for rework which can contribute to the efficiency and effectiveness and as it enables interactive and interdisciplinary collaboration. BIM is "a process focused on the development, use and transfer of a digital information model of a building project to improve the design, construction, and operations of a project or portfolio of facilities." (Computer Integrated Construction Research Group [CICRG], 2010, p. 1) In other words, BIM is defined as a "process of designing, constructing or operating a building or infrastructure asset using electronic object-oriented information" (The British Standards Institution, 2013, p. 3). It requires skilled employees competed to use BIM. For this reason, project managers need to be able to cope with the dynamism and uncertainty of the construction projects. Universities need to keep their curriculum up-to-date to graduate future professionals able to deal with the changing requirements of and skills needed in the construction industry. Graduate future professionals equipped with necessary knowledge and skills can be hired with relatively high wages as there is "..., strong positive returns to education in terms of employment and wages" (Kyui, 2016, 68). Furthermore, there is a need for reducing the environmental footprint of construction project management and processes as well as of the materials used, and of the built environment as the construction industry is one of the industries adversely affecting the environment as a result of construction processes as well as outputs (e.g. constructions). Increased competition and the need for reducing environmental footprint require construction companies to transform their processes into lean ones. Additionally, increased competition leads the companies to accelerate their processes and to deliver high-quality constructions within shortest possible time and to accomplish the constructions as cheap as possible. Companies' competitiveness and success depend on their ability to deal with innovation challenges and effective use of resources (Kotulic, Huttmanova, Vozarova, & Nagy, 2015, p. 1590). Construction industry benchmarks from other industries' processes and management principles (e.g. aviation, automobile industries) to enhance its processes. For example, off-site construction can lead to minimization of waste, reduction in costs (Davies Langdon & Everest, 2009; Cambridge & Oxford Brookes Universities, 2013; DEFRA, 2013, p. 7), and acceleration of the construction process (DEFRA, 2013, p. 7) affecting employment requirements.

Majority of the construction professionals, all over the world, work for small and medium size companies mainly due to volatility in the construction market and low entry barriers to the construction industry. Majority of construction companies are small organizations (Sunindijo, 2015, p. 109). Even if large construction companies are "responsible for a significant and increasing share of output", their employment rate is decreasing as they tend to be "increasingly removed from the construction site and construction workers" and as they tend to rely on "a stable core workforce, consisting mainly of white-collar workers" (ILO, 2001, pp. 22-23). As a result, quantity of large construction companies is decreasing, and small subcontractors, as well as labor contractors, became the main employers of the construction workforce (ILO, 2001, p. 23). Contractors can prefer to subcontract or outsource parts of the construction work contracted. They generally do not subcontract their core competency related activities to keep their competitiveness. Their decision whether or not to outsource various parts of the work depends on the asset specificity of the subcontracted work items as it influences subcontractors' profit margin as well as the transaction cost of subcontracting. Subcontracting and "outsourcing" of labor requirements, however, are widely used in the construction industry as subcontracting provides flexibility in the labor recruitment as well as enables the construction companies to cope with a volatile economy and heterogeneous skills needed in construction projects (ILO, 2001, pp. 15-24). Subcontracting also enables specialization and division of work which can enhance productivity. Furthermore, subcontracted construction labor provides construction companies to delegate the responsibility for supervision and to reduce costs by avoiding restrictive labor legislation and welfare regulations (ILO, 2001, p. 24).

Throughout the world, the construction industry is not successful in attracting young and skilled workers. Demographic situation affects the availability of young construction workers locally. "The aging population also has implications for the construction sector workforce and supply of skills in the sector. Key skills can be lost through retirement and there is a need to inspire and attract younger workers to the industry in order to replace lost skills (UKCES, 2012)." (DEFRA, 2013, p. 5) The average age of construction workers increases in many countries (e.g. in Korea) mainly due to the reluctance of young generation in working in the construction industry as they tend to perceive construction industry as difficult, dirty, dangerous, and incapable of satisfying their needs resulting in scarcity of workforce which is tried to be compensated by hiring of foreign workers (Kim et al., 2015, p. 1534) and/or by mechanization of the production (ILO, 2001, pp. 40-43). Failure of the construction industry in attracting young construction workers/professionals can have an adverse impact on the health and safety performance of the construction industry. Construction workers' age influences the accident types as Choi (2015, p. 151)'s study on identification of injury type trends based on age and trade of construction workers revealed that younger workers tend to suffer mainly from finger/hand/wrist injuries due to cuts/lacerations and contusion, whereas older workers tend to suffer from sprains/strains injuries to the ankle/foot/toes, knees/lower legs, and multiple body parts due to falls from a higher level or overexertion." (Choi, 2015, p. 151)

SOLUTIONS AND RECOMMENDATIONS

Employment contributes to the peace, social welfare and development of the countries. Unemployment is idle workforce preventing the effective growth of the countries. Unemployment does have not only economic impacts to the countries but also social impacts as unemployed workforce's happiness level and hope for future can be low. For this reason, the skills of the construction workforce capable of working need to match with the skills required in the workforce in the industry. As construction industry is one the industries capable of providing job and contributing the employment rate of the countries, it is important that construction workforce is equipped with the skills required in the construction industry. Universities, higher education institutions, and vocational schools need to collaborate with the construction industry in educating and training of skilled construction professionals able to work globally. Their collaboration can contribute to the elimination of the scarcity of skilled construction professional and to the solutions of the global talent challenges problems. Construction professionals need to be able to work within multilingual and multicultural working teams in different countries as construction activities have been globalized. They need to be equipped with relevant IT skills as innovation rate tends to be accelerated and new managerial processes are benchmarked from other industries. Education of construction project management professionals is important as there is a need for skilled project managers who are competent in dealing with uncertain and dynamic nature of the construction projects in different countries as project success is influenced by project manager's competency (Hwang & Ng, 2013, p. 272). Furthermore, as construction industry contributes to the employment rate of the countries all over the world, future construction professionals should be equipped with entrepreneurial skills. For example, in Tunisia, the entrepreneurship education provided to young university students fostered the self-employment (Premand, Brodmann, Almeida, Grun, & Barouni, 2016, p. 311).

Construction industry's ability to attract young and competent workers need to be enhanced throughout the world. ILO (2001, p. 43) emphasizes that construction industry's working conditions need to be improved with respect to: provided rights at work (e.g. joining trade unions, elimination of discriminations) and fair conditions of employment; enhanced income or social security especially for construction workers under 'temporary employment status'; enhanced social dialogue through strengthened workers' and employers' organizations; and overcoming scarcity of skilled labour. O'Brien and Williams (2007, pp. 258-259) recommend core labor standards to be part of the World Trade Organization and the workers' rights abuses to be propagated in the media so that necessary precautions can be taken. As construction industry has poor health and safety performance all over the world, enhancing health and safety conditions can influence young workers' decision to work in the construction industry. Proactive health and safety precautions (e.g. effective training) can contribute to the health and safety performance in the construction industry.

As construction workforce tends to consist of local, and foreign workers, the construction industry is attractive for immigrants and peasants who generally do not have relevant experience and skill. Construction companies and their partners in the supply chain need to accommodate as well as to adapt foreign workers, immigrants, and peasants who are working within their organization. Language barrier needs to be overcome as this barrier has the potential for increasing the risk of emergence of accidents.

Human resources are key strategic competitive advantages of the construction companies all over the world. Construction companies, which can survive economic crises, can keep their employees within their organization and provide employment opportunities for other construction professionals. For this reason, effective strategic management plays an important role in the survival of the construction companies in the competitive and uncertain market as well as in their contribution to the employment rate of the countries. Effective strategic management can contribute to construction companies' survival in the economic crises as a threat does not always mean that companies will lose money or their market share. The magnitude of the threat and its consequences depend on how well and successful companies cope with the crises. Their proactive actions can enable them to increase their market share even under economic crisis conditions. For example, international construction companies operating in at least two different countries can get benefit from the growing market opportunity in one country despite the shrinkage in another market in another country. This portfolio management approach to the markets has potential for companies to enable risk allocation in different markets. Furthermore, even if construction market grows in a country demand for certain construction types might still be decreasing due to changes in the lifestyles, purchasing powers, and demographic structure. Similarly, even if a construction market shrinks in a country demand for certain construction types might be increasing due to changes in lifestyles, purchasing powers, and demographic structure.

Construction companies' decision on which market to operate can influence their success and demand for employment. The decision on market selection need to be based on economics and political stability, local laws, and regulations, potential market growth, availability of materials in the vicinity of the construction sites, availability of local competent workers, their salaries with respect to their efficiencies, and purchasing power of local inhabitants as well as local demographic situation. Demographic situation influences average age of construction workforce locally. Furthermore, demographic situation influences demand for construction type as in the countries where there is aging population there is demand for hospitals, and healthcare facilities whereas in the countries where there is young population there is demand for more schools, and accommodation buildings (DEFRA, 2013, p.5). For this reason, global construction companies' strategic decision on which markets to operate needs to be based on consideration of the demographic situations of potential markets to comply with their specialization field to have a competitive advantage.

Competent and experienced key human resources need to be kept within the construction company as they can provide a competitive advantage to their organizations. Especially skilled employees, however, might wish to leave the construction company voluntarily. Top managers of the construction companies need to keep their staff motivated (especially their key and skilled staff) and try to reduce their voluntary turnover by observing their symptoms for leaving the company. According to the unfolding model of voluntary turnover of construction professionals, construction professionals potential pattern of leaving the company consists of the different combinations of the following constructs (Jones, Ross, & Sertyesilisik, 2010, p. 272, Lee & Mitchell, 1994; Lee, Mitchell, Holtom, McDaniel, & Hill, 1999; Niederman, Summer, & Maertz, 2007): shock, engaged script, image violation, satisfaction, search and evaluation of alternatives, offer in hand. Managers can try to motivate their key staff for staying in the construction company based on their observation on key staff's symptoms related to these constructs.

Enhanced competitiveness of the construction companies can contribute to their survival, to keep their employees within the company, to get the bids, and to provide employment opportunities. As project teams may change from project to project, experience and expertise gained in each project should be stored within the company. Construction company's competitiveness can be enhanced with the help of its transformation into a learning organization. Construction companies need to be learning organizations which can enable the experience and expertise gained in one project and/or in one country to be kept within the company and tacit knowledge to be transformed into implicit knowledge. In other words, experience should not remain only on the employees' brains, and it should become institutionalized. Construction company's organization type can have an impact on retaining employees within the company even under the economic crisis situation. Construction companies can have matrix type organization to be able to adapt their organization to the changing requirements (e.g. increased or decreased project quantities, changes in the economy). Matrix organization and subcontracting can provide flexibility to the global construction companies, especially in the economic crisis periods. Construction companies can retain their employees in case they can reduce adverse impacts of economic volatility. Furthermore, construction companies can focus on construction projects having relatively inelasticity of demand so that they can increase their chance of survival under economic crisis. Elasticity of demand for different construction projects can be different. Construction companies can prefer to specialize in the construction project types for which demand is relatively inelastic as demand for inelastic goods can be sustained even in the economic crises. Optimum integration of labor- and capital-intensive production techniques can result in reduced cost and employer turnover, and it can support construction companies to keep their talented construction workforce within the company. Construction employment opportunities, working conditions, and skills needed depend on labor- or capital-intensive production techniques used in the construction industry. Construction companies can have different labor-intensive or capital-intensive production combinations in different markets and projects mainly based on the availability of expert construction professionals and workers, man-hour wages and efficiencies, the frequency of getting new projects, and their project sizes influencing economies of scale.

FUTURE RESEARCH DIRECTIONS

Unemployment in a specific country reveals that country cannot be developed as fast as it could due to inefficient production level and idle workforce. Furthermore, unemployment affects happiness and social welfare adversely. For this reason, construction industry plays a vital role in contributing to the employment rate and the welfare of the society all over the world. Construction industry's labour-intensive nature contributes to the employment rate of the countries, especially of the developing countries. Construction labor is an important factor of production in construction. Changes in the construction labour market are observed due to global trends (e.g. globalization of the labour market, innovations affecting construction processes, poor working conditions resulting in increased average age in construction labour market, global talent challenges due to lack of skilled construction professionals who are capable of and competent in matching construction labour profile demanded, changing employment profile due to immigrants and peasants involvement in the construction process).

Further research is recommended to be carried out on how to enhance working conditions in the construction industry so that construction industry can be transformed into an attractive one for young and skilled construction professionals throughout the world. Globalization of construction activities resulted in multilingual and multicultural construction teams. As construction labor profile tends to consist of more and more immigrants and peasants, their adaptation to the construction project, and to the language used on site as well as improvement of their living and working conditions are important. For this reason, further research is recommended to be carried out on how to solve problems of the immigrants and peasants as construction workers.

CONCLUSION

This chapter investigated global trends in the employment of construction professionals in construction projects in the global construction industry. With this aim, this chapter focused on: construction industry's contribution to the employment rate of the countries; global trends in the employment in the construction industry; their impacts on the employment as well as on the changes in the professionals' skills and talents needed in the construction industry; ways of adaptation of the construction workforce to the changes in the global trends.

Global construction industry contributes to the employment rate and development of the countries and of the world. Construction industry influences construction employees' welfare, living, and working conditions. Construction employees' skills and talents need to be adapted to the changes in the employees' profile demanded by the construction industry. Globalization of the construction labor market resulted in changing labor profile as well as in the emergence of the multilingual and multicultural project and construction teams. Globalization of the construction industry increased opportunities and expanded markets where construction labor can work.

Employment rate and conditions in the construction industry are affected by the global trends which include: globalization, volatility in the economy, tendency of increase in quantities of small and medium-sized construction companies, tendency of increased subcontracting and outsourcing activities, site based and project based nature of the construction industry, innovations influencing construction project management processes and constructions, increase in the average age of the construction employees in the construction labour market in various countries.

Construction employees' skills and talents should comply with the changing global trends in the industry. For this reason, universities, higher education institutes, and vocational schools play an important role in solving global talent challenges by training and educating future construction professionals equipped with the necessary skills and talents. Furthermore, construction companies can allocate budget to enable their staff to get relevant training and education as human resources are key competitive advantages of the construction companies. Labor markets' skills and talents, as well as their adaptation to the global trends in the construction industry can contribute to the sustainability of the construction labor market and to the competitiveness of the construction companies globally.

Politicians' and policies' role in encouraging the development of the construction industry, can foster global employment rate, and development. Economic development policies fostering construction industry

Table 2. Key global trends, their potential impacts on construction employment as well as ways of, drivers for and barriers against adapting construction workforce to the key global changes

Global Trends	Global Trends' Potential Impacts on/Challenges for Construction Employment	Ways of Adapting Construction Workforce to the Global Trends	Drivers for Adaptation of the Construction Workforce to the Changes in the Global Trends	Barriers against Adaptation of the Construction Workforce to the Changes in the Global Trends
Globalization of the construction labor market	• Multilingual and multicultural working teams • Language barriers affecting accident rates and quality • Immigrants as construction workforce having poor working conditions	• Enhancing standards for working conditions and work environment and encouraging countries to align their standards with enhanced requirements (ILO can play an active role) • Effective health and safety training • Multilingual site safety manager and team • Collaboration of universities and construction industry in updating education and training programs curriculum to equip future construction professionals with skills and talents needed to deal with the challenges of globalization of the construction labor market	Increased market size provides opportunities for employment	• Resistance of the countries to collaborate in raising working conditions and work environment. • Construction companies' reluctance in investing in the training of their human resources due to the project-based and changing nature of the construction teams. • Construction companies' potential reluctance in hiring multilingual site safety manager and team due to their relative higher salaries compared to non-multilingual professionals
Innovations affecting construction processes	• Decrease in demand for employment in certain work packages • Increase in demand for employment in certain work packages • Changes in the employment skills needed	• Investing in research and development as well as in adapting innovations to the construction companies • Providing training and education to the staff so that they are capable of using new technology/innovation • Hiring staff capable of using the new technology/innovation • Adapting companies in the supply chain to the new technology/innovation so that they become capable of using new technology/innovation • Encouraging companies in the supply chain to invest in new technology/innovation and to training their staff via partnership agreements.	• New work packages introduced as a result of innovations providing employment opportunities for construction workforce equipped with the relevant talents and skills required. • Innovations enhancing productivity and competitiveness of the construction companies can enable construction companies implementing these innovations to get new projects and to provide new employment opportunities.	• Resistance of the construction companies in allocating budget for research and development • Resistance of the construction workforce to adapt themselves to the changes and to become equipped with the new skills needed. • Companies failing to adopt innovations enhancing productivity and competitiveness might lose their market share and ability to provide new employment. • Supply chain companies' reluctance in investing in new technology/innovation and in training their staff as supply chain can consist of different companies due to the project-based nature of construction projects.

continued on following page

Table 2. Continued

Global Trends	Global Trends' Potential Impacts on/Challenges for Construction Employment	Ways of Adapting Construction Workforce to the Global Trends	Drivers for Adaptation of the Construction Workforce to the Changes in the Global Trends	Barriers against Adaptation of the Construction Workforce to the Changes in the Global Trends
Perception of the construction industry as an industry providing poor working and living conditions of the employees	• Increase in the average age of construction workers due to reluctance of young generation preference in working in the construction industry • Foreign workers as construction workforce • Living conditions and language barriers as well as skills gaps in construction workforce	• Strengthening labor organizations • Providing vocational training and language education to foreign workers • Enhancing standards for working conditions and work environment	Enhanced working conditions in the construction industry can contribute to the quality and enable construction industry to attract competent professionals	Political and legal difficulties
Changes in the skills needed	• Global talent challenges due to lack of skilled construction professionals who are capable of and competent in matching construction labor profile demanded • Need for managers to try to minimize voluntary turnover rate among talented and successful staff.	Collaboration of universities/ higher education institutes/ vocational schools and construction industry in updating education and training programs' curriculums to equip future construction professionals with skills and talents needed to deal with the changes in the construction industry	• Demand for employment equipped with certain talent and skills reveals employment opportunities for construction workforce equipped with the relevant talents and skills required. • Competitive advantage based on human resources	Need for construction companies' investment in training their staff
Increase in the quantities of small and medium size construction companies and increase in the tendency for subcontracting/ outsourcing	Increase in the construction workforce as "Temporary employment status"	Enhancing standards for working conditions	Potential increase in the construction workers' productivity, happiness, and living conditions	Increase in construction companies' costs due to enhanced standards for working conditions

can contribute to the employment rate and development of the countries. These economic development policies need to be supported by the education policies so that labor productivity is enhanced, and labor is equipped with skills needed.

Key global trends affecting construction professionals' employment, their potential impacts on construction employment as well as ways of adapting construction workforce to the key global changes have been summarized in Table 2.

This chapter is expected to contribute to the literature with respect to the challenges construction industry will face due to the global trends as well as with respect to the changes in the workforce profile, skills, and talents in the construction industry. This chapter will be beneficial for academics, practitioners, institutions and organizations concerned with construction labor market, as well as for politics.

REFERENCES

Ajayi, S. O., Oyedele, L. O., Akinade, O. O., Bilal, M., Owolabi, H. A., Alaka, H. A., & Kadiri, K. O. (2016). Reducing waste to landfill: A need for cultural change in the UK construction industry. *Journal of Building Engineering*, *5*, 185–193. doi:10.1016/j.jobe.2015.12.007

Ascalon, M. E., Schleicher, D. J., & Born, M. P. (2008). Cross-cultural social intelligence: An assessment for employees working in cross-national contexts. *Cross Cultural Management: An International Review*, *15*(2), 109–130. doi:10.1108/13527600810870570

Australian Industry Group. (2015). *Australia's construction industry*. Retrieved May 30, 2016, from http://www.aigroup.com.au/portal/binary/com.epicentric.contentmanagement.servlet.ContentDeliveryServlet/LIVE_CONTENT/Economic%2520Indicators/Construction%2520Survey/2015/Construction%2520industry%2520profile%2520and%2520Outlook.pdf

Bel-Air, F. (2014). *Demography, migration, and labour market in Qatar Gulf labour markets and migration*. GLMM - EN - No. 8/2014. Retrieved August 26, 2016, from http://cadmus.eui.eu/bitstream/handle/1814/32431/GLMM_ExpNote_08-2014.pdf?sequence=1

Building Economics Research Unit. (1972). *Construction and development: A framework for research and action. Paper prepared for the International Bank for Reconstruction and Development*. London: University College Environmental Research Group.

Cai, W., Mu, Y., Wang, C., & Chen, J. (2014). Distributional employment impacts of renewable and new energy–A case study of China. *Renewable & Sustainable Energy Reviews*, *39*, 1155–1163. doi:10.1016/j.rser.2014.07.136

Cameron, L., & Zwaan, B. (2015). Employment factors for wind and solar energy technologies: A literature review. *Renewable & Sustainable Energy Reviews*, *45*, 160–172. doi:10.1016/j.rser.2015.01.001

Campolieti, M., Gefang, D., & Koop, G. (2014). A new look at variation in employment growth in Canada: The role of industry, provincial, national and external factors. *Journal of Economic Dynamics & Control*, *41*, 257–275. doi:10.1016/j.jedc.2014.02.005

Cetin, M., & Egrican, N. (2011). Employment impacts of solar energy in Turkey. *Energy Policy*, *39*(11), 7184–7190. doi:10.1016/j.enpol.2011.08.039

Chiang, Y. H., Tao, L., & Wong, F. K. W. (2015). Causal relationship between construction activities, employment and GDP: The case of Hong Kong. *Habitat International*, *46*, 1–12. doi:10.1016/j.habitatint.2014.10.016

Choi, S. D. (2015). Aging workers and trade-related injuries in the US construction industry. *Safety and Health at Work*, *6*(2), 151–155. doi:10.1016/j.shaw.2015.02.002 PMID:26106517

Computer Integrated Construction Research Group. (2010). *BIM operate. construct. design plan. Project execution planning guide version 2.0*. Retrieved from http://engr. Psu.edu/bim/PxP

Cooper, S., Skelton, A. C. H., Owen, A., Densley-Tingley, D., & Allwood, J. M. (2016). A multi-method approach for analysing the potential employment impacts of material efficiency. *Resources, Conservation and Recycling, 109*, 54–66. doi:10.1016/j.resconrec.2015.11.014

Davies, Langdon, & Everest. (2009). *Cost model: off-site manufacturing*. Retrieved May 26, 2016, from http://www.building.co.uk/cost-model-off-site-manufacture/3042466.article

Department for Business Innovation and Skills. (2013). *UK construction an economic analyses of the sector*. Retrieved May 26, 2016, from https://www.gov.uk/government/uploads/system/uploads/attachment_data/file/210060/bis-13-958-uk-construction-an-economic-analysis-of-sector.pdf

Dong, K., & Liu, Y. (2010). Cross-cultural management in China. *Cross Cultural Management: An International Journal, 17*(3), 223–243. doi:10.1108/13527601011068333

Engel, D., & Daniel, M. (2009). *Green jobs and the clean energy economy*. Copenhagen Climate Council.

Ernst, E., & Sarabia, M. (2015). *The role of construction as an employment provider: A world-wide input-output analysis*. ILO Employment working paper no. 186. Employment Policy Department Development and Investment Branch. Retrieved August 26, 2016, from http://www.ilo.org/wcmsp5/groups/public/---ed_emp/---emp_policy/---invest/documents/publication/wcms_444326.pdf

European Commission. (2011). *The roadmap to a resource efficient Europe* (COM(2011) 571). Retrieved October 21, 2016, from http://ec.europa.eu/environment/resource_efficiency/about/roadmap/index_en.htm

Fontaine, R. (2007). Cross-cultural management: Six perspectives. *Cross Cultural Management: An International Journal, 14*(2), 125–135. doi:10.1108/13527600710745732

Ge, Y., & Zhi, Q. (2016). Literature review: The green economy, clean energy policy and employment. *Energy Procedia, 88*, 257–264. doi:10.1016/j.egypro.2016.06.159

Go, S. G., Park, M. K., Kim, Y. S., Lim, C. W., & Kim, C. D. (2009, November). A study about the plan of foreign construction worker's safety management. *Proceedings of Korea Institute of Construction Engineering and Management,* 36–39.

Haerer, D., & Pratson, L. (2015). Employment trends in the U.S. electricity sector, 2008–2012. *Energy Policy, 82*, 85–98. doi:10.1016/j.enpol.2015.03.006

Harrod, J., & O'Brien, R. (Eds.). (2002). *Global unions? Theory and strategy of organised labour in the global political economy*. London: Routledge.

Henriques, C. O., Coelho, D. H., & Cassidy, N. L. (2016). Employment impact assessment of renewable energy targets for electricity generation by 2020—An IO LCA approach. *Sustainable Cities and Society, 26*, 519–530. doi:10.1016/j.scs.2016.05.013

Horta, I. M., Camanho, A. S., & Costa, J. M. (2012). Performance assessment of construction companies: A study of factors promoting financial soundness and innovation in the industry. *International Journal of Production Economics, 137*(1), 84–93. doi:10.1016/j.ijpe.2012.01.015

Hwang, B. G., & Ng, W. J. (2013). Project management knowledge and skills for green construction: Overcoming challenges. *International Journal of Project Management*, *31*(2), 272–284. doi:10.1016/j.ijproman.2012.05.004

Ibis World. (2012). *Report top 10 fastest growing industries*. Retrieved May 26, 2016, from http://www.newstatesman.com/sites/default/files/files/Fastest%20Growing%20Industries.pdf

International Labour Organization. (2001). *The construction industry in the twenty-first century: Its image, employment prospects and skill requirements*. Retrieved May 26, 2016, from http://www.ilo.org/public/english/standards/relm/gb/docs/gb283/pdf/tmcitr.pdf

International Labour Organization. (2014). *Global employment trends 2014: Risk of a jobless recovery?* Retrieved August 21, 2016, from http://www.ilo.org/wcmsp5/groups/public/---dgreports/---dcomm/---publ/documents/publication/wcms_234107.pdf

International Renewable Energy Agency. (2011). *IRENA working paper: renewable energy jobs: status, prospects & policies*. Abu Dhabi: International Renewable Energy Agency.

International Renewable Energy Agency. (2014). *Renewable energy and jobs – annual review 2014*. Abu Dhabi: International Renewable Energy Agency.

Ji-ying, Z., & Yao, W. (2015). Investigation and study on employment status of migrant workers in Heilongjiang Province.[English Edition]. *The Journal of Northeast Agricultural University*, *22*(1), 83–90. doi:10.1016/S1006-8104(15)30011-8

Jones, S. M., Ross, A., & Sertyesilisik, B. (2010). Testing the unfolding model of voluntary turnover on construction professionals. *Construction Management and Economics*, *28*(3), 271–285. doi:10.1080/01446191003587737

Jude, C., & Silaghi, M. (2016). Employment effects of foreign direct investment: New evidence from Central and Eastern European countries. *Inter Economics*, *145*, 32–49. doi:10.1016/j.inteco.2015.02.003

Kim, D., & Jeong, J. (2016). Electricity restructuring, greenhouse gas emissions efficiency and employment reallocation. *Energy Policy*, *92*, 468–476. doi:10.1016/j.enpol.2016.02.009

Kim, S., Kim, J. D., Shin, Y., & Kim, G. H. (2015). Cultural differences in motivation factors influencing the management of foreign laborers in the Korean construction industry. *International Journal of Project Management*, *33*(7), 1534–1547. doi:10.1016/j.ijproman.2015.05.002

Kotulic, R., Huttmanova, E., Vozarova, I. K., & Nagy, J. (2015). The structural analysis of the sectors of Slovak economy and employment in times of global change and the subsequent development. *Procedia Economics and Finance*, *23*, 1590–1595. doi:10.1016/S2212-5671(15)00363-9

Kunapatarawong, R., & Martínez-Ros, E. (2016). Towards green growth: How does green innovation affect employment? *Research Policy*, *45*(6), 1218–1232. doi:10.1016/j.respol.2016.03.013

Kyui, N. (2016). Expansion of higher education, employment and wages: Evidence from the Russian Transition. *Labour Economics*, *39*, 68–87. doi:10.1016/j.labeco.2016.01.001

Labour Market Statistics. (2005-2015a). *Employment by activity agriculture / construction / industry including construction / manufacturing / services, thousand persons, 2005 – 2015.* Author.

Labour Market Statistics. (2005-2015b). *Employment rate total, thousand persons, 2005 – 2015.* Author.

Lee, T. W., & Mitchell, T. R. (1994). An alternative approach: The unfolding model of employee turnover. *Academy of Management Review*, *19*, 51–89.

Lee, T. W., Mitchell, T. R., Holtom, B. C., McDaniel, L. S., & Hill, J. W. (1999). The unfolding model of voluntary turnover: A replication and extension. *Academy of Management Journal*, *42*(4), 450–462. doi:10.2307/257015

Liu, C. Y., & Edwards, J. (2015). Immigrant employment through the Great Recession: Individual characteristics and metropolitan contexts. *The Social Science Journal*, *52*(3), 405–414. doi:10.1016/j.soscij.2014.03.013

Mazhar, N., & Arain, F. (2015). Leveraging on work integrated learning to snhance Sustainable design practices in the construction industry. *Procedia Engineering, 118*, 434 – 441.

Mirasgedis, S., Tourkolias, C., Pavlakis, E., & Diakoulaki, D. (2014). A methodological framework for assessing the employment effects associated with energy efficiency interventions in buildings. *Energy and Building*, *82*, 275–286. doi:10.1016/j.enbuild.2014.07.027

Niederman, F., Summer, M., & Maertz, C. P. Jr. (2007). Testing and extending the unfolding model of voluntary turnover to IT professionals. *Human Resource Management*, *46*(3), 331–347. doi:10.1002/hrm.20167

O'Brien, R., & Williams, M. (2007). *Global political economy evolution and dynamics (2nd ed.).* New York: Palgrave MacMillan.

Organisation for Economic Co-operation and Development. (2016a). *Employment by activity (indicator).* Retrieved August 23, 2016, from https://data.oecd.org/emp/employment-by-activity.htm#indicator-chart

Organisation for Economic Co-operation and Development. (2016b). *Employment rate (indicator).* Retrieved August 23, 2016, from https://data.oecd.org/emp/employment-rate.htm#indicator-chart

Organisation for Economic Co-operation and Development. (2016c). *Foreign-born employment (indicator). Foreign-born employment Total / Women / Men, % of foreign-born population, 2014.* Retrieved August 23, 2016, from https://data.oecd.org/migration/foreign-born-employment.htm

Premand, P., Brodmann, S., Almeida, R., Grun, R., & Barouni, M. (2016). Entrepreneurship education and entry into self-employment among university graduates. *World Development*, *77*, 311–327. doi:10.1016/j.worlddev.2015.08.028

Rhodes, C. (2015). *Construction industry: Statistics and policy.* House of Commons Library. Retrieved May 30, 2016, from http://researchbriefings.files.parliament.uk/documents/SN01432/SN01432.pdf

Rutovitz, J., & Atherton, A. (2009). *Energy sector jobs to 2030: A global analysis.* Sydney: The Institute for Sustainable Futures, University of Technology.

Scholte, J. A. (2000). *Globalization: A critical introduction*. New York: St Martin's.

Schuler, R. S., Jackson, S. E., & Tarique, I. (2011). Global talent management and global talent challenges: Strategic opportunities for IHRM. *Journal of World Business*, *46*(4), 506–516. doi:10.1016/j.jwb.2010.10.011

Stalker, P. (2001). *The no-nonsense guide to international migration*. Oxford, UK: New Internationalist.

Sun, Y., Mitra, P., & Simone, A. (2013). *The driving force behind the boom and bust in construction in Europe*. IMF Working paper WP/13/181. Retrieved October 21, 2016, from https://www.imf.org/external/pubs/ft/wp/2013/wp13181.pdf

Sunindijo, R. Y. (2015). Improving safety among small organisations in the construction industry: Key barriers and improvement strategies. *Procedia Engineering, 125*, 109 – 116.

The British Standards Institution. (2013). *Specification for information management for the capital/delivery phase of construction projects using building information modeling*. PAS 1192-2:2013.

The World Bank. (2016). *Employment in industry (% of total employment)*. Retrieved May 26, 2016, from http://data.worldbank.org/indicator/SL.IND.EMPL.ZS/countries?display=graph

Timmer, M. (Ed.). (2012). *The world input-output database(WIOD): "Contents, sources and methods"*. Working Paper No. 10. Brussels: European Commission.

UKCES. (2012). *Sector skills insights: Construction*. Retrieved May 26, 2016, from https://www.gov.uk/government/uploads/system/uploads/attachment_data/file/304475/Sector_Skills_Insights_Construction_evidence_report_50.pdf

United Nations Environment Programme. (2011). Towards a green economy: Pathways to sustainable development and poverty eradication - A synthesis for policy makers. Nairobi, Kenya: Author.

University of Cambridge, Oxford Brookes University and Construction Industry Council. (2013). *Off-site housing review*. Retrieved May 26, 2016, from http://architecture.brookes.ac.uk/research/resources/offsite-housing-review-feb-2013-for-web.pdf

Zuo, W., Wang, Q., & Yang, P. (2012). Research on the current situation of peasant-workers in construction industry based on AHP. *Systems Engineering Procedia*, *5*, 405–411. doi:10.1016/j.sepro.2012.04.062

KEY TERMS AND DEFINITIONS

Capital-Intensive Production: Production relying more on machinery and equipment rather than on manpower.

Construction Workforce: White and blue collar construction professionals.

Economic Fluctuation: Shrinkages and expansions in the economy affecting supply and demand.

Employment Rate: Ratio of employed labor force to the total labor force.

Expertise: Knowledge, valid experience, and capability for doing something.

Immigrant Labour Force: Labor force working outside of their home country.

Labour Force: Workforce capable of working consisting of employed and unemployed people.

Labour-Intensive Production: Production relying more on manpower rather than on machinery and equipment.

Subcontracting: Outsourcing parts of contracted work to subcontractors.

Supply Chain: Production/construction and value creation chain consisting of all subcontractors/suppliers etc. taking part in the production/construction process.

Talent: Someone's capability of doing something good.

Unemployment: Unemployment refers to idle workforce and mismatch between employment demand and employment supply.

Chapter 16
The Effects of Economic Structural Transformation on Employment:
An Evaluation in the Context of Economic Complexity and Product Space Theory

Muhlis Can
Hakkari University, Turkey

Buhari Doğan
Süleyman Demirel University, Turkey

ABSTRACT

Structural transformation concept emphasized by countless numbers of policy makers and scholars. Structural transformation affects not only countries' income levels but also a number of their economic parameters. Employment is one of the most significant of these parameters because the success of structural transformation is measured by the contributions of agriculture, manufacturing, and the service sector to growth and employment. In this chapter, the changing effects of economic complexity (as a major indicator of structural transformation) on employment, and the visual representation of this complexity, which is called product space, are studied using samples from South Korea and Japan. As a result of research, it is found out that increased complexity of a country's economy (increased intensity of the product space center) will lead to a decrease in the employment in agriculture and manufacturing, an increase in the employment in the services sector.

INTRODUCTION

In today's world, countries are competing with one another economically in ways that they have not before. While some compete through their cheap workforce, others keep up with the competition through their sophisticated product manufacturing capabilities. This competition is also reflected in the incomes of countries. The question is whether countries can outmatch the competition by more products in general

DOI: 10.4018/978-1-5225-2008-5.ch016

or manufacturing more sophisticated products. According to Rodrik (2006), the number of products a country sells is not significant anymore. What is more important is what type of product the country sells. For example, both Singapore and Pakistan sell 133 different sorts of products to the world market. However, when compared in terms of per capita income, the case of each country is quite different. Singapore is 38 times richer than Pakistan (Hausmann et al., 2011, p. 22). If this is the case, what contributes to this striking difference? The answer to this question takes us to the "structural transformation" concept emphasized by countless numbers of policy makers and scholars.

The first studies on structural transformation were carried out by Prebisch (1950), Singer (1950), Lewis (1954), and Hirschman (1958). The mutual point underlined by all these studies is that countries which specialize in primary products and have a limited export basket might experience problems in terms of trade in the long run. Moreover, these studies suggest that countries should move from selling traditional products to more complex ones (Petralia, Balland, & Morrison, 2015). Additionally, in their studies, Rostow (1959) and Kaldor (1967) emphasized that knowledge and skills, structural transformation, forward and backward linkage among sectors, and productivity growth are significant for countries that aim to grow over the long term. These studies also strongly underlined that structural transformation can significantly contribute to output and employment growth. Furthermore, structurally transformed countries have the capability to overcome macro-economic shocks more easily (De Bandt & Vigna, 2008). In general terms, structural transformation can be defined as changing the manufacturing structure of a country from one of agriculture to industry and then from industry to service.

Structural transformation affects not only countries' income levels but also a number of their economic parameters. Employment is one of the most significant of these parameters because the success of structural transformation is measured by the contributions of agriculture, manufacturing, and the service sector to growth and employment (Srinivasan, 2013, p. 54). Transformation generally formed out of the growth of a country results initially in the workforce moving from agriculture to the manufacturing industry and then to the service sector. Increased economic growth also leads to urban migration from rural areas (De Brauw, Muller, & Lee, 2014, p. 33). The most significant reason for migration is the higher life standards provided by larger cities (The United Nations Human Settlements Programme [UN-HABITAT], 2011, p. 13). Also, when compared with the agriculture sector, wages in the manufacturing and service sectors are higher.

In this chapter, the changing effects of economic complexity (as a major indicator of structural transformation) on employment, and the visual representation of this complexity, which is called product space, are studied using samples from South Korea and Japan. The underlying reason for selecting these two countries as samples is their achievement of structural transformation through conscious policies. The chapter begins with a discussion of economic complexity and product space theory. The effects of structural transformation on employment in agriculture, manufacturing, and the service sector in South Korea and Japan are then examined separately.

ECONOMIC COMPLEXITY

Economic structural transformation, which has been referred to quite often in economic literature in recent years, influences countries in many ways. Countries' features underlie this transformation. The variety (or scarcity) of these features (capabilities) has a determining role in the increase (or decrease) of countries' incomes. Moreover, turning toward sectors other than agriculture is of high significance in increasing income because agriculture is a low-productivity sector (McMillan, Rodrik, & Verduzco-Gallo, 2014, p. 11). In these terms, structural transformation is regarded as redistribution of input used for manufacturing in the economy from the low-productive agriculture sector to non-agricultural sectors (Lee & Malin, 2013). Structural transformation first requires transformation from agriculture to manufacturing and then from manufacturing to service (Gilmann, 2011). To realize structural transformation, a shift of focus to high-productivity areas is needed. This provides more rapid growth of the economy (Hausmann, Hwang, & Rodrik, 2007). This also means that the productive economic structures determine the countries' welfare (Hidalgo, 2009, p. 2).

Products are composed of the aggregation of inputs that are different in terms of content. Some of these inputs are non-tradable (Hausmann & Hidalgo, 2011, p. 310). These include a country's human and physical capital, the legal system, institutions and infrastructure. Each one of these can be defined as a "capability" of the country (Hidalgo, 2009; Hidalgo & Hausmann, 2009). "Knowledge" itself is a type of capability. In this context, the factors of production, technology level, and a country's other capabilities play a significant role in producing a product. Increasing these capabilities means increasing the variety of the production basket (Hausmann & Hidalgo, 2011, p. 310). In other words, increasing the qualifications of the country's human capital, improving the legal system, protecting intellectual property rights, increasing the quality of infrastructure, and increasing physical capital can provide the country with the ability to manufacture more sophisticated products. For example, let's assume that each capability can be represented by one letter and that each word composed of these letters represents one product. The words with more letters symbolize complex products, while the ones with fewer letters represent products that do not require complex knowledge and skills to produce. We shall choose the following letters for this example: D, E, V, E, L, O, and P. In this assortment of letters, the most sophisticated product will be DEVELOP. If the country can increase its capabilities and provide M, E, N, and T inputs as capabilities, it can manufacture a DEVELOPMENT product, which will be more sophisticated than the DEVELOP product. However, if the country has the letters (capabilities) M, E, and N letters, it can only manufacture MEN (or the other combinations of these letters). More precisely, the more the capability level (letters) of a country is increased, the more sophisticated and complex the products (words) that can be manufactured.[1]

Figure 1 represents manufacturing capabilities in the way described above. As can be inferred from the figure, the A, B, and C countries have different capabilities. The country with the highest number of capabilities is A. The fact that this country has the most diverse set of capabilities means that it can manufacture three different products using its different capabilities. Country B has a more limited set of capabilities in comparison with country A. Country B can manufacture two different types of products with its existing capabilities. Country C has the most limited set of capabilities, which means that it can manufacture only one type of product. It cannot manufacture the most sophisticated product manufactured by country A. In order for country C to manufacture the products produced by country A, it needs to increase its capabilities. In other words, it is necessary for country C to increase its human capital, improve its legal system, resolve infrastructure problems, protect intellectual property rights, and increase physical capital.

Limited capabilities forcibly lead the country to focus on simple products that do not require complex knowledge and skills to produce. If the country has limited knowledge and skills, it is quite challenging for it to manufacture nuclear reactors or technologically advanced machines of even low quality (Schetter, 2015). Nations that hold complex knowledge are able to make complex or sophisticated products that cannot be made in countries with only basic knowledge. Therefore, there is a causal relationship between

Figure 1. Capabilities and products

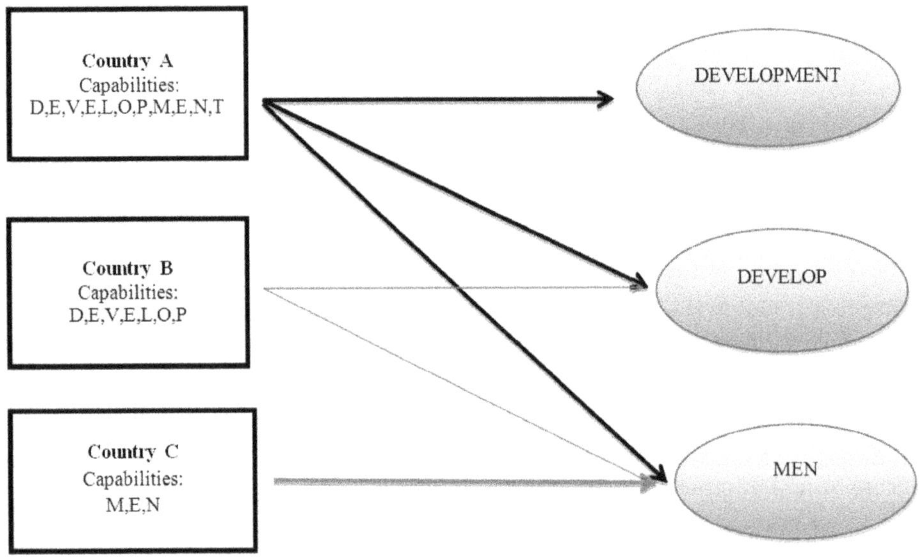

knowledge and development (Yameogo, Nabassaga, & Ncube, 2014, p. 402). Diversity of productive knowledge, however, is not enough. In order to put knowledge into productive use, societies need to reassemble these distributed bits of knowledge through teams, organizations, and markets (Hausmann et al., 2011, p. 7). What's more, capabilities require individual and social quality, information efficiency, and experience. These features lead to the improvement of a firm's technological and organizational skills (Andreoni, 2011, p. 1). Economically, this can be defined as productivity growth. For productivity growth, companies must spend money on research and development (R&D), prioritize mechanization, and train their workforce (Chang, Andreoni, & Kuan, 2013, p. 14). It is clear that this process cannot be accomplished in a short time. In other words, a long and continuous process is necessary for ensuring productivity growth in the economy as a whole. Hidalgo and Hausmann (2009) stated that the most prominent factor affecting a country's productivity level is non-tradable capabilities. According to Hidalgo and Hausmann, the basis of the difference in income among countries is a difference in capabilities.

If this is the case, how can one identify the capabilities (including knowledge) of a country? In other words, how can one determine how complex a country's economy is? Hidalgo and Haussmann (2009) claimed that the most suitable way to find out about the capabilities of a country is to look at its export basket. According to these scholars, the export basket is, in fact, the best indicator of to what extent a country is capable of manufacturing knowledge-skills-involved products. According to Lall (2000), the strength of a country's production capabilities is reflected in the manufactured products. If the country is able to manufacture sophisticated products, this shows the extent of its human capital, physical capital, institutions, and other capabilities. The capabilities of countries can be divided into general and private. While some capabilities (general ones such as institutions, infrastructure, etc.) are necessary for the manufacturing of all products, other capabilities are needed for specific products. From this point of view, what is more significant for countries is that they have general capabilities because such capabilities make it more possible for countries to manufacture new products. However, countries that are deprived of general capabilities will find it less possible to produce new products (Boschma & Capone, 2015, p. 4).

Today, countries are exporting many products of various content. Scholars create different indexes to measure export baskets. The most commonly used are the Herfindahl-Hirchman and entropy indexes. However, these indexes do not contain data on the quantity and types of product a country exports. In these indexes, there is no difference between an export basket consisting of 10% banana and 90% mango and one consisting of 10% motorcycle and 90% aircraft engine (Hausmann & Hidalgo, 2011, p. 316). What is more significant for the above-mentioned indexes is the diversity of exported products. The economic complexity index is different from the other two in this regard. This index emphasizes the diversity of product content. Product diversity is the most prominent indicator of the income level of a country.

So, what does economic complexity mean? Arthur (2013) stated that it is more than a theory involving efforts to understand how the elements of a system work. Economic complexity can instead be defined as the efforts of individuals who come together to create a new model (Arthur, 2013). According to Hidalgo (2009), on the other hand, complexity is the effect of a country's capabilities and qualifications on the economy. If the products manufactured by a country are produced by many others—*if the products are common everywhere*—the knowledge and skill level of a country is regarded to be present in many other countries as well. Minondo and Requena-Silvente (2013) defined complexity as the whole of knowledge and skills that are used in manufacturing. Ferrarini and Scaramozzino (2016) underlined that product variety and the ubiquity of the manufactured products are indicators of a country's economic complexity. According to Lall (2000), turning toward complex sectors is important for structural transformation, technological advancement, modernization, and development. For instance, in Malaysia and Chile in 2012, per capita income and gross enrollment were almost similar. In the same period, Chile was ranked 72nd in economic complexity in the world, while Malaysia was in 24th place. The most important reason for this is that Malaysia focuses on the manufacturing of electronic and mechanical products that require complex knowledge and skills to produce. Conversely, Chile predominantly specializes in copper, fish, and fruit production, which do not require complex knowledge and skills (Hartmann, Guevara, Jara-Figueroa, Aristaran, & Hidalgo, 2015). Commodity exporter countries intensify the production of less sophisticated products because of the Dutch disease. As these sectors are mainly physical capital intensive, they lead to less employment and fewer spillover effects (Daude, Nagengast, & Perea, 2015, p. 3).

Lall (2000) expressed that knowledge- and skills-intensive (technology-intensive) product manufacturing plays an important role in the growth of countries. The most significant reason for this is that these types of products have high income elasticity. Knowledge-intense manufacturing also affects other sectors via a spillover effect. For example, let's assume that engineers in the chemistry industry develop a product that functionally decreases energy loss in vehicles by 20%. So, will this product be used only in the automotive industry? The answer is no. We can predict that this product will swiftly expand into other sectors. It will be used in each product in which energy loss through friction occurs (e.g., aircrafts, trains, washing machines, refrigerators, etc.). Another example can be given from the medicine industry. Cancer is one of today's most challenging health problems. We know that different types of cancer exist. Let's assume that a country has developed a medicine for 10 types of cancer and that this drug has a 100% success ratio. In your opinion, would it be easy to develop an imitation of this product? The answer is absolutely not because long studies were carried out on this drug, a number of experiments were done, and scientists from different disciplines (biology, chemistry, pharmaceuticals, etc.) were employed. The country that discovered this medicine will export it to a number of other countries and earn a serious amount of revenue. This will increase the income differences of manufacturer country and other countries. The above scenario is an example of what Hidalgo and Haussmann mean when they speak of economic complexity. If a product requires a variety of knowledge and skills in its manufacturing procedure and can be exported by very few countries, this is an indication of how sophisticated and unique the product is (Özgüzer &Binatlı, 2015).

Various knowledge and skills are needed for the manufacturing of complex products. If a country has limited knowledge and skills, it will experience difficulty in finding the resources to manufacture such products. However, if a country has a vast scale of knowledge and skills, it will not experience such hardship (Daude et al., 2015, p. 3). Having advanced and efficient knowledge-skills enables countries to manufacture high-value-added and sophisticated products. Furthermore, a country's knowledge-skills provide significant advantages for manufacturing new products (Hartmann & Pyka, 2013). Today, it is clear that developed countries are the ones with extensive knowledge and skills. It is because of these knowledge and skills that this group of countries is ranked at the top of the economic complexity index. Additionally, the biggest advantage these countries have is their ability to combine the small differences in qualifications among the workforce in their manufacturing process (Minondo & Requena-Silvente, 2013, pp. 929-930).

Table 1 shows the world's economic complexity index (ECI) rankings. As can be inferred from the table, Japan has the most complex economy in the world. Switzerland, Germany, and Sweden follow, in second, third, and fourth place, respectively. When the 2011, 2012, and 2013 tables are compared, the top 10 countries are more or less the same. These countries are also in the World Bank's high-income countries group which can be regarded as a reflection of capability differences on income level.

PRODUCT SPACE THEORY

It was once quite difficult to assess the economic complexity and knowledge and skill levels of countries. By means of product space theory, however, these phenomena have become observable (Ferrarini & Scaramozzino, 2016). Product space theory was introduced by Hausmann and Klinger (2006) and developed by Hidalgo, Klinger, Barabasi, and Hausmann (2007). Later, Hidalgo and Hausmann (2009) and Hidalgo (2009) contributed more significant studies to product space theory. Product space theory

Table 1. Economic complexity index rankings

Rank(2011)	Countries	ECI	Rank (2012)	Countries	ECI	Rank (2013)	Countries	ECI
1	Japan	2.31	1	Japan	2.23	1	Japan	2.29
2	Switzerland	2.04	2	Switzerland	1.97	2	Switzerland	2.16
3	Germany	1.96	3	Germany	1.84	3	Germany	1.95
4	Sweden	1.86	4	Sweden	1.71	4	Sweden	1.83
5	South Korea	1.80	5	South Korea	1.70	5	England	1.72
6	Austria	1.80	6	Czech Republic	1.62	6	Czech Republic	1.71
7	Czech Republic	1.80	7	England	1.61	7	South Korea	1.70
8	Finland	1.73	8	Finland	1.59	8	Finland	1.64
9	England	1.57	9	Singapore	1.59	9	Austria	1.64
10	USA	1.54	10	Austria	1.57	10	Singapore	1.63

Source: Atlas Media Database

provides the opportunity to observe economic complexity in a visual way.[2]Hidalgo et al. (2007) tried to visually represent products whose manufacture and knowledge and skill level were similar. Hidalgo et al. (2007) and Hausmann et al. (2007) defined the product space as the relatedness of products that are subject to world trade. This means that product space is the network between products. In this network, products requiring similar knowledge, skills, and capabilities are grouped together. A new product that is similar to those in the existing product group is more likely to be added to the production basket. Therefore, countries tend to expand and diversify in sectors that are strongly related to their current activities (Boschma & Capone, 2015, p. 2). For instance, let's suppose that country A does not manufacture anything related to machinery equipment products, while country B manufactures machinery tools for different fields. Accordingly, in which country is it more possible to produce a new jet engine? (Hidalgo, 2011, p. 1). In such a context, it is essential for the country to consider the previously manufactured products in their efforts to produce the new one. If this new product requires similar infrastructures, physical factors, and organizations to products produced in the past, it will be more likely to be produced (Hidalgo et al., 2007). This fact is supported by empirical studies as well. For example, in their industry-based studies, Klepper (2002) and Klepper and Simons (2000) discovered that the success of companies who start to manufacture in new sectors/industries is built on their previous experience in a similar industry and their use of this experience in their new industry by means of knowledge, skills, and capabilities.

Using classifications by STIC of 1006 products (4-digit level of desegregation), Hausmann and Klinger (2007) first assessed the comparative advantages of a country from a given product. They then checked the relationship of this product to the remaining 1005 products. The more the product was connected to the other products, the more central its position in the product space.

Figure 2 demonstrates this phenomenon. "Vehicle parts" is located in the center of the product space. It is connected to 27 products. Some of these products are as follows: other iron products, lifting machinery, rubber pipes, cars, valves, steam turbines, and metalworking machine parts. If a country can manufacture vehicle parts, it is highly likely that it can produce the 27 other products. This was explained in detail in the economic complexity section. What is more significant for countries are whether they can manufacture the products that are in the center of the product space and that have extensive network connections.

In product space theory, each circle represents one product. The size of this circle shows the product's weight in terms of world trade. In accordance with Leamer's (1984) classification scheme, each color represents a product group. Leamer's classification scheme consists of 10 different product groups. The lines connecting the circles reveal the relatedness of the products. This relatedness does not indicate physical similarity between products but rather a country's likelihood of exporting a product on the basis of its export of a similar one (Felipe, Kumar, & Abdon, 2010, p. 3). In the product space, the outermost products are the non-sophisticated ones that do not require much knowledge and skills to produce (Hidalgo, 2011, pp. 3-4). The center of the product space is mostly occupied by machinery, chemical, and metal products, whereas petroleum, raw materials, vegetable and animal products, and labor- and capital-intensive goods (except metal products) are located on the outer border. The closer the products a country manufactures to the center (core), the easier it is to manufacture new goods because the existing capabilities can be redeployed to realize this production (Felipe et al., 2010, p. 4). Hausmann and Klinger (2006) symbolized each product in the product space as a tree, the product basket of a country as a forest, and the country's knowledge and skills as monkeys. The closer the trees are to one another, the higher the likelihood of the monkeys jumping from one tree to another. Moreover, the more individual connections the products in the product space have, the higher the possibility of the country facing frequent and longer recessions (Hausmann & Klinger, 2006).

Figure 2. Backward-forward connections in product space
Source: Atlas Media Database.

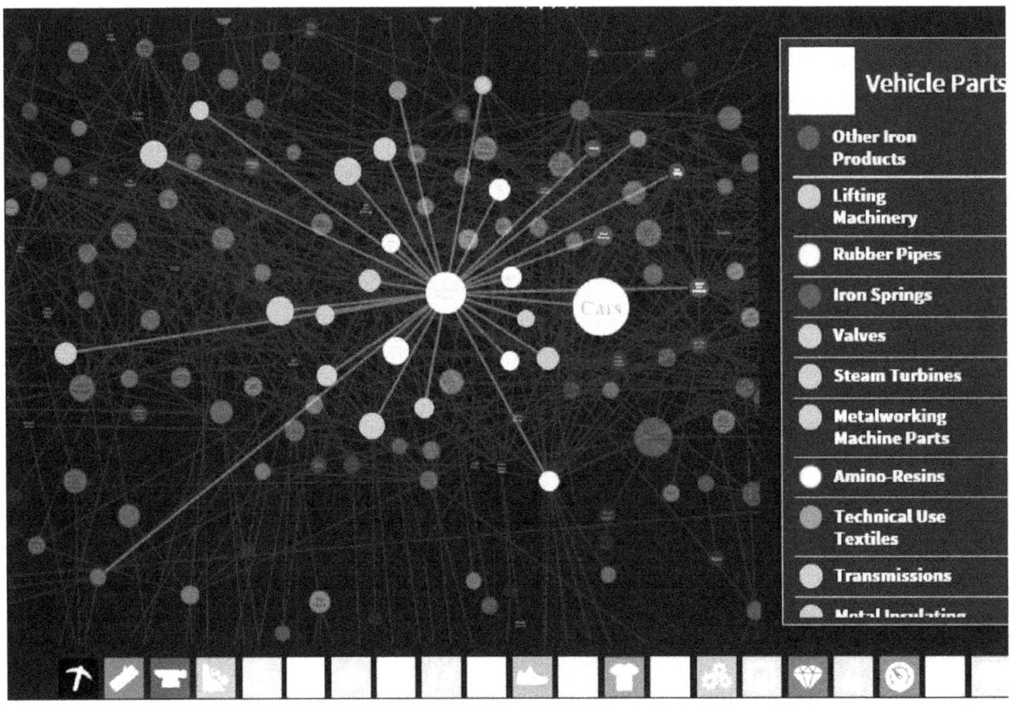

Figure 3. A sample of product space
Source: The Atlas of Economic Complexity and Hausmann et al. (2011, p. 45).

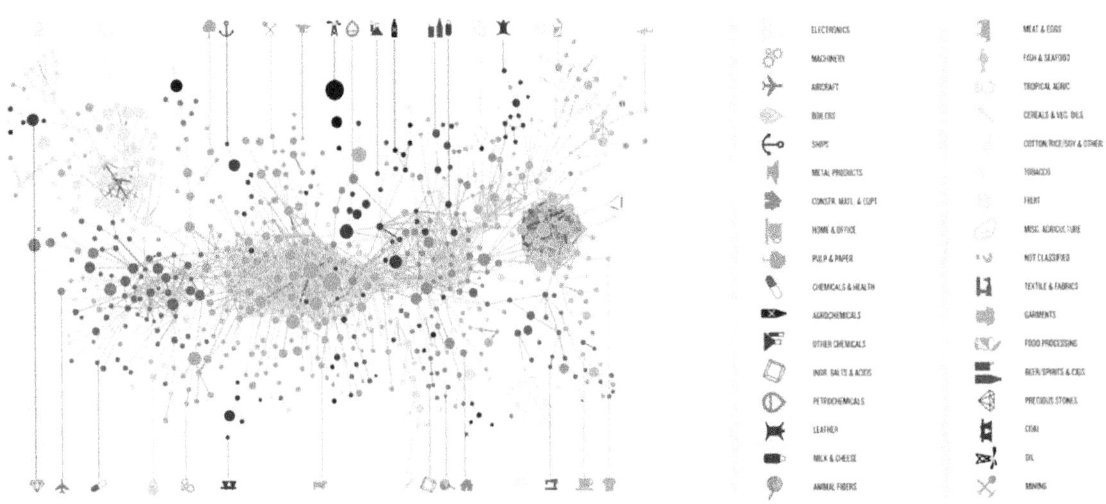

Product space is reviewed from left to right. As can be inferred from Figure 3, the products located on the right-hand side of the space consist of agriculture and clothing products, which mostly require less knowledge and skills. On the other hand, products on the left-hand side of the space are sophisticated products that require advanced knowledge and skills (Stafforte & Tamberi, 2012, p. 101). Complex products with a high spillover effect are located in the center of the space. Human capital also has a crucial role in the product space. Quality human capital makes the manufacturing of products that are close to one another easier. In other words, the more qualified the human capital of the country, the easier it is for the country to head toward the other areas in the product space. It has been observed that products sometimes become intensified in specific areas. Such intensification is the most significant indicator of the comparative advantages of a country (Hausmann & Klinger, 2007).

THE EFFECTS OF ECONOMIC COMPLEXITY AND PRODUCT SPACE THEORY ON EMPLOYMENT

In today's modern economies, the most basic productivity growth source is the manufacturing industry. In essence, the manufacturing industry contributes greatly to the productivity of other sectors by producing intermediate inputs such as machinery and chemicals. Furthermore, the industry is regarded as the first area in which new organizational abilities appear. Productivity growth, especially in the last two centuries, cannot be explained solely by technological advancement. It is a well-known fact that the new organizational abilities that have appeared in the manufacturing industry have had a considerable role in productivity growth (Chang et al., 2013, p. 11). However, it is almost impossible to claim that this productivity growth has had a positive impact on employment in the manufacturing industry. Quite the contrary, productivity growth is one of the factors contributing to decreased employment in this industry (Harrison, Jaumandreu, Mairesse, & Peters, 2014, p. 30). As they grow, companies add new technologies (automation, computerization, etc.) to their production lines in order to decrease their costs. These types of applications negatively affect the low-skilled workforce. In countries that have completed their structural transformation, it has been observed that low-skilled occupations have started to disappear. On the other hand, the same structural transformation period leads to the emergence of high-skilled occupations. This has been specifically observed in the information technology industry (Gesthuizen & Wolbers, 2010).

It is essential to discuss this phenomenon in the context of economic complexity and product space theory. One can comfortably assert that new employment opportunities emerge as economic complexity increases because transformation from the lower productivity of agriculture to sectors with higher productivity also results in the creation of new jobs. Intensity in the center of the product space means increased employment (number of persons) in the manufacturing industry. However, industries such as textiles, which are significant in the initial stages of development and create new employment opportunities, are also part of the manufacturing industry. From this point of view, the intensity in the center of the product space of a country (showing an increase in economic complexity) might affect areas such as textiles negatively. For example, it is expected that employment will decrease in related industries. When evaluated in general, even though intensity in the product space means an increase in the number of people employed in the manufacturing industry, it can be claimed that the manufacturing industry's share in the total employment of the country could decrease. This may vary depending on the industrialization stage of the country that is being studied. If a country cannot complete the industrialization process in the relevant period, the total share of employment in the manufacturing sector is expected to increase initially and then to decrease.

Established companies in high-income countries tend to move their production lines to countries with lower production costs, and this leads to changes in the existing production structure of the world. In this context, countries' previous expertise differentiates them from one another (Corcoles, Diaz-Mora, & Gandoy, 2014, p. 33). For instance, a century ago, textile products were manufactured in today's developed countries, including England, Germany, Japan, and Korea. However, today it is not possible to claim the same thing. Nowadays, it is a well-known fact that textile manufacturing has moved to countries with lean production in East Asia and other parts of the world. The most prominent underlying reasons for this are increased production costs and high wages in the developed countries.

In order to manufacture sophisticated products of increased economic complexity, a serious amount of R&D spending is needed. What companies are trying to create here is "innovation." One example of this is smartphones. Let's assume that a company invested a great deal of money in a new application that is to be used on smartphones. The company needs to form a team to develop this application, which means increasing employment in the service sector. Moreover, to launch this application, the company might need to receive service support from other firms with no prior connections to the company. This new application will, therefore, contribute to employment both in the company itself and in other firms in the same sector. The company might also invest more money to develop the specifications of this smartphone application in order to compete with its competitors in the market. It can be suggested that when this company researches new software that makes playing games on smartphones easier, both the company and other companies in the sector will increase the number of their employees. Acquired innovation can be said to have a positive impact on employment because new products manufactured as a result of this innovation lead to the emergence of new employment opportunities. Additionally, the increasing market demand for new products has an active role in increasing employment (Harrison et al., 2014, pp. 29–30). Another industry that has caused increases in the service sector is the pharmaceutical industry. This industry intensively requires knowledge and skills. Scientists perform various tests on the manufacturing of a drug for years, and therefore manufacturers work with a number of different teams. For example, let's assume that a medicine manufacturer invests in R&D for a drug that has not been produced previously. In this case, it will not be possible for this manufacturer to develop a new drug with its existing team. The company has to form a new team for this new drug, and this will lead to increased employment in the service sector.

The financial and education sectors both have a huge impact on the formation of complex economic structures (Cristelli, Tacchella, & Pietronero, 2015). The reason for this is that companies are unable to produce new complex products with their own capital. Therefore, companies might need support from bank loans. As the economic complexity in the country increases, the number of people who are employed in finance is expected to increase too. It is possible to claim the same thing about the education field. Human capital is one of the key factors in the increase of economic complexity. Educational investments made in qualified human capital play an important role in the increase of employment in the service industry. In the agricultural industry, farmers whose education levels increase begin to use advanced farming equipment in agricultural production (Cochrane, 1993). This leads to a decrease in the use of old methods of production in the agricultural industry, leading to a decrease in employment in the industry as a whole.

It would not be right to claim that increased employment in the service sector can be maintained only through innovation and knowledge-skills-based production. Structural changes also lead to the introduction of low-skilled service jobs, mainly in the catering and cleaning industries (Gesthuizen & Wolbers, 2010). Call center jobs, which require fewer qualifications, are also an example of such a job. Call center employees have the ability to speak properly, which is an important skill for people employed in the service sector. These employees may have good knowledge and skills in physics, chemistry, and mathematics, but such knowledge is not important in the context of their sector.

Moreover, the increase in retail stores, especially in the last 20 years, also lies behind the employment increase in the service sector. These stores are operated by national and international companies. They offer a wide range of products at cheap prices to consumers, which have led to the emergence of new employment opportunities. This phenomenon has affected not only developed countries but also the other country groups (Cho, Chun, & Lee, 2015, pp. 559–560). Increasing a country's economic complexity (increasing the intensity in the center of the product space) leads to an increase in per capita income in the country, which is a factor that has paved the way for the opening of many different retail stores. In other words, an increase in economic complexity in the country will result in the opening of more retail stores, and the number of people employed in the service sector will grow. In addition, increased economic complexity makes a significant contribution to the expansion of the country's export markets and the increase of its exports, which in turn cause an increase of employment in the transport sector.

According to Hallak (2006), complex and more sophisticated goods are generally purchased by high-income countries and, within countries, by those segments of consumers that have been less exposed to external shocks and may guarantee a more stable demand. Moreover, as the substitution of complex products is also quite difficult, it would not be wrong to claim that countries that specialize in complex product groups could have some advantages. Countries specialized in more complex goods are less exposed to external shocks and have higher stability in their overall sales (Maggioni, Turco, & Gallegati, 2014). When this is considered in terms of employment, big fluctuations are not expected to result from the impact of external shocks. However, the impact of external shocks to the agricultural sector is different because the income elasticity of agricultural products is very solid. Even if their prices decline, there will not be a big change in the demand for agricultural products. What is significant here is that if prices rise in countries that manufacture agricultural products, purchasing countries are then directed to where they can get cheaper products, which might also negatively affect the employment structure in the country specializing in agricultural products. Also, being exposed to the seasonal impacts of the agricultural sector is a major disadvantage in terms of employment.

Structural Transformation of South Korea Economy: A Brief Overview

Korea is a well-known case of successful economic catch-up achieved through state-sponsored manufacturing and export-oriented strategy. Korea is one of the few recent examples of a country that has managed to rapidly transform its agriculture-based economy to the extent of becoming a leading industrial power (Organisation for Economic Co-operation and Development [OECD], 2014, p. 32; Chung, 2010; Chen & Suh, 2007, p. 4). The main focus of South Korean industrial development shifted from light to heavy and high-tech industry in the 2000s. The Korean form of catch-up was shaped by strong state leadership, a state-controlled banking system, and the dominance of the chaebol—large, highly diversified family-owned companies[3] (Organisation for Economic Co-operation and Development [OECD], 2009, p. 13, 60).

The origins of many of the larger chaebol can be traced to the period after Japanese colonialism. Most of these companies started small; however, the South Korean government from 1961 to 1987 actively supported chaebol operations through successive strategies and policies as a means of pursuing the government's industrialization objectives. The chaebol has therefore played a central role in Korea's economic development (OECD, 2009, p. 62).

It is necessary to focus primarily on the processes of South Korea's economic transformation in the 1960s and 1970s. In the literature, there is a widespread belief that many institutional and economic changes occurred that led to fast growth during this period. The three main periods of South Korea's economic transformation are as follows: first, the imitation era of import substitution/ protectionist policies that encouraged exports (the 1960s and 1970s); secondly, the transformation era, during which structural arrangements were made, liberalization policies were promoted, and the private sector established its own R&D structure (1980s); and third, the innovation era, during which policies in favor of technological development were encouraged, and rather than large R&D-based companies, dynamic and innovative SMEs gained importance (the 1990s onwards) (OECD, 2009, pp. 173–176).

Park Chung Hee, who rose to power after a military coup d'état in 1961, spearheaded two developments. First, he encouraged companies' exports by transferring foreign aid to the entrepreneurial firms. Second, he initiated a shift from light industry to heavy manufacturing and high-tech industry (Kim, 2000). In the 1960s, South Korea began developing its agriculture (e.g., rice) and labor-intensive light manufacturing industries (e.g., textiles and bicycles) (Chen & Suh, 2007, 7; OECD, 2009, p. 58). In this process, the realization of the country's export-oriented production efforts occurred. Export-oriented policies have contributed to the fall in the unemployment rate and the opening of new manufacturing companies throughout the country. Initially, the development of basic industry for the promotion of exports (cement, fertilizer, etc.), light industry based on manpower (textiles, footwear, etc.), and basic infrastructure (communications, electricity, etc.) was encouraged (Chung, 2007). South Korea's biggest problems in this process were inadequate technological capabilities and inadequate domestic capital. Therefore, capital accumulation was encouraged, and the government made significant investments in education. These investments allowed a gradual transition toward more sophisticated products. The key to this transition was the acquisition of new technologies through foreign licensing and the adaptation of them to domestic manufacturing (Chen & Suh, 2007, p. 7; OECD, 2009, p. 58).

Selection and assimilation of appropriate technology required a reasonable level of local R&D capacity and S&T (science and technology) infrastructure. To address these needs, in the 1960s research institutes[4] such as the Korea Institute of Science and Technology (KIST) were established. These institutes aimed to carry out R&D in key technological fields, with a view to supporting the industrial upgrading strategy, facilitating the adoption of new technologies in industry, and developing projects for private companies (OECD, 2014, p. 32; OECD, 2009, p. 58). Furthermore, in order to investigate export opportunities in foreign markets, Korea Trade Promotion Corporation (KOTRA) was founded (Lee, 2000, p. 145). Subsequently, the Ministry of Science and Technology (MOST) was established, and the Science and Technology Promotion Law was enacted. In this process, foreign direct investment (FDI) played an important role in the transfer of technology (Ernst, 2000). Strong commitment to economic independence led to economic policies based on long-term loans to finance industrial development instead of FDI. These loans were then allocated to the South Korean government to make direct investments in selected sectors. This process led to the import of a significant proportion of foreign capital goods. Later, reverse engineering methods were used to obtain the necessary technologies (Chung, 2010).

In the 1970s, Park Chung Hee made efforts toward the establishment of high technology and heavy industry. At the same time, the state continued to encourage research to meet the needs of industry. In this process, foreign- owned companies were given limited access to the South Korean market. In other words, mostly protectionist policies were implemented in the country during this period (OECD, 2009,

p. 58; Park, 1997). In the mid-1970s, the government's use of a well-targeted industrial policy resulted in a major shift toward the development of heavy industries (e.g., chemicals, shipbuilding). Along with industrial targeting, policies were enacted to further improve technological capabilities, together with improving access to and quality of technical and vocational training (Chen & Suh, 2007, p. 7). The government also played a key role in developing domestic R&D capability by establishing industry-oriented government research institutes (GRIs) in areas such as machinery, electronics, chemistry, and shipbuilding (OECD, 2009, p. 58). For this reason, it is possible to claim that the role of government as a major planner of strategic industrial policy was very important in South Korea's industrialization process (Park, 1997).

In the 1980s, South Korean industry dependence on imports of technology and increasingly expensive domestic labor made it difficult to compete in international markets. To overcome this situation, South Korea created a new domestic center for research and innovation (Bartzokas, 2007). Additionally, the first national R&D program initiated by MOST was introduced in 1982. Shortly afterward, similar R&D programs were set up in various institutions. In particular, a separate directorate to support industrial R&D was set up inside the Ministry of Industry. In addition to public funding of R&D, the private sector was encouraged to actively engage in absorbing and improving technologies from countries operating at the technological frontier (OECD, 2014, p. 33).

South Korea continued to pursue high-value-added manufacturing in the 1990s by promoting domestic high-technology innovation (Chen & Suh, 2007, p. 7; OECD, 2009, p. 59). Since the second half of the 1990s, the Korean government has been pressured to change its catch-up-oriented industrial development policy, which is based on extensive labor and capital input, and to seek new growth engines. Economic growth, which averaged more than 8% a year from 1960 to 1997, has slowed from the mid-1990s to a yearly average of 5%. The Asian financial crisis in 1998 caused negative Gross Domestic Product (GDP) growth and led to a high increase in mass unemployment (Chen & Suh, 2007, p. 13; OECD, 2014, pp. 33-34).

In the post-2000 period, South Korea underwent a comprehensive and innovation-oriented transformation in all areas. Its Vision 2025 program proposed the following fundamental shifts in technology policy (OECD, 2014, p. 35):

1. Moving from a government-led and development-oriented innovation system to a private-industry-led and diffusion-oriented innovation system,
2. Moving from a closed R&D system to a globally networked R&D system,
3. Moving from a supply-dominated investment enhancement strategy to an efficient utilization and investment-distribution strategy,
4. Moving from a short-term technology-development strategy to a long-term market-creating innovation strategy,
5. Moving toward a science-and-technology-led national innovation system.

In brief, several factors appear to be behind South Korea's achievements. In particular, state-oriented plans for the realization of economic development efforts can be regarded as the roots of the South Korean miracle. In addition, these plans have been revised according to the circumstances and needs of a given period. Strict adherence to these strategies could be the underlying reason for the high likelihood of coming across a South Korean product in most of today's houses.

South Korea's Economic Complexity and Product Space: An Evaluation in the Context of Employment

This section examines South Korea's economic complexity and product space. In addition, the effects of the transformations encountered in economic complexity and product space on employment are discussed. Figure 4 shows the development of South Korea's economic complexity. Economic complexity index values, except for those in the 2010–2013 period, have been calculated as five-year averages.[5] When South Korea's economic complexity is analyzed, we observe that its index value during the period 1970–1974 is below one. The index values of 1975–1979, 1980–1984, and 1985–1989 are above one. The 1990–1994 period, however, shows a significant decline in South Korea's economic complexity. This is because products produced by South Korea in previous periods began to be manufactured by many other countries in this period. But as can be seen from the chart, the manufacturing structure during the period between 1995 and 1999 recovered and complex production increased. This rise accelerated in the 2000–2004, 2005–2009, and 2010–2013 periods. In the most recent period, South Korea's economic complexity index value was over 1.6.

South Korea's economic complexity world rankings in the above-mentioned periods can be seen in the table. According to Atlas Media Database, South Korea ranked 23rd in economic complexity in 1970, 18th in 1980, 24th in 1990, 22nd in 2000, and 7th in 2013.

In addition to its evolving economic complexity, South Korea's product space changes should be examined. In 1970, as seen in Figure 5 (part "a"), the product space is mostly concentrated on the right-hand side (in the large white circle). Additionally, the left-hand side and the center of the product space are almost empty. The most conspicuous product group on the left side is miscellaneous manufactured goods (in the upper left corner). The right-hand side of the product space consists of knit clothing accessories, footwear, embroidery, pharmaceutical flora, silk-woven fabrics, dried vegetables, crustaceans,

Figure 4. South Korea's economic complexity index
Note: Economic complexity is calculated as five-year averages.

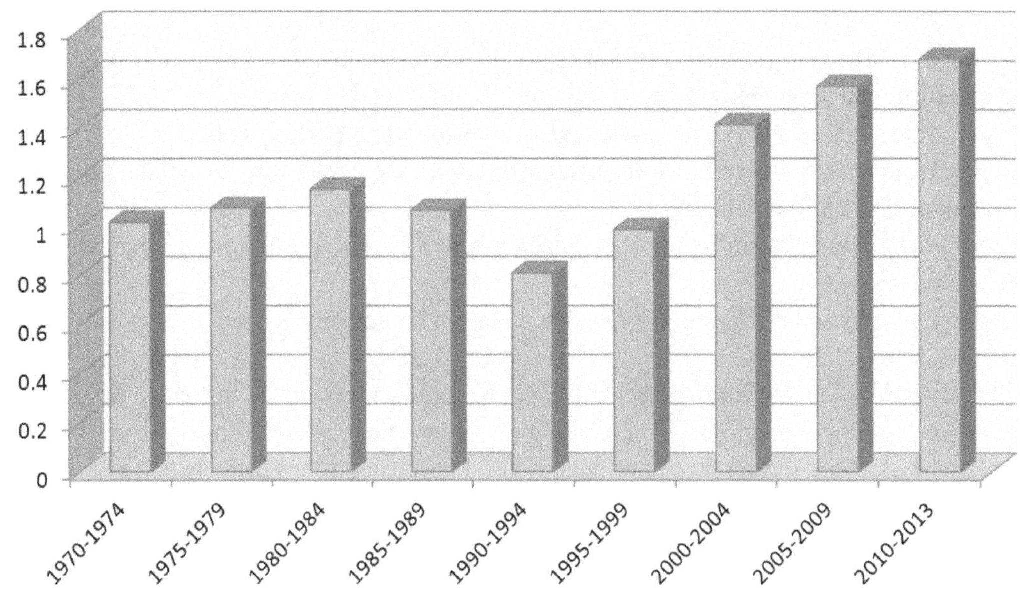

Figure 5. South Korea's product space in 1970 / 1990 / 2013
Source: Atlas Media Database. Please note that (a), (b) and (c) represent 1970, 1990 and 2013 respectively.

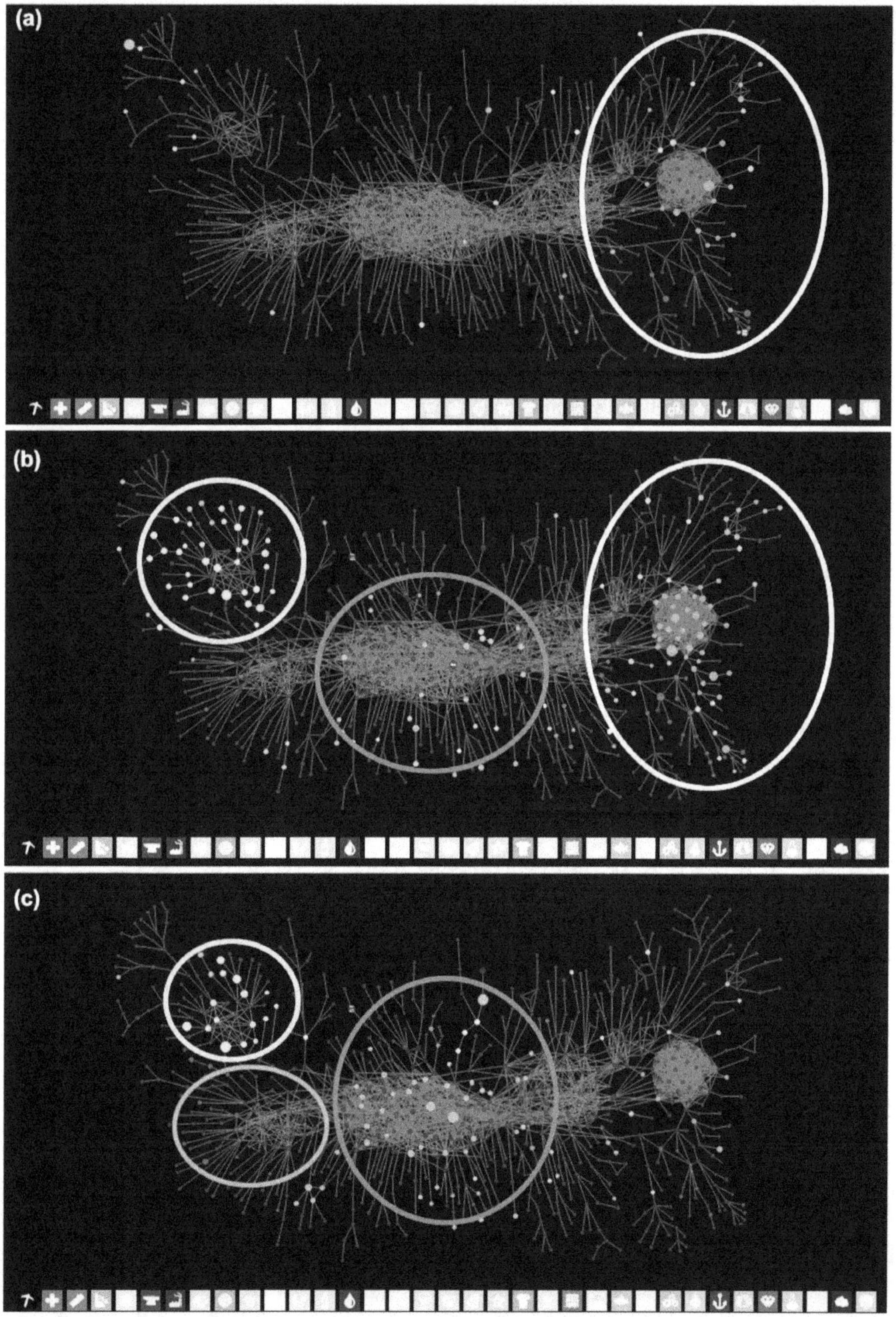

and mollusks, etc. On the basis of this data, we can claim that South Korea had a mainly textile manufacturing structure in the 1970s and specialized in agricultural products.

In the 1990s, South Korea's product space was divided into three main sections, as seen in Figure 5 (part "b"). What is significant is that less sophisticated products, which mainly comprise textile and agriculture products, are centered on the right-hand side of the product space (see white circle). Especially when compared with the 1970s, there is a visible increase in this section. In addition to the products from the 1970s on this side, there is a concentration of the products of leather accessories, miscellaneous men's outerwear, knitted outerwear, synthetic woven fabrics, frozen fish, and temporarily preserved fruit.

We can see that more new products started to appear in South Korea's product space in 1990 in comparison with the 1970s. This section is indicated by the red circle. Among these products are cars, fasteners, electric heating devices, car tires, and metal cables. Almost nonexistent in 1970, the products on the left-hand side of the product space in 1990 are indicated by a yellow circle. This area represents the production of complex products whose spillover effect is limited to spread to other sectors. Some of these products are electronic microcircuits, color TVs, computer peripherals, telecom parts and accessories, toys and games, and vehicle stereos.

There are significant differences in South Korea's product space in 2013 compared to 1990. As seen in Figure 5 (part "c"), in 2013, the products that were located on the right-hand side of the product space have disappeared. Additionally, there are relatively fewer products compared to 1990 in the upper-left side of the product space, which is composed of electronic products and indicated by a yellow circle. Two condensation areas are seen at the center of the product space. These areas are those in which backward and forward connections among the sectors are strong. There are also important changes in the area marked by the red circle when compared with the 1990s. In addition to the products manufactured in the 1990s, the country started to specialize in construction machinery, circuit breakers and panels, air pumps and compressors, vehicle parts and accessories, piston engine parts, miscellaneous heating and cooling equipment, and miscellaneous machinery products. Another major development occurred in the area marked by the blue circle involving chemicals and health-related products. This section is not included in the previous periods. However, it is believed that South Korea's space expanded into this area because of past R&D investments. Remarkable products in this section are polymerization products, synthetic rubber, acrylic polymers, cyclic hydrocarbons, silicones, and polycarboxylic acids.

All in all, it can be said that the South Korean economy was based on agriculture in the early development phase. In the 1970s and 1990s, it can be understood from the product space that the South Korean economy attached importance to industrialization. We have observed that South Korea focused on the textile industry, especially in the 1970s and 1990s. However, the textile industry was subsequently abandoned in the manufacturing area. This can be ascertained from the concentration of products in the center and left-hand side of the product space. When this process is evaluated in terms of employment, initially increasing and then decreasing percentages of people employed can be expected in the manufacturing sector. Moreover, while the tendency toward complex manufacturing in the product space negatively affects the number of people employed in the agriculture sector, it brings a remarkable increase in the service sector.

The Effects of Structural Transformation on South Korea's Employment

The structural transformation of the South Korean economy has been discussed in the previous sections. It is obvious that this structural transformation would have economic effects as well. In this chapter, the effects of structural transformation on employment in South Korea's economy will be evaluated in the context of economic complexity and product space.

As can be seen from Figure 6, the agricultural sector was significantly superior in the 1970s in terms of the number of people employed. During this period, the number of people employed is understood from the graph to be around five million. However, in the 1980s, we can see that a downward trend in the number of people employed in agriculture started. This process continued regularly until the 2010–2012 period. The development of this process is easily understood from the graph. Whereas there was around a 50% share of the agricultural sector in total employment in the 1970s, Figure 7 shows that this share was around 5% in the period 2010–2012. This is supported by the South Korean product space as well. As you recall, the right-hand side of the product space in the 1970s was dominated by agriculture-oriented textile manufacturing and consisted of mostly agriculture-based products. However, in the following years, this trend changed, and this section on the right side of the product space disappeared.

The number of people employed in the manufacturing area seems to have steadily increased until the period 1990–1994. This is clear from Figure 7 with regard to the share of the manufacturing sector in total employment. The most important factor in the emergence of this trend is the production structure based on the textile industry. As you recall, there was a serious increase in the concentration on the right-hand side of the product space in the 1990s. This situation had an effect on employment as well. With the increased concentration in the center of product space in the following period, we can deduce that the number of people employed in the manufacturing industry decreased. These industries require mostly complex knowledge and skills and are areas in which automation and computerization are necessary instead of manpower.

Considering Figure 6 and Figure 7 in terms of the service sector, we are faced with a very different picture from the other two sectors. It can be inferred from both Figure 6 and Figure 7 that the number

Figure 6. Number of employed people by sector in South Korea (Thousands)
Note: Numbers are considered as averages. Data sets were obtained from the Bureau of Labor Statistics.

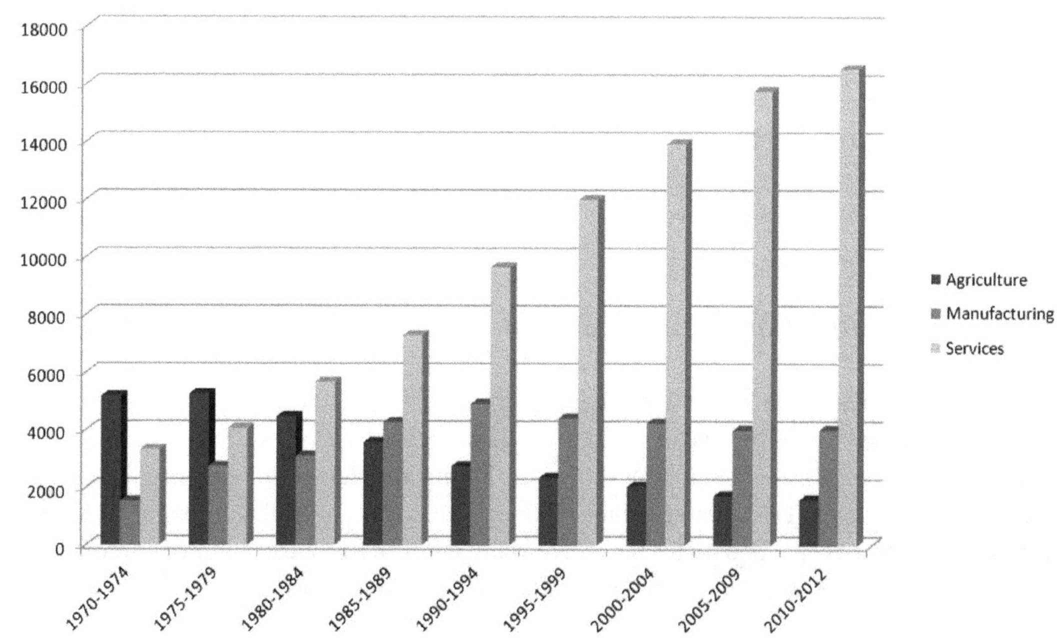

Figure 7. South Korea's sector shares in total employment (%)
Note: Numbers are considered as averages. Data sets were obtained from the Bureau of Labor Statistics.

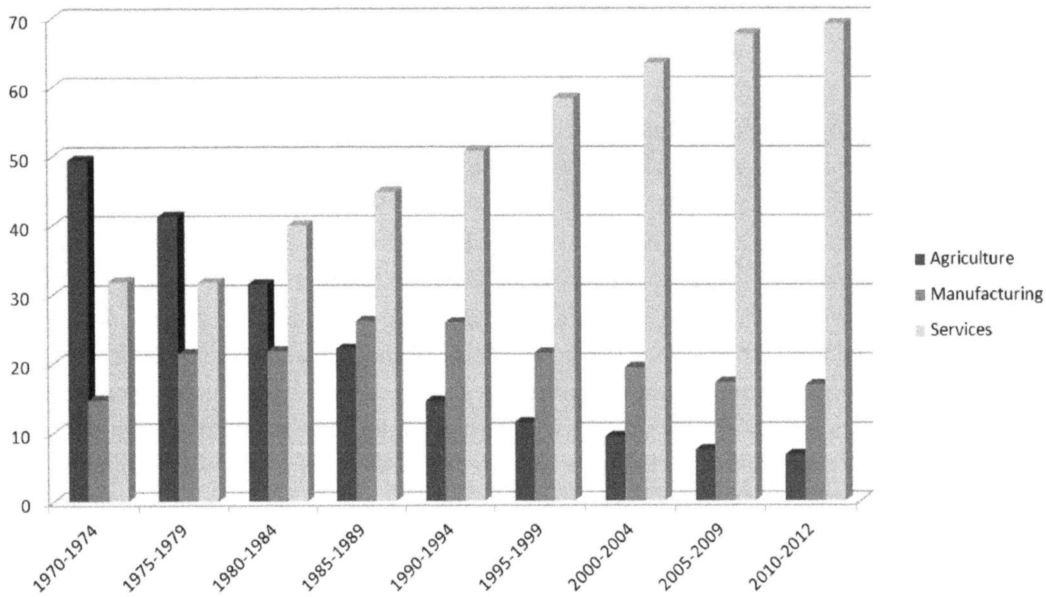

of people employed in the service sector consistently increased between the years 1970 and 2012. This trend is seen in South Korea's product space too, if you recall the parts marked with yellow and red circles in 1990. The industries in this sector require knowledge and skills, and intensive research and development. In addition to the concentration in these two areas, in the 2013 product space, we have a blue marked area comprising health-related products. This area is among the main reasons for the increase of employment in the service sector, as serious research and development activities must be carried out for production to be made in this field.

When evaluated in general terms, the structural transformation of the South Korean economy was also reflected in employment. This transformation process has been observed primarily in the steady decline of the agricultural sector. The manufacturing sector initially experienced an increase and then a decrease. The biggest reason for this was the use of automation instead of labor in the manufacturing sector, along with technological progress. On the other hand, the service sector experienced steady growth in the number of people employed because of the greater need for knowledge and skills with the increase in economic complexity (represented by intensity in the center of the product space).

Structural Transformation of the Japanese Economy: A Brief Overview

Contrary to common belief, the Japanese miracle did not start after World War II. The main foundations of the process were laid in the 18th and 19th centuries. Japan realized its most striking transformation in the 1540–1856 (Edo) and 1868—1914 (Meiji) periods. During the Edo period, Japan adopted a practice of isolation from the world. The country banned entrances and exits, and all commercial relations were operated only from Nagasaki. Also in this period, developments in European countries were closely followed, and new discoveries were transferred to Japan. In particular, a strong industrial infrastructure was formed during this closed economic period by absorbing and assimilating many technical innovations from China, which were imported through South Korea (Derya, 2015).

In the 1850s, Western states made great efforts toward Japan's adoption of liberal economic policies. With the development of international trade, Japan was forced to restart trade relations with the West as a result of the need for its ports to meet demands for water and steam for steamships. Using their military power, the U.S. and other Western countries signed a number of trade agreements[6] with Japan, indicating that these countries had achieved a number of privileges (Fletcher, 1996). Once the country was free of the unequal treaties in 1913, there was a major switch in Japan's trade policy. Japan gained full autonomy because of this change in policy (Hunter, 1998, p. 86).

Japan's economic development process started at the beginning of the Meiji Restoration. During this time, the government embarked on a plan to create a modern infrastructure. Investments were carried out by the state or state-aided private sectors. The origins of "sector selection," which can be regarded as the basis for Japan's industrial policy, can also be traced back to the Meiji period (Derya, 2015). The textile industry, which is the pioneer of the industrialization process, is an example of sector selection because the state invested in this industry and played a direct role in its development. Public policies contributed to the formation of the necessary human resources for the development of this industry. Within nearly 40 years of the Meiji period of recovery/development policies, Japan had achieved economic and social transformation. The country also achieved trade surpluses in this process (Ito, 1996).

After the First World War, despite Japan's greater industrialization compared to other Asian countries, Western countries still viewed Japan as an agricultural country. During this period, Japan dominated a large part of the Asian market by filling the industrial gap that had emerged in the world with its modern and effective institutions (Derya, 2015). In the 1900s, Japan's productivity, technology, and industrial infrastructure were clearly inferior to that of the West. However, receiving a strong impetus and pressure from abroad, Japan made earnest efforts to mobilize its civil service and people to catch up (Ohno, 2003, p. 38).

The Japanese economy expanded at an average annual rate of about 3 percent for more than a half century before the Second World War. This long period of sustained growth was accompanied by rapid structural change from an agrarian to an industrialized economy (Ito, 1996). The agricultural sector played an important role at the beginning of this period of high growth in Japan. The increase in productivity in the agricultural sector and the mobility of the workforce contributed significantly to this process. Labor productivity in Japan doubled[7] during the Meiji Restoration (1881–1920) (Asian Development Bank, 2013, p. 9). However, after the Second World War, the Japanese economy entered a very troublesome phase. As productive resources had been either diverted to military use or destroyed in the war, real output fell by half from 1944 to 1946. Recovery was quick, however. By the mid-1950s, GDP had regained its 1943 level, and by 1960, it was at the level predicted by its prewar trend. In the post-war period, the economy shifted from labor-intensive sectors to capital-intensive heavy industry (Ito, 1996).

Japan experienced a period of rapid export-led growth from 1953 to 1973 (Yülek, 1997). Until the oil crisis of 1973–1974, the main purpose of industrialization in Japan was to increase wealth. In the process of industrialization, the Japanese government acted by connecting trade, finance, and industry policies (Yülek, 2013, p. 4). In 20 years' time, the country had become a highly industrialized country with more complex (sophisticated) technology. Japan's annual growth rate in the postwar years was around 10%. The determining factor in the rapid growth of Japan was its concrete support of promising industries (Ito 1996; Ifo Institute for Economic Research, 1997, p. 46; Beason & Weinstein, 1996). In this process, the country focused on heavy industry products. But by the 1970s, Japan's priority was no longer capital-intensive heavy industry. During this period, the country focused on research-intensive high-tech products. Automobile manufacturing and electrical machinery production, in which technology plays a decisive role, gained importance. On the other hand, the intermediate products (e.g., iron and steel) provided by the labor-intensive textile industry and heavy industry lost their significance (Kohama, 1990).

The growth trend of the 1960s slowed suddenly after the first oil crisis, in 1973–74. Possible reasons for this abrupt decline are the Japanese economy's transition to different industries leading to a reduction in high-yield investments; high oil prices; pollution prevention arrangements.[8] Additionally, the annual growth rate from 1975 to 1990 was roughly half of that achieved in the previous two decades. Another interesting feature of this period was the sharp nominal increase in the value of the Japanese yen: its value tripled from 1970 to 1995. However, the growth rate did not rise above 1 percent between 1992 and 1995 (Ito, 1996).

In Japan's Meiji and other rapid growth periods, strengthening the industries' implementation of traditional industrial policy and the state's direct intervention in the market played an important role in economic transformation. In later periods, rather than managing coordination and dissemination of information through government intervention, Japan found a better way. After the 1980s, a transition to policies based on technology and innovation occurred. Thereafter, liberal policies in Japan gained weight, and traditional policies were dropped from the agenda. Transformation taking place alongside the liberalization experienced in recent years has been shaped around "new generation" policies. These policies and the government's role in shaping them are different from the traditional industrial policies. Innovation in sophisticated production structures and R&D stand out in the new generation policies (Yülek, 2013, p. 22). Hence, structural transformation is expected to play a significant role in leading the Japanese economy to be among the modern industrial and service economies in the 21st century as well (Asian Development Bank, 2013, p. 59).

Japan's Economic Complexity and Product Space: An Evaluation in the Context of Employment

In this section, Japan's economic complexity and the changes in its product space will be discussed. In addition, the possible effects of changes in economic complexity and product space on employment will be evaluated. Innovation is an important stage in the creation of a complex production structure. The unit of analysis is the national economy, and the major players involved in innovation are the government, universities, government-sponsored laboratories, and private companies. While companies and laboratories endeavor to develop new products, universities contribute to this process by educating scientists and engineers. The government is among the actors in the process that leads to technological development. Japan is considered to be one of the most successful countries in terms of innovation, and this success is thought to be closely linked to the country's innovation system. Thanks to harmony in innovation, the country has achieved a considerable growth rate (Lee & Han, 2002).

Looking at Japan's economic complexity index, we observe that the index value is under two in the 1970s. Figure 8 shows that this index value exceeded two in the 1980s and maintained stability until the end of this period. The period 2000–2004 was when Japan had the most complex economy. The index value was over 2.5 during this period.

Japan's economic complexity rankings for the period between 1970 and 2013 can be found in the Atlas Media Database. In 1970, Japan was ranked third for economic complexity. It ranked first between

Figure 8. Japan's economic complexity index
Note: Economic complexity is calculated as five-year averages.

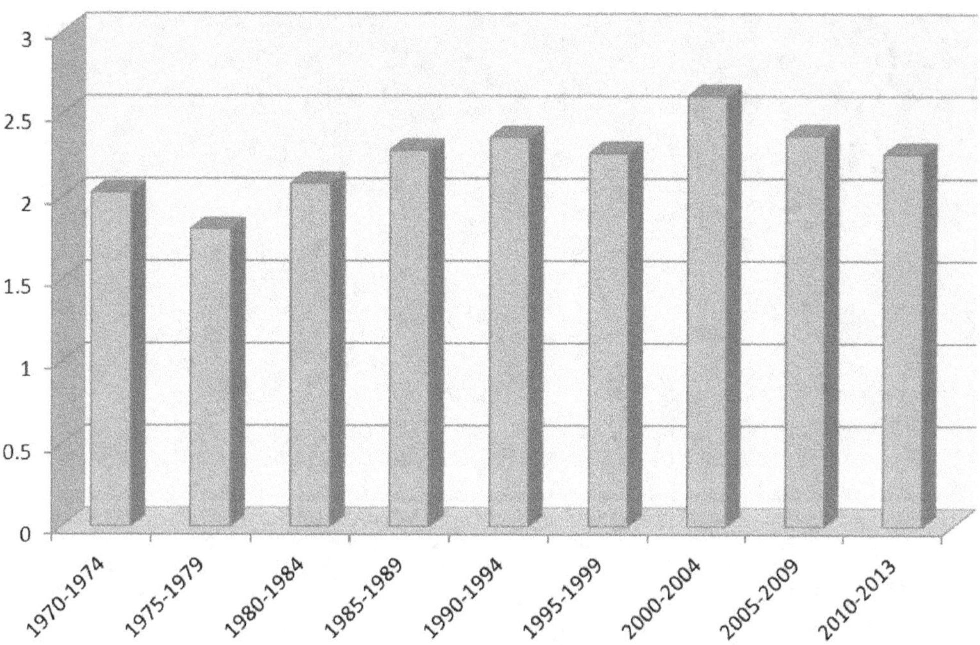

the years 1972 and 1990. Between the years 1990 and 2000, the country's ranking varied between 1st and 3rd. From 2000 to 2013, Japan was ranked 1st.

We shall now have a look at the country's product space. As can be seen from Figure 9 (part "a"), in 1970, manufactured products were concentrated in three main areas. The white circle represents weak complexity areas, including agriculture and agro-based industries. Some of these products are footwear, linens, blouses, embroidery, finished cotton fabrics, rice, pasta, silk-woven fabrics, prepared fruit, and temporarily preserved fruit.

In the same period, there were also many products in the center of the product space. This situation is an indicator of Japan's ability to produce many complex products in the 1970s. Some of the manufactured products marked by the red circle include cars, trucks and vans, seamless iron tubes, motorcycles, railway track fixtures and fittings, roller bearings, fasteners, metal cables, thin iron sheets, and iron coils. In the same year, there is a concentration marked by a yellow circle in the top left corner of the product space. This area includes cameras, calculating machines, clocks, sporting goods, and toys and games. When evaluated in general, Japan's economy in 1970 was mainly based on both agriculture and manufacturing (including agro-textiles).

There were dramatic changes to Japan's product space in 1990 (Figure 9, part "b"). For instance, the area marked by the white circle in 1970, which represented agricultural manufacturing, disappeared. This can be interpreted as arising from the decline of the share of manufacturing and agriculture in total employment. In comparison with 1970, there is an increase in density in the red and yellow areas. The causes of increased density in the red zone are vehicles parts and accessories, valves, pulley system parts, motor vehicles piston engines, construction machinery, DC motors, car tires, and miscellaneous parts of stream power units. The reasons for the increased density in the yellow zone are color TVs, TV tubes

Figure 9. Japan's product space in 1970/1990/2013
Source: Atlas Media Database. Please note that (a), (b) and (c) represent 1970, 1990 and 2013 respectively.

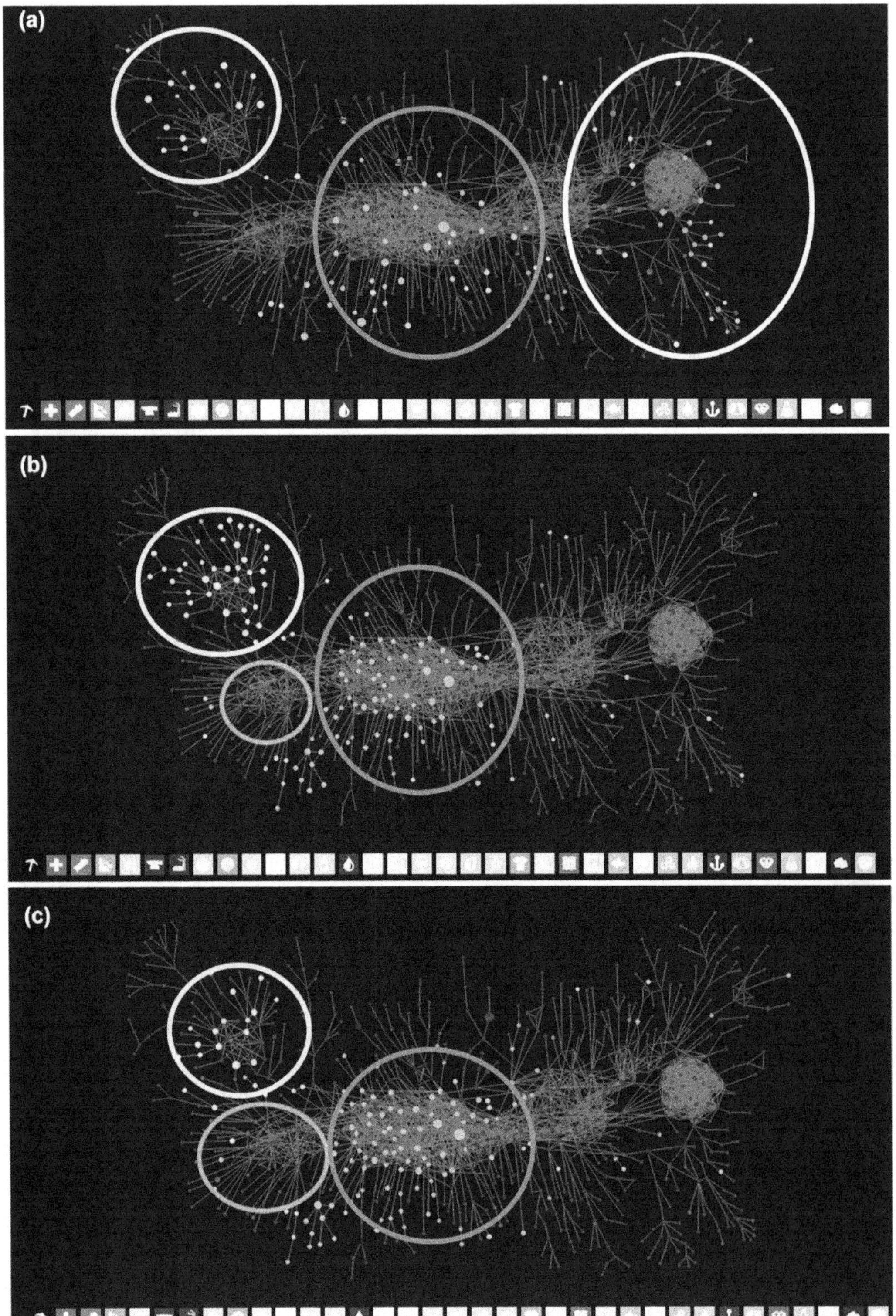

and cathode rays, computer parts and accessories, computer peripherals, video and sound recorders, miscellaneous electrical machinery, telecom parts and accessories, and printed circuits. Additionally, there is a newly added blue circle, which was non-existent in 1970. This area consists of health-related products. Some of the manufactured products included in this area are synthetic rubber, monocarboxylic acids, photographic film, x-ray equipment, cyclic alcohols, heterocyclic compounds, medical instruments, and regenerated fiber. We can infer that Japan began to manufacture new products. This meant the emergence of new business opportunities in the service sector and the manufacturing industry in terms of employment. In this context, the manufacturing industry in the 1990s could be expected to increase the number of people employed. However, it seems that there might have been a decline in the share of the manufacturing sector in total employment, because instead of labor automation, computerization became more important in the center of product space. It is also possible that there was an increase in the number of people employed in the service sector and an increase in the share of total employment in the service sector.

When Japan's product space in 2013 is assessed (Figure 9, part "c"), greater density in the red-marked area is observed in comparison with the 1990s. The underlying reason for this is that more new products were being manufactured compared to the 1990s. Some of these products are transmission belts, miscellaneous centrifuge and filtering machinery, miscellaneous pump parts, electrical insulators, control instruments of gas or liquid, and valves. Moreover, there is also a significant reduction in the yellow area when compared with the 1990s. The reason for this may be the shifting of manufacturing in this area to different regions across the world. For example, today, even though the originating country of cameras and digital cameras is Japan, most of them are manufactured in China. This could be the underlying reason for the decline in the yellow area. Furthermore, the blue area in the product space is denser in comparison with the 1990s. Some of the new products appearing in this area are regenerated fiber, photographic chemicals, photographic film, chemical products, ethers and acetyls, inorganic esters, printing ink, analog instruments for physical analysis, and glycosides and vaccines.

We can conclude that overall, the Japanese economy was well structured in terms of the agriculture, manufacturing, and service sectors in the 1970s. However, in the 1990s, agriculture and agro-based manufacturing sector production disappeared. This led to a decline of the manufacturing sector's percentage share in total employment. There was also a higher concentration in the product space in the areas involving complex manufacturing. This situation is an indication of the emergence of new business opportunities in the manufacturing and service sectors. In 2013, we can deduce from the figure that there was a decrease in the production of electronic devices while there was an expansion in the production of health-related products. This signifies an employment increase in the service sector but a decline (both in terms of percentage share of employment and number of people employed) in the manufacturing industry.

The Effects of Structural Transformation on Japan's Employment

The structural transformation of the Japan economy has been discussed in the previous sections. It is obvious that this structural transformation would have economic effects as well. In this chapter, the effects of structural transformation on employment in Japan's economy will be evaluated in the context of economic complexity and product space.

As can be understood from Figure 10, agricultural employment in Japan in the period 1970–1974 was over five million. A steady decrease is observed in the number of people employed in agriculture in subsequent periods. This was also observed in Japan's product space in the 1970s and 1990s. As you

Figure 10. Number of employed people by sector in Japan (thousands)
Note: Numbers are considered as averages. Data sets were obtained from the Bureau of Labor Statistics.

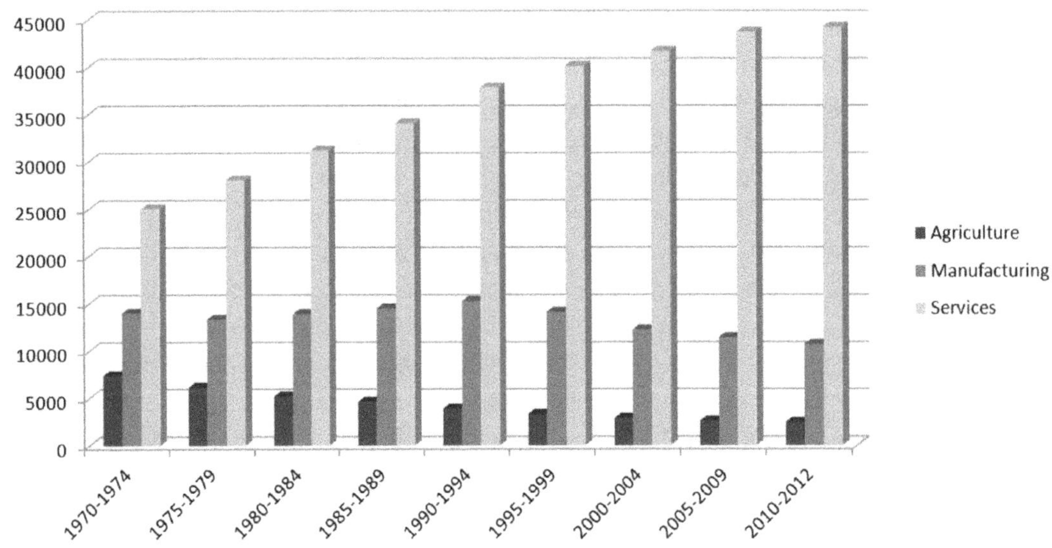

recall, agro-production, which was on the right-hand side of the product space (marked by the white circle) in 1970, disappeared 20 years later, in 1990. The effects of this are also reflected in the number of employed people, which can be seen in Figure 11. For instance, the percentage share of agriculture in total employment was around 15% between the years 1970 and 1974 but decreased to 4% in the 2010–2012 period.

In terms of the manufacturing sector, both the agro-based textile industry (white circle) and the other manufacturing sectors (red and yellow circles) were present in the product space in the 1970s. It can be inferred from Figure 10 that the number of people employed in manufacturing in 1970 was around 14 million. Moreover, Figure 11 shows that the manufacturing sector's share in total employment was around 28% in the 1970–1974 period. However, in the 1990s, there was a concentration mainly in the red and yellow areas of the product space. This is also reflected in the number of people employed in these areas. Approximately 15 million people were employed in the manufacturing industry from 1990 to 1994. The share of the manufacturing sector in total employment is close to that of the previous period. In the 2010–2012 period, on the other hand, there was a significant decline in the number of people employed in the manufacturing industry compared to the previous period. During this period, the total number of people employed was around 10 million. The manufacturing sector's share of total employment was around 17% in this period. This can be explained by comparing the product spaces of 1990 and 2013. As you remember, we saw that there was a concentration in the yellow area in 1990. This area primarily consisted of electrical and electronic equipment. However, in 2013, the country abandoned the manufacturing of the products in this area, which was an important factor in the decline in employment in the manufacturing sector. Besides, when compared with 1990, more products were manufactured in the blue circle area in 2013. We previously mentioned that this area was knowledge-skills intensive.

Figure 10 shows that the total number of people employed in the service sector in the 1970–1974 period was around 25 million. Furthermore, Figure 11 indicates that the share of the service sector in total employment was approximately 49% during this period. The same table also shows that this share

Figure 11. Japan's sector shares in total employment (%)
Note: Numbers are considered as averages. Data sets were obtained from the Bureau of Labor Statistics.

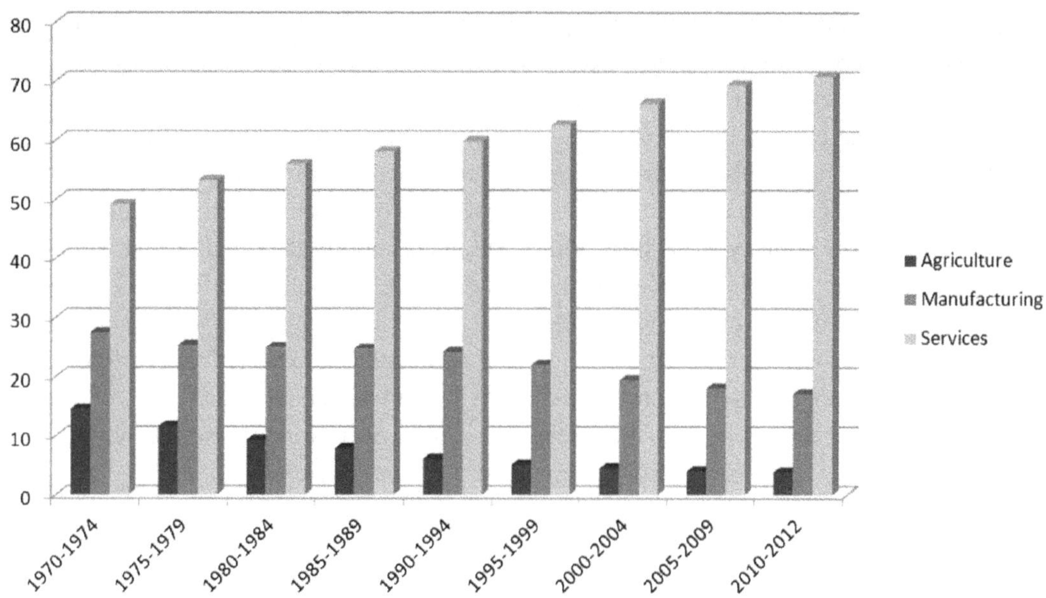

in employment continually increased over time. In 2010–2013, the total number of people employed in the service sector was 45 million. Also during this period, the share of the service sector in total employment climbed to 70%. These developments can be observed in the product space too. For example, we observed that the Japanese product space in 1970 and 1990 was mainly composed of the red and yellow circled areas, which mean R&D had a significant role in the manufacturing of these products. Besides, there was a significant increase in the manufacturing of health-related products (marked by the blue circle) in 1990 and 2013. In line with this development, it is possible to claim that the concentration in red, yellow, and blue areas, where knowledge- and skills-intensive manufacturing is performed, had an impact on the employment increase in the service sector.

When Japanese structural transformation is evaluated with regard to employment, it is obvious that there has been a steady decline in the agricultural sector. The underlying reason for this is that the increase in economic complexity has led to increased productivity in the agricultural sector. Additionally, the manufacturing industry has experienced a steady decrease in employment (of a percentage basis). This situation can be interpreted as a negative effect of automation on the manufacturing industry. In the service sector, on the other hand, there has been an increase both with regard to people employed and in percentage terms. This can be interpreted as a positive contribution of knowledge- and skills-intensive manufacturing to the service sector.

CONCLUSION

Structural transformation is a concept often discussed in today's economic literature. To realize sustainable growth and development objectives, countries have to succeed in structural transformation. Success in structural transformation has the power to influence many economic parameters, one of which is the employment structure of the country. In this chapter, changes in the employment structure of South Korea and Japan, both of whom have successfully completed the structural transformation, were studied in terms of economic complexity and product space theory. Economic complexity refers to a country's knowledge and skills production structure. The product space, on the other hand, is a visual representation of economic complexity. As a result of our research, we found out that increased complexity of a country's economy (increased intensity of the product space center) first affects agriculture. The basic dynamic of structural transformation is to shift from agriculture to other industries. However, the process of employment in the manufacturing industry differs depending on the development level of the country. If industrialization of the country is not fully completed, then initially there may be an increase in employment in the manufacturing industry, followed by a decrease through the effects of automation and computerization. On the other hand, if industrialization of the country is fully completed, then a decline in employment in the manufacturing sector on a regular basis may be expected. By contrast, growth in economic complexity may lead to an increase in the service sector. In other words, concentration in the center of the product space may lead to an increase in employment in the service sector both in terms of percentage share in total employment and the number of people employed.

REFERENCES

Andreoni, A. (2011). *Productive capabilities indicators for industrial policy design.* UNIDO, Development Policy, Statistics and Research Branch, Working Paper 17.

Arthur, W. B. (2013). *Complexity economics: A different framework for economic thought.* Santa Fe Institute, Working Paper, 2013-01-012.

Asako, K., Ito, T., & Sakamoto, K. (1991). The rise and fall of deficit in Japan, 19651990. *Journal of the Japanese and International Economies*, *5*(4), 451–472. doi:10.1016/0889-1583(91)90008-E

Asian Development Bank. (2013). *Asia's economic transformation: Where to, how, and how fast? Key Indicators for Asia and the Pacific*. Manila, Philippines: Asian Development Bank.

Atlas Media Database. (n.d.). Retrieved January 02, 2016, from http://atlas.media.mit.edu/en/

Bartzokas, A. (2007). *Monitoring and analysis of policies and public financing instruments conducive to higher levels of R&D investments: The policy mix project.* Case Study, South Korea, A study funded by the European Commission – DG Research.

Beason, R., & Weinstein, D. E. (1996). Growth, economies of scale, and targeting in Japan (19551990). *The Review of Economics and Statistics*, *78*(2), 286–295. doi:10.2307/2109930

Boschma, R., & Capone, G. (2015). Relatedness and diversification in the European Union (EU-27) and European Neighbourhood Policy countries. *Environment and Planning C*, *20*, 1–21.

Bureau of Labor Statistics. (n.d.). Retrieved March 15, 2016, from http://www.bls.gov/ilc/

Chang, H., Andreoni, A., & Kuan, M. L. (2013). *International industrial policy experiences and the lessons for the UK. Future of Manufacturing Project: Evidence Paper 4*. Government Office for Science.

Chen, D. H. C., & Suh, J. (2007). Introduction. In Korea as a Knowledge Economy: Evolutionary Process and Lessons Learned (pp. 1-16). WBI Development Studies. Washington, DC: World Bank.

Cho, J., Chun, H., & Lee, Y. (2015). How does the entry of large discount stores increase retail employment? Evidence from Korea. *Journal of Comparative Economics*, *43*(3), 559–574. doi:10.1016/j.jce.2015.04.004

Chung, H. H. (2007). *Lessons from the Korean venture industry development.* World Bank Working Paper, 39379.

Chung, S. (2010). Innovation, competitiveness and growth: Korean experiences. In J. Y. Lin & B. Pleskovic (Eds.), *Lessons from east asia and the global financial crisis* (pp. 333-358). Annual Word Bank Conference on Development Economics.

Cochrane, W. W. (1993). *The development of American agriculture: A historical perspective* (2nd ed.). Minneapolis, MN: University of Minneapolis Press.

Corcoles, D., Diaz-Mora, C., & Gandoy, R. (2014). Product sophistication: A tie that binds partners in international trade. *Economic Modelling*, *44*, 33–41. doi:10.1016/j.econmod.2013.12.009

Cristelli, M., Tacchella, A., & Pietronero, L. (2015). The heterogeneous dynamics of economic complexity. *PLoS ONE*, *10*(2), e0117174. doi:10.1371/journal.pone.0117174 PMID:25671312

Daude, C., Nagengast, A., & Perea, J. R. (2015). Productive capabilities: An empirical analysis of their drives. *The Journal of International Trade & Economic Development*, *25*(4), 504–535. doi:10.1080/09638199.2015.1073342

De Bandt, O., & Vigna, O. (2008). The macroeconomic impact of structural reforms. *Banque de France Bulletin Digest,* 0169.

De Brauw, A., Muller, V., & Lee, H. L. (2014). The role of rural-urban migration in structural transformation of Sub-Saharan Africa. *World Development*, *63*, 33–42. doi:10.1016/j.worlddev.2013.10.013

Derya, H. (2015). Almanya ve Japonya'nın sanayileşme sürecinde korumacı politikaların önemi. *Akademik Bakış Dergisi*, *48*, 97–117.

Ernst, D. (2000). *Catching up and post-crisis industrial upgrading: Searching for new sources of growth in Korea's electronics industry.* East-West Center Working Paper 2, East-West Center, Honolulu.

Felipe, J., Kumar, U., & Abdon, A. (2010). *As you saw so shall you reap: From capabilities to opportunities.* The Levy Economics Institute, Working Paper Collection, 613.

Ferrarini, B., & Scaramozzino, P. (2016). Production Complexity, adaptability and economic growth. *Structural Change and Economic Dynamics*, *37*, 52–61. doi:10.1016/j.strueco.2015.12.001

Fletcher, M. W. (1996). The Japan spinners association: Creating industrial policy in Meiji Japan. *Journal of Japanese Studies*, *22*(1), 49–75. doi:10.2307/133046

Gesthuizen, M., & Wolbers, M. H. J. (2010). Employment transition in the Netherlands, 19802004: Are low educated men subject to structural or cyclical crowding out? *Research in Social Stratification and Mobility*, *28*(4), 437–451. doi:10.1016/j.rssm.2010.06.001

Gillman, M. (2011). *A simple theory of structural transformation.* Cardiff Business School, Working Paper Series, E2011/4.

Hahm, J. H. (2003). The government, the chaebol and financial ınstitutions before the economic crisis. In S. Haggard, W. Lim, & E. Kim (Eds.), *Economic crisis and corporate restructuring in Korea: Reforming the Chaebol* (pp. 79–101). Cambridge, UK: Cambridge University Press. doi:10.1017/CBO9781139085083.006

Hallak, J. C. (2006). Product quality and the direction of trade. *Journal of International Economics, 68*(1), 238–265. doi:10.1016/j.jinteco.2005.04.001

Harrison, R., Jaumandreu, J., Mairesse, J., & Peters, B. (2014). Does innovation stimulate employment? A firm-level analysis using comparable micro-data from four European countries. *International Journal of Industrial Organization, 35*, 29–43. doi:10.1016/j.ijindorg.2014.06.001

Hartmann, D., Guevara, M. R., Jara-Figueroa, C., Aristaran, M., & Hidalgo, C. A. (2015). Linking *economic complexity, institutions and income inequality*. Retrieved November 2, 2015, from http://arxiv.org/abs/1505.07907

Hartmann, D., & Pyka, A. (2013). *Innovation, economic diversification and human development.* FZID Discussion Papers, 65-2013.

Hausmann, R., & Hidalgo, C. A. (2011). The network structure of economic output. *Journal of Economic Growth, 16*(4), 309–342. doi:10.1007/s10887-011-9071-4

Hausmann, R., Hidalgo, C. A., Bustos, S., Coscia, M., Chung, S., Jimerez, J., & Yıldırım, M. A. et al. (2011). *The atlas of economic complexity: Mapping paths to prosperity. Center for International Development at Harvard University and Macro Connections MIT Media Lab*. Cambridge, MA: Puritan Press.

Hausmann, R., Hwang, J., & Rodrik, D. (2007). What you export matters. *Journal of Economic Growth, 12*(1), 1–25. doi:10.1007/s10887-006-9009-4

Hausmann, R., & Klinger, B. (2006). *Structural transformation and patterns of comparative advantage in the product space.* CID Working paper, 128.

Hausmann, R., & Klinger, B. (2007). *The structure of the product space and the evolution of comparative advantage.* CID Working Paper, Harvard University, 146.

Hidalgo, C., Klinger, B., Barabasi, A. L., & Hausmann, R. (2007). The product space conditions the development of nations. *Science, 317*(5827), 482–487. doi:10.1126/science.1144581 PMID:17656717

Hidalgo, C. A. (2009). *The dynamics of economic complexity and the product space over a 42 year period.* CID Working Paper, Harvard University, 189.

Hidalgo, C. A. (2011). *Discovering southern and east Africa's industrial opportunities*. GMF Economic Policy Paper Series.

Hidalgo, C. A., & Hausmann, R. (2009). The building of economic complexity, proceedings of the national academy of sciences of the United States of America. *Proceedings of the National Academy of Sciences of the United States of America, 106*(26), 10570–10575. doi:10.1073/pnas.0900943106 PMID:19549871

Hirschman, A. O. (1958). *The strategy of economic development.* New Haven, CT: Yale University Press.

Hunter, J. (1998). The Japanese experience of economic development. In P. O'Brien (Ed.), *Industrialisation: Critical perspectives on the world economy* (pp. 71–141). London: Routledge.

Ifo Institute for Economic Research. (1997). *A comparative analysis of Japanese and German economic success*. Sakura Institute of Research, Springer.

Ito, T. (1992). *The Japanese economy*. Cambridge, MA: MIT Press.

Ito, T., & Weinstein, D. E. (1996). Japan and the Asian economies: A Miracle in transition. *Brookings Papers on Economic Activity*, *2*(2), 205–272. doi:10.2307/2534622

Kaldor, N. (1967). Strategic factors in economic development. New York: Ithaca.

Kim, L. (2000). The dynamics of technological learning in industrialization. *International Social Science Journal*, *53*(168), 297–308. doi:10.1111/1468-2451.00316

Kim, L., & Nelson, R. (2000). *Technology, learning, and innovation: Experiences of newly industrializing economies*. Cambridge, UK: Cambridge University Press.

Klepper, S. (2002). The capabilities of new firms and the evolution of the US automobile industry. *Industrial and Corporate Change*, *11*(4), 645–666. doi:10.1093/icc/11.4.645

Klepper, S., & Simons, K. L. (2000). Dominance by birthright: Entry of prior radio producers and competitive ramifications in the U.S. television receiver industry. *Strategic Management Journal*, *21*(10-11), 997–1016. doi:10.1002/1097-0266(200010/11)21:10/11<997::AID-SMJ134>3.0.CO;2-O

Kohama, H. (1990). Japans economic development and foreign trade. In L. Chung & Y. Ippei (Eds.), *The economic development of Japan and Korea: A parallel with lessons* (pp. 3–18). New York: Praeger.

Lall, S. (2000). *The technological structure and performance of developing country manufactured exports, 1985-1998.* Quenn Elizabeth House University of Oxford Working Paper Series, 44.

Leamer, E. (1984). *Sources of international comparative advantage: Theory and evidence*. Cambridge, MA: MIT Press.

Lee, C. H. (2000). Institutions and economic development. In U. Hiemenz (Ed.), *Growth and competition in the new global economy* (pp. 137–156). Paris: OECD Publishing.

Lee, H., & Han, S. Y. (2002). The evolution of the national innovation system in the Korean mobile telecommunication industry. *Communications & Stratégies*, *48*, 161–186.

Lee, S., & Malin, B. A. (2013). Educations role in Chinas structural transformation. *Journal of Development Economics*, *101*, 148–166. doi:10.1016/j.jdeveco.2012.10.006

Lewis, W. A. (1954). Economic development with unlimited supplies of labour. *The Manchester School*, *22*(2), 139–191. doi:10.1111/j.1467-9957.1954.tb00021.x

Maggioni, D., Turco, A. L., & Gallegati, M. (2014) Does export complexity matter for firms' output volatility?. *Università Politecnica Dellemarche, Dipartimento di Scienze Economiche e Sociali*. Quaderni Dı Ricerca.

McMillan, M., Rodrik, D., & Verduzco-Gallo, I. (2014). Globalization, structural change, and productivity growth, with an update on Africa. *World Development*, *63*, 11–32. doi:10.1016/j.worlddev.2013.10.012

Minami, R. (1994). *The economic development of Japan: A quantitative study* (2nd ed.). New York: St. Martin's Press. doi:10.1007/978-1-349-23221-5

Minondo, A., & Requena-Silvente, F. (2013). Does complexity explain the structure of trade? *The Canadian Journal of Economics. Revue Canadienne dEconomique*, *46*(3), 928–955. doi:10.1111/caje.12033

Ohno, K. (2003). *East Asian growth and Japanese aid strategy*. GRIPS Development Forum.

Organisation for Economic Co-operation and Development. (2009). *OECD Reviews of Innovation Policy: Korea 2009*. Paris: OECD Publishing.

Organisation for Economic Co-operation and Development. (2014). *Industry and technology policies in Korea*. OECD Publishing.

Özgüzer, G. E., & Binatlı, A. O. (2015). *Economic convergence in the EU: A complexity approach.* RePec Working Paper Series, 15/03.

Park, S. C. (1997). The transformation of the South Korean economy and international economic development in East and Southeast Asia. *International Planning Studies*, *2*(2), 241–255. doi:10.1080/13563479708721681

Petralia, S., Balland, P.-A., & Morrison, A. (2015). *Climbing the ladder of technological development.* DRUID Academy Conference in Aalborg.

Prebisch, R. (1950). The economic development of Latin America and its principal problems. New York: United Nations (UN).

Rodrik, D. (2006). What's so special about China's exports? *China&World Economy*, *14*(5), 1–19.

Rostow, W. W. (1959). The stages of economic growth. *The Economic History Review*, *12*(1), 1–16. doi:10.1111/j.1468-0289.1959.tb01829.x

Schetter, U. (2015). *Comparative advantages with product complexity and product quality.* Retrieved January 15, 2016, from http://www.etsg.org/ETSG2015/Papers/372.pdf

Simoes, A. J. G., & Hidalgo, C. A. (2011). *The economic complexity observatory: An analytical tool for understanding the dynamics of economic development.* Workshops at the Twenty-Fifth AAAI Conference on Artificial Intelligence.

Singer, H. W. (1950). U.S. foreign investment in underdeveloped areas: The distribution of gains between investing and borrowing countries. *The American Economic Review*, *40*(2), 473–485.

Srinivasan, P. V. (2013). Dynamics of structural transformation in South Asia. *Asia-Pacific Development Journal*, *20*(2), 53–88. doi:10.18356/82da9007-en

Stafforte, S., & Tamberi, M. (2012). Italy in the space (of Products). *Economia Marche Journal of Applied Economics*, *31*(1), 90–113.

The Atlas of Economic Complexity. (n.d.). Retrieved February 23, 2016, from http://atlas.cid.harvard.edu/

United Nations Human Settlements Programme. (2011). *UN-HABITAT annual report 2010* (R. Rollnick & T. Naudin, Eds.). Nairobi, Kenya: UNON Publishing Services Section.

Yameogo, N. D., Nabassaga, T., & Ncube, M. (2014). Diversification and sophistication of livestock products: The case of African countries. *Food Policy*, *49*, 398–407. doi:10.1016/j.foodpol.2014.10.005

Yülek, M. A. (1997). On the financial repression in Japan during the high growth period (1953-73). *METU Studies in Development*, *24*(4), 575–595.

Yülek, M. A. (2013). Kalkınma tartışmalarında Japon modelinin yükselişi, düşüşü ve tekrar yükselişi. In K. A. Akkemik & S. Ünay (Eds.), *Doğu Asyanın politik ekonomisi: Japonya Çin ve Güney Kore'de kalkınma siyaset ve jeostrateji* (pp. 1–27). İstanbul: Boğaziçi Üniversitesi Yayınları.

KEY TERMS AND DEFINITIONS

Capabilities: Abilities of a country including human and physical capital, legal system, institutions and infrastructure.

Economic Complexity: A country's whole knowledge and skills used in manufacturing.

Employment: An agreement between an employer and an employee that the employee will provide certain services on the job.

Japan: An island country in East Asia.

Product Space: Relatedness of products which are subject to world trade.

Production: A process to transform tangible and intangible inputs into goods or services.

Sophisticated Product: A product which needs more knowledge, experience or education for being manufactured.

South Korea: A country in the southern part of the Korean peninsula.

Structural Transformation: The reallocation of resources across the agriculture, manufacturing, and services.

ENDNOTES

1 Hausmann et al., (2011: 20) example was re-adapted.

2 See for details Simoes & Hidalgo (2011).

3 See Hahm (2003).

4 Institutes established by the Korean government in order to adapt to the technologies brought in from foreign countries are as follows: Korea Institute of Machinery and Metals, Electronics and Telecommunications Research Institute, Korea Research Institute of Chemical Technology, Korea Research Institute of Standards and Science, Korea Institute of Energy Research, and Korea Ocean Research Institute (See Kim &Nelson, 2000).

5 The economic complexity index for 1962-2013 is available in the Atlas Media Database.

6 These agreements are known as "the unequal treaties" because Japan was forced to sign them under military pressure from western powers despite the agreements' inclusion of articles against Japan.

7 See Minami (1994).

8 See Ito (1992). That the growth trend is downward is because the government encouraged excessive fiscal in the second half of the 1970s. See Ito (1992, chapter 6) and Asako, Ito, & Sakamoto (1991).

Chapter 17
Major Macroeconomic Dynamics for Labor Market in Turkey:
A Causality Analysis

Mustafa Karabacak
Uşak University, Turkey

Oytun Meçik
Eskişehir Osmangazi University, Turkey

ABSTRACT

The relationship among inflation, unemployment, and economic growth can be treated as a trade-off in general. When the economy is in recession, inflationary pressures are expected to decrease while unemployment is increasing. On the contrary, a decrease is expected while inflationary pressures are rising. Thus the relation between these twin macroeconomic variables and their relation to economic growth are a focal point for developing countries. The aim of this study is analyzing the relationship among unemployment, inflation, and economic growth in Turkey by alternative methods. Thus the causality among these variables is tested with modified Wald statistic developed by Toda-Yamamoto. Findings obtained from causality test will provide policy recommendations for Turkish economy on a macroeconomic level.

INTRODUCTION

As the basic economic indicators of modern economic conditions, the concepts of unemployment, inflation, and economic growth are macroeconomic variables which are often analyzed and of which relations among themselves are studied in detail in the context of interaction. Whereas an economic growth could occur as a result of financial activity level in an economy, an inflationary setting and/or high unemployment rates could also be observed.

To the extent that the mutual trade-off among those principal macroeconomic variables has generally been accepted, the likelihood of being subject to the different type of interaction in the whole country or different time period is stronger. Hence, it is needed to analyze the relationship among mentioned variables by focusing on especially the country and period which are wanted to be studied.

DOI: 10.4018/978-1-5225-2008-5.ch017

Regarding the recent past of the Turkish economy, high unemployment, inflation and low economic growth keep remaining on the agenda as the common problems. Beyond any doubt, ensuring a sustainable economic growth in an economy is based on primarily ensuring economic stabilization. Like Turkey's, in an economy which is equipped with both powerful and treating features in terms of labor force, the interaction demonstrated by those three outstanding variables gains great importance.

In the present chapter, it is aimed to analyze the relationship among variables about annual economic growth in the period of 1960-2014, inflation rate and unemployment data in Turkey through modified Wald statistics developed by Toda-Yamamoto[1] and to present political suggestions in the level of macroeconomy for the economy of Turkey in the light of those findings. Accordingly, the literature review about causality relation of those three major macroeconomic variables mentioned in the present study was given, the macroeconomic developments in the related period were analyzed, and the findings of causality analysis which was conducted in the light of data were presented.

LITERATURE REVIEW

Being major macroeconomic variables of an economy, unemployment, inflation, and economic growth relation are often discussed in the literature, though they might be in the characteristic of variability from period to period. Like all of the other economies in the world, it is seen that the literature searching the causality relation among those factors which regard financial and real dimensions of the economy as well as in Turkey supports the stated evaluation. Focusing the literature in terms of unemployment, inflation, economic growth and the constraint of Turkish economy; the outstanding findings could be summarized as:

Uysal and Erdoğan (2003, p. 45) focused on the relation between the unemployment rates and price level in Turkey between 1980 and 2002. In the study, the related time period was evaluated according to different periods. Hereunder, the fact that there is a positive relation among variables in the 80s whereas there is a negative between 1990 and 2002 is remarkable. Karaca (2003, p. 254) searched the relation between inflation and growth in Turkey using quarterly data for the period of 1987-2002 and observed the existence of one-way Granger causality from inflation to growth. It is emphasized that the inflation in the economy of Turkey in the related period downgraded the growth rate.

Berber and Artan (2004, p. 115) analyzed the relation between inflation and economic growth in Turkey for the period of 1987-2003 and they found out one-way causality relation from inflation to economic growth. Furthermore, it is also a remarkable finding that inflation influences economic growth negatively. On the other hand, Terzi and Oltulular (2004, p. 31) analyzed the relation between the inflation and growth rates at the sectoral level in the economy of Turkey with annual data in the period of 1923-2003. The findings point out a negative causality relation from inflation to sectoral growth. Considering those findings, it is emphasized that inflation is a considerable obstacle to growth and price stabilization is significant in this respect.

Göktaş Yılmaz (2005, p. 74) performed Granger and Hsiao causality tests in order to specify the causality relation between the growth and unemployment rates in Turkey in the period of 1978-2004. The findings show that the causality relation is only from unemployment rate to growth rate. Thereby, for the related periods, unemployment is among the factors influencing economic growth and in response to this, it is seen that economic growth cannot decrease unemployment rate. On the other hand, Yapraklı (2007, p. 297) analyzed the relation between inflation and economic growth in Turkey with the quarterly data for the period of 1987-2007 by using Granger causality test. Accordingly, in the related period, inflation influences economic growth while economic growth does not affect inflation.

Uysal, Mucuk, and Alptekin (2008, p. 66) found out that there is a one-way Granger causality from inflation to economic growth in the period of 1950-2006 according to the results of Granger causality test analyzing the relation between inflation and economic growth in Turkey. Karaçor, Şaylan, and Üçler (2009, p. 71) conducted Granger causality test by using quarterly data of the 1990-2005 period of the Turkish economy and reached the conclusion that there is a double way interaction between growth and inflation rates.

Şentürk and Akbaş (2014, p. 9) analyzed the relation between economic growth and unemployment rate represented with industrial production index in the economy of Turkey from 2005 to 2012 and inflation rate by using Toda-Yamamoto causality test. Accordingly, it is seen that there is a two-way causality relation between the industrial production index and the unemployment rate in the related period and inflation rate. Süleymanov and Nadirov (2014, p. 123) studied the inflation-growth relation in the Turkish economy in the period of 2003-2013, and they found a one-way causality relation from growth to inflation. Similarly, Akan and Kanca (2015, p. 17) reached a finding of one-way causality relation from growth rate to inflation in the period of 1980-2013 in the Turkish economy.

Focusing on the literature, as stated commonly in the studies supported by empirical findings, it is seen that the relationship among unemployment, inflation, and economic growth variables may vary according to studied period. Hence, analyzing the relations among those variables through a different and new method for the Turkish economy has a great significance in terms of empowering the information scale in the literature as well.

THREE MAJOR MACROECONOMIC VARIABLES IN TURKEY

In the economy of Turkey, the observation of macroeconomic developments for the period of 1960-2014 will end up with some evaluations. The most significant of all is, no doubt, the Turkish economy which suffered from high inflation in a considerable part of this period and which came up against more fragility as its own integration to global economy got stronger.

In Figure 1, the process of inflation, unemployment and economic growth series as the three major macroeconomic variables of Turkish economy in the period of 1960-2014 is shown. The process of inflation and economic growth in the figure points out a significant relation between those macroeconomic variables in the related period. Likewise, while there is an inflationary process going on in an economy, and annual gross domestic product (GDP) is growing in real terms, it is possible to mention growth with inflation. And it stands out that there is that kind of relation for a considerable period except for the years in which some crisis effects are observed for the Turkish economy. It could be stated that the process of the unemployment rate in the related period is more stable than the other variables.

Since Figure 1 reflects a long period of time, it enables to specify the developments which end up with dramatic results clearly in the economy as well. For instance, the fact that the oil crisis which broke out as a result of oil embargo declared by Organization of Arab Petroleum Exporting Countries [OAPEC][2] on 15th October 1973, caused an increase in the world oil price and peaked in 1979 caused one of the most dramatic inflation increases in the economy of Turkey reflects the graphic. This period took its place on the stage of history as a time in which the world experienced stagflation at the same time, questioned the aspect of 'activist government interventionism' and new alternative trends came out.

The year 1980 represents a process in which the economy of Turkey came to the new path and the drift in the financial politics differentiated from the previous periods with the experienced paradigm shift. The effects of fluctuation and developments observed in the world economy as a result of constraint abolition on the capital movements in 1989 were started to be seen in the economy extremely. 1993 and 1994 were the years of devaluation and economic crisis. 1999 corresponds to the effects of great Marmara earthquake which stroke breeder power directly and 2000-02 correspond to the periods in which backstopping negotiations were being made with International Monetary Fund (IMF), and economic crisis were observed.

Since the declaration of "Transition to the Strong Economy Program" in 2001, great structural reforms, which first interest financial sector and aim radical changes and transformations in the medium-long terms, have been made (Taşar, 2012, p. 84). It is possible to associate the general level of prices and positive progress in the economic growth in the 2000s to the acquisitions in the same period. However, it is not possible to state that the positive developments in GDP, industrial production, the rates of capacity utilization and foreign trade created a significant acceleration for the indicators to employment (Kol & Karaçor, 2012, p. 392).

The developments related to prices in Turkey for the period of 1960-2014 are seen in Figure 2. It is observed that increasing inflation in the economy of Turkey with the stagflation atmosphere which the world economy came across in the 1970s starts to influence the growth in a negative way. Thus, Turkey met two digit inflation in the 1970s and in the following process, due to the rapid increase in the inflation, economic and social uncertainties came out, which ended up with a regression in the potential revenue of the economy. During this process, the fact that the inflation reached three digit numbers in February-October 1980, January 1998 and the period between April 1994 and March 1995 reflected the history books. However, in return for this, it could be expressed that crazy inflations which marked the parts of Latin American and European countries have not been seen in any periods of Turkish economy (Özatay, 2011, p. 248).

Figure 1. Three major macroeconomic variables in Turkey: 1960-2014
Source: Republic of Turkey Ministry of Development, Turkstat, Organization for Economic Co-operation and Development [OECD] Statistics.

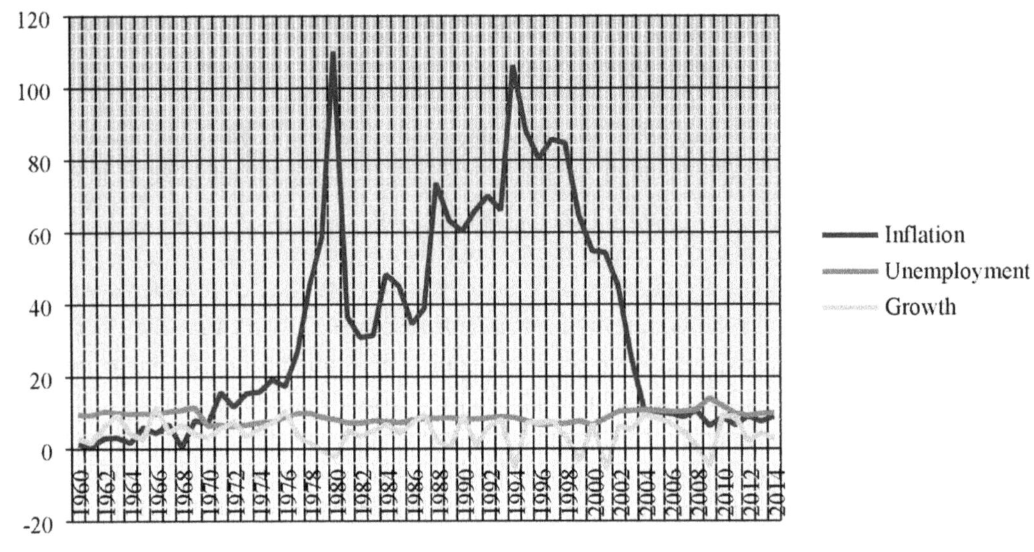

Figure 2. Inflation rate in Turkey: 1960-2014
Source: OECD Statistics.

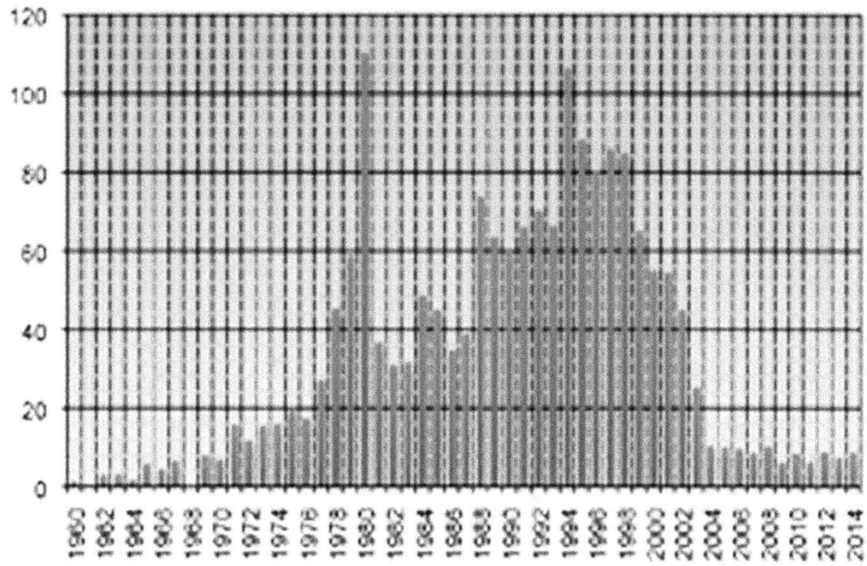

After Turkey had experienced the transition process to the inflation targeting in the period of 2002-2005, it went into inflation targeting period. Thus, a process in which direct inflation was aimed by the Central Bank of the Republic of Turkey (CBRT) without using any intermediate objective started (Kara & Orak, 2008, p. 60). The main aim of practicing inflation targeting process in the economy of Turkey is to provide price stabilization and from this point of view, economic stabilization. It is discussed that inflation targeting process which has been in practice in Turkey recently results in an average inflation decrease which has positive effects on economic growth with its dimensions of financial sector development and financial deepening (Meçik & Karabacak, 2011).

Inflation targeting regime, for the period after 2002 in which political stabilization was enabled with convenient global economic developments, ensured the inflation separated from the previous periods and approached one digit levels. However, it is hard to say that monetary authority was successful when descending to the particulars of inflation targeting process. Yet, as seen clearly in the graphic, it is possible to say that the process of inflation which did not show fluctuation relatively in the 2000s is a significant acquirance compared to the previous periods.

The unemployment rates in the related period are available in Figure 3. It is seen that the unemployment rate has relatively a low process between the 1970s and the 2000s. When this period is evaluated with the movement resulted from the increase in the general prices level in Figure 2, the trade-off relation between inflation and unemployment is striking. The inference made with the annual average data for Turkey reminds the theoretical relation which is framed with Phillips curve[3].

It is seen that the ability of Turkey to generate employment did not change especially after the 1980s and consequently the developments which could decrease unemployment did not occur. Beyond any doubt, monetary and fiscal policies have a great role for this reality. Likewise, the fact that monetary authority adopted inflation targeting regime and the fact that fiscal policies focused on budget deficits and creating primary surplus caused a significant decrease in the generation of employment power (Köksel and Fisunoğlu, 2013, p. 45).

Figure 3. Unemployment rate in Turkey: 1960-2014
Source: OECD Statistics.

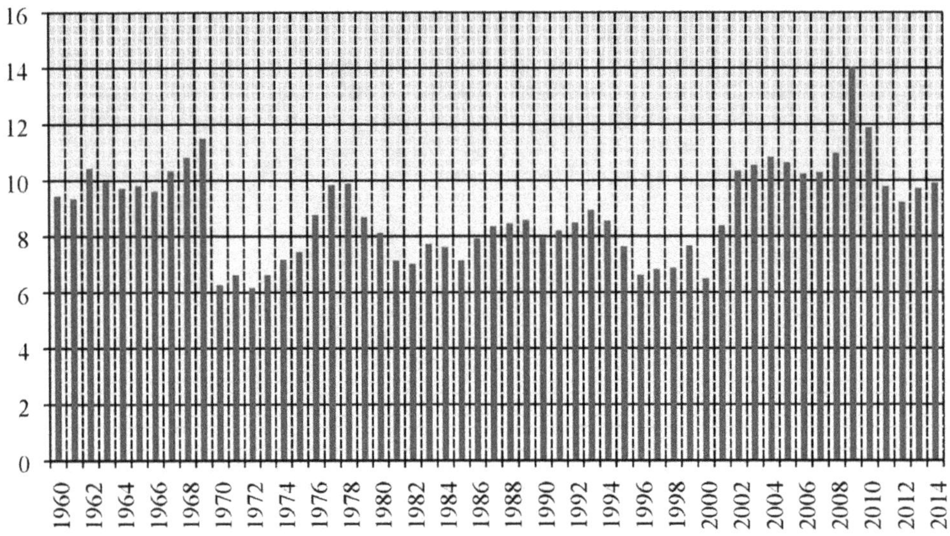

The fact that unemployment in the Turkish economy displays a non-decreasing characteristic requires the questioning of the traditional politics aimed to solve this problem. In this context, it should be noted that the politics which could decrease unemployment should require the sustainability of economic growth. It should be emphasized that first of all there should be a paradigm shift in the labor force market and a process which includes education policies aiming flexible employment and decrease in cost burden at micro level and aiming increase in the quality at macro level (Türk Sanayicileri ve İşadamları Derneği [TUSİAD], 2002, p. 235).

Economic growth, defined as the positive increase in the GDP and per capita GDP from one year to the other, reflects the Figure 4 as below for the period 1960-2014 in Turkey. According to this, on a yearly basis, it stands out that economic growth has a floating and low potential process in general.

The paradigm shift in 1980 and the drift in economic policies distinguished this period from the previous ones and the effects of fluctuation and developments observed in the world after the abolition of constraints on capital movements in 1989 on the economy were started to be felt considerably. As a result, in this process, it is seen that economy went into an unsteady growth process with fluctuation in capital movements at an increasing level (Boratav, 2008, p. 172). As well as the fact that Turkey started to face instability more often under international capital movements with the free capital mobility of Turkey increased the fragility in the economy, it also caused discussions about applications like Tobin tax[4] (Meçik, 2014, p. 362). However, the most significant condition, in order to empower the economic growth in Turkey, should be rendering sustainable growth. Likewise, the recent empirical findings remark joint relation of economic growth and employment. Especially, the fact that the countries with high-income level reach a better employment level and the role of economic growth in this reality is emphasized (Ghose, Majid, & Ernst, 2010, p. 99). It is a well-accepted reality that a sustainable economic growth is based on the technology keeping up with the present era and also the production of technology (Kepenek & Yentürk, 2005, p. 636).

Figure 4. Economic growth rate in Turkey: 1960-2014
Source: Republic of Turkey Ministry of Development, Turkstat.

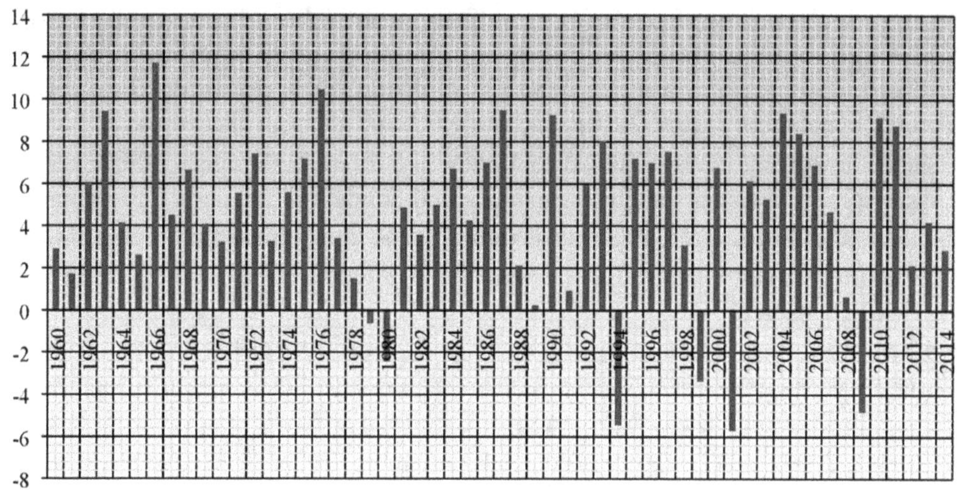

Evaluating the Turkish economy for the period of 1960-2014 in terms of macroeconomic variables such as unemployment, inflation, and economic growth; it is possible to state that the introvert, protective and interfering industrialization model of the 1930s yielded to opening foreign countries in the frame of market-friendly neoliberal politics after 1980. During this period, it is seen that the average growth speed of Turkish economy resembled the developing countries while macroeconomic performance did not develop significantly in spite of paradigm change and political choices (Pamuk, 2014, p. 346).

The Turkish economy is in a period of change related to sectoral based labor productivity which is under the effect of not only global developments but also development acceleration of the economy. Therefore, it is seen that the percentage of the agricultural sector in the revenue and employment regressed while the percentage of the service sector came into prominence. In the same process, while the sectoral distribution of labor force was getting changed, resistance seen in the rates of unemployment in spite of all developments leads to inferences on jobless growth[5] (Meçik & Afşar, 2014, p. 19).

THE MODEL

Data

In the empirical analysis; the data of annual inflation rate, unemployment rate, and economic growth were used as three major macroeconomic variables for the Turkish economy in the 1960-2014 period. Whereas inflation rate data (INF) was taken as the general level of prices rate of increase series which was calculated by OECD[6] for the base year 2010 Consumer Price Index (CPI) series, the unemployment rate data (UN) was provided from the series presented in the OECD Statistics database. The economic growth series is the numbers of growth speed taken from Republic of Turkey Ministry of Development web page and calculated for GDP series harmonized with Turkish Statistical Institute (Turkstat) data.

Methodology

The methodology in the present chapter was developed according to Granger causality testing which a statistical hypothesis is testing in order to find out whether a time series is useful in forecasting another time series. Such cause and effect relations among economic variables are analyzed with causality tests in a frame of economic theory (Tarı, 2010, p. 437).

Even though the applicability of the causality test developed by Granger (1969) is high, there is a need to make some pre-testings about stationarity and cointegration. The Granger methodology is highly sensitive to the characteristics such as stationarity and cointegration of series. Since series with unit root do not have standard distribution as stated in Gujarati (1995), F test procedure and Granger methodology will not be valid.

On the other hand, dynamic causality test developed by Granger (1988) which enables to test the causality through a vector error correction mechanism, requires all of the series to be integrated I(1) order one. It does not allow testing the causality among the series at different integration orders (Büyükakın, Bozkurt & Cengiz, 2009, p. 111). Hence, Toda and Yamamoto (1995) developed a test which provides an analysis of causality relation without regarding the integration orders of series and the existence of cointegration relation.

Toda-Yamamoto test developed according to a VAR model requires the estimation of VAR ($p+d$) model given in equation (1) while p is the optimal lag length and d is maximum integration order[7]. In the equation (1), A represents parameters matrix while x a vector consist of k variable and ε and v represent error terms vector and constants vector respectively (Akçay, 2011, p. 84).

$$x_t = v + A_1 x_{t-1} + \ldots + A_p x_{t-p} + \ldots + A_{p+1} x_{t-p-d} + \varepsilon \qquad (1)$$

The null hypothesis on the non-existence of Granger causality is tested by practicing a constraint supposing the first p parameter in the equation (1) equals to zero. MWALD (Modified Wald) statistics obtained from the estimation equation (1) has an asymptotic chi-square distribution (Kar, Nazlıoğlu, & Ağır, 2014, p. 69). However, Hacker and Hatemi-J (2006) suggested applying the test based on bootstrap distribution instead of standard chi-square distribution since the performance of MWALD statistics with standard chi-square standard is weak when the sample size is small. Likewise, bootstrap distribution displays a better performance when applied to both small and big samples compared to asymptotic chi-square distribution.

Empirical Evidence

There is no precondition for the variables in leveraged bootstrap Toda-Yamamoto causality test developed by Hacker and Hatemi-J (2006) such as being stationary or cointegrated. However, maximum integration order of the variables should be known in order to apply the test (Büyükakın, Bozkurt & Cengiz, 2009, p. 111). Because of it, Augmented Dickey-Fuller and Phillips-Perron unit root tests were applied in order to find out the integration order of the variables involved in the analysis. According to the results acquired from the Unit root test, the maximum integration order of the variables was defined as “1”.

Table 1. Unit root test results

INF	Level				First Difference			
	Constant	Trend	Constant	Trend	Constant	Trend	Constant	Trend
ADF	-2.0542	[0.2636]	-1.8942	[0.6440]	-8.8262	[0.0000]	-4.2400	[0.0000]
PP	-1.8728	[0.3425]	-1.6486	[0.7603]	-9.0051	[0.0000]	-9.5579	[0.0000]
UN	**Level**				**First Difference**			
	Constant	**Trend**	**Constant**	**Trend**	**Constant**	**Trend**	**Constant**	**Trend**
ADF	-2.6335	[0.0926]	-2.7443	[0.2238]	-7.0722	[0.0000]	-7.0164	[0.0000]
PP	-2.7074	[0.0793]	-2.7467	[0.2230]	-8.1007	[0.0000]	-8.3253	[0.0000]
Growth	**Level**				**First Difference**			
	Constant	**Trend**	**Constant**	**Trend**	**Constant**	**Trend**	**Constant**	**Trend**
ADF	-1.6469	[0.4520]	-1.4336	[0.8396]	-5.9688	[0.0000]	-5.7576	[0.0001]
PP	-1.7287	[0.4113]	-1.3995	[0.8501]	-6.4024	[0.0000]	-11.041	[0.0000]

The values in brackets are the probability values.

AS stated beforehand, the causality analysis developed by Hacker and Hatemi-J (2006) is based on a VAR ($p+d$) model estimation. Thereby, first of all, a VAR (p) model should be specified providing stability condition and necessary assumptions in order to analyze the causality between variables. In this context, after necessary testings, it was concluded that VAR (10) model is appropriate for the analysis of relation between inflation and economic growth; VAR (3) model for the analysis of relation between unemployment and inflation and again VAR (10) model for the analysis of relation between inflation and unemployment.

According to the results given in Table 2 about causality analysis, there is only one-way causality from economic growth to inflation. Since MWALD statistics obtained from causality tests applied for the other variables are smaller than the bootstrap critic values, the null hypothesis cannot be rejected. That is, it is not possible to refer to causality between unemployment and inflation.

Table 2. Causality test results

	MWALD Stat.	Bootstrap Critical Values		
		% 1	% 5	% 10
INF ⇒ GROWTH	6.791	30.649	22.003	18.312
GROWTH ⇒ INF	29.094	31.842	22.106	18.329
GROWTH ⇒ UN	3.013	12.786	8.510	6.653
UN ⇒ GROWTH	0.457	12.734	8.424	6.544
UN ⇒ INF	5.289	33.461	23.679	18.943
INF ⇒ UN	7.537	35.873	24.852	20.235

CONCLUSION

Unemployment, inflation and economic growth could be listed as the most significant indicators of an economy at the macroeconomic level. It is known that there exists some trade-off among those variables proposed in the theoretical framework. According to this, while unemployment rate decreases in an economy, it could be expected that inflationary pressures may increase.

In the present chapter, it is aimed to analyze the relation among the economic growth, unemployment rate and inflation variables for the period of 1960-2014 in Turkey and in consideration of the findings, to present some policy suggestions at macroeconomic level for the Turkish economy.

As emphasized in the literature, since those relationships could vary from period to period, analyzing this relation through different and new methods has a supportive quality to empower the knowledge in the literature. Though findings of the analysis suggest that there is one-way causality from economic growth to inflation, it is not possible to state that there is a causality relation between unemployment and growth; and unemployment and inflation. So, like the statement in the literature and emphasized commonly in the studies about unemployment, inflation and economic growth relation; the relation among unemployment, inflation, and economic growth variables could vary from period to period; and the findings of the present study about the 1960-2014 period of Turkish economy could be taken confirmatory since they are parallel to the findings of the studies about the same period performed by Süleymanov and Nadirov (2014) and Akan and Kanca (2015).

In accordance with the findings of the analysis, it is possible to speculate that the growth process in the related period is in the manner of creating inflation and corresponds to an inflationary growth process as a characteristic. Additionally, it is also observed that the conditions created by the global economic crisis in the last period of Turkish economy cyclically changed the mentioned relation for a while.

In the light of the findings acquired from the time series analysis, it is possible to emphasize that policymakers should be in an approach regarding the structural features of the economic growth dynamics in the framework of price stability. Therefore, the need for structural reforms which has been discussed very often recently in the Turkish economy should be highlighted once more. Likewise, the present situation shows that the economic growth process should well-analyzed in terms of problem solutions such as unemployment and inflation.

In order to keep the growth process sustainable, the economy of Turkey should be built in a manner of promoting growth dynamics; based on technology and meanwhile not only importing technology but also producing it. It is obvious that it will bring new requirements in the context of the labor market, quality and productivity increase.

It is expected that bringing about sustainable economic growth will be effective to empower the economy in terms of finance; to support price stability and to diminish unemployment problem. Thus, it could be noted that permanent political designs which are for medium or long terms should be formed for the economy of Turkey instead of short term solutions.

ACKNOWLEDGMENT

This chapter is the updated and extended version of the paper presented in the EUREFE'16 on July 14th-16th 2016 in Aydın/Turkey organized by Adnan Menderes University.

REFERENCES

Akan, Y., & Kanca, O. C. (2015). Türkiye'de dış borçlanma, büyüme ve enflasyon ilişkisi: VAR yaklaşımı (1980-2013). *Hacettepe Üniversitesi İktisadi ve İdari Bilimler Fakültesi Dergisi*, *33*(3), 1–22.

Akçay, S. (2011). Causality relationship between total r&d investment and economic growth: Evidence from United States. *Süleyman Demirel Üniversitesi İktisadi ve İdari Bilimler Fakültesi Dergisi*, *16*(1), 79–92.

Berber, M., & Artan, S. (2004). Türkiye'de enflasyon-ekonomik büyüme ilişkisi (teori, literatür ve uygulama). *Atatürk Üniversitesi İktisadi ve İdari Bilimler Fakültesi Dergisi*, *18*(3-4), 103–117.

Boratav, K. (2008). *Türkiye iktisat tarihi 1908-2007*. Ankara: İmge Kitabevi.

Büyükakın, F., Bozkurt, H., & Cengiz, V. (2009). Türkiye'de parasal aktarımın faiz kanalının granger nedensellik ve Toda-Yamamota yöntemleri ile analizi. *Erciyes Üniversitesi İktisadi ve İdari Bilimler Fakültesi Dergisi*, *33*, 101–118.

Ghose, A. K., Majid, N., & Ernst, C. (2010). *Küresel istihdam sorunu* (G. Aykaç & S. Kayan, Eds., Ö. F. Çolak, Trans.). Ankara: Efil Yayınevi.

Göktaş Yılmaz, Ö. (2005). Türkiye ekonomisinde büyüme ile işsizlik oranları arasındaki nedensellik ilişkisi. *İstanbul Üniversitesi İktisat Fakültesi Ekonometri ve İstatistik Dergisi, 2*, 11-29.

Granger, C. W. J. (1969). Investigating causal relation by econometric and cross-sectional method. *Econometrica*, *37*(3), 424–438. doi:10.2307/1912791

Granger, C. W. J. (1988). Some recent developments in the concept of causality. *Journal of Econometrics*, *39*(1-2), 199–211. doi:10.1016/0304-4076(88)90045-0

Gujarati, D. N. (1995). *Basic Econometrics*. New York: McGraw-Hill.

Hacker, R. S., & Hatemi-J, A. (2006). Tests for causality between integrated variables using asymptotic and bootstrap distributions: Theory and application. *Applied Economics*, *38*(13), 1489–1500. doi:10.1080/00036840500405763

Kar, M., Nazlıoğlu, Ş., & Ağır, H. (2014). Trade openness, financial development and economic growth in Turkey: Linear and nonlinear causality analysis. *BDDK Bankacılık ve Finansal Piyasalar*, *8*(1), 63–86.

Kara, A. H., & Orak, M. (2008, October). *Enflasyon hedeflemesi*. Paper presented at the meeting of the Ekonomik Tartışmalar Konferansı, İstanbul, Turkey.

Karaca, O. (2003). Türkiye'de enflasyon-büyüme ilişkisi: Zaman serisi analizi. *Doğuş Üniversitesi Dergisi*, *4*(2), 247–255.

Karaçor, Z., Şaylan, Ş., & Üçler, G. (2009). Türkiye ekonomisinde enflasyon ve ekonomik büyüme ilişkisi üzerine eşbütünleşme ve causality analizi (1990-2005). *Niğde Üniversitesi İİBF Dergisi*, *2*(2), 60–74.

Kepenek, Y., & Yentürk, N. (2005). *Türkiye ekonomisi*. İstanbul: Remzi Kitabevi.

Köksel, B., & Fisunoğlu, H. M. (2013). Türkiye'de işsizlik ve istihdam politikası önerileri. In H. Atik (Ed.), *Prof. Dr. Cihan Dura'ya armağan 2000'li yıllarda Türkiye ekonomisi: Yapısal dönüşümler, ana sorunlar ve çözüme dönük politika önerileri* (pp. 23–48). Ankara: Nobel Yayıncılık.

Kol, E. N., & Karaçor, Z. (2012). 2001 güçlü ekonomiye geçiş programı ve istihdam üzerine etkileri. *Maliye Dergisi*, *162*, 379–395.

Meçik, O. (2014). Uluslararası sermaye akımları ve vergilendirilmesi: Türkiye ekonomisi üzerine bir değerlendirme. In E. Gümüş, A. Çelikkaya, E. Ferhatoğlu, M. Aslan, E. Gümüş, S. Bilge, & M. Çildir (Eds.), *Prof. Dr. Fazıl TEKİN'e armağan* (pp. 343–367). Eskişehir: Eskişehir Osmangazi Üniversitesi Basımevi.

Meçik, O., & Afşar, M. (2014). Türkiye ekonomisinde yapısal dönüşümler ve işgücü piyasasındaki gelişmeler. *Optimum Ekonomi ve Yönetim Bilimleri Dergisi*, *1*(2), 1–23.

Meçik, O., & Karabacak, M. (2011, June). *Türkiye'de enflasyon, finansal derinleşme ve büyüme ilişkisi*. Paper presented at the meeting of the Anadolu Uluslararası İktisat Kongresi II. Eskişehir: Anadolu Üniversitesi.

Organization for Economic Co-operation and Development. (2016). *Statistics*. Retrieved May 21, 2016, from http://stats.oecd.org/

Organization of Arab Petroleum Exporting Countries. (2016). *Organization of Arab Petroleum Exporting Countries*. Retrieved April 15, 2016, from www.oapecorg.org

Özatay, F. (2011). *Parasal iktisat: Kuram ve politika*. Ankara: Efil Yayınevi.

Pamuk, Ş. (2014). *Türkiye'nin 200 yıllık iktisadi tarihi, büyüme, kurumlar ve bölüşüm*. İstanbul: Türkiye İş Bankası Kültür Yayınları.

Phillips, A. W. (1958). The relationship between unemployment and the rate of change of money wages in the United Kingdom 1861-1957. *Economica*, *25*(100), 283–299.

Republic of Turkey Ministry of Development. (2016). *Statistics*. Retrieved May 21, 2016, from http://www.mod.gov.tr/Pages/index.aspx

Şentürk, M., & Akbaş, Y. E. (2014). İşsizlik-enflasyon ve ekonomik büyüme arasındaki karşılıklı ilişkinin değerlendirilmesi: Türkiye örneği. *Journal of Yasar University*, *9*(34), 5820–5832. doi:10.19168/jyu.43548

Süleymanov, E., & Nadirov, O. (2014). Türkiye örneğinde enflasyonla ekonomik büyüme arasında ilişki. *Journal of Qafqaz University-Economics and Administration*, *2*(2), 119–125.

Tarı, R. (2010). *Ekonometri*. Kocaeli: Umuttepe Yayınları.

Taşar, M. O. (2012). *Küresel kriz ve Türkiye ekonomisinin yapısal dönüşümü*. Konya: Palet Yayınları.

Terzi, H., & Oltulular, S. (2004). Türkiye'de ekonomik büyüme-enflasyon süreci: Sektörler itibariyle ekonometrik bir analiz. *Bankacılar Dergisi*, *50*, 19–33.

Toda, H. Y., & Yamamoto, T. (1995). Statistical inference in vector autoregressions with possibly integrated processes. *Journal of Econometrics*, *66*(1-2), 225–250. doi:10.1016/0304-4076(94)01616-8

Türk Sanayicileri ve İşadamları Derneği. (2002). *Türkiye'de işgücü piyasası ve işsizlik (Yayın No: TÜSİAD-T/2002/12-354)*. İstanbul: Lebib Yalkın Yayımları.

Turkstat. (2016). *Statistics*. Retrieved May 20, 2016, from http://www.turkstat.gov.tr/Start.do

Uysal, D., & Erdoğan, S. (2003). Enflasyon ile işsizlik oranı arasındaki ilişki ve Türkiye örneği (1980-2002). *SÜ İİBF Sosyal ve Ekonomik Araştırmalar Dergisi*, *6*, 35–47.

Uysal, D., Mucuk, M., & Alptekin, V. (2008). Türkiye ekonomisinde vektör otoregresif model ile enflasyon-büyüme ilişkisinin analizi. *ZKÜ Sosyal Bilimler Dergisi*, *4*(8), 55–71.

Yapraklı, S. (2007). Enflasyon ve ekonomik büyüme arasındaki ilişki: Türkiye için eş-bütünleşme ve nedensellik analizi. *Atatürk Üniversitesi Sosyal Bilimler Enstitüsü Dergisi*, *10*(2), 287–301.

KEY TERMS AND DEFINITIONS

Economic Growth: The increase in an economy's production possibilities frontier over time. There are three main causes of economic growth: increases in the stock of capital; technological progress embodied in new capital equipment; and growth in labor input due primarily to population growth, immigration, and changes in participation rates.

Granger Causality: The Granger causality test is a statistical hypothesis test for determining whether one time series is useful in forecasting another, first proposed in 1969. The intuition behind the Granger causality test is the quite straightforward. Ordinarily, regressions reflect "mere" correlations, but C. Granger argued that causality in economics could be tested for by measuring the ability to predict the future values of a time series using prior values of another time series.

Inflation Rate: The annual percentage increase of the cost of living as measured by the consumer price index. Consumer price indices are based on a representative basket of goods and services purchased by consumers in an economy. Composition and relative weights of the basket are reviewed periodically.

Inflation Targeting: Inflation targeting is a monetary policy in which a central bank has an explicit target inflation rate for the medium term and announces this inflation target to the public. The assumption is that the best that monetary policy can do to support the long-term growth of the economy is to maintain price stability. The central bank uses interest rates as its main short-term monetary instrument.

Phillips Curve: The Phillips curve is a single-equation empirical model, named after A. W. Phillips. Phillips curve states the negative correlation between the unemployment rate and rate of inflation. The decreases in unemployment will end up higher rates of inflation.

Unemployment Rate: Unemployment rate is the number of unemployed people as a percentage of the labor force, where the latter consists of the unemployed plus those in paid or self-employment.

ENDNOTES

1. For further information: Toda and Yamamoto (1995).
2. OAPEC is a regional Arab organization of an international character specializes in the affairs of oil. For further information: www.oapecorg.org.

3 For further information: Phillips (1958).

4 A means of taxing spot currency conversions that was originally suggested by James Tobin. The Tobin tax was developed with the intention of penalizing short-term currency speculation, and to place a tax on all spot conversions of currency.

5 Growth without creation of proportionate employment opportunities is called "jobless growth". Machinery and capital when displaces labor (and not helps it) in production, results in an increase in unemployment and causes "jobless growth".

6 The mission of the OECD is to promote policies that will improve the economic and social well-being of people around the world.

7 Maximum lag of the series should not exceed the optimal lag of count of VAR model. Otherwise Toda-Yamamoto causality test should not be applied.

Chapter 18
Employment in Innovation Performance:
Comparison of Turkey and EU Countries

Nuray Girginer
Eskişehir Osmangazi University, Turkey

Aslışah Şenak
Eskişehir Osmangazi University, Turkey

ABSTRACT

This study aims to determine the innovation performance of Turkey and EU countries in terms of human resources and employment indicators. Firstly, 28 EU countries' and Turkey's innovation efficiency is analyzed with Data Envelopment Analysis (DEA) technique. An output-oriented DEA model was used with 4 inputs (government R&D % of GDP, at least upper secondary educational attainment, science and technology graduates, employment in knowledge-intensive service sectors) and 4 outputs (high-tech patent applications to the European Patent Office, high-tech exports as a share of total exports, UNDP Human Development Index and WIPO Innovation Index). DEA helps to determine where to look to improve DMU efficiency, but it is not possible to rank the efficient DMUs through DEA. Consequently, efficient countries and innovation indicators with respect to their impact on performances are ranked with Gray Relation Analysis (GRA). As a result of GRA, Sweden has been the first ranked country among efficient countries. Most important performance indicator has been found to be human development index.

INTRODUCTION

Over the last centuries, capability to develop technology has led to reduced production costs, increased quality and accelerated globalization. Due to globalization, levels of competition increased dramatically both in domestic and foreign markets. In today's highly competitive technological markets, innovation plays a substantial role in countries' strategies as it is the most important factor for sustainable development and competitive superiority.

DOI: 10.4018/978-1-5225-2008-5.ch018

Innovation has been defined as creating economic value by introduction or improvement of a new product and production process (Nafziger, 2006). The notion of innovation here addresses not only technological innovation that may be defined as new product and services of 'technological nature of economics', but also organizational and institutional non-technological innovations (Ünlükaplan, 2009).

Innovation is an important driving force that boosts the productivity of both physical and human capital. Successful implementation of creative ideas and innovation are essential for countries to sustain economic development and improve competitive advantage.

The more efficient innovation activities are conducted, the more innovation output will be obtained. Innovation efficiency can be defined as the ability to translate innovation inputs into innovation outputs. (Hollanders & Celikel-Esser, 2007). The key to designing effective policies with the purpose of a positive influence on a country's technologic innovation performance is to explore which are the factors that have an impact on innovation.

Research in innovation efficiency may aid policy makers in understanding how innovation, information technology, new business practices and intangible organizational investments can lead to higher profits, economic growth and a greater standard of living. (Brynjolfsson & Saunders, 2009). The concept of innovation efficiency may be a useful tool for guiding policy decisions (Hollanders & Celikel-Esser, 2007), as one of the key interests of policy makers is the return on investment of public funding for science & technology for the good of society. (Litan, Wyckoff, & Fealing, 2012).

This chapter aims to assess the innovation performances of European Union (EU) countries and Turkey to determine prominent drivers that affect the innovative activity of innovation efficient countries. Moreover, authors rank the efficient countries among themselves, detect where to implement performance improvements and suggest that the factors that play a major role in innovation performances of efficient countries are mainly related to human capital and labor market.

As mentioned in the methodology section of the chapter, a Data Envelopment Analysis (DEA) model is used first to measure innovation efficiency of countries with a combination of commonly used inputs and output variables in literature. Then Grey Relational Analysis (GRA) is applied to rank both the countries that are found to be efficient and to the factors that affect innovation performances of countries. Results show that human capital and employment related drivers (human development index, educational attainment, graduates in science & technology and employment in high and medium-high technology manufacturing and knowledge-intensive service) are the factors that foster innovation efficiency the most on a cross country level compared to research and development (R&D) expenditure, intellectual property rights, application, infrastructure and environmental indicators, within most innovation efficient EU countries.

There are numerous studies that measure innovation efficiency of countries by using DEA method, and there is one study in literature that applies GRA together with DEA to provide cross-national innovation policy analysis for leading innovation efficient countries. Most of the studies comparing the efficiency of countries do not focus on the weight of efficiency determining factors. Others that test the relationship between innovation drivers and innovation do not take into account efficiency on a country level in general. They are either firm-based or regional studies. Differently than most of the prior ones, this study ranks the efficient countries and also identifies factors that are affecting innovation the most, within parameters taken into account.

This chapter is organized as follows. In literature review section, drawing from various literatures, it is presented how the theoretical framework for the analysis is developed. Then the research methods and data used are described, the parameters are defined. Subsequently, empirical results are presented and their implications are discussed before drawing conclusions.

LITERATURE REVIEW

In the literature, a large number of studies have been concluded to measure innovation efficiency, but most of them do not investigate the weight of parameters that affect efficiency or do not rank countries that are found efficient. Many of these studies are mentioned here followed by a list of main input and output variables they have used.

In his publication, Kotsemir (2013) provides a comprehensive review of 11 empirical studies on cross-country analysis of national innovation systems efficiency with DEA technique. The review covers a major part of previous DEA studies conducted to measure innovation efficiency of countries. The studies analyzed with the insight from Kotsemir (2013) are Wang (2007), Guan and Chen (2012), Hsu (2011), Cai (2011), Abbasi, Hajihoseini, and Haukka (2011), Pan, Hung and Lu (2010), Öztürk (2010), Cullmann, Schmidt-Ehmcke and Zloczysti (2009), Sharma and Thomas (2008), Hollanders and Celikel-Esser (2007), Nasierowski and Arcelus (2003), Rousseau and Rousseau (1997), Rousseau and Rousseau (1998). Studies on innovation efficiency in the current literature mostly apply DEA. There have been very few studies employing combined techniques with DEA to rank the efficient units according to their performances. The only researcher that uses both GRA and DEA together to measure the efficiency of R&D activities is Hsu (2011) according to our literature review.

Researchers have used different sets of input and output variables to measure innovation efficiency. Main input and output variables used in reviewed studies are: R&D expenditures conducted by business enterprises, government and higher education sectors, R&D expenditures per capita, percentage of R&D performed by the government, total education expenditure, youth education attainment level, number of full-time researchers, number of employed people that have master's and doctoral degree, employment in technology intensive companies, share of enterprises receiving public funding for innovation as inputs and the number of scientific publications, number of international scientific and technical articles, number of patents registered in domestic patent offices, number of patents registered in foreign patent offices, high-technology exports (% of manufactured exports), mobile phone users, internet users, PC penetration as outputs (Girginer & Şenak, 2016).

As mentioned above, Hsu (2011) runs GRA and DEA together in his paper. He uses European Commission (2005) indicators that are categorized under 3 innovation input dimensions covering 15 indicators and 2 innovation output dimensions covering 10 indicators. Those 3 input dimensions are namely:

- **Innovation Drivers:** (S&E graduates per 1000 population, population with tertiary education per 100 population, broadband penetration rate, number of broadband lines, participation in life-long learning per 100 population; % of population aged 20-24 having completed at least upper secondary education),
- **Knowledge Creation:** (Public R&D expenditures (% of gross domestic product (GDP), business R&D expenditures (% of GDP), share of medium-high-tech and high-tech R&D (% of manufacturing R&D expenditures), share of enterprises receiving public funding for innovation), and

- **Innovation and Entrepreneurship:** (Small and medium-sized enterprises (SMEs) innovating in-house (% of all SMEs), innovative SMEs co-operating with others (% of all SMEs), innovation expenditures (% of total turnover), early-stage venture capital (% of GDP), information and communication technology (ICT) expenditures (% of GDP); SMEs using organizational innovation (% of all SMEs)).

Output variables were cumulated under following two dimensions:

- **Application:** (Employment in high-tech services (% of total workforce), exports of high technology products as a share of total exports, sales of new-to-market products (% of total turnover), sales of new-to-firm products (% of total turnover), employment in medium-high and high-tech manufacturing (% of total workforce) and
- **Intellectual Property:** (European Patent Office (EPO) patents per million population, the United States Patent and Trademark Office (USPTO) patents per million population, triad patents per million population, community trademarks per million population, community designs per million population) (European Commission, 2005).

Applying GRA, Hsu (2011) ranks countries according to each of these input and output variable categories.

Hsu (2011) then evaluates the innovation efficiency using DEA for 33 countries (including 25 EU Member States in 2005, Bulgaria, Romania, Turkey, Iceland, Norway, Switzerland, the United States and Japan). He lists Denmark, Germany, Ireland, Luxemburg, Malta and Switzerland as the most efficient among 33 countries and provides cross-national innovation policy analysis in his study for leading innovation efficient countries.

With studies indicated above, we do not have an insight on which drivers have a bigger impact on innovation efficiency among country-level variables evaluated. According to our research studies comparing factors that affect innovation are examined within manufacturing and/or service sectors, a region or a specific country with very few exceptions. We also noted that studies examining innovation performances and factors that affect innovation in general look at correlations and regressions rather than efficiency comparison. Therefore our study contributes to the literature by examining affective factors within innovation efficient countries with GRA.

In their annual report, European Bank for Reconstruction and Development (EBRD, 2014) discusses the causes for the difference in levels of innovation of countries and sectors. It is one of the few studies examining internal and external drivers of innovation within both firm and country level. Firm level analysis findings suggest that human capital differences in a particular industry do not explain much of the remaining differences in innovation activity. Similarly, after regression analysis conducted in country-level, measures of human capital including the percentage of the population that has completed secondary or tertiary education, the average number of years of schooling and the average number of years of tertiary education are not consistently found to be significant determinants of innovation. However, it is discussed in the report that the weak correlation may be due to the fact that educational atteinment indicators measure not the quality but the quantity of education.

Concordantly, the report includes the positive correlation between the average performances of 15-year-old students in the Programme for International Student Assessment (PISA) assessment and innovation. PISA is an international standardized assessment of 15-year-old students' abilities in the areas of reading, mathematics, and science. Higher average scores among students in above-mentioned subjects generally refer to a higher quality of education in a given country. A significant correlation was found between the quality of education and innovation both in terms of patent output and the innovation intensity of exports (EBRD, 2014).

There are studies that consider the role of human capital in innovation or the relationships among human capital, innovation, and economic growth. But most of these studies capture only specific regions, industries, small and medium-sized enterprises (SMEs) or country-specific cases. An exemplary study by Lee, Florida, and Gates (2002), supports the correlation between innovation and human capital in a regional level. They argue that innovation is a joint product of human capital and creativity. They test the joint effects of R&D expenditure, human capital, creativity/diversity, and industry mix on regional innovation. They also introduce new measures of creativity (the bohemian index) and diversity (the gay index) to evaluate creativity and diversity. The findings suggest that innovation at the regional level is positively and significantly associated with human capital and creativity. (Lee et al., 2002)

Our analysis, differently, makes a cross-country comparison of the factors affecting innovation. The purpose of our study is not only to identify innovation performances of Turkey and EU countries but also to rank the efficient countries and the innovation efficiency parameters employed by using DEA together with GRA, which is a multi-criteria decision making method. We aim to evaluate innovation efficiency through a different perspective with a combination of input and output variables never used together previously. This study is among the first studies ranking both efficient countries and efficiency influencing factors of innovation.

MATERIAL AND METHODS

Data Envelopment Analysis (DEA) is applied in this study to determine the efficiency scores for innovation performance levels of EU-28 and Turkey. Indicators classified as input and output variables are determined based on the scope of the study and on the previously used variables in similar studies. Besides comparing 29 countries in terms of innovation performances, the purpose is to make suggestions to ineffective countries about where improvements can take place within input and output indicators to reach the efficiency frontier, as DEA is a suitable method for achieving this target.

In the second part of the study, countries that are assessed efficient with DEA are ranked by applying GRA. DEA can introduce performance improvement suggestions for inefficient units but does not provide details concerning efficient ones. This paper addresses this issue and evaluates the efficiency taking into account input and output variables used, and then it employs GRA also to rank the efficient units with respect to their performances. Further, differently from prior studies, this study also ranks the indicators that affect performances of efficient countries using GRA and identifies the factors that play a major role in country-level innovation performances.

DETERMINING THE INNOVATION EFFICIENCY OF COUNTRIES USING DATA ENVELOPMENT ANALYSIS

The mathematical structure of the DEA model was first introduced as a fractional programming model by Charnes, Cooper, and Rhoders (1978). DEA is a "data-oriented" approach for evaluating the performance of a set of peer entities called Decision Making Units (DMUs) which convert multiple inputs into multiple outputs. There is a variety of DMUs in use in evaluating the performances of many different kinds of entities engaged in many different activities and in many different contexts. Over the years, DEA applications have used DMU's of various forms to evaluate the performance of entities such as hospitals, universities, cities, countries, etc. (Cooper, Seiford, & Zhu, 2004).

DEA technique, based on linear programming, seeks to measure the relative performance of the decision units in cases where inputs and outputs measured by multiple scales pose challenges in the execution of the comparison (Cooper, Seiford, & Tone, 2007). Analyzed decision units need to have similar functions, focus on the same objective and operate under the same market circumstances. Unit size and intensity do not need to be same, but factors identifying efficiencies need to be identical. Additionally, all inputs and outputs should be represented by positive numbers; and there should be no null input or output (Kuosmanen, 2003).

DEA compares identical production units to identify the best unit as efficiency frontier. Other observations are assessed by reference to this frontier. For each decision unit, the inefficiency level, roots and causes are identifiable by applying DEA. This helps management in decision making and in deciding whether to increase the amount of inputs and/or decrease in the amount of outputs (Banker & Thrall, 1992). DEA models are either input-oriented or output-oriented. As we employed an output-oriented DEA model in the present study, a general formulation of this DEA model is given below:

Objective function:

$$Enbh_k = \sum_{r=1}^{s} u_{rk} y_{rk} \; ; k=1,2,3,\ldots,n$$

Restrictive conditions:

$$\sum_{r=1}^{s} u_{rk} y_{rj} - \sum_{i=1}^{m} v_{ik} x_{ij} \leq 0 \; ; j=1,2,3,\ldots,n$$

$$\sum_{i=1}^{m} v_{ik} x_{ik} = 1$$

$$u_{rk} \geq 0 \; ; r = 1,2,3,\ldots,s$$

$$v_{ik} \geq 0 \; ; i = 1,2,3,\ldots,m$$

m: number of inputs,
s: number of outputs,
n: number of decision units,
x_{ij} : amount of *i*. input used by the *j*th decision making unit

y_{rj} : amount of r. output produced by the jth decision making unit

u_{rk} , v_{ik} : Weight of decision making unit for i. inputs and r. outputs

The DEA conduct the below steps to measure relative efficiency (Yolalan, 1993):

1. Determination of the best observation (or the decision-making units on the efficiency frontier) that generates the largest composition of output by use of the least combination of input within a given observation group.
2. Radial measurement of the distance of the inefficient decision-making units to the identified frontier, considered as the reference point.

For applying DEA to our research, countries are determined as decision-making units due to their ability to turn similar inputs into similar outputs. A different set of input and output variables than those used in prior studies are selected in accordance with the aim of this chapter, to investigate the weight of different drivers. Apart from educational attainment, labor skills and employment aspects of labor market related innovation drivers (at least upper secondary educational attainment, science and technology graduates, employment in high-tech sectors), infrastructural, environmental and social aspects were also taken into consideration in this study by using human development and innovation indices as well as knowledge creation, property rights and application dimensions that include governmental R&D expenditure in business sector, number of patent applications and high-tech exports variables.

Data used in the analysis is obtained from online sources of Statistical Office of the European Union (EUROSTAT, 2016b), United Nations Development Programme (UNDP, 2012), and WIPO Statistics Database (World Intellectual Property Organization [WIPO] & Institut Européen d'Administration des Affaires [INSEAD], 2012).

It is well known that large numbers of inputs and outputs compared to the number of DMUs may diminish the discriminatory power of DEA. The suggested number of DMUs is at least twice the number of inputs and outputs combined (Golany & Roll, 1989). Banker, Charnes, Cooper, Swarts, and Thomas (1989) on the other hand state that the number of DMUs should be at least three times the number of inputs and outputs combined (Zhu, 2009). The number of DMUs (29 countries) in this study provides these suggestions related with the number of inputs (4) and outputs (4) combined. Aforementioned input and output variables are shown in Table 1.

Table 1. Input and output variables

Input Variables	Output Variables
X1: R&D expenditure by government sector in business enterprise sector (% of Gross Domestic Product (GDP))	*X5*: High-tech patent applications to the EPO by priority year (per million inhabitants)
X2: At least upper secondary educational attainment, 25-64 (%)	*X6*: High-tech exports - Exports of high technology products as a share of total exports
X3: Science & technology graduates (per 1000 inhabitants aged between 20-29)	*X7*: Human Development Index by UNDP
X4: Employment in high- and medium-high technology manufacturing and knowledge-intensive service sectors (% of total employment)	*X8*: Innovation Index by World Intellectual Property Organization

First input variable taken is 'R&D expenditures performed by the government sector in business enterprise sector'. Research and experimental development (R&D) comprise creative work undertaken on a systematic basis in order to increase the stock of knowledge, including knowledge of man, culture, and society and the use of this stock of knowledge to devise new applications. (OECD, 2002). R&D expenditures by government sector include expenditures for R&D performed by government within the business enterprise sector in a given country during a given period. Data is provided as a percentage of GDP (Statistical Office of the European Union [EUROSTAT], 2016f).

'At least upper secondary educational attainment 25-64' input variable is defined as the percentage of people aged 25-64 who have successfully completed at least upper secondary education. This educational attainment refers to ISCED (International Standard Classification of Education) 1997 level 3-6. The indicator is based on the EU Labour Force Survey. The indicator measures the share of the population that have the minimum qualifications required to participate in social and economic life actively. It should be noted that completion of upper secondary education can be achieved in European countries after varying lengths of study, according to different national educational systems (Statistical Office of the European Union [EUROSTAT], 2016a).

'Tertiary graduates in science & technology per 1.000 inhabitants aged 20-29 years' indicator includes new tertiary graduates in a calendar year from both public and private institutions completing graduate and postgraduate studies compared to an age group that corresponds to the typical graduation age in most countries (Statistical Office of the European Union [EUROSTAT], 2016g).

'Employment in high and medium-high technology manufacturing sectors and knowledge-intensive service sectors' data shows the employment in high and medium-high technology manufacturing sectors and in knowledge-intensive service sectors as a share of total employment. Data source is the European Labor Force Survey (LFS) (Statistical Office of the European Union [EUROSTAT], 2016c).

'High-tech patent applications to the EPO by priority year' parameter data refers to the ratio of patent applications made directly to the EPO or via the Patent Cooperation Treaty and designating the EPO, in the field of high-technology patents per million inhabitants of a region. The definition of high-technology patents uses specific subclasses of the International Patent Classification (IPC) as defined in the trilateral statistical report of the EPO, Japan Patent Office (JPO) and USPTO (Statistical Office of the European Union [EUROSTAT], 2016e).

'Exports of high technology products as a share of total exports' dataset that contains shares of exports of high technology products as a share of total exports of a given country is used as one of the four outputs selected (Statistical Office of the European Union [EUROSTAT], 2016d).

Two out of the four output variables were taken as indices. Below is a brief explanation on these two indices.

'The Human Development Index (HDI)' developed by the UNDP, is a summary measure of average achievement in key dimensions of human development: a long and healthy life, being knowledgeable and have a decent standard of living. The HDI is the geometric mean of normalized indices for each of the three dimensions (average life expectancy, the number of literate adults, and income per capita (in US Dollar) (United Nations Development Programme [UNDP], 2015).

The Global Innovation Index (GII) aims to explore the conditions in which innovation flourishes and documents which countries are most successful in fostering those conditions. There are 84 indicators included in the GII to rank the countries, that are grouped under 7 pillars;

1. **Institutions:** (That captures indicators such as ease of starting a business, resolving insolvency, paying taxes),
2. **Human Capital and Research:** (Including quality of scientific research institutions, gross expenditure on R&D (GERD), researchers, Expenditure on education etc.),
3. **Infrastructure:** (With indicators such as environmental performance, electricity consumption, government's online service index etc.),
4. **Market Sophistication:** (Taking into account exports/imports of goods and services, applied tariff rate, ease of getting credit etc.),
5. **Business Sophistication:** (Capturing foreign direct investment net inflows, computer and communications service imports, hi-tech imports, share of patents with foreign inventor, joint ventures strategic alliance deals, GERD performed by business enterprise, employment in knowledge-intensive services indicators etc.),
6. **Knowledge and Technology Outputs:** (Indicators used under that dimension are high-tech exports, royalty and license fees receipts, ISO 9001 quality certificates, total computer software spending, national office patent applications, etc.) and
7. **Creative Outputs:** (With indicators such as new uploads on YouTube, Wikipedia monthly edits, creative services exports, creative goods exports, daily newspapers' circulation, generic top-level domains, national office trademark registrations etc. (WIPO & INSEAD, 2012).

The GII is formed by two sub-indices, the Innovation Input and the Innovation Output Sub-Indices, each built around pillars. Institutions, human capital and research, infrastructure, market sophistication, and business sophistication are taken as enabler pillars in Input Sub-Index, which can be considered as the environmental aspects of a country. Innovation outputs instead are considered as the results of innovative activities within the economy. There are two output pillars used in GII: knowledge and technology outputs and creative outputs. Output Sub-Index has the same weight in calculating the overall GII scores as the Input Sub-Index (World Intellectual Property Organization [WIPO] & Institut Européen d'Administration des Affaires [INSEAD], 2016).

The entire process for GII followed four steps; 1- Conceptual consistency, 2- Data checks, 3-Statistical coherence, 4- Qualitative review. The Applied Statistics Unit at the European Commission Joint Research Centre (JRC) analysis suggests that the GII 2012 is not dominated by any pillar or sub-pillar, therefore is statistically coherent and balanced (WIPO & INSEAD, 2012).

While gross domestic expenditure on R&D performed by government in business sector is more pertinent to financial aspects of innovation, educational attainment, science & technology graduates and HDI can be considered as human capital indicators. Human capital refers to the skills, abilities, and knowledge of individuals (Becker, 1964; van Uden, Knoben, & Vermeulen, 2014). In general, it has been argued that human capital is an important source of competitive advantages for firms and nations (Dakhli & De Clercq, 2004; van Uden et al., 2014).

This chapter investigates whether human capital is a prominent driver in most innovation efficient EU countries when analyzed within a model taking other aspects of innovation into account such as intellectual property rights (number of patent applications), application (share of high-tech exports to total exports), infrastructural, social and environmental indicators (HDI and GII).

The findings and the composite of inputs and outputs used in this study are valid for 2012. It should be emphasized that DEA is a technique measuring relative performance. Thus, the evaluation will be affected by different input-output combinations and subsets of observations. It is required to choose one of the optimization models of Data Envelopment Analysis and the returns to scale types, such as input minimization or output maximization. In the analysis, countries are assumed to maximize output rather than minimizing input, and both variable returns to scale BCC model (introduced by and named after the initial letters of Banker, Charnes and Cooper (1984)) and constant return to scale CCR model (named after the model was introduced by Charnes, Cooper and Rhodes (1978)) were used together.

Overall efficiency by input oriented CCR model and technical efficiency by input oriented BCC model were calculated with the Frontier Analyst Professional software. The main distinction between the CCR model and the BCC model is that the λ js are now restricted to summing to one. This has the effect of removing the constraint in the CCR model that DMUs must be scale efficient. Consequently, the BCC model allows variable returns to scale and measures only technical efficiency for each DMU. That is, for a DMU to be considered as CCR efficient, it must be both scale and technically efficient. For a DMU to be considered BCC efficient, it only needs to be technically efficient (Bowlin, 1998).

In Table 2 the efficiency status of Turkey with the EU countries in the scope of innovation is presented. According to the CCR model in Table 2, while 15 countries are successful in terms of the parameters involved in the analysis, the 14 other countries are not deemed efficient. The countries which are not efficient in innovation according to the CCR model; France (98.53%), Germany) (98.32%) and Greece (75.38%) which has the lowest performance, are not efficient with respect to their patent quantity, exportation, HDI and innovation index. In other words, those countries which are not efficient according to CCR model, fail to provide the double output quantity in return for the double input they invest in innovation.

Table 2 also shows 18 efficient and 11 inefficient countries that obtain less output in return to double input in innovation when BCC model is applied. 15 countries which are efficient with CCR model are also efficient with BCC model.

As these countries can succeed to provide double output in return for doubled input, evidently they are also successful in obtaining less than double output over double input. An increase is expected in innovation performance of countries that are inefficient in innovation except for France. For France, a decreased innovation performance is observed.

It is assumed that both reference units and inefficient units have the same organizational structure according to DEA. Hence, an inefficient unit can become efficient by conducting complying activities to the organizational structure of the reference units.

The number of being identified as a reference for inefficient units demonstrates that these units are strong in their activity structure. Accordingly, Turkey (12), Romania (7) and Malta (7), in CCR model and the Czech Republic (6), Romania (5), Netherlands and Austria (5) in BCC model are the strongest countries in terms of innovation activity structure due to the frequency of being referred. In both models, Romania is the country which is referred the most. It can be interpreted as these countries are the ones that conduct innovation activities in the most appropriate way by generating the maximum outputs by the available inputs. On the contrary, Portugal, even though found to be efficient in both models, is not taken as a reference by any other country.

DEA not only provides an efficiency score for each unit but also indicates by how much and in what areas an inefficient unit needs to improve in order to be efficient. Inefficient units are assumed to reach the same efficiency level of relatively effective units by employing similar methods.

Table 3 includes potential improvement values for all 11 countries that are found to be inefficient with BCC model.

It is seen in Table 3 that the performance of all the countries that cannot reach the efficiency frontier is above 90%. Based on DEA model, these countries are all close to efficiency frontier. The "Potential

Table 2. Innovation efficiency of countries

Countries	CCR Model (Overall Efficiency)			BCC Model (Technical Efficiency)			Scale Efficiency	Scale (CCR/ BCC)
	Efficiency Score	Efficiency	Reference Counts	Efficiency Score	Efficiency	Reference Counts		
Denmark	100%	Efficient	1	100%	Efficient	2	1	Constant
Portugal	100%	Efficient	0	100%	Efficient	0	1	Constant
Finland	100%	Efficient	1	100%	Efficient	0	1	Constant
Sweden	100%	Efficient	4	100%	Efficient	2	1	Constant
Luxembourg	100%	Efficient	5	100%	Efficient	1	1	Constant
Cyprus	100%	Efficient	3	100%	Efficient	2	1	Constant
Turkey	100%	Efficient	12	100%	Efficient	1	1	Constant
Romania	100%	Efficient	7	100%	Efficient	5	1	Constant
Austria	100%	Efficient	2	100%	Efficient	5	1	Constant
Hungary	100%	Efficient	2	100%	Efficient	1	1	Constant
Czech	100%	Efficient	2	100%	Efficient	6	1	Constant
Ireland	100%	Efficient	1	100%	Efficient	1	1	Constant
Malta	100%	Efficient	7	100%	Efficient	4	1	Constant
Netherlands	100%	Efficient	6	100%	Efficient	5	1	Constant
Estonia	100%	Efficient	5	100%	Efficient	2	1	Constant
France	98,53%	Inefficient	0	98,54%	Inefficient	0	99,99%	Decrease
Germany	98,32%	Inefficient	0	100%	Efficient	1	98,32%	Constant
UK	91,30%	Inefficient	0	99,63%	Inefficient	0	91,64%	Increase
Belgium	89,93%	Inefficient	0	98,41%	Inefficient	0	91,38%	Increase
Italy	84,60%	Inefficient	0	100	Efficient	8	84,60%	Constant
Latvia	83,39%	Inefficient	0	92,52%	Inefficient	0	90,13%	Increase
Slovenia	83,34%	Inefficient	0	99,30%	Inefficient	0	83,92%	Increase
Bulgaria	82,44%	Inefficient	0	92,79%	Inefficient	0	88,85%	Increase
Spain	81,60%	Inefficient	0	100	Efficient	0	81,60%	Constant
Slovakia	80,38%	Inefficient	0	97,25%	Inefficient	0	82,65%	Increase
Croatia	79,80%	Inefficient	0	95,71%	Inefficient	0	83,37%	Increase
Lithuania	79,20%	Inefficient	0	95,85%	Inefficient	0	82,63%	Increase
Poland	78,82%	Inefficient	0	98,09%	Inefficient	0	79,69%	Increase
Greece	75,38%	Inefficient	0	98,24%	Inefficient	0	76,73%	Increase

Improvement" column shows how much, in percentage terms, inefficient countries' use of inputs or production of outputs needs to change by in order for them to be efficient. It can be noted that no performance improvement suggestion is made for employment and R&D expenditure inputs. The suggestions to reduce inputs are mostly on the number of upper secondary educational attainment and science & technology graduates. This reduction suggestion for fewer inputs is to be interpreted in terms of qualification and not in quantity. Suggestions to improve output performances are mostly on the number of patents and

Table 3. Potential improvement ratios and reference groups for inefficient countries (BCC model)

Countries	Factors		Actual	Target	Potential Improvement (%)	Reference Groups
United Kingdom 99,63%	Input	R&D	0,13	0,13	00,00	Ireland Luxembourg Malta Netherlands Sweden
		At least upper secondary education	77,90	77,51	-00,50	
		Science & Technology graduates	19,80	18,27	-07,73	
		Employment	48,50	48,50	00,00	
	Output	No. of patents	14,74	40,22	172,94	
		High-tech exports	17,40	17,46	00,37	
		Human development index	0,90	0,90	00,37	
		Innovation index	61,20	61,43	00,37	
Slovenia 99,30%	Input	R&D	0,34	0,34	00,00	Czech Germany Italy
		At least upper secondary education	85,0	85,00	00,00	
		Science & Technology graduates	19,30	15,99	-17,17	
		Employment	35,20	35,20	00,00	
	Output	No. of patents	3,16	11,66	268,71	
		High-tech exports	5,20	13,94	168,15	
		Human development index	0,88	0,88	00,70	
		Innovation index	49,90	51,11	02,43	
France 98,54%	Input	R&D	0,29	0,20	-31,37	Malta Netherlands Romania Sweden
		At least upper secondary education	72,50	67,15	-07,38	
		Science & Technology graduates	22,90	11,09	-51,56	
		Employment	44,50	44,50	00,00	
	Output	No. of patents	26,00	26,39	01,48	
		High-tech exports	20,00	20,30	01,48	
		Human development index	0,89	0,90	01,48	
		Innovation index	51,80	59,02	13,94	
Belgium 98,41%	Input	R&D	0,19	0,19	00,00	Denmark Malta Netherlands
		At least upper secondary education	71,60	71,60	00,00	
		Science & Technology graduates	13,00	12,16	-06,48	
		Employment	47,60	45,96	-03,45	
	Output	No. of patents	28,64	30,16	05,30	
		High-tech exports	8,60	17,94	108,58	
		Human development index	0,90	0,91	01,62	
		Innovation index	54,30	60,07	10,63	

continued on following page

Table 3. Continued

Countries		Factors	Actual	Target	Potential Improvement (%)	Reference Groups
Greece 98,24%	Input	R&D	0,17	0,17	00,00	Denmark Italy Cyprus Netherlands Austria
		At least upper secondary education	65,80	65,80	00,00	
		Science & Technology graduates	13,90	13,90	00,00	
		Employment	36,30	36,30	00,00	
	Output	No. of patents	1,14	12,48	997,85	
		High-tech exports	3,20	9,08	183,74	
		Human development index	0,86	0,88	01,79	
		Innovation index	35,30	48,57	37,59	
Poland 98,09%	Input	R&D	0,25	0,25	00,00	Czech Italy Romania
		At least upper secondary education	89,60	75,24	-16,02	
		Science & Technology graduates	17,90	15,68	-12,42	
		Employment	30,60	30,60	00,00	
	Output	No. of patents	1,49	2,62	75,95	
		High-tech exports	6,00	10,41	73,49	
		Human development index	0,84	0,85	01,95	
		Innovation index	40,40	45,41	12,41	
Slovakia 97,25%	Input	R&D	0,20	0,20	00,00	Czech Italy Austria Romania
		At least upper secondary education	91,70	67,90	-25,95	
		Science & Technology graduates	17,90	14,94	-16,52	
		Employment	31,90	31,90	00,00	
	Output	No. of patents	1,22	6,36	421,74	
		High-tech exports	8,20	8,43	02,83	
		Human development index	0,84	0,86	02,83	
		Innovation index	41,40	45,24	09,28	
Lithuania 95,85%	Input	R&D	0,18	0,18	00,00	Czech Italy Austria Romania
		At least upper secondary education	93,30	64,06	-31,34	
		Science & Technology graduates	23,0	14,25	-38,06	
		Employment	33,60	33,60	00,00	
	Output	No. of patents	4,35	8,39	92,89	
		High-tech exports	5,80	7,83	34,93	
		Human development index	0,83	0,87	04,33	
		Innovation index	44,00	45,91	04,33	

continued on following page

Table 3. Continued

Countries		Factors	Actual	Target	Potential Improvement (%)	Reference Groups
Croatia 95,71%	Input	R&D	0,21	0,21	00,00	Czech Italy Romania
		At least upper secondary education	80,50	65,56	-18,56	
		Science & Technology graduates	17,40	14,81	-14,88	
		Employment	30,80	30,80	00,00	
	Output	No. of patents	0,12	3,55	2936,45	
		High-tech exports	7,20	7,62	05,85	
		Human development index	0,82	0,85	04,48	
		Innovation index	40,70	43,75	07,48	
Bulgaria 92,79%	Input	R&D	0,18	0,18	00,00	Czech Estonia Italy Austria Turkey
		At least upper secondary education	81,00	60,01	-25,91	
		Science & Technology graduates	13,30	13,30	00,00	
		Employment	29,90	29,90	00,00	
	Output	No. of patents	0,57	5,34	839,03	
		High-tech exports	3,80	7,71	102,96	
		Human development index	0,78	0,84	07,77	
		Innovation index	40,70	43,86	07,77	
Latvia 92,52%	Input	R&D	0,18	0,18	00,00	Estonia Italy Cyprus Netherlands Austria
		At least upper secondary education	89,10	71,69	-19,54	
		Science &Technology graduates	13,50	13,50	00,00	
		Employment	36,50	36,50	00,00	
	Output	No. of patents	3,58	13,16	267,01	
		High-tech exports	6,40	11,18	74,62	
		Human development index	0,81	0,88	08,09	
		Innovation index	47,00	50,80	08,09	

high-tech exports. It may be beneficiary for those inefficient countries to find ways to increase their high-tech patents and high-tech exports without change in given inputs.

As an example, findings show that the UK with 99.63% efficiency score can perform (%172.94) better in the number of patent applications and (%00.37) better in exports, human development and innovation indices. If also decreases upper secondary educational attainment levels and the number of science & technology graduates by (%00.5) and (%07.73) respectively, while not conducting any change in employment and R&D expenditure, UK can become fully innovation efficient.

Latvia, the least efficient country according to BCC model (with 92.52% efficiency), needs to decrease the upper secondary educational attainment level by 19.54% and increase number of patents (267.01%), high-tech exports (74.62%), human development and innovation indices (08.09%) to perform fully efficient.

RANKING EFFICIENT COUNTRIES AND PERFORMANCE VARIABLES USING GREY RELATIONAL ANALYSIS

'The Grey System Theory', introduced by Deng is supplementary to limited conventional statistical methods. By GRA the correlations between the reference factor and other factors can be identified and compared (Deng, 1988). Contrary to traditional statistical techniques, GRA captures quantitative and qualitative relationships among complex variables despite inconclusive data. Without sufficient information, it is difficult to achieve required confidence levels with traditional methods. GRA can be used to determine significant correlations among factors of a system with less data. That makes GRA preferred to generate satisfactory results using a relatively small amount of data or with a high variability of factors (Li et al., 1997).

The procedure for calculating the GRA is as follows:

Firstly, let X_0 be the referential series with k entities (or criteria such as innovation indicators in this study) of $X_1, X_2, \ldots, X_i, \ldots, X_N$ (or N measurement criteria). The grey relation coefficient between the compared series X_i and the referential series of X_0 at the j-th entity is defined as:

$$\gamma_{0i}(j) = \frac{\Delta \min + \Delta \max}{\Delta_{0i}(j) + \Delta \max} \tag{1}$$

where $\Delta_{0i}(j)$ is the absolute value of difference between X_0 and X_i at the j.th entity, that is $\Delta_{0i}(j) = \left| x_0(j) - x_i(j) \right|$, and $\Delta_{\max} = Max_i \max_j \Delta_{0i}(j)$, $\Delta_{\min} = Min_i \min_j \Delta_{0i}(j)$

The grey relational grade (GRG) for series of X_i is given as:

$$\Gamma_{0i} = \sum_{j=1}^{K} w_j \gamma_{0i}(j) \tag{2}$$

where w_j is the weight of j-th entity. Whereas the weight is not applied, take $\omega_j = \frac{1}{K}$ as an average.

Prior to calculating grey relation coefficients the data series can be treated based on the linearity of data normalization and the following three options to prevent distorting the normalized data (Hsia & Wu, 1997). Options are;

1. **Benefit Target:** Upper-bound effectiveness measuring (i.e. larger-the-better)

$$x_i^*(j) = \frac{x_i(j) - \min_j x_i(j)}{\max_j x_i(j) - \min_j x_i(j)} \tag{3}$$

2. **Cost Target:** Lower bound effectiveness measuring (i.e. smaller-the-better)

$$x_i^*(j) = \frac{\max_j x_i(j) - x_i(j)}{\max_j x_i(j) - \min_j x_i(j)} \tag{4}$$

3. **Medium Target:** Moderate effectiveness measuring (i.e. nominal-the- best)

If $\max_j x_i(j) \leq x_{ob}(j)$, then

$$x_i^*(j) = \frac{x_i(j) - \min_j x_i(j)}{x_{ob}(j) - \min_j x_i(j)} \tag{5}$$

If $\min_j x_i(j) \leq x_{ob}(j) \leq \max_j x_i(j)$, then

$$x_i^*(j) = \frac{\left| x_i(j) - x_{ob}(j) \right|}{\max_j x_i(j) - \min_j x_i(j)} \tag{6}$$

If $x_{ob}(j) \leq \min_j x_i(j)$, then

$$x_i^*(j) = \frac{\max_j x_i(j) - x_i(j)}{\max_j x_i(j) - x_{ob}(j)} \tag{7}$$

where x_{ob} *(j)* is the objective value of entity *j*.

GRA calculation steps explained above have been applied as shown below in compliance with the purpose of the study.

Step 1: Establishing decision-making matrix: A decision-making matrix was established with the set of data obtained by the variables used in DEA for 29 countries.

Step 2: Normalizing Data: Data Normalization was computed using Equation 3 for all variables. Established referential series can be $X_0 = \{1.00, \ldots, 1.00\}$.

Step 3: Computing absolute values [$\Delta_{0i}(j)$]: $\Delta_{0i}(j)$, is the absolute value of difference X_0 (differential series) and Xi at the j-th factors.

Step 4: Computing Grey Relation Coefficients [$\gamma_{0i}(j)$]: The relational coefficients, $\gamma_{0i}(j)$, were computed using Equation 1.

Step 5: Computing Grey Relation Grade: Equation 2 was applied for each country as the sum of the grey relation coefficients. Table 4 summarizes these results.

Table 4. Grey relation coefficient $\gamma_{0i}(j)$

Countries	Innovation Indicators							
	Inputs				Outputs			
	X1	*X2*	*X3*	*X4*	*X5*	*X6*	*X7*	*X8*
Romania	0,447	0,643	0,722	0,337	0,334	0,376	0,383	0,362
Hungary	0,425	0,746	0,431	0,459	0,347	0,533	0,457	0,456
Malta	0,333	0,362	0,464	0,606	0,337	1	0,475	0,638
Finland	0,630	0,8	0,925	0,594	0,872	0,386	0,679	0,836
Netherlands	0,486	0,617	0,456	0,615	0,477	0,565354	0,988	0,781
Sweden	0,406	4	0,5994	0,7732	1	0,455	0,829	1
Estonia	0,447	0,925	0,514	0,458	0,343	0,475	0,556	0,618
Denmark	0,333	0,6784	0,727	0,705	0,471	0,410	1	0,758
Austria	0,378	0,762	0,618	0,478	0,424	0,455	0,690	0,567
Turkey	0,354	0,333	0,443	0,333	0,333	0,333	0,333	0,333
Cyprus	0,333	0,671	0,422	0,471	0,336	0,439	0,545	0,476
Portugal	0,333	0,358	0,761	0,434	0,335	0,348	0,467	0,440
Luxembourg	0,773	0,684	0,333	1	0,359	0,849	0,714	0,684
Spain	0,515	0,449	0,588	0,471	0,349	0,364	0,637	0,466
Czech	0,68	1	0,629	0,427	0,336	0,509	0,604	0,504
Ireland	0,34	0,632	1	0,614	0,382	0,612	0,882	0,716
Germany	1	0,839	0,609	0,529	0,461	0,478	0,932	0,641
Italy	0,436	0,466	0,514	0,446	0,348	0,377	0,627	0,431

As presented in Table 5, Sweden has a better performance in comparison to other efficient countries with respect to the grey relational distinguished coefficient.

Sweden stands out as the strongest country in terms of activity structure and enhances output performance the best with current innovation inputs. Turkey instead, raises concern as it shows the lowest performance compared to other countries included in the analysis.

Table 6 demonstrates that the HDI factors play the most substantial role in innovation performances of efficient countries. The least significant factor is determined to be the number of high-tech patent applications. The assessment indicates that the factors that affect the innovation performance the most are those related to human capital (human development index, at least upper secondary educational attainment, the number of science & technology graduates and factors related to employment).

CONCLUSION

Innovation remains a priority for countries as it enables countries to achieve better economic performance and boosts the productivity of both physical and human capital. Therefore it has been one of the main concerns of EU countries since the beginning of the last century.

Table 5. Performances of countries

Countries	Γ_{0i}	Rank
Romania	45.05%	16
Hungary	48.17%	12
Malta	52.69%	11
Finland	71.54%	2
Netherlands	62.29%	7
Sweden	72.66%	1
Estonia	54.21%	10
Denmark	63.54%	6
Austria	54.67%	9
Turkey	34.96%	18
Cyprus	46.16%	14
Portugal	43.46%	17
Luxembourg	67.46%	4
Spain	47.98%	13
Czech	58.63%	8
Ireland	64.73%	5
Germany	68.62%	3
Italy	45.57%	15

Table 6. Grey relation grades and ranks of indicators in model

Factors	Γ_{0i}	Rank
Governmental R&D expenditure in business sector	48.05%	7
At least upper secondary education	65.11%	2
Science & Technology graduates	59.74%	3
Employment in high-tech	54.15%	5
No. Of Patents	43.58%	8
High-tech Exports	49.82%	6
Human development index	65.56%	1
Innovation Index	59.49%	4

This chapter provides efficiency scores for innovation performances of Turkey and 28 EU countries, ranks the countries that are found to be efficient, captures the factors that affect efficiency the most and aims to guide inefficient countries to improved performances. Consequently, it is discussed that the human capital and employment related drivers are the most important innovation efficiency drivers on a cross-country level.

Primarily efficiency scores were obtained by measuring the relative innovation performance of countries. Using those DEA findings, it was then illustrated by how much and in what areas inefficient countries need to improve in order to be efficient as the ones that conduct the best practice.

DEA is commonly used to provide performance improvement propositions to inefficient units and to set appropriate targets. Yet, it is also important to be able to assess efficiency among efficient units and rank efficient units according to their performances. Therefore, countries proven to be efficient with DEA were ranked by applying GRA with the same input and output variables. The number of prior studies in ranking efficient innovation performances is limited in the literature. This study contributes to the literature not only by ranking the factors contributing to the efficient countries' performances but also by ranking countries found to be efficient.

Results show that Sweden pioneers the innovation efficiency ranking conducted by GRA. This finding complies with Hsu's prior study that compares 33 countries and determines Sweden as the number one country as per innovation driver dimension.

Based on GRA, among aspects of physical and human capital, human resources related factors are found to be more influential on innovation performance. Thus, Sweden can be considered as a reference among analyzed countries and can be followed closely in terms of innovation activities, with a focus on human development indicators, educational, and employment structure.

It should be emphasized that the countries like Turkey and Portugal which are not provided as a reference even though found to be efficient with DEA, ranked among lowest countries in the list. That can be explained both due to structural differences between efficient countries and inefficient ones and to not strong enough performances of those countries to be taken as references. Further research may discuss the relation between the frequency of referrals and ranking of efficient countries.

In the potential improvement findings for inefficient countries provided with DEA, no reduction is required in employment, in high technology and knowledge intensive sectors. Inefficient countries are recommended to increase not input but output parameters which are the number of patent applications, share of high-tech exports, human development index and innovation index.

Even though some of these factors were found to rank lowest in the GRA analysis, DEA results imply the need to generate more high-tech patents and exports with given governmental R&D expenditure in business sector, educational qualification of human resources and high-tech employment related inputs for improving innovation performance of inefficient countries.

It should be mentioned here that a part of patent applications and high-tech exports may be shifted to other countries where labor and production costs are lower. Likewise, a part of patents and exports in examined countries may belong to foreign direct investors. More nuanced examinations on contract manufacturing in other countries, on foreign direct investments and their impacts on patents and exports can clarify whether such shifting yield different outcomes.

Despite the fact that highly ranked innovation factors with GRA display strength in human resources related dimensions (human development index, at least upper secondary education attainment, science & technology graduates, and employment factors), the results may change accordingly with countries or sub-sectors covered in the analysis.

EU countries, in general, have high scores in human resources related ratings such as human development index, at least upper secondary educational attainment, etc. However, including countries with higher governmental gross domestic expenditure on R&D in the investigation may change weights and ranking of innovation factors.

On the other hand, when the assessment is conducted in firm-level, the impact of human capital is found fairly small relative to the effect of other firm-level characteristics in previous studies (EBRD, 2014). Thus, different framework and models including different input and output variables give different outcomes.

Considering the substantial role innovation efficiency plays for nations, further research addressing similar questions and nuanced studies using continuously updated data on the subject is essential.

Nevertheless, among EU countries and Turkey on a cross-country level, our findings suggest that increased human development index scores and structural support to improve the quality of human capital related inputs such as educational attainment, science & technology graduates and employment in high–tech industries will help to boost innovation efficiency.

REFERENCES

Abbasi, F., Hajihoseini, H., & Haukka, S. (2011). Use of virtual index for measuring efficiency of innovation systems: A cross-country study. *International Journal of Technology Management and Sustainable Development*, *9*(3), 195–212. doi:10.1386/tmsd.9.3.195_1

Banker, R. D., Charnes, A., & Cooper, W. (1984). Models for Estimation of Technical and Scale Inefficiencies in Data Envelopment Analysis. *Management Science*, *30*(9), 1078–1092. doi:10.1287/mnsc.30.9.1078

Banker, R. D., Charnes, A., Cooper, W. W., Swarts, J., & Thomas, D. (1989). An introduction to data envelopment analysis with some of its models and their uses. *Research in Government and Nonprofit Accounting*, *5*, 125–163.

Banker, R. D., & Thrall, R. M. (1992). Estimation of returns to scale using data envelopment analysis. *European Journal of Operational Research*, *62*(1), 74–84. doi:10.1016/0377-2217(92)90178-C

Becker, G. (1964). *Human capital*. New York: National Bureau of Economic Research.

Bowlin, W. F. (1998). Measuring performance: An introduction to data envelopment analysis (DEA). *Journal of Cost Analysis*, *15*(2), 3–27. doi:10.1080/08823871.1998.10462318

Brynjolfsson, E., & Saunders, A. (2009). *Wired for innovation: How information technology is reshaping the economy*. Cambridge, MA: MIT Press.

Cai, Y. (2011). *Factors affecting the efficiency of the BRICSs' national innovation systems: A comparative study based on DEA and Panel Data Analysis*. Economics Discussion paper, (2011-52).

Charnes, A., Cooper, W., & Rhodes, E. (1978). Measuring the efficiency of decision making units. *European Journal of Operational Research*, *2*(6), 429–444. doi:10.1016/0377-2217(78)90138-8

Cooper, W. W., Seiford, L. M., & Tone, K. (2007). *Data envelopment analysis: A comprehensive text with models, applications, references and DEA-solver software* (2nd ed.). New York: Springer.

Cooper, W. W., Seiford, L. M., & Zhu, J. (2004). Data envelopment analysis: History, models and interpretations. In *Handbook on data envelopment analysis* (pp. 1–39). New York: Springer. doi:10.1007/1-4020-7798-X_1

Cullmann, A., Schmidt-Ehmcke, J., & Zloczysti, P. (2009). *Innovation, R&D efficiency and the impact of the regulatory environment: A two stage semi-parametric DEA approach.* Discussion Papers of DIW Berlin 883, DIW Berlin. doi:10.2139/ssrn.1460709

Dakhli, M., & De Clercq, D. (2004). Human capital, social capital, and innovation: A multi-country study. *Entrepreneurship & Regional Development, 16*(2), 107–128. doi:10.1080/08985620410001677835

Deng, J. L. (1988). Properties of relational space for grey system. In *Essential topics on grey system theory and applications* (pp. 1–13). Beijing: China Ocean.

European Bank for Reconstruction and Development. (2014). Drivers of innovation. In *Transition Report 2014: Innovation in Transition* (pp. 44-63). Retrieved from http://www.ebrd.com/downloads/research/transition/tr14.pdf

European Commission. (2005). *European innovation scoreboard 2005: Comparative analysis of innovation performance.* Maastricht Economic Research Institute on Innovation and Technology (MERIT) and the Joint Research Centre (Institute for the Protection and Security of the Citizen) of the European Commission.

Girginer, N., & Şenak, A. (2016). *A data envelopment analysis application for comparing R&D efficiency of G7 countries and Turkey.* EconWorld 2016 working paper at London.

Golany, B., & Roll, Y. (1989). An application procedure for DEA. *Omega, 17*(3), 237–250. doi:10.1016/0305-0483(89)90029-7

Guan, J., & Chen, K. (2012). Modeling the relative efficiency of national innovation systems. *Research Policy, 41*(1), 102–115. doi:10.1016/j.respol.2011.07.001

Hollanders, H., & Celikel-Esser, F. (2007). Measuring innovation efficiency. INNO Metrics 2007 report, European Commission, DG Enterprise, Brussels.

Hsia, K. H., & Wu, J. H. (1997). A study on the data preprocessing in grey relational analysis. *Journal of Chinese Grey System, 1*, 47–53.

Hsu, Y. (2011). Cross national comparison of innovation efficiency and policy application. *African Journal of Business Management, 5*(4), 1378–1387.

Kotsemir, M. N. (2013). *Measuring national innovation systems efficiency - A review of DEA approach.* Higher School of Economics Research Paper No. WP BRP, 16.

Kuosmanen, T. (2002). *Modeling blank data entries in data envelopment analysis.* Econ-WPA working paper at Wustl.

Lee, S. Y., Florida, R., & Gates, G. J. (2002). *Innovation, human capital, and creativity.* Working Paper, Software Industry Center, Carnegie Mellon University, Pittsburgh.

Li, P., Tan, T. C., & Lee, J. Y. (1997). Grey relational analysis of amine inhibition of mild steel corrosion in acids. *Corrosion*, *53*(3), 186–194. doi:10.5006/1.3280459

Litan, R. E., Wyckoff, A. W., & Fealing, K. H. (Eds.). (2012). *Improving measures of science, technology, and innovation: Interim report*. National Academies Press.

Nafziger, E. W. (2006). *Economic development*. New York: Cambridge University Press.

Nasierowski, W., & Arcelus, F. J. (2003). On the efficiency of national innovation systems. *Socio-Economic Planning Sciences*, *37*(3), 215–234. doi:10.1016/S0038-0121(02)00046-0

Organization for Economic Co-operation and Development. (2002). *Frascati manual 2002: Proposed standard practice for surveys on research and experimental development*. OECD.

Öztürk, S. P. (2010). *OECD ülkelerinin AR-GE etkinliklerinin sıralı AHP/VZA metodu ile belirlenmesi* (Unpublished master's thesis). Gazi Universitesi, Ankara.

Pan, T. W., Hung, S. W., & Lu, W. M. (2010). DEA performance measurement of the national innovation system in Asia and Europe. *Asia-Pacific Journal of Operational Research, 27*(3), 369-392.

Rousseau, S., & Rousseau, R. (1997). Data envelopment analysis as a tool for constructing scientometric indicators. *Scientometrics*, *40*(1), 45–56. doi:10.1007/BF02459261

Rousseau, S., & Rousseau, R. (1998). The scientific wealth of European nations: Taking effectiveness into account. *Scientometrics*, *42*(1), 75–87. doi:10.1007/BF02465013

Sharma, S., & Thomas, V. (2008). Inter-country R&D efficiency analysis: An application of data envelopment analysis. *Scientometrics*, *76*(3), 483–501. doi:10.1007/s11192-007-1896-4

Statistical Office of the European Union. (2016a). *At least upper secondary educational attainment, age group 25-64 by sex* (Dataset). Retrieved from http://ec.europa.eu/eurostat/en/web/products-datasets/-/TPS00065

Statistical Office of the European Union. (2016b). *Database*. Retrieved from http://ec.europa.eu/eurostat/data/database

Statistical Office of the European Union. (2016c). *Employment in high- and medium-high technology manufacturing sectors and knowledge-intensive service sectors* (Dataset). Retrieved from http://ec.europa.eu/eurostat/web/products-datasets/-/tsc00011

Statistical Office of the European Union. (2016d). *High-tech exports - Exports of high technology products as a share of total exports (from 2007, SITC Rev. 4)* (Dataset). Retrieved from http://ec.europa.eu/eurostat/web/products-datasets/-/htec_si_exp4

Statistical Office of the European Union. (2016e). *High-tech patent applications to the European patent office (EPO) by priority year* (Dataset). Retrieved from http://ec.europa.eu/eurostat/web/products-datasets/-/tsc00010

Statistical Office of the European Union. (2016f). *Research and development expenditure, by sectors of performance* (Dataset). Retrieved from http://ec.europa.eu/eurostat/en/web/products-datasets/-/TSC00001

Statistical Office of the European Union. (2016g). *Science and technology graduates by sex* (Dataset). Retrieved from http://ec.europa.eu/eurostat/en/web/products-datasets/-/TPS00188

United Nations Development Programme. (2012). *United Nations Development Programme's human development reports, 2012*. Retrieved from http://hdr.undp.org/en/composite/trends

United Nations Development Programme. (2015). *Human development index* (HDI) (Dataset). Retrieved from http://hdr.undp.org/en/content/human-development-index-hdi

Ünlükaplan, İ. (2009). Avrupa Birliği üyesi ülkelerde iktisadi kalkınma, rekabetçilik ve inovasyon ilişkilerinin kanonik korelasyon analizi ile belirlenmesi. *Maliye Dergisi, 157*, 235–250.

van Uden, A., Knoben, J., & Vermeulen, P. (2014). *Human capital and innovation in developing countries: A firm level study*. DFID Working Paper.

Wang, E. C. (2007). R&D efficiency and economic performance: A cross-country analysis using the stochastic frontier approach. *Journal of Policy Modeling, 29*(2), 345–360. doi:10.1016/j.jpolmod.2006.12.005

World Intellectual Property Organization & Institut Européen d'Administration des Affaires. (2012). *The global innovation index (GII) 2012: Stronger innovation linkages for global growth.* Retrieved from https://www.globalinnovationindex.org/userfiles/file/gii-2012-report.pdf

World Intellectual Property Organization & Institut Européen d'Administration des Affaires. (2016). *The Global Innovation Index (GII) Conceptual Framework* (Annex). Retrieved from http://www.wipo.int/edocs/pubdocs/en/wipo_pub_gii_2016-annex1.pdf

Yolalan, R. (1993). *İşletmeler arası göreli etkinlik ölçümü*. Ankara: Milli Prodüktivite Merkezi Yayınları.

Zhu, J. (2014). *Quantitative models for performance evaluation and benchmarking: Data envelopment analysis with spreadsheets* (3rd ed.). New York: Springer. doi:10.1007/978-3-319-06647-9

KEY TERMS AND DEFINITIONS

Competitive Advantage: A concept that causes superior performance of a nation, an institution, an individual or an organization compared to its competitors.

Cross-National: Involving more than one country.

EU-28: The EU-28 is the abbreviation of European Union (EU) which consists a group of 28 countries (Belgium, Bulgaria, Czech Republic, Denmark, Germany, Estonia, Ireland, Greece, Spain, France, Croatia, Italy, Cyprus, Latvia, Lithuania, Luxembourg, Hungary, Malta, Netherlands, Austria, Poland, Portugal, Romania, Slovenia, Slovakia, Finland, Sweden, United Kingdom) that operates as an economic and political block.

Global Innovation Index (GII): An index prepared by Cornell University, INSEAD (Institut Européen d'Administration des Affaires), and the World Intellectual Property Organization that ranks innovation performance of 128 countries aiming to explore the conditions in which innovation flourishes.

Human Capital: An input of production consisting human resources.

Human Development Index (HDI): An index prepared annually by United Nations Development Programme (UNDP), that measures average achievement of human development with indicators concerning health, knowledge and standard of living aspects.

Innovation: Creation and implementation of value adding methods into a way of doing something.

Innovation Drivers: Anything that contributes into producing incremental innovation.

Innovation Efficient: Performing or functioning in the best possible way in innovation related activities and matters with the least waste of resources.

Intellectual Property: Possessions not based on physical property but based on creations of the mind and intelligence.

Knowledge Creation: Formation of new ideas through interactions between organizations, institutions or individuals.

Physical Capital: A factor of production that consists of physical assets.

Research and Development: An initiation that involves research, design, development and application seeking to achieve an advance in science or technology.

Chapter 19
Economic Growth, Labor Market Segmentation, and Labor Productivity:
A Story from Indonesia

Tulus T. H. Tambunan
Center for Industry, SME, and Business Competition Studies, Indonesia

ABSTRACT

This chapter examines economic growth, labor market segmentation, informal employment, and labor productivity in Indonesia from 1990-2015. It shows four important facts. First, Indonesia was ever among countries in Southeast Asia with the highest economic growth before the country was severely hit by the Asian financial crisis in 1997/98. In 1999, the country started to recover, and since then, the economy has performed exceptionally well until these days. Second, total employment increased continuously, although as a percentage of total labor force, it tends to decline. Second, total labor productivity also continued to increase. Third, employment is still dominated by the informal sector. This chapter also discusses labor market policy in Indonesia. This chapter concludes that there are many factors that simultaneously determine directly or indirectly the growth of labor productivity, including good macro-economic management and effective labor market policies.

INTRODUCTION

During the 'New Order' era (1966-1998), Indonesia was among countries with the highest economic growth in Southeast Asia. Only in 1998, when it was severely hit by the Asian financial crisis, the country experienced a negative economic growth up to 13 percent. In 1999 Indonesia started to recover, and since then the economy performed well. This was also the reason why during the 2008/09 global financial crisis, the economy was not seriously impacted, although exports of some commodities dropped as the crisis affected the economy mainly through export channel. However, economic growth has been moderated in recent years, which is expected to grow only by 5 percent by the end of 2016. This decline in

DOI: 10.4018/978-1-5225-2008-5.ch019

economic growth rate was caused by a combination of the following factors: weakening world demand for Indonesian exports, low investment growth related, a certain extent, to lower international prices for some commodities, and heightened regulatory uncertainty and lack of infrastructure in the country. The good performance of the economy, except in 1998, has a positive impact on employment as it continued to increase; although the rate of the increase varies by sector.

The main aim of this chapter is to examine the Indonesian experience with economic growth and changes in labor market segmentation and labor productivity for the period 1990-2015. It is beyond the scope of this paper to identify links between the variables such as economic growth, market segmentation, informal employment, and labor productivity with econometric or regression analyses. Rather, the goal here is to assess changes in these variables during that particular period and to highlight the likely main causes behind the changes, and the relationship between the changes of the variables. More specific, this chapter has the following three questions to deal with:

- How was the pattern of Indonesia's economic growth during that particular period and what were the likely factors behind that?
- How was the labor productivity growth during that period and what were the likely main determinants?
- How has labor market segmentation changed since the early 1990s and what is the likely implication of labor market segmentation on the country's economic growth?

The rationale of analyzing this topic is to contribute to the understanding of economic growth, labor productivity, and labor market segmentation in a developing country like Indonesia. This topic is particularly important for Indonesian economic growth for two main reasons. First, along with accumulation in physical investment and technology progress (including innovation), labor productivity growth is also a major determinant of long-term economic growth. Thus, understanding the dynamic of long-term labor productivity growth and its main determinants are crucial. Second, like in other developing countries, the labor market in Indonesia is also segmented with a large share of informal workers, and it may have a negative impact on the country's economic growth. Therefore, understanding this labor market phenomenon in the course of continued economic growth is crucial. For this purpose, this chapter has eight sections as follows. Section 1: Introduction. Section 2: Literature review. Section 3: Review of key previous studies in Indonesia. Section 4: Economic growth during 1990-2015 in three important phases. Section 5: Labor market segmentation and the importance of informal labor market. Section 6: Labor productivity and main determinant factors. Section 7: Labor market policy. Section 8: Conclusion.

LITERATURE REVIEW

The Relationship between Labor Productivity and Economic Growth

Firms use a combination of labor and capital, called production factors, to produce their output. To increase their output, firms have three options: by increasing the number of one of their production factors (e.g. use more machines or hire more people) or both; by increasing productivity of one of their production factors (i.e. partial factor productivity) or both (i.e. total factor productivity), or by combining these two options. The growth of output in all firms determines economic growth in the long run. In other words, through sustained output growth in all firms, there is a positive long-term relationship between labor productivity growth and economic growth (e.g. Solow, 2000; Stiroh, 2001).

The increase in labor productivity is referred to as labor productivity growth. Many factors that determine, directly as well as indirectly, labor productivity, can be grouped into two categories, namely internal and external factors. Internal factors are those inside a firm, and in the literature, it is often stated that there are three key internal determinants of labor productivity growth. The first one is human capital or skill improvement, which is the increased knowledge, skills or expertise of workers obtained from education, training or long time experience. Typically, the level of education of labor force is positively related to the accumulation of human capital and level of labor productivity. The second factor inside a firm is capital accumulation or technological change. Technological change is putting advances in knowledge (i.e. invention) in a new product or service (i.e. innovation). The third internal factor is economies of scale which are, on the one hand, negatively related to average costs of production due to the size of production, and, on the other hand, positively related to the level of labor productivity (International Labour Organization [ILO], 2004, 2013; Landmann, 2004).

Among these internal factors, especially in developing countries such as Indonesia, most attention has been given to skills or education of workers. It is generally accepted that skill or education of workers is the most crucial factor in determining their performance. As stated by International Labour Organization (ILO), education and training are both at the core of any effort to increase a country's productivity and to improve people's likelihood not only of accessing employment at all but of accessing good quality employment. The educational attainment and skills base of the workforce have a clear impact not only at the individual level but also at the national level (International Labour Organization [ILO], 2015).

At the national level, there is a positive link between the proportion of highly educated adults in the labor force in a given country and the country's income per capita (e.g. Holland, Liadze, Rienzo, & Wilkinson, 2013). A study involving 18 developing countries found that in most of the countries analyzed, an increase in national literacy rates was accompanied by a higher rate of national economic growth. That is, human capital has a statistically significant positive impact on economic growth or overall productivity (Vinod & Kaushik, 2007).

At the sector level or firm level, a link exists between skill or education level of workers and labor productivity: A greater proportion of the labor force with a tertiary education is associated with higher level of labor productivity (ILO, 2015).

However, McMillan and Rodrik (2012) argue that the productivity of labor can increase not only within a sector (as result of, for instance, capital accumulation, or the use of new technologies, or the improvement of the quality of employees, or reduction of misallocation across plants), but also through the shift of workers across sectors, from those with low productivity (e.g. agriculture) to sectors with high-productivity (e.g. industry manufacturing), which led overall labor productivity in the economy to increase. McMillan and Rodrik (2012) expressed this second cause of labor productivity growth by using the following decomposition:

$$\Delta Y_t = \sum_{i=n} q_{i,t} - k\Delta y_{i,t} + \sum_{i=n} y_{i,t}\Delta q_{i,t} \quad (1)$$

where:

Y_t : Economy-wide productivity level,
$y_{i,t}$: Sectoral labor productivity level,
$q_{i,t}$: The share of employment in sector *i*,
Δ : Operator denotes the change in productivity or employment shares between *t-k* and *t*.

The first term of the equation, called 'the within component of productivity growth', is the weighted sum of the change in productivity within individual sectors or firms, where the weights are the employment share of each sector at the beginning of the time period. The second term of the equation called 'the structural change term, is the productivity effect of labor shifts across sectors, with a change in the total number of workers across sectors. When this term of structural change is positively correlated with labor productivity, it will be positive because the overall growth of labor productivity will increase.

The external determinant factors of labor productivity growth, on the other hand, are those that cannot be influenced or controlled by a firm. The most important ones from this category are access to financing and lending interest rate; labor market condition and regulations; level of infrastructure development, not only related to quality of roads, railroads, ports, and air transport, but also in the areas of telecommunications, transport systems and facilities and the availability of electricity and clean water; access to market and competition among firms; availability of technological information and support services; and government policies which influence business or investment climate (Firdausy, 2005).

The Relationship between Labor Market Segmentation and Economic Growth

A labor market is segmented if it consists of different sub-groups with little or no crossover capability, or if the labor market is divided into separate sub-markets or segments, distinguished by different characteristics and behavioral rules. For instance, differences in wage, health benefit, social and job securities, grade, and status. Lewis (as cited in Hull, 2009), who was among the first scholars to study the segmented labor market phenomenon in developing countries, identified a dual labor market in which those who could not find jobs in the formal sector did any kind of work in a free entry unregulated informal sector that provides them with certain, though minimum or unstable incomes.

According to ILO, labor market segmentation may arise from particularities of labor market institutions, such as governing contractual arrangements (segmentation along permanent/temporary nature of employment contracts), from lack of enforcement (segmentation along formal/informal line), as well as types of workers concerned (such as migrant and non-migrant workers) (ILO, 2016).

A common feature of labor market segmentation in developing countries is the presence of a sprawling informal sector, which employs a large share of the total workforce but is characterized by low productivity and low or unstable earnings, relative to the formal sector (Maloney, 1999). According to many studies, e.g. Bacchetta, Ernst, and Bustamante (2009), Sharma (2013), and ILO (2013), between 50 to 80 percent of workers in many developing countries across Latin America, Asia, and Africa are employed in the informal sector; moreover, this share has remained largely unchanged in the last few decades, even as many of these countries have experienced rapid economic growth and rapid increase in income per capita.

The informal sector in developing countries has traditionally been analyzed in the context of labor market segmentation due to institutional factors or barriers such as labor unions and minimum wage legislation. The formal segment of the labor market has been envisaged as a modern, urban sector characterized by such as high productivity and earnings. The informal labor market, on the other hand, is seen as traditional, often rural sector characterized by low productivity and low or unstable earnings. According to Sharma (2013), institutional barriers generate large earnings differentials between similar workers in both sectors.

According to Hull (2009), labor market segmentation will have a negative effect on the overall rate of economic growth in countries where labor markets are segmented. Their economic growth is likely to be lower than in countries with fully integrated labor markets because a segmented labor market inhibits the efficient flow of labor force participants between different jobs.

A REVIEW OF PREVIOUS KEY STUDIES IN INDONESIA

Labor Productivity

As labor productivity has always been among important economic policy issues in Indonesia since the country started its national economic development at the beginning of "New Order" era in 1969, many studies have been conducted which come with two common conclusions. First, labor productivity has shown a sustained growth and has, partly, contributed to economic growth in Indonesia. For instance, through various tests, Hossain (2012) finds that the relationship between labor productivity and economic growth has remained stable since 1969 up to recently. From his research for his Master of Arts in development studies, Ariwanto (2012) finds that Indonesian productivity growth in term of labor productivity and total factor productivity had shown a relatively stable trend in the last 40 years, except in the late 1990s when an economic crisis occurred. Furthermore, compared to GDP, productivity growth of Indonesia shows a similar trend.

All these studies suggest that labor productivity growth has a positive impact on economic growth. The Indonesia's labor productivity gain has come from both productivity improvements within sectors as well as through a shift of workers from relatively low productivity sectors such as agriculture to other higher productivity sectors including manufacturing industry. However, some studies come to different conclusions. For instance, from their in-depth analysis, Oberman, Dobbs, Budiman, Thompson, & Rossé (2012) found that the majority of labor productivity gain in Indonesia has come not from the movement of labor from the unregulated informal sector to the regulated formal sector, but from productivity improvements within industries or companies in the formal sector. While, a most recent study by Lindsay, Goldmark, Hansen, Fawcett, and Wang (2016) indicates that labor productivity in Indonesia has gained in all sectors, and employment shifts across sectors explain much of the recent economic growth in Indonesia. Each Indonesian worker is now contributing on average more to GDP than ever before.

However, as the second common conclusion, gains in labor productivity in Indonesia are still much lower in comparison with many other countries including in Southeast Asia particularly Malaysia, Singapore, and Thailand. The main problem still facing Indonesia today is that the quality of its labor force or "human resource", determined by formal education, training and skill levels, is still relatively low. This despite the fact that, as shown by a report made by Lindsay et al. (2016) on the education of manpower in Indonesia, educational attainment across all levels has increased significantly in past 20 years, and the government through the Ministry of Education has pushed and provided various facilities to increase vocational training. This achievement has contributed to the labor productivity growth in Indonesia in the past decades. Another most recent study on the labor market in Indonesia by the Asian

Development Bank (Allen, 2016) may have the answer for this. It shows that increased investment in education since the beginning of the 'new order' era in the early 1970s has indeed increased the number of educated workers in Indonesia. But, still, it has not resulted in a significant gain in labor productivity. High qualified workers are still in short supply in the country, and this will be a serious challenge for Indonesia for many years to come.

Labor Market Segmentation

Indonesia is a very interesting example of a rapidly transforming and fast-growing economy that continues to have a large informal sector contribution to both GDP and employment. This is the most important phenomenon of labor market segmentation in Indonesia, which has been studied by many including Bacchetta et al. (2009), Alatas and Newhouse (2010), Organisation for Economic Co-operation and Development (OECD, 2011), Comola and de Mello (2011, 2013), Sharma (2013), and Allen (2016). The analysis of some of these studies (e.g. Comola & de Mello 2011, 2013; Sharma, 2013) focuses on earning differentials between similar workers in the informal and formal sectors. For instance, Allen's (2016) analysis of wage in Indonesia shows that workers in the informal sector earned much lower than those employed in the formal sector. By using data 2015 on wage by the status of employment, Allen found that casual workers in agriculture earned average monthly wage around Rp 0.8 million, non-agricultural workers Rp 1.3 million, and casual employees Rp 1.4 million; while that of regular employees was Rp 2.1 million on average.

While, some other studies tried to identify key factors behind this phenomenon and its likely implication on the labor market in Indonesia. For instance, according to OECD (2011), the large informal sector distorts the labor market in Indonesia, which may have a negative effect on economic growth. Therefore, an appropriate reform of labor regulations is very needed to enhance the shift of workers from low-income generating activities in the informal sector too much better-paid jobs in the formal sector. Also as emphasized by Allen (2016), free movement of labor from low-income jobs such as in agriculture to higher earning jobs in the formal sector such as manufacturing industry and services is critical to boosting incomes and labor productivity and hence economic growth. Thus, these studies may suggest that there is a trade-off between the degree of labor market segmentation and economic growth.

ECONOMIC GROWTH IN THREE PHASES DURING 1990-2015

High Performing Period: 1990-1996

When Suharto came to power in 1966, the beginning of the 'New Order' era, he began first with reconstruction and rehabilitation and then started development of the country's economy, which suffered from hyperinflation, high poverty, and heavy foreign debt burden during Sukarno era (1945-1966). The process of economic development was guided by subsequent five-year development plans (REPELITA), started in 1969. Also in his first few years in power, Suharto began with modernization in agriculture ('green revolution') to increase productivity, and as a result, in the early 1970s output in the sector started to increase, and it continued steadily. Pushed by green revolution technologies and modern methods of production, rice production outer islands also increased rapidly.

Suharto also promoted industrialization which begun first with the development of labor-intensive substituting industries (so-called import substitution policies), including automotive and consumer goods, and followed later on by the development of export-oriented industries (export promotion policies) with the focus on textile and garment, footwear, and wood-based products industries.

As a result, Indonesia experienced annual high growth rates of gross domestic products (GDP). Especially the period 1990-96, which was not only marked by high average growth rate of real GDP (Figure 1), but also known as the period of export-led growth that begun in the early 1980s with the implementation of the first package of deregulations in 1983 including new measures to liberalize the national banking sector and external trade (albeit not completely), to improve the investment climate for private investors, and to encourage domestic companies to export (such as the exemption of import duties and another devaluation of the rupiah).

At the beginning of the mid-1980s, soon after the fall of oil prices in international markets, the government redirected its focus of attention towards exports of manufactured goods. With various special measures and supported by the above-mentioned first package of deregulations, the government promoted labor-intensive manufactured exports, particularly, textiles, clothing, footwear, toys, furniture and other products soared. Industries producing these goods provided many jobs, especially for relatively low educated/skilled workers, and established a conduit for the introduction of new technologies (Radelet, 1999). This has also contributed to the increase in real GDP per capita (Figure 2).

This first package of deregulations and followed by the second one in the early 1990s also encouraged the inflows of foreign direct investments (FDIs) into the country. Between the late 1980s and early 1990s, foreign investment barriers in some sectors were rapidly removed. Although, in that time the government still had a long negative list, i.e. sectors or group of industries not open for FDIs or open with strong preconditions. Especially export-oriented FDIs were very welcomed. However, FDI to GDP ratio in that period was relatively small, with the highest ratio in 1996 at around 3 percent of the country's real GDP.

With huge inflows of export-oriented FDI supported by export-promotion policies to promote export-oriented industries in combination with import-substitution policies to promote domestic industries servicing domestic markets, and with social and political stability, this period was also marked by high

Figure 1. Real GDP growth rates in Indonesia during the export-led growth and deregulation measures period: 1991-1996 (%)

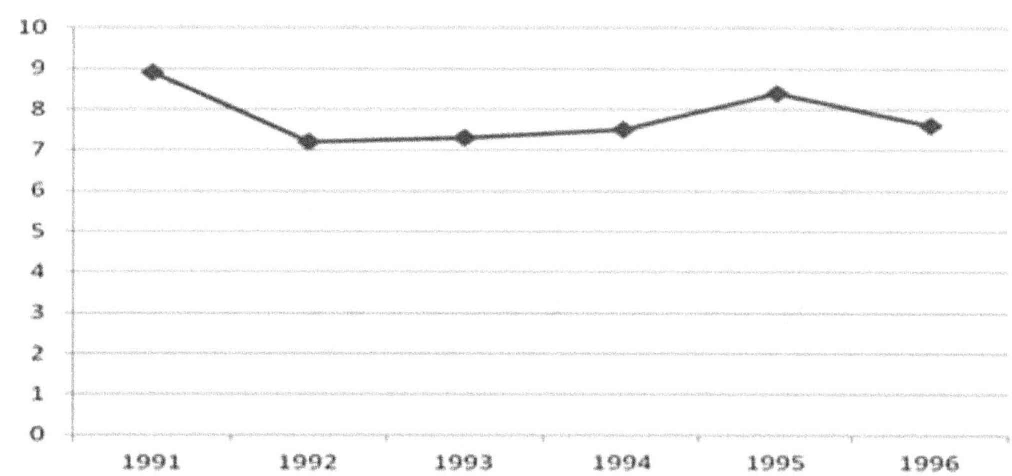

Figure 2. Real GDP per capita, 1990-1996 (million Rp)

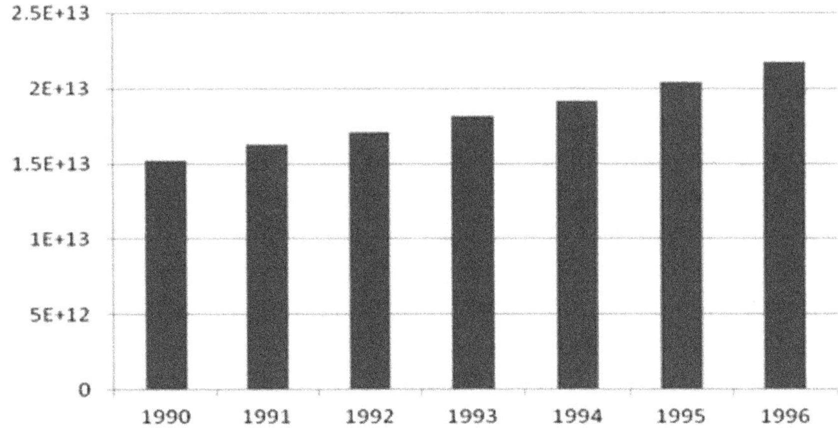

growing output in many domestic industries. Although the average GDP share of industry was lower at around 37 to slightly over 40 percent per year than that of services at around 41 to 42 percent per year (Figure 3), but with higher output growth rate than those of the other two key sectors, industry had the largest contribution to the national GDP growth during the period (Figure 4).

Especially for labor-intensive industries in which Indonesia has comparative advantages (e.g. abundance of the labor force) such as textiles and garments, leather products, tobacco, footwear, and furniture, and also automotive industries, this period was the best era they ever had since the beginning of the New Order. During that period, as a whole, the industrial sector had the highest year-on-year (y-o-y) growth rate than agriculture and services, ranged from the lowest level at around 8.2 percent in 1992 to the highest above 11 percent in some years (Figure 5).

Figure 3. Shares of three key economic sectors in total real GDP during the export-led growth and deregulation measures period: 1990-1996 (%)

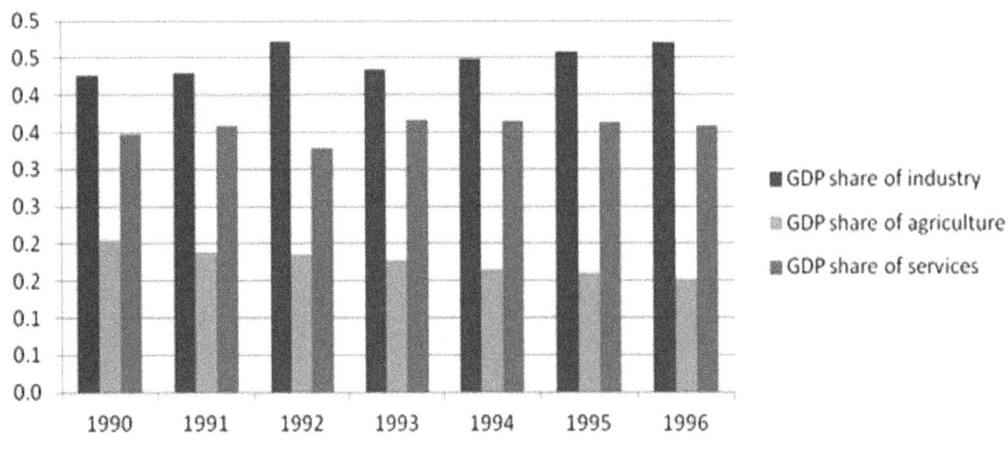

Figure 4. Contributions of three key economic sectors to real GDP growth during the export-led growth and deregulation measures period: 1991-1996 (%)[1]

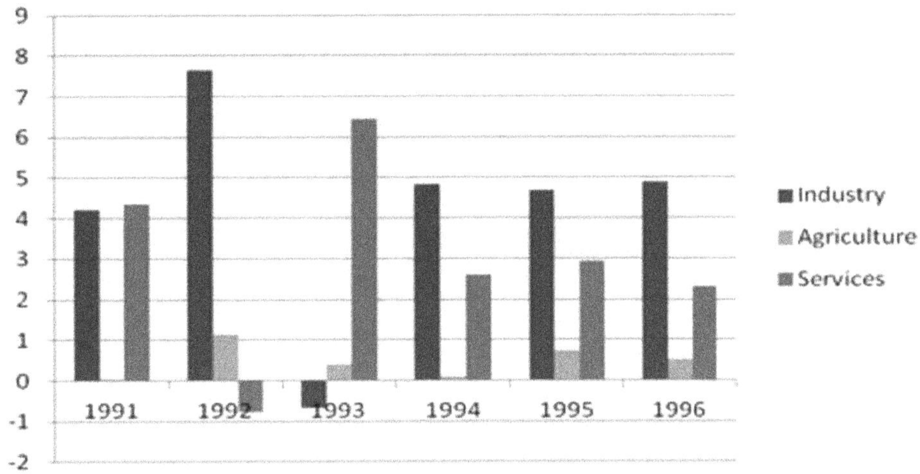

Figure 5. Real value added growth rates in three key economic sectors and total in Indonesia during the export-led growth and deregulation measures period: 1990-1996 (%)

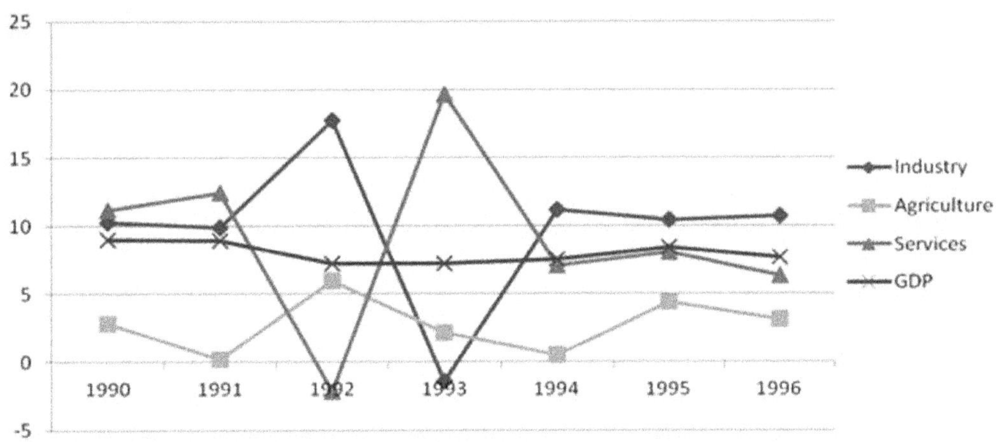

Asian Financial Crisis Period: 1997-1998 and the Recovery Period: 1999-2007

Indonesia was severely affected by this crisis, which pushed its economy into a deep recession in 1998 with a negative economic growth at minus around 13 percent (Figure 6). Aggregating all economic sectors into three key sectors shows that industry was the most severely affected which led output of the sector dropped by around 14 percent in 1998, followed by services at 16.5 percent, and agriculture experienced a decline of 1.3 percent (Figure 7). But, the contribution of the service sector to the negative growth of GDP in 1998 was the largest at around 6.52 percent, followed by the industrial sector 6.9 percent and the smallest agriculture at 0.2 percent (Figure 8).

Figure 6. Real GDP growth rates during the Asian financial crisis and the recovery periods, 1997-2007 (%)

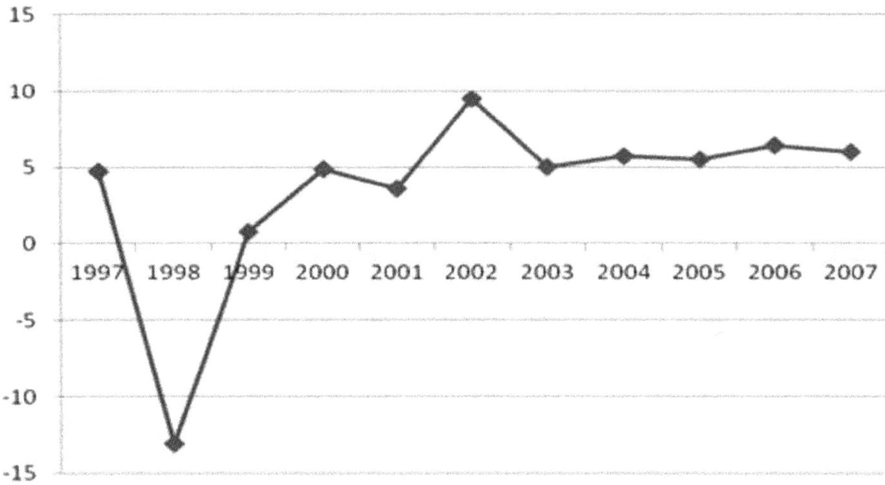

Figure 7. Real value added growth rates of three key sectors during the Asian financial crisis and the recovery periods, 1997-2007 (%)

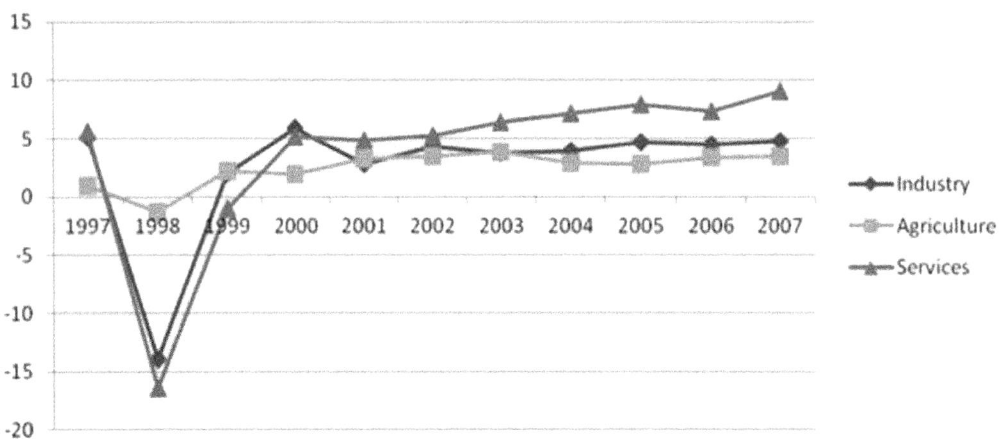

Not only negative economic growth but also domestic prices (including prices for food and other basic needs) raised significantly, which resulted in the general inflation rate at 78 percent in 1998, caused by money supply expansion and rupiah depreciation. In response to this development, students in many universities in various cities, including the capital, Jakarta, started to demonstrate in early 1998, followed soon by riots in Jakarta and some other big cities such as Solo (in the Central Java province), and Medan (in the North Sumatera Province) in May 1998, which led to the resignation of President Soeharto in the same month, who had been in power since 1966.

In 1999, with the improvement of macroeconomic management where Indonesia had implemented wide-ranging policy reforms in many areas including bureaucracy, law on foreign investments, and price regulations, and in key sectors including manufacturing, agriculture and trade since the crisis, in combination with a prudent monetary and fiscal policies, a sound banking system, and a more flexible

Figure 8. Contributions of three key economic sectors to real GDP growth during the Asian financial crisis and the recovery period: 1997-2007 (%) [2]

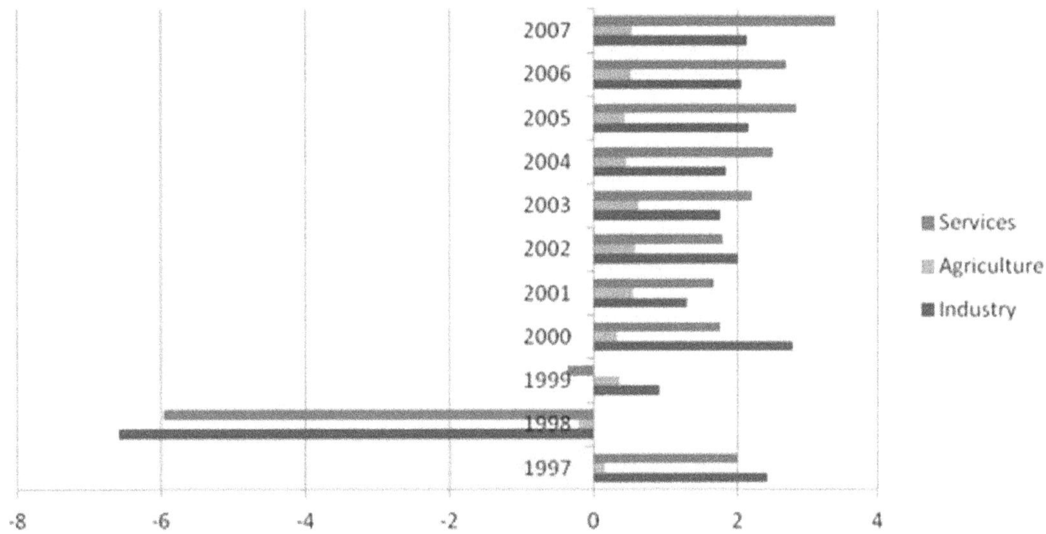

exchange rate, Indonesian economy started to recover. Since that year up to 2007, the country's economic growth shows a positive trend.

One important characteristic of the Indonesian economy in the post 1997/98 crisis recovery was a structural shift took place from the relative dominance of industry to services. As can be seen in Figure 7, from 2001 onwards the value added growth rate of services was higher than those of industry and agriculture, and the gap tended to enlarge. Sorts of services which gained in the recovery were travel, transportation and communications, and hotel and restaurants (Elias & Noone, 2011; Suryahadi, Hadiwidjaja, & Sumarto, 2012).

Global Financial Crisis Period 2008-2009 and Beyond

Compared to other neighboring countries, Indonesia was lucky that shown no significant effects of the crisis. The most severely impacted countries in the region were Singapore, Malaysia, and Thailand. Singapore which is fully integrated with the global economy through goods and services and financial markets, its economy suffered almost minus 9 percent in the first quarter 2009. In that same period, the Thai economy was contracted by 7.11 percent and Malaysia by slightly above 6 percent. Meanwhile, Indonesia was managed to keep its economy with positive growth although at a declining rate during that period (Figure 9).

Although some domestic industries such as textile and garment, and furniture had experienced a decline in their export orders from United States (US), Japan, and other crisis-affected countries of destination, which led total growth rate of industrial output to decline during the crisis period, no evidence of negative growth rates. Also, other two key sectors managed to keep positive growth rates although at lower levels than before the crisis (Figure 10). Also, the contributions of especially industry and service to GDP growth started to increase again in 2010 (Figure 11).

Figure 9. Real GDP growth rates during the 2008-09 global financial crisis and beyond (%)

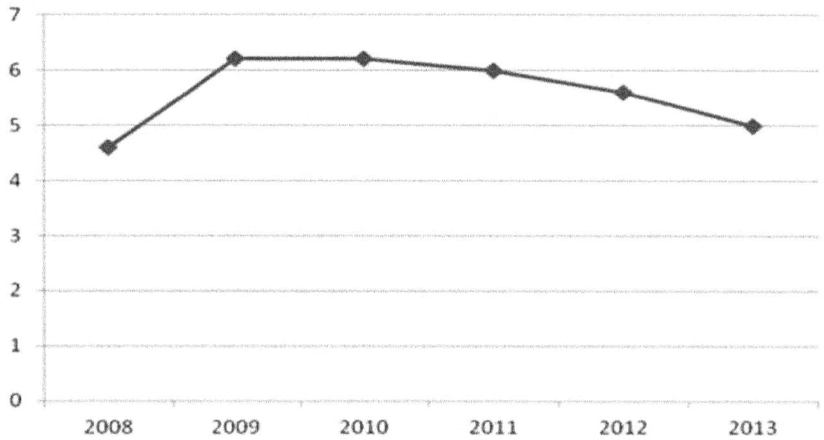

Figure 10. Real value added growth rates of three key sectors in Indonesia during the 2008-09 global financial crisis and beyond (%)

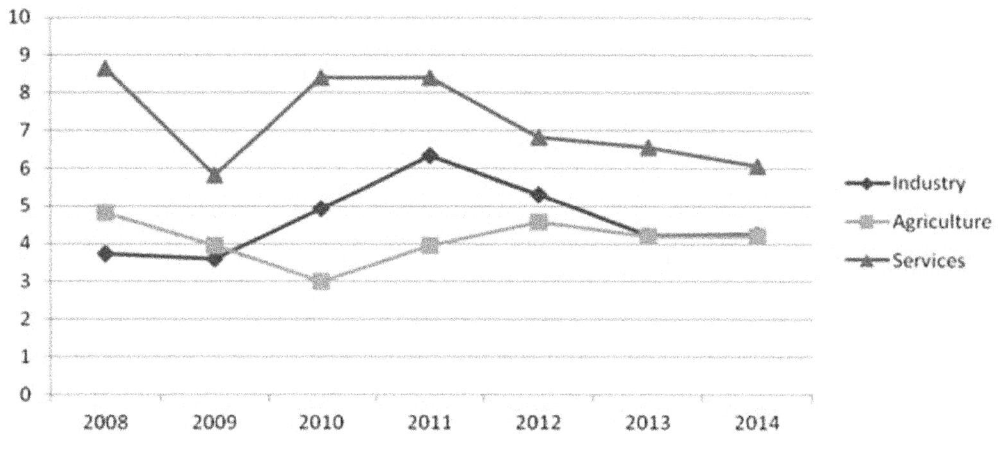

Figure 11. Contributions of three key economic sectors to real GDP growth during the 2008-09 global financial crisis and beyond (%)[3]

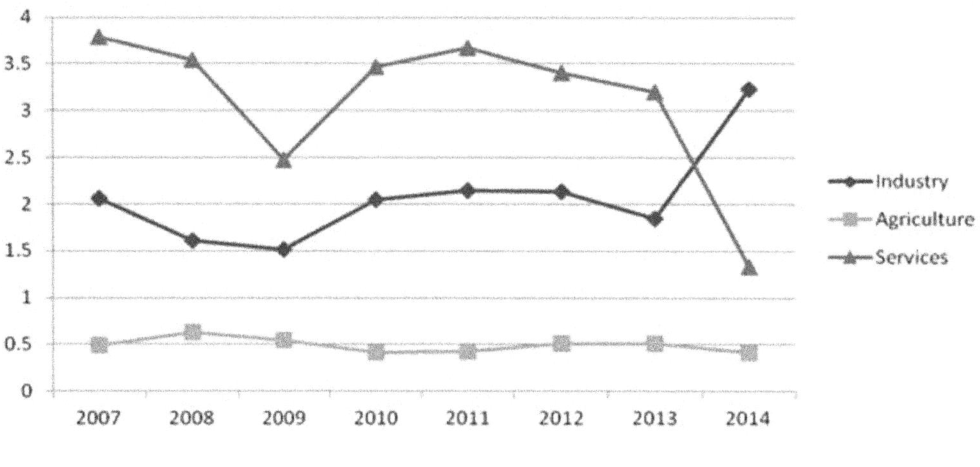

LABOR MARKET SEGMENTATION AND THE IMPORTANCE OF INFORMAL EMPLOYMENT

When talking about labor market segmentation in a developing country like in Indonesia, one important question always being asked is: how significant is informal employment or how many people fully depend on the informal sector for their primary income? If more and more people working in the informal sector, measured as a percentage of total employment, it means that the sector becomes more important in the economy, simply because more people earned their incomes not from the formal sector but from the informal sector.

For Indonesia, to answer this question, there are only two types of data are available that can be used to estimate the importance of informal labor market or informal employment in the country. First, data on total employment by size-category of enterprises. In Indonesia, the majority of employed people are found in micro and small enterprises (MSEs). These enterprises mostly operate in the informal sector; especially micro enterprises (MIEs) in Indonesia (as a normally observed phenomenon in developing/ low-income/poor countries), including self-employment and income-generating own-account activities, are operated in the informal sector. Obviously, these tiny enterprises have different characteristics than medium and large enterprises (MLEs) in the formal sector (Table 1). Thus, total workers employed in the MIEs, as a percentage of total employment in all enterprises of all sizes can be used as an indication of the importance of informal employment.

The MSEs in Indonesia are very numerous, amounting to 57,843,615 units, compared to only 57,172 MLEs in 2013. MSEs have always been the main drivers of domestic economic activities, and they provide employment opportunities for over 90 percent of the country's workforce (Figure 12). Especially MIEs, they generate a significant amount of not only primary but also in many cases, secondary income sources for low-income/poor households. For instance, in many small or poor farm households, men

Table 1. Main characteristics of MSEs and MEs in Indonesia

Key Aspect	MSEs	MLEs
Formality	• Operating in the informal sector • Not registered • Pay no taxes	• Operating in the formal sector, • Registered • Pay taxes
Location	Mainly in rural areas/villages	Mostly in urban areas/cities
Organization & management	• Run by the owner • No internal labor division • No formal management • Not use formal/modern accounting system (bookkeeping)	• Use professional managers, • Adopt labor division, • Have a formal organizational structure • Use a formal accounting system
Nature and condition of employment	• Many use unpaid family members • Hire workers without an official contract, • Many use casual and seasonal workers with low paid • No social and job security, and pension • Bad working condition and no safety regulation • Most hired workers have low formal education • Low labor productivity	• Use permanent employees with good monthly salaries • Hired employees have high formal education • Have a formal recruitment system • Have social and job security, and pension • Have good working condition and safety regulations • Have on-the-job training for employees • Have good promotion prospects • High labor productivity

Figure 12. Total employment in MSEs and MLEs in Indonesia, 2005-2013

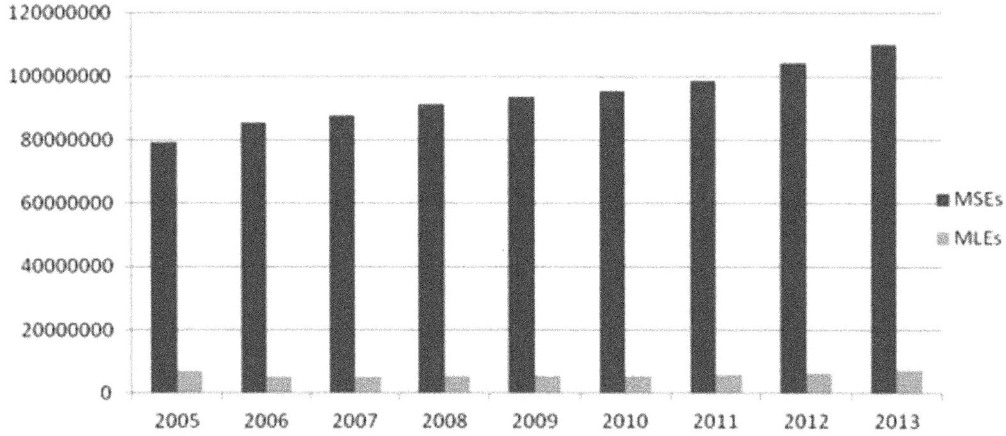

(husband) work in the field while women (their wives) own small businesses at home making simple handicraft items or food products or running small shops selling basic need items.

Second, data on labor market by the status of employment. In Indonesia, according to the National Statistics Agency (BPS), since 2001, status of employment has seven types: (i) own-account workers, (ii) employers assisted by temporary workers/unpaid workers; (iii) employers assisted by permanent workers/paid workers; (iv) wage-paid permanent employees; (v) casual agricultural employee; (vi) non-agricultural casual employee; and (vii) family/unpaid workers. Own-account workers, casual employees (in agriculture and non-agriculture), and family/unpaid workers are categorized as informal employees.

Based on the above classification of employment by formality, dualism in employment in Indonesia is obvious. Based on annual National Labor Survey (SAKERNAS) from BPS, the share of formal employment, although it varies by year, is between minimum 52 percent and maximum 60 percent (Figure 13). This may suggest that the informal sector, although less than half of total employment, still plays an exceptionally large role in Indonesia's economy today, especially on employment creation.

Further, Table 2 shows changes in total informal and formal workers by sub-category (status) during the two crisis periods. As can be seen, during the 1997/98 crisis, among the subcategories of informal employment, only self-employed steadily increased in 1998 and 1999; while family or unpaid workers only went up in 1998 but then dropped in 1999. Aaron et al. (2004) observed indeed that during that crisis, total employment in Indonesia did not drop simply because many displaced wage-paid people from such as manufacturing, mining, and construction opened their own small activities just to earn some money to maintain their minimum level of income.

Ghose, Majid, and Ernst (2008) argued that in countries like Indonesia with this kind of labor market characteristic (dualism), improvement of employment condition should be reflected by simultaneous increase in the share of the formal employment in total employment (or the growth rate of formal employment must larger than that of labor force/supply), and decline in the share of the informal employment or decline of underemployment in the informal sector either by movement of many workers from the informal sector or output increases in the sector. Figure 43 may suggest that after the global economic crisis, the employment condition in Indonesia started to improve.

Figure 13. Formal employment share as percentage of total employment, Indonesia, 1990-2015

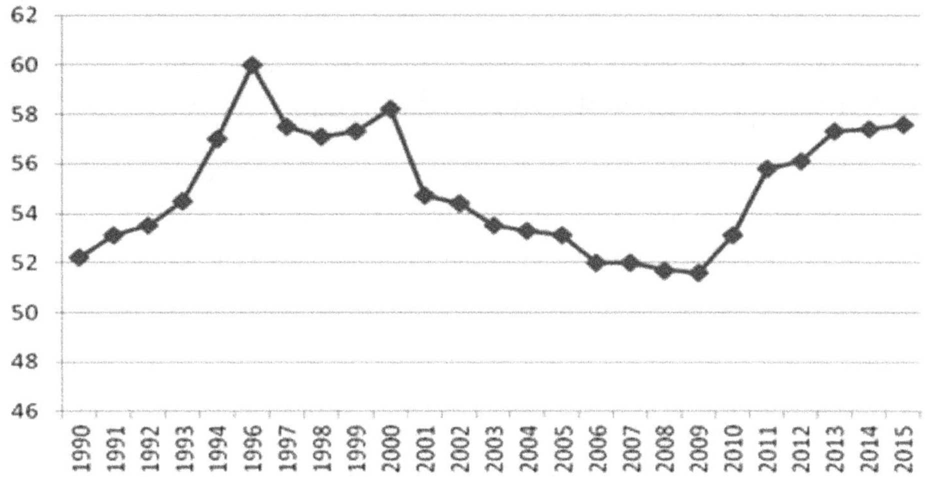

Table 2. Total informal and formal workers by sub-category during the 1997/98 and 2008/2009 crises (people)

Status of Employment	1997	1998	1999	2007	2008	2009
Self employed	19978117	20523338	21707778	20324527	20921567	21046007
Casual workers in agriculture	17055557	17128006	16258228	5917400	5991493	5878894
Casual non-agricultural workers				4458772	5292262	5670709
Family/unpaid workers				17278999	17375335	18194246
Employers with non-fixed/unpaid workers	18046722	19690059	18914502	21024297	21772994	21933546
Employers with fixed/paid workers	1480154	1525625	2552803	2883832	3015326	3033220
Wage-paid employees	30489206	28805421	29383548	28042390	28183773	29114041
Total	87049756	87672449	88816859	99930217	102552750	104870663

Sources: BPS: SAKERNAS 1990 to 2015; in 2015 is February; for other years: August.
Note: until 2000, BPS adopted only five categories of workers, n which family or unpaid workers included casual workers.

Ghose et al. (2008) give an alternative way to measure employment in the informal sector or the degree of dualism in the labor market, by using data or estimates of output and employment shares of three broad sectors, namely agriculture, industry, and services, with the following formula:

$$\left(Y_i / Y\right) / \left(E_i / E\right) = \left(Y_i / E_i\right) / \left(Y / E\right) \qquad (2)$$

where E and E_i are, respectively, total employment in the economy and employment in sector i (i = agriculture, industry, and services) and Y and Y_i are, respectively, total output (GDP) and output in sector i. Thus

$$\left(Y_i / Y\right) / \left(E_i / E\right) = \left(Y_i / E_i\right) / \left(Y / E\right)$$

is the ratio of output per worker in sector *i* to output per worker in the economy.

By using this method with national data on total GDP and total employment, and distributions of GDP and employment by the three major sectors, Indonesian case shows that agriculture is predominantly non-formal because its ratio is less than unity, i.e., the output per worker in the sector is less than that in the economy, and industry is predominantly formal as its ratio is above the unity, i.e. the output per worker in the sector is more than that in the economy (Figure 14). The ratio of labor productivity in agriculture to that in industry, i.e. $\left(Y_a / E_a\right) / \left(Y_i / E_i\right)$ is around minimum 10 percent and maximum 18 percent in 2014 (Figure 15).

Figure 14. Employment dualism (i.e. the ratio of sectoral labor productivity to national labor productivity) in Indonesia, 1990-2014

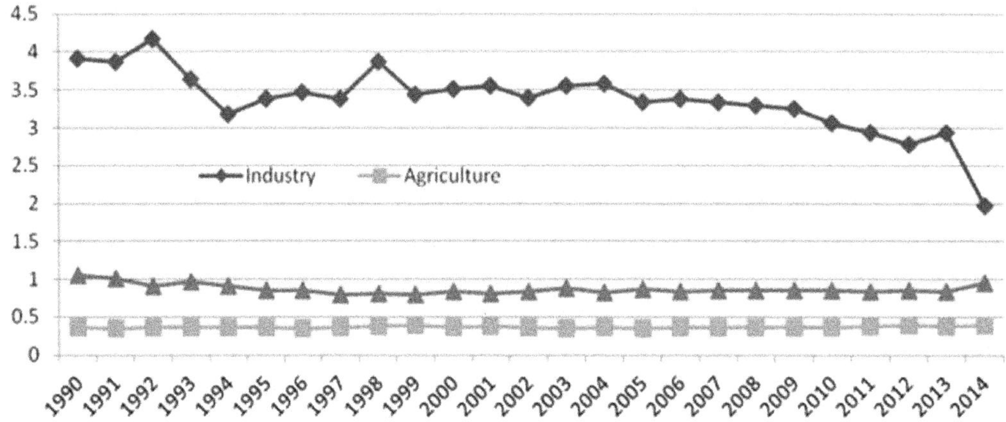

Figure 15. Gap in labor productivity in agriculture and industry (i.e. ratio of labor productivity in agriculture to that in industry), 1990-2014

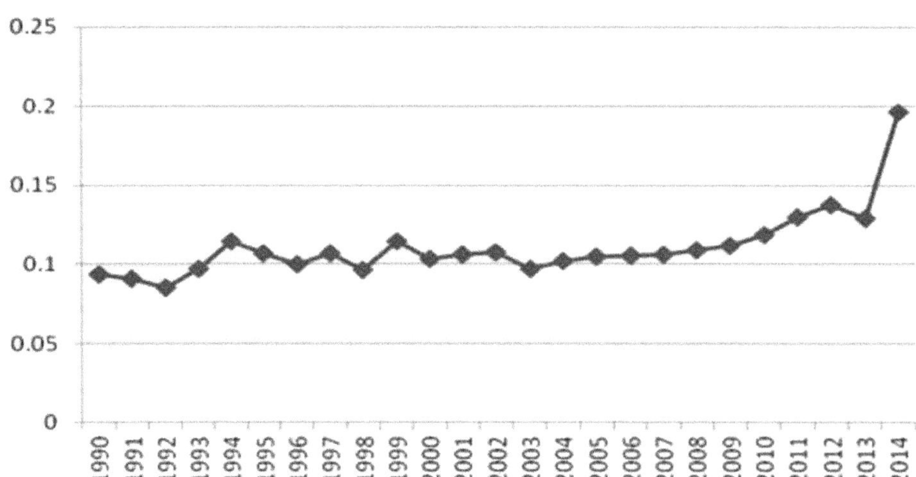

As already discussed in Section 2, countries with segmented labor markets may have lower economic growth rates than those with fully integrated labor markets. However, it is hard to support this view for Indonesia. Because informal employment has always been there even during the "new order" era, when Indonesia reached the highest average economic growth rate ever experienced since its independence in 1945.

LABOR PRODUCTIVITY AND MAIN DETERMINANT FACTORS

As shown in Figure 16, the ratio of total real GDP to total employment, referred as total labor productivity, in Indonesia increased annually. This sustained increase in labor productivity, no doubt, has made an important contribution to the country's sustained economic growth during the period reviewed, except during the Asia financial crisis 1997-98. As already discussed in Section 3, many previous studies on labor productivity and its contribution to GDP growth in Indonesia support this view.

However, based on Asian Productivity database, labor productivity in Indonesia in US dollar is lower than those in many other countries including in Southeast Asia such as Thailand, Malaysia and especially Singapore (Figure 17). Next, Figure 18 show labor productivities in the three main sectors.

Based on the formula introduced by McMillan and Rodrik (2012) as explained before in Section 2 (see equation 1), Figures 19, 20 and 21 show the overall labor productivity with its two components in Indonesia for the three important phases during 1991-2014, respectively. It is obvious that especially after the 1997/98 crisis period, within components of labor productivity growth has become the most important driven for the overall labor productivity growth in Indonesia.

Although Indonesia has proved adept at exploiting its mineral wealth and its economy continues to grow, its human resources are lagging behind. Indonesia is still facing this manpower problem and, therefore, the government needs to take necessary but appropriate measures, in co-operation with the private sector, to improve the competitiveness of its human resources. Otherwise, the labor force in Indonesia will not able to compete both at home and abroad, especially in the ASEAN integrated region. As presented in Table 3, data from the BPS on the composition of Indonesian workers show that almost

Figure 16. Total labor productivity in Indonesia, 1990-2014 (trillion IDR)

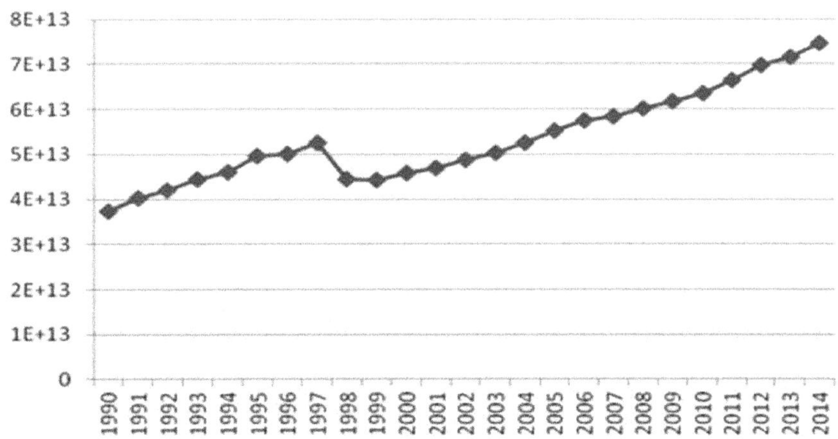

Figure 17. Labor productivity in some selected Asian countries, 2012 (thousand US$)

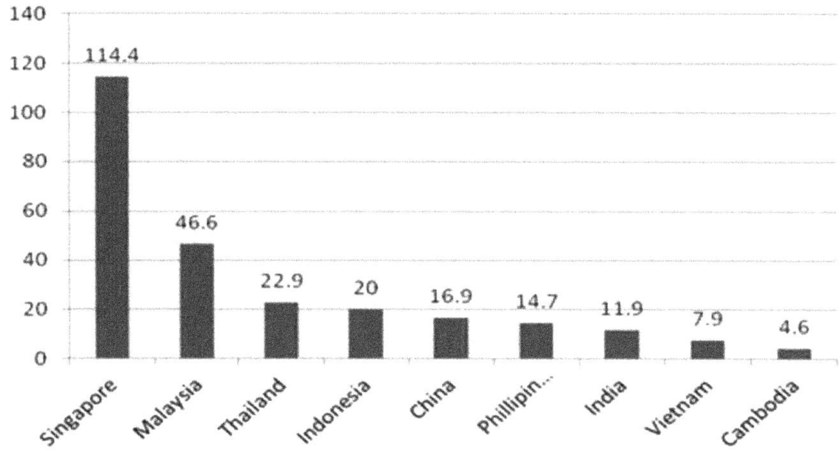

Figure 18. Labor productivity by the three key economic sectors in Indonesia during the three important phases, 1990-2014 (IDR trillion per worker)

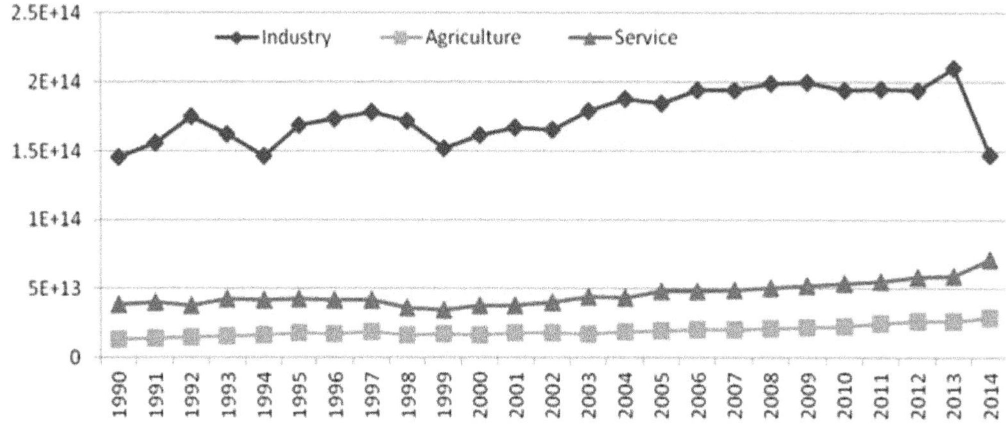

Figure 19. Labor productivity decomposition in three key economic sectors during the export-led growth and deregulation measures period: 1991-1996 (%)

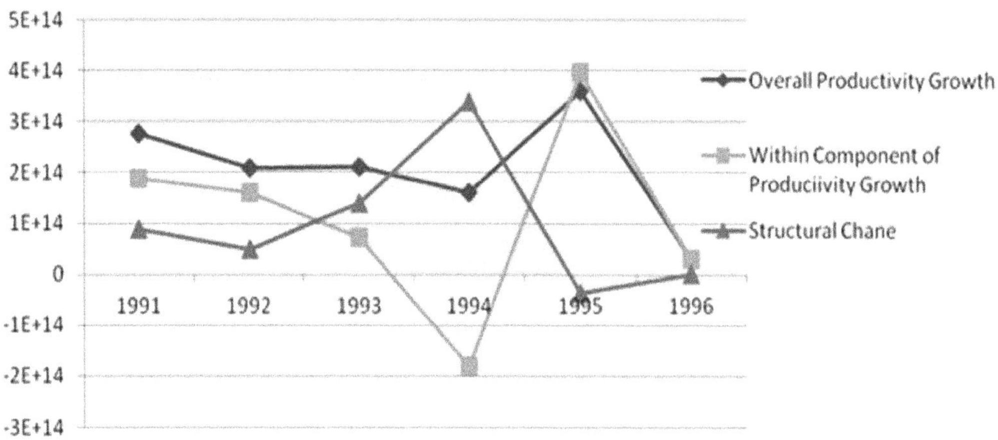

Figure 20. Labor productivity decomposition in three key economic sectors during the Asian financial crisis and the recovery period: 1997-2007 (%)

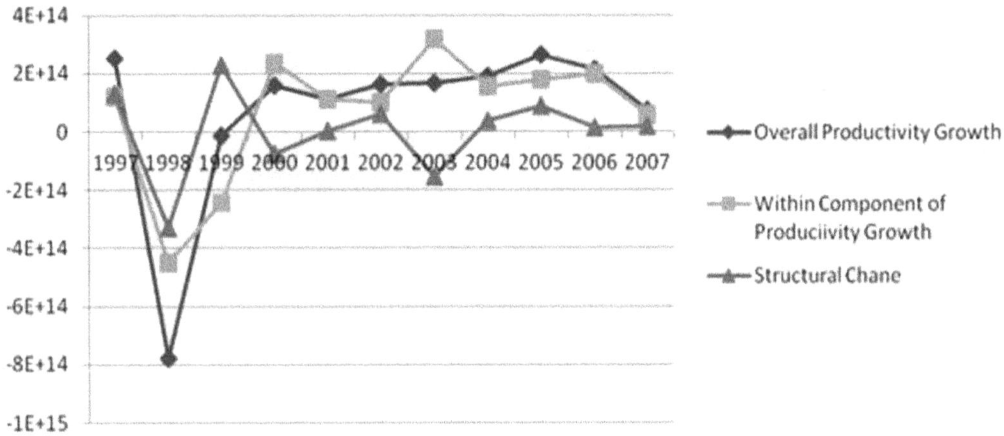

Figure 21. Labor productivity decomposition in three key economic sectors during the global financial crisis and beyond: 2008-2014 (%)

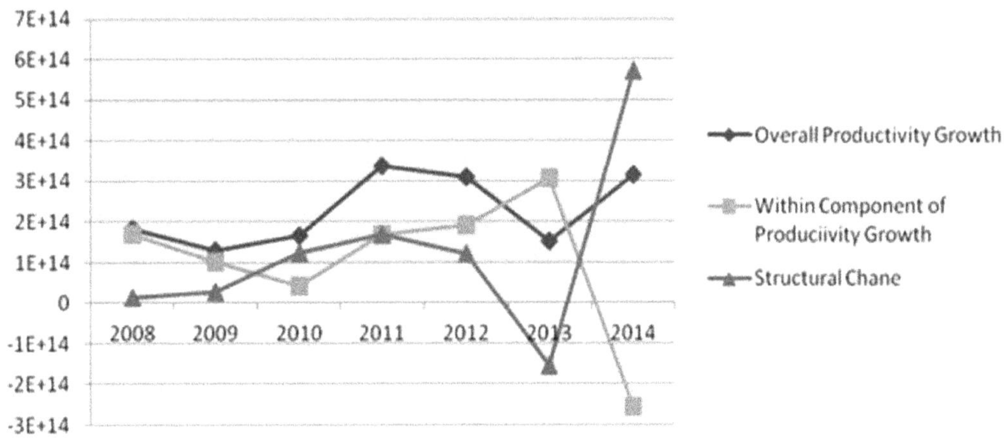

51 million of them or around 44.0 percent have no education or had elementary school education (and many of them not finished it).

The annual human development report from the United Nations for Development Program (UNDP) also confirms this labor condition in Indonesia with respect to the level of formal education. As well known, UNDP publishes every year the Human Development Index (HDI), which gives an assessment of long-term progress achieved by communities in countries all over the world in three basic dimensions of human development, namely a long and healthy life (measured by life expectancy), knowledge level (measured by mean years of education among the adult population aged 25 years and older, and expected years of schooling for children of school-entry age) and a decent standard of living (measured by Gross National Income (GNI) per capita). As can be seen in Table 4, the world rank of Indonesia is 110, or number five in ASEAN.

Table 3. Labor force by level of formal education in Indonesia, August 2015

Item	Employed	Unemployment	Total Labor Force
No education	4,387,904	55,554	4,443,458
Not finished elementary school	14,951,112	371,542	15,322,654
Elementary school	31,487,578	1,004,961	32,492,539
Junior high school	20,698,644	1,373,919	22,072,563
Senior high school	30,650,622	3,849,719	34,500,341
Academy	3,086,444	251,541	3,337,985
University	9,556,895	653,586	10,210,481
Total	114,819,199	7,560,822	122,380,021

Source: BPS (2015).

Table 4. Human Development Index rank of ASEAN countries, 2014

Member Countries	World Rank	ASEAN Rank
Singapore	11	1
Brunei Darussalam	31	2
Malaysia	62	3
Thailand	93	4
Indonesia	110	5
Philippines	115	6
Viet Nam	116	7
Lao People's Democratic Republic	141	8
Cambodia	143	9
Myanmar	148	10

Source: United Nations for Development Program (UNDP, 2015).

LABOR MARKET POLICIES

The government of Indonesian is faced with two most important tasks, namely to increase or maintain long-term high economic growth, and to tackle the problems of unemployment and underemployment, and low labor productivity as well as poverty. The government does not intend to increase employment and improve labor productivity by, at the same time, eliminating the informal sector. Because the government is fully aware that the existence of informal employment in the country is a direct consequence of, on the one hand, the lack of formal employment opportunities and the shortage of skilled labor demanded by companies in the formal sector on the other hand. In the condition like this, it would be an unwise political decision or even impossible, to eliminate the informal sector, especially in countries like Indonesia which do not have a special public financial scheme to support unemployed people. On the contrary, the sector will grow naturally.

In dealing with this problem, the Indonesian government has done a lot of things with two main goals, namely to support the growth of existing businesses and to encourage new businesses in the formal sector, and to enhance the movement of workers from the informal sector to the formal sector. In the meantime, while labor movement from the informal sector to the formal sector is not an overnight process (instead it will take many years or even more than one generation especially if barriers are still there), the government has also implemented a variety of measures to support the existence of the informal sector, including the launch of a special credit guarantee scheme for micro and small enterprises in 2007, called Community Business Credit (or KUR). For the unemployed people and/or low-paid formal employees (lowest-ranked civil servants, taxi drivers, bus drivers, hotel cleaners, teachers, etc.), the sector is considered as their "last resort"; for the unemployed people, the informal sector is their alternative primary source of income, and for low-paid employees in the formal sector, the informal sector is their secondary source of income

To reach the first goal, the most important policy actions in the past two decades are including simplified the procedure to get new business, import and export licenses; launched a new investment law to encourage inflows of foreign direct investments; and implemented various programs to encourage new young entrepreneurs. In addition to those policy measures, the government has launched various programs to generate employment creation and to enhance the quality and productivity of workers, with the aim (i) to eliminate labor market rigidities through appropriate regulations, (ii) to reduce unemployment by regulations friendly to investment, (iii) to revitalize and renew existing programs aiming to generate employment, (iv) to increase the quality of labor, (v) to restore regulations on migrations, (vi) to develop other necessary labor market policies, and (vii) to set-up social protection system for workers in order to increase their welfare (Hasoloan, 2006; Sumadilaga, 2012).

Two key government employment programs are (1) productivity and training, and (2) employment placement (Allen, 2016, p. 30). The first program has four elements: (i) increasing labour productivity through setting standards for the skills and competencies of trainers and programs of entrepreneurship training in public and private training institutions, and by promoting the independent operation of certification authorities; (ii) developing and improving facilities in public and private training institutions; (iii) promoting employment for young people through apprenticeship programs that provide classroom learning and on-the-job training; and (iv) supporting the development of entrepreneurship by providing supports for strengthening productivity of employees in enterprises, providing entrepreneurship trainings, and identifying best practices interventions.

The second program has five elements: (i) to provide job matching and employment counseling services (not only by government agencies but also by private agencies including universities and business associations); (ii) to develop an information system on current labour market development; (iii) to provide short-term work opportunities for such as vulnerable groups, particularly the unemployed, underemployed, and poor; (iv) to support Indonesian migrant worker placements; and (v) to regulate foreign workers by improving the efficiency of foreign worker licensing and associated regulation compliance, and utilization of the foreign workers' training levy fund for financing capacity building of Indonesian workers. To reach the second goal, various vocational training has been provided to improve the quality of workers in the informal sector.

Although employment creation, improvement of labor productivity and workers mobility from the informal to the formal sector depend on many factors, which mean that all parties especially technical ministries have an important role to play, labor or employment policy in Indonesia is under the responsibility of the Ministry of Manpower and Transmigration. The ministry has the task to formulate a strategic policy for manpower and transmigration development in Indonesia, including the field of vocational training, productivity, entrepreneurship, manpower placement, industrial relation and social security, labor inspection, and the development of transmigration area. In the field of training and productivity, the Ministry has the goal to improve the quality of Indonesian manpower to be competent, productive, and competitive in facing global competition through technical and vocational education and training (TVET).

To achieve that, the Ministry is managing 20 training centers which are spread throughout the country in order to train Indonesia manpower. Training centers that are owned and managed by the Ministry can be divided into 3 types, i.e.: (1) Vocational Training Centers (BBPLKLN Cevest Bekasi, BBPLKDN Bandung, BBLKI Serang, BBLKI Medan, BBLKI Surakarta, BLKI Aceh, BLKI Padang, BLKI Semarang, BLKI Makassar, BLKI Samarinda, BLKI Ternate, BLKI Kendari, and BLKI Sorong); (2) Transmigration Training Centers (BBPLK Jakarta, BBLK Yogyakarta, Balatrans Pekanbaru, Balatrans Bali, Balatrans Makassar, and Balatrans Banjarmasin); and (3) Productivity Training Center (BBPP Bekasi) (indonesia.go.id/en/ministries/ministers/ministry-of-manpower).

To ensure the effectiveness of government's efforts to increase the quality of manpower and hence to improve labor productivity, the Indonesian government has developed a national training system, and in co-operation with the private sector, particularly the Indonesian Chamber of Commerce and Industry (Kadin Indonesia), has set up the National Board for Professional Certification aiming to develop accreditation, certification, licensing, and training standardization. The government's efforts in improving labor quality cover many programs with the aim: (i) to develop "link and match" between business community or those who demand for skilled workers and education/training institutions as the suppliers of skilled workers; (ii) to develop "three in one program" consisting three key activities namely training, certification, and placement; (iii) to develop training institutions; and (iv) to improve work ethics of workers and to increase their awareness that they must have high productivity and (Hasoloan, 2010).

CONCLUSION

Economic growth and employment increases have been the main concern in Indonesia since the beginning of the New Order era (1966-1998). When Suharto came to power as the Indonesian second president, he launched in 1969 the first five-year economic plan (Repelita) with the aim to boost the economy with the hope it would have positive effects on employment and hence would reduce poverty. However, the government's attention on "pro-job growth" was emerged long after that, namely during the era of President Susilo Bambang Yudiono (SBY) who launched the so-called "the inclusive economic development", which explicitly stated in the country's Medium Term National Development Plan (RPJMN) 2010-2014.

This chapter aims to examine economic growth, labor market segmentation and labor productivity growth in Indonesia from 1990-2015. It shows three important facts. First, total employment increased continuously, with services as the leading employment generation sector; although as a percentage of total labor force, it tends to decline. Second, total labor productivity also continued to increase, with industry as the leading sector; and third, employment is still dominated by informal sector which is concentrated in agriculture. In addition, this chapter also shows that through many programs, labor market policy in Indonesia not only aimed to create employment but also to enhance quality and productivity of labor.

However, as explained before, due to the fact that there are many factors which determine directly or indirectly the growth of productive employment, therefore, the successful of Indonesian government efforts to achieve full and productive employment will depend on good macroeconomic management to create a good business environment that encourages more investment and hence economic growth and more demand for labor, and, on the other hand, on effective labor policy with the aim to achieve full and productive employment.

REFERENCES

Aaron, C., Kenward, L., Bird, K., Desai, M., Aswicahyono, H., Basri, C. M., & Tubagus, C. (2004). *Strategic approaches to job creation and employment in Indonesia.* Report prepared for the United States Agency for International Development, Jakarta Mission. Retrieved from http://pdf.usaid.gov/pdf_docs/Pnada948.pdf

Alatas, V., & Newhouse, D. (2010). *Indonesia jobs report: Towards better jobs and security for all.* Policy Research Working Paper. Washington, DC: The World Bank.

Allen, E. R. (2016). *Analysis of trends and challenges in the Indonesian labor market (ADB Papers on Indonesia No.16, March).* Manila: Asian Development Bank.

Ariwanto, D. A. (2012). *Infrastructure role on productivity in manufacturing sector in Indonesia* (Unpublished master's thesis). International Institute of Social Studies, The Hague.

Bacchetta, M., Ernst, E., & Bustamante, J. P. (2009). *Globalization and informal jobs in developing countries: A joint study of the International Labour Office and the Secretariat of the World Trade Organization.* Geneva: Services des publications de l'OMC and Organisation Mondiale du Commerce.

BPS. (2015). *Survei angkatan kerja nasional (Sakernas).* Jakarta: Badan Pusat Statistik.

Comola, M., & De Mello, L. (2011). How does decentralized minimum wage setting affect employment and informality? The case of Indonesia. *Review of Income and Wealth*, *57*, 79–99. doi:10.1111/j.1475-4991.2011.00451.x

Comola, M., & De Mello, L. (2013). Salaried employment and earnings in Indonesia: New evidence on the selection bias. *Applied Economics*, *45*(19), 2808–2816. doi:10.1080/00036846.2012.667551

Elias, S., & Noone, C. (2011). The growth and development of the Indonesian economy. *RBA Bulletin*, 33-43. Retrieved from http:// www.rba.gov.au/publications/bulletin/2011/dec/pdf/bu-1211-4.pdf

Firdausy, C. M. (2005). *Productivity performance in developing countries, country case studies: Indonesia.* Report for the United Nations Industrial Development Organization. Retrieved from https://www.unido.org/uploads/tx_ templavoila/Productivity_performance_in_DCs_Indonesia.pdf

Ghose, A. K., Majid, N., & Ernst, C. (2008). The global employment challenge. Geneva: International Labour Organisation. Retrieved from http://www.amazon.com/Global-Employment-Challenge-Ajit-Ghose/dp/9221203050

Hasoloan, M. A. (2006). Country report the Indonesian labor market. In *Forum on the Restated OECD Jobs Strategy in Tokyo, Tokyo.* Retrieved from http://www.oecd.org/fr/els/emp/37873500.pdf

Holland, D., Liadze, I., Rienzo, C., & Wilkinson, D. (2013). The relationship between graduates and economic growth across countries. *BIS Research Paper, 110.*

Hossain, A. A. (2012). *Macroeconomic and monetary policy issues in Indonesia*. London: Routledge.

Hull, K. (2009). Understanding the relationship between economic growth, employment and poverty reduction. In Promoting pro-poor growth: Employment (pp. 69–94). Paris: Organization for Economic Cooperation and Development. Retrieved from https://www.oecd.org/dac/ povertyreduction/43280288.pdf

International Labour Organization. (2004). *World employment report 2004-2005: Employment, productivity and poverty reduction*. Geneva: International Labour Organization.

International Labour Organization. (2013). *Global employment trends 2013: Recovering from a second jobs dip*. Geneva: International Labour Organization.

International Labour Organization. (2015). *Key indicators of the labour market*. Geneva: International Labour Organization.

International Labour Organization. (2016). *Labour market segmentation*. Geneva: International Labour Organisation. Retrieved from http://www.ilo.org/global/topics/ employment-security/labour-market-segmentation/lang--en/index.htm

Kompas. (2015, July 10). Penguatan productivitas (strengthening productivity). *Ekonomi, 17.*

Landmann, O. (2004). Employment, productivity and output growth. *Employment Trends Unit, Employment Strategy Department Employment Strategy Papers, 17*, 1-61. Retrieved from http://www.ilo.int/ wcmsp5/groups/public/---ed_emp/---emp_elm/documents/publication/wcms _114299. pdf

Lindsay, J., Goldmark, L., Hansen, A., Fawcett, C., & Wang, E. (2016). Workforce connections: Analysis of skills demand in Indonesia. Jakarta: United States Agency for International Development (USAID) and FHI360.

Maloney, W. F. (1999). Does informality imply segmentation in urban labor markets? Evidence from sectoral transitions in Mexico. *The World Bank Economic Review*, *13*(2), 275–302. doi:10.1093/wber/13.2.275

McMillan, M. S., & Rodrik, D. (2012). *Globalization, structural change and productivity growth* (IFPRI Discussion Paper 01160, February). Washington, DC: Development Strategy and Governance Division, International Food Policy Research Institute.

Ministry of Manpower and Transmigration, Republic of Indonesia. (n.d.). Retrieved from indonesia. go.id/en/ministries/ministers/ministry-of-manpower

Oberman, R., Dobbs, R., Budiman, A., Thompson, F., & Rossé, M. (2012). *The archipelago economy: Unleashing Indonesia's potential*. McKinsey Global Institute. Retrieved fromhttp://www.mckinsey.com/ global-themes/asia-pacific/the-archipelago-economy

Organisation for Economic Co-operation and Development. (2011). *Southeast Asian economic outlook 2011/12*. Paris: OECD Publishing.

Radelet, S. (1999). *Indonesia: Long road to recovery*. Harvard Institute for International Development. Retrieved from http://www.cid.harvard.edu/ archive/ hiid/ papers/indonesia.pdf

Sharma, A. (2013). *Informality, firm size and labour market segmentation in Indonesia*. September, Centre for the Study of African Economies (CSAE) and Department of Economics, University of Oxford. Retrieved from https://editorialexpress.com/cgi-bin/conference/download.cgi?db_name=CSAE2014&paper_id=771

Solow, R. M. (2000). *Growth theory: An exposition* (2nd ed.). New York: Oxford University Press.

Stiroh, K. J. (2001). What drives productivity growth. *Economic Policy Review, 7*(1), 37–59.

Sumadilaga, C. K. (2012). *Employment policies and strategies. As a respond to "Toward inclusive growth in Indonesia: Improving trade and employment"*. Jakarta: Minister of National Development Planning for Poverty, Labor and SMEs. Retrieved from http://www.ilo.org/wcmsp5/groups/public/---asia/---ro-bangkok/---ilo-jakarta/documents/ presentation/wcms_203899.pdf

Suryahadi, A., Hadiwidjaja, G., & Sumarto, S. (2012). *Economic growth and poverty reduction in Indonesia before and after the Asian financial crisis.* Working Paper. Jakarta: SMERU Research Institute. Retrieved from http://www.smeru.or.id/sites/ default/files/publication/econgrow2.pdf

United Nations for Development Program. (2015). *Human development report 2015: Work for human development*. New York: United Nations Development Program.

Vinod, H. D., & Kaushik, S. K. (2007). Human capital and economic growth: Evidence from developing countries. *The American Economist, 51*(1), 29–39. doi:10.1177/056943450705100103

KEY TERMS AND DEFINITIONS

Asian Financial Crisis: This was a period of the worst financial crisis ever occurred in Southeast Asia. The crisis started first in Thailand in around mid. 1997 which led the Thai baht to collapse. Then, just in few months, the crisis also impacted several other countries in the region such as Indonesia and South Korea.

Community Business Credit: This is a credit scheme designed by the Indonesian government specifically dedicated to micro, small and medium enterprises and cooperatives, where they are unable to meet certain requirements set by banks (not yet bankable). In Indonesian, it is known as *Kredit Usaha Rakyat.*

Export-Led Growth: This is a trade or an industrialization policy adopted by many developing countries, including Indonesia, with the aim to speed up their industrialization process by exporting manufactured goods for which they have comparative advantages.

Global Financial Crisis: This was the financial crisis occurred in the period 2007–09, caused by a high default rate in the subprime home mortgage sector in the United States of America. The crisis is considered by many economists as the worst financial crisis the world ever experienced since the Great Depression of the 1930s.

Green Revolution: This term was first used in the late 1960s by former US Agency for International Development (USAID) director William Gaud, who noted the spread of the new technologies in agriculture that increased agricultural production worldwide, particularly in developing countries.

Informal Employment: It is employment which includes all jobs in enterprises or units of production considered as 'not-formal' or unregistered income generating activities.

New Order Era: It is the term coined by the second Indonesian President Suharto to characterize his regime as he came to power in 1966. The period before that, during the first Indonesian President Sukarno (1945-1966), is termed as "Old Order" era.

ENDNOTES

1 There are different ways to calculate the contributions of sectors to GDP growth. For Figure 4, the contributions of the three sectors are calculated as the followings. Supposed the GDP share of industry in 2012 is 14 percent and its output growth in 2013 (from 2012) is 100 percent. So, the GDP growth contribution of industry in 2013 is 14% x 100%. The same way of calculation for agriculture and services, and the sum of the GDP contributions of the three sectors is the GDP growth rate in 2013.

2 As explained before, there are different ways to calculate the contributions of sectors to GDP growth. For Figure 9, the contributions of the three sectors are calculated with the same way as for Figure 4; see endnote 1.

3 See endnote 1 for the way of calculating the contributions of sectors to GDP growth.

Chapter 20
Trade Openness and Unemployment in Transition Economies:
A Dynamic Heterogeneous Panel Data Analysis

Esin Kılıç
Eskişehir Osmangazi University, Turkey

Erol Kutlu
Anadolu University, Turkey

ABSTRACT

Liberalization of foreign trade and foreign exchange regimes of the countries in transition from planned economies to liberal economies, which are called transition economies in the literature, constitutes one of the crucial pillars of the process. The effect of foreign trade liberalization process on the workforce markets, however, has been a matter of ongoing dispute in the literature. For this reason, the long-term relationship between trade openness and unemployment in 17 transition economies between years 1998-2014 is researched in this study, using dynamic heterogeneous panel data analysis methods. As a result of the econometrical analysis, it has been found that there is a significant relationship between trade openness and the rate of unemployment and that trade openness has a reducing effect on unemployment.

INTRODUCTION

Transition economy is the technical term used for the economies in transition from centrally planned economy to liberal economy. Transition economies shift to an environment where the prices are determined by the free market instead of a central organization during the process of economic liberalization. In this process, removal of trade barriers, privatization of state-owned enterprises and trade liberalization policies will be applied. Though it may differ from country to country, this process either came to

DOI: 10.4018/978-1-5225-2008-5.ch020

fruition or is still going on in China, former Soviet Union countries, former Warsaw members and many other developing countries.

The Central and Eastern European countries and former Union of Soviet Socialist Republics (USSR) countries take the dominant place in the International Monetary Fund (IMF) classification of transition economies. These countries and their classifications are as follows (Güler, 2012):

1. Central and Eastern European States: Albania, Bulgaria, Croatia, Czechia, Macedonia, Hungary, Romania, Slovak Republic, and Slovenia,
2. Baltic States: Estonia, Latvia, and Lithuania,
3. Former Soviet Union States: Russian Federation, Azerbaijan, Belarus, Armenia, Georgia, Kazakhstan, Kyrgyzstan, Moldova, Uzbekistan, Tajikistan, Turkmenistan, and Ukraine.

When the emergence process of transition economies - the definition and scope of which are given above – is analyzed; it can be seen that the breakthrough in Poland (the workers' strike in 1988, the change of the system of government and Poland's break from the influence area of the Soviet Union) had evolved into a gigantic movement. Following this example; other European countries' progress in the same direction, some with bloody conflicts (Romania) and some with peaceful means (Hungary), achieved similar results and they also switched to the market economy after the collapse of communism. The process did not stop there. With the Baltic States gaining their independence, which can be counted as European states rather than Soviet Republics, the Soviet Union became a federal structure. The final link in this chain was the establishment of the Commonwealth of Independent States (CIS), which took the place of the USSR after the gathering of the presidents of Russia, Kazakhstan, and Belarus on December 30, 1991. The CIS also fell apart later, and the member states applied for integration with the western institutions, just like the former members of the Warsaw Pact. All the economies which involved in this process are termed transition economies in the literature (Kutlu & Eşkinat, 2014, p. 197).

International institutions –World Trade Organization (WTO), IMF and the World Bank in particular – have engaged in promotive practices and gave training services and technical assistance in order to liberalize the foreign trade and exchange regimes of the transition economies which have adopted the western economy models (Seyidoğlu, 2015, pp. 231, 850). The purpose of these aids was the transition of the countries to an open market. These practices achieved significant results, as all of the transition countries adopted the free market economy model and started using the arguments of this model.

With the liberalization of foreign trade, which is one of the most important arguments of this model, a rapid increase was observed in the trade openness ratios of the transition economies. A country's openness ratio is generally calculated as the ratio of the foreign trade volume to the GDP. Another indicator that approximates trade openness is the foreign dependency ratio, which is the ratio of exports to the GDP. In the most general sense, it can be said that the higher these ratios are, the more open that economy is. To improve the trade openness, barriers to foreign trade -customs duties, quotas, non-tariff barriers, etc.- must be removed.

The liberalization process in the transition economies (especially the ones that are focused in this chapter), which has started post-1990, is going on rapidly. Though the economic growth of these countries varies, it is observed that the growth is bigger than the pre-1990 period. The growth rates, which were usually negative at the start of the 1990s, were seen to improve as the result of the rapid foreign expansion efforts in the second half of the 1990s and have passed the average rate of 5% before the last global economic crisis. Economic growth is associated with the increase in employment in the economic literature

(Okun's Law). With the economic growth expanding the labor markets during the periods when these countries follow open trade policies, significant drops took place in the unemployment rates. However, the theoretical and empirical literature on the relationship between trade openness and unemployment is open to debate at the point of the existence of this relationship and the direction of it, if it exists.

This chapter studies the relationship between trade openness and unemployment, using data from 17 transition economies between the period of 1998 and 2014 with dynamic panel data analysis methods. The chapter firstly touches upon the theoretical and empirical literature on the trade openness – unemployment relationship. Then, the variables and data analysis methods of the model used in the econometric analysis are introduced. The final part of the chapter covers the econometric analysis results and their interpretations.

TRADE OPENNESS AND UNEMPLOYMENT

The basis of the relationship between foreign trade and unemployment lies at the Heckscher-Ohlin Theory, which is based on David Ricardo's Comparative Advantages Theory. This theory suggests that the primary determinant of the foreign trade is different factor endowments of countries. The theory, which is also called the factor endowment theory, argues that foreign trade will be profitable when labor-abundant countries export labor-intensive products and the countries that have more capital export capital-intensive products. When a labor-abundant country opens up to foreign trade, the labor demand in the labor-intensive sectors will increase since most of the exports will be carried by these sectors. Because of this, the Heckscher-Ohlin Theory may be interpreted in a way that trade openness has a positive impact on the employment of the countries which have abundant labor.

The Heckscher-Ohlin Theory uses the assumption of full employment. By relaxing this assumption, Brecher (1974), studied the effects of trade liberalization on welfare and unemployment for a small country with a minimum wage (this practice may also cause unemployment in the economy) in a two-country and two-commodity Heckscher-Ohlin model. This study, in accordance with the deduction of Heckscher-Ohlin Theory, found that unemployment in the labor-abundant countries will decrease and unemployment in the capital-abundant countries, however, increases after trade openness. Another assumption of the Heckscher-Ohlin Theory is that there is perfect competition in the labor and good markets. Besides, Brecher's results on the trade liberalization-unemployment relationship are found under the assumption of a small country. Davis (1998), on the other hand, researched the effects of the trade flows between the flexible-wage U.S. and rigid-wage Europe (which are large enough to affect the terms of foreign trade) on unemployment within the frame of Brecher (1974) model. According to the results of this study, "in a benchmark case, a move from autarky to free trade doubles European unemployment" (Davis, 1998, p. 478). These studies put forth the connection between the findings of Heckscher-Ohlin Theory on the trade-unemployment relationship with the assumptions of the model.

Today, contrary to the implication of the Heckscher-Ohlin Theory, unemployment rates in the labor-abundant countries that have adopted a free trade regime are observed to be higher than the unemployment rates of capital-abundant countries. Krueger (1983, p. 9) states that the relationship between trade regime and unemployment can arise in three different ways:

1. A trade strategy with a rapid economic growth due to the optimal allocation of resources in the whole economy can raise the employment rates.

2. Whether an import substitution or export oriented strategy is followed, a trade strategy in which the growth in the labor-intensive sector is high will provide a larger increase in the employment rates.
3. The foreign trade regime in effect can change the capital/labor ratio and production techniques in the industries. For example, when a rigid import substitution policy on capital goods is followed, employment may be affected negatively because of the increase in the capital intensity.

This three-alternative relationship of Krueger (1983) also puts forth the uncertainty of the presence and the direction of trade openness-employment relationship. Carrere, Fugazza, Olarreaga, and Robert-Nicoud (2014), on the other hand, empirically shows the ambiguity of the trade-unemployment relationship using panel data analysis with the data from 98 different countries in the period of 1995-2009. According to the findings of the study, the determinant of the trade-unemployment relationship is the covariance between comparative advantage and sector level labor market frictions. In the case where the covariance is positive, trade liberalization has a reducing effect on unemployment.

The results of empirical studies on the trade-unemployment relationship in the literature also differ from one another. Especially, the studies on developed countries have found that trade openness reduces unemployment rates. Felbermayr, Prat, and Schmerer (2011) have found, in a panel data analysis they conducted on 20 OECD countries using different measures of trade openness, that a 10% increase in trade openness reduces unemployment by about 1%, directly by itself and indirectly by the effect of total factor productivity. Gözgör (2014), who has conducted an econometric analysis of the trade openness-unemployment relationship in the G7 countries using four different trade openness measures, has found that foreign trade openness reduces unemployment in the developed countries. However, studies on the U.S. generally find that trade increases unemployment. For example, Sachs, Shatz, Deardorff, and Hall (1994) has reached the conclusion that foreign trade increases skilled labor employment while decreasing unskilled labor employment. The findings of Janiak (2006) show, considering labor market with search frictions, that foreign trade in America creates job destruction rather than job creation. Pierce and Schott (2012) have stated that the sharp fall in the employment rates of the U.S. manufacturing sector that started in 2001 was the result of the lifting of import tariffs applied on China. Autor, Dorn, and Hanson (2013), from their analysis of the period of 1990-2007, have also reached the conclusion that 1/4 of the fall in the employment rates of the U.S. manufacturing sectors is because of the import substitution strategy of China.

The findings on the countries which have started their trade liberalization process later than the developed countries show that trade openness affects the labor demand rather negatively. Revenga (1997), states that the trade liberalization process in Mexico between 1985 and 1987 has reduced the industrial production and labor demand, resulting in a downside pressure on employment and wages. Moreira and Najberg (2000) have concluded that the trade openness process of the 1990-1997 period in Brazil, another country that is going through trade liberalization, has a low employment cost in the short term but high in the long term. Menezes-Filho and Muendler (2011) have also reached the conclusion that trade liberalization has increased unemployment in Brazil during the 1990s due to less workers employed in the comparative-advantage, and thus exporting, sectors than in the average businesses. Sandalcılar and Yalman (2012) have found in their econometric analysis on Turkey, which started its liberalization process in the 1980s, that the decrease in employment was the result of trade openness. Özel, Topkaya, and Kurt (2012) have concluded that there is no trade openness-unemployment relationship in the long run in Turkey, but that trade openness results in a decrease in the unemployment rates in the short run.

Though the trade openness-unemployment relationship in different countries with varying development levels has been studied; it is remarkable that the investigation of this relationship in the transition economies has not found itself a notable place in the literature, since these countries have taken radical trade liberalization steps in relatively shorter periods. Because of this, the study on trade openness-unemployment relationship focuses on the transition economies in this chapter. The following section will cover the introduction of the data and the econometric model that will be used in the research of this relationship in transition economies.

DATA AND MODEL

This study researches the relationship between trade openness and unemployment in 17 transition economies using the annual data from the period of 1998-2014. The countries that are included in the study on the base of data availability are given in Table 1. Some other transition economies like Azerbaijan and Belarus are excluded from the analysis due to lack of data.

The general form of the econometric model used in the study is given in equation (1).

$$unemp_{it} = \beta_0 + \beta_1 open_{it} + \beta_2 growthrate_{it} + \beta_3 lnpop_{it} + \beta_4 tfp_{it} + u_{it} \quad (1)$$

The *i* subscript denotes the country and *t* subscript denotes the time. β_0 is the constant, and u_{it} is the error term. Trade openness, which is shown with *open* in the general form, will be included in the analysis with two different openness measures, nominal trade openness (*nto*) and real trade openness (*rto*). *nto* is reached by the ratio of the foreign trade volume (export + import) to the nominal GDP. The export and import data and the current GDP of the 17 transition economies used to reach the nominal trade openness figures are in current USD and have been obtained from World Development Indicator.

The most commonly used traditional openness measures in the literature are import/nominal GDP (import trade intensity), export/nominal GDP (export trade intensity), and import+export/nominal GDP (trade intensity that is shown with *nto* in this study). For instance, Jin (2000) included import trade intensity to the empirical model in his study on the openness-growth relationship in the Eastern Asia countries. Heid and Larch (2012), Sandalcılar and Yalman (2012), Özel et al. (2012), Türedi (2013), Menyah, Nazlıoğlu, and Wolde-Rufael (2014), and Neogi (2016) are some of the recent studies that trade intensity is used as a measure of openness in econometric analysis. Yanıkkaya (2003), on the other hand, has used various trade liberalization measures like average tariff rates together with trade shares,

Table 1. Sample of countries

Baltics	Central Europe	CIS	Southeast Europe	Central Asia
Estonia	Czechia	Moldova	Bulgaria	Armenia
Latvia	Hungary	Russia	Croatia	Kazakhstan
Lithuania	Poland	Ukraine	Romania	Kyrgyz Republic
	Slovak Republic			
	Slovenia			

export shares, and import shares in GDP when studying the relationship between trade liberalization and economic growth. Alcalá and Ciccone (2001), however, have shown that when the demand for non-tradable goods is inelastic, the expected increase in the productivity of tradable goods via foreign trade may lower the nominal trade openness of the country concerned, since this increase in productivity may increase the relative prices of non-tradable goods. Accordingly, using *nto* as a trade openness measure in the econometric analysis may be misleading. Alcalá and Ciccone (2001, p. 614) propose the use of real openness rate which is calculated as import ($)+export ($)/GDP (purchasing power parity $) instead of nominal openness rate, in order to eliminate the relative differences in the price of non-tradable goods among various countries. Because of this, *rto* is used as a second measure of trade openness in the study. Gözgör (2014) also included real openness as a trade openness measure into the econometric model along with the nominal openness variable when researching the relationship between trade openness and unemployment in the G7 countries.

Data for unemployment rate, which is shown with *unemp* in the model, annual GDP growth rate (*growthrate*) and population (*pop*) used as control variables are obtained from World Bank World Development Indicator. Unemployment rate estimated by International Labor Organization (ILO) is calculated as the ratio of the unemployed people searching for work to the 15+ active population. The population variable takes place in the model in a logarithmic form.

Data for total factor productivity (*tfp*), another control variable used in the study, is obtained from Penn World Tables 9.0 and are created by Feenstra, Inklaar, and Timmer (2015). Feenstra et al. (2015, p. 3166) state that the values obtained by the ratio of the observed differences in real GDP between the countries to the Törnqvist quantity index of factor endowments[1] are significant measures for the productivity differences between countries. The total factor productivity value of the U.S. (at current PPPs) in the data created by Feenstra et al. (2015) is 1. In other words, the total factor productivity value is the relative productivity of a given country compared to the U.S., and thus is suitable for the comparisons between the countries in question.

The descriptive statistics for the data sets of the variables used in the study are given in Table 2.

Theoretical expectation regarding the sign of the β_2, which is the coefficient of the independent variable of *growthrate*, is negative – as pointed out by Okun's Law. In periods when economic growth is limited, the low economic growth will have an increasing effect on the unemployment rate since the demand for labor also decreases. An increase in population will also increase the unemployment rate, in a case where labor participation rate also increases with the population and the economy cannot create sufficient new job opportunities. Thus, the potential expectation for the sign of the β_3 coefficient will also be negative.

Table 2. Descriptive statistics

Variables	Obs	Mean	Std. Dev.	Min	Max
unemp	289	10.55536	5.027036	3.400000	35.90000
nto	289	104.2284	31.89762	48.43506	183.4276
rto	289	53.02816	29.86595	12.96299	127.4287
growthrate	289	3.725462	4.757814	-14.81416	14.04080
lnpop	289	15.88195	1.221894	14.08900	18.81050
tfp	289	0.527102	0.168827	0.157260	0.944424

There is not a clear theoretical expectation regarding the sign of the β_4, coefficient of the *tfp* variable, the coefficient may be negative or positive. In Pissarides and Vallanti (2007), where the effects of total factor productivity increase on steady-state unemployment are examined, it is stated that the direction of the relationship between total factor productivity and unemployment depends on the new technologies used in the new job opportunities created in the economy. The net effect of total factor productivity on unemployment is determined by the greater one of the following: "capitalization effect", in which the transition to a new technology creates an increase in labor demand, and "creative destruction effect", which takes place when the new technology cannot be implemented and thus reducing the demand for labor (Pissarides and Vallanti, 2007, p. 608). In a case where the sign of *tfp* coefficient is negative (positive), the conclusion will be that the effect of an increase in total factor productivity will reduce (increase) the unemployment rate.

The sign of β_1, coefficient of trade openness variable (*open*), and its statistical significance constitute the basic question of this study.

PANEL UNIT ROOT TEST AND METHODOLOGY

When the trade openness-unemployment relationship in 17 transition economies is researched in this chapter, a balanced panel data set that is composed of observations of the variables in the model between the years of 1998-2014 is used. In order to determine the method of the study using the relevant data set, first, it is needed to establish that whether the data set contains unit root or not. There are many panel unit root tests for this purpose, such as Harris and Tzavalis (1999), Maddala and Wu (1999), Hadri (2000), Levin, Lin and Chu, (2002), and Im, Pesaran, and Shin (2003). The common point of these tests, which are called first generation panel unit root tests, is that they use the hypothesis of cross-sectional independency as their base. However, second generation panel unit root tests that take into consideration cross-sectional dependence, defined as "the interaction between cross-sectional units" in Baltagi, Feng, and Kao (2012, p. 164), have been developed recently. Because of this, cross section dependence tests have been applied to the panel data set of this study before executing the panel unit root test.

For the purpose of testing the cross-sectional dependence of the data for the variables in the model, the general form of which was given in equation (1), CD test by Pesaran (2004) and bias-corrected scaled LM test by Baltagi et al. (2012) have been used. These cross section dependence tests are based on the correlation tests between error terms. In other words, these tests examine cross section dependence by testing the hypothesis of H_0: $Corr(u_{it}, u_{jt}) = \rho_{ij} = 0, i \neq j$ when the panel data model is $y_{it} = \alpha_i + \beta_i x_{it} + u_{it}$, where, *i* denotes cross sections, *t* denotes time-periods, and x_{it} denotes (k×1) explanatory variables vector. These tests may be applied on the error terms obtained from the model and also variables in the model.

The Pesaran (2004) CD test statistic is developed using the average of the correlation coefficient ρ_{ij}'s, as shown in equation (2).

$$CD = \sqrt{\frac{2}{N\left(N-1\right)}\sum_{i=1}^{N-1}\sum_{j=i+1}^{N} T_{ij}\hat{\rho}_{ij}} \rightarrow N\left(0,1\right) \tag{2}$$

The test statistic for Baltagi et al. (2012) bias-corrected scaled LM test is as in equation (3):

$$LM = \sqrt{\frac{1}{N\left(N-1\right)}}\sum_{i=1}^{N-1}\sum_{j=i+1}^{N}(T_{ij}\hat{\rho}_{ij}^{2}-1)-\frac{N}{2T-1}\rightarrow N\left(0,1\right) \quad (3)$$

The null hypothesis for both tests is the existence of cross-sectional independency. Cross section dependence test results are given in Table 3.

According to the Pesaran CD and bias-corrected scale LM test results in Table 3, the null hypothesis is rejected for all the variables in equation (1). Thus, a unit root test that takes into consideration the existence of cross section dependence is also included into the study. Before deciding the methodology to be used in the research, panel unit root testing procedure is conducted using Maddala and Wu (1999) first generation unit root test and Pesaran (2007) cross-sectionally augmented Dickey-Fuller (CADF) second generation unit root test.

Pesaran (2007), developed a panel unit root test that takes into consideration the cross-sectional dependence, including the unobserved common effect into the Augmented Dickey-Fuller (ADF) unit root test model that will be applied for each cross section. The ADF unit root test model to be applied for each cross-section i in the panel dataset is given in equation (4).

$$\Delta y_{it} = \alpha_{i} + \beta_{i}y_{i,t-1} + u_{it},\ i = 1,2,\ldots,N; t = 1,2,\ldots,T \quad (4)$$

Pesaran (2007, p. 268) divides the error term u_{it} in the model into two parts: "unobserved common effect" and "individual-specific error". Equation (4) is rewritten in equation (5), this time f_t showing the unobserved common effect and ε_{it} showing the individual-specific error.

$$\Delta y_{it} = \alpha_{i} + \beta_{i}y_{i,t-1} + \theta f_{t} + \varepsilon_{it} \quad (5)$$

For the unobserved common effect in equation (5), when u_{it} is serially uncorrelated, cross section mean ($\bar{y}_{t-1}$) and its lagged values are used as proxy and a CADF model, which can be estimated by ordinary least squares (OLS) and shown in equation (6), is developed in Pesaran (2007, p. 269).

Table 3. Cross section dependence test results

Variables	Pesaran CD Test	Prob.	Bias-Corrected Scaled LM Test	Prob.
uemp	11.35288	0.000	25.49554	0.000
nto	18.00733	0.000	49.92684	0.000
rto	58.03968	0.000	145.8461	0.000
growthrate	31.98606	0.000	48.57946	0.000
lnpop	7.267984	0.000	128.8380	0.000
tfp	11.27152	0.000	73.53696	0.000

$$\Delta y_{it} = \alpha_i + \beta_i y_{i,t-1} + \delta_i \overline{y}_{t-1} + \gamma_i \Delta \overline{y}_t + \varepsilon_{it} \tag{6}$$

The null hypothesis for the CADF panel unit root test is $\beta_i = 0$ for all i, and the alternative hypothesis is H_1: $\beta_i < 0, i = 1, 2, \ldots, N_1$ or H_1: $\beta_i = 0, i = N_1 + 1, N_1 + 2, \ldots, N$.

Maddala and Wu (1999) unit root test is a non-parametric Fisher-type test and uses the P values developed by combining probability (p) values from the unit root test applied to each cross section. The calculation of the P test statistic, where N denotes the number of the cross-section, is given in equation (7).

$$P = -2\sum_{i=1}^{N} \ln p_i \rightarrow \chi^2(2N) \tag{7}$$

The advantage of this test is that it lets us individually determine the lag lengths in the Augmented Dickey-Fuller test that is used to obtain the p_i values for each cross section and that it is also suitable for the unbalanced panel data sets. In this test, the null hypothesis, each individual cross-section has a unit root, is tested against the alternative hypothesis of some cross sections without unit root.

In this study, the existence of unit root for the variables in the panel data set are tested with both trend and no trend models, using the Maddala and Wu and Pesaran CADF tests. Table 4 shows the unit root test results obtained using these two methods.

Table 4 shows that, according to Maddala and Wu unit root test applied using a trend model, all the variables are stationary, in other words, they do not have a unit root. No-trend model test resulted with all variables stationary, except for the *rto* variable. However, according to the cross section dependence test results in Table 3, cross-sectional dependence exists for all the variables in the model. According to the Pesaran CADF test results that take this into consideration, the no-trend model shows that all variables except *rto* are stationary. However, the trend model gives us different results. Graphs of the variables are used in order to determine which of the two models is suitable, and it was seen that the variables

Table 4. Unit root test results

Variables	Model I Maddala and Wu (No Trend)	Model II Maddala and Wu (Trend)	Model III Pesaran (CADF) (No Trend)	Model IV Pesaran (CADF) (Trend)	Unit Root
unemp	76.240***	102.532***	-1.735**	-0.228	I(1)
Δunemp	275.118***	209.386***	-8.406***	-6.219***	
nto	64.801**	90.433***	-3.198***	-0.495	I(1)
Δnto	246.381***	179.252***	-6.380***	-3.946***	
rto	18.962	57.187*	0.554	3.473	I(1)
Δrto	295.178***	204.224***	-7.828***	-6.212***	
growthrate	108.248***	96.046***	-4.437***	-1.319*	I(0)
lnpop	113.156***	168.376***	-2.346***	-3.396***	I(0)
tfp	26.246	50.398**	-2.064**	0.849	I(1)
Δtfp	216.012***	150.346***	-7.797***	-5.017***	

Note:*, **, and *** indicate significance at 10%, ** at 5% and *** at 1%.

unemp, nto, rto, and *tfp* have a significant trend. Thus, it is concluded that *growthrate* and *lnpop* are variables without unit root according to Pesaran CADF test results. The variables *unemp, nto, rto*, and *tfp* are non-stationary. When the test is repeated taking first differences of the variables with a unit root, all the variables became stationary. As a result, it can be said that the *growthrate* and *lnpop* variables are level stationary (I(0)), while other variables are first difference stationary (I(1)).

Because some of the variables are level stationary while others are first difference stationary, the study uses heterogeneous panel data methods as for the research. Pesaran and Smith (1995) and Pesaran, Shin, and Smith (1997, 1999) provide dynamic heterogeneous panel data methods that can be applied in panel data sets that I(0) and I(1) regressors are both a part of. These methods are based on the calculation of long term parameters and the speed of adjustment toward equilibrium, i. e. error correction term, using the appropriate autoregressive distribution lag (ARDL(p, q_1, ..., q_k)) model. Pesaran and Shin (1998) show that whether the variables are I(0) or I(1) is not important in the application of ARDL technique.

Where i is cross-section unit, t is time, and X_{it} is (k×1) explanatory variable matrix, the basic form of ARDL (p, q_1, ..., q_k) model is given in equation (8) (Blackburne & Frank, 2007, p. 198).

$$y_{it} = \mu_i + \sum_{j=1}^{p} \theta_{ij} y_{i,t-j} + \sum_{j=0}^{q} \gamma_{ij}^{'} X_{i,t-j} + \varepsilon_{it}, i = 1,2,\ldots,N, t = 1,2,\ldots,T \quad (8)$$

In equation (8), μ_i denotes group-specific effect and γ_{ij} denotes (k×1) coefficient vector. In the case where the variables in equation (8) are cointegrated, error terms obtained for each i cross section unit become I(0). This means that the short-run dynamics of the variables in the error correction model are affected from the deviations from equilibrium. Error correction form of equation (8) can be written as in equation (9).

$$\Delta y_{it} = \mu_i + \varphi_i \left(y_{i,t-1} - \delta_i^{'} X_{it} \right) + \sum_{j=1}^{p-1} \theta_{ij}^{*} \Delta y_{i,t-j} + \sum_{j=0}^{q-1} \gamma_{ij}^{*'} \Delta X_{i,t-j} + \varepsilon_{it}, i = 1,2,\ldots,N, t = 1,2,\ldots,T \quad (9)$$

Here

$$\varphi_i = -\left(1 - \sum_{j=1}^{p} \theta_{ij} \right);$$

$$\delta_i = \sum_{j=0}^{q} \gamma_{ij} \,/\, (1 - \sum_{k} \theta_{ik});$$

$$\theta_{ij}^{*} = - \sum_{h=j+1}^{p} \theta_{ih}, j = 1,2,\ldots,p-1;$$

$$\gamma_{ij}^{*} = -\sum_{h=j+1}^{q} \gamma_{ih}, j = 1,2,\ldots,q-1.$$

φ_i, denotes the speed of adjustment toward equilibrium. In the case where $\varphi_i \neq 0$, it can be argued that there is a long-term relationship and it is expected for φ_i to result negative, indicating that the variables are directed toward long-term equilibrium (Blackburne & Frank, 2007, pp. 198-199).

In this study, the error correction model is estimated by using dynamic fixed effect (DFE), Mean Group (MG) developed by Pesaran and Smith (1995) and pooled mean group (PMG) developed by Pesaran et al. (1997, 1999) estimators. The maximum likelihood estimation method is used in all of these methods.

DFE carries the restrictions of all short-term and long-term coefficients (except for intercept) and the speed of adjustment toward equilibrium being the same for all cross-sections. MG, on the other hand, is a method that calculates the unweighted mean of coefficients that are estimated using separate estimations for each cross section in the panel dataset (Pesaran and Smith, 1995). This method lets both the short term and the long term coefficients to be heterogeneous for a cross section. In order to obtain consistent estimation, the data set for each cross section must be large enough. PMG lets the short term coefficients and error variances to be determined cross-section specific, but this method is limited in the way that long-term coefficients must be identical. "There are often good reasons to expect the long-run equilibrium relationships between variables to be similar across groups, due to budget or solvency constraints, arbitrage conditions or common technologies influencing all group in a similar way" (Pesaran et al., 1999, p. 621). When the short-term coefficients are allowed to be heterogeneous, a different dynamic specification can be established for each cross-section, so PMG is an intermediate estimator that includes the pooling procedure in DFE and the averaging procedure in MG. All three estimators are used for estimating error correction form of equation (1), in order to compare the results obtained from the econometric analysis conducted to establish the trade openness-unemployment relationship in the transition economies.

ECONOMETRIC ANALYSIS

In this chapter, where the relationship between trade openness and unemployment in the transition economies is researched, two alternative models that include either nominal trade openness (*nto*) or real trade openness (*rto*) as measures of openness are used. The control variables included in both models are the same. The models are estimated in ARDL (1,1,1,1,1) form. ARDL dynamic panel model specification was selected according to Akaike Information Criterion (AIC). For the model where *nto* is included as the measure of trade openness, results obtained using the PMG, MG, and DFE estimators are shown in Table 5.

Error correction term resulted negative and significant at %1 level, according to the estimation results obtained by using all three estimators in Table 5. This implies that the variables in the model show a return to a long-run equilibrium. Short term results indicate that the coefficient of $\Delta growthrate$ variable is positive for all three models and statistically significant. A significant relationship between other variables and unemployment in the short term could not be found. In the long term relationships, the results of estimations using different estimators vary from each other. According to the DFE estimation

Table 5. PMG, MG and DFE estimation results (Trade openness measure: Nominal trade openness)

Dependent Variable: unemp	PMG		MG		DFE	
Variables	**Long Run**	**Short Run**	**Long Run**	**Short Run**	**Long Run**	**Short Run**
Error Correction		-0.179*** (0.027)		-0.575*** (0.094)		-0.285*** (0.042)
Δnto		0.0323 (0.045)		0.018 (0.053)		-0.012 (0.016)
Δgrowthrate		0.095** (0.047)		0.061** (0.029)		0.127*** (0.029)
Δlnpop		-54.711 (39.986)		218.295 (154.346)		-43.353 (28.668)
Δtfp		-13.134 (17.026)		-2.769 (9.176)		5.925 (5.277)
cons		-34.228*** (5.401)		1351.608 (1009.44)		-121.214** (59.825)
nto	-0.134*** (0.0233)		0.606 (0.838)		-0.058** (0.027)	
growthrate	-1.512*** (0.207)		-0.607*** (0.183)		-0.978*** (0.198)	
lnpop	15.195 (12.737)		-65.742 (131.444)		28.804** (13.784)	
tfp	-32.059*** (5.849)		-152.114 (128.803)		-24.148*** (5.447)	
Hausman Test	$\chi^2(4)=4.56$ Prob=0.336					

Note:*, **, and *** indicate significance at 10%, ** at 5% and *** at 1%.

results, all coefficients of the variables included in the model are statistically significant. The coefficient of *lnpop* variable is positive while other variable coefficients are negative, and the coefficient signs are consistent with the theoretical expectations. MG estimations have found that the variables other than economic growth have no significant relationship with the unemployment rate in the long term and the coefficient signs also diverge from theoretical expectations. This situation may be because that the cross-section dimensions in the panel dataset are inadequate for an efficient MG estimation. PMG estimation results show that long-term *growthrate and tfp* coefficients are statistically significant at 1% level and have negative signs; thus, it can be said that the increases in economic growth and total factor productivity decrease the unemployment rate. The *lnpop* coefficient, while positive in accordance with theoretical expectations, is not statistically significant. The coefficient of the *nto* variable, which denotes nominal trade openness, is also found to be negative and statistically significant at 1% significance level. According to these results, it can be seen that there is a negative relationship between nominal trade openness and unemployment in the long run.

The Hausman test has been applied in order to determine which of the PMG and MG estimates is consistent (even if the coefficients estimated with MG found to be divergent from the theoretical expectations) since the PMG estimation is made under the restriction of the long-term coefficients being homogenous. When the Hausman test results show the existence of long run slope homogeneity, the

PMG estimator is consistent and efficient. The Hausman test is used to examine the null hypothesis that the coefficients obtained from PMG and MG estimators are equal. In the case of the null hypothesis being rejected (prob<0.05), the assumption that the long-term coefficients that are obtained for cross sections are homogenous becomes invalid, and the cross sections need to be modeled separately. The probability value for Hausman test statistic in Table 5 is 0.336, then the null hypothesis cannot be rejected, and the assumption of homogeneity is valid. Because of this, it can be said - based on the PMG and DFE estimates - that there is a significant and negative relationship between nominal trade-openness and unemployment in the long run for transition economies.

For robustness check, the estimation procedure is repeated by using real trade openness (*rto*) proposed by Alcalá and Ciccone (2001), instead of nominal trade openness (*nto*), in the model. The results are shown in Table 6.

The results in Table 6 show that the error correction terms estimated with all three estimators are negative and statistically significant, just like the previous model. As a result of the estimations, the coefficient of the $\Delta growthrate$ variable is also statistically significant at the significance level of 1%. The PMG estimation showed a weak relationship between *rto* and unemployment in the short run. Long run coefficients show that the PMG method has estimated statistically significant coefficients, which

Table 6. PMG, MG, and DFE estimation results (trade openness measure: real trade openness)

Dependent Variable: unemp	PMG		MG		DFE	
Variables	Long Run	Short Run	Long Run	Short Run	Long Run	Short Run
Error Correction		-0.248*** (0.034)		-0.651*** (0.097)		-0.301*** (0.042)
Δrto		-0.096* (0.056)		-0.651 (0.097)		-0.022 (0.019)
Δgrowthrate		0.142*** (0.035)		0.102*** (0.033)		0.119*** (0.026)
Δlnpop		-96.425* (52.486)		57.538 (108.601)		-42.373 (28.246)
Δtfp		-12.335 (15.119)		1.229 (8.400)		4.478 (5.241)
cons		-110.461*** (14.408)		1096.278 (842.041)		-103.509*** (60.634)
rto	-0.055*** (0.012)		-0.028 (0.134)		-0.061** (0.025)	
growthrate	-0.902*** (0.116)		-0.664** (0.312)		-0.873*** (0.181)	
lnpop	30.198*** (8.380)		-26.430 (103.304)		23.282* (13.146)	
tfp	-18.860*** (3.490)		2.721 (34.851)		-18.229*** (5.198)	
Hausman Test	$\chi^2(4)=0.76$ Prob=0.944					

Note:*, **, and *** indicate significance at 10%, ** at 5% and *** at 1%.

are in accordance with theoretical expectations, at the significance level of 1%. The DFE estimation also results in statistically significant and theoretically expected coefficients for all variables. The MG estimator could not determine a long-term relationship between *rto* and *lnpop* and unemployment. Since the results from Hausman test, which is applied to test long run slope homogeneity, cannot reject the null hypothesis, the homogeneity assumption is valid, and the PMG estimator is efficient and consistent. As a result, the model that uses real trade openness as a trade openness measure also points to a significant and negative relationship between trade openness and unemployment in the long run.

CONCLUSION

The countries which are in transition from a centrally planned economic structure to a free market economy, termed transition economies in the literature, also take steps toward the liberalization of foreign trade during this process. With the barriers to foreign trade like tariffs and quotas eliminated, there has been a rapid increase in the trade openness rates, which can be calculated as the ratio of the foreign trade volume to the GDP, of these countries. It was also observed that the unemployment rates in these countries have fallen during the course of economic liberalization. But while the Heckscher-Ohlin Theory points to the potential reducing effects of foreign trade on unemployment, the existence of trade openness and unemployment relationship and the direction of this relationship, if it exists, are ambiguous in the light of the findings from the theoretical and empirical literature on the subject.

This chapter investigated the relationship between trade openness and unemployment using dynamic heterogeneous panel data analysis with the data of 17 transition economies between 1998 and 2014. Two trade openness measures, those being nominal and real openness rate, have been used in the econometric analysis. The analysis results obtained by using pooled mean group, mean group and dynamic fixed effect estimators point to a statistically significant and negative relationship between trade openness and unemployment in the long run. In other words, increases in these countries' trade openness rates have a reducing effect on the unemployment rates. This can be interpreted as the positive effect of commercial liberalization on the labor market of transition economies in terms of employment.

REFERENCES

Alcalá, F., & Ciccone, A. (2001). Trade and productivity. *The Quarterly Journal of Economics*, *119*(2), 613–646. doi:10.1162/0033553041382139

Autor, D. H., Dorn, D., & Hanson, G. H. (2013). The China syndrome: Local labor market effects of import competition in the United States. *The American Economic Review*, *103*(6), 2121–2168. doi:10.1257/aer.103.6.2121

Baltagi, B. H., Feng, Q., & Kao, C. (2012). A Lagrange multiplier test for cross-sectional dependence in a fixed effects panel data model. *Journal of Econometrics*, *170*(1), 164–177. doi:10.1016/j.jeconom.2012.04.004

Blackburne, E. F., & Frank, M. W. (2007). Estimation of nonstationary heterogeneous panels. *The Stata Journal*, *7*(2), 197–208.

Brecher, R. A. (1974). Minimum wage rates and the pure theory of international trade. *The Quarterly Journal of Economics*, *88*(1), 98–116. doi:10.2307/1881796

Carrere, C., Fugazza, M., Olarreaga, M., & Robert-Nicoud, F. (2014). *Trade in unemployment*. CEPR Discussion Paper, No. DP9916.

Davis, D. R. (1998). Does European unemployment prop up American wages? National labor markets and global trade. *The American Economic Review*, *88*, 478–494.

Feenstra, R. C., Inklaar, R., & Timmer, M. P. (2015). The next generation of the Penn World Table. *The American Economic Review*, *105*(10), 3150–3182. Retrieved from www.ggdc.net/pwt doi:10.1257/aer.20130954

Felbermayr, G., Prat, J., & Schmerer, H. J. (2011). Trade and unemployment: What do the data say? *European Economic Review*, *55*(6), 741–758. doi:10.1016/j.euroecorev.2011.02.003

Gözgör, G. (2014). The impact of trade openness on the unemployment rate in G7 countries. *The Journal of International Trade & Economic Development*, *23*(7), 1018–1037. doi:10.1080/09638199.2013.827233

Güler, E. (2012). Geçiş ekonomileri ve Yeni Kurumsal İktisat'ın yeniden yükselişi. *Doğuş Üniversitesi Dergisi*, *13*(1), 52–68.

Hadri, K. (2000). Testing for stationarity in heterogeneous panel data. *The Econometrics Journal*, *3*(2), 148–161. doi:10.1111/1368-423X.00043

Harris, R. D., & Tzavalis, E. (1999). Inference for unit roots in dynamic panels where the time dimension is fixed. *Journal of Econometrics*, *91*(2), 201–226. doi:10.1016/S0304-4076(98)00076-1

Heid, B., & Larch, M. (2012). Migration, trade and unemployment. *Economics: The Open-Access, Open-Assessment E-Journal*, *6*(4), 1-40. Retrieved from10.5018/economics-ejournal.ja.2012-4

Im, K. S., Pesaran, M. H., & Shin, Y. (2003). Testing for unit roots in heterogeneous panels. *Journal of Econometrics*, *115*(1), 53–74. doi:10.1016/S0304-4076(03)00092-7

Janiak, A. (2006). *Does trade liberalization lead to unemployment? Theory and some evidence*. Universite Libre de Bruxelles.

Jin, J. C. (2000). Openness and growth: An interpretation of empirical evidence from East Asian countries. *The Journal of International Trade & Economic Development*, *9*(1), 5–17. doi:10.1080/096381900362517

Krueger, A. O. (1983). *Trade and employment in developing countries: Synthesis and conclusions* (Vol. 3). University of Chicago Press.

Kutlu, E., & Eşkinat, R. (2014). *Dünya ekonomisi*. Ankara: Nisan Kitabevi.

Levin, A., Lin, C. F., & Chu, C. S. J. (2002). Unit root tests in panel data: Asymptotic and finite-sample properties. *Journal of Econometrics*, *108*(1), 1–24. doi:10.1016/S0304-4076(01)00098-7

Maddala, G. S., & Wu, S. (1999). A comparative study of unit root tests with panel data and a new simple test. *Oxford Bulletin of Economics and Statistics*, *61*(S1), 631–652. doi:10.1111/1468-0084.61.s1.13

Menezes-Filho, N. A., & Muendler, M. A. (2011). *Labor reallocation in response to trade reform (No. w17372)*. National Bureau of Economic Research. doi:10.3386/w17372

Menyah, K., Nazlıoğlu, S., & Wolde-Rufael, Y. (2014). Financial development, trade openness and economic growth in African countries: New insights from a panel causality approach. *Economic Modelling*, *37*, 386–394. doi:10.1016/j.econmod.2013.11.044

Moreira, M. M., & Najberg, S. (2000). Trade liberalisation in Brazil: Creating or exporting jobs? *The Journal of Development Studies*, *36*(3), 78–99. doi:10.1080/00220380008422629

Neogi, C. (2016). Productivity convergence and Asian trade blocks. In R. Das (Ed.), *Handbook of research on global indicators of economic and political convergence* (pp. 92–118). Hershey, PA: Business Science Reference. doi:10.4018/978-1-5225-0215-9.ch005

Özel, H. A., Topkaya, Ö., & Kurt, S. (2012). Ticari açıklık ve işsizlik ilişkisi: Türkiye örneği. *Kamu-İş*, *12*(4), 29–54.

Pesaran, M. H. (2004). *General diagnostic tests for cross section dependence in panels*. University of Cambridge, Faculty of Economics, Cambridge Working Papers in Economics, No. 0435.

Pesaran, M. H. (2007). A simple panel unit root test in the presence of cross-section dependence. *Journal of Applied Econometrics*, *22*(2), 265–312. doi:10.1002/jae.951

Pesaran, M. H., & Shin, Y. (1998). An autoregressive distributed-lag modelling approach to cointegration analysis. *Econometric Society Monographs*, *31*, 371–413.

Pesaran, M. H., Shin, Y., & Smith, R. P. (1997). *Pooled estimation of long-run relationships in dynamic heterogeneous panels*. University of Cambridge, Department of Applied Economics.

Pesaran, M. H., Shin, Y., & Smith, R. P. (1999). Pooled mean group estimation of dynamic heterogeneous panels. *Journal of the American Statistical Association*, *94*(446), 621–634. doi:10.1080/01621459.1999.10474156

Pesaran, M. H., & Smith, R. (1995). Estimating long-run relationships from dynamic heterogeneous panels. *Journal of Econometrics*, *68*(1), 79–113. doi:10.1016/0304-4076(94)01644-F

Pierce, J. R., & Schott, P. K. (2012). *The surprisingly swift decline of US manufacturing employment (No. w18655)*. National Bureau of Economic Research. doi:10.3386/w18655

Pissarides, C. A., & Vallanti, G. (2007). The impact of tfp growth on steady-state unemployment. *International Economic Review*, *48*(2), 607–640. doi:10.1111/j.1468-2354.2007.00439.x

Revenga, A. (1997). Employment and wage effects of trade liberalization: The case of Mexican manufacturing. *Journal of Labor Economics*, *15*(S3), S20–S43. doi:10.1086/209875

Sachs, J. D., Shatz, H. J., Deardorff, A., & Hall, R. E. (1994). Trade and jobs in US manufacturing. *Brookings Papers on Economic Activity*, *1994*(1), 1–84. doi:10.2307/2534630

Sandalcılar, A. R., & Yalman, İ. N. (2012). Türkiye'de dış ticaretteki serbestleşmenin işgücü piyasaları üzerindeki etkileri. *Eskişehir Osmangazi Üniversitesi İktisadi ve İdari Bilimler Dergisi*, *7*(2), 49–65.

Seyidoğlu, H. (2015). *Uluslararası iktisat teori politika ve uygulama*. Ankara: Güzem Can Yayınları.

Türedi, S. (2013). The effect of economic freedom on economic growth: A panel data analysis for 12 Islamic countries. *International Research Journal of Finance and Economics*, *107*, 154–162.

Yanıkkaya, H. (2003). Trade openness and economic growth: A cross-country empirical investigation. *Journal of Development Economics*, *72*(1), 57–89. doi:10.1016/S0304-3878(03)00068-3

KEY TERMS AND DEFINITIONS

Cross-Section Dependence: The interaction between the cross-sections in a panel data set.

Dynamic Fixed Effect (DFE): The estimator that is restricted by the short-term (except for intercept) and long-term coefficients and the speed of adjustment toward equilibrium being the same for all cross-sections.

Heterogeneous Panel Data Model: The panel data model where the coefficients in the model differ for each cross-section in the panel dataset.

Mean Group (MG): The estimator that calculates the unweighted average of the estimated coefficients, making separate estimations for each cross-section in the panel dataset.

Nominal Openness Rate: Trade openness measure that is the ratio of the sum of export and import of a country to its nominal GDP.

Pooled Mean Group (PMG): The estimator that lets the short term coefficients and error variances to be determined cross-section specific, but this method is limited by the long-term coefficients being identical.

Real Openness Rate: Trade openness measure that is the ratio of the sum of export and import of a country to its purchasing power parity GDP.

Transition Economies: The technical term for the economies that are in transition from a centrally planned economy to a liberal economy.

Unemployment: Presence of active population that is ready to work at the current wage level and looks for work but is not employed in an economy.

ENDNOTE

1 For further information, please see Feenstra et al. (2015).

Chapter 21
The Labor Market Effects of Immigration

Özlem İnanç-Tunçer
Işık University, Turkey

ABSTRACT

This chapter discusses the effects of immigration on the labor market of receiving countries, focusing on employment. The effect of immigration on the welfare of native population is an important issue in public debate. The common perception is, at least in the short run, because of immigration, unemployment rates would increase in the host countries, or that immigrants would depress wages of native workers. However, these perceptions do not find confirmation in the previous research on this literature. According to Jean and Jimenez (2011), the evidence is, at best, mixed. Although the magnitude of the impact depends on time and space, in general, results of the previous literature indicate that immigration has only very small or no effect on employment and wages of resident workers. The aim of this chapter is to provide an overview of immigration-labor market relation for different countries and time intervals with some significant policy implications with regards to state officials.

INTRODUCTION

Though the immigration phenomenon is regarded as a demographic one, reasons for both its emergence and consequences are intimately linked with the economy. Especially the possible unfavorable effects of immigration on the employment and wage rates of the native population are one of the much-debated subjects on economic theory. Research on the area is divided into three main areas: Concerns of the domestic residents that immigrant workers would increase competition for jobs, and therefore wages will fall and unemployment will rise, concern that immigrants would affect the social security system of the receiving country negatively, and finally the prospect of rising migration would affect wealth distribution (Dustmann & Glitz, 2005)

This chapter is about an analysis of the relation between the immigration and the labor market of receiving countries, specifically focusing on employment and wages.

DOI: 10.4018/978-1-5225-2008-5.ch021

There is vast empirical literature for the US and the other traditionally immigrant-receiving countries. There is a common perception that, at least in the short run, immigrants would substitute the native workers and increase unemployment in the host country, or that immigrant would accept lower wages than the natives, and therefore may create downward pressure on the wage rates of the native workers. These perceptions are one of the reasons for more conservative migration policies enforced by governments. However, these perceptions do not find confirmation in the previous research on this literature. According to Jean and Jimenez (2011), the evidence is, at best, mixed.

The effect of the immigrants on the welfare of the native population is a fundamental issue in the public debate. There is a vast empirical literature for the US and the other traditional countries of immigration. However, most European countries experienced large-scale immigration more recently than for countries like Australia, the US, or Canada. Moreover, the US and European experience are very different from each other since the composition and size of the immigrants are specific to the each receiving country. Therefore results of one empirical analysis are unlikely to hold for another one (Dustmann & Frattini, 2011).[1]

Immigration can affect the host countries' economy, through different channels, such as changes in output structure, technology and competitiveness, and complementarities and additions to the skill base (Dustmann, Frattini, & Glitz, 2007). For instance, immigration may affect the composition of goods and services produced in the economy and the structure of the labor market. Or immigration may alter the technology in a specific sector. (Gaston & Nelson, 2000; Hanson & Slaughter, 2002; Lewis, 2004; Gonzales & Ortega, 2007; Dustmann & Glitz, 2008). In addition to these, the impacts of immigration on the wage rates and employment levels of the native workers also depend on to what extent migrant's skills are complements or substitutes to the skills of native workers (Borjas, 1995). If the skills of migrants and native workers are substitutes, in the short-run, immigration may increase competition and decrease the wages in the labor market. Should, on the other hand, the skills of migrants be complementary to native workers, productivity in the economy shall increase, and this, in turn, may lead a rise in the wages of all workers. All of these cases shall have different impacts on the labor market.

Immigration affects the economy from both demand and supply sides. Therefore, in the medium-run and/or long-run, immigration may increase labor demand as well as labor supply. Migrants increase demand for goods and services, and immigration may lead higher level of investment in the long-run. Both of these effects create higher demand for labor and thus higher level of wages and employment. In other words, immigration may increase competition for existing jobs in the short- run, but it can also create new job opportunities for all workers in the entire economic system of the host country. Besides, immigrants fill vacancies for jobs that could not otherwise be filled by native workers. (Dustmann & Glitz, 2005). The speed to which investment and labor demand respond to immigration depends on the characteristics of the economy. For instance, during an economic recession, labor demand may respond to immigration more slowly.

However, although the effect of immigration on wages and unemployment is the most intensive research area on this phenomenon, measuring, testing and quantifying of these impacts are not easy tasks. Although there are some common trends in the empirical findings, still there is no consensus on the type and the size of the effect of immigration on the labor market. According to Dustmann and Glitz (2005), different empirical analysis technique requires different (and most of the time strong and debatable) assumptions, all methods may have some problems, and they may provide different results. Besides, unavailability of sufficient quality data would lead to imprecise and ambiguous empirical findings. Moreover, immigration differs across countries in terms of intensity, timing, skill, composition and duration, and, the impact of immigration-related with the economic and social conditions of the receiving economy.

The structure of the chapter is as follows: In Section 2, some background information will be provided. Then early literature in the area will be summarized. Section 3 summarizes the recent data on labor market for OECD and EU. In Section 4, the recent refugee flow from Syria will be discussed, mainly concentrating on the effect of refugee flow on the labor market in Turkey. Section 5 concludes.

THEORY AND LITERATURE REVIEW

Theoretical Approach

Economic theory offers more than one set of predictions since in theory, the impacts of immigration on the labor market contingent upon many factors, such as the composition and size of the immigrants, characteristics of the host economy, and the relation between the skills of migrants and native workers. Among the channels by which immigration has an impact on the economy of the host economy, the most analyzed one is through wages and unemployment.

In general, models that analyze effects of immigration on wages and employment are equilibrium models. These base models are helpful to gain important insight regarding the problem. However as these models start off in an equilibrium situation, their predictions may not necessarily hold in reality. Because data indicates that full employment equilibrium often not the situation in which immigration occurs. For instance, in Europe, periods of large immigration, such as immigration flow in 1960's to Germany, often characterized by a high number of vacancies in the receiving economy (Dustmann & Glitz, 2005).

Theoretical models differ from each other in assumptions on the number of goods produced and therefore in the flexibility of the economy to adapt through changes in the mix of outputs, and in the openness of the goods sector to trade and therefore in the extent to which output prices are set locally or on world markets.[2]

Early literature on the area assumes a closed economy, with homogenously skilled labor, and capital and labor are complementary to each other. Immigration will affect wages and unemployment in the host country if it *changes* the skill mix of the economy. If immigrants and native workers' skills are not differing from each other, there will be no impact on the labor market of the host economy. On the other hand, if labor is not homogeneous, different worker groups will be affected asymmetrically from the immigration; some workers might benefit, but some others might lose. Therefore skill groups of immigrants and how particular skill endowments differ from the resident population should be taken into account. One of the earliest study Grossmann (1982)'s idea that immigrants and natives might be different factors of production have been utilized in the more recent literature, which assumes that immigrants and natives are imperfect substitutes within skill groups (see Borjas, 2003; Ottaviano & Peri, 2006).

According to Borjas (1995), the impacts of immigration on wages and employment of domestic workers depend on migrant's skills endowment and whether their skills are complements or substitutes to the skills of native workers. If the skills of migrants and native workers are substitutes, in the short-run, immigration may increase competition in the labor market and depress the wages. Should, on the other hand, the skills of migrants be complementary to native workers, productivity in the economy shall increase, and this, in turn, may lead higher wages in the market. Similarly, Lalonde and Topel (1991) assumes immigrant and non-immigrant workers are different labor types. Therefore the distributional effects depend on the level of substitutability between the groups.

In the basic models, immigration affects the host country's labor market via increasing the labor supply. These models assume one industry, produces output using capital, skilled and unskilled labor both are completely inelastic to wages and constant returns to scale in the production. Immigrants are different in their skill composition from native workers; so after the immigration, the skill composition in the labor market of the host country will be changed. The elasticity of capital is an important determinant of the distribution of the gains and losses from migration. In this very basic model, the supply elasticity of capital is infinite; therefore capital owners will neither loses nor gains from the immigration. In the case of perfectly inelastic capital supply, the capital owners shall receive all of the gains from the immigration. If on the other hand, the supply of capital is between zero and one, then the elasticity of substitution among the immigrant workers and the natives will determine the distribution of the gains and the losses.

And finally, models assume that the labor market is at the equilibrium before the immigration.

If we consider the simplest form of the model with the perfectly elastic capital supply, results indicate that the immigration shall put downward pressure on the wages of native workers who are substitute to immigrants and increase wages of native workers who are complements to them, so gains and losses of migration are not uniformly distributed in the host country. For example, if all immigrants are unskilled labor, then the proportion of unskilled workers increases and the excess supply of unskilled workers will be created at the pre-immigration wage rate. This decreases the wages of unskilled workers but increases the wages of skilled workers due to relative scarcity. Since the wage rate for unskilled workers decreases, the demand for this type of labor will increase. Because both immigrants and natives are insensitive to wage rate[3], all unskilled workers will be employed and equilibrium restored but at a lower wage rate than the pre-immigration rate. In the short-run, absorption of the new workers and restoration of the equilibrium in the labor market will create changes in the wages and unemployment levels. In this scenario, skilled workers will gain, but unskilled workforce will lose. (Dustmann & Glitz, 2005).

In short, in this simple base model, the economy can be adjusted to the changes in the labor market composition only through changes in the wage structure. Whether effects on wages and employment are permanent or not depends on the structure of the receiving economy. More specifically it depends on the possibilities of the economy to adjust to the changes in the labor market condition. In such models with limited flexibility in a close economy, immigration will have long run wage and employment effect (Borjas, 1999; Card, 2001). Different assumptions about the structure of the host economy may lead to differences in the long run effects of immigration on labor market outcomes of the native workforce. In the simplest case, the economy produces one good only, and any adjustment to a change in the skill composition of the labor force immigration will be through wages. However, if the economy has more than one sector, then, adjustment to changes in skill composition of labor market can also take place through the changes in the relative composition of goods produced (Dustmann, Fabbri, & Preston, 2005; Dustmann & Preston, 2012; Altonji & Card, 1991; Borjas, 1995; Friedberg & Hunt, 1995; Borjas, 1999; Gaston & Nelson, 2000; Card, 2001; Glitz, 2006).

In these more realistic models, the economy is small and open with usually two sectors and each sector produces single good. One of the sectors produces unskilled labor intensive product and the other one use the skilled labor more intensively. Prices of tradable goods are set on the international markets. For simplicity, labor supply is assumed inelastic to wages.[4] Finally, assume that all immigrant workers are unskilled workers. In this case, those sectors produce the unskilled labor-intensive product may be expanded without affecting relative wages. Because, immigration will create unskilled labor surplus in the receiving economy and by holding the output ratio fixed, immigration will decrease the wage rate for unskilled labor as in one sector model. However, this will increase the profit in the sector that produces unskilled worker-intensive products. As a result, this sector will increase the level of production, which in turn increases demand for unskilled labor in the labor market. Wages of unskilled labor will then again increase. Although the proportion of unskilled labor increases due to immigration, composition of output in the economy will be adjusted and wages will be kept on the pre-immigration level. In such an economy, in contrast to the simple one-sector model, there will be no wage effects and also no welfare effects in the long run.

Under the assumption of continuous production in all traded goods sector in equilibrium, while the immediate effect of immigration is a decrease in the wages of unskilled labor, in the long- run they will back to pre-immigration levels. In other words, the long-run effects of immigration will be seen in the output mix, not on wages. This is called "hypothesis of factor price insensitivity" by Leamer and Levinshon (1995). In the literature of immigration, this situation is referred as the "structural hypothesis, meaning that the immigration changes the industry structure in the host economy, rather than the wage structure (Dustmann & Glitz, 2005).

To sum up, the size of the traded good sector, and the flexibility of the economy are important determinants of the effect of immigration on the host economy's labor market outcome. If the economy is flexible enough and its traded goods sector is large and heterogeneous, employment and wages may be insensitive to immigration, at least in the long run, because the impact of immigration on employment and wages is absorbed by changes in the traded goods composition. However, if the economy is less flexible and traded good sector is not heterogeneous enough to absorb the changes caused by immigration, the long-run impact of immigration on the labor market will be larger (Kuhn & Wooton, 1991; Hanson & Slaughter, 2002; Gaston & Nelson, 2000, 2001). Despite, in the short-run, disequilibria can exist, and wages might be affected, in the long-run, wage rate shall return to its pre-immigration level since lower wages lead to positive profits being earned in sectors using intensively labor types which become cheaper, and as a result, expand the level of production and labor demand.

According to the analysis of labor market and economy in general, conditions in the United States are more flexible than European countries. Angrist and Kugler (2003) argue that immigration has a greater negative impact on the employment level of the less flexible economies and parallel to this, findings of the previous literature indicate that the impact of immigration on wages and employment are stronger in European countries than the United States. Many studies in the literature suggest that in the US, adjustment of the economy restored through the changes in the output composition

Alternatively, economies can adjust through technology, by adopting technologies that the relatively more abundant type of labor is used more intensively. Lewis (2004) provides empirical evidence for his hypothesis for the US.

Empirical Approach

Empirical works in the area utilize different approaches in order to evaluate the effects of immigration on the level of employment and wages in the host countries. The prevalent approach for estimating such models is the "spatial correlations" approach (Borjas, 1999). In this approach, the host country is divided into two spatial units, and only one of these areas receives immigrant workers. Then the average wages of the native workforce in both units are computed before and after immigration and explain differences in wages by differences in immigrant population.

Nevertheless, there exist some problems related to the spatial correlations approach. First of all, in order to build metrics for the regional concentration of immigrants, spatial information is necessary. Although typical studies regress employment (or wages) of natives in a relative quantity of immigrants, immigrant influxes are the outcome of economic decisions. Putting it the other way around, levels of the relative quantities of immigrants and levels of labor market turnaround might be spatially correlated due to some other common fixed effects, such as the level of economic welfare of the area, or historical settlement choices of prior immigrants from the same countries. If this is the case, spatial correlation approach will show a relation between the variables of interest, even in the absence of a real correlation. In order to alleviate this problem, models are estimated by using "fixed effect" technique; either by estimating the relation in "differences" or by using "within group" estimation technique which is tantamount to incorporating a whole set of dummy variables into the model for the each geographical units.

Another problem regarding with the spatial correlations approach is measurement error and may occur due to a small sample size. In contrast to the first problem, it may cause finding no effect even when one indeed exists. The instrumental variable technique may offer a remedy for this problem.

Simultaneity is another problem on the spatial correlations approach. Although models aim to explain the level (or changes) in the labor market outcomes for natives by the level (or changes) in the relative size of immigrants, the directionality of causality between immigrant influxes and labor market turnarounds is not limpid. Since immigrants tend to go those areas with high level of wages and/or welfare level (Zachariadis, 2012), it is not only that immigration cause changes in the outcomes in labor market of host countries, but also the labor market outcomes cause immigrant inflows. This problem leads to an upwardly biased estimate of the model. As for the measurement problem, the instrumental variable technique may offer a solution to the simultaneity problem. In literature, pre-existing immigrant concentrations from the same source country is the most preferred instrument.

The last but not the least, because immigration depresses the wages, there may be an outflow of native workers from the spatial units. If this is the case, then estimated coefficient will underestimate the effects of immigration on the native workforce. Adding a number of workers that are moved from the receiving units directly to a model can be a solution. But since native worker outflow may be related with shocks to current economic variables, this may create simultaneity problem. Therefore instrumental variable technique is needed. Unlike to abovementioned simultaneity problem, there is no clear instrument for that. Generally lagged value is preferred.

The outflow of native workers due to immigration has been discussed in many researches in US literature. Results conflict; according to Borjas (1999), Frey (1995, 1996), and Filer (1992) argue that this is a serious issue in the US labor market. However, Card and di Nardo (2000), and Card (2001) claim the opposite.

Hatton and Tani (2005) analyze the same issue for the UK labor market by using internal migration information. Authors study net internal migration between eleven regions of Britain over two decades and find consistently negative displacement effects, yet their magnitude and significance vary. The effects are stronger in the regions where immigration from abroad is concentrated. Authors conclude that internal migration is one of the mechanisms by which regional labor markets adjust to immigrant shocks. Wage and employment effects of immigration may not be observed at the local level if native workers move out of regions due to immigration then but the effect may still be important for the entire economy.

There are many papers in the literature that use spatial correlations approach in order to estimate the effect of immigration on the labor market outcomes of the cost country. One of the most influential studies in this area, Card (1990) analyzes the effect of the Cuban immigration (Mariel Boatlift event) to the US unskilled labor force. Altonji and Card (1991), Lalolende and Topel (1991), Card (2001), Peri (2008), and Peri and Sparber (2008) are another examples of the literature that utilize the spatial correlation approach.

Simulation-based approach and the skill cell correlation approach are two other methods that are used by researchers in this area. The simulation-based approach creates a counterfactual simulation based on structural economic model and pre-estimated parameters instead of direct estimation (Borjas, Freeman, & Katz, 1997). In this approach, results are sensitive to chosen model and parameters. Borjas, Freeman and Katz (1992, 1996, 1997), Jeager (1996), and Chassamboulli and Peri (2015) are examples of the simulation-based approach in the literature.

Skill cell correlation approach considers the entire national economy and distinguishes between different age, education, and experience cells. Perfect substitutability between native workers and immigrants that are located in the same cell is an important assumption in this method. Later Manacorda, Manning, and Wadsworth (2006) and Ottaviano and Peri (2006) analyze the validity of this assumption for the UK and the US respectively. According to the findings of both studies, natives and immigrants are not perfect substitutes for each other, but partly complement. With the assumption of imperfect substitutability between native workforce and immigrants, results indicate that the most affected group due to immigration flows are the previous immigrants in the host countries. Other studies from the literature that can be cited for skill cell correlation approach are Borjas(2003), Cohen-Goldner and Paserman (2004), Borjas, Grogger, and Hanson (2008), Borjas (2006), Bratsberg, Raaum, and Roed (2010), Llull (2014), and Fogged and Peri (2015).

Another important assumption of the skill cell correlation approach is that the possibility of allocation of the immigrants according to their observable characteristics (Dustmann et al., 2007). This is problematic since immigrants downgrade after their arrival to the receiving country (Dustmann, Frattini, & Preston, 2007).

In general, the empirical evidence in the literature suggests that there is zero or small negative impacts on wages. Only a few studies find positive effects. For the US, most studies find no, or small to moderate effects of immigration on wages and employment of native groups. Similarly, for the Europe, the majority of studies finds no or small to moderate effects. Studies that concentrate specifically on the UK labor market do not find negative wage effects. However, in all empirical literature, it is valid that Labor market effects may occur only if the skill composition of immigrant labor differs from that of the native workforce.

There exists a vast amount of empirical research on the impact of immigrants on the labor markets of host countries.[5] Most of these studies are concentrated on the effects of immigration on the US labor market.[6] There are some other works, which focus on European countries. Pischke and Velling (1994, 1997), de New and Zimmermann (1994), Bauer (1998), Haisken DeNew and Zimmermann (1999), D'Amuri, Ottaviano and Peri (2010) and Glitz (2012) analyze effects of immigration on the German labor market. Hunt (1992) concentrates on France whereas Carrington and Lima (1996) concentrate on Portugal. Venturini (1999) examines the Italian case. For Norway, Bratsberg, Raaum, Roed, and Schone (2010) and Bratsberg, Raaum, and Roed (2016) can be given as examples. Fogged and Peri (2015) analyzes labor market in Denmark. For Austria Winter-Ebmer and Zweimuller's (1996, 1999) studies can be cited. Friedberg (2001) and Cohen and Hsieh (2001) analyze the topic for Israel. Carrasco, Jimeno, and Ortega (2008) investigates the effects on the Spanish labor market, and there are some recent research on the United Kingdom, such as Manacorda (2006), Dustmann et al. (2005), Dustmann et al. (2007), and Dustmann, Glitz, and Frattini (2008). In addition to single country studies, Hartog and

Zorlu (2005) for the Netherlands, the UK and Norway, Angrist, and Kugler (2001) for Western Europe, Jauer, Liebig, Martin, and Puhani (2014) for the EU and the US, Llull (2014) for the US and Canada, Dustmann, Glitz, and Vogel (2010) for the UK and Germany, and Longhi, Nijkamp, and Poot (2005), Jean and Jimenez (2011) and Docquier, Ozden, and Peri (2014) for OECD countries are examples of studies on country groups.

UNEMPLOYMENT AND MIGRATION: RECENT DEVELOPMENTS

As it is demonstrated in Table 1, the share of the migrant population increased during the years in OECD countries; not only for traditional countries of immigration, like Australia, the US, or Canada but for also most of the European countries. Especially for some European countries, like Ireland, the UK, Spain and Italy, the increase is more appreciable. This development raises the concerns of the domestic residents on the impact of immigrant workers on the labor markets.

On the last one and a half decade, for both OECD and the EU countries, there are no significant differences between the labor force participation rates of natives and immigrants. However, as it is shown in Figure 1 and Figure 2, on the average, probability of being unemployed is higher for migrant workers in both group of countries. This fact is more significant for the EU countries than OECD. In EU countries, due to the economic crisis started at the end of 2009, the unemployment rate has increased for both natives and immigrant workers.

In Table 2, the unemployment rate for natives and migrants in some OECD countries are provided. As data indicate that, only with a few exceptions in each year, the percentage of unemployed migrant workers are higher than the percentages of natives. As it was mentioned above, the absorption capacity of the immigrant workers of the receiving countries is specific to time and places. For example, during the economic slowdown in the EU countries, the share of unemployed people in total immigrants has increased. Especially for the countries that affected from the crisis dramatically, such as Greece, Spain, Portugal and Ireland, there are considerable raise in the above-mentioned rate. For instance, before the crisis in Spain, the share of unemployed people in the respective populations was around 10% for both natives and immigrants. However, at the end of 2010, this rate increased to18% to natives. At the same year about 30% of immigrants were classified as unemployed. In 2013 and 2014 share of unemployed people were around 24% and 35% for natives and immigrants, respectively.

FORCED IMMIGRATION FROM SYRIA AND ITS EFFECTS ON RECEIVING COUNTRIES' LABOR MARKETS

According to Ruiz and Vargas-Siva (2015), forced migration is one of the major consequences of civil conflicts. Data indicates that due to the magnitude and frequency forced migration has important humanitarian and economic impacts on both immigrants' welfare and also host countries' labor markets. However, the literature mainly concentrated on the results of voluntary migration, and the effects of forced migration on the labor markets of the receiving countries are generally go unnoticed.

Ruiz and Vargas-Siva (2013) and Mabiso, Hirvonen and Vandercasteelen (2014) argue that the forced migration situations have certain characteristics that could facilitate the identification of causal relationships. As it was discussed in detail above, immigrant inflows would themselves be the outcome

Table 1. Foreign-born population OECD (%in total population)

	2000	2005	2010	2013
Australia	23.40	24.10	26.60	27.60
Austria	10.39	14.50	15.70	16.70
Belgium	10.33	12.10	14.90	15.50
Canada	17.36	18.70	19.90	20.00
Czech Republic	4.20	5.10	6.30	7.10
Denmark	5.78	6.50	7.70	8.50
Estonia	18.42	16.90	16.00	10.10
Finland	2.63	3.40	4.60	5.60
France	10.13	11.30	11.70	11.90(1)
Germany	12.48	12.60	13.00	12.80
Greece	10.26(2)	...	7.40	6.60(3)
Hungary	2.88	3.30	4.50	4.50
Iceland	6.02	8.30	10.90	11.50
Ireland	8.66	12.60	17.00	16.40
Italy	3.91(4)	...	8.90	9.40(5)
Luxembourg	33.24	36.20	40.50	43.70
Mexico	0.50	0.50	0.80	0.80
Netherlands	10.14	10.60	11.20	11.60
New Zealand	17.19	20.30	27.30	28.20
Norway	6.79	8.20	11.60	13.90
Portugal	5.11	7.10	8.10	8.30(6)
Slovak Republic	2.21(7)	4.60	...	3.20
Slovenia	...	0.00	11.20	16.10
Spain	4.89	11.10	14.30	13.40
Sweden	11.31	12.50	14.80	16.00
Switzerland	21.86	23.80	26.50	28.30
United Kingdom	7.92	9.20	11.20	12.30
USA	11.02	12.10	12.90	13.10

Source: Organisation for Economic Co-operation and Development (OECD) http://data.oecd.org/migration
Notes: (1) (3) and (6): 2011 value, (2), (4) and (7): 2001 value
...: No data

of economic decisions; migrants typically prefer to places with better economic conditions. Nonetheless, since violence is the main driver of forced migration, at least in the short run, choice of destination is unrelated to the economic conditions of the receiving area. Therefore, results of the forced migration are free from the simultaneity problem from that respect and cause an exogenous increase in the labor supply of the host country.

The recent movement of Syrian refugees is one of the largest population movements in history. Due to a civil war that was started in the first quarter of 2011, the Syrian people started to migrate from their

Figure 1. Share of unemployment in OECD countries

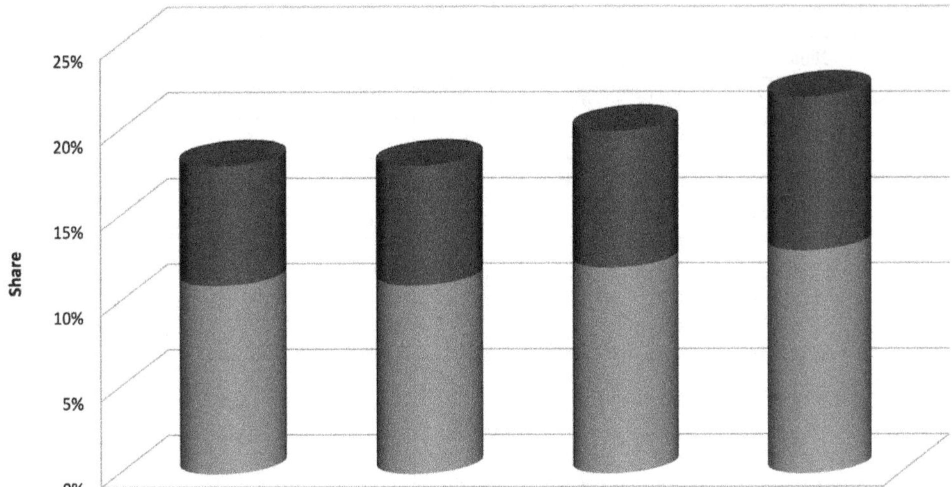

	2000	2005	2010	2013
native	7%	7%	8%	9%
Migrant	11%	11%	12%	13%

Figure 2. Share of unemployment in EU-28 countries

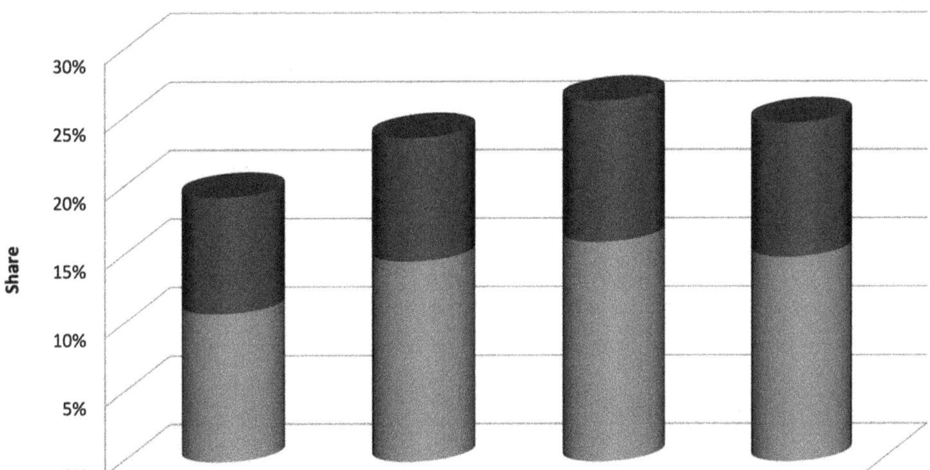

	2005	2010	2013	2014
native	8.50%	9%	10.30%	9.80%
Migrant	10.80%	14.60%	16%	14.90%

homes in search of security. António Guterres, the United Nations High Commissioner for Refugees (UNHCR), point to *as the Syrian crisis has become the biggest humanitarian emergency of our era, yet the world is failing to meet the needs of refugees and the countries hosting them.*

According to UNHCR, most of the refugees remain in countries neighboring Syria, with the highest concentrations in Lebanon, Jordan, Iraq, and Turkey. As it can be seen from Figure 3 and Table 3, although the number of Syrian refugees arriving in European countries continues to increase as of April

Table 2. Foreign-born and native unemployment in OECD (%in foreign-born and native population, respectively)

	2000		2005		2010		2013		2014	
	Native	Migrant	Native	Migrant	Native	Migrant	Native	Migrant	Native	Migrant
Australia	6.3	6.7	5.0	5.3	5.2	5.5	5.7	5.9	6.2	6.1
Austria	4.3	8.0	4.2	10.6	3.7	8.2	4.0	9.3	4.7	10.1
Belgium	5.6	15.8	7.4	17.0	6.9	17.1	6.8	17.2	6.9	17.6
Canada	...	...	...	...	7.6	9.9	6.9	8.1	6.7	7.9
Czech Repub.	...	8.8	7.9	12.2	7.4	7.2	7.0	7.8	6.2	7.0
Denmark	4.3	8.6	4.6	9.6	6.9	13.8	6.5	12.4	6.0	12.3
Estonia	13.7	12.2	7.6	10.5	16.4	22.8	8.6	11.0	7.3	9.3
Finland	11.1	31.7	9.3	22.6	8.3	13.8	8.0	14.3	8.3	16.8
France	9.4	16.7	8.2	14.4	8.6	14.5	9.1	16.0	9.1	16.0
Germany	7.4	10.6	10.0	17.5	6.6	10.8	4.8	8.6	4.5	7.9
Greece	11.3	14.7	10.0	10.3	12.3	16.2	26.5	38.0	25.8	34.5
Hungary	6.6	4.1	7.3	4.6	11.3	7.5	10.3	9.9	7.8	6.0
Iceland	1.9	0.8	2.6	2.5	7.2	13.5	5.1	7.5	4.7	7.6
Ireland	4.3	5.7	4.1	6.0	13.4	16.9	12.7	15.7	11.0	13.5
Italy	10.9	12.2	7.6	10.0	8.1	11.5	11.7	16.7	12.3	16.4
Luxembourg	2.0	2.9	3.6	5.6	2.9	6.0	4.0	7.9	4.4	7.2
Mexico	...	...	3.7	3.1	5.6	6.8	5.1	6.9	5.0	6.8
Netherlands	2.3	6.2	4.0	10.4	4.0	8.2	5.8	13.2	6.1	12.0
New Zealand	...	...	3.7	4.5	6.5	7.4	6.6	6.2	5.9	6.3
Norway	3.3	6.1	3.9	10.6	3.1	7.9	2.7	8.3	2.9	7.9
Poland	...	16.6	18.0	12.3	9.7	11.6	10.4	12.2	9.1	12.1
Portugal	3.9	6.4	8.0	9.4	11.0	15.0	16.5	21.8	14.2	16.9
Slovak Repub.	...	19.1	16.2	22.2	14.4	11.8	14.3	10.7	13.3	7.4
Slovenia	6.8	9.0	6.6	6.9	7.2	9.6	9.7	15.3	9.6	13
Spain	13.8	15.2	8.9	11.2	17.8	30.5	24.5	34.7	22.8	33.3
Sweden	4.7	12.4	6.9	14.4	7.3	16.4	6.2	16.4	6.5	16.4
Switzerland	...	2.7	3.1	8.6	3.4	7.8	3.2	7.6	3.3	7.7
Turkey	...	...	...	...	10.8	12.8	8.9	10.7	10.0	12.0
U.K	5.4	8.9	4.3	7.3	8.0	8.0	7.6	8.4	6.1	7.1
USA	4.1	4.3	5.3	4.8	9.9	9.8	7.7	7.0	6.5	5.8

Source: OECD, http://data.oecd.org/migration.
Note:...: No data

2011, it remains still low compared to neighboring countries. Table 4 provides the most recent data of the number of Syrian refugees in the four neighbor countries of Syria. Numbers indicate that Lebanon and Turkey single-handedly accommodate more than the total number of refugees in Europe. In total Syria's four neighbor countries Turkey, Lebanon, Iraq, and Jordan house approximately 5 million refugees.

Jordan has been hosting refugees from the other Middle East countries for many years. The Syrian immigration to Jordan due to the civil war started to increase after the second half of 2012. According to the report prepared by Orhan (2014), there are both positive and negative ramifications of Syrian refugees on Jordan's economy. Although the reduction in trade by Syria hurts the economy, immigrants bring dynamism into the economic life in Jordan by increasing efforts in entrepreneurship. From the point of the labor market, a labor surplus is created by the immigration since about forty percent of the refugees are between the ages of 18-49. Immigrants are settled for lower wages than the natives. Therefore job opportunities of the natives diminish. Although this creates concerns among the native workforce, lower qualified labor cost can also be considered as a positive impact on the economy as a whole (Orhan, 2014).

Lebanon hosts second highest number of Syrian refugees in the area. According to UNHCR there are about 1 million refugees are registered in the country; however, with the addition of illegal entries, this number is much higher. Syrian refugees constitute about 20% of the population; inevitably this creates a surplus in the labor market as it happens in Jordan. Due to the fragile political and economic structure and the relative size of the immigrants, a tension between the natives and immigrants has increased.

Likewise, problems can be observed in another neighbor: Iraq. In Iraq, as of March 2014, more than half of the refugees prefer to live outside of the designated camps. As in Jordan and Lebanon, immigrants in Iraq also provide cheap labor in labor-intensive sectors, for example, construction and services. This

Figure 3. Number of Syrian refugees in Europe

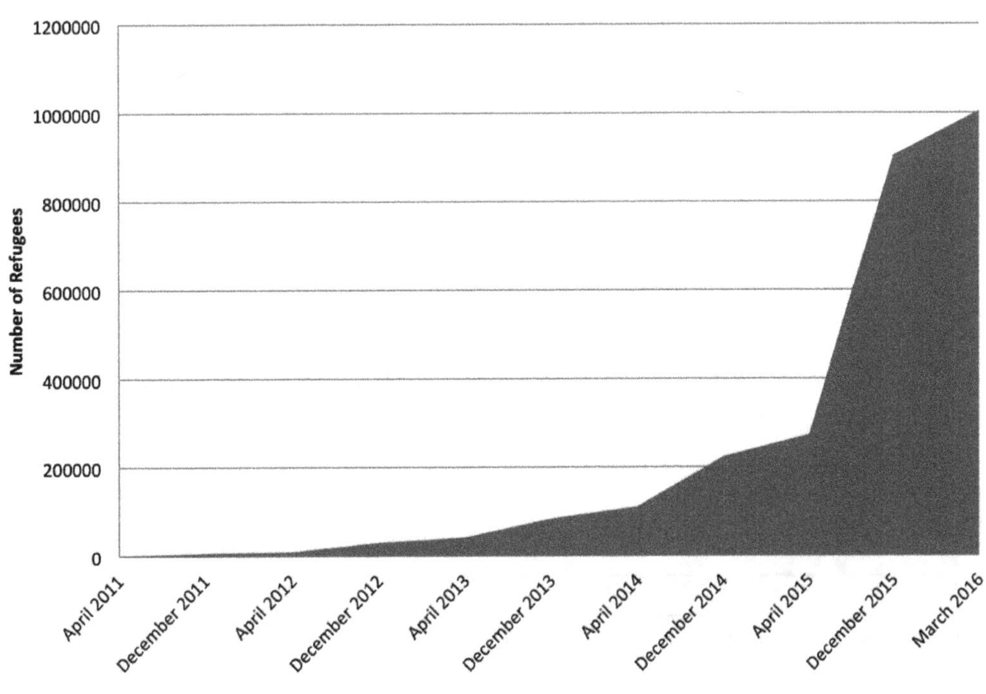

Table 3. The number of Syrian refugees in Europe (April 2011-March2016)

Host Country	Number of Syrian Refugees
Albania	190
Austria	38385
Belgium	15744
Bosnia and Herzegovina	104
Bulgaria	17527
Croatia	386
Cyprus	3464
Czech Republic	387
Denmark	19433
Estonia	42
Finland	1581
Former Yug.Rep.of Macedonia	2150
France	11402
Germany	306703
Greece	5615
Hungary	72505
Iceland	55
Ireland	178
Italy	2538
Latvia	93
Lithuania	34
Luxembourg	865
Malta	1312
Montenegro	2975
Netherlands	30698
Norway	13993
Poland	771
Portugal	206
Romania	2525
Serbia(+Kosovo)	313314
Slovakia	63
Slovenia	324
Spain	8697
Sweden	107966
Switzerland	12822
UK	9292
TOTAL	1 004345

Source: United Nations High Commissioner for Refugees (UNHCR). http://data.unhcr.org/syrianrefugees/asylum.php.

Table 4. Number of registered Syrian refugees in neighboring countries

Host Country	Number of Registred Syrian Refugees	Date of Record
Egypt	120491	04/30/2016
Iraq	246589	04/30/2016
Jordan	651114	05/16/2016
Lebanon	1048275	03/31/2016
Turkey	2 748 367	05/05/2016

Source: United Nations High Commissioner for Refugees (UNHCR), http://data.unhcr.org/syrianrefugees/asylum.php.

trend diminishes as the number of job opportunities for natives that immigrants can become a substitute for them.

Turkey hosts the largest population of Syrian refugees in the world. Immigration of the Syrian refugees began in April 2011 when 252 Syrian immigrants *entered* to Turkey from Hatay and had been continuing at an increasing rate since then. In mid-2016, about 2.7 million Syrians are residing in Turkey, and a number of refugees account for approximately 4% of the population of the country. For a country that has never experienced this kind of large and sudden inflow of people, demographic changes in the size and composition of the population and labor force generate important and unprecedented implications (Azevedo, Yang, & Inan, 2016).

According to Azevedo et al. (2016), the Turkish government has provided a tremendous amount of support to refugees in camps. However, because of the limited amount of funds, the physical capacity of camps have been exhausted, and refugees face problems that will persist over the long-term. As a result, the proportion of Syrian refugees that prefers to live outside of the designated camps significantly increased over time. Table 5 provides the information on the temporary refugee camps designated in different cities of Turkey. As it can be seen from the data of Republic of Turkey Prime Ministry Disaster and Emergency Management (AFAD), the number of refugee lives in camps does not change significantly between October 2014 and May 2016. As of May 2016, the number of refugees resides in camps is only about 10% of the total Syrian refugee population in Turkey. Although the majority of refugees prefer to stay in cities near the Syrian border, such as Gaziantep, Kilis, and Hatay, the dispersion of Syrian across the country expanded, especially in big cities like Istanbul and Ankara.

Refugee inflow from Syria causes distress on the social and economic environment in Turkey.

These problems are more intense in the cities that attract more immigrants due to the closeness to the Syrian border, like Kilis, Gaziantep, Osmaniye, and Hatay. From the point of the labor market, a spread of illegal workers and child labor creates unfair competition between natives and Syrian immigrants. Until January 2016[7], about 95% of the immigrants were under temporary protection, and due to the practice of law on refugee classification in Turkey, immigrants from Syria considered as "guest", none of them received a work permit.

Del Carpio and Wagner (2015) analyze the impact of immigrants on Turkish labor market by utilizing two years of Turkish Household Labor Force Survey (LFS); 2011 and 2014. Authors argue that without any legal work permit all refugees employed in the informal area. This type of shock to the labor market enables a more direct test of predictions of the theoretical model. The results show that the inflow of informally employed refugees causes a large-scale displacement of native Turkish workers among all gender, age and education level. In addition to this, refugees affected the propensity of legally employed

Table 5. Number of Syrian immigrants resides in temporary refugee camps in Turkey

City	Number of Camp	Number of Syrian Refugees	
Hatay	6	October 2014	14669
		October 2015	14803
		May 2016	18588
Gaziantep	5	October 2014	33213
		October 2015	52277
		May 2016	47021
Şanlıurfa	5	October 2014	78411
		October 2015	104890
		May 2016	103094
Kilis	2	October 2014	37623
		October 2015	33651
		May 2016	33131
Mardin	3	October 2014	2890
		October 2015	15740
		May 2016	13057
Kahramanmaraş	1	October 2014	16954
		October 2015	17853
		May 2016	18414
Osmaniye	1	October 2014	6806
		October 2015	9160
		May 2016	9173
Adıyaman	1	October 2014	10016
		October 2015	9599
		May 2016	9669
Adana	1	October 2014	11208
		October 2015	10598
		May 2016	10232
Malatya	1	October 2014	7349
		October 2015	7813
		May 2016	7790
Total	26	October 2014	219169
		October 2015	276384
		May 2016	270169

Source: AFAD, Republic of Turkey Prime Ministery Disaster and Emergency Management Presidency, http://www.afag.gov.tr/en/2602/Current-Status-in-AFAD-Temporary-Protection-Centres

Turkish male workers with less than high school education since lower wages created by the competition in informal sector result substitution of legal workers with illegal ones. Simultaneously, lower wages decrease production costs and output will increase. In that case, Turkish took advantage of new job opportunities in the related sectors. Results of this study are parallel with Ceritoglu, Yunculer, Torun, and Tumen (2015), which also addresses the impact of Syrian immigrants on Turkish labor market by using data for 2012-2013.

Native workers in receiving cities believe that newcomers have taken job opportunities away from them. Ozturkler and Goksel (2015) conducted a survey in four cities in Turkey that immigrants are attracted to; Şanlıurfa, Gaziantep, Kilis, and Hatay. Results indicate that the highest rate of job loss created by the refugees is in Hatay (18%), and in Şanlıurfa (16%). However in all cities natives blame refugees on this issue. For instance, Kilis has the lowest job loss rate, but almost 100% of respondents believe that this situation is created by the immigrants' entry into the market. Results of the survey indicate that more than half of the sample blames refugees for wage decline. Although Gaziantep has the second lowest job loss rate half of the population believes that existence of refugees in job market increases the probability of job loss for natives. This rate is 40% at Kilis, which has the lowest job loss rate. Herein, the share of Syrian immigrants in the total population may have an impact on the beliefs of the natives. In Kilis the ratio of immigrants-natives is close to 90% in 2015, and higher visibility of refugees in a city may be a reason for biased opinion of the native workers.

Orhan and Senyucel-Gundogar (2015) mention some positive impacts of Syrian refugees on their report prepared for the Center for Middle Eastern Strategic Studies According to this report; Syrian workers meet the labor demand in areas where native workers are not willing to work in. In addition to this, from the demand side, Syrian refugees increase demand for some products then create new investment opportunities and increase in production. And finally, Syrian investors move their firms to the cities close to the border. In Gaziantep, for instance, the registered number of Syrian companies increased about 30% after the civil war.

FUTURE RESEARCH DIRECTIONS

On 11 January 2016, registered Syrian refugees have the gain right to obtain a work permit in Turkey. Now, it is too early to evaluate the impact of this legislation on the labor market outcomes in Turkey. Prospective research in this field should concentrate on the effect of work permit on labor supply as well as labor demand not only for immigrants but also for the natives.

CONCLUSION

The effect of immigration on the welfare of the native population is an important issue in public debate. Economic theory offers more than one set of predictions since in theory, impacts of immigration on the labor market contingent upon many factors, such as the composition and size of the immigrant population, characteristics of the host economy, more specifically the flexibility of the economy and the tradability of its output on world markets, and the relation between the skills of migrants and native workers. Amongst the channels by which immigration has an impact on the economy of the host economy, the most analyzed one is through wages and unemployment. Although the magnitude of the impact depends on time and place, in general, the results of previous literature indicate that immigration has the only minute or no effect on employment and wages of resident workers.

According to Ruiz and Vargas-Siva (2015), forced migration is one of the major consequences of civil conflicts. According to United Nations High Commissioner for Refugees (UNHCR), the scale of the challenge is larger than ever with approximately 60 million people has to move from their home due to conflicts across the world. The recent movement of Syrian refugees is one of the largest population movements in history. Most of the refugees remain in countries neighboring Syria, with the highest concentrations in Lebanon, Jordan, Iraq, and Turkey. Among these countries, Turkey hosts the largest population of Syrian refugees in the world. For a country that has never experienced this kind of large and sudden inflow of people, demographic changes in the size and composition of the population and labor force generate important and unprecedented implications (Azevedo et al., 2016). Refugee inflow from Syria causes distress on the social and economic environment in Turkey. These problems are more intense in the cities that attract more immigrants due to the closeness to the Syrian border, like Kilis, Gaziantep, Osmaniye, and Hatay.

The initial presence of Syrian refugees was considered temporary at the beginning of the crisis, but now it becomes a permanent one (Orhan & Senyucel-Gundogar, 2015). Since registered refugees can obtain a work permit as of January 2016, it can be expected that the number of refugees in the legal labor force will increase. This may intensify the competition among natives and immigrants. According to OECD data, in 2014 labor force participation rate for migrants were higher than natives in Turkey. Similarly, the employment rate for immigrants was found to be higher than the natives'.

Interviews conducted in destination cities point out that natives already blame refugees for job loss and decrease in wage rate, although this is not the case in reality. With the higher number of people contributing to the workforce and increasing competition for limited jobs, a tension between natives and immigrants is inevitable.

In conclusion, immigration may have both positive and negative impacts on the labor market. In host countries, investments to increase job opportunities especially in the sectors within which immigrants work intensively are necessary. Should capacity and the growth rate of the economy can be expanded, both natives and immigrants shall obtain benefit, and positive impacts of migration mentioned by some researchers shall be realized. This outcome can be made more visible for the natives, thus might decrease the tension between the natives and the newcomers.

REFERENCES

AFAD. (n.d.). *Republic of Turkey Prime Ministery Disaster and Emergency Management Presidency.* Retrieved December, 2015, and May, 2016 from http://www.afag.gov.tr/en/2602/Current-Status-in-AFAD-Temporary-Protection-Centres

Altonji, J. G., & Card, D. (1991). The effects of immigration on the labor market outcomes of less-skilled natives. In R. Freeman (Ed.), *Immigration, trade and the labor market* (pp. 201–234). Chicago: University of Chicago Press and NBER.

Angrist, J. D., & Kugler, A. D. (2001). *Labor market institutions and the impact of immigrants on natives: Evidence from Western Europe.* Mimeo.

Angrist, J. D., & Kugler, A. D. (2003). Protective or counter-productive? Labour market institutions and the effect of immigration on EU natives. *The Economic Journal, 113*(488), F302–F331. doi:10.1111/1468-0297.00136

Azevedo, J. P., Yang, J. S., & Inan, O. K. (2016). *What are the impacts of Syrian refugees on host community welfare in Turkey? A subnational poverty analysis.* World Bank Policy Research Working Paper, 7542.

Bauer, T. (1998). *Do immigrants reduce natives' wages? Evidence from Germany.* Departmental Working Papers, 1998/02, Rutgers University.

Borjas, G. J. (1994). The economics of immigration. *Journal of Economic Literature, 32*(4), 1667–1717.

Borjas, G. J. (1995). Assimilation and changes in cohort quality revisited: What happened to immigrant earnings in the 1980s? *Journal of Labor Economics, 13*(2), 201–245. doi:10.1086/298373 PMID:12291239

Borjas, G. J. (1999). The economic analysis of immigration. Handbook of Labor Economics, 3, 1697-1760.

Borjas, G. J. (2003). The labor demand curve is downward sloping: Reexamining the impact of immigration on the labor market. *The Quarterly Journal of Economics, 118*(4), 1335–1374. doi:10.1162/003355303322552810

Borjas, G. J. (2006). Native internal migration and the labor market impact of immigration. *The Journal of Human Resources, 41*(2), 221–258. doi:10.3368/jhr.XLI.2.221

Borjas, G. J., Freeman, R. B., & Katz, L. F. (1992). On the labor market effects of immigration and trade. In G. J. Borjas & R. B. Freeman (Eds.), *Immigration and the work force: Economic consequences for the United States and source areas* (pp. 213–244). Chicago: University of Chicago Press. doi:10.7208/chicago/9780226066707.001.0001

Borjas, G. J., Freeman, R. B., & Katz, L. F. (1996). *Searching for the effect of immigration on the labor market.* NBER Working Paper, No. 5454.

Borjas, G. J., Freeman, R. B., Katz, L. F., DiNardo, J., & Abowd, J. M. (1997). How much do immigration and trade affect labor market outcomes? *Brookings Papers on Economic Activity, 1997*(1), 1–90. doi:10.2307/2534701 PMID:12321914

Borjas, G. J., Grogger, J., & Hanson, G. H. (2008). *Imperfect substitution between immigrants and natives: A reappraisal.* NBER Working Paper, No. 13887.

Bratsberg, B., Raaum, O., & Roed, M. (2010). When minority labor migrants meet the welfare state. *Journal of Labor Economics, 28*(3), 633–676. doi:10.1086/650546

Bratsberg, B., Raaum, O., & Roed, M. (2016). *Job loss and immigrant labor market performance.* CReAM Discussion Paper Series, 02/16.

Bratsberg, B., Raaum, O., Roed, M., & Schaum, P. (2010). *Immigration wage impacts by origin.* CReAM Discussion Paper Series, 30/10.

Card, D. (1990). The impact of the Mariel boatlift on the Miami labor market. *Industrial & Labor Relations Review, 43*(2), 245–257. doi:10.1177/001979399004300205

Card, D. (2001). Immigration inflows, native outflows, and the local labor market impacts of higher immigration. *Journal of Labor Economics*, *19*(1), 22–64. doi:10.1086/209979

Card, D., & DiNardo, J. (2000). Do immigrant inflows lead to native outflows? *The American Economic Review*, *90*(2), 360–367. doi:10.1257/aer.90.2.360

Carrasco, R., Jimeno, J. F., & Ortega, A. A. (2008). The effects of immigration on the employment opportunities of native born workers: Some evidence for Spain. *Journal of Population Economics*, *21*, 627–648. doi:10.1007/s00148-006-0112-9

Carrington, W. J., & De Lima, P. J. (1996). The impact of 1970s repatriates from Africa on the Portuguese labor market. *Industrial & Labor Relations Review*, *49*(2), 330–347. doi:10.1177/001979399604900210

Ceritoglu, E., Yunculer, H. B. G., Torun, H., & Tumen, S. (2015). *The impact of Syrian refugees on natives' labor market outcomes in Turkey: Evidence from a quasi-experimental design.* MPRA Paper, 61503.

Chassamboulli, A., & Peri, G. (2015). *The labor market effects of reducing the number of illegal immigrants.* CReAM Discussion Paper Series, 06/15.

Cohen, S., & Hsieh, C. T. (2001). *Macroeconomic and labor market impact of Russian immigration in Israel.* Department of Economics Working Papers, 105, Bar-Ilan University.

Cohen-Goldner, S., & Paserman, M. D. (2004). *The dynamic impact of immigration on natives' labor market outcomes: Evidence from Israel.* IZA Discussion Paper, No. 1315.

DAmuri, F., Ottaviano, G. I. P., & Peri, G. (2010). The labor market impact of immigration in Western Germany in the 1990s. *European Economic Review*, *54*(4), 550–570. doi:10.1016/j.euroecorev.2009.10.002

Del Carpi, X. V., & Wagner, M. (2015). *The impact of Syrian refugees on Turkish labor market.* World Bank Policy Research Working Paper Series, 7402.

DeNew, J. P., & Zimmermann, K. F. (1994). Native wage impacts of foreign labor - A random effects panel analysis. *Journal of Population Economics*, *7*(2), 177–192. doi:10.1007/BF00173618 PMID:12345483

Docquier, F., Ozden, C., & Peri, G. (2014). The labor market impact of immigration and emigration in OECD countries. *The Economic Journal*, *124*(579), F1106–F1145. doi:10.1111/ecoj.12077

Duncan, B., & Trejo, S. J. (2009). *Immigration and the U.S. labor market.* CReAM Discussion Paper Series, 08/09.

Dustmann, C., Fabbri, F., & Preston, I. (2005). The impact of immigration on the British labor market. *The Economic Journal*, *115*(507), 324–341. doi:10.1111/j.1468-0297.2005.01038.x

Dustmann, C., & Frattini, T. (2011). *Immigration: The European experience.* CReAM Discussion Paper Series, 22/11.

Dustmann, C., Frattini, T., & Glitz, F. (2007). *The impact of migration: A review of the economic evidence.* CReAM Discussion Paper Series, 102.

Dustmann, C., Frattini, T. & Preston, I. (2007). *A study of migrant workers and the national minimum wage and enforcement issues that arise*. Report for the Low Pay Commission.

Dustmann, C., & Glitz, A. (2005). *Immigration, jobs and wages: Theory, evidence and opinion*. London: Centre for Economic Policy Research.

Dustmann, C., & Glitz, A. (2008). *How do industries and firms respond to changes in local labour supply?* Mimeo.

Dustmann, C., Glitz, F., & Frattini, T. (2008). The labor market impact of immigration. *Oxford Review of Economic Policy*, *24*(3), 477–494. doi:10.1093/oxrep/grn024

Dustmann, C., Glitz, F., & Vogel, T. (2010). Employment, wages and the economic cycle: Differences between immigrants and natives. *European Economic Review*, *54*(1), 1–17. doi:10.1016/j.euroecorev.2009.04.004

Dustmann, C., & Preston, I. (2012). Estimating the effect of immigration on wages: A Comment. *Journal of the European Economic Association*, *10*(1), 216–223. doi:10.1111/j.1542-4774.2011.01056.x

Filer, R. K. (1992). The effect of immigrant arrivals on migratory patterns of native workers. In G. J. Borjas & R. B. Freeman (Eds.), *Immigration and the work force: Economic consequences for the united states and Source Areas* (pp. 245–269). Chicago, IL: University of Chicago Press.

Foged, M., & Peri, G. (2015). *Immigrants' effect on native workers: New analysis on longitudinal data.* CReAM Discussion Paper Series, 07/15.

Frey, W. H. (1995). Immigration and internal migration flight—A California case study. *Population and Environment*, *16*(4), 353–375. doi:10.1007/BF02208119

Frey, W. H. (1996). Immigration, domestic migration, and demographic balkanization in America: New evidence for the 1990s. *Population and Development Review*, *22*(4), 741–763. doi:10.2307/2137808

Friedberg, R. M. (2001). The impact of mass migration on the Israeli labor market. *The Quarterly Journal of Economics*, *116*(4), 1373–1408. doi:10.1162/003355301753265606

Friedberg, R. M., & Hunt, J. (1995). The impact of immigration on host country wages, employment and growth. *The Journal of Economic Perspectives*, *9*(2), 23–44. doi:10.1257/jep.9.2.23

Gaston, N., & Nelson, D. (2000). Immigration and labour-market outcomes in the United States: A political-economy puzzle. *Oxford Review of Economic Policy*, *16*(3), 104–114. doi:10.1093/oxrep/16.3.104

Gaston, N., & Nelson, D. (2001). *The employment and wage effects of immigration: Trade and labour economics perspectives.* University of Nottingham, Leverhulme Centre for Research on Globalization and Economic Policy Research Paper, 2001/28.

Gaston, N., & Nelson, D. (2002). The employment and wage effects of immigration: Trade and labour economics perspectives. In D. Greenaway, R. Upward, & K. Wakelin (Eds.), *Trade, investment, migration and labour market adjustment* (pp. 201–235). Palgrave Macmillan, UK. doi:10.1057/9781403920188_12

Glitz, A. (2006). *The labour market impact of immigration: Quasi-experimental evidence.* CReAM Discussion Paper, No. 12/06.

Glitz, A. (2012). The labor market impact of immigration: A quasi-experiment exploiting immigrant location rules in Germany. *Journal of Labor Economics*, *30*(1), 175–213. doi:10.1086/662143

Gonzalez, L., & Ortega, F. (2007). *How do very open economies adjust to large immigration flows? Recent evidence from Spanish regions.* Universitat Pompeu Fabra Working Paper, 1059.

Grossman, J. B. (1982). The substitutability of natives and immigrants in production. *The Review of Economics and Statistics*, *64*(4), 596–603. doi:10.2307/1923944

Haisken DeNew, J. P., & Zimmerman, K. F. (1999). Wage and mobility effects of trade and migration. In M. Dewatripont & A. Sapir (Eds.), International trade and employment: The European experience (pp. 139-160). Oxford University Press. doi:10.1093/0198293607.003.0008

Hanson, G. H., & Slaughter, M. J. (2002). Labor-market adjustment in open economies: Evidence from US States. *Journal of International Economics*, *57*(1), 3–29. doi:10.1016/S0022-1996(01)00138-6

Hartog, J., & Zorlu, A. (2005). The effect of immigration on wages in three European countries. *Journal of Population Economics*, *18*(1), 113–151. doi:10.1007/s00148-004-0204-3

Hatton, T. J., & Tani, M. (2005). Immigration and inter-regional mobility in the UK, 1982–2000. *The Economic Journal*, *115*(507), F342–F358. doi:10.1111/j.1468-0297.2005.01039.x

Hunt, J. (1992). The impact of the 1962 repatriates from Algeria on the French labor market. *Industrial & Labor Relations Review*, *45*(3), 556–572. doi:10.1177/001979399204500310

Jauer, J., Leibig, T., Martin, J. P., & Puhani, P. A. (2014). *Migration as an adjustment mechanism in the crisis? A comparison of Europe and the United States.* CReAM Discussion Paper Series, 10/14.

Jeager, D. (1996). *Skill differences and the effect of immigrants on the wages of natives.* US Bureau of Labor Statistics Working Paper, 273.

Jean, S., & Jiménez, M. (2011). The unemployment impact of immigration in OECD countries. *European Journal of Political Economy*, *27*(2), 241–256. doi:10.1016/j.ejpoleco.2010.11.006

Kuhn, P., & Wooton, I. (1991). Immigration, international trade and the wages of native workers. In J. M. Abowd & R. B. Freeman (Eds.), *Immigration, trade, and the labor market* (pp. 285–304). Chicago: University of Chicago Press.

LaLonde, R. J., & Topel, R. H. (1991). Labor market adjustments to increased immigration. In J. M. Abowd & R. B. Freeman (Eds.), *Immigration, trade and the labor market* (pp. 167–199). Chicago: University of Chicago Press.

Leamer, E. E., & Levinsohn, J. (1995). International trade theory: The evidence. In G. Grossman & K. Rogoff (Eds.), *Handbook of international economics* (Vol. 3, pp. 1339–1394). North- Holland.

Lewis, E. G. (2004). *Local open economies within the US: How do industries respond to immigration.* Federal Reserve Bank of Philadelphia Working Paper, 04-1.

Llull, J. (2014). *The effect of immigration on wages: exploiting exogenous variation at the national level.* CReAM Discussion Paper Series, 36/14.

Longhi, S., Nijkamp, P., & Poot, J. (2005). The meta-analytic assessment of the effect of immigration on wages. *Journal of Economic Surveys*, *19*(3), 451–477. doi:10.1111/j.0950-0804.2005.00255.x

Mabiso, A., Maystadt, J.-F., Hirvonen, K., & Vandercasteelen, J. (2014). *Refugees and food security in host communities: A review of impacts and policy options to enhance resilience. International Food Policy Research Institute*. IFPRI.

Manacorda, M., Manning, A., & Wadsworth, J. (2006). *The impact of immigration on the structure of male wages: Theory and evidence from Britain.* CReAM Discussion Papers, 08/06. Organisation for Economic Co-operation and Development. Retrieved from http:// data.oecd.org/migration

Orhan, O. (2014). The situation of Syrian refugees in the neighboring countries: Findings, conclusions, and recommendations. Center for Middle Eastern Strategic Studies Reports, 189.

Orhan, O., & Senyucel-Gundogar, S. (2015). Effects of the Syrian refugees on Turkey. Center for Middle Eastern Strategic Studies Reports, 195.

Ottaviano, G. I., & Peri, G. (2006). *The effects of immigration on wages.* NBER Working Papers, 12497.

Ozturkler, H., & Goksel, T. (2015). The economic effects of Syrian refugees on Turkey: A synthetic modelling. Center for Middle Eastern Strategic Studies Reports, 196.

Peri, G. (2007). *Immigrants' complementarities and native wages: Evidence from California.* NBER Working Paper, 12956.

Peri, G. (2008). *Immigration accounting: U.S. States 1960-2006.* CReAM Discussion Paper Series, 05/08.

Peri, G., & Sparber, C. (2008). *The fallacy of crowding-out: A note on 'native internal migration and the labor market impact of immigration.* Manuscript, UC Davis.

Peri, G., & Sparber, C. (2009). Task specialization, immigration, and wages. *American Economic Journal. Applied Economics*, *1*(3), 135–169. doi:10.1257/app.1.3.135

Pischke, J. S., & Velling, J. (1994). *Wage and employment effects of immigration to Germany: An analysis based on local labor markets.* CEPR Discussion Paper, 935.

Pischke, J. S., & Velling, J. (1997). Employment effects of immigration to Germany: An analysis based on local labor markets. *The Review of Economics and Statistics*, *79*(4), 594–604. doi:10.1162/003465397557178

Ruiz, I., & Vargas-Silva, C. (2013). The economics of forced migration. *The Journal of Development Studies*, *49*(6), 772–784. doi:10.1080/00220388.2013.777707

Ruiz, I., & Vargas-Silva, C. (2015). The labor market impacts of forced migration. *AER:Papers & Proceedings*, *105*(5), 581–586.

United Nations High Commissioner for Refugees. (n.d.a). Retrieved April, 2016 from data.unhcr.org/syrianrefugees/country.php

United Nations High Commissioner for Refugees. (n.d.b). Retrieved April, 2016 from http://www.unhcr.org/news/latest/2014/8/53ff76c99/needs-soar-number-syrian-refugees-tops-3-million.html

Venturini, A. (1999). Do immigrants working illegally reduce the natives legal employment? Evidence from Italy. *Journal of Population Economics*, *12*(1), 135–154. doi:10.1007/s001480050094 PMID:12295037

Winter-Ebmer, R., & Zweimuller, J. (1996). Immigration and the earnings of young native workers. *Oxford Economic Papers*, *48*(3), 473–491. doi:10.1093/oxfordjournals.oep.a028579

Winter-Ebmer, R., & Zweimuller, J. (1999). Do immigrants display young native workers: The Austrian experience. *Journal of Population Economics*, *12*(2), 320–340. doi:10.1007/s001480050102

Zachariadis, M. (2012). Immigration and international prices. *Journal of International Economics*, *87*(2), 298–311. doi:10.1016/j.jinteco.2012.01.004

KEY TERMS AND DEFINITIONS

Forced Migration: An involuntary migration movement due to threats to life and livelihood, whether from natural or human-made factors.

Host Country: Destination country of the immigrants.

Immigration: A process of moving into a country for the purpose of settlement.

Labor Demand: A concept that describes the amount of labor that employers in an economy are willing to employ at a given real wage rate.

Labor Supply: A concept that describes the total hours that workers in an economy wish to work at a given real wage rate.

Syrian Refugees: Citizens of Syria who have to be forced to leave their home country since the onset of the Syrian Civil War in 2011.

Unemployment: A situation where someone of the adult population is would like to be employed but not able to find a job at a given real wage rate.

Work Permit: A document which gives to the holder the permission to take a job within a foreign country.

ENDNOTES

1 For more information about the historical immigration experience for Europe, see Dustmann and Frattini (2011).

2 Because of this assumption, there will be no welfare redistribution among workers and capital owners. For detail, please see Borjas (1995).

3 If labor supply is not completely inelastic to wages, at the new lower wage rate, some workers may prefer to remain as unemployed. For further discussion please see Dustmann and Glitz (2005).

4 If labor supply is not perfectly inelastic, there may be both employment and wage effects in the short run, before the adjustment of output mix. For the detailed discussion, please see Dustman and Glitz (2005).

5 Please see Borjas (1994. 1999), Friedberg and Hunt (1995), Gaston and Nelson (2002), and Dustmann et al. (2007).

6 For example Card (1990), Altonji and Card (1991), Kuhn and Wooton (1991), Lalonde and Topel (1991), Borjas, Freeman, and Katz (1996), Card (2001), Ottaviano and Peri (2006), Peri (2007), Peri (2008), Peri and Sparber (2009), Duncan and Trejo (2009), and Chassamboulli and Peri (2015).

7 On 11 January 2016, registered Syrian refugees have gain right to obtain a work permit in Turkey. According to new legislation, employers can hire Syrian workers up to 10% of their total number of employees, and immigrant can have vocational training under the Turkish Employment Agency. Seasonal workers are exempted from the work permit and the wage rate for the immigrants cannot be lower than the minimum wage.

Compilation of References

Aaron, C., Kenward, L., Bird, K., Desai, M., Aswicahyono, H., Basri, C. M., & Tubagus, C. (2004). *Strategic approaches to job creation and employment in Indonesia.* Report prepared for the United States Agency for International Development, Jakarta Mission. Retrieved from http://pdf.usaid.gov/pdf_docs/Pnada948.pdf

Abbasi, F., Hajihoseini, H., & Haukka, S. (2011). Use of virtual index for measuring efficiency of innovation systems: A cross-country study. *International Journal of Technology Management and Sustainable Development*, *9*(3), 195–212. doi:10.1386/tmsd.9.3.195_1

Abbott, K. (2006). A review of employment relations theories and their application. *Problems and Perspectives in Management*, *1*, 187–199.

Abduh, M., Brahim, S., & Omar, M. A. (2012). A study on finance-growth nexus in dual financial countries: Evidence from Bahrain. *World Applied Science Journal*, *20*(8), 1166–1174.

Abduh, M., & Chowdhury, N. T. (2012). Islamic banking – economic growth nexus: Evidence from Bangladesh. *Journal of Islamic Economics. Banking and Finance*, *8*(3), 104–113.

Abduh, M., & Omar, M. A. (2012). Islamic banking and economic growth: The Indonesian experience. *International Journal of Islamic and Middle Eastern Finance and Management*, *5*(1), 35–47. doi:10.1108/17538391211216811

Abdulrazzak, N. L. (2014). *My rights are divine: A closer look at children's rights in the Muslim Arab world.* Bloomington, IN: AuthorHouse.

Abedelo, R. (n.d.). *The impact of Lifelong Learning Policies On the Inclusion of Vulnerable Groups.* Retrieved from http://www.prismanet.gr/LLL/downloads/LLL-report.pdf

AFAD. (n.d.). *Republic of Turkey Prime Ministery Disaster and Emergency Management Presidency.* Retrieved December, 2015, and May, 2016 from http://www.afag.gov.tr/en/2602/Current-Status-in-AFAD-Temporary-Protection-Centres

Aghion, P., Burgess, R., Redding, S., & Zilibotti, F. (2008). The unequal effects of liberalisation: Evidence from dismantling the license raj in India. *The American Economic Review*, *94*(4), 1397–1412. doi:10.1257/aer.98.4.1397

Ahmed, A. (2010). Global financial crisis: An Islamic finance perspective. *International Journal of Islamic and Middle Eastern Finance and Management*, *3*(4), 306–320. doi:10.1108/17538391011093252

Aidt, T., & Tzannatos, Z. (2005). *The cost and benefits of collective bargaining: A survey.* Cambridge Working Papers in Economics, No 0541. Cambridge: Cambridge University.

Ajayi, S. O., Oyedele, L. O., Akinade, O. O., Bilal, M., Owolabi, H. A., Alaka, H. A., & Kadiri, K. O. (2016). Reducing waste to landfill: A need for cultural change in the UK construction industry. *Journal of Building Engineering*, *5*, 185–193. doi:10.1016/j.jobe.2015.12.007

Akan, Y., & Kanca, O. C. (2015). Türkiye'de dış borçlanma, büyüme ve enflasyon ilişkisi: VAR yaklaşımı (1980-2013). *Hacettepe Üniversitesi İktisadi ve İdari Bilimler Fakültesi Dergisi*, *33*(3), 1–22.

Akçay, S. (2011). Causality relationship between total r&d investment and economic growth: Evidence from United States. *Süleyman Demirel Üniversitesi İktisadi ve İdari Bilimler Fakültesi Dergisi*, *16*(1), 79–92.

Akın, H. B., & Eren, O. (2012). OECD ülkelerinin eğitim göstergelerinin kümeleme analizi ve çok boyutlu ölçekleme analizi ile karşılaştırmalı analizi. *Öneri*, *10*(37), 175-181.

Akküçük, U. (2011). A study on the competitive positions of countries using cluster analysis and multidimensional scaling. *European Journal of Economics, Finance and Administrative Sciences*, *37*, 17–26.

Aksoy, T., & Gönel, F. (2016). Revisiting FDI-led growth hypothesis: The role of sector characteristics. *The Journal of International Trade & Economic Development*, *25*(8), 1144–1166. doi:10.1080/09638199.2016.1195431

Alatas, V., & Newhouse, D. (2010). *Indonesia jobs report: Towards better jobs and security for all.* Policy Research Working Paper. Washington, DC: The World Bank.

Albayrak, A. N., & Erkut, G. (2010). Türkiye'de bölgesel rekabet gücü analizi. *Megaron*, *5*(3), 137–148.

Alcalá, F., & Ciccone, A. (2001). Trade and productivity. *The Quarterly Journal of Economics*, *119*(2), 613–646. doi:10.1162/0033553041382139

Al-Faruqi, I. R., & Al-Banna, G. (1985). *Towards Islamic labour and unionism: Three papers.* Cairo: International Islamic Confederation of Labor.

Al-Jarhi, M. A. (2009). *Islamic finance an efficient & equitable option.* Islamic Development Bank, The Islamic Research and Training Institute. Retrieved April 20, 2016, from http://www.iefpedia.com/english/wp-content/uploads/2009/11/ISLAMIC-FINANCE-AN-EFFICIENT-EQUITABLE-OPTION.pdf

Alkan, D. (1995). *Women's employment and income distribution by gender in Turkey* (Unpublished master's thesis). Middle East Technical University, Ankara, Turkey.

Allen, E. R. (2016). *Analysis of trends and challenges in the Indonesian labor market (ADB Papers on Indonesia No.16, March).* Manila: Asian Development Bank.

Almeida, R., Ridao-Cano, C., Levent, A., & McKenzie, D. (2011). *İŞKUR vocational trainees: Profile, job-search behavior and expectations. Baseline report.* Washington, DC: World Bank.

Al-Samadi, A. A.-M. A., Hamdan, F., & Almsafir, M. K. (2013). Islamic banking vs. conventional banking, during the global financial crisis: Malaysia as a case. *Journal of Islamic and Human Advanced Research*, *3*(1), 27–40.

Altan, Ş., & Ersöz, A. (1994). *Kadının çifte yükümlülüğü* (Vol. 2). Kadın ve Sosyal Hizmetler Müsteşarlığı Kadın Statüsü ve Sorunları Genel Müdürlüğü Bülteni.

Altonji, J. G., & Card, D. (1991). The effects of immigration on the labor market outcomes of less-skilled natives. In R. Freeman (Ed.), *Immigration, trade and the labor market* (pp. 201–234). Chicago: University of Chicago Press and NBER.

Amorós, J. E., & Bosma, N. (2013). *Global entrepreneurship monitor 2013.* Retrieved December 20, 2014, from http://www.gemconsortium.org/report

Anderson, D. F. (1984). *An introduction to multivariate statistical methods* (2nd ed.). New York: John Wiley and Sons.

Andor, L. (2014). *Labor mobility in the EU: Challenges and perspectives for a genuine European labor market.* Press Release. Retrieved May 1, 2016, from http://europa.eu/rapid/press-release_SPEECH-14-491_en.htm

Andreoni, A. (2011). *Productive capabilities indicators for industrial policy design.* UNIDO, Development Policy, Statistics and Research Branch, Working Paper 17.

Angrist, J. D., & Kugler, A. D. (2001). *Labor market institutions and the impact of immigrants on natives: Evidence from Western Europe*. Mimeo.

Angrist, J. D., & Kugler, A. D. (2003). Protective or counter-productive? Labour market institutions and the effect of immigration on EU natives. *The Economic Journal, 113*(488), F302–F331. doi:10.1111/1468-0297.00136

Anner, M., & Caraway, T. (2010). International institutions and workers rights: Between labor standards and market flexibility. *Studies in Comparative International Development, 45*(2), 151–169. doi:10.1007/s12116-010-9064-x

Aras, O. N., & Öztürk, M. (2011). Reel ekonomiye katkıları bakımından katılım bankalarının kullandırdığı fonların analizi. *Ekonomi Bilimleri Dergisi, 3*(2), 167–179.

Ariwanto, D. A. (2012). *Infrastructure role on productivity in manufacturing sector in Indonesia* (Unpublished master's thesis). International Institute of Social Studies, The Hague.

Arslan, N., & Tatlıdil, H. (2012). Defining and measuring competitiveness: A comparative analysis of Turkey with 11 potential rivals. *International Journal of Basic and Applied Sciences LJBAS-LJENS, 12*(2), 31–43.

Arthur, W. B. (2013). *Complexity economics: A different framework for economic thought.* Santa Fe Institute, Working Paper, 2013-01-012.

Asako, K., Ito, T., & Sakamoto, K. (1991). The rise and fall of deficit in Japan, 19651990. *Journal of the Japanese and International Economies, 5*(4), 451–472. doi:10.1016/0889-1583(91)90008-E

Ascalon, M. E., Schleicher, D. J., & Born, M. P. (2008). Cross-cultural social intelligence: An assessment for employees working in cross-national contexts. *Cross Cultural Management: An International Review, 15*(2), 109–130. doi:10.1108/13527600810870570

Asian Development Bank. (2013). *Asia's economic transformation: Where to, how, and how fast? Key Indicators for Asia and the Pacific*. Manila, Philippines: Asian Development Bank.

Aslan, O. E. (2006). Cumhuriyet ve kadın memurlar. *Amme İdaresi Dergisi, 39*(4), 117–149.

Associated Chambers of Commerce of India. (2014). *Rise of contract workers by 39% in 2013.* Retrieved 31 November, 2015, from http://www.assocham.org/newsdetail.php?id=4379

Atlas Media Database. (n.d.). Retrieved January 02, 2016, from http://atlas.media.mit.edu/en/

Auer, P., Berg, J., & Coulibaly, E. I. (2005). Une main-d'œuvre stable est-elle bonne pour la productivité?. *Revue internationale du Travail, 144*(3), 335-361.

Australian Industry Group. (2015). *Australia's construction industry.* Retrieved May 30, 2016, from http://www.aigroup.com.au/portal/binary/com.epicentric.contentmanagement.servlet.ContentDeliveryServlet/LIVE_CONTENT/Economic%2520Indicators/Construction%2520Survey/2015/Construction%2520industry%2520profile%2520and%2520Outlook.pdf

Autor, D. H., Dorn, D., & Hanson, G. H. (2013). The China syndrome: Local labor market effects of import competition in the United States. *The American Economic Review, 103*(6), 2121–2168. doi:10.1257/aer.103.6.2121

Autor, D. H., Kerr, W. R., & Kugler, A. D. (2007). Does employment protection reduce productivity? Evidence from US States. *The Economic Journal, 117*(521), 189–217. doi:10.1111/j.1468-0297.2007.02055.x

Aydın, D. (2013). Bankaların 2012 yılı sermaye yeterlilik rasyolarına göre kümeleme analizi ve çok boyutlu ölçekleme sonucu sınıflandırılma yapıları. *Bankacılık ve Sigortacılık Araştırmaları Dergisi, 1*(5-6), 29–47.

Azevedo, J. P., Yang, J. S., & Inan, O. K. (2016). *What are the impacts of Syrian refugees on host community welfare in Turkey? A subnational poverty analysis.* World Bank Policy Research Working Paper, 7542.

Bacchetta, M., Ernst, E., & Bustamante, J. P. (2009). *Globalization and informal jobs in developing countries: A joint study of the International Labour Office and the Secretariat of the World Trade Organization.* Geneva: Services des publications de l'OMC and Organisation Mondiale du Commerce.

Bacchetta, M., Ekkehard, E., & Bustamante, J. P. (2009). *Globalization and informal jobs in developing countries: A joint study of the International Labour Office and the Secretariat of the World Trade Organization.* Geneva: International Labour Organization and World Trade Organization.

Bacha, O. I. (2004). Dual banking systems and interest rate risk for Islamic banks. *The Journal of Accounting, Commerce & Finance – Islamic Perspective, Working Paper, MPRA 12763, 8*(1), 1-42.

Bäckman, O., & Nilsson, A. (2011). Pathways to Social Exclusion-A Life-Course Study. *European Sociological Review, 27*(1), 107–123. doi:10.1093/esr/jcp064

Bäckman, O., & Nilsson, A. (2016). Long-term consequences of being not in employment, education or training as a young adult. Stability and change in three Swedish birth cohorts. *European Societies, 18*(2), 136–157. doi:10.1080/14616696.2016.1153699

Badan Pusat Statistik. (2016a). *Data masyarakat yang berusia 15 tahun atau lebih dan aktivitas mereka dari tahun 2004-2014.* Retrieved February 28, 2016, from http://www.bps.go.id/linkTabelStatis/view/id/969

Badan Pusat Statistik. (2016b). *Laju pertumbuhan produk domestik bruto per kapita beberapa negara menurut harga konstan (persen).* Retrieved September 4, 2016, from https://www.bps.go.id/linkTabelStatis/view/id/1244

Badan Pusat Statistik. (2016c). *Persentase penduduk miskin September 2015 mencapai 11.13%.* Retrieved September 6, 2016, from https://www.bps.go.id/brs/view/id/1227

Badan Pusat Statistik. (2016d). *Persentase penduduk usia 15 tahun ke atas menurut* jenis *kegiatan seminggu yang lalu 2009-2012.* Retrieved on March 3, 2016, from http://www.bps.go.id/linkTabelStatis/view/id/1608

Badan Pusat Statistik. (2016e). *Tingkat pengangguran berdasarkan tingkat pendidikan.* Retrieved March 10, 2016, from http://www.bps.go.id/linkTabelStatis/view/id/972

Baggio, S., Iglesias, K., Deline, S., Studer, J., Henchoz, Y., Mohler-Kuo, M., & Gmel, G. (2015). Not in education, employment, or training status among young Swiss men. Longitudinal associations with mental health and substance use. *The Journal of Adolescent Health, 56*(2), 238–243. doi:10.1016/j.jadohealth.2014.09.006 PMID:25620308

Balassa, B. (1961). *The theory of economic integration.* Homewood, IL: Richard D. Irwin.

Bales, K. (2010, February). *How to combat modern slavery?* Retrieved from http://www.ted.com/talks/kevin_bales_how_to_combat_modern_slavery

Bales, K. (2002). *"Kullanılıp atılanlar": Küresel ekonomide yeni kölelik* (P. Öğünç, Trans.). İstanbul: Çitlembik Yayınları. (Original work published 2000)

Baltagi, B. H., Feng, Q., & Kao, C. (2012). A Lagrange multiplier test for cross-sectional dependence in a fixed effects panel data model. *Journal of Econometrics, 170*(1), 164–177. doi:10.1016/j.jeconom.2012.04.004

Baltagi, B. H., & Wu, P. X. (1999). Unequally spaced panel data regressions with AR(1) disturbances. *Econometric Theory*, *15*(06), 814–823. doi:10.1017/S0266466699156020

Baltagi, B., Baskaya, Y. S., & Hulagu, T. (2013). How different are the wage curves for formal and informal workers? Evidence from Turkey. *Papers in Regional Science*, *92*(2), 271–283. doi:10.1111/j.1435-5957.2012.00478.x

Bank Indonesia. (2016). *Undang-undang Republik Indonesia no. 20 tahun 2008 tentang usaha kecil, mikro, dan menengah.* Retrieved March 10, 2016, from http://www.bi.go.id/id/tentang-bi/uu-bi/Documents/UU20Tahun2008UMKM.pdf

Banker, R. D., Charnes, A., & Cooper, W. (1984). Models for Estimation of Technical and Scale Inefficiencies in Data Envelopment Analysis. *Management Science*, *30*(9), 1078–1092. doi:10.1287/mnsc.30.9.1078

Banker, R. D., Charnes, A., Cooper, W. W., Swarts, J., & Thomas, D. (1989). An introduction to data envelopment analysis with some of its models and their uses. *Research in Government and Nonprofit Accounting*, *5*, 125–163.

Banker, R. D., & Thrall, R. M. (1992). Estimation of returns to scale using data envelopment analysis. *European Journal of Operational Research*, *62*(1), 74–84. doi:10.1016/0377-2217(92)90178-C

Barslund, M., Busse, M., & Schwarzwälder, J. (2015). *Labor mobility in Europe: An untapped resource?*. CEPS Policy Brief, No. 327, March.

Bartelsman, E., Bassanini, A., Haltiwanger, J., Jarmin, R., & Scarpetta, S. (2002). *The spread of ICT and productivity growth: Is Europe really lagging behind in the new economy?* Oxford, UK: Oxford University Press.

Bartzokas, A. (2007). *Monitoring and analysis of policies and public financing instruments conducive to higher levels of R&D investments: The policy mix project.* Case Study, South Korea, A study funded by the European Commission – DG Research.

Baskaya, Y. S., & Hulagu, T. (2011). *Informal-formal worker wage gap in Turkey: Evidence from a semi-parametric approach* (Central Bank of Turkey Working Paper 11/15). Retrieved from http://www.tcmb.gov.tr/wps/wcm/connect/TCMB+EN/TCMB+EN/Main+Menu/PUBLICATIONS/Research/Working+Paperss/2011/11-15

Basu, K. (1999). Child labor: Cause, consequence, and cure, with remarks on international labor standards. *Journal of Economic Literature*, *37*(3), 1083–1119. doi:10.1257/jel.37.3.1083

Bauer, T. (1998). *Do immigrants reduce natives' wages? Evidence from Germany.* Departmental Working Papers, 1998/02, Rutgers University.

Bayraktar, S., & İncekara, A. (2013). Tükiye'nin genç işsizlik profili. *Çalışma İlişkileri Dergisi*, *4*(1), 15-38.

Bayraktar, S., & İncekara, A. (2013). Profile of youth unemployment in Turkey. *Journal of Labor Relations*, *4*(1), 15–38.

Beason, R., & Weinstein, D. E. (1996). Growth, economies of scale, and targeting in Japan (19551990). *The Review of Economics and Statistics*, *78*(2), 286–295. doi:10.2307/2109930

Becker, G. (1964). *Human capital.* New York: National Bureau of Economic Research.

Becker, G. S. (1991). *A treatise on the family.* Harvard University Press.

Beck, T., Levine, R., & Loayza, N. (2000). Finance and the sources of growth. *Journal of Financial Economics*, *58*(1-2), 261–300. doi:10.1016/S0304-405X(00)00072-6

Bel-Air, F. (2014). *Demography, migration, and labour market in Qatar Gulf labour markets and migration.* GLMM - EN - No. 8/2014. Retrieved August 26, 2016, from http://cadmus.eui.eu/bitstream/handle/1814/32431/GLMM_ExpNote_08-2014.pdf?sequence=1

Belet, N. (2013). Kriz olgusunun kadına yönelik algıya ve kadın işgücüne etkisi. *Gazi Üniversitesi İİBF Dergisi, 15*(1), 1–28.

Bell, D. N. F., & Blanchflower, D. G. (2010). *Youth unemployment: Déjà vu?* (IZA Discussion Paper No. 4075). Retrieved from http://ftp.iza.org/dp4705.pdf

Belot, M., Boone, J., & Van Ours, J. (2007). Welfare effects of employment protection. *Economica, 74*(295), 381–396. doi:10.1111/j.1468-0335.2006.00576.x

Belser, P. (2005). *Forced labour and human trafficking: Estimating the profits*. Geneva: International Labour Office.

Benjet, C., Hernández-Motoya, D., Borges, G., Méndez, E., Medina-Mora, M. E., & Aguilar-Gaxiola, S. (2012). Youth who neither study nor work: Mental health, education and employment. *Salud Pública de México, 54*(4), 410–417. doi:10.1590/S0036-36342012000400011 PMID:22832833

Bentolila, S., Boeri, T., & Cahuc, P. (2010). *Ending the scourge of dual labour markets in Europe*. VoxEU.org.

Berber, M., & Yılmaz Eser, B. (2008). Türkiye'de kadın istihdamı: Ülke ve bölge düzeyinde sektörel analiz. *İş Güç Endüstri İlişkileri ve İnsan Kaynakları Dergisi, 10*(2), 1-16.

Berber, M., & Artan, S. (2004). Türkiye'de enflasyon-ekonomik büyüme ilişkisi (teori, literatür ve uygulama). *Atatürk Üniversitesi İktisadi ve İdari Bilimler Fakültesi Dergisi, 18*(3-4), 103–117.

Berber, M., & Eser, B. Y. (2008). Türkiye'de kadın istihdamı: Ülke ve bölge düzeyinde sektörel analizi. *İş, Güç. Endüstri İlişkileri ve İnsan Kaynakları Dergisi, 10*(2), 1–16.

Bernstein, H. (2007). *Capital and labour from centre to margins*. Paper prepared for the Living on the Margins conference, Stellenbosch.

Besamusca, J., Tijdens, K., Keune, M., & Steinmetz, S. (2015). Working women worldwide. Age effects in female labor force participation in 117 countries. *World Development, 74*, 123–141. doi:10.1016/j.worlddev.2015.04.015

Besley, T., & Burgess, R. (2004). Can labour regulation hinder economic performance? - Evidence from India. *The Quarterly Journal of Economics, 119*(1), 91–134. doi:10.1162/003355304772839533

Betcherman, G., & Whitehead, T. (2002). Règlementations de protection d'emploi: Règles d'embauche et de licenciement. *Banque Mondiale: Cahiers de la politique de l'emploi, 1*, 1-8.

Beyhan Acar, A. (2013). İşgücü piyasası temel göstergeleri bakımından çok boyutlu ölçekleme analizi ile Türkiye ile diğer OECD ülkelerinin karşılaştırılması. *İstanbul Üniversitesi İşletme Fakültesi İşletme İktisadı Enstitüsü Yönetim Dergisi, 24*(75), 121-144.

Bhalla, S. (2003). *The restructuring of unorganized sector in India*. Planning Commission, Government of India.

Bharat Heavy Electricals Ltd. vs. State of Uttar Pradesh. (2003). *Supreme Court Cases (SCC) 528*.

Bhargava, A., Franzini, L., & Narendranathan, W. (1982). Serial correlation and the fixed effects model. *The Review of Economic Studies, 49*(4), 533–549. doi:10.2307/2297285

Blackburne, E. F., & Frank, M. W. (2007). Estimation of nonstationary heterogeneous panels. *The Stata Journal, 7*(2), 197–208.

Black, S., Devereux, P., & Salvanes, K. (2008). Staying in the classroom and out of the maternity ward? The effect of compulsory schooling laws on teenage births. *The Economic Journal, 118*(530), 1025–1034. doi:10.1111/j.1468-0297.2008.02159.x

Blanchard, O., & Tirole, J. (2003). *Protection de l'emploi et procédures de licenciement*. Paris: La documentation française.

Blanchard, O., & Wolfers, J. (2000). The role of shocks and institutions in the rise of European unemployment: The aggregate evidence. *The Economic Journal, 110*(462), 1–33. doi:10.1111/1468-0297.00518

Block, R. N. (2007). Indicators of labour standards: An overview and comparison. In D. Kucera (Ed.), *Qualitative Indicators of Labour Standards* (pp. 27–56). Dordrecht, Netherlands: Springer. doi:10.1007/978-1-4020-5310-8_2

Block, R. N., Berg, P., & Roberts, K. (2003). Comparing and quantifying labour standards in the United States and the European Union. *International Journal of Comparative Labour Law and Industrial Relations, 19*(4), 441–468.

Blomström, M., & Kokko, A. (2003). *Human capital and inward FDI.* EIJS Working Papers Series, 167. Stockholm: The European Institute of Japanese Studies.

Bloom, D. E., Canning, D., & Fink, G. (2011). *Implications of population aging for economic growth* (NBER Working Paper No. 16705). Retrieved from http://www.nber.org/papers/w16705

Boeri, T., & Garibaldi, P. (2007). Two tier reforms of employment protection: A honeymoon effect? *The Economic Journal, 117*(521), 357–385. doi:10.1111/j.1468-0297.2007.02060.x

Boeri, T., Helppie, B., & Macis, M. (2008). *Labor regulations in developing countries: a review of the evidence and directions for future research.* World Bank.

Boeri, T., & Jimeno, J. (2005). The effects of employment protection: Learning from variable enforcement. *European Economic Review, 49*(8), 2057–2077. doi:10.1016/j.euroecorev.2004.09.013

Bonin, H., Eichhorst, W., Florman, C., Hansen, M. O., Skiöld, L., Stuhler, J., . . . Zimmermann, K. F. (2008). *Geographic mobility in the European Union: Optimising its economic and social benefits,* IZA Research Report No.19. Bonn: Institute for the Study of Labor.

Boratav, K. (2008). *Türkiye iktisat tarihi 1908-2007.* Ankara: İmge Kitabevi.

Borjas, G. J. (1999). The economic analysis of immigration. Handbook of Labor Economics, 3, 1697-1760.

Borjas, G. J., Freeman, R. B., & Katz, L. F. (1996). *Searching for the effect of immigration on the labor market.* NBER Working Paper, No. 5454.

Borjas, G. J., Grogger, J., & Hanson, G. H. (2008). *Imperfect substitution between immigrants and natives: A reappraisal.* NBER Working Paper, No. 13887.

Borjas, G. J. (1994). The economics of immigration. *Journal of Economic Literature, 32*(4), 1667–1717.

Borjas, G. J. (1995). Assimilation and changes in cohort quality revisited: What happened to immigrant earnings in the 1980s? *Journal of Labor Economics, 13*(2), 201–245. doi:10.1086/298373 PMID:12291239

Borjas, G. J. (2003). The labor demand curve is downward sloping: Reexamining the impact of immigration on the labor market. *The Quarterly Journal of Economics, 118*(4), 1335–1374. doi:10.1162/003355303322552810

Borjas, G. J. (2006). Native internal migration and the labor market impact of immigration. *The Journal of Human Resources, 41*(2), 221–258. doi:10.3368/jhr.XLI.2.221

Borjas, G. J., Freeman, R. B., & Katz, L. F. (1992). On the labor market effects of immigration and trade. In G. J. Borjas & R. B. Freeman (Eds.), *Immigration and the work force: Economic consequences for the United States and source areas* (pp. 213–244). Chicago: University of Chicago Press. doi:10.7208/chicago/9780226066707.001.0001

Borjas, G. J., Freeman, R. B., Katz, L. F., DiNardo, J., & Abowd, J. M. (1997). How much do immigration and trade affect labor market outcomes? *Brookings Papers on Economic Activity*, *1997*(1), 1–90. doi:10.2307/2534701 PMID:12321914

Borrero, M. (2014). Psychological and Emotional Impact of Unemployment. *Journal of Sociology and Social Welfare*, *7*(6), 916–934. Retrieved from http://scholarworks.wmich.edu/jssw/vol7/iss6/12?utm_source=scholarworks.wmich.edu%2Fjssw%2Fvol7%2Fiss6%2F12&utm_medium=PDF&utm_campaign=PDFCoverPages

Boschma, R., & Capone, G. (2015). Relatedness and diversification in the European Union (EU-27) and European Neighbourhood Policy countries. *Environment and Planning C*, *20*, 1–21.

Botero, J., Djankov, S., La Porta, R., Lopez-de-Silanes, F., & Shleifer, A. (2005). The regulation of labor. *The Quarterly Journal of Economics*, *119*(4), 1339–1382. doi:10.1162/0033553042476215

Bottai, M. (2003). Confidence regions when the Fisher information is zero. *Biometrika*, *90*(1), 73–84. doi:10.1093/biomet/90.1.73

Bowlin, W. F. (1998). Measuring performance: An introduction to data envelopment analysis (DEA). *Journal of Cost Analysis*, *15*(2), 3–27. doi:10.1080/08823871.1998.10462318

BPS. (2015). *Survei angkatan kerja nasional (Sakernas)*. Jakarta: Badan Pusat Statistik.

Bratsberg, B., Raaum, O., & Roed, M. (2016). *Job loss and immigrant labor market performance.* CReAM Discussion Paper Series, 02/16.

Bratsberg, B., Raaum, O., Roed, M., & Schaum, P. (2010). *Immigration wage impacts by origin.* CReAM Discussion Paper Series, 30/10.

Bratsberg, B., Raaum, O., & Roed, M. (2010). When minority labor migrants meet the welfare state. *Journal of Labor Economics*, *28*(3), 633–676. doi:10.1086/650546

Brecher, R. A. (1974). Minimum wage rates and the pure theory of international trade. *The Quarterly Journal of Economics*, *88*(1), 98–116. doi:10.2307/1881796

Breslin, D. A. (1999). *On the ethics of outsourcing: a philosophical look at A-76.* Defence Acquisition Industry.

Breusch, T. S., & Pagan, A. R. (1980). The lagrange multiplier test and its applications to model specification in econometrics. *The Review of Economic Studies*, *47*(1), 239–253. doi:10.2307/2297111

British Broadcasting Corporation. (2014). *French riots: Amiens buildings torched in clashes.* Retrieved September 25, 2014, from http://bbc.in/QxxkGm

Brooks, R. L. (2014). Postconflict justice in the aftermath of modern slavery. *The George Washington International Law Review*, *46*(2), 243–303.

Brown, D. K., Deardorff, A. V., & Stern, R. M. (2008). Child labor: Theory, evidence, and policy. In K. Basu (Ed.), *International labor standards: History, theory, and policy options.* Hoboken, NJ: Blackwell Publishing Ltd.

Brown, F. (2000). *Tourism reassessed: Blight or blessing?* Oxford, UK: Butterworth Heinemann.

Brynjolfsson, E., & Saunders, A. (2009). *Wired for innovation: How information technology is reshaping the economy.* Cambridge, MA: MIT Press.

Building Economics Research Unit. (1972). *Construction and development: A framework for research and action. Paper prepared for the International Bank for Reconstruction and Development.* London: University College Environmental Research Group.

Bülbül, S., & Köse, A. (2010). Türkiye'de bölgelerarası iç göç hareketlerinin çok boyutlu ölçekleme yöntemi ile incelenmesi. *İstanbul Üniversitesi İşletme Fakültesi Dergisi, 39*(1), 75-94.

Bulut, Y., & Sayin, E. (2010). An evaluation of entrepreneurship characteristics of university students: An empirical investigation from the faculty of economic and administrative sciences in Adnan Menderes University. *International Journal of Economic Perspectives, 4*(3), 559–568.

Burawoy, M. (2010). From Polanyi to Pollyanna: The false optimism of global labor studies. *Global Labour Journal, 1*(2), 301–313. doi:10.15173/glj.v1i2.1079

Bureau of Labor Statistics. (n.d.). Retrieved March 15, 2016, from http://www.bls.gov/ilc/

Burgard, S. A., Brand, J. E., & House, J. S. (2007). Toward a better estimation of the effect of job loss on health. *Journal of Health and Social Behavior, 48*(4), 369–384. doi:10.1177/002214650704800403 PMID:18198685

Burrows, S. (2013). Precarious work, neo-liberalism and young peoples experiences of employment in the Illawarra region. *Economic and Labour Relations Review, 24*(3), 380–396. doi:10.1177/1035304613498189

Büyükakın, F., Bozkurt, H., & Cengiz, V. (2009). Türkiye'de parasal aktarımın faiz kanalının granger nedensellik ve Toda-Yamamota yöntemleri ile analizi. *Erciyes Üniversitesi İktisadi ve İdari Bilimler Fakültesi Dergisi, 33*, 101–118.

Bynner, J., & Parsons, S. (2002). Social exclusion and the transition from school to work: The case of young people not in employment, education or training (NEET). *Journal of Vocational Behavior, 60*, 289–309. doi:10.1006/jvbe.2001.1868

Çağatay, N., & Berik, G. (1990). Transition to export-led growth in Turkey: Is there a feminization of employment? *The Review of Radical Political Economics, 22*(1), 115–134. doi:10.1177/048661349002200110

Çağatay, N., & Özler, Ş. (1995). Feminization of the labor force: The effects of long- term development and structural adjustment. *World Development, 23*(11), 1883–1894. doi:10.1016/0305-750X(95)00086-R

Cahayani, A., Gunawan, A. S., & Isololipu, K. (2016, July). The dimension of entrepreneurial characteristics in young entrepreneurs in the creative industry field in Jakarta. *China-USA Business Review, 15*(7), 319–329. doi:10.17265/1537-1514/2016.07.00

Cahuc, P., Carcillo, S., Rinne, U., & Zimmermann, K. F. (2013). *Youth unemployment in old Europe: The polar cases of France and Germany* (IZA Discussion Paper No. 7490). Retrieved from http://ftp.iza.org/dp7490.pdf

Cahuc, P., Carcillo, S., Rinne, U., & Zimmermann, K. F. (2013). *Youth unemployment in old Europe: The polar cases of France and Germany.* IZA Discussion Paper No. 7490.

Cai, Y. (2011). *Factors affecting the efficiency of the BRICSs' national innovation systems: A comparative study based on DEA and Panel Data Analysis.* Economics Discussion paper, (2011-52).

Cai, L. (2010). The relationship between health and labour force participation: Evidence from a panel data simultaneous equation model. *Labour Economics, 17*(1), 77–90. doi:10.1016/j.labeco.2009.04.001

Cai, W., Mu, Y., Wang, C., & Chen, J. (2014). Distributional employment impacts of renewable and new energy–A case study of China. *Renewable & Sustainable Energy Reviews, 39*, 1155–1163. doi:10.1016/j.rser.2014.07.136

Çakır Zeytinoğlu, F., & Sadıç, Ç. (2013). Türkiye'deki illerin turizm verileri açısından çok boyutlu ölçekleme analizi ile incelenmesi. *Trakya Üniversitesi Sosyal Bilimler Dergisi, 15*(2), 77–94.

Çakır, M. T., Sözen, A., & Yücesu, H. S. (2009). Türkiye'nin sosyo-ekonomik göstergeleri ile enerji göstergeleri arasındaki ilişkinin çok değişkenli veri analizi ile irdelenmesi. *Uluslararası İlişkiler, 5*(20), 27–56.

Calderon, C., & Liu, L. (2002). *The direction of causality between financial development and economic growth.* Working Paper No. 184, Central Bank of Chile, Santiago.

Caliendo, M., & Schmidl, R. (2016). Youth unemployment and active labor market policies in Europe. *IZA Journal of Labor Policy*, *5*(1), 1. doi:10.1186/s40173-016-0057-x

Cameron, L., & Zwaan, B. (2015). Employment factors for wind and solar energy technologies: A literature review. *Renewable & Sustainable Energy Reviews*, *45*, 160–172. doi:10.1016/j.rser.2015.01.001

Campolieti, M., Gefang, D., & Koop, G. (2014). A new look at variation in employment growth in Canada: The role of industry, provincial, national and external factors. *Journal of Economic Dynamics & Control*, *41*, 257–275. doi:10.1016/j.jedc.2014.02.005

Canetta, E., Fries-Tersch, E., & Mabilia, V. (2014). *Annual report on statistics on Intra-EU movers.* Network Statistics FMSSFE.

Card, D. (1990). The impact of the Mariel boatlift on the Miami labor market. *Industrial & Labor Relations Review*, *43*(2), 245–257. doi:10.1177/001979399004300205

Card, D. (2001). Immigration inflows, native outflows, and the local labor market impacts of higher immigration. *Journal of Labor Economics*, *19*(1), 22–64. doi:10.1086/209979

Card, D., & DiNardo, J. (2000). Do immigrant inflows lead to native outflows? *The American Economic Review*, *90*(2), 360–367. doi:10.1257/aer.90.2.360

Card, D., Kluve, J., & Weber, A. (2010). Active labour market policy evaluation: A meta- analysis. *The Economic Journal*, *120*(548), 452–477. doi:10.1111/j.1468-0297.2010.02387.x

Carrasco, R., Jimeno, J. F., & Ortega, A. A. (2008). The effects of immigration on the employment opportunities of native born workers: Some evidence for Spain. *Journal of Population Economics*, *21*, 627–648. doi:10.1007/s00148-006-0112-9

Carrere, C., Fugazza, M., Olarreaga, M., & Robert-Nicoud, F. (2014). *Trade in unemployment.* CEPR Discussion Paper, No. DP9916.

Carrington, W. J., & De Lima, P. J. (1996). The impact of 1970s repatriates from Africa on the Portuguese labor market. *Industrial & Labor Relations Review*, *49*(2), 330–347. doi:10.1177/001979399604900210

Çelik, Ş. (2015). Çok boyutlu ölçekleme analizi ile hayvancılık açısından Türkiye'de illerin sınıflandırılması. *Erciyes Üniversitesi Fen Bilimleri Enstitüsü Dergisi*, *31*(4), 159–164.

Ceritoglu, E., Yunculer, H. B. G., Torun, H., & Tumen, S. (2015). *The impact of Syrian refugees on natives' labor market outcomes in Turkey: Evidence from a quasi-experimental design.* MPRA Paper, 61503.

Cetin, M., & Egrican, N. (2011). Employment impacts of solar energy in Turkey. *Energy Policy*, *39*(11), 7184–7190. doi:10.1016/j.enpol.2011.08.039

Çevik, S., & Charap, J. (2011). *The behaviour of conventional and Islamic bank deposit returns in Malaysia and Turkey.* Working Paper, IMF 11/156. International Monetary Fund.

Ceylan, S., & Şahin, B. Y. (2010). Asymmetry in the relationship between unemployment and economic growth. *Journal of Dogus University*, *11*(2), 157–165.

Chakrabarti, S. (2009). *Gender dimensions of the informal sector and informal employment in India.* Global Forum on Gender Statistics.

Chang, H., Andreoni, A., & Kuan, M. L. (2013). *International industrial policy experiences and the lessons for the UK. Future of Manufacturing Project: Evidence Paper 4*. Government Office for Science.

Chapra, M. U. (2008). *The global financial Crisis: Can Islamic finance help minimize the severity and frequency of such a crisis in the future?* Conference Paper, Islamic Development Bank, Forum on the Global Financial Crisis.

Charnes, A., Cooper, W., & Rhodes, E. (1978). Measuring the efficiency of decision making units. *European Journal of Operational Research*, *2*(6), 429–444. doi:10.1016/0377-2217(78)90138-8

Chassamboulli, A., & Peri, G. (2015). *The labor market effects of reducing the number of illegal immigrants.* CReAM Discussion Paper Series, 06/15.

Chatterji, P., Alergria, M., Lu, M., & Takeuchi, D. (2007). Psychiatric disorders and labor market outcomes: Evidence from the national Latino and Asian American study. *Health Economics*, *16*(10), 1069–1090. doi:10.1002/hec.1210 PMID:17294497

Chen, D. H. C., & Suh, J. (2007). Introduction. In Korea as a Knowledge Economy: Evolutionary Process and Lessons Learned (pp. 1-16). WBI Development Studies. Washington, DC: World Bank.

Cheung, K. W., & So, H. C. (2005). A multidimensional scaling framework for mobile location using time-of-arrival measurements. *IEEE Transactions on Signal Processing*, *53*(2), 460–470. doi:10.1109/TSP.2004.840721

Chiang, Y. H., Tao, L., & Wong, F. K. W. (2015). Causal relationship between construction activities, employment and GDP: The case of Hong Kong. *Habitat International*, *46*, 1–12. doi:10.1016/j.habitatint.2014.10.016

Choi, S. D. (2015). Aging workers and trade-related injuries in the US construction industry. *Safety and Health at Work*, *6*(2), 151–155. doi:10.1016/j.shaw.2015.02.002 PMID:26106517

Cho, J., Chun, H., & Lee, Y. (2015). How does the entry of large discount stores increase retail employment? Evidence from Korea. *Journal of Comparative Economics*, *43*(3), 559–574. doi:10.1016/j.jce.2015.04.004

Chong, B. S., & Liu, M.-H. (2009). Islamic banking: Interest-free or interest- based? *Pacific-Basin Finance Journal*, *17*(1), 125–144. doi:10.1016/j.pacfin.2007.12.003

Choudry, M. T., Marelli, E., & Signorelli, M. (2012). Youth unemployment rate and impact of financial crises. *International Journal of Manpower*, *33*(1), 76–95. doi:10.1108/01437721211212538

Cho, Y., & Newhouse, D. (2012). How did the Great Recession affect different types of workers? Evidence from 17 middle-income countries. *World Development*, *41*, 31–50. doi:10.1016/j.worlddev.2012.06.003

Chung, H. H. (2007). *Lessons from the Korean venture industry development.* World Bank Working Paper, 39379.

Chung, S. (2010). Innovation, competitiveness and growth: Korean experiences. In J. Y. Lin & B. Pleskovic (Eds.), *Lessons from east asia and the global financial crisis* (pp. 333-358). Annual Word Bank Conference on Development Economics.

Çınar, M. (1994). Unskilled urban migrant women and disguised employment: Home-working women in İstanbul, Turkey. *World Development*, *22*(3), 369–380. doi:10.1016/0305-750X(94)90128-7

Ciputra. (2008). *Ciputra quantum leap.* Jakarta: PT. Elex Media Komputindo.

Çitçi, O. (1982). *Kadın sorunu ve kamu kesiminde kadın.* Ankara: Todaie Yayınları.

Clancy, M. J. (1999). Tourism and development: Evidence from Mexico. *Annals of Tourism Research*, *26*(1), 1–20. doi:10.1016/S0160-7383(98)00046-2

Clark, A. E., & Oswald, A. (1994). Unhappiness and unemployment. *The Economic Journal, 104*(424), 648–659. doi:10.2307/2234639

Clark, A., Knabe, A., & Ratzel, S. (2011). Boon or bane? Others unemployment, well-being and job insecurity. *Labour Economics, 17*(1), 52–61. doi:10.1016/j.labeco.2009.05.007

Clark, K., & Drinkwater, S. (2007). *Ethnic minorities in the labour market. Dynamics and diversity*. York: JRF.

Cochrane, W. W. (1993). *The development of American agriculture: A historical perspective* (2nd ed.). Minneapolis, MN: University of Minneapolis Press.

Cohen, S., & Hsieh, C. T. (2001). *Macroeconomic and labor market impact of Russian immigration in Israel.* Department of Economics Working Papers, 105, Bar-Ilan University.

Cohen-Goldner, S., & Paserman, M. D. (2004). *The dynamic impact of immigration on natives' labor market outcomes: Evidence from Israel.* IZA Discussion Paper, No. 1315.

Comola, M., & De Mello, L. (2011). How does decentralized minimum wage setting affect employment and informality? The case of Indonesia. *Review of Income and Wealth, 57*, 79–99. doi:10.1111/j.1475-4991.2011.00451.x

Comola, M., & De Mello, L. (2013). Salaried employment and earnings in Indonesia: New evidence on the selection bias. *Applied Economics, 45*(19), 2808–2816. doi:10.1080/00036846.2012.667551

Computer Integrated Construction Research Group. (2010). *BIM operate. construct. design plan. Project execution planning guide version 2.0.* Retrieved from http://engr. Psu.edu/bim/PxP

Çondur, F., & Bölükbaş, M. (2014). A study on labor market and the relationship between youth unemployment and economic growth in Turkey. *Public Administration Journal, 47*(2), 77–93.

Çondur, F., & Bölükbaş, M. (2014). Türkiye'de işgücü piyasası ve genç işsizlik büyüme ilişkisi üzerine bir inceleme. *Amme Idaresi Dergisi, 47*(2), 77–93.

Connelly, R. (1992). The effect of child care costs on married womens labor force participation. *The Review of Economics and Statistics, 74*(1), 83–90. doi:10.2307/2109545

Cooper, S., Skelton, A. C. H., Owen, A., Densley-Tingley, D., & Allwood, J. M. (2016). A multi-method approach for analysing the potential employment impacts of material efficiency. *Resources, Conservation and Recycling, 109*, 54–66. doi:10.1016/j.resconrec.2015.11.014

Cooper, W. W., Seiford, L. M., & Tone, K. (2007). *Data envelopment analysis: A comprehensive text with models, applications, references and DEA-solver software* (2nd ed.). New York: Springer.

Cooper, W. W., Seiford, L. M., & Zhu, J. (2004). Data envelopment analysis: History, models and interpretations. In *Handbook on data envelopment analysis* (pp. 1–39). New York: Springer. doi:10.1007/1-4020-7798-X_1

Corcoles, D., Diaz-Mora, C., & Gandoy, R. (2014). Product sophistication: A tie that binds partners in international trade. *Economic Modelling, 44*, 33–41. doi:10.1016/j.econmod.2013.12.009

Crane, A. (2012). Modern slavery as a management practice: Exploring the conditions and capabilities for human exploitation. *Academy of Management Review, 38*(1), 49–69. doi:10.5465/amr.2011.0145

Cristelli, M., Tacchella, A., & Pietronero, L. (2015). The heterogeneous dynamics of economic complexity. *PLoS ONE, 10*(2), e0117174. doi:10.1371/journal.pone.0117174 PMID:25671312

Cullmann, A., Schmidt-Ehmcke, J., & Zloczysti, P. (2009). *Innovation, R&D efficiency and the impact of the regulatory environment: A two stage semi-parametric DEA approach.* Discussion Papers of DIW Berlin 883, DIW Berlin. doi:10.2139/ssrn.1460709

Dahduli, M. S. (2009). Islamic banking and economic development. *SSRN Electronic Journal*. doi: 10.2139/ssrn.1616624

Dakhli, M., & De Clercq, D. (2004). Human capital, social capital, and innovation: A multi-country study. *Entrepreneurship & Regional Development, 16*(2), 107–128. doi:10.1080/08985620410001677835

Daly, K. A. (2013). *Managing the contingent work force: lessons for success.* Queen's University Industrial Relations Centre.

DAmuri, F., Ottaviano, G. I. P., & Peri, G. (2010). The labor market impact of immigration in Western Germany in the 1990s. *European Economic Review, 54*(4), 550–570. doi:10.1016/j.euroecorev.2009.10.002

Darby, J., Hart, R. A., & Vecchi, M. (2001). Labour force participation and the business cycle: A comparative analysis of France, Japan, Sweden and United States. *Japan and the World Economy, 13*(2), 113–133. doi:10.1016/S0922-1425(00)00049-9

Dar, H. A., & Presley, J. R. (2000). Lack of profit loss sharing in Islamic banking: Management and control imbalances. *International Journal of Islamic Financial Services, 2*, 1–9.

Daude, C., Nagengast, A., & Perea, J. R. (2015). Productive capabilities: An empirical analysis of their drives. *The Journal of International Trade & Economic Development, 25*(4), 504–535. doi:10.1080/09638199.2015.1073342

Davies, Langdon, & Everest. (2009). *Cost model: off-site manufacturing.* Retrieved May 26, 2016, from http://www.building.co.uk/cost-model-off-site-manufacture/3042466.article

Davies, R. B., & Vadlamannati, K. C. (2013). A race to the bottom in labor standards? An empirical investigation. *Journal of Development Economics, 103*, 1–14. doi:10.1016/j.jdeveco.2013.01.003

Davis, D. R. (1998). Does European unemployment prop up American wages? National labor markets and global trade. *The American Economic Review, 88*, 478–494.

Dayıoğlu, M., & Kırdar, M. (2010). *The determinants of and trends in labor force participation of women in Turkey.* Working Paper, No. 5. Ankara: State Planning Organization of the Republic of Turkey/World Bank.

Dayıoğlu, M. (2000). Labor force participation of women in Turkey. In F. Acar & A. Güneş-Ayata (Eds.), *Gender and identity construction: Women of Central Asia, the Caucasus and Turkey* (pp. 44–73). Leiden: Brill.

Dayıoğlu, M., & Kasnakoğlu, Z. (1997). Kentsel kesimde kadın ve erkeklerin işgücüne katılımları ve kazanç farklılıkları. *METU Studies in Development, 24*(3), 329–361.

Dayıoğlu, M., & Tunalı, I. (2003). *Falling behind while catching up: Changes in the female-male wage differential in urban Turkey, 1988 to 1994. Manuscript.* Koç University.

De Bandt, O., & Vigna, O. (2008). The macroeconomic impact of structural reforms. *Banque de France Bulletin Digest,* 0169.

De Brauw, A., Muller, V., & Lee, H. L. (2014). The role of rural-urban migration in structural transformation of Sub-Saharan Africa. *World Development, 63*, 33–42. doi:10.1016/j.worlddev.2013.10.013

Deakin, S., Armour, J., & Singh, A. (2009). Law, finance and development indices, 1970-2005. UK Data Service. SN: 6260.

Dedeoğlu, S., & Öztürk, M. Y. (2010). *Kapitalizm, ataerkillik ve kadın emeği Türkiye örneği.* İstanbul: Sav Yayıncılık.

Del Carpi, X. V., & Wagner, M. (2015). *The impact of Syrian refugees on Turkish labor market.* World Bank Policy Research Working Paper Series, 7402.

Demetriades, P. O., & Hussein, A. K. (1996). Does financial development cause economic growth? Time-series evidence from 16 countries. *Journal of Development Economics, 51*(2), 387–411. doi:10.1016/S0304-3878(96)00421-X

Demiray Erol, E. (2013). Türkiye ve Avrupa Birliği üyesi ülkelerin sosyoekonomik gelişmişlik düzeylerinin karşılaştırmalı analizi. *Sosyal ve Beşeri Bilimler Dergisi, 5*(1), 198–208.

Demir, F. (2007). Atatürk dönemi çalışma hayatımız. *TÜHİS İş Kanunu ve İktisat Dergisi, 20*(4), 1–20.

DeNew, J. P., & Zimmermann, K. F. (1994). Native wage impacts of foreign labor - A random effects panel analysis. *Journal of Population Economics, 7*(2), 177–192. doi:10.1007/BF00173618 PMID:12345483

Deng, J. L. (1988). Properties of relational space for grey system. In *Essential topics on grey system theory and applications* (pp. 1–13). Beijing: China Ocean.

Department for Business Innovation and Skills. (2013). *UK construction an economic analyses of the sector.* Retrieved May 26, 2016, from https://www.gov.uk/government/uploads/system/uploads/attachment_data/file/210060/bis-13-958-uk-construction-an-economic-analysis-of-sector.pdf

Derya, H. (2015). Almanya ve Japonya'nın sanayileşme sürecinde korumacı politikaların önemi. *Akademik Bakış Dergisi, 48*, 97–117.

Desai, S., & Waite, L. (1991). Womens employment during pregnancy and after the first birth: Occupational characteristics and work commitment. *American Sociological Review, 56*(4), 551–566. doi:10.2307/2096274

Deslauriers, J., Dostie, B., & Gagné, R. (2009). L'impact économique de la législation du marché du travail. *Centre sur la productivité et la prospérité*, 1-42.

Detik. (2016). *ILO: Pekerja perempuan masih alami diskriminasi.* Retrieved March 10, 2016, from http://news.detik.com/bbc/3160381/ilo-pekerja-perempuan-masih-alami-diskriminasi

Devereux, P. J. (2004). Changes in relative wages and family labor supply. *The Journal of Human Resources, 39*(3), 696–722. doi:10.2307/3558993

Devlet Planlama Teşkilatı. (2006). *Orta vadeli program 2007-2009.* Ankara: DPT. Retrieved from http://ekutup.dpt.gov.tr/program/2007-09.pdf

Dhéret, C., Lazarowicz, A., Nicoli, F., Pascouau, Y., & Zuleeg, F. (2013). *Making progress towards the completion of the Single European Labor Market. EPC Issue Paper No. 75.* Brussels: European Policy Centre.

Di Tella, R., & MacCulloch, R. (2005). The consequences of labor market flexibility: Panel evidence based on survey data. *European Economic Review, 49*(5), 1225–1259. doi:10.1016/j.euroecorev.2003.11.002

Dietrich, H., & Moller, J. (2016). Youth unemployment in Europe – business cycle and institutional effects. *International Economics & Economic Policy, 13*(1), 5–15. doi:10.1007/s10368-015-0331-1

Djankov, S., & Ramalho, R. (2009). Employment laws in developing countries. *Journal of Comparative Economics, 37*(1), 3–13. doi:10.1016/j.jce.2008.10.003

Djohanputro, B. (2006). *Prinsip-prinsip ekonomi makro. General Series No. 10.* Jakarta: PPM.

Docquier, F., Ozden, C., & Peri, G. (2014). The labor market impact of immigration and emigration in OECD countries. *The Economic Journal, 124*(579), F1106–F1145. doi:10.1111/ecoj.12077

Doepke, M., & Zilibotti, F. (2009). International labor standards and the political economy of child-labor regulation. *Journal of the European Economic Association, 7*(2-3), 508–518. doi:10.1162/JEEA.2009.7.2-3.508

Dong, K., & Liu, Y. (2010). Cross-cultural management in China. *Cross Cultural Management: An International Journal, 17*(3), 223–243. doi:10.1108/13527601011068333

Dooley, D., & Prause, J. (2004). *The social costs of underemployment: Inadequate employment as disguised unemployment.* Cambridge: Cambridge University Press.

Duanmu, J. L. (2014). A race to lower standards? Labor standards and location choice of outward FDI from the BRIC countries. *International Business Review, 23*(3), 620–634. doi:10.1016/j.ibusrev.2013.10.004

Duncan, B., & Trejo, S. J. (2009). *Immigration and the U.S. labor market.* CReAM Discussion Paper Series, 08/09.

Dunlop, J. T. (1958). *Industrial relations systems.* New York: Holt Rinehart and Winston.

Dustmann, C., & Frattini, T. (2011). *Immigration: The European experience.* CReAM Discussion Paper Series, 22/11.

Dustmann, C., Frattini, T. & Preston, I. (2007). *A study of migrant workers and the national minimum wage and enforcement issues that arise.* Report for the Low Pay Commission.

Dustmann, C., Frattini, T., & Glitz, F. (2007). *The impact of migration: A review of the economic evidence.* CReAM Discussion Paper Series, 102.

Dustmann, C., Fabbri, F., & Preston, I. (2005). The impact of immigration on the British labor market. *The Economic Journal, 115*(507), 324–341. doi:10.1111/j.1468-0297.2005.01038.x

Dustmann, C., & Glitz, A. (2005). *Immigration, jobs and wages: Theory, evidence and opinion.* London: Centre for Economic Policy Research.

Dustmann, C., & Glitz, A. (2008). *How do industries and firms respond to changes in local labour supply?* Mimeo.

Dustmann, C., Glitz, F., & Frattini, T. (2008). The labor market impact of immigration. *Oxford Review of Economic Policy, 24*(3), 477–494. doi:10.1093/oxrep/grn024

Dustmann, C., Glitz, F., & Vogel, T. (2010). Employment, wages and the economic cycle: Differences between immigrants and natives. *European Economic Review, 54*(1), 1–17. doi:10.1016/j.euroecorev.2009.04.004

Dustmann, C., & Preston, I. (2012). Estimating the effect of immigration on wages: A Comment. *Journal of the European Economic Association, 10*(1), 216–223. doi:10.1111/j.1542-4774.2011.01056.x

Dwyer, C. J. (2012). *Contingent workforce management: The next-generation guidebook to managing the modern contingent workforce umbrella.* Aberdeen Group.

Dwyer, C. J. (2013). *The state of contingent workforce management 2014: A framework for success.* Ardent Partners.

Ecevit, Y. (1988). *Küreselleşme, yapısal uyum ve kadın emeğinin kullanımında değişmeler.* İstanbul: KSSGM ve İnsan Haklarını Geliştirme Vakfı.

Ecevit, Y. (1995). Kentsel üretim sürecinde kadın emeğinin konumu ve değişen biçimleri. In Ş. Tekeli (Ed.), *Kadın bakış açısından kadınlar.* İstanbul: İletişim Yayınları.

Ecevit, Y. (2008). İşgücüne katılım ve istihdam. In *Türkiye'de toplumsal cinsiyet eşitsizliği: Sorunlar, öncelikler ve çözüm önerileri.* İstanbul: TÜSİAD-KAGİDER.

Edwards, T., & Kuruvilla, S. (2005). International HRM: National business systems, organizational politics and the international division of labour in MNCs. *International Journal of Human Resource Management*, *16*(1), 1–21. doi:10.1080/0958519042000295920

El Badaoui, E., Strobl, E., & Walsh, F. (2008). Is there an informal employment wage penalty? Evidence from South Africa. *Economic Development and Cultural Change*, *56*(3), 683–710. doi:10.1086/533550

Elias, S., & Noone, C. (2011). The growth and development of the Indonesian economy. *RBA Bulletin*, 33-43. Retrieved from http:// www.rba.gov.au/publications/bulletin/2011/dec/pdf/bu-1211-4.pdf

Elsaman, R. (2011). Corporate social responsibility in Islamic law: Labor and employment. *Yonsei Law Journal*, *2*(1), 64–93.

Emerson, J. (2011). Unemployment and labor force participation in the United States. *Economics Letters*, *111*(3), 203–206. doi:10.1016/j.econlet.2011.02.022

Engel, D., & Daniel, M. (2009). *Green jobs and the clean energy economy*. Copenhagen Climate Council.

England, P., Gornick, J., & Shafer, E. F. (2012). Women's employment, education, and the gender gap in 17 countries. *Monthly Labor Review*, *13*(4), 3–12.

English, J. (1970). Not as a patient: Psychological development in a job training program. *The American Journal of Orthopsychiatry*, *40*(1), 142–150. doi:10.1111/j.1939-0025.1970.tb00688.x PMID:5410676

Ergeç, E. H., & Arslan, B. G. (2013). Impact of interest rates on Islamic and conventional banks: The case of Turkey. *Applied Economics*, *45*(17), 2381–2388. doi:10.1080/00036846.2012.665598

Ergeç, E. H., & Kaytancı, B. G. (2014). The causality between returns of interest-based banks and interest free banks: The case of Turkey. *International Journal of Islamic and Middle Eastern Finance and Management*, *7*(4), 443–456. doi:10.1108/IMEFM-07-2014-0072

Erman, T. (2001). Rural migrants and patriarchy in Turkish cities. *International Journal of Urban and Regional Research*, *25*(1), 118–133. doi:10.1111/1468-2427.00301

Ernst & Young. (2016). *World Islamic Banking Competitiveness Report-2016*. Retrieved April 20, 2016, from http://www.ey.com/Publication/vwLUAssets/ey-world-islamic-banking-competitiveness-report-2016/$FILE/ey-world-islamic-banking-competitiveness-report-2016.pdf

Ernst, D. (2000). *Catching up and post-crisis industrial upgrading: Searching for new sources of growth in Korea's electronics industry*. East-West Center Working Paper 2, East-West Center, Honolulu.

Ernst, E., & Sarabia, M. (2015). *The role of construction as an employment provider: A world-wide input-output analysis*. ILO Employment working paper no. 186. Employment Policy Department Development and Investment Branch. Retrieved August 26, 2016, from http://www.ilo.org/wcmsp5/groups/public/---ed_emp/---emp_policy/---invest/documents/publication/wcms_444326.pdf

Ersöz, F. (2009). Avrupa inovasyon göstergeleri (EIS) ışığında Türkiye'nin konumu. *İstanbul Teknik Üniversitesi Sosyal Bilimler Dergisi*, *6*(1), 3-16.

Ersöz, T., Türkoğlu Elitaş, M. N., & Ersöz, F. (2015). OECD ülkelerinde biyokütle enerji üretiminin çok boyutlu ölçekleme analizi ile incelenmesi. *TÜBAV Bilim*, *8*(3), 1–11.

Ersungur, Ş. M., Kızıltan, A., & Polat, Ö. (2007). Türkiye'de bölgelerin sosyo-ekonomik gelişmişlik sıralaması: Temel bileşenler analizi. *Atatürk Üniversitesi İktisadi ve İdari Bilimler Dergisi*, *21*(2), 55–66.

Eser Yılmaz, B., & Terzi, H. (2008). The employment problem in Turkey and European employment strategy. *Erciyes University Faculty of Economics and Administrative Sciences Journal*, *30*, 229–250.

Etheredge, K., Dorf, S., & Thakkar, T. (2009). Optimize your contract labor. *Supply Chain Management Review*, *13*(5), 50–51.

Eurofound. (2012). *NEETs – Young people not in employment, education or training: Characteristics, costs and policy responses in Europe*. Luxembourg: Publications Office of the European Union.

Eurofound. (2014). *Labor mobility in the EU: Recent trends and policies*. Publications Office of the European Union. Luxembourg: European Commission.

European Bank for Reconstruction and Development. (2014). Drivers of innovation. In *Transition Report 2014: Innovation in Transition* (pp. 44-63). Retrieved from http://www.ebrd.com/downloads/research/transition/tr14.pdf

European Commission. (1985). *White Paper on completing the internal market*. COM (85) 310, 14 June. Brussels: European Commission.

European Commission. (2005). *European innovation scoreboard 2005: Comparative analysis of innovation performance*. Maastricht Economic Research Institute on Innovation and Technology (MERIT) and the Joint Research Centre (Institute for the Protection and Security of the Citizen) of the European Commission.

European Commission. (2010). *Geographical and labor market mobility. Special Eurobarometer, 337/Wave 72.5*. Brussels: European Commission.

European Commission. (2011). *The roadmap to a resource efficient Europe* (COM(2011) 571). Retrieved October 21, 2016, from http://ec.europa.eu/environment/resource_efficiency/about/roadmap/index_en.htm

European Commission. (2012). *Single Market Act II–Together for new growth. Communication from the Commission to the European Parliament, the Council, the European Economic and Social Committee and the Committee of the Regions, COM(2012) 573 final*. Brussels: European Commission.

European Commission. (2013). *Labor market developments in Europe 2013. European Economy Series 6/2013*. Brussels: European Commission.

European Commission. (2014). *Labor mobility within the EU*. MEMO, Press Release Database 25 September. Retrieved May 1, 2016, from http://europa.eu/rapid/press-release_MEMO-14-541_en.htm

European Commission. (2015). *Labor mobility in the EU: Facts, figures and the labor mobility package*. DG Employment, Social Affairs and Inclusion Free Movement of Workers and Coordination of Social Security Systems.

Ewing, K. D. (2005). The function of trade unions. *Industrial Law Journal*, *34*(1), 1–22. doi:10.1093/ilj/34.1.1

Eyüboğlu, A., Özar, Ş., & Tanrıöver, H. T. (2000). *Kentlerde kadınların iş yaşamına katılım sorunlarının sosyo-ekonomik ve kültürel boyutları*. Ankara: T. C. Başbakanlık KSSGM.

Fagan, C., Kanjuo-Mrcela, A., & Norman, H. (2012). Work young adults navigating European labour markets: Old and new social risks and employment policies. In T. Knijin (Ed.), *Work, family policies and transitions to adulthood in Europe* (pp. 130–154). London: Palgrave Macmillan. doi:10.1057/9781137284198_6

Feenstra, R. C., Inklaar, R., & Timmer, M. P. (2015). The next generation of the Penn World Table. *The American Economic Review*, *105*(10), 3150–3182. Retrieved from www.ggdc.net/pwt doi:10.1257/aer.20130954

Felbermayr, G., Prat, J., & Schmerer, H. J. (2008). *Globalization and labor market outcomes: Wage bargaining, search frictions and firm heterogeneity.* IZA Discussion Paper, 3363. Retrieved from http://digital.csic.es/bitstream/10261/44732/3/Globalization%20and%20labor%20market.pdf

Felbermayr, G., Prat, J., & Schmerer, H. J. (2011). Trade and unemployment: What do the data say? *European Economic Review*, *55*(6), 741–758. doi:10.1016/j.euroecorev.2011.02.003

Felipe, J., Kumar, U., & Abdon, A. (2010). *As you saw so shall you reap: From capabilities to opportunities.* The Levy Economics Institute, Working Paper Collection, 613.

Ferguson, A., & Folbre, N. (1981). The unhappy marriage of patriarchy and capitalism. In L. Sargent (Ed.), *Women and revolution: A discussion of the unhappy marriage of Marxism and feminism* (pp. 313–339). Boston: South End Press.

Feron, A. (2004). *Poverty and social exclusion in Europe and Greece: Notions, perceptions, policies.* Athens: Sakkoulas. (in Greek)

Ferrarini, B., & Scaramozzino, P. (2016). Production Complexity, adaptability and economic growth. *Structural Change and Economic Dynamics*, *37*, 52–61. doi:10.1016/j.strueco.2015.12.001

Fevre, R. (1984). *Cheap Labour and Racial Discrimination.* Cambridge: Gower.

Fields, G. (1975). Rural-urban migration, urban unemployment and underemployment, and job search activity in LDCs. *Journal of Development Economics*, *2*(2), 165–187. doi:10.1016/0304-3878(75)90014-0 PMID:12265914

Filer, R. K. (1992). The effect of immigrant arrivals on migratory patterns of native workers. In G. J. Borjas & R. B. Freeman (Eds.), *Immigration and the work force: Economic consequences for the united states and Source Areas* (pp. 245–269). Chicago, IL: University of Chicago Press.

Firdausy, C. M. (2005). *Productivity performance in developing countries, country case studies: Indonesia.* Report for the United Nations Industrial Development Organization. Retrieved from https://www.unido.org/uploads/tx_templavoila/Productivity_performance_in_DCs_Indonesia.pdf

Fletcher, M. W. (1996). The Japan spinners association: Creating industrial policy in Meiji Japan. *Journal of Japanese Studies*, *22*(1), 49–75. doi:10.2307/133046

Flinn, C. J. (2006). Minimum wage effects on labor market outcomes under search, matching, and endogenous contact rates. *Econometrica*, *74*(4), 1013–1062. doi:10.1111/j.1468-0262.2006.00693.x

Foged, M., & Peri, G. (2015). *Immigrants' effect on native workers: New analysis on longitudinal data.* CReAM Discussion Paper Series, 07/15.

Fontaine, R. (2007). Cross-cultural management: Six perspectives. *Cross Cultural Management: An International Journal*, *14*(2), 125–135. doi:10.1108/13527600710745732

Foster, K. (2012). *Youth employment and un(der) employment in Canada-more than a temporary problem. In Behind the Numbers* (pp. 1–6). Ottawa: Canadian Center for Policy Alternatives.

Fougere, D., Kramarz, F., & Pouget, J. (2009). Youth unemployment and crime in France. *Journal of the European Economic Association*, *7*(5), 909–938. doi:10.1162/JEEA.2009.7.5.909

Freitag, T. G. (1994). Enclave tourism development: For whom the bell tolls? *Annals of Tourism Research*, *21*(3), 538–554. doi:10.1016/0160-7383(94)90119-8

French, M., & Zarkin, G. (1998). Mental health, absenteeism and earnings at a large manufacturing worksite. *The Journal of Mental Health Policy and Economics*, *1*(4), 161–172. doi:10.1002/(SICI)1099-176X(199812)1:4<161::AID-MHP21>3.0.CO;2-I PMID:11967394

Frey, W. H. (1995). Immigration and internal migration flight—A California case study. *Population and Environment*, *16*(4), 353–375. doi:10.1007/BF02208119

Frey, W. H. (1996). Immigration, domestic migration, and demographic balkanization in America: New evidence for the 1990s. *Population and Development Review*, *22*(4), 741–763. doi:10.2307/2137808

Friedberg, R. M. (2001). The impact of mass migration on the Israeli labor market. *The Quarterly Journal of Economics*, *116*(4), 1373–1408. doi:10.1162/003355301753265606

Friedberg, R. M., & Hunt, J. (1995). The impact of immigration on host country wages, employment and growth. *The Journal of Economic Perspectives*, *9*(2), 23–44. doi:10.1257/jep.9.2.23

Fryer, D. (1992). Psychological or material deprivation: Why does unemployment have mental health consequences. In E. McLaughlin (Ed.), *Understanding Unemployment. New perspectives on active labour market policies* (pp. 103–125). London: Routledge. doi:10.4324/9780203061459.ch6

Furlong, A. (2006). Not a very NEET solution: Representing problematic labour market transitions among early school-leavers. *Work, Employment and Society*, *20*(3), 553–569. doi:10.1177/0950017006067001

Furqani, H., & Mulyany, R. (2009). Islamic banking and economic growth: Empirical evidence from Malaysia. *Journal of Economic Cooperation and Development*, *30*, 59–74.

Fyfe, J. (1978). Youth unemployment: An international perspective. *International Journal of Social Economics*, *5*(1), 51–62. doi:10.1108/eb013820

Gartside, D., Silverstone, Y., Farley, C., & Cantrel, S. M. (2013). *Trends reshaping the future of HR: The rise of the extended workforce*. Accenture.

Gaston, N., & Nelson, D. (2001). *The employment and wage effects of immigration: Trade and labour economics perspectives.* University of Nottingham, Leverhulme Centre for Research on Globalization and Economic Policy Research Paper, 2001/28.

Gaston, N., & Nelson, D. (2000). Immigration and labour-market outcomes in the United States: A political-economy puzzle. *Oxford Review of Economic Policy*, *16*(3), 104–114. doi:10.1093/oxrep/16.3.104

Gaston, N., & Nelson, D. (2002). The employment and wage effects of immigration: Trade and labour economics perspectives. In D. Greenaway, R. Upward, & K. Wakelin (Eds.), *Trade, investment, migration and labour market adjustment* (pp. 201–235). Palgrave Macmillan, UK. doi:10.1057/9781403920188_12

Geiger, J. J. (1999). The new emerging temporary workforce. In *Proceedings of the Academy of Strategic and Organisational leadership.*

Gesthuizen, M., & Wolbers, M. H. J. (2010). Employment transition in the Netherlands, 19802004: Are low educated men subject to structural or cyclical crowding out? *Research in Social Stratification and Mobility*, *28*(4), 437–451. doi:10.1016/j.rssm.2010.06.001

Gevrekçi, Y., Ataç, F. E., Takma, Ç., Akbaş, Y., & Taşkın, T. (2011). Koyunculuk açısından Batı Anadolu illerinin sınıflandırılması. *Kafkas Üniversitesi Veterinerlik Fakültesi Dergisi*, *17*(5), 755–760.

Ge, Y., & Zhi, Q. (2016). Literature review: The green economy, clean energy policy and employment. *Energy Procedia, 88*, 257–264. doi:10.1016/j.egypro.2016.06.159

Ghose, A. K., Majid, N., & Ernst, C. (2008). The global employment challenge. Geneva: International Labour Organisation. Retrieved from http://www.amazon.com/Global-Employment-Challenge-Ajit-Ghose/dp/9221203050

Ghose, A. K., Majid, N., & Ernst, C. (2010). *Küresel istihdam sorunu* (G. Aykaç & S. Kayan, Eds., Ö. F. Çolak, Trans.). Ankara: Efil Yayınevi.

Gibson, N. (2015). *Five ways employers can better manage contingent workers.* Retrieved 15 March, 2016, from http://www.thestaffingstream.com/2015/09/01/five-ways-employers-can-better-manage-contingent-workers/

Giddens, A. (2013). *Sosyoloji* (7th ed.). İstanbul: Kırmızı Yayınları.

Gillman, M. (2011). *A simple theory of structural transformation.* Cardiff Business School, Working Paper Series, E2011/4.

Girginer, N., & Şenak, A. (2016). *A data envelopment analysis application for comparing R&D efficiency of G7 countries and Turkey.* EconWorld 2016 working paper at London.

Givord, P., & Marbot, C. (2015). Does the cost of child care affect female labor market participation? An evaluation of a French reform of childcare subsidies. *Labour Economics, 36*, 99–111. doi:10.1016/j.labeco.2015.07.003

Glaeser, E., & Shleifer, A. (2002). Legal origins. *The Quarterly Journal of Economics, 117*(4), 1193–1229. doi:10.1162/003355302320935016

Glitz, A. (2006). *The labour market impact of immigration: Quasi-experimental evidence.* CReAM Discussion Paper, No. 12/06.

Glitz, A. (2012). The labor market impact of immigration: A quasi-experiment exploiting immigrant location rules in Germany. *Journal of Labor Economics, 30*(1), 175–213. doi:10.1086/662143

Go, S. G., Park, M. K., Kim, Y. S., Lim, C. W., & Kim, C. D. (2009, November). A study about the plan of foreign construction worker's safety management. *Proceedings of Korea Institute of Construction Engineering and Management,* 36–39.

Goaied, M., & Sassi, S. (2011). Financial development, Islamic banking and economic growth evidence from MENA region. *International Journal of Business and Management Science, 4*(2), 105–128.

Göksel, İ. (2013). Female labor force participation in Turkey: The role of conservatism. *Womens Studies International Forum, 41*, 45–54. doi:10.1016/j.wsif.2013.04.006

Göktaş Yılmaz, Ö. (2005). Türkiye ekonomisinde büyüme ile işsizlik oranları arasındaki nedensellik ilişkisi. *İstanbul Üniversitesi İktisat Fakültesi Ekonometri ve İstatistik Dergisi, 2*, 11-29.

Göktaş Yılmaz, O. (2005). The causality relationship between growth and unemployment rates in the Turkish economy. *Economie & Statistique, 2*, 11–29.

Golany, B., & Roll, Y. (1989). An application procedure for DEA. *Omega, 17*(3), 237–250. doi:10.1016/0305-0483(89)90029-7

Gong, X., & Van Soest, A. (2002). Wage differentials and mobility in the urban labour market: A panel data analysis for Mexico. *Labour Economics, 9*(4), 513–529. doi:10.1016/S0927-5371(02)00045-3

Gonzalez, L., & Ortega, F. (2007). *How do very open economies adjust to large immigration flows? Recent evidence from Spanish regions.* Universitat Pompeu Fabra Working Paper, 1059.

Gordon, M. (1979). *Youth education and unemployment problems: an international perspective*. New York: Carnegie Council on Policy Studies in Higher Education.

Government of Bangladesh. (2002). *National information and communication technology (ICT) policy*. Dhaka: Ministry of Science and Information and Communication Technology.

Gower, M., & Hawkins, O. (2013). *Ending of transitional restrictions for Bulgarian and Romanian workers*. Standard Note SN/HA/06606, House of Commons Library.

Gözgör, G. (2014). The impact of trade openness on the unemployment rate in G7 countries. *The Journal of International Trade & Economic Development*, *23*(7), 1018–1037. doi:10.1080/09638199.2013.827233

Granger, C. W. J. (1969). Investigating causal relations by econometric models and cross-spectral methods. *Econometrica*, *37*(3), 424–438. doi:10.2307/1912791

Granger, C. W. J. (1980). Testing for causality: A personal viewpoint. *Journal of Economic Dynamics & Control*, *2*, 329–352. doi:10.1016/0165-1889(80)90069-X

Granger, C. W. J. (1988). Some recent developments in the concept of causality. *Journal of Econometrics*, *39*(1-2), 199–211. doi:10.1016/0304-4076(88)90045-0

Greene, W. (2000). *Econometric Analysis*. Upper Saddle River, NJ: Prentice-Hall.

Greenwood, J., & Jovanovic, B. (1990). Financial development, growth and the distribution of income. *Journal of Political Economy*, *98*(5), 1076–1107. doi:10.1086/261720

Gregg, P., & Tominey, E. (2005). The wage scar from male youth unemployment. *Labour Economics*, *12*(4), 487–509. doi:10.1016/j.labeco.2005.05.004

Griffith, R., & Macartney, G. (2014). Employment protection legislation, multinational firms, and innovation. *The Review of Economics and Statistics*, *96*(1), 135–150. doi:10.1162/REST_a_00348

Grossman, J. B. (1982). The substitutability of natives and immigrants in production. *The Review of Economics and Statistics*, *64*(4), 596–603. doi:10.2307/1923944

Guan, J., & Chen, K. (2012). Modeling the relative efficiency of national innovation systems. *Research Policy*, *41*(1), 102–115. doi:10.1016/j.respol.2011.07.001

Gujarati, D. N. (1995). *Basic Econometrics*. New York: McGraw-Hill.

Güler, E. (2012). Geçiş ekonomileri ve Yeni Kurumsal İktisat'ın yeniden yükselişi. *Doğuş Üniversitesi Dergisi*, *13*(1), 52–68.

Gumelar, G. (2016). *BPS: Laju ekonomi 2015 banyak terganjal faktor eksternal*. Retrieved September 4, 2016, from http://www.cnnindonesia.com/ekonomi/20160205135559-78-109139/bps-laju-ekonomi-2015-banyak-terganjal-faktor-eksternal/

Gündüz-Hoşgör, A., & Smits, J. (2006). *Variation in labor market participation of married women in Turkey*. Nijmegen: Radboud University.

Günsoy, G., & Özsoy, C. (2012). Türkiye'de kadın işgücü, eğitim ve büyüme ilişkisinin VAR analizi. *Finans Politik & Ekonomik Yorumlar*, *49*(568), 21–39.

Gustafsson, S., & Jacobsson, R. (1985). Trends in female labor-force participation in Sweden. *Journal of Labor Economics*, *3*(1), 256–274. doi:10.1086/298084 PMID:12267649

Gustavsson, M., & Osterholm, P. (2006). The informational value of unemployment statistics: A note on the time series properties of participation rates. *Economics Letters*, *92*(3), 428–433. doi:10.1016/j.econlet.2006.03.032

Hacker, R. S., & Hatemi-J, A. (2006). Tests for causality between integrated variables using asymptotic and bootstrap distributions: Theory and application. *Applied Economics*, *38*(13), 1489–1500. doi:10.1080/00036840500405763

Hadri, K. (2000). Testing for stationarity in heterogeneous panel data. *The Econometrics Journal*, *3*(2), 148–161. doi:10.1111/1368-423X.00043

Haerer, D., & Pratson, L. (2015). Employment trends in the U.S. electricity sector, 2008–2012. *Energy Policy*, *82*, 85–98. doi:10.1016/j.enpol.2015.03.006

Haghighat, E. (2002). Culture, development and female labor force participation: Disaggregating different sectors. *International Review of Sociology*, *12*(3), 343–362. doi:10.1080/0390670022000041376

Hahm, J. H. (2003). The government, the chaebol and financial ınstitutions before the economic crisis. In S. Haggard, W. Lim, & E. Kim (Eds.), *Economic crisis and corporate restructuring in Korea: Reforming the Chaebol* (pp. 79–101). Cambridge, UK: Cambridge University Press. doi:10.1017/CBO9781139085083.006

Hair, J. F., Anderson, R. E., Tahtam, R. L., & Black, W. C. (1998). *Multivariate data analysis*. Prentice-Hall.

Haisken DeNew, J. P., & Zimmerman, K. F. (1999). Wage and mobility effects of trade and migration. In M. Dewatripont & A. Sapir (Eds.), International trade and employment: The European experience (pp. 139-160). Oxford University Press. doi:10.1093/0198293607.003.0008

Hallak, J. C. (2006). Product quality and the direction of trade. *Journal of International Economics*, *68*(1), 238–265. doi:10.1016/j.jinteco.2005.04.001

Haltiwanger, J., Scarpetta, S., & Schweiger, H. (2014). Cross country differences in job reallocation: The role of industry, firm size and regulations. *Labour Economics*, *26*, 11–25. doi:10.1016/j.labeco.2013.10.001

Hanson, G. H., & Slaughter, M. J. (2002). Labor-market adjustment in open economies: Evidence from US States. *Journal of International Economics*, *57*(1), 3–29. doi:10.1016/S0022-1996(01)00138-6

Harding, S. (1981). What is the real material base of patriarchy and capital? In L. Sargent (Ed.), *Women and revolution: A discussion of the unhappy marriage of Marxism and feminism* (pp. 15–164). Boston: South End Press.

Härdle, W. K., & Simar, L. (2012). Applied multivariate statistical analysis (3rd ed.). Springer. doi:10.1007/978-3-642-17229-8

Hardt, M., & Negri, A. (2001). *Empire*. Cambridge, MA: Harvard University Press.

Hare, D. (2016). What accounts for the decline in labor force participation among married women in urban China. 1991–2011? *China Economic Review*, *38*, 251–266. doi:10.1016/j.chieco.2016.01.004

Haron, S., & Ahmad, N. (2000). The effects of conventional interest rates and rate of profits on funds deposited with Islamic banking system in Malaysia. *International Journal of Islamic Financial Services*, *1*(4), 1–7.

Harrison, R., Jaumandreu, J., Mairesse, J., & Peters, B. (2014). Does innovation stimulate employment? A firm-level analysis using comparable micro-data from four European countries. *International Journal of Industrial Organization*, *35*, 29–43. doi:10.1016/j.ijindorg.2014.06.001

Harris, R. D., & Tzavalis, E. (1999). Inference for unit roots in dynamic panels where the time dimension is fixed. *Journal of Econometrics*, *91*(2), 201–226. doi:10.1016/S0304-4076(98)00076-1

Harrod, J., & O'Brien, R. (Eds.). (2002). *Global unions? Theory and strategy of organised labour in the global political economy*. London: Routledge.

Hartmann, D., & Pyka, A. (2013). *Innovation, economic diversification and human development.* FZID Discussion Papers, 65-2013.

Hartmann, D., Guevara, M. R., Jara-Figueroa, C., Aristaran, M., & Hidalgo, C. A. (2015). Linking *economic complexity, institutions and income inequality*. Retrieved November 2, 2015, from http://arxiv.org/abs/1505.07907

Hartmann, H. (1992). Marksizm'le Feminizm'in mutsuz evliliği. In G. A. Savran & N. Tura (Eds.), *Kadının görünmeyen emeği: Maddeci bir feminizm üzerine* (G. Aygen, Trans.). (pp. 128–170). İstanbul: Kardelen.

Hartog, J., & Zorlu, A. (2005). The effect of immigration on wages in three European countries. *Journal of Population Economics*, *18*(1), 113–151. doi:10.1007/s00148-004-0204-3

Harvey, D. (2005). *A brief history of neoliberalism*. New York: Oxford University Press.

Harvey, D. (2010). *The enigma of capital: And the crises of capitalism*. London: Profile.

Hasan, M. M., & Dridi, J. (2010). *The effects of the global crisis on Islamic and conventional banks: A comparative study*. Working Paper, IMF 10-201. International Monetary Fund.

Hasan, R., Mitra, D., & Ural, B. (2007a). Trade liberalisation, labour market institutions and poverty reduction: Evidence from India states. *India Policy Forum, 3*, 71-122.

Hasan, R., Mitra, D., & Ramaswamy, K. (2007b). Trade reforms, labor regulations, and labor-demand elasticities: Empirical evidence from India. *The Review of Economics and Statistics*, *89*(3), 466–481. doi:10.1162/rest.89.3.466

Hasoloan, M. A. (2006). Country report the Indonesian labor market. In *Forum on the Restated OECD Jobs Strategy in Tokyo, Tokyo*. Retrieved from http://www.oecd.org/fr/els/emp/37873500.pdf

Hassan, A., & Burns, P. (2014). Tourism policies of Bangladesh – A contextual analysis. *Tourism Planning and Development*, *11*(4), 463–466. doi:10.1080/21568316.2013.874366

Hatton, T. J., & Tani, M. (2005). Immigration and inter-regional mobility in the UK, 1982–2000. *The Economic Journal*, *115*(507), F342–F358. doi:10.1111/j.1468-0297.2005.01039.x

Hausman, J. A. (1978). Specification tests in econometrics. *Econometrica*, *46*(6), 1251–1271. doi:10.2307/1913827

Hausmann, R., & Klinger, B. (2006). *Structural transformation and patterns of comparative advantage in the product space*. CID Working paper, 128.

Hausmann, R., & Klinger, B. (2007). *The structure of the product space and the evolution of comparative advantage*. CID Working Paper, Harvard University, 146.

Hausmann, R., Tyson, L. D., & Zahidi, S. (2012). *The global gender gap report*. Geneva: The World Economic Forum.

Hausmann, R., & Hidalgo, C. A. (2011). The network structure of economic output. *Journal of Economic Growth*, *16*(4), 309–342. doi:10.1007/s10887-011-9071-4

Hausmann, R., Hidalgo, C. A., Bustos, S., Coscia, M., Chung, S., Jimerez, J., & Yıldırım, M. A. et al. (2011). *The atlas of economic complexity: Mapping paths to prosperity. Center for International Development at Harvard University and Macro Connections MIT Media Lab*. Cambridge, MA: Puritan Press.

Hausmann, R., Hwang, J., & Rodrik, D. (2007). What you export matters. *Journal of Economic Growth*, *12*(1), 1–25. doi:10.1007/s10887-006-9009-4

Heid, B., & Larch, M. (2012). Migration, trade and unemployment. *Economics: The Open-Access, Open-Assessment E-Journal, 6*(4), 1-40. Retrieved from10.5018/economics-ejournal.ja.2012-4

Heinz, F. F., & Warmedinger, W. M. (2006). *Cross-border labor mobility within an enlarged EU.* ECB Occasional Paper Series No. 52. Frankfurt: European Central Bank.

Henriques, C. O., Coelho, D. H., & Cassidy, N. L. (2016). Employment impact assessment of renewable energy targets for electricity generation by 2020—An IO LCA approach. *Sustainable Cities and Society, 26*, 519–530. doi:10.1016/j.scs.2016.05.013

Henson, R. (2008). Contingent workforce: beyond the four walls. In K. V. Beaman (Ed.), *HR frontiers: Shifting borders and changing boundaries* (pp. 211–226). IHRIM Press: Futura Publishing.

Hidalgo, C. A. (2009). *The dynamics of economic complexity and the product space over a 42 year period.* CID Working Paper, Harvard University, 189.

Hidalgo, C. A. (2011). *Discovering southern and east Africa's industrial opportunities.* GMF Economic Policy Paper Series.

Hidalgo, C. A., & Hausmann, R. (2009). The building of economic complexity, proceedings of the national academy of sciences of the United States of America. *Proceedings of the National Academy of Sciences of the United States of America, 106*(26), 10570–10575. doi:10.1073/pnas.0900943106 PMID:19549871

Hidalgo, C., Klinger, B., Barabasi, A. L., & Hausmann, R. (2007). The product space conditions the development of nations. *Science, 317*(5827), 482–487. doi:10.1126/science.1144581 PMID:17656717

Hill, C., Corbett, C., & Rose, A. (2010). *Why So Few? Women in Science, Technology, Engineering, and Mathematics.* Washington, DC: AAUW.

HireRight. (2015). *Employment screening benchmarking report.* Retrieved 24 January, 2016, from http://www.hireright.com/benchmarking

Hirschman, A. O. (1958). *The strategy of economic development.* New Haven, CT: Yale University Press.

Hoffman, N. (2011). *Schooling the in the Workplace – How Six of the World's Best Vocational Education Systems Prepare Young People for Jobs and Life.* Cambridge, MA: Harvard Education Press.

Holland, D., Liadze, I., Rienzo, C., & Wilkinson, D. (2013). The relationship between graduates and economic growth across countries. *BIS Research Paper, 110.*

Hollanders, H., & Celikel-Esser, F. (2007). Measuring innovation efficiency. INNO Metrics 2007 report, European Commission, DG Enterprise, Brussels.

Honda, Y. (1985). Testing the error components model with non-normal disturbances. *The Review of Economic Studies, 52*(4), 681–690. doi:10.2307/2297739

Hornstein, A., & Lubik, T. A. (2010). *The rise in long-term unemployment: Potential causes and implications.* Richmond, VA: Federal Reserve Bank of Richmond. Retrieved March 8, 2016, from http://search.proquest.com/docview/874210915?accountid=48149

Horta, I. M., Camanho, A. S., & Costa, J. M. (2012). Performance assessment of construction companies: A study of factors promoting financial soundness and innovation in the industry. *International Journal of Production Economics, 137*(1), 84–93. doi:10.1016/j.ijpe.2012.01.015

Hoşgör, S., & Tansel, A. (2010). *2050'ye doğru nüfusbilim ve yönetim: Eğitim, işgücü, sağlık ve sosyal güvenlik sistemine yansımalar (Yayın No: TUSIAD-T/2010/11/505)*. İstanbul: Türkiye Sanayicileri ve İşadamları Derneği ve Birleşmiş Milletler Nüfus Fonu.

Hossain, A. A. (2012). *Macroeconomic and monetary policy issues in Indonesia*. London: Routledge.

Hotz, V. J., Klerman, J. A., & Willis, R. J. (1997). The economics of fertility in developed countries. In M. R. Rosenzweig & O. Stark (Eds.), *Handbook of population and family economics* (pp. 275–347). Amsterdam: Elsevier. doi:10.1016/S1574-003X(97)80024-4

Hsia, K. H., & Wu, J. H. (1997). A study on the data preprocessing in grey relational analysis. *Journal of Chinese Grey System, 1*, 47–53.

Hsu, Y. (2011). Cross national comparison of innovation efficiency and policy application. *African Journal of Business Management, 5*(4), 1378–1387.

Hull, K. (2009). Understanding the relationship between economic growth, employment and poverty reduction. In Promoting pro-poor growth: Employment (pp. 69–94). Paris: Organization for Economic Cooperation and Development. Retrieved from https://www.oecd.org/dac/ povertyreduction/43280288.pdf

Hunter, J. (1998). The Japanese experience of economic development. In P. O'Brien (Ed.), *Industrialisation: Critical perspectives on the world economy* (pp. 71–141). London: Routledge.

Hunt, J. (1992). The impact of the 1962 repatriates from Algeria on the French labor market. *Industrial & Labor Relations Review, 45*(3), 556–572. doi:10.1177/001979399204500310

Hur, J., & Zhao, L. (2009). Labor standards, labor-management bargaining and international rivalry. *Journal of Economic Behavior & Organization, 71*(2), 259–272. doi:10.1016/j.jebo.2009.04.002

Hwang, B. G., & Ng, W. J. (2013). Project management knowledge and skills for green construction: Overcoming challenges. *International Journal of Project Management, 31*(2), 272–284. doi:10.1016/j.ijproman.2012.05.004

Hyman, R. (2007). How can trade unions act strategically? *Transfer: European Review of Labour and Research, 13*(2), 193–210. doi:10.1177/102425890701300204

Ibis World. (2012). *Report top 10 fastest growing industries*. Retrieved May 26, 2016, from http://www.newstatesman.com/sites/default/files/files/Fastest%20Growing%20Industries.pdf

İçduygu, A. (2012). Demography and immigration/emigration. In M. Heper & S. Sayarı (Eds.), *The Routledge handbook of modern Turkey* (pp. 328–338). London: Routledge.

Ifo Institute for Economic Research. (1997). *A comparative analysis of Japanese and German economic success*. Sakura Institute of Research, Springer.

ILO. (2008). Global employment trends for youth. Geneva: ILO (International Labour Organization).

Im, K. S., Pesaran, M. H., & Shin, Y. (2003). Testing for unit roots in heterogeneous panels. *Journal of Econometrics, 115*(1), 53–74. doi:10.1016/S0304-4076(03)00092-7

India Brand Equity Foundation. (2016). *Indian consumer durables and FMCG industry analysis*. Retrieved 22 February, 2016, from http://www.ibef.org/industry/fmcg-presentation

India Business Insight. (2014). *India ranks second in contingent workforce availability (stands at the top in cost efficiency)*. Informatics India Limited.

Institute for Human Development. (2014). *India labour and employment report 2014: Workers in the era of globalization*. New Delhi: Academic Foundation.

International Airports Authority Employees Union vs. Airport Authority of India, (1997). *Supreme Court Cases (SCC) 754*.

International Labour Office. (2011). *Global employment trends for youth: 2011 update*. Geneva: ILO.

International Labour Office. (2015). *World employment and social outlook: Trends 2015*. Geneva: ILO.

International Labour Organization. (1930). *Forced labour convention* (No.29). Retrieved from http://www.ilo.org/dyn/normlex/en/f?p=NORMLEXPUB:12100:0:NO:12100:P12100_INSTRUMENT_ID:312174:NO

International Labour Organization. (1957). *Abolition of Forced Labour Convention* (No.105). Retrieved from http://www.ilo.org/dyn/normlex/en/f?p=NORMLEXPUB:12100:0:NO:12100:P12100_INSTRUMENT_ID:312250:NO

International Labour Organization. (1998). *About the declaration*. Retrieved from http://www.ilo.org/declaration/thedeclaration/lang--en/index.htm

International Labour Organization. (1998). *Declaration on Fundamental Principles and Rights at Work: Declaration overview*. Retrieved from http://www.ilo.org/wcmsp5/groups/public/---ed_norm/---declaration/documents/publication/wcms_095898.pdf

International Labour Organization. (1999). *Worst Forms of Child Labour Convention* (No.182). Retrieved from http://www.ilo.org/dyn/normlex/en/f?p=NORMLEXPUB:12100:0:NO:12100:P12100_INSTRUMENT_ID:312327:NO

International Labour Organization. (2001). *Stopping forced labour*. Geneva: International Labour Office.

International Labour Organization. (2001). *The construction industry in the twenty-first century: Its image, employment prospects and skill requirements*. Retrieved May 26, 2016, from http://www.ilo.org/public/english/standards/relm/gb/docs/gb283/pdf/tmcitr.pdf

International Labour Organization. (2004). *World employment report 2004-2005: Employment, productivity and poverty reduction*. Geneva: International Labour Organization.

International Labour Organization. (2008). *Child labor - causes*. United Nations.

International Labour Organization. (2011). *Policies and regulations to combat precarious employment*. Retrieved from September 25, 2016, from http://www.ilo.org/wcmsp5/groups/public/---ed_dialogue/---actrav/documents/meetingdocument/wcms_164286.pdf

International Labour Organization. (2012a). *21 million people are now victims of forced labour, ILO says*. Retrieved 28 January, 2016, from http://www.ilo.org/global/about-the-ilo/newsroom/news/WCMS_181961/lang--en/index.htm

International Labour Organization. (2012b). *Measurement of forced labour: Opportunities and challenges*. Geneva: International Labour Office.

International Labour Organization. (2012c). Global estimate of forced labour: Results and methodology (Special Action Programme to Combat Forced Labour [SAP-FL]). Geneva: International Labour Office.

International Labour Organization. (2013). *Global employment trends 2013: Recovering from a second jobs dip*. Geneva: International Labour Organization.

International Labour Organization. (2013). *Women and men in the informal economy: A statistical picture*. Geneva: International Labour Office, Employment Sector.

International Labour Organization. (2014). *Global employment trends 2014: Risk of a jobless recovery?* Retrieved August 21, 2016, from http://www.ilo.org/wcmsp5/groups/public/---dgreports/---dcomm/---publ/documents/publication/wcms_234107.pdf

International Labour Organization. (2014a). *Profits and poverty: The economics of forced labour*. Geneva: International Labour Office.

International Labour Organization. (2014b). *The Protocol to the Forced Labour Convention*. Retrieved from http://www.ilo.org/wcmsp5/groups/public/---ed_norm/---declaration/documents/publication/wcms_321414.pdf

International Labour Organization. (2014c). *ILO calls for urgent investment in youth work opportunities*. Retrieved from September 25, 2012, from http://bit.ly/QX0Rd2

International Labour Organization. (2015). *Key indicators of the labour market*. Geneva: International Labour Organization.

International Labour Organization. (2015). *Ratifications of fundamental conventions by country*. Retrieved from http://www.ilo.org/dyn/normlex/en/f?p=NORMLEXPUB:10011:0:NO:P10011_DISPLAY_BY,P10011_CONVENTION_TYPE_CODE:1,F

International Labour Organization. (2016). *Key Indicators of the labour market* (8th ed.).

International Labour Organization. (2016). *Labour market segmentation*. Geneva: International Labour Organisation. Retrieved from http://www.ilo.org/global/topics/ employment-security/labour-market-segmentation/lang--en/index.htm

International Monetary Fund. (2013). *Women, work, and the economy: Macroeconomic gains from gender equity*. IMF Staff Discussion Note, SDN/13/10.

International Renewable Energy Agency. (2011). *IRENA working paper: renewable energy jobs: status, prospects & policies*. Abu Dhabi: International Renewable Energy Agency.

International Renewable Energy Agency. (2014). *Renewable energy and jobs – annual review 2014*. Abu Dhabi: International Renewable Energy Agency.

İpekçi Çetin, E. (2003). Çok değişkenli analizlerin pazarlama ile ilgili araştırmalarda kullanımı: 1995-2002 arası yazın taraması. *Akdeniz İ.İ.B.F. Dergisi*, *5*, 32–47.

Iqbal, Z. (1997). Islamic financial systems. *Finance & Development*, (June), 42–45.

Ito, T. (1992). *The Japanese economy*. Cambridge, MA: MIT Press.

Ito, T., & Weinstein, D. E. (1996). Japan and the Asian economies: A Miracle in transition. *Brookings Papers on Economic Activity*, *2*(2), 205–272. doi:10.2307/2534622

Janiak, A. (2006). *Does trade liberalization lead to unemployment? Theory and some evidence*. Universite Libre de Bruxelles.

Jauer, J., Leibig, T., Martin, J. P., & Puhani, P. A. (2014). *Migration as an adjustment mechanism in the crisis? A comparison of Europe and the United States*. CReAM Discussion Paper Series, 10/14.

Jauer, J., Liebig, T., Martin, J. P., & Puhani, P. A. (2014). *Migration as an adjustment mechanism in the crisis? A comparison of Europe and the United States*. IZA Discussion Paper No. 7921. Bonn: Institute for the Study of Labor.

Jeager, D. (1996). *Skill differences and the effect of immigrants on the wages of natives*. US Bureau of Labor Statistics Working Paper, 273.

Jean, S., & Jiménez, M. (2011). The unemployment impact of immigration in OECD countries. *European Journal of Political Economy*, *27*(2), 241–256. doi:10.1016/j.ejpoleco.2010.11.006

Jin, J. C. (2000). Openness and growth: An interpretation of empirical evidence from East Asian countries. *The Journal of International Trade & Economic Development*, *9*(1), 5–17. doi:10.1080/096381900362517

Ji-ying, Z., & Yao, W. (2015). Investigation and study on employment status of migrant workers in Heilongjiang Province. [English Edition]. *The Journal of Northeast Agricultural University*, *22*(1), 83–90. doi:10.1016/S1006-8104(15)30011-8

Joardar, A., Wu, S., & Chen, S. (2014). The impact of national culture and type of entrepreneurs on outsourcing. *The International Entrepreneurship and Management Journal*, *10*(3), 643–659. doi:10.1007/s11365-012-0247-y

Jobson, J. D. (1992). *Applied multivariate data analysis*. New York: Springer-Verlag. doi:10.1007/978-1-4612-0921-8

Johnson, R. A., & Wichern, D. A. (2007). *Applied multivariate statistical analysis* (6th ed.). Englewood Cliffs, NJ: Prentice-Hall.

Jones, S. M., Ross, A., & Sertyesilisik, B. (2010). Testing the unfolding model of voluntary turnover on construction professionals. *Construction Management and Economics*, *28*(3), 271–285. doi:10.1080/01446191003587737

Jovanovic, M. N. (1998). *International economic integration: Limits and prospects*. London: Routledge.

Jovanovic, M. N. (2009). *Evolutionary economic geography: Location and production and the European Union*. Oxfordshire, UK: Routledge.

Jude, C., & Silaghi, M. (2016). Employment effects of foreign direct investment: New evidence from Central and Eastern European countries. *Inter Economics*, *145*, 32–49. doi:10.1016/j.inteco.2015.02.003

Jung, W. S. (1986). Financial development and economic growth: International evidence. *Economic Development and Cultural Change*, *34*(2), 336–346. doi:10.1086/451531

Kabaklarlı, E., Er, P. H., & Buluş, A. (2011). *Economic determinants of Turkish youth unemployment problem: Co integration analysis*. Retrieved from http://kastoria.teikoz.gr/icoae2/wordpress/wp-content/uploads/2011/10/028.pdf

Kabaklarlı, E., Er, P. H., & Buluş, A. (2011). Economic determinants of Turkish youth unemployment problem: Cointegration analysis.*International Conference on Applied Economics – ICOAE*, (pp. 267-272).

Kabeer, N. (2003). *Gender mainstreaming in poverty eradication and the Millennium Development Goals*. London: The Commonwealth Secretariat, the International Development Research Center, and the Canadian International Development Agency. doi:10.14217/9781848598133-en

Kalaycı, Ş. (2005). *SPSS uygulamalı çok değişkenli istatistik teknikleri* (2nd ed.). Ankara: Asi l Yayın Dağıtım Ltd. Şti.

Kaldor, N. (1967). Strategic factors in economic development. New York: Ithaca.

Kaleem, A., & Isa, M. M. (2003). Causal relationship between Islamic and conventional banking instruments in Malaysia. *International Journal of Islamic Financial Services*, *4*(4), 1–8.

Kalleberg, A. L. (2009). Precarious Work, Insecure Workers: Employment Relations in Transition. *American Sociological Review*, *74*(1), 11–22. doi:10.1177/000312240907400101

Kapusuzoğlu, A., & İbicioğlu, M. (2013). Portföy çeşitlemesi: İMKB'de sektörel endeksler üzerine bir analiz. *Muhasebe ve Finansman Dergisi,* 119-138.

Kara, A. H., & Orak, M. (2008, October). *Enflasyon hedeflemesi*. Paper presented at the meeting of the Ekonomik Tartışmalar Konferansı, İstanbul, Turkey.

Karacaer, S., & Kapusuzoğlu, A. (2010). İMKB turizm sektöründe entellektüel sermayenin firma değeri üzerindeki etkisinin analizi. *Anatolia: Turizm Araştırmaları Dergisi*, *21*(1), 98–108.

Karaca, O. (2003). Türkiye'de enflasyon-büyüme ilişkisi: Zaman serisi analizi. *Doğuş Üniversitesi Dergisi*, *4*(2), 247–255.

Karaçor, Z., Şaylan, Ş., & Üçler, G. (2009). Türkiye ekonomisinde enflasyon ve ekonomik büyüme ilişkisi üzerine eşbütünleşme ve causality analizi (1990-2005). *Niğde Üniversitesi İİBF Dergisi*, *2*(2), 60–74.

Karamesini, M. (2004). Unemployment, poverty and social exclusion in Greece. In M. Petmezidou & C. Papatheodorou (Ed.), Poverty and Social Exclusion (pp. 399-438). Athens: Exantas. (in Greek)

Karantinos, D. (2012). *The Impact of the Crisis on the Greek Labour Market*. European Employment Observatory, Ad Hoc Paper.

Kar, M., Nazlıoğlu, Ş., & Ağır, H. (2014). Trade openness, financial development and economic growth in Turkey: Linear and nonlinear causality analysis. *BDDK Bankacılık ve Finansal Piyasalar*, *8*(1), 63–86.

Kasnakoğlu, Z., & Dayıoğlu, M. (1997). Female labor force participation and earnings differentials between genders in Turkey. In J. M. Rives & M. Yousefi (Eds.), *Economic dimensions of gender inequality: A global perspective* (pp. 95–117). Westport, CT: Praeger.

Kasnakoğlu, Z., & Dayıoğlu, M. (2002). Measuring the value of home production in Turkey. In T. Bulutay (Ed.), *The new developments in national accounts*. Ankara: DİE.

Kasri, R. A., & Kassim, S. H. (2009). Empirical determinants of saving in the Islamic Banks: Evidence from Indonesia. *Journal of King Abdulaziz University: Islamic Economics*, *22*(2), 181–201.

Kassim, S., Majid, M. A., & Yusof, R. M. (2009). Impact of monetary policy shocks on conventional and Islamic banks in a dual banking system: Evidence from Malaysia. *Journal of Economic Cooperation and Development*, *30*, 41–58.

Keep, E. (2012). *Youth Transitions, the Labour Market and Entry into Employment: Some Reflections and Questions*. SKOPE Research Paper No. 108. Cardiff, UK: Cardiff University.

Kepenek, Y., & Yentürk, N. (2005). *Türkiye ekonomisi*. İstanbul: Remzi Kitabevi.

Kesici, M. R. (2010). In high growth phase of Turkey economy employment and unemployment. *The Journal of Industrial Relations & Human Resources*, *12*(3), 7–26.

Kessler, R. C., House, J. S., & Turner, J. B. (1987). Unemployment and health in a community sample. *Journal of Health and Social Behavior*, *28*(1), 51–59. doi:10.2307/2137140 PMID:3571906

Kessler, R., & Frank, R. (1997). The impact of psychiatric disorders on work loss days. *Psychological Medicine*, *27*(4), 861–873. doi:10.1017/S0033291797004807 PMID:9234464

Khan, M. (1986). Islamic interest-free banking: A theoretical analysis. *Staff Papers - International Monetary Fund. International Monetary Fund*, *33*(1), 1–27. doi:10.2307/3866920

Kia, A., & Darrat, A. F. (2003). *Modeling money demand under the profit-sharing banking scheme: Evidence on policy invariance and long-run stability*. Working Paper, Department of Economics, Carleton University. Retrieved April 20, 2016, from http://www.mafhoum.com/press7/193E13.pdf

Killingsworth, M., & Heckman, J. (1986). Female labor supply: A survey. In O. Ashenfelter & R. Layard (Eds.), *Handbook of labor economics* (Vol. 1, pp. 103–204). Amsterdam: North- Holland.

Kim, D., & Jeong, J. (2016). Electricity restructuring, greenhouse gas emissions efficiency and employment reallocation. *Energy Policy*, *92*, 468–476. doi:10.1016/j.enpol.2016.02.009

Kim, L. (2000). The dynamics of technological learning in industrialization. *International Social Science Journal*, *53*(168), 297–308. doi:10.1111/1468-2451.00316

Kim, L., & Nelson, R. (2000). *Technology, learning, and innovation: Experiences of newly industrializing economies*. Cambridge, UK: Cambridge University Press.

Kim, S., Kim, J. D., Shin, Y., & Kim, G. H. (2015). Cultural differences in motivation factors influencing the management of foreign laborers in the Korean construction industry. *International Journal of Project Management*, *33*(7), 1534–1547. doi:10.1016/j.ijproman.2015.05.002

Kınalı, F. (2012). *Faizsiz sistemde bankacılık anlayışı ve kredi işlemleri* (Unpublished master's thesis). T.C. Selçuk Üniversitesi Sosyal Bilimler Enstitüsü İşletme Anabilim Dalı Muhasebe Finansman Bilim Dalı, Konya.

King, M. L., & Wu, P. X. (1997). Locally optimal one sided tests for multiparameter hypotheses. *Econometric Reviews*, *16*(2), 131–156. doi:10.1080/07474939708800379

King, R. G., & Levine, R. (1993). Finance and growth: Schumpeter might be right. *The Quarterly Journal of Economics*, *108*(3), 717–737. doi:10.2307/2118406

Kinoshita, Y., & Guo, F. (2015). *What can boost female labor force participation in Asia?* IMF Working Paper, WP/15/56.

Kirat, T. (2006). *Les indicateurs de protection de l'emploi (OCDE et Banque Mondiale)*. Document de travail pour le Projet « Évaluation du droit du travail ».

Kırdar, M. G., Tayfur, M. D., & Koç, İ. (2009). *The impact of schooling on the timing of marriage and fertility: Evidence from a change in compulsory schooling law*. Ankara: Department of Economics, Middle East Technical University.

Klepper, S. (2002). The capabilities of new firms and the evolution of the US automobile industry. *Industrial and Corporate Change*, *11*(4), 645–666. doi:10.1093/icc/11.4.645

Klepper, S., & Simons, K. L. (2000). Dominance by birthright: Entry of prior radio producers and competitive ramifications in the U.S. television receiver industry. *Strategic Management Journal*, *21*(10-11), 997–1016. doi:10.1002/1097-0266(200010/11)21:10/11<997::AID-SMJ134>3.0.CO;2-O

Kluve, J. (2010). The effectiveness of European active labor market programs. *Labour Economics*, *17*(6), 904–918. doi:10.1016/j.labeco.2010.02.004

Knabe, A., & Rätzel, S. (2011). Scarring or scaring? The psychological impact of past unemployment and future unemployment risk. *Economica*, *78*(310), 283–293. doi:10.1111/j.1468-0335.2009.00816.x

Kochhar, K., Mitra, P., & Nayar, R. (2012). More jobs, better jobs. *Finance & Development*, *49*(2), 48–51.

Kohama, H. (1990). Japans economic development and foreign trade. In L. Chung & Y. Ippei (Eds.), *The economic development of Japan and Korea: A parallel with lessons* (pp. 3–18). New York: Praeger.

Köksel, B., & Fisunoğlu, H. M. (2013). Türkiye'de işsizlik ve istihdam politikası önerileri. In H. Atik (Ed.), *Prof. Dr. Cihan Dura'ya armağan 2000'li yıllarda Türkiye ekonomisi: Yapısal dönüşümler, ana sorunlar ve çözüme dönük politika önerileri* (pp. 23–48). Ankara: Nobel Yayıncılık.

Kol, E. N., & Karaçor, Z. (2012). 2001 güçlü ekonomiye geçiş programı ve istihdam üzerine etkileri. *Maliye Dergisi*, *162*, 379–395.

Kompas. (2013). *Wapres imbau dunia usaha menjangkau wirausaha muda*. Kompas, January 18, 2013. Retrieved September, 2016, from http://nasional.kompas.com/read/2013/01/18/04034059/wapres.imbau.dunia.usaha.menjangkau.wirausaha.muda on September 10, 2016.

Kompas. (2015, July 10). Penguatan productivitas (strengthening productivity). *Ekonomi, 17*.

Koray, M. (1992). Çalışma yaşamında kadın gerçekleri. *Amme İdaresi Dergisi, 25*(1), 25–40.

Koray, M., Demirbilek, S., & Demirbilek, T. (2000). *Gıda işkolunda çalışan kadınların koşulları ve geleceği*. Ankara: T.C. Başbakanlık KSSGM.

Korgaokar, C., & Myrstad, G. (1997). *Protecting children in the world of work*. International Labour Organization.

Korkmaz, M., Alacahan, N. D., Cesim, D. T., Yücel, A. S., & Aras, G. (2013). Türkiyede kadın istihdamının Amerika Birleşik Devletlerindeki kadın istihdamı ile karşılaştırılması. *Turkish Studies, 8/9*(Summer), 1845–1863. doi:10.7827/TurkishStudies.5494

Kotsemir, M. N. (2013). *Measuring national innovation systems efficiency - A review of DEA approach*. Higher School of Economics Research Paper No. WP BRP, 16.

Kotulic, R., Huttmanova, E., Vozarova, I. K., & Nagy, J. (2015). The structural analysis of the sectors of Slovak economy and employment in times of global change and the subsequent development. *Procedia Economics and Finance, 23*, 1590–1595. doi:10.1016/S2212-5671(15)00363-9

Kountentakis, F. (2012). *Unemployment Dynamics in the Greek Crisis*. University of Crete, Working Paper.

Krause, A., Rinne, U., & Zimmermann, K. F. (2014). *How far away is a Single European Labor Market?* IZA Discussion Paper No. 8383. Bonn: Institute for the Study of Labor.

Kretsos, L. (2011). Union responses to the rise of precarious youth employment in Greece. *European Journal of Industrial Relations, 9*(1), 453–472. doi:10.1111/j.1468-2338.2011.00634.x

Krueger, A. O. (1983). *Trade and employment in developing countries: Synthesis and conclusions* (Vol. 3). University of Chicago Press.

Kugler, A., & Saint-Paul, G. (2004). How do firing costs affect worker flows in a world with adverse selection. *Journal of Labor Economics, 22*(3), 553–584. doi:10.1086/383107

Kuhn, P., & Wooton, I. (1991). Immigration, international trade and the wages of native workers. In J. M. Abowd & R. B. Freeman (Eds.), *Immigration, trade, and the labor market* (pp. 285–304). Chicago: University of Chicago Press.

Kulshreshtha, A. C. (2011). Measuring the unorganized sector in India. *Review of Income and Wealth, 57*, 123–134.

Kunapatarawong, R., & Martínez-Ros, E. (2016). Towards green growth: How does green innovation affect employment? *Research Policy, 45*(6), 1218–1232. doi:10.1016/j.respol.2016.03.013

Kuosmanen, T. (2002). *Modeling blank data entries in data envelopment analysis*. Econ-WPA working paper at Wustl.

Kuratko, D. F., & Hodgetts, R. M. (2007). *Entrepreneurship: Theory, process, practice* (7th ed.). Ohio: Thomson South-Western.

Kurtuluş, K. (1998). Pazarlama araştırmaları (6th ed.). İstanbul: İstanbul Üniv., İşletme Fakültesi Yayınları, No: 28.

Kutlu, E., & Eşkinat, R. (2014). *Dünya ekonomisi*. Ankara: Nisan Kitabevi.

Kyridis, A. (2014). Social vulnerability and social cohesion. The asymptote of a relation. In A. Kyridis (Ed.), *Vulnerable social groups and Lifelong Learning*. Athens: Gutenberg. (in Greek)

Kyui, N. (2016). Expansion of higher education, employment and wages: Evidence from the Russian Transition. *Labour Economics*, *39*, 68–87. doi:10.1016/j.labeco.2016.01.001

La Porta, R., Lopez-de-Silanes, F., Shleifer, A., & Vishny, R. W. (1997). Legal determinants of external finance. *The Journal of Finance*, *52*(3), 1131–1150. doi:10.1111/j.1540-6261.1997.tb02727.x

La Porta, R., Lopez-de-Silanes, F., Shleifer, A., & Vishny, R. W. (1998). Law and finance. *Journal of Political Economy*, *106*(6), 1113–1155. doi:10.1086/250042

Labour Market Statistics. (2005-2015a). *Employment by activity agriculture / construction / industry including construction / manufacturing / services, thousand persons, 2005 – 2015*. Author.

Labour Market Statistics. (2005-2015b). *Employment rate total, thousand persons, 2005 – 2015*. Author.

Lall, S. (2000). *The technological structure and performance of developing country manufactured exports, 1985-1998*. Quenn Elizabeth House University of Oxford Working Paper Series, 44.

LaLonde, R. J., & Topel, R. H. (1991). Labor market adjustments to increased immigration. In J. M. Abowd & R. B. Freeman (Eds.), *Immigration, trade and the labor market* (pp. 167–199). Chicago: University of Chicago Press.

Lamprianidis, L. (2011). *Investing in Getaway*. Athens: Kritiki. (in Greek)

Landmann, O. (2004). Employment, productivity and output growth. *Employment Trends Unit, Employment Strategy Department Employment Strategy Papers, 17*, 1-61. Retrieved from http://www.ilo.int/wcmsp5/groups/public/---ed_emp/---emp_elm/documents/publication/wcms _114299. pdf

Lawless, P., Martin, R., & Hardy, S. (Eds.). (1998). *Unemployment and Social Exclusion: Landscapes of Labour Inequality*. London: Jessica Kingsley Publishers Ltd & Regional Studies Association.

Layard, R., Nickell, S. J., & Jackman, R. (1991). *Unemployment: Macroeconomic performance and the labour market*. Oxford, UK: Oxford University Press.

Lazear, E. P. (1990). Job security provisions and employment. *The Quarterly Journal of Economics*, *105*(3), 699–726. doi:10.2307/2937895

Leamer, E. (1984). *Sources of international comparative advantage: Theory and evidence*. Cambridge, MA: MIT Press.

Leamer, E. E., & Levinsohn, J. (1995). International trade theory: The evidence. In G. Grossman & K. Rogoff (Eds.), *Handbook of international economics* (Vol. 3, pp. 1339–1394). North- Holland.

LeBleu, R., & Sobkowiak, R. (1995). New workforce competency models. *Information Systems Management*, *12*(3), 7–12. doi:10.1080/07399019508962980

Lechman, E., & Kaur, H. (2015). Economic growth and female labor force participation- verifying the u-feminization Hypothesis. New evidence for 162 countries over the period 1990-2012. *Economia e Sociologia (Evora, Portugal)*, *8*(1), 246–257.

Lee, S. Y., Florida, R., & Gates, G. J. (2002). *Innovation, human capital, and creativity*. Working Paper, Software Industry Center, Carnegie Mellon University, Pittsburgh.

Lee, C. H. (2000). Institutions and economic development. In U. Hiemenz (Ed.), *Growth and competition in the new global economy* (pp. 137–156). Paris: OECD Publishing.

Lee, H., & Han, S. Y. (2002). The evolution of the national innovation system in the Korean mobile telecommunication industry. *Communications & Stratégies*, *48*, 161–186.

Lee, S., & Malin, B. A. (2013). Educations role in Chinas structural transformation. *Journal of Development Economics*, *101*, 148–166. doi:10.1016/j.jdeveco.2012.10.006

Lee, T. W., & Mitchell, T. R. (1994). An alternative approach: The unfolding model of employee turnover. *Academy of Management Review*, *19*, 51–89.

Lee, T. W., Mitchell, T. R., Holtom, B. C., McDaniel, L. S., & Hill, J. W. (1999). The unfolding model of voluntary turnover: A replication and extension. *Academy of Management Journal*, *42*(4), 450–462. doi:10.2307/257015

Levin, A., Lin, C. F., & Chu, C. S. J. (2002). Unit root tests in panel data: Asymptotic and finite-sample properties. *Journal of Econometrics*, *108*(1), 1–24. doi:10.1016/S0304-4076(01)00098-7

Levine, R., Loayza, N., & Beck, T. (2000). Financial intermediation and growth: Causality and causes. *Journal of Monetary Economics*, *46*(1), 31–77. doi:10.1016/S0304-3932(00)00017-9

Lewis, E. G. (2004). *Local open economies within the US: How do industries respond to immigration.* Federal Reserve Bank of Philadelphia Working Paper, 04-1.

Lewis, W. A. (1954). Economic development with unlimited supplies of labour. *The Manchester School*, *22*(2), 139–191. doi:10.1111/j.1467-9957.1954.tb00021.x

L'Haridon, O., & Malherbet, F. (2003). Protection de l'emploi et performance du marché du travail. *Revue française d'économie, 17*(4), 21-83.

Licht, A., Goldschmidt, C., & Schwartz, S. H. (2005). Culture, law and corporate governance. *International Review of Law and Economics*, *25*(2), 229–255. doi:10.1016/j.irle.2005.06.005

Lim, J. Y. (2000). The effects of the East Asian crisis on the employment of women and men: The Philippine case. *World Development*, *28*(7), 1285–1306. doi:10.1016/S0305-750X(00)00023-1

Lindbeck, A., & Snower, D. J. (2001). Insiders versus outsiders. *The Journal of Economic Perspectives*, *15*(1), 165–188. doi:10.1257/jep.15.1.165

Lindberg, S. M., Hyde, J. S., Petersen, J. L., & Linn, M. C. (2010). New Trends in Gender and Mathematics Performance: A Meta Analysis. *Psychological Bulletin*, *136*(6), 1123–1135. doi:10.1037/a0021276 PMID:21038941

Lindsay, J., Goldmark, L., Hansen, A., Fawcett, C., & Wang, E. (2016). Workforce connections: Analysis of skills demand in Indonesia. Jakarta: United States Agency for International Development (USAID) and FHI360.

Linn, M. (2007). Women in science: Can evidence inform the debate? *Science*, *317*(5835), 199–200. doi:10.1126/science.1141569

Li, P., Tan, T. C., & Lee, J. Y. (1997). Grey relational analysis of amine inhibition of mild steel corrosion in acids. *Corrosion*, *53*(3), 186–194. doi:10.5006/1.3280459

Litan, R. E., Wyckoff, A. W., & Fealing, K. H. (Eds.). (2012). *Improving measures of science, technology, and innovation: Interim report.* National Academies Press.

Liu, C. Y., & Edwards, J. (2015). Immigrant employment through the Great Recession: Individual characteristics and metropolitan contexts. *The Social Science Journal*, *52*(3), 405–414. doi:10.1016/j.soscij.2014.03.013

Liu, D.-C. (2014). The link between unemployment and labor force participation rates in Japan: A regional perspective. *Japan and the World Economy*, *30*, 52–58. doi:10.1016/j.japwor.2014.02.004

Llull, J. (2014). *The effect of immigration on wages: exploiting exogenous variation at the national level.* CReAM Discussion Paper Series, 36/14.

Longhi, S., Nijkamp, P., & Poot, J. (2005). The meta-analytic assessment of the effect of immigration on wages. *Journal of Economic Surveys*, *19*(3), 451–477. doi:10.1111/j.0950-0804.2005.00255.x

Mabiso, A., Maystadt, J.-F., Hirvonen, K., & Vandercasteelen, J. (2014). *Refugees and food security in host communities: A review of impacts and policy options to enhance resilience. International Food Policy Research Institute*. IFPRI.

Machin, S., & Manning, A. (1998). *The Causes and Consequences of Long – Term Unemployment in Europe* (Vol. 3, pp. 3085–3139). Elsevier Handbook of Labor Economics.

Maddala, G. S., & Wu, S. (1999). A comparative study of unit root tests with panel data and a new simple test. *Oxford Bulletin of Economics and Statistics*, *61*(S1), 631–652. doi:10.1111/1468-0084.61.s1.13

Maggioni, D., Turco, A. L., & Gallegati, M. (2014) Does export complexity matter for firms' output volatility?. *Università Politecnica Dellemarche, Dipartimento di Scienze Economiche e Sociali.* Quaderni Dı Ricerca.

Majid, S. A., & Kassim, S. (2010, August). *Islamic finance and economic growth: The Malaysian experience.* Conference paper, Kuala Lumpur Islamic Finance Forum, Kuala Lumpur.

Makal, A. (2010). Türkiye'de erken cumhuriyet döneminde kadın emeği. *Çalışma ve Toplum, 25*(2), 13–41.

Maloney, W. F. (1999). Does informality imply segmentation in urban labor markets? Evidence from sectoral transitions in Mexico. *The World Bank Economic Review*, *13*(2), 275–302. doi:10.1093/wber/13.2.275

Manacorda, M., Manning, A., & Wadsworth, J. (2006). *The impact of immigration on the structure of male wages: Theory and evidence from Britain.* CReAM Discussion Papers, 08/06. Organisation for Economic Co-operation and Development. Retrieved from http:// data.oecd.org/migration

Mankiw, N. G. (2007). *Principles of economics* (4th ed.). Ohio: Thomson South-Western.

ManpowerGroup Solutions. (n.d.). *Valuable contributors to contingent workforce management.* White Paper.

Margiman. (2008). *Quo vadis kewirausahaan di Indonesia*. Retrieved November 30, 2009, from http://www.ciputra.org/node/95/quo-vadis-kewirausahaan-di-indonesia.htm

Margolis, D., & Fougère, D. (1999). *Moduler les cotisations employeurs à l'assurance-chômage: Le système américain de l'experience rating*. Rapport au Commissariat Général du Plan.

Mariniello, M., Sapir, A., & Terzi, A. (2015). *The long road towards the European Single Market.* Bruegel Working Paper, 2015/01.

Martin, J., Du Marais, B., & Dehaze, A. (2013). *Mise en perspective des difficultés dans la mesure du droit du travail, Direction générale du Trésor.* Retrieved from http://www.tresor.economie.gouv.fr/File/405741

Mazhar, N., & Arain, F. (2015). Leveraging on work integrated learning to snhance Sustainable design practices in the construction industry. *Procedia Engineering, 118*, 434 – 441.

MBO Partners. (2013). *The state of independence in America.* Third Annual Independent Workforce Report.

McCormick, J. (2008). *Understanding the European Union: A concise introduction* (4th ed.). Palgrave Macmillan.

McCrudden, C., & Davies, A. (2000). A perspective on trade and labor rights. *Journal of International Economic Law*, *3*(1), 43–62. doi:10.1093/jiel/3.1.43

McKee-Ryan, F. M., Song, Z., Wanberg, C. R., & Kinicki, A. J. (2005). Psychological and physical well-being during unemployment: A meta-analytic study. *The Journal of Applied Psychology*, *90*(1), 53–76. doi:10.1037/0021-9010.90.1.53 PMID:15641890

McMillan, M. S., & Rodrik, D. (2012). *Globalization, structural change and productivity growth* (IFPRI Discussion Paper 01160, February). Washington, DC: Development Strategy and Governance Division, International Food Policy Research Institute.

McMillan, M., Rodrik, D., & Verduzco-Gallo, I. (2014). Globalization, structural change, and productivity growth, with an update on Africa. *World Development*, *63*, 11–32. doi:10.1016/j.worlddev.2013.10.012

McNamara, M., Bohle, P., & Quinlan, M. (2011). Precarious employment, working hours, work-life conflict and health in hotel work. *Applied Ergonomics*, *42*(2), 225–232. doi:10.1016/j.apergo.2010.06.013 PMID:20643398

Meçik, O., & Karabacak, M. (2011, June). *Türkiye'de enflasyon, finansal derinleşme ve büyüme ilişkisi*. Paper presented at the meeting of the Anadolu Uluslararası İktisat Kongresi II. Eskişehir: Anadolu Üniversitesi.

Meçik, O. (2014). Uluslararası sermaye akımları ve vergilendirilmesi: Türkiye ekonomisi üzerine bir değerlendirme. In E. Gümüş, A. Çelikkaya, E. Ferhatoğlu, M. Aslan, E. Gümüş, S. Bilge, & M. Çildir (Eds.), *Prof. Dr. Fazıl TEKİN'e armağan* (pp. 343–367). Eskişehir: Eskişehir Osmangazi Üniversitesi Basımevi.

Meçik, O., & Afşar, M. (2014). Türkiye ekonomisinde yapısal dönüşümler ve işgücü piyasasındaki gelişmeler. *Optimum Ekonomi ve Yönetim Bilimleri Dergisi*, *1*(2), 1–23.

Menezes-Filho, N. A., & Muendler, M. A. (2011). *Labor reallocation in response to trade reform (No. w17372)*. National Bureau of Economic Research. doi:10.3386/w17372

Menyah, K., Nazlıoğlu, S., & Wolde-Rufael, Y. (2014). Financial development, trade openness and economic growth in African countries: New insights from a panel causality approach. *Economic Modelling*, *37*, 386–394. doi:10.1016/j.econmod.2013.11.044

Miah, M. M. R., & Mizan, A. N. (1995). Labor force participation and fertility: A study of married women in Bangladesh. In M. S. Das & V. K. Gupta (Eds.), *Social status of women in developing countries* (pp. 125–140). New Delhi: M D Publications PVT Ltd.

Michael, R. T. (1985). Consequences of the rise in female labor force participation rates: Questions and probes. *Journal of Labor Economics*, *3*(1), 117–146. doi:10.1086/298078

Mies, M. (1994). Gender and global capitalism. In L. Sklair (Ed.), *Capitalism and development* (pp. 107–122). London: Routledge. doi:10.4324/9780203201961_chapter_6

Millán, A., Millán, J. M., Román, C., & Van Stel, A. (2013). How does employment protection legislation influence hiring and firing decisions by the smallest firms? *Economics Letters*, *121*(3), 444–448. doi:10.1016/j.econlet.2013.09.021

Mills, P. S., & Presley, J. R. (1999). *Islamic finance: Theory and practice*. London: Macmillan. doi:10.1057/9780230288478

Minami, R. (1994). *The economic development of Japan: A quantitative study* (2nd ed.). New York: St. Martin's Press. doi:10.1007/978-1-349-23221-5

Mincer, J. (1958). Investment in human capital and personal ıncome distribution. *Journal of Political Economy*, *66*(4), 281–302. doi:10.1086/258055

Ministry of A Cooperative and Small and Medium Enterprise. (2016). *Data usaha mikro, kecil, dan menengah (UMKM) dan usaha besar (UB).* Retrieved March 3, 2016, from http://www.depkop.go.id/berita-informasi/data-informasi/data-umkm/

Ministry of Finance Department of Strategic Development. (2011). *Research Report, Problems of the labor market in Turkey and recommendations for solution.* Department of Economic and Sectorial Analysis. Retrieved August 7, 2016, from http://www.maliye.gov.tr

Ministry of Manpower and Transmigration, Republic of Indonesia. (n.d.). Retrieved from indonesia.go.id/en/ministries/ministers/ministry-of-manpower

Ministry of Statistics and Programme Implementation. (2014). *Labour and employment statistics.* Government of India.

Minondo, A., & Requena-Silvente, F. (2013). Does complexity explain the structure of trade? *The Canadian Journal of Economics. Revue Canadienne dEconomique, 46*(3), 928–955. doi:10.1111/caje.12033

Mirasgedis, S., Tourkolias, C., Pavlakis, E., & Diakoulaki, D. (2014). A methodological framework for assessing the employment effects associated with energy efficiency interventions in buildings. *Energy and Building, 82*, 275–286. doi:10.1016/j.enbuild.2014.07.027

Moors, A. (1999). Debating Islamic family law: Legal texts and social practices. In M. L. Meriwether & J. E. Tucker (Eds.), *A social history of women and gender in the modern Middle East* (pp. 141–176). Boulder, CO: Westview Press.

Moreira, M. M., & Najberg, S. (2000). Trade liberalisation in Brazil: Creating or exporting jobs? *The Journal of Development Studies, 36*(3), 78–99. doi:10.1080/00220380008422629

Moulton, B. R., & Randolph, W. C. (1989). Alternative tests of the error components model. *Econometrica, 57*(3), 685–693. doi:10.2307/1911059

Moussis, N. (2011). Access to European Union: Law, economics, policies (19th ed.). Rixensart.

Muana, N. (2005). Makro ekonomi: Teori, masalah, dan kebijakan (2nd ed.). Jakarta: PT. Raja Grafika Persada.

Muller, L., & Berger, D. P. (2013). The impact of a country's employment protection legislation on its economic prosperity. *International Journal of Humanities and Social Science, 3*(12), 1–13.

Mundell, R. A. (1961). A theory of optimum currency areas. *The American Economic Review, 51*, 657–665.

Murat, S., & Şahin, L. (2011). Gençlerin istihdamı/işsizliği bakımından Türk eğitim sisteminin değerlendirilmesi. *Çalışma ve Toplum, 3*, 93-135.

Murphy, G. C., & Athanasou, J. A. (1999). The effect of unemployment on mental health. *Journal of Occupational and Organizational Psychology, 72*(1), 83–99. doi:10.1348/096317999166518

Murphy, K. M., & Topel, R. (1997). Unemployment and nonemployment. *The American Economic Review, 87*, 295–300.

Nafziger, E. W. (2006). *Economic development.* New York: Cambridge University Press.

Nasierowski, W., & Arcelus, F. J. (2003). On the efficiency of national innovation systems. *Socio-Economic Planning Sciences, 37*(3), 215–234. doi:10.1016/S0038-0121(02)00046-0

National Statistical Commission. (2012). *Report of the committee on unorganised sector statistics.* Government of India.

National Thermal Power Corporation Ltd. v. Karri Pothuraju. (2003). *Supreme Court Cases (SCC) 384.*

Nawangpalupi, C. B., Pawitan, G., Gunawan, A., Widyarini, M., & Iskandarsjah, T. (2014). *Global entrepreneurship monitor 2013, Indonesia report.* Bandung: Universitas Katolik Parahyangan.

Neogi, C. (2016). Productivity convergence and Asian trade blocks. In R. Das (Ed.), *Handbook of research on global indicators of economic and political convergence* (pp. 92–118). Hershey, PA: Business Science Reference. doi:10.4018/978-1-5225-0215-9.ch005

Niederman, F., Summer, M., & Maertz, C. P. Jr. (2007). Testing and extending the unfolding model of voluntary turnover to IT professionals. *Human Resource Management*, *46*(3), 331–347. doi:10.1002/hrm.20167

Niel, S. (2009). Comment développer un plan de départ volontaire pour motif économique?. *Les cahiers du DRH, 155*, 27-33.

Noorbakhsh, F., Paloni, A., & Youssef, A. (2001). Human capital and FDI inflows to developing countries: New empirical evidence. *World Development*, *29*(9), 1593–1610. doi:10.1016/S0305-750X(01)00054-7

O'Brien, R., & Williams, M. (2007). *Global political economy evolution and dynamics (2nd ed.)*. New York: Palgrave MacMillan.

O'Higgins, N. (2015). *Youth unemployment* (IZA Policy Paper No.103). Retrieved from http://ftp.iza.org/pp103.pdf

Oberman, R., Dobbs, R., Budiman, A., Thompson, F., & Rossé, M. (2012). *The archipelago economy: Unleashing Indonesia's potential*. McKinsey Global Institute. Retrieved fromhttp://www.mckinsey.com/global-themes/asia-pacific/the-archipelago-economy

Ochel, W. (2009). Employment protection: Concepts and measurement. *CESifo DICE Report*, *7*(2), 30–38.

Oğuzlar, A. (1995). Çok boyutlu ölçekleme ve kümeleme analizi arasındaki ilişkiler. *Uludağ Üniversitesi İ.İ.B.F. Dergisi, 18*(2).

Ohno, K. (2003). *East Asian growth and Japanese aid strategy*. GRIPS Development Forum.

Önder, N. (2013). Türkiye'de kadın işgücünün görünümü. *ÇSGB Çalışma Dergisi, 1*(1), 35-61.

Oracle. (2010). *Successfully executing and managing a contingent workforce strategy*. E-Business Suite Human Resources Management System.

Oren, K., & Şahverdioğlu, H. (2016). Turkiye'de genç işsizliği ve genç işsizliğinin giderilmesinde aktif istihdam politikaları. *Gençlik Araştırmaları Dergisi*, *5*(1), 5–37.

Organisation for Economic Co-operation and Development. (2007). *Des emplois plus nombreux, mais moins productifs? L'impact des politiques du marché du travail sur la productivité. In Perspective de l'emploi de l'OCDE 2007*. Éditions OCDE.

Organisation for Economic Co-operation and Development. (2008). Declaring work or staying underground: Informal employment in seven OECD countries. In *OECD employment outlook 2008*. OECD Publishing.

Organisation for Economic Co-operation and Development. (2009). *OECD Employment Outlook 2009: Tackling the jobs crisis*. Paris: OECD Publishing. doi:10.1787/empl_outlook-2009-en

Organisation for Economic Co-operation and Development. (2009). *OECD Reviews of Innovation Policy: Korea 2009*. Paris: OECD Publishing.

Organisation for Economic Co-operation and Development. (2010). *OECD Employment Outlook 2010: Moving beyond the jobs crisis*. Paris: OECD Publishing. doi:10.1787/empl_outlook-2010-en

Organisation for Economic Co-operation and Development. (2011). *Southeast Asian economic outlook 2011/12*. Paris: OECD Publishing.

Organisation for Economic Co-operation and Development. (2013). *Protéger l'emploi, renforcer la flexibilité: Un nouveau regard sur la législation sur la protection de l'emploi. In Perspectives de l'emploi de l'OCDE 2013*. Éditions OCDE.

Organisation for Economic Co-operation and Development. (2014). *Industry and technology policies in Korea*. OECD Publishing.

Organisation for Economic Co-operation and Development. (2014). *Les indicateurs de l'OCDE sur la protection de l'emploi*. Retrieved from http://www.oecd.org/fr/emploi/emp/lesindicateursdelocdesurlaprotectiondelemploi.htm

Organisation for Economic Co-operation and Development. (2014). Promoting better labor market outcomes for the youth. Report on youth employment and apprenticeships prepared for the G20 Labour and Employment Ministerial Meeting, Melbourne, Australia.

Organisation for Economic Co-operation and Development. (2015). *OECD employment outlook 2015*. Paris: OECD Publishing. doi:10.1787/empl_outlook-2015-en

Organisation for Economic Co-Operation and Development. (2015a). *Education at a glance interim report: Update of employment and educational attainment indicators*. Retrieved from www.oecd.org/edu/eag-interim-report.htm

Organisation for Economic Co-Operation and Development. (2015c). *OECD factbook 2015-2016: Economic, environmental and social statistics*. Paris: OECD Publishing. doi:10.1787/factbook-2015-en

Organisation for Economic Co-Operation and Development. (2015e). *OECD online employment database*. Retrieved from http://www.oecd.org/employment/emp/onlineoecdemploymentdatabase.htm

Organisation for Economic Co-operation and Development. (2016). *OECD labour force statistics 2015*. Paris: OECD Publishing. doi:10.1787/oecd_lfs-2015-en

Organisation for Economic Co-operation and Development. (2016). *Population with tertiary education* (indicator). doi: 10.1787/0b8f90e9-en

Organisation for Economic Co-operation and Development. (2016a). *Employment by activity (indicator)*. Retrieved August 23, 2016, from https://data.oecd.org/emp/employment-by-activity.htm#indicator-chart

Organisation for Economic Co-operation and Development. (2016a). Skills matter: Further results from the survey of adult skills. *OECD Skills Studies*. Paris: OECD Publishing. 10.1787/9789264258051-en

Organisation for Economic Co-operation and Development. (2016b). *Employment rate (indicator)*. Retrieved August 23, 2016, from https://data.oecd.org/emp/employment-rate.htm#indicator-chart

Organisation for Economic Co-operation and Development. (2016b). Skills matter: Further results from the survey of adult skills. *Country note Turkey*. Retrieved August 22, 2016, from http://www.oecd.org/skills/piaac/

Organisation for Economic Co-operation and Development. (2016c). *Foreign-born employment (indicator). Foreign-born employment Total / Women / Men, % of foreign-born population, 2014*. Retrieved August 23, 2016, from https://data.oecd.org/migration/foreign-born-employment.htm

Organisation for Economic Co-operation and Development. (n.d.). *Data set of youth statistics*. Retrieved from www.oecd.org/youth.htm

Organization for Economic Co-operation and Development. (2002). *Frascati manual 2002: Proposed standard practice for surveys on research and experimental development*. OECD.

Organization for Economic Co-operation and Development. (2016). *Statistics*. Retrieved May 21, 2016, from http://stats.oecd.org/

Organization of Arab Petroleum Exporting Countries. (2016). *Organization of Arab Petroleum Exporting Countries*. Retrieved April 15, 2016, from www.oapecorg.org

Orhan, O. (2014). The situation of Syrian refugees in the neighboring countries: Findings, conclusions, and recommendations. Center for Middle Eastern Strategic Studies Reports, 189.

Orhan, O., & Senyucel-Gundogar, S. (2015). Effects of the Syrian refugees on Turkey. Center for Middle Eastern Strategic Studies Reports, 195.

Osterholm, P. (2010). Unemployment and labour-force participation in Sweden. *Economics Letters*, *106*(3), 205–208. doi:10.1016/j.econlet.2009.12.002

Ottaviano, G. I., & Peri, G. (2006). *The effects of immigration on wages*. NBER Working Papers, 12497.

Özar, Ş., & Günlük-Şenesen, G. (1998). Determinants of female (non) participation in the urban labour force in Turkey. *METU Studies in Development*, *25*(2), 311–328.

Özatay, F. (2011). *Parasal iktisat: Kuram ve politika*. Ankara: Efil Yayınevi.

Özdamar, K. (1999). *Paket programlarla istatistiksel veri analizi*. Eskişehir: Kaan Kitabevi.

Özdemir, S., Ersöz, H. Y., & Sarıoğlu, I. (2006). *Supporting SMEs for tackling the unemployment problem*. İstanbul: İstanbul Trade Chamber.

Özel, H. A., Topkaya, Ö., & Kurt, S. (2012). Ticari açıklık ve işsizlik ilişkisi: Türkiye örneği. *Kamu-İş*, *12*(4), 29–54.

Özer, M., & Biçerli, K. (2004). Türkiye'de kadın işgücünün panel veri analizi. *Anadolu Üniversitesi Sosyal Bilimler Dergisi*, *3*(1), 55–86.

Özgüzer, G. E., & Binatlı, A. O. (2015). *Economic convergence in the EU: A complexity approach*. RePec Working Paper Series, 15/03.

Öztürk, S. P. (2010). *OECD ülkelerinin AR-GE etkinliklerinin sıralı AHP/VZA metodu ile belirlenmesi* (Unpublished master's thesis). Gazi Universitesi, Ankara.

Ozturkler, H., & Goksel, T. (2015). The economic effects of Syrian refugees on Turkey: A synthetic modelling. Center for Middle Eastern Strategic Studies Reports, 196.

Öztürk, M., & Çetin, B. I. (2009). Dünyada ve Türkiye'de yoksulluk ve kadınlar. *Journal of Yaşar University*, *3*(11), 2661–2698.

Pages, C., & Stampini, M. (2009). No education, no good jobs? Evidence on the relationship between education and labor market segmentation. *Journal of Comparative Economics*, *37*(3), 387–401. doi:10.1016/j.jce.2009.05.002

Pamuk, Ş. (2014). *Türkiye'nin 200 yıllık iktisadi tarihi, büyüme, kurumlar ve bölüşüm*. İstanbul: Türkiye İş Bankası Kültür Yayınları.

Pan, T. W., Hung, S. W., & Lu, W. M. (2010). DEA performance measurement of the national innovation system in Asia and Europe. *Asia-Pacific Journal of Operational Research*, *27*(3), 369-392.

Pancaroğlu, N. S. (2006). *Problems of women participation in labor force and employment in urban areas: The case of İzmit* (Unpublished master's thesis). Kocaeli Üniversitesi, Kocaeli.

Park, S. C. (1997). The transformation of the South Korean economy and international economic development in East and Southeast Asia. *International Planning Studies*, *2*(2), 241–255. doi:10.1080/13563479708721681

Patrick, H. T. (1966). Financial development and economic growth in underdeveloped countries. *Economic Development and Cultural Change*, *14*(2), 174–189. doi:10.1086/450153

Peksen, D., & Blanton, R. G. (2016). The impact of ILO conventions on worker rights: Are empty promises worse than no promises? *The Review of International Organizations*. doi:10.1007/s11558-015-9241-9

Pereira, B. (2010). Libéralisation du marché du travail: Vers une flexisécurité à la française. *Management & Avenir*, *4*(34), 81–106. doi:10.3917/mav.034.0081

Peri, G. (2007). *Immigrants' complementarities and native wages: Evidence from California*. NBER Working Paper, 12956.

Peri, G. (2008). *Immigration accounting: U.S. States 1960-2006.* CReAM Discussion Paper Series, 05/08.

Peri, G., & Sparber, C. (2008). *The fallacy of crowding-out: A note on 'native internal migration and the labor market impact of immigration.* Manuscript, UC Davis.

Peri, G., & Sparber, C. (2009). Task specialization, immigration, and wages. *American Economic Journal. Applied Economics*, *1*(3), 135–169. doi:10.1257/app.1.3.135

Pesaran, M. H. (2004). *General diagnostic tests for cross section dependence in panels.* University of Cambridge, Faculty of Economics, Cambridge Working Papers in Economics, No. 0435.

Pesaran, M. H. (2007). A simple panel unit root test in the presence of cross-section dependence. *Journal of Applied Econometrics*, *22*(2), 265–312. doi:10.1002/jae.951

Pesaran, M. H., & Shin, Y. (1998). An autoregressive distributed-lag modelling approach to cointegration analysis. *Econometric Society Monographs*, *31*, 371–413.

Pesaran, M. H., Shin, Y., & Smith, R. P. (1997). *Pooled estimation of long-run relationships in dynamic heterogeneous panels.* University of Cambridge, Department of Applied Economics.

Pesaran, M. H., Shin, Y., & Smith, R. P. (1999). Pooled mean group estimation of dynamic heterogeneous panels. *Journal of the American Statistical Association*, *94*(446), 621–634. doi:10.1080/01621459.1999.10474156

Pesaran, M. H., & Smith, R. (1995). Estimating long-run relationships from dynamic heterogeneous panels. *Journal of Econometrics*, *68*(1), 79–113. doi:10.1016/0304-4076(94)01644-F

Petralia, S., Balland, P.-A., & Morrison, A. (2015). *Climbing the ladder of technological development.* DRUID Academy Conference in Aalborg.

Phillips, A. W. (1958). The relationship between unemployment and the rate of change of money wages in the United Kingdom 1861-1957. *Economica*, *25*(100), 283–299.

Pierce, J. R., & Schott, P. K. (2012). *The surprisingly swift decline of US manufacturing employment (No. w18655).* National Bureau of Economic Research. doi:10.3386/w18655

Pillinger, J. (2001). *European Foundation for the Improvement of Living and Working Conditions, Quality in social public services.* Luxembourg: Office for Official Publications of the European Communities.

Pischke, J. S., & Velling, J. (1994). *Wage and employment effects of immigration to Germany: An analysis based on local labor markets.* CEPR Discussion Paper, 935.

Pischke, J. S., & Velling, J. (1997). Employment effects of immigration to Germany: An analysis based on local labor markets. *The Review of Economics and Statistics*, *79*(4), 594–604. doi:10.1162/003465397557178

Pissarides, C. A., & Vallanti, G. (2007). The impact of tfp growth on steady-state unemployment. *International Economic Review*, *48*(2), 607–640. doi:10.1111/j.1468-2354.2007.00439.x

Planning Commission of India. (2007). *Labour laws and other labour regulations*. The Government of India.

Pocock, B. (2003). *The work/life collision: What work is doing to Australians and what to do about it*. Annandale: Federation Press.

Poschke, M. (2009). Employment protection, firm selection, and growth. *Journal of Monetary Economics*, *56*(8), 1074–1085. doi:10.1016/j.jmoneco.2009.10.013

Postel-Vinay, F., & Saint-Martin, A. (2004). Comment les salariés perçoivent-ils la protection de lemploi? *Economie & Statistique*, *372*(1), 41–59. doi:10.3406/estat.2004.7266

Praditya, I. I. (2015, October 5). Tekan pengangguran: Joko Widodo luncurkan program padat karya. Retrieved September 4, 2016, from http://bisnis.liputan6.com/read/2332754/tekan-pengangguran-jokowi-luncurkan-program-padat-karya

Prebisch, R. (1950). The economic development of Latin America and its principal problems. New York: United Nations (UN).

Premand, P., Brodmann, S., Almeida, R., Grun, R., & Barouni, M. (2016). Entrepreneurship education and entry into self-employment among university graduates. *World Development*, *77*, 311–327. doi:10.1016/j.worlddev.2015.08.028

Press Trust of India. (2012). Maruti's Manesar plant GM(HR) burned to death, 91 workers arrested; government says business confidence intact. *The Times of India*.

Prieto-Rodriguez, J., & Rodriguez-Gutierrez, C. (2003). Participation of married women in the European labor markets and the added worker effect. *Journal of Socio-Economics*, *32*(4), 429–446. doi:10.1016/S1053-5357(03)00050-7

Psacharopoulos, G., & Tzannatos, Z. (1993). Economic and demographic effects on working women in Latin America. *Journal of Population Economics*, *6*(4), 293–315. doi:10.1007/BF00599040 PMID:12286863

Quinlan, M. (2012). The pre-invention of precarious employment: The changing world of work in context. *Economic and Labour Relations Review*, *23*(4), 3–24. doi:10.1177/103530461202300402

Radelet, S. (1999). *Indonesia: Long road to recovery*. Harvard Institute for International Development. Retrieved from http://www.cid.harvard.edu/ archive/ hiid/ papers/indonesia.pdf

Rajan, G. R., & Zingales, L. (1998). Financial dependence and economic growth. *The American Economic Review*, *88*, 559–586.

Reardon, G. (2011). *How to manage contingent workers*. Littler Mendelson, P.C.

Regulation on the Working Conditions of Pregnant and Nursing Women, Nursing Rooms and Child Care Homes. (2004). Official Gazette, No: 25522. Retrieved from http://www.resmigazete.gov.tr/eskiler/2004/07/20040714.htm#5

Republic of Turkey Ministry of Development. (2016). *Statistics*. Retrieved May 21, 2016, from http://www.mod.gov.tr/Pages/index.aspx

Republika. (2015). *Jumlah pengusaha Indonesia hanya 16,5%*. Retrieved September 6, 2016, from http://www.republika.co.id/berita/nasional/umum/15/03/12/nl3i58-jumlah-pengusaha-indonesia-hanya-165-persen

Revenga, A. (1997). Employment and wage effects of trade liberalization: The case of Mexican manufacturing. *Journal of Labor Economics*, *15*(S3), S20–S43. doi:10.1086/209875

Rhodes, C. (2015). *Construction industry: Statistics and policy*. House of Commons Library. Retrieved May 30, 2016, from http://researchbriefings.files.parliament.uk/documents/SN01432/SN01432.pdf

Rica, S., & Ferrero, M. D. (2003). The effect of fertility on labor force participation: The Spanish evidence. *Spanish Economic Review*, *5*(2), 153–172.

Riessman, F. (1967). New interventions for disadvantaged youth. *The American Journal of Psychiatry*, *123*(7), 880–882. doi:10.1176/ajp.123.7.880 PMID:6066740

Rindfuss, R. R., & Brewster, K. L. (1996). Childrearing and fertility. *Population and Development Review*, *22*, 258–289. doi:10.2307/2808014

Robertson, M., Collins, A., Medeira, N., & Slater, J. (2003). Barriers to start-up and their effect on aspirant entrepreneurs. *Education + Training*, *45*(6), 308–316. doi:10.1108/00400910310495950

Robson, P. (1998). The economics of international integration (4th ed.). London: Routledge.

Rodrik, D. (2006). What's so special about China's exports? *China&World Economy*, *14*(5), 1–19.

Rosly, S. A. (1999). Al-bay Bithaman Ajil financing: Impacts on Islamic banking performance. *Thunderbird International Business Review*, *41*(4-5), 461–480. doi:10.1002/tie.4270410410

Rostow, W. W. (1959). The stages of economic growth. *The Economic History Review*, *12*(1), 1–16. doi:10.1111/j.1468-0289.1959.tb01829.x

Rousseau, S., & Rousseau, R. (1997). Data envelopment analysis as a tool for constructing scientometric indicators. *Scientometrics*, *40*(1), 45–56. doi:10.1007/BF02459261

Rousseau, S., & Rousseau, R. (1998). The scientific wealth of European nations: Taking effectiveness into account. *Scientometrics*, *42*(1), 75–87. doi:10.1007/BF02465013

Ruiz, I., & Vargas-Silva, C. (2013). The economics of forced migration. *The Journal of Development Studies*, *49*(6), 772–784. doi:10.1080/00220388.2013.777707

Ruiz, I., & Vargas-Silva, C. (2015). The labor market impacts of forced migration. *AER:Papers & Proceedings*, *105*(5), 581–586.

Rutovitz, J., & Atherton, A. (2009). *Energy sector jobs to 2030: A global analysis*. Sydney: The Institute for Sustainable Futures, University of Technology.

Ruwanpura, K. N., & Rai, P. (2004). *Forced labour: Definitions, indicators and measurement*. Geneva: International Labour Office.

Sachs, J. D., Shatz, H. J., Deardorff, A., & Hall, R. E. (1994). Trade and jobs in US manufacturing. *Brookings Papers on Economic Activity*, *1994*(1), 1–84. doi:10.2307/2534630

Sadler, K., Akister, J., & Burch, S. (2014). Who are the young people who are not in education, employment or training? An application of the risk factors to a rural area in the UK. *International Journal of Social Work*, *58*(4), 508–520. doi:10.1177/0020872813515010

Şahin, A., Abay, C., & Miran, B. (2008). Tarımsal ve sosyo ekonomik özellikler açısından Türkiye'nin AB'ne uyum olanaklarının değerlendirilmesi: Bir MDS uygulaması. *Finans Politik ve Ekonomik Yorumlar Dergisi*, *45*(5), 17–59.

Saint-Paul, G. (1996). Labor market institutions and the cohesion of the middle class. *International Tax and Public Finance*, *3*(3), 385–395. doi:10.1007/BF00418951

Saint-Paul, G. (2002). Employment protection, international specialization, and innovation. *European Economic Review*, *46*(2), 375–395. doi:10.1016/S0014-2921(01)00093-9

Salimath, M. S., & Cullen, J. B. (2010). Formal and informal institutional effects on entrepreneurship: A synthesis of national-level research. *The International Journal of Organizational Analysis*, *18*(3), 358–385. doi:10.1108/19348831011062175

Sandalcılar, A. R., & Yalman, İ. N. (2012). Türkiye'de dış ticaretteki serbestleşmenin işgücü piyasaları üzerindeki etkileri. *Eskişehir Osmangazi Üniversitesi İktisadi ve İdari Bilimler Dergisi*, *7*(2), 49–65.

Sanusi, A. (2007). Perbandingan laju pertumbuhan ekonomi dan laju pertumbuhan penduduk. *Widya: Majalah Ilmiah*, *24*(240), 36-42. Retrieved August 30, 2016, from http://www.atmajaya.ac.id/web/WebHost.aspx?cid=library code: MM47-25 V24 N260 200705 p36 optim.pdf

Sarwer, M. S., Ramzan, M., & Ahmad, W. (2013). Does Islamic banking system contributes to economy development. *Global Journal of Management and Business Research Version 1.0*, *13*(2), 61-68.

Sayın, F. (2011). Türkiye'de 1988-2010 döneminde eğitim ve büyümenin genç işsizliğine etkisinin analizi. *Dokuz Eylül Üniversitesi Sosyal Bilimler Enstitüsü Dergisi*, *13*(4), 33–53.

Schetter, U. (2015). *Comparative advantages with product complexity and product quality.* Retrieved January 15, 2016, from http://www.etsg.org/ETSG2015/Papers/372.pdf

Schilderman, T. (2002). *Strengthening the knowledge and information systems of the urban poor*. Massachusetts: ITDG.

Scholte, J. A. (2000). *Globalization: A critical introduction*. New York: St Martin's.

Schoon, I., & Silberstein, R. K. (2009). Conceptualising school-towork transitions in context. In Transitions to Work – Globalization, Individualization and Patterns of Delivery. Cambridge, UK: Cambridge University Press.

Schuler, R. S., Jackson, S. E., & Tarique, I. (2011). Global talent management and global talent challenges: Strategic opportunities for IHRM. *Journal of World Business*, *46*(4), 506–516. doi:10.1016/j.jwb.2010.10.011

Sen, K., Saha, B., & Maiti, D. (2010). *Labour market institution and flexibility in Indian manufacturing*. University of Manchester.

Şentürk, M., & Akbaş, Y. E. (2014). The evaluation of mutual relationship among unemployment-inflation and economic growth: The case of Turkey. *Journal of Yasar University*, *9*(34), 5820–5832. doi:10.19168/jyu.43548

Seyidoğlu, H. (2015). *Uluslararası iktisat teori politika ve uygulama*. Ankara: Güzem Can Yayınları.

Shah, N. M., & Al-Qudsi, S. S. (1990). Female work roles in a traditional, oil economy: Kuwait. *Research in Human Capital and Development*, *6*, 213–246.

Shahstree, A. (2013). *Contract Labour (R&A) Act, 1970: Practices, problems & perspectives with respect to manufacturing industry.* Legal Services India. Retrieved 15 December, 2015, from http://www.legalservicesindia.com/article/article/perspectives-on-contract-labour-act-1452-1.html

Sharma, A. (2013). *Informality, firm size and labour market segmentation in Indonesia*. September, Centre for the Study of African Economies (CSAE) and Department of Economics, University of Oxford. Retrieved from https://editorialexpress.com/cgi-bin/conference/download.cgi?db_name=CSAE2014&paper_id=771

Sharma, S. (1996). *Applied multivariate techniques*. New York: John Wiley & Sons Inc.

Sharma, S., & Thomas, V. (2008). Inter-country R&D efficiency analysis: An application of data envelopment analysis. *Scientometrics*, *76*(3), 483–501. doi:10.1007/s11192-007-1896-4

Shimada, H., & Higuchi, Y. (1985). An analysis of trends in female labor-force participation in Japan. *Journal of Labor Economics*, *3*(1), 355–374. doi:10.1086/298089 PMID:12267652

Sığırlı, D., Ediz, B., Cangür, Ş., Ercan, İ., & Kan, İ. (2006). Türkiye ve Avrupa Birliği'ne üye ülkelerin sağlık düzeyi ölçütlerinin çok boyutlu ölçekleme analizi ile incelenmesi. *İnönü Üniversitesi Tıp Fakültesi Dergisi, 13*(2), 81-85.

Sikumbang, Z. (2014). *Menkop: jumlah koperasi dan UMKM terus meningkat.* February 1, 2014. Retrieved March 27, 2016, from http://www.antaranews.com/berita/416949/menkop-jumlah-a cooperative-dan-umkm-terus-meningkat

Simoes, A. J. G., & Hidalgo, C. A. (2011). *The economic complexity observatory: An analytical tool for understanding the dynamics of economic development.* Workshops at the Twenty-Fifth AAAI Conference on Artificial Intelligence.

Singer, H. W. (1950). U.S. foreign investment in underdeveloped areas: The distribution of gains between investing and borrowing countries. *The American Economic Review*, *40*(2), 473–485.

Smith, D. (1974). *Racial Disadvantage in Employment.* London: Political and Economic Planning.

Smith, D. (1980). How unemployment makes the poor poorer. *Policy Studies*, *1*(1), 20–26. doi:10.1080/01442878008423299

Smith, D., Gartside, D., Sloman, C., & Marshall, B. (2014). *Managing the extended workforce: A skills strategy for business agility. Outlook Point of View*. Accenture.

Smith-Lovin, L., & Tickamyer, A. (1978). Nonrecursive models of labor force participation, fertility behavior, and sex role attitudes. *American Sociological Review*, *43*(4), 541–557. doi:10.2307/2094778 PMID:707913

Solow, R. M. (2000). *Growth theory: An exposition* (2nd ed.). New York: Oxford University Press.

Srinivasan, P. V. (2013). Dynamics of structural transformation in South Asia. *Asia-Pacific Development Journal*, *20*(2), 53–88. doi:10.18356/82da9007-en

Stafforte, S., & Tamberi, M. (2012). Italy in the space (of Products). *Economia Marche Journal of Applied Economics*, *31*(1), 90–113.

Stalker, P. (2001). *The no-nonsense guide to international migration*. Oxford, UK: New Internationalist.

Standing, G. (2011). *The precariat: The new dangerous class*. London: Bloomsberg.

Statistical Office of the European Union. (2016a). *At least upper secondary educational attainment, age group 25-64 by sex* (Dataset). Retrieved from http://ec.europa.eu/eurostat/en/web/products-datasets/-/TPS00065

Statistical Office of the European Union. (2016b). *Database*. Retrieved from http://ec.europa.eu/eurostat/data/database

Statistical Office of the European Union. (2016c). *Employment in high- and medium-high technology manufacturing sectors and knowledge-intensive service sectors* (Dataset). Retrieved from http://ec.europa.eu/eurostat/web/products-datasets/-/tsc00011

Statistical Office of the European Union. (2016d). *High-tech exports - Exports of high technology products as a share of total exports (from 2007, SITC Rev. 4)* (Dataset). Retrieved from http://ec.europa.eu/eurostat/web/products-datasets/-/htec_si_exp4

Statistical Office of the European Union. (2016e). *High-tech patent applications to the European patent office (EPO) by priority year* (Dataset). Retrieved from http://ec.europa.eu/eurostat/web/products-datasets/-/tsc00010

Statistical Office of the European Union. (2016f). *Research and development expenditure, by sectors of performance* (Dataset). Retrieved from http://ec.europa.eu/eurostat/en/web/products-datasets/-/TSC00001

Statistical Office of the European Union. (2016g). *Science and technology graduates by sex* (Dataset). Retrieved from http://ec.europa.eu/eurostat/en/web/products-datasets/-/TPS00188

Stevens, J. P. (2009). *Applied multivariate statistics for the social sciences* (5th ed.). Taylor & Francis Group.

Stiroh, K. J. (2001). What drives productivity growth. *Economic Policy Review*, *7*(1), 37–59.

Stone, E. (1992). Investing in the poor. *Asian Business, April*, 24-32.

Studer, R. (2015). How important is an integrated European market? Some insights from history, Perspectives on Europe. *Autumn, 45*(2), 14-19. Retrieved May 13, 2016, from http://councilforeuropeanstudies.org/files/Perspectives/Autumn%20 2015/s4_Studer.pdf

Stycos, J. M., & Weller, R. H. (1967). Female working roles and fertility. *Demography*, *4*(1), 210–217. doi:10.2307/2060362 PMID:21279773

Subandi. (2006). *Sistem ekonomi Indonesia*. Bandung: ALFABETA.

Suedekum, J., & Ruehmann, P. (2003). Severance payments and firm-specific human capital. *Labour*, *17*(1), 47–62. doi:10.1111/1467-9914.00221

Sukmana, R., & Kassim, S. H. (2010). Roles of the Islamic banks in the monetary transmission process in Malaysia. *International Journal of Islamic and Middle Eastern Finance and Management*, *3*(1), 7–19. doi:10.1108/17538391011033834

Süleymanov, E., & Nadirov, O. (2014). Türkiye örneğinde enflasyonla ekonomik büyüme arasında ilişki. *Journal of Qafqaz University-Economics and Administration*, *2*(2), 119–125.

Sumadilaga, C. K. (2012). *Employment policies and strategies. As a respond to "Toward inclusive growth in Indonesia: Improving trade and employment*". Jakarta: Minister of National Development Planning for Poverty, Labor and SMEs. Retrieved from http://www.ilo.org/wcmsp5/groups/public/---asia/---ro-bangkok/---ilo-jakarta/documents/ presentation/ wcms_203899.pdf

Sun, Y., Mitra, P., & Simone, A. (2013). *The driving force behind the boom and bust in construction in Europe*. IMF Working paper WP/13/181. Retrieved October 21, 2016, from https://www.imf.org/external/pubs/ft/wp/2013/wp13181.pdf

Sunindijo, R. Y. (2015). Improving safety among small organisations in the construction industry: Key barriers and improvement strategies. *Procedia Engineering, 125*, 109 – 116.

Sürücü, M. (2014). *Passive employment policies to fight against unemployment: The cases of Germany and Turkey. Thesis of Expertise*. Ministry of Labor and Social Security Directorate General of External Affairs and Services for Workers Abroad. Retrieved September 1, 2016, from https://www.csgb.gov.tr/media/1785/mustafasueruecue.pdf

Suryahadi, A., Hadiwidjaja, G., & Sumarto, S. (2012). *Economic growth and poverty reduction in Indonesia before and after the Asian financial crisis*. Working Paper. Jakarta: SMERU Research Institute. Retrieved from http://www.smeru.or.id/sites/ default/files/publication/econgrow2.pdf

Swaminathan, M. (1991). *Understanding the informal sector: A survey*. WIDER Working Papers.

Takım, A. (2015). The relation between economic growth and unemployment in Turkey: Granger causality test. *Dumlupinar University Journal of Social Sciences*, *27*, 315–325.

Tansel, A. (1999). *Formal versus informal sector choice of wage earners and their wages in Turkey* (Economic Research Forum Working Paper no. 9927). Retrieved from http://papers.ssrn.com/sol3/papers.cfm?abstract_id=263469

Tansel, A. (1999). *Public-private employment choice, wage differentials and gender in Turkey.* Yale University Economic Growth Center Discussion Paper, No. 797.

Tansel, A. (2001). *Economic development and female labor force participation in Turkey: Time-series evidence and cross-province estimates.* ERC Working Paper, 01/05.

Tansel, A., & Kan, E. O. (2012). *Labor mobility across the formal/informal divide in Turkey: Evidence from individual level data* (IZA Discussion Paper No.6271). Retrieved from http://ftp.iza.org/dp6271.pdf

Tansel, A. (1994). Wage employment, earnings and returns to schooling for men and women in Turkey. *Economics of Education Review*, *13*(4), 305–320. doi:10.1016/S0272-7757(05)80054-8

Tarı, R. (2010). *Ekonometri.* Kocaeli: Umuttepe Yayınları.

Taşar, M. O. (2012). *Küresel kriz ve Türkiye ekonomisinin yapısal dönüşümü.* Konya: Palet Yayınları.

Tasci, M., & Zenker, M. (2011). *Labor market rigidity, unemployment, and the Great Recession.* Federal Reserve Bank of Cleveland, Economic Commentary.

Tatlıdil, H. (2002). *Uygulamalı çok değişkenli istatistiksel analiz.* Ankara: Ziraat Matbaacılık A.Ş.

Taylor, F. W. (2011). *Scientific management.* New York: Harper Row.

Terzi, H., & Oltulular, S. (2004). Türkiye'de ekonomik büyüme-enflasyon süreci: Sektörler itibariyle ekonometrik bir analiz. *Bankacılar Dergisi*, *50*, 19–33.

Tetteh, V. A. (2016). Management of human resources. *Research Starters Business,* 1-5.

Tezcan, N. (2014). OECD ve BRIC ülkelerinin enerji göstergeleri açısından çok boyutlu ölçekleme analizi ile karşılaştırılması. *İstanbul Üniversitesi İşletme Fakültesi İşletme İktisadı Enstitüsü Yönetim Dergisi, 25*(77), 119-134.

The Atlas of Economic Complexity. (n.d.). Retrieved February 23, 2016, from http://atlas.cid.harvard.edu/

The British Standards Institution. (2013). *Specification for information management for the capital/delivery phase of construction projects using building information modeling.* PAS 1192-2:2013.

The Daily Mail. (2014). *News.* Retrieved December 18, 2014, from http://bit.ly/nBHBst

The Daily Star. (2014). *Tourism: Next job creator.* Retrieved August 7, 2014, from http://bit.ly/GPTuBw

The World Bank. (2016). *Employment in industry (% of total employment).* Retrieved May 26, 2016, from http://data.worldbank.org/indicator/SL.IND.EMPL.ZS/countries?display=graph

Theodoropoulos, D., Kyridis, A., Zagkos, Ch., & Konstantinidou, Z. (2015). The "Brain Drain" Phenomenon in Greece: Young Greek scientists on their Way to Immigration, in an era of "crisis". Attitudes, Opinions and Beliefs towards the Prospect of Migration. *Journal of Education and Human Development*, *3*(4), 229–248. doi:10.15640/jehd.v3n4a21

Timmer, M. (Ed.). (2012). *The world input-output database(WIOD): "Contents, sources and methods".* Working Paper No. 10. Brussels: European Commission.

Tobing, E. (2005). *Pengangguran tenaga kerja terdidik.* Jakarta: The Prospect.

Toda, H. Y., & Yamamoto, T. (1995). Statistical inference in vector autoregressions with possibly integrated processes. *Journal of Econometrics*, *66*(1-2), 225–250. doi:10.1016/0304-4076(94)01616-8

Toksöz, G. (2007b). İşgücü piyasasının toplumsal cinsiyet perspektifinden analizi ve bölgeler arası dengesizlikler. *Çalışma ve Toplum Dergisi, 4*, 57-79.

Toksöz, G. (2015). *Bin Yıl Kalkınma Hedefleri açısından Türkiye'de çalışma yaşamında kadınların durumu* [PowerPoint slides]. Retrieved May 10, 2016, from http://www.halksagligi.hacettepe.edu.tr/sunumlar_ve_seminerler/20mart_Sempozyum/GToksoz_trde_calismayasaminda_kadinlar.pdf

Toksöz, G. (2007a). *Türkiye'de kadın istihdamı durum raporu*. Ankara: Uluslararası Çalışma Örgütü Yayını.

Tsani, S., Paroussos, L., Fragiadakis, C., Charalambidis, I., & Capros, P. (2013). Female labour force participation and economic growth in the South Mediterranean countries. *Economics Letters, 120*(2), 323–328. doi:10.1016/j.econlet.2013.04.043

Tumen, S. (2015). Skill acquisition in the informal economy and schooling decisions: Evidence from emerging economies. *Labour, 29*(3), 270–290. doi:10.1111/labr.12059

Tunalı, I. (1997). To work or not to work: An examination of female labor force participation in urban Turkey.*Proceedings of the 4th Annual Conference of the Economic Research Forum.*

Tunalı, I., & Ercan, H. (1998). Labor market segmentation in Turkey. In T. Bulutay (Ed.), *Main characteristics and trends in the Turkish labor market* (pp. 85–127). Ankara: Turkish Statistical Institute.

Türedi, S. (2013). The effect of economic freedom on economic growth: A panel data analysis for 12 Islamic countries. *International Research Journal of Finance and Economics, 107*, 154–162.

Türk Sanayicileri ve İşadamları Derneği. (2002). *Türkiye'de işgücü piyasası ve işsizlik (Yayın No: TÜSİAD-T/2002/12-354)*. İstanbul: Lebib Yalkın Yayımları.

Turkish Banking Law. No: 5411. (2005). *Official Gazette of the Republic of Turkey, 25983 (bis)*. Retrieved April 20, 2016, from https://www.bddk.org.tr/websitesi/turkce/Mevzuat/Bankacilik_Kanunu/15405411_sayili_bankacilik_kanunu.pdf

Turkish Statistical Institute. (2014). Youth in statistics (Istatistiklerle Gençlik), 2013. Haber Bülteni, No.16055, Ankara.

Turkish Statistical Institute. (2015). *Labor force statistics*. Retrieved July 17, 2016, from http://www.tuik.gov.tr/PreHaberBultenleri.do?id=18627

Turkish Statistical Institute. (2015). *Youth in statistics (Istatistiklerle Gençlik), 2014*. Retrieved from http://www.tuik.gov.tr/Kitap.do?metod=KitapDetay&KT_ID=11&KITAP_ID=251

Turkish Statistical Institute. (2016). *Labor force statistics*. Retrieved July 17, 2016, from http://www.tuik.gov.tr/PreHaberBultenleri.do?id=21572

Turkish Statistical Institute. (2016). Youth in statistics (Istatistiklerle Gençlik), 2015. Haber Bülteni, No.21517, Ankara.

Turkish Statistical Institute. (n.d.). *Data set of labor statistics*. Retrieved from www.tuik.gov.tr/Dinamik Sorgulama/Isgucu Istatistikleri

Türkiye Katılım Bankaları Birliği. (2015). *Katılım Bankaları 2015*. İstanbul: Türkiye Katılım Bankaları Birliği. Retrieved April 20, 2016, from http://www.tkbb.org.tr/Documents/Yonetmelikler/KATILIM_2015_TR_final.pdf

Türkiye Katılım Bankaları Birliği. (2015, March). *Türkiye katılım bankacılığı strateji belgesi 2015 – 2025 (No: 5)*. İstanbul: Türkiye Katılım Bankaları Birliği.

Türkiye Katılım Bankaları Birliği. (n.d.). *Katılım Bankacılığı Nedir? Nasıl Çalışır?* Retrieved April 20, 2016, from http://www.tkbb.org.tr/Documents/Yonetmelikler/KATILIM_BANKACILIGI-NEDIR-NASIL-CALISIR.pdf

Turkstat. (2016). *Statistics*. Retrieved May 20, 2016, from http://www.turkstat.gov.tr/Start.do

UKCES. (2012). *Sector skills insights: Construction.* Retrieved May 26, 2016, from https://www.gov.uk/government/uploads/system/uploads/attachment_data/file/304475/Sector_Skills_Insights_Construction_evidence_report_50.pdf

United Nations Development Programme. (2012). *United Nations Development Programme's human development reports, 2012*. Retrieved from http://hdr.undp.org/en/composite/trends

United Nations Development Programme. (2014). *Rio + 20: National report on sustainable development*. Dhaka: Ministry of Environment and Forests, Peoples Republic of Bangladesh.

United Nations Development Programme. (2015). *Human development index* (HDI) (Dataset). Retrieved from http://hdr.undp.org/en/content/human-development-index-hdi

United Nations Environment Programme. (2011). Towards a green economy: Pathways to sustainable development and poverty eradication - A synthesis for policy makers. Nairobi, Kenya: Author.

United Nations for Development Program. (2015). *Human development report 2015: Work for human development*. New York: United Nations Development Program.

United Nations High Commissioner for Refugees. (n.d.a). Retrieved April, 2016 from data.unhcr.org/syrianrefugees/country.php

United Nations High Commissioner for Refugees. (n.d.b). Retrieved April, 2016 from http://www.unhcr.org/news/latest/2014/8/53ff76c99/needs-soar-number-syrian-refugees-tops-3-million.html

United Nations Human Settlements Programme. (2011). *UN-HABITAT annual report 2010* (R. Rollnick & T. Naudin, Eds.). Nairobi, Kenya: UNON Publishing Services Section.

United Nations, Department of Economic and Social Affairs, Population Division. (2013). *World population aging 2013* (ST/ESA/SER.A/348).

United Nations. (2012). *The millennium development goals report 2012*. New York: United Nations.

University of Cambridge, Oxford Brookes University and Construction Industry Council. (2013). *Offsite housing review*. Retrieved May 26, 2016, from http://architecture.brookes.ac.uk/research/resources/offsite-housing-review-feb-2013-for-web.pdf

Ünlükaplan, İ. (2009). Avrupa Birliği üyesi ülkelerde iktisadi kalkınma, rekabetçilik ve inovasyon ilişkilerinin kanonik korelasyon analizi ile belirlenmesi. *Maliye Dergisi*, *157*, 235–250.

Uyar Bozdağlıoğlu, E. Y. (2008). The characteristics of unemployment in Turkey and the policies for fighting it. *Journal of Social Sciences*, *20*, 45–65.

Uysal, D., & Erdoğan, S. (2003). Enflasyon ile işsizlik oranı arasındaki ilişki ve Türkiye örneği (1980-2002). *SÜ İİBF Sosyal ve Ekonomik Araştırmalar Dergisi*, *6*, 35–47.

Uysal, D., Mucuk, M., & Alptekin, V. (2008). Türkiye ekonomisinde vektör otoregresif model ile enflasyon-büyüme ilişkisinin analizi. *ZKÜ Sosyal Bilimler Dergisi*, *4*(8), 55–71.

Van Schaik, T., & Van de Klundert, T. (2013). Employment protection legislation and catching-up. *Applied Economics*, *45*(8), 973–981. doi:10.1080/00036846.2011.613784

van Uden, A., Knoben, J., & Vermeulen, P. (2014). *Human capital and innovation in developing countries: A firm level study*. DFID Working Paper.

Vatsa, K. S. (2004). Risk, vulnerability, and asset-based approach to disaster risk management. *International Journal of Sociology and Social Research*, *24*(10/11), 1–48.

Vecchio, N., Mihala, G., Sheridan, J., Hilton, M. F., Whiteford, H., & Scuffham, P. A. (2014). A link between labor participation, mental health and class of medication for mental well-being. *Economic Analysis and Policy*, *44*(4), 376–385. doi:10.1016/j.eap.2014.11.006

Venturini, A. (1999). Do immigrants working illegally reduce the natives legal employment? Evidence from Italy. *Journal of Population Economics*, *12*(1), 135–154. doi:10.1007/s001480050094 PMID:12295037

Verick, S. (2009). *Who is hit hardest during a financial crisis? The vulnerability of young men and women to unemployment in an economic downturn* (IZA Discussion Paper No.4359). Retrieved from http://ftp.iza.org/dp4359.pdf

Verick, S. (2014). *Female labor force participation in developing countries*. IZA World of Labor.

Viner, J. (1992). Turkey, the EEC and labor law: Is harmonization possible. *Northwestern Journal of International Law & Business*, *13*(2), 445–476.

Vinod, H. D., & Kaushik, S. K. (2007). Human capital and economic growth: Evidence from developing countries. *The American Economist*, *51*(1), 29–39. doi:10.1177/056943450705100103

Vlasbom, J. D., & Schippers, J. J. (2004). Increases in female labor force participation in Europe: Similarities and differences. *European Journal of Population*, *20*(4), 375–392. doi:10.1007/s10680-004-5302-0

Vosko, L. F. (2011). *Managing the margins: Gender, citizenship and the international regulation of precarious employment*. New York: Oxford University Press.

Walk Free Foundation. (2016). *The Global Slavery Index 2016*. Walk Free Foundation Publications.

Waluyo, A. (2015, September 9). *Jokowi umumkan paket kebijakan ekonomi*. Retrieved September 3, 2016, from http://www.voaindonesia.com/a/jokowi-umumkan-paket-kebijakan-ekonomi-/2953846.html

Wang, E. C. (2007). R&D efficiency and economic performance: A cross-country analysis using the stochastic frontier approach. *Journal of Policy Modeling*, *29*(2), 345–360. doi:10.1016/j.jpolmod.2006.12.005

Willis, R. K. (1987). What have we learned from the economics of the family? *The American Economic Review*, *77*(2), 68–81.

Wilson, W. J. (1996). *When work disappears: The world of the new urban poor*. New York: Alfred A. Knopf.

Winkelmann, L., & Winkelmann, R. (1998). Why are the unemployed so unhappy? Evidence from panel data. *Economica*, *65*(257), 1–15. doi:10.1111/1468-0335.00111

Winter-Ebmer, R., & Zweimuller, J. (1996). Immigration and the earnings of young native workers. *Oxford Economic Papers*, *48*(3), 473–491. doi:10.1093/oxfordjournals.oep.a028579

Winter-Ebmer, R., & Zweimuller, J. (1999). Do immigrants display young native workers: The Austrian experience. *Journal of Population Economics*, *12*(2), 320–340. doi:10.1007/s001480050102

Wooldridge, J. M. (2002). *Introductory econometrics: A modern approach* (2nd ed.). South-Western Cengage Learning.

World Bank & International Monetary Fund. (2014). *Global monitoring report 2014/2015: Ending poverty and sharing prosperity*. Retrieved September 10, 2016, from http://www.worldbank.org/content/dam/Worldbank/gmr/gmr2014/GMR_2014_Full_Report.pdf

World Bank. (2006). *Turkey - Labor market study*. Washington, DC: World Bank. Retrieved from http://documents.worldbank.org/curated/en/869781468310746230/Turkey-Labor-market-study

World Bank. (2009). *Female labor force participation in Turkey: Trends, determinants and policy framework*. Washington, DC: World Bank Group. Retrieved from http://documents.worldbank.org/curated/en/201081468111238047/Female-labor-force-participation-in-Turkey-trends-determinants-and-policy-framework

World Bank. (2013). *Final report*. Washington, DC: World Bank Group. Retrieved from http://documents.worldbank.org/curated/en/2013/08/19151577/turkey-evaluating-impact-İŞKURs-vocational-training-programs-vol-1-2-final-report

World Bank. (2016). *World Development Indicators 2016*. Retrieved February 15, 2016, from http://databank.worldbank.org/data/reports.aspx?source=world-development-indicators

World Bank. (n.d.). *Data set of country statistics (Turkey)*. Retrieved from www.worldbank.org

World Economic Forum. (2015). *Global gender gap report 2015*. Retrieved September 6, 2016, from http://www3.weforum.org/docs/GGGR2015/cover.pdf

World Economic Forum. (2015). *Global gender gap report*. Geneva: WEF. Retrieved from http://reports.weforum.org/global-gender-gap-report-2015/

World Intellectual Property Organization & Institut Européen d'Administration des Affaires. (2012). *The global innovation index (GII) 2012: Stronger innovation linkages for global growth*. Retrieved from https://www.globalinnovationindex.org/userfiles/file/gii-2012-report.pdf

World Intellectual Property Organization & Institut Européen d'Administration des Affaires. (2016). *The Global Innovation Index (GII) Conceptual Framework* (Annex). Retrieved from http://www.wipo.int/edocs/pubdocs/en/wipo_pub_gii_2016-annex1.pdf

World Travel and Tourism Council. (2014). *Bangladesh-key facts at a glance*. Retrieved August 7, 2014, from http://bit.ly/hHqb5P

Xu, B. (2000). Multinational enterprises, technology diffusion, and host country productivity growth. *Journal of Development Economics*, *62*(2), 477–493. doi:10.1016/S0304-3878(00)00093-6

Yaman Öztürk, M. (2008). *Kapitalist toplumda kadının ezilmesinin koşulları: Martha Gimenez'e yanıt*. Manuscript.

Yameogo, N. D., Nabassaga, T., & Ncube, M. (2014). Diversification and sophistication of livestock products: The case of African countries. *Food Policy*, *49*, 398–407. doi:10.1016/j.foodpol.2014.10.005

Yanıkkaya, H. (2003). Trade openness and economic growth: A cross-country empirical investigation. *Journal of Development Economics*, *72*(1), 57–89. doi:10.1016/S0304-3878(03)00068-3

Yapraklı, S. (2007). Enflasyon ve ekonomik büyüme arasındaki ilişki: Türkiye için eş-bütünleşme ve nedensellik analizi. *Atatürk Üniversitesi Sosyal Bilimler Enstitüsü Dergisi*, *10*(2), 287–301.

Yates, S., & Payne, M. (2006). Not a very NEET solution: Representing problematic labour market transitions among early school-leavers. *Journal of Youth Studies*, *20*(3), 553–569.

Yazdan, G. F., & Dastan, M. (2013). Analysis of Islamic banks financing and economic growth: A panel cointegration approach. *International Journal of Islamic and Middle Eastern Finance and Management*, *6*(2), 156–172. doi:10.1108/17538391311329842

Yazdan, G. F., & Hossein, S. S. M. (2012). Analysis of Islamic bank's financing and economic growth: Case study Iran and Indonesia. *Journal of Economic Cooperation and Development*, *33*(4), 1–24.

Yenilmez, F., & Girginer, N. (2016). Comparison of indicators of womens labour between Turkey and EU member states by employing multidimensional scaling analysis and clustering analysis. *Applied Economics*, *48*(13), 1229–1239. doi:10.1080/00036846.2015.1096005

Yenilmez, F., & Işıklı, B. (2010). The comparison of labor force participation rate of women in Turkey with the world country groups. *Anadolu University Journal of Social Sciences*, *10*(3), 77–92.

Yentürk, N., & Başlevent, C. (2007). *Youth unemployment in Turkey*. Youth Research Unit Research Report No 2.

Yolalan, R. (1993). *İşletmeler arası göreli etkinlik ölçümü*. Ankara: Milli Prodüktivite Merkezi Yayınları.

Yülek, M. A. (1997). On the financial repression in Japan during the high growth period (1953-73). *METU Studies in Development*, *24*(4), 575–595.

Yülek, M. A. (2013). Kalkınma tartışmalarında Japon modelinin yükselişi, düşüşü ve tekrar yükselişi. In K. A. Akkemik & S. Ünay (Eds.), *Doğu Asyanın politik ekonomisi: Japonya Çin ve Güney Kore'de kalkınma siyaset ve jeostrateji* (pp. 1–27). İstanbul: Boğaziçi Üniversitesi Yayınları.

Yusof, R. M., & Bahlous, M. (2013). Islamic banking and economic growth in GCC & East Asia countries: A panel cointegration analysis. *Journal of Islamic Accounting and Business Research*, *4*(2), 151–172. doi:10.1108/JIABR-07-2012-0044

Zachariadis, M. (2012). Immigration and international prices. *Journal of International Economics*, *87*(2), 298–311. doi:10.1016/j.jinteco.2012.01.004

Zainol, Z., & Kassim, S. H. (2010). An analysis of Islamic banks' exposure to rate of return risk. *Journal of Economic Cooperation and Development*, *31*(1), 59–84.

Zarqa, M. A. (2009). Stability in an interest-free Islamic economy: A note. In *Issues in the international financial crisis* (pp. 227–235). Jeddah: King Abdulaziz University, Islamic Economic Research Center.

Zhu, J. (2014). *Quantitative models for performance evaluation and benchmarking: Data envelopment analysis with spreadsheets* (3rd ed.). New York: Springer. doi:10.1007/978-3-319-06647-9

Zimmermann, K. F. (2009). *Labor mobility and the integration of European Labor Markets*. IZA Discussion Paper No. 3999. Bonn: Institute for the Study of Labor.

Zimmermann, K. F. (2004). *European labor lobility: Challenges and potentials. IZA Policy Paper No. 69*. Bonn: Institute for the Study of Labor.

Zuo, W., Wang, Q., & Yang, P. (2012). Research on the current situation of peasant-workers in construction industry based on AHP. *Systems Engineering Procedia*, *5*, 405–411. doi:10.1016/j.sepro.2012.04.062

About the Contributors

Füsun Yenilmez was born in Afyon/Emirdağ in 1969. She graduated from Faculty of Economics and Administrative Sciences of Anadolu University in 1992. She was graduated from Ph.D. program of Social Sciences Institute of Anadolu University in 2004. She worked as a Research assistant from 1994 to 2004 and as an Assistant Professor from 2004 to 2013 at International Economics in Economics and administrative Sciences Faculty of Eskişehir Osmangazi University. She is currently an Associate Professor at the same university. She is interested in studies on Theories of International Economics, Turkey-EU foreign trade, sectoral analysis, health economics, and Women's Employment. She was appointed as Research Assistant Chairman of the Board Representation of Osmangazi University in 2003. She worked as Deputy Head of the Department of Economics between 2007 and 2009. She is the head of Turkish Association of University Woman since 2014. She is a member of Economic Council of Turkey. She is married and has two boys.

Esin Kılıç was born in Eskişehir. She completed her primary, secondary and high school education in Eskişehir. She has two Bachelor's degrees — in statistics and in economics— from the Anadolu University. After then, she started the Integrated Doctoral Education Program at Anadolu University. Her doctoral education is funded by The Scientific and Technological Research Council of Turkey (TÜBİTAK). She earned her Ph. D. degree in economics from Anadolu University in 2013. She started to work at Eskişehir Osmangazi University as a research assistant in 2010. Since 2015, she is working as an assistant professor at the same university. Her main research areas are international trade, exchange rate, and sectoral economic studies.

* * *

Tolga Aksoy is an Assistant Professor of Economics at the Yıldız Technical University, Department of Economics where he teaches Statistics, World Economy, and Theories of Financial Crises. He received his Ph.D. in Economics from the Bocconi University, his MA in Economics from the Marmara University and his BS in Economics from the Yıldız Technical University. His main area of research is macroeconomics, labor economics, and empirical political economy. His research has focused on macroeconomics of labor and product market imperfections, economic growth and electoral consequences of structural reforms. Recently, in addition to the above research, he has started a number of projects related to applied microeconomics.

Samir Amine is a full-professor of economics at the Department of labor and industrial relations of the University of Québec in Canada. He is also Fellow (Senior Researcher) at The Interuniversity Center of Public Policies (CIRANO). Labor economics specialist, his work focuses on the evaluation of public policies and on the development of income inequalities. His research has been funded by the Quebec Fund for Research on Society and Culture (FQRSC) and by The Social Sciences and Humanities Research Council of Canada (SSHRC). He is a member of the editing board of several journals such as Theoretical Economics Letters. He is Member of The Society of Labor Economists (SOLE), of The European Association of Labour Economists (EALE) and of The Eurasian Economics Society.

Ati Cahayani has a doctoral degree in education management from Jakarta State University, Indonesia. She has been a lecturer since 1998 especially on organization theory, human resource, and also entrepreneurship. She has written books on human resource, organization theory, and also entrepreneurship. She translated some books, especially on human resource, psychology, leadership, and management, from English to Bahasa Indonesia. She wrote some articles, either in English or Bahasa Indonesia, on entrepreneurship, human resource, management, education, and leadership. As a lecturer who has deep concern towards the welfare of the community, she also conducted a number of activities to empower the community, particularly related to entrepreneurship, management, or leadership, as a facilitator.

Muhlis Can is an assistant professor at Hakkari University in Department of Economics and Finance. He holds a BA from Atatürk University in 2003. Thereafter, he started his career in the private sector. He has 6 years experience in various areas of the private sector, including marketing, export, and import. In 2011, he completed MA in Süleyman Demirel University. In 2015, he completed his Ph.D. at the same university. He writes on issues of international trade, energy, tourism, and globalization. He has collaborated actively with researchers in different universities around the world. In recent years, he has focused on econometric modeling. His researches were published in different peer-reviewed journals (indexing in SSCI, ESCI, Econlit) including Environmental Science and Pollution Research, Eurasian Business Review, International Journal of Alanya Faculty of Business, Akdeniz University Journal of The Faculty of Economics and Administrative Sciences.

Fatih Çemrek was born in Konya in 1977. He graduated from Arts and Science Faculty of Osmangazi University in 1998. From this time to 2001, he attended Master's program in Institutes of Science of Osmangazi University and graduated from Ph.D. Program of Institutes of Science of Eskişehir Osmangazi University in 2006. To date from 1999, he is working as a faculty member of Applied Statistics in Arts and Science Faculty of Eskişehir Osmangazi University. He is interested in studies of Time Series Analysis, Econometric Time Series Analysis, Multivariate Statistical Analysis, and Applied Statistics. He became an assistant professor in 2008 and became an associate professor in 2015. He is married and has one girl.

Banu Demirhan was born in Ankara in 1975. He received the B.E., M.E., and Ph.D. degrees from Afyon Kocatepe University, Afyonkarahisar, Turkey, in 1999, 2006, and 2014, respectively. Since 2006, he has been with the Department of Economics, where he is currently a Lecturer. His main areas of research interest are monetary policy, econometric modeling, and applied economics.

Erdal Demirhan was born in Afyonkarahisar in 1970. He received the B.E., degree from Erciyes University, Kayseri, Turkey, in 1991, and M.E., and Ph.D. degrees from Afyon Kocatepe University, Afyonkarahisar, Turkey, in 1995 and 1998, respectively. Since 1994, he has been with the Department of Economics, where he is currently a Professor. His main areas of research interest are monetary policy, econometric modeling, and applied economics.

Buhari Doğan was born in Isparta in 1985. He completed his primary and secondary education in Egirdir and Isparta. Then, he holds BA from Kocaeli University, Department of Economics of the Faculty of Economics and Administrative Sciences. He completed his MA in Department of Econometrics at Süleyman Demirel University, and then he completed his Ph.D. education in Department of Economics at the same university. Currently, he is working as Research Assistant in the Faculty of Economics and Administrative Sciences in Süleyman Demirel University. He writes on issues of energy, economic growth, and globalization. He was awarded in the category of the best academic paper in the International Conference of European Union Relations, Economics, Finance and Econometrics. His researches were published in different peer-reviewed journals (indexing in Econlit, Scopus).

Yahya Can Dura has worked for Ministry of Interior for more than 13 years in the Department of Strategy Development as Planning Expert. He has also "Certified Government Auditing Professional (CGAP) Certification". He holds bachelor's degree in Finance from Ankara Gazi University and master of science degree in International Economy from Ankara Gazi University. Also, he has been studying as a Ph.D. student in Eskişehir Osmangazi University-Economy Department. His proficiency subjects are "investment planning, strategical planning and management, performance management, public administrative institution, local and regional development, political economy and international economy". So far, his 9 academic articles, 10 popular articles, and one book have been published.

Etem Hakan Ergeç is an associate professor in Department of Economics at İstanbul Medeniyet University in Istanbul, Turkey. He mainly teaches Monetary Theory and Policy (MBA, BA), Financial Economics (BA) Monetary Theory and Policy (BA) and Money and Capital Market (BA). His interest topics are monetary policy, financial system, and Islamic banking. His recent research includes monetary policy, development of Islamic banking and finance in Turkey, Islamic banking and finance, customers of Islamic banks in Turkey and the empirical aspects of Islamic banking and finance. His articles on his research interests have appeared in various journals.

Nikos Fotopoulos is an Assistant Professor of Sociology in the field of Cultural and Educational Practices at the University of Western Macedonia, and he currently is Head of Department for Planning and Innovation of KANEP/GSEE. He has participated in a significant number of national and European expert committees and has participated in the planning and implementation of research, educational and cultural courses in the field of lifelong learning, culture and education policy. He has served as a member of the Board of Experts «European Training Foundation (ETF) - Advisory Forum» on matters related to policy development for Education and Lifelong Learning in Central and Eastern Europe and as a member of National Committee for Lifelong Learning - Ministry of Education. He has been involved as a National Representative of the social partners in the Advisory Group on the European Qualifications

Framework, and he has also worked for the implementation of ECVET in Greece as a part of national team of experts. He has published a lot of articles in pedagogical, political and social and journals both in Greece and abroad. abroad.

Nuray Girginer was born in Eskişehir in 1967. She graduated from Department of Statistics, Faculty of Science at Anadolu University in 1992. She received her master's degree in 1994 and Ph.D. degree in 2001 from Department of Quantitative Methods, Institute of Social Science, Anadolu University. Since 1994, she has been working as a faculty member at Eskişehir Osmangazi University, Faculty of Economics and Administrative Sciences, Department of Business. She continued her academic career as an associated professor during 2009-2014, and she has been working as a professor since 2014 at the same university. She is head of Department of Business and vice-dean of Faculty of Economics and Administrative Sciences, Eskişehir Osmangazi University. Her major fields are operations research, mathematical modeling, quantitative methods, multivariate statistical analysis, data analysis, and econometric analysis.

Azizul Hassan is a member of the Tourism Consultants Network of the UK Tourism Society, and is currently working towards a PhD at Cardiff Metropolitan University. His main areas of research are: technology-supported marketing in tourism; innovative marketing dynamics; destination branding in tourism; cultural heritage tourism; heritage interpretation; and sustainable management/marketing alternatives for cultural heritage industries. He is a regular reviewer of Tourism Management Perspectives, International Journal of Tourism Cities, Tourism Analysis, the International Journal of Human Resource Management, the International Journal of Ecotourism, the eReview of Tourism Research (eRTR), and The International Interdisciplinary Business-Economics Advancement Journal.

Özlem İnanç-Tunçer was born in Waldbröl-Germany in the year 1975. She has obtained her BS degree in Economics in 1998, and MA degree in Economics in 2001 from Hacettepe University. Thereafter, she obtained her MS in Economics in 2003, and Ph.D. degree in the same field from LSU in 2007. Her doctoral work was on the effect of trade cost on the PPP deviations in the European countries. Between January 2007 and May 2007, she has worked as a visiting assistant professor at Northern Michigan University. During 2007-2010, she was an instructor at Işık University Department of Economics. She was appointed to an assistant professorship in 2010 at the same department. Dr. İnanç-Tunçer received the TÜBİTAK National Young Scientist Career Development Program Award in 2011. Her research interest primarily lies in the macroeconomic aspects of international trade and finance. Other research interests include economic growth, tourism economics, and economic geography. She is fluent in English.

Zeynep Kaplan is an assistant Professor in division of Economic Development and International Economics at the Faculty of Economics and Business Administration, Yıldız Technical University. She holds a B.A and M.A degree on Economics from Yıldız Technical University, Ph.D. degree on Economics of the European Union from Marmara University. Her current research interests are in the area of International Economics, Economic Integration, Economics of the European Union and Innovation Policy. At the university, she teaches International Economics, International Trade and Finance and Economics of European Integration. Her publications include a number of articles related to international economics and European economic integration.

Mustafa Karabacak was born in Eskişehir. He graduated from Anadolu University, Faculty of Economics and Administrative Sciences, Department of Economics in 2008. He started his academic career as a Research Assistant at Uşak University, Faculty of Economics and Administrative Sciences, Department of Economics in 2009. He completed his graduate degree at Anadolu University, Department of Economics in 2010 and he finished his Ph.D. studies at Anadolu University in 2016. Then he continued his academic career as an Assistant Professor in 2016 at Uşak University, Faculty of Economics and Administrative Sciences, Department of Economics. He is interested in studies on monetary Policy, education economics and labor market.

Yavuz Hürol Karabilgin has worked for Turkish Revenue Administration for more than 10 years in the Department of EU and Foreign Affairs and OECD Ankara Multilateral Tax Centre as State Revenue Expert. He holds bachelor's degree in Finance from Ankara Gazi University and master of science degree in Administrative Studies, Innovation & Technology and Multinational Commerce concentrations from Boston University. He is also the co-writer of "Dexterity in Global Business: A Cross-Dimensional Analysis" published in 2014. Innovation, entrepreneurship, growth and taxation are the focal points of his studies. His proficiency subjects are "tax, state revenues, multilateral tax, public finance, economy".

Bengül Gülümser Kaytancı is an assistant professor in Department of Economics at Anadolu University, Eskişehir, Turkey. She mainly teaches Monetary Theory and Policy (MBA, BA), Financial Economics (BA) and Monetary Theory and Policy (BA). Her recent research includes monetary policy, development of Islamic banking and finance in Turkey, Islamic banking and finance, customers of Islamic banks in Turkey and the empirical aspects of Islamic banking and finance. Her articles on his research interests have appeared in various journals.

Eda Kılıç was born in Eskişehir in 1983. She completed his primary and secondary education in Eskişehir. Then, she earned a bachelor's degree from Department of Sociology, Faculty of Science and Literature, Uludağ University. She received her master's degree from Department of Labour Economics and Industrial Relationship, Institute of Social Science, Uludağ University, and she continues her Ph.D. education in the same department at the same university. Currently, she is a columnist for a local newspaper. She writes on issues of organizational commitment, organizational alienation, women in working life, gender inequality, and motherhood.

Erol Kutlu was born in 1961. He graduated from Department of Economics and Administrative Sciences of Anadolu University in 1985. He continued his academic career and completed his M.A. and Ph.D. degrees at Anadolu University. He became an Assistant Professor in 1992 and an associate professor in 2002 at Department of Economics, Anadolu University. He currently works as a professor at the same department and university since 2008. He was the head of the department of economic development and international economics between the year 2009-2010. His main research areas are international trade, economics, knowledge, and economy. He is married and has two children.

Argyris Kyridis is a professor of Sociology of Education at the Department of Early Childhood Education (S.E.C.E.), Faculty of Education, of Aristotle University in Thessaloniki. He obtained an undergraduate degree in Politics from the Department of Political Science and Public Administration of the University of Athens (1988) and an M.Sc. degree in Politics and Sociology from the University of

London – Birkbeck College in 1989. In 1994 he was awarded a Ph.D. degree in Sociology from University of Athens. His research is focused on aspects that concern sociology of education, culture, ethnicity, political sociology and sociology of new technologies. He has published 5 books as single author, 19 books as co-author and 26 of his works have been included in books –three of them in English. He has published 215 articles in scientific journals and conferences proceedings - 95 of them in international journals and proceeding of international conferences. There are 420 citations of his works – 150 of them in international journals and conferences proceedings.

Özge Kama Masala is an assistant Professor in division of Economic Theory at the Faculty of Economics and Business Administration, Yıldız Technical University. She holds a B.A degree from Istanbul University, M.A and Ph.D. degrees from Yıldız Technical University. Her current research interests are in the area of Institutional Economics, Sustainable Growth, Public Finance and Labor Economics. At the university, she teaches Institutional Economics and Public Finance. Her publications include a number of articles related to institutional economics and public policies.

Oytun Meçik was born in Eskişehir in 1985. He graduated from Eskişehir Osmangazi University, Faculty of Administrative and Economic Sciences, Department of Economics in 2008. In the same year, he began his academic career as a Research Assistant at Uşak University, Faculty of Administrative and Economic Sciences, Department of Economics and he completed his graduate degree at Uşak University. He completed his Ph.D. studies at Anadolu University, Department of Economics in 2014. Dr. Meçik became an assistant professor in the same year at Uşak University. He has been working at Eskişehir Osmangazi University, Faculty of Administrative and Economic Sciences, Department of Economics since 2015. Dr. Meçik's main research fields of study, labor market, social capital, and structural transformations.

Halise Duygu Özalp received her bachelor degree both Sociology and Labour Economics and Industrial Relations Department at Anadolu University. During her bachelor education, she studied at Jagiellonian University Institute of Sociology in Krakow-Poland. After getting the bachelor degrees, she started to integrated Ph.D. program at Ankara University Institute of Social Sciences in Labor Economics and Industrial Relations Department and still continues her Ph.D. education. Also, she is working in University of Turkish Aeronautical Association (UTAA) as a lecturer. Her academic research interests include industrial sociology and new forms of work.

Maria Pavlis Korres obtained a university degree in Political Science in Athens (1981). From 1983 until today she works on Adult Education in the Greek Ministry of Education. She has participated as an expert in the first research on Roma Education conducted by the European Council (1985-1986), and she has participated in educational and research projects on Roma education implemented in Greece. Since 2005 her research interests are focused on e-learning, and she obtained her Ph.D. with honors from the Computer Science Department of the University of Alcalá in 2010. The subject of her Ph.D. is "Development of an e-education framework for the education of educators of special groups in order to improve their compatibility with their learners". Since 2012 she is a member of the scientific staff of Hellenic Open University and teaches in the Adult Education postgraduate program. Her current interests are focused on design, development, and evaluation of adult education programs, face to face and e-learning, as well as the group dynamics in an online environment.

Aslışah Şenak holds a Bachelor degree in Business Administration from Anadolu University and a Master's degree in International Relations from Galatasaray University. She started her career in the marketing department of an international company and has been involved in business development projects. She lived and worked in Frankfurt, Milano, and Paris before starting her own company in business development back in Turkey. She speaks English, French and Italian. She is currently a Ph.D. student in Business Administration at Osmangazi University in Eskişehir and has made studies on effects of globalization on small and medium-sized enterprises, R&D efficiency and innovation efficiency.

Begüm Sertyeşilışık is an Assoc. Prof. in the Department of Architecture at the Istanbul Technical University. She has been awarded her PhD in the field of construction contracts at the Middle East Technical University in 2007. She obtained an MSc in project management in 2003, an MBA in 2003 and a BSc in Architecture in 2001 at the Istanbul Technical University. She has been specialized in the areas of project management, sustainability, sustainable built environment, strategic management, health and safety, lean and agile management, construction contracts, contract and dispute management. She has international publications in these areas. She contributes to international scientific conferences as international scientific member and to international scientific journals as reviewer.

Shaurya Sharma is a chemical engineer who is currently pursuing his Master of Business Administration at XLRI - Xavier School of Management, India, he has an avid interest in academic writing and debating. He seeks to pursue research in the field of public policy and sustainable development. In addition, he has undertaken various entrepreneurial ventures and is presently developing an online platform that strives to enhance social awareness. Lastly, he is passionate about adventure sports and his love for nature has made him travel across the world.

Shivankar Sharma, Advocate, is a graduate of NALSAR University of Law (2014) and has been working at Shardul Amarchand Mangaldas, Delhi, where he advises on matters of Indian corporate law, private equity and mergers and acquisitions. He has a keen interest in contemporary questions revolving around the development of the law and the interplay of law and society.

Z. Bilgen Susanlı is an assistant professor of Economics at Işık University. She has taught courses in labor economics, statistics, microeconomics, and game theory. Her research interests include the labor market outcomes of the youth and women. She has also written papers on topics such as education, subjective well-being, and child labor. She received a B.A. in Economics in 2001, and Master of Business Administration from Boğaziçi University in 2003. She then received her Master's and a Ph.D. degree in Economics from Georgetown University in 2005 and 2009, respectively. In 2009, she joined the Department of Economics at Işık University.

Tulus T. H. Tambunan received his Ph.D. in economics from the University of Erasmus in Rotterdam, the Netherlands. He is currently a professor in the Faculty of Economics and the director of the Center for Industry, Small and Medium Enterprises, and Business Competition Studies at the University of Trisakti in Jakarta, Indonesia. The Center has just launched a new international journal of Small and Medium Enterprises and Business Sustainability (http://www.usakti-cisbucs.com). His interests of research areas are especially the development of small and medium enterprises, economic crisis, industrialization and international trade. Since 1995 he has been the country researcher representing Indonesia for the World Economic Forum (WEF) in Geneva, which publishes, annually, the Global Competitiveness Report.

Christos D. Tourtouras was born in Xanthi (Greece) in 1966. He has studied Pedagogy at graduate level (B.Ed.) in Larissa (Pedagogical Academy) and Thessaloniki (Department of Primary Education of Aristotle University), as well as Psychology in Thessaloniki (Department of Psychology of Aristotle University). He also holds a Ph.D. in Education from the Department of Primary Education of Aristotle University of Thessaloniki, concerning especially the sector of "minorities and educational/social exclusion" in Greece. He used to be a primary school teacher in Greek state/public education for 22 years (from 1989-90 up to 2010-11). Now, he serves as an Assistant Professor of Pedagogy in the Pedagogical Department of Primary Education of Aristotle University. The phenomena of "school failure" and "social and educational exclusion" (causes and factors) as well as the Intercultural and Anti-racist Education are the main fields of his scientific interests. Mr. Tourtouras offers the courses: 1. "School failure" (Winter - 1st semester). 2. "Introduction to Pedagogy" (Winter - 1st semester). 3. "Introduction to Pedagogy" (Spring - 2nd semester). 4. "Social exclusion and education" (Spring - 4th semester).

Christos Zagkos is a researcher in the Center of Educational Policy Development (KANEP/GSEE). He studied Balkan Studies at the Aristotle University of Thessaloniki and he obtained his postgraduate studies in International Relations and International Law at the University of Lancaster, U.K. He holds a Ph.D. degree from the University of Western Macedonia in the field of Political Sociology and he has published more than forty papers in Greek, European and American scientific journals. His research is focused on aspects that concern political sociology, educational policy, ethnicity and vulnerable social groups.

Index

A

B

C

D

E

F

M

N

O

P

R

S

T

U

W

Y

www.ingramcontent.com/pod-product-compliance
Lightning Source LLC
LaVergne TN
LVHW060352300926
849162LV00006B/1253
* 9 7 8 1 5 2 2 5 2 0 0 8 5 *